2ND CLASS
FCC ENCYCLOPEDIA

2ND CLASS FCC ENCYCLOPEDIA

Complete Study Guide to the Commercial Radiotelephone Exam

By Kendall Webster Sessions

TAB BOOKS

Blue Ridge Summit, Pa. 17214

Foreword

There aren't many who can sit down and take an exam as comprehensive as the FCC Second Class radiotelephone test without a little prior cramming. Regardless of how much you know about electronics, and radio in particular, you can't be expected to have all the answers to all the questions right off the top of your head. If you're going to take the exam to upgrade your existing license status, you'll need to refresh yourself on some of the FCC Rules. If you're going to go for the Second Class ticket right from scratch, you need to know what the FCC examiners have in store for you.

That's what this handbook is all about. There is no shortage of FCC question-and-answer books, nor are simple study guides difficult to find. The fare currently available, however, has some serious shortcomings that could slow your learning or leave you in doubt about certain aspects of the examination procedure.

The first section in this book contains basic information: how to apply for your license, where to take the test, what each of the tests is composed of, and the field offices and dates on which the exams are administered.

The remainder of the book is separated into sections, each representing an official FCC categorical element or group of elements. The second section, for example, contains questions and answers for the radiotelephone Third Class operator permit (FCC Elements 1 and 2). Section 3 contains questions, answers, and backup information pertaining to Element 9 (broadcast endorsement). Section 4 contains basic questions and answers relating to Second Class radiotelephone operator licenses (Element 3). Section 5 contains supplemental questions and answers for Element 3; these questions represent material designed to update the study guide material originally issued by the FCC.

The final section, on troubleshooting, will help prepare you for "diagram" questions relating to this subject.

I wish to acknowledge the cooperation of the U.S. Government during preparation of this book, not only for supplying the applicable rules and study questions but for providing many volumes of technical research material as well.

The index for this book has been made especially comprehensive to help you through areas where you yourself have discovered a weakness in your knowledge.

Kendall Webster Sessions

Contents

Basic License Information

You want to go into the two-way radio service business because you have a strong background in radio and a healthy knowledge of electronics. How do you go about getting an FCC license so that you can legally work on transmitters? You're a disc jockey with the chance to advance—but you need a higher class of license than you now hold. What do you do?

The FCC publishes several pamphlets that are designed to help you get all the information you need to apply for an FCC radiotelephone operator's permit. Like most official publications and forms, those from the FCC can be confusing. You'll fare a sight better all the way down the line if you know exactly what you require and from whom, and how much money you must pay and for what. That information is given next.

FCC EXAMINATION

For all classes of radiotelephone operator authority other than *restricted*, you'll have to take a written test at a participating FCC field office. The FCC's battery of tests includes nine discrete categories, or *elements*. Table 1-1 lists the *classes of licenses* along with the FCC exam elements applicable to them.

Table. 1-1. License Classes and Exams.

LICENSE OR PERMIT CATEGORY	EXAM ELEMENTS APPLICABLE
Restricted Radiotelephone Operator Permit	None
Radiotelephone Third Class Operator Permit	1 and 2
Radiotelephone Second Class Operator License	1, 2, and 3
Radiotelephone First Class Operator License	1, 2, 3, and 4
Radiotelegraph Third Class Operator Permit	1, 2, and 5[1]
Radiotelegraph Second Class Operator License	1, 2, 5, and 6[1]
Radiotelegraph First Class Operator License	1, 2, 5, and 6[2]

[1]A code test is given wherein applicant must demonstrate ability to send and copy sixteen 5-digit code groups per minute, as well as 20 words per minute of plain language.
[2]Applicant must demonstrate ability to copy and send 20 code groups per minute and 25 words per minute of plain language.

Table 1-2. FCC Test Elements.

FCC Element	No. & Type of Questions	Description
1	20 Multiple Choice	Provisions of laws, treaties, and regulations with which every operator should be familiar.
2	20 Multiple Choice	Operating procedures and practices generally followed or required in communicating by radiotelephone stations.
3	100 Multiple Choice	Technical, legal, and other matters applicable to operating radiotelephone stations other than broadcast.
4	50 Multiple Choice	Advanced technical, legal, and other matters particularly applicable to operating various classes of broadcast stations.
5	50 Multiple Choice	Radio-operating procedures and practices generally followed or required in communicating by radiotelegraph stations other than in the maritime mobile services of public correspondence.
6	100 Various Types	Technical, legal, and other matters applicable to operating all classes of radiotelegraph stations, including: maritime mobile services of public correspondence, message traffic routing and accounting, radio navigational aids, etc.
7	100 Multiple Choice	Special endorsement on radiotelegraph First and Second Class operator licenses. Theory and practice in operation of radio communication and navigational systems in use on aircraft.
8	50 Multiple Choice	Special endorsement on First or Second Class operator licenses. Specialized theory and practice applicable to proper installation, servicing, and maintenance of ship radar equipment for marine navigation.
9	20 Multiple Choice	Special endorsement on radiotelephone Third Class operator license. Specialized elementary theory and practice in operation of standard AM and FM broadcast stations.

Once you determine the class of license you need, consult the table to learn the elements you must study for.

The elements themselves are described in Table 1-2. Note that every FCC examination includes the first two elements. When you take your test, you will be required to answer 20 multiple-choice questions regarding basic operating practice and 20 relating to radio law. The questions in these two elements will be of the same level of difficulty regardless of the class of license or permit you are applying for.

The table also includes information applicable to radio*telegraph* examinations, even though questions relating to licenses and permits in that category are not included in this book.

BASIC REQUIREMENTS OF APPLICANT

An applicant for any commercial radio operator license or permit must normally be a citizen or national of the United States. Under certain circumstances, U.S. nationality may be waived for alien aircraft pilots and citizens of a U.S. "trust territory."

For all licenses and permits other than restricted radiotelephone operator, you must submit, in advance, a completed application Form 756 and appropriate fee to the office that will administer the examination. If the examination is to be taken at an FCC office, the forms may be obtained and completed at the time of the examination. To request a restricted radiotelephone operator permit (for which no examination is required), submit FCC application Form 753 and fee by mail to Commission's office at Gettysburg, Pa. 17325. A schedule of fees for all U.S. radio licenses and permits is given in Table 1-3.

The Commission has not established any age limit for applicants for commercial radio operator licenses, except as follows:

Radiotelegraph First Class operator licenses may not be issued to applicants under 21 years of age; applicants for an aircraft radiotelegraph endorsement must be at least 18 years of age; and applicants for the restricted radiotelephone operator permit must be at least 14 years of age.

Each radio operator application form inquires as to the applicant's criminal record (if any), the status of his citizenship, and his physical ability to perform the duties of a radio operator.

There are no educational or training requirements.

Table 1-3. FCC License Fee Schedule.

Radio Service	Classification	Fee, $
Commercial	First Class (new, duplicate, renewal, replacement)	5
	Third Class (new, duplicate, renewal, replacement)	3
	Second Class (new, duplicate, renewal, replacement)	4
	Provisional certificate for Third Class (phone) with broadcast endorsement	2
	License verification card	2
	Posting statements in lieu of permit or license)	2
	Separate application for endorsement of license	2
	Restricted radio telephone operator (new or replacement)	
	Lifetime permit (for U.S. citizen)	8
	One-year (renewable) permit (for alien)	2
Amateur	Novice	None
	Initial license, renewal, duplicate, or new class	9
	Modification of license without renewal	4
	Modification of license with renewal	9
	Special call sign (does not include other applicable fees per above schedule)	25
Aviation	Microwave stations (new, renewal, or assignment)	75
	All other applications	20
Citizens Band	Station license	20
Industrial, Land Transportation, and Public Safety	Initial license, renewal, or assignment	20
	Microwave station (new, renewal, or assignment)	75
	Microwave station (modification without renewal)	20
	Microwave station (yearly renewal)	15
Marine	Interim ship license (includes subsequent license)	25
	Microwave (new, renewal, or assignment)	75
	Common carrier and public coastal stations (new, renewal, or assignment)	75
	All other applications (including exemptions from ship radio requirements)	20
Safety and Special Radio Services	Duplicate licenses	6

Examinations for commercial radio operator licenses are conducted at each radio district office of the Commission on the days designated by the local engineer in charge. In addition to the radio district offices of the Commission, examinations are held in certain other cities on dates designated by the engineer in charge of the radio district in which these cities are located. A list of designated examination points appears in Table 1-4. Specific dates and times of examinations should be obtained from the engineer in charge at the office concerned. Table 1-4 is a basic exam schedule listing the time and dates of examinations at the FCC field engineering offices. Table 1-5 contains a list of additional FCC offices where exams are conducted. While the months of exams are shown for these additional offices, the exact dates may vary, so check with the appropriate office before scheduling a trip.*

The holder of a license who applies for another class of license or special endorsement will be required to pass only the additional written examination elements applicable to new class of license. Applicants should bring with them and present any licenses, permits, and verification cards they may hold. If the holder of a license qualifies for higher class of license in the same group, the license held will be canceled and returned to the licensee upon issuance of the new license.

An applicant who fails an examination element will be ineligible for a period of 2 months to take an examination for any class of license requiring that element. Examination elements will be graded in the order listed (not necessarily the same day completed), and an applicant may, without further application, be issued the class of license or permit for which he qualifies. A score of 75% is the passing grade for written examination elements.

Filing fees must accompany applications for radio operator licenses and permits. Fees must be paid by check or money order payable to the Federal Communications Commission. If an examination is to be taken at a place away from a field office, the application and fee should be filed, in advance, at the field office administering the examination.

Table 1-4. FCC Field Offices and Exam Schedules*.

FCC FIELD OFFICE	EXAMINATION SCHEDULE
ALABAMA, Mobile 439 Federal Building & U. S. Courthouse 113 St. Joseph Street Mobile, Alabama 36602 Phone: Area Code 205 690-2808	By appointment only. Call for an appointment Monday of the week of the examination.
ALASKA, Anchorage U. S. Post Office Building Room G63 4th & G Street, P. O. Box b44 Anchorage, Alaska 99510 Phone: Area Code 907 272-1822	Commercial Radiotelephone Examinations **Monday through Friday - 8:00 AM to 3:30 PM** Amateur Examinations **Requiring code - Monday through Friday by appointment only Not requiring code - Monday through Friday 8:00 AM to 3:30 PM**
CALIFORNIA, Los Angeles U. S. Courthouse, Room 1754 312 North Spring Street Los Angeles, California 90012 Phone: Area Code 213 688-3276	Commercial Radiotelephone Examinations **Tuesday and Thursday - 9:00 AM and 1:00 PM** Amateur Examinations **Wednesday - 9:00 AM and 1:00 PM**

* The FCC is currently conducting a temporary experiment to provide better service for exams. This schedule is provided in Appendix A.

Table 1-4. Con't.

FCC FIELD OFFICE	EXAMINATION SCHEDULE
CALIFORNIA, San Diego Fox Theatre Building 1245 Seventh Avenue San Diego, California 92101 Phone: Area Code 714 293-5460	Wednesday by appointment only. Appointment should be made one week in advance.
CALIFORNIA, San Francisco 323A Customhouse 555 Battery Street San Francisco, California 94111 Phone: Area Code 415 556-7700	Commercial Radiotelephone Examinations Monday and Tuesday - 8:00 AM Amateur Examinations Extra Class Friday 8:30 AM Others requiring code Friday 10:00 AM Code not required Friday 8:30 AM
COLORADO, Denver 504 U.S. Customhouse 19th St. between California & Stout Sts. Denver, Colorado 80202 Phone: Area Code 303 837-4054	Commercial Radiotelephone Examinations Tuesday and Thursday - 8:30 AM to 1:00 PM Amateur Examinations First and Second Wednesday of each month 8:30 AM
DISTRICT OF COLUMBIA WASHINGTON 1919 M Street N. W. Room 411 Washington, D. C. 20554 Phone: Area Code 202 632-7000	Commercial Radiotelephone Examinations Tuesday and Friday - 8:30 AM to 2:00 PM Amateur Examinations Friday - 9:00 AM and 10:30 AM
FLORIDA, Miami 919 Federal Building 51 S. W. First Avenue Miami, Florida 33130 Phone: Area Code 305 350-5541	Commercial Radiotelephone Examinations Tuesday and Wednesday - 8:00 AM to 1:00 PM Amateur Examinations Requiring code - Thursday - 9:00 AM Not requiring code - Tuesday and Wednesday 8:00 AM to 1:00 PM
FLORIDA, Tampa 738 Federal Building 500 Zack Street Tampa, Florida 33602 Phone: Area Code 813 228-2605	By appointment only. Appointment should be made one week in advance.
GEORGIA, Atlanta 1602 Gas Light Tower 235 Peachtree Street, N. E. Atlanta, Georgia 30303 Phone: Area Code 404 526-6381	Commercial Radiotelephone Examinations Tuesday and Friday - 8:30 AM to 12:00 Noon Amateur Examinations Requiring code - Friday - 8:30 AM Not requiring code - Tuesday and Friday 8:30 AM to 12:00 Noon.
GEORGIA, Savannah 238 Federal Office Bldg. and Courthouse Bull and State Streets P.O. Box 8004 Savannah, Georgia 31402 Phone: Area Code 912 232-4321 ext. 320	By appointment only. Appointment should be made one week in advance.
HAWAII, Honolulu 502 Federal Building P. O. Box 1021 Honolulu, Hawaii 96808 Phone: Area Code 808 546-5640	Commercial Radiotelephone Examinations Tuesday and Thursday - 8:00 AM Other times by appointment Amateur Examinations Wednesday - 8:00 AM Other times by appointment.

Table 1-4. Con't.

FCC FIELD OFFICE	EXAMINATION SCHEDULE
ILLINOIS, Chicago 3935 Federal Building 230 South Dearborn Street Chicago, Illinois 60604 Phone: Area Code 312 353-5386	Commercial Radiotelephone Examinations **Wednesday and Thursday - 8:45 AM and 1:00 PM** Amateur Examinations **Friday - 8:45 AM**
LOUISIANA, New Orleans 829 Federal Building South 600 South Street New Orleans, Louisiana 70130 Phone: Area Code 504 589-2094	Commercial Radiotelephone Examinations **Tuesday and Wednesday - 8:30 AM to 12:00 Noon** Amateur Examinations **Requiring code - Tuesday - 8:00 AM** **Not requiring code - Tuesday and Wednesday** **8:30 AM to 12:00 Noon**
MARYLAND, Baltimore George M. Fallon Federal Building Room 823 31 Hopkins Plaza Baltimore, Maryland 21201 Phone: Area Code 301 962-2727	Commercial Radiotelephone Examinations **Monday and Friday - 8:30 AM to 12:00 Noon** Amateur Examinations **Monday - 8:30 AM**
MASSACHUSETTS, Boston 1600 Customhouse India & State Streets Boston, Massachusetts 02109 Phone: Area Code: 617 223-6608	Commercial Radiotelephone Examinations **Tuesday and Wednesday - 9:00 AM to 11:00 AM** Amateur Examinations **Wednesday - 9:00 AM**
MICHIGAN, Detroit 1054 Federal Building 231 W. Lafayette Street Detroit, Michigan 48226 Phone: Area Code 313 226-6077	Commercial Radiotelephone Examinations **Tuesday and Thursday - 9:00 AM** Amateur Examinations **Friday - 9:00 AM**
MINNESOTA, St. Paul 691 Federal Building 316 N. Robert Street St. Paul, Minnesota 55101 Phone: Area Code 612 725-7819	Commercial Radiotelephone Examinations **Thursday - 8:45 AM** Amateur Examinations **Friday - 8:45 AM**
MISSOURI, Kansas City 1703 Federal Building 601 East 12th Street Kansas City, Missouri 64106 Phone: Area Code 816 374-5526	Commercial Radiotelephone Examinations **Wednesday and Thursday - 9:00 AM** Amateur Examinations **Thursday - 1:00 PM**
NEW YORK, Buffalo 1305 Federal Building 111 W. Huron Street at Delaware Ave. Buffalo, New York 14202 Phone: Area Code 716 842-3216	Commercial Radiotelephone Examinations **Thursday - 9:00 AM to 11:00 AM** Amateur Examinations **Friday - 9:00 AM** **Groups of eight or more, by appointment.**
NEW YORK, New York 748 Federal Building 641 Washington Street New York, New York 10014 Phone: Area Code 212 620-5746	Commercial Radiotelephone Examinations **Tuesday and Thursday - 9:00 AM to 12:00 Noon** Amateur Examinations **Wednesday - 9:00 AM**

Table 1-4. Con't.

FCC FIELD OFFICE	EXAMINATION SCHEDULE
OREGON, Portland 314 Multnomah Building 319 S. W. Pine Street Portland, Oregon 97204 Phone: Area Code 503 221-3097	Commercial Radiotelephone Examinations **Tuesday and Wednesday - 8:45 AM** Amateur Examinations **Friday - 8:45 AM**
PENNSYLVANIA. Philadelphia 1005 U. S. Customhouse 2nd & Chestnut Streets Philadelphia, Pennsylvania 19106 Phone: Area Code 215 597-4410	Commercial Radiotelephone Examinations **Monday, Tuesday, and Wednesday - 10:00 AM to** **12:00 Noon** Amateur Examinations **Requiring code - Tuesday and Wednesday** **8:00 AM to 9:00 AM** **Not requiring code - Monday, Tuesday, and** **Wednesday - 10:00 AM to 12:00 Noon**
PUERTO RICO, San Juan U. S. Post Office and Courthouse Room 323 P. O. Box 2987 San Juan, Puerto Rico 00903 Phone: Area Code 809 722-4562	Commercial Radiotelephone Examinations Thursday and Friday - 8:30 AM (or 1:00 PM by appointment only). Amateur Examinations **Requiring Code - Friday - 10:00 AM** **Not Requiring code - Thursday and Friday** **8:30 AM (or 1:00 PM** **by appointment only).**
TEXAS, Beaumont Room 323 Federal Building 300 Willow Street Beaumont, Texas 77701 Phone: Area Code 713 838-0271	By appointment only. Appointment should be made one week in advance.
TEXAS, Dallas Federal Building - U.S. Courthouse Room 13E7, 1100 Commerce Street Dallas, Texas 75202 Phone: Area Code 214 749-3243	Commercial Radiotelephone Examinations **Tuesday and Thursday - 8:00 AM to 11:00 AM** Amateur Examinations **Tuesday - 9:00 AM**
TEXAS, Houston 5636 Federal Building 515 Rusk Avenue Houston, Texas 77002 Phone: Area Code 713 226-4306	Commercial Radiotelephone Examinations **Thursday - 10:00 AM to 12:00 Noon** **Friday - 8:00 AM to 12:00 Noon** Amateur Examinations **Requiring code - Thursday - 9:00 AM** **Not requiring code - Friday - 8:00 AM to** **12:00 Noon**
VIRGINIA, Norfolk Military Circle 870 North Military Highway Norfolk, Virginia 23502 Phone: Area Code 804 420-5100	Commercial Radiotelephone Examinations **Wednesday and Friday - 9:00 AM to 12:00** **Noon** Amateur Examinations **Thursday - 9:00 AM**
WASHINGTON, Seattle 8012 Federal Office Building 909 First Avenue Seattle, Washington 98174 Phone: Area Code 206 442-7653	Commercial Radiotelephone Examinations **Tuesday and Wednesday - 8:00 AM to 11:00 AM** Amateur Examinations **Friday - 8:45 AM**

Table. 1-5. Exam Points and Administering Schedule.

STATE	CITY	MONTH IN WHICH EXAMINATION ADMINISTERED	FCC OFFICE ADMINISTERING EXAMINATION
ALABAMA	Birmingham	MAR, SEP	Atlanta, Georgia
	Montgomery	JUN, DEC	,, ,,
*ALASKA	Adak	JAN, JUL	Anchorage, Alaska
	Fairbanks	JAN, APR, JUL, OCT	,, ,,
	Juneau	JAN, JUL	,, ,,
	Ketchikan	FEB, AUG	,, ,,
	Kodiak	MAR, SEP	,, ,,
	Nome	FEB, AUG	,, ,,
	Seward	JUN, DEC	,, ,,
	Sitka	APR, OCT	,, ,,
ARIZONA	Phoenix	JAN, APR, JUL, OCT	Los Angeles, California
	Tucson	APR, OCT	,, ,,
ARKANSAS	Little Rock	FEB, MAY, AUG, NOV	New Orleans, Louisiana
CALIFORNIA	Bakersfield	MAY	Los Angeles, California
	Fresno	MAR, JUN, SEP, DEC	San Francisco, California
CONNECTICUT	Hartford	JAN, APR, JUL, OCT	Boston, Massachusetts
FLORIDA	Jacksonville	APR, OCT	Miami, Florida
GEORGIA	Albany	FEB, AUG	Atlanta, Georgia

* See Appendix

18

			Honolulu, Hawaii
*GUAM	Agana	FEB, MAY, AUG, NOV	Honolulu, Hawaii
*HAWAII	Hilo	JAN, APR, JUL, OCT	'' ''
	Kaunakakai	FEB, MAY, AUG, NOV	'' ''
	Lihue	JAN, APR, JUL, OCT	'' ''
	Wailuku	MAR, JUN, SEP, DEC	'' ''
*IDAHO	Boise	APR, OCT	Portland, Oregon
	Lewiston	MAR, JUN, SEP, DEC	Seattle, Washington
*ILLINOIS	Decatur	JAN, APR, JUL, OCT	Chicago, Illinois
	Rock Island	EVERY MONTH	'' ''
*INDIANA	Evansville	MAR, JUN, SEP, DEC	Chicago, Illinois
	Fort Wayne	EVERY MONTH	'' ''
	Indianapolis	'' ''	'' ''
IOWA	Des Moines	MAR, JUN, SEP, DEC	Kansas City, Missouri
KANSAS	Wichita	MAR, SEP	Kansas City, Missouri
*KENTUCKY	Ashland	MAR, JUN, SEP, DEC	Detroit, Michigan
	Frankfort	FEB, AUG	'' ''
	Harlan	MAY, NOV	'' ''
	Hazard	FEB, AUG	'' ''
	Lexington	EVERY MONTH	'' ''
	London	MAR, SEP	'' ''
	Louisville	EVERY MONTH	Chicago, Illinois
	Maysville	JAN, APR, JUL, OCT	Detroit, Michigan

19

STATE	CITY	MONTH IN WHICH EXAMINATION ADMINISTERED	FCC OFFICE ADMINISTERING EXAMINATION
*Kentucky - Cont.			
	Pikeville	APR, OCT	Detroit, Michigan
	Richmond	JUN, DEC	" "
	Somerset	JAN, JUL	" "
MAINE	Bangor	MAY, NOV	Boston, Massachusetts
	Portland	APR, OCT	" "
*MICHIGAN	Adrian	JAN, APR, JUL, OCT	Detroit, Michigan
	Alpena	JAN, JUL	" "
	Ann Arbor	MAR, JUN, SEP, DEC	" "
	Battle Creek	JAN, APR, JUL, OCT	" "
	Bay City	FEB, MAY, AUG, NOV	" "
	Benton Harbor	FEB, MAY, AUG, NOV	" "
	Big Rapids	JAN, JUL	" "
	East Tawas	MAR, SEP	" "
	Flint	EVERY MONTH	" "
	Grand Rapids	EVERY MONTH	" "
	Jackson	FEB, MAY, AUG, NOV	" "
	Kalamazoo	EVERY MONTH	" "
	Lansing	EVERY MONTH	" "
	Manistee	MAR, SEP	" "
	Marquette	MAY	St. Paul, Minnesota
	Muskegon	FEB, MAY, AUG, NOV	Detroit, Michigan
	Petoskey	FEB, AUG	" "
	Pontiac	EVERY MONTH	" "
	Port Huron	MAR, JUN, SEP, DEC	" "

State	City	Months	Location
	Saginaw	MAR, JUN, SEP, DEC	,, ,,
	Traverse City	JAN, APR, JUL, OCT	,, ,,
MISSISSIPPI	Jackson	JUN, DEC	New Orleans, Louisiana
MISSOURI	St. Louis	FEB, MAY, AUG, NOV	Kansas City, Missouri
*MONTANA	Billings	FEB, MAY, AUG, NOV	Seattle, Washington
	Glasgow	MAR, SEP	,, ,,
	Havre	JAN, JUL	,, ,,
	Helena	MAR, JUN, SEP, DEC	,, ,,
	Kalispell	FEB, AUG	,, ,,
	Miles City	APR, OCT	,, ,,
	Missoula	JAN, APR, JUL, OCT	,, ,,
NEBRASKA	Omaha	JAN, APR, JUL, OCT	Kansas City, Missouri
NEVADA	Las Vegas	JAN, JUL	Los Angeles, California
	Reno	APR, OCT	San Francisco, California
NEW MEXICO	Albuquerque	APR, OCT	Denver, Colorado
NEW YORK	Albany	MAR, JUN, SEP, DEC	New York, New York
	Syracuse	JAN, APR, JUL, OCT	Buffalo, New York
NORTH CAROLINA	Wilmington	JUN, DEC	Norfolk, Virginia
	Winston-Salem	FEB, MAY, AUG, NOV	,, ,,

STATE	CITY	MONTH IN WHICH EXAMINATION ADMINISTERED	FCC OFFICE ADMINISTERING EXAMINATION
NORTH DAKOTA	Jamestown	OCT	St. Paul, Minnesota
*OHIO	Akron	EVERY MONTH	Detroit Michigan
	Ashtabula	JAN, APR, JUL, OCT	,,
	Athens	MAY, NOV	,,
	Canton	EVERY MONTH	,,
	Chillicothe	MAR, JUN, SEP, DEC	,,
	Cincinnati	EVERY MONTH	,,
	Cleveland	,, ,,	,,
	Columbus	,, ,,	,,
	Dayton	,, ,,	,,
	Elyria	FEB, MAY, AUG, NOV	,,
	Findlay	,, ,, ,, ,,	,,
	Greenville	,, ,, ,,	,,
	Hamilton	MAR, JUN, SEP, DEC	,,
	Lima	JAN, APR, JUL OCT	,,
	Mansfield	,, ,, ,,	,,
	Marietta	MAR, JUN, SEP, DEC	,,
	Marion	,, ,, ,,	,,
	Napoleon	JUN, DEC	,,
	Newark	MAR, JUN, SEP, DEC	,,
	Painesville	MAY, NOV	,,
	Portsmouth	FEB, MAY, AUG, NOV	,,
	Sandusky	JAN, APR, JUL, OCT	,,
	Springfield	MAR, JUN, SEP, DEC	,,
	Steubenville	MAR, JUN, SEP, DEC	,,

STATE	City	EVERY MONTH	
	Toledo	" "	" "
	Youngstown	," ,"	" "
	Zanesville	JAN, APR, JUL, OCT	" "
OKLAHOMA	Oklahoma City	JAN, APR, JUL, OCT	Dallas, Texas
	Tulsa	FEB, MAY, AUG, NOV	" "
OREGON	Klamath Falls	MAY	Portland, Oregon
PENNSYLVANIA	Pittsburgh	FEB, MAY, AUG, NOV	Buffalo, New York
	Williamsport	MAR, SEP	" "
SOUTH CAROLINA	Columbia	MAY, NOV	Atlanta, Georgia
SOUTH DAKOTA	Rapid City	MAY	Denver, Colorado
	Sioux Falls	MAR, JUN, SEP, DEC	St. Paul, Minnesota
TEXAS	Corpus Christi	JUN, DEC	Houston, Texas
	El Paso	," ,"	Dallas, Texas
	Lubbock	MAR, SEP	" "
	San Antonio	FEB, MAY, AUG, NOV	Houston, Texas
TENNESSEE	Knoxville	MAR, JUN, SEP, DEC	Atlanta, Georgia
	Memphis	JAN, APR, JUL, OCT	" "
	Nashville	FEB, MAY, AUG, NOV	" "
UTAH	Salt Lake City	MAR, JUN, SEP, DEC	Denver, Colorado
VIRGINIA	Salem	APR, OCT	Norfolk, Virginia

STATE	CITY	MONTH IN WHICH EXAMINATION ADMINISTERED	FCC OFFICE ADMINISTERING EXAMINATION
*WASHINGTON	Bellingham	JAN, APR, JUL, OCT	Seattle, Washington
	Olympia	FEB, MAY, AUG, NOV	" "
	Spokane	EVERY MONTH	" "
	Wenatchee	MAR, JUN, SEP, DEC	" "
	Yakima	JAN, APR, JUL, OCT	" "
*WEST VIRGINIA	Beckley	JAN, APR, JUL, OCT	Detroit, Michigan
	Bluefield	MAR, JUN, SEP, DEC	" "
	Charleston	EVERY MONTH	" "
	Huntington	" "	" "
	Lewisburg	JUN, DEC	" "
	Parkersburg	JAN, APR, JUL, OCT	" "
	Wheeling	EVERY MONTH	" "
	Williamson	JUN, DEC	" "
*WISCONSIN	Madison	MAR, JUN, SEP, DEC	Chicago, Illinois
	Milwaukee	EVERY MONTH	" "

VERIFICATION OF LICENSE HOLDING

Operators holding a radio operator license of the diploma form (other than restricted radiotelephone operator permit) may obtain a *verification card*, FCC Form 758-F, attesting to license holding. Verification cards may be carried on the person of the operator in lieu of the license when operating a station at which the posting of an operator license is not required. When such verification cards are used, the original license or permit must be readily accessible for inspection by an authorized government representative.

If an operator is required to post his license at more than one station, he may post the original at one station and post *verified statements*, FCC Form 759, at the other stations.

Verification cards or verified statements may be obtained by filing a properly completed application Form 756. The license or permit must accompany the request for verification. In lieu of the license or permit the operator must exhibit a signed copy of the application that has been submitted by him until action is taken on the request.

RENEWALS, DUPLICATES, AND REPLACEMENTS

An operator whose license or permit of the diploma form (other than restricted radiotelephone operator permits) has been lost, mutilated, or destroyed, must immediately notify the Commission. An application Form 756 for a duplicate may be submitted to the *office issuing the original license or permit*. A replacement restricted radiotelephone operator permit may be requested by filing application Form 753 and the required fee with the Gettysburg, Pa. office.

The holder of any license or permit whose name is legally changed may make application for a replacement document to indicate the new legal name by submitting a properly completed application and the required fee to the office of original issue, accompanied by the license or permit affected.

Licenses are normally renewable at any time within the last year of the license term or within one year after the date of expiration. During this grace period, an expired license is not valid. It is not necessary to show service under a license to be renewed. Renewal applications, when accompanied by the expiring license, should be filed at the nearest district office. If the expiring license has been lost, destroyed, or mutilated, the application should be filed at the office which issued the original document. Applications may be made by mail, using FCC Form 756.

When a duplicate or replacement operator license or permit has been requested or a request has been made for renewal or endorsement, in lieu of the license or permit the operator must exhibit a signed copy of the application which has been submitted by him.

OPERATOR PRIVILEGES

All licenses and permits other than amateur are considered to be *commercial* licenses and permits. Radio operator license requirements are usually governed by the type of emission involved and whether the operator's duties include making adjustments to transmitters.

The Commission does not issue licenses for radio engineers, television engineers, television cameramen, radio mechanics, radio announcers, or studio console operators. Persons who are employed at these jobs are required to hold operator licenses only if their duties include the operation of radio-frequency transmitting equipment.

Restricted radiotelephone operator permits are normally issued for the lifetime of the holder. Commercial operator licenses and permits of other classes are normally issued for a term of 5 years.

The minimum requirement of a person wishing to obtain employment as an operator at a standard AM or FM broadcast station is a radiotelephone Third Class operator permit with the basic broadcast endorsement (examination elements 1,2, and 9). A nonrenewable *provisional radio operator certificate*, which carries all the authority now embraced by a Third Class operator permit endorsed for broadcast use, may be obtained by mail without examination. The holder is expected to fulfill the examination requirements within the one-year term of the certificate. Application may be made on FCC Form 756-C.

Holders of restricted radiotelephone operator and Third Class operator permits are, in general, prohibited from making adjustments that may result in improper transmitter operation. The FCC Rules require that equipment operated by holders of these operator permits shall be so designed that none of the operations performed during the normal course of service may cause off-frequency operation or any unauthorized radiation. Any needed adjustments to transmitters operated by holders of the *restricted* and Third Class operator permits should be made by or in the presence of the holder of the proper higher class license.

In general, anyone wishing to obtain employment as an operator at a ship radiotelegraph station should hold a radiotelegraph First or Second Class operator license.

Restricted radiotelephone operator permits are valid for the normal operation of radiotelephone equipment installed in most aircraft, at certain ground stations, and on most boats where radio equipment is not mandatory.

The class of commercial radio operator license that is normally required as sufficient authority to install, service, and maintain radiotelephone transmitting equipment on board aircraft and small boats and most radio transmitting equipment in the land-mobile services is the *radiotelephone Second Class operator license*.

EMPLOYMENT

Persons interested in securing information regarding employment with agencies of the federal government should communicate with the Civil Service Commission, Washington, D.C. 20415. In most instances, government radio stations are not required to employ licensed radio operators. With respect to employment in privately owned radio stations, the FCC requires only that properly licensed operators be on duty in accordance with its rules. This does not preclude an employer from establishing additional qualifications if he so desires. Employment at such stations is a matter of agreement between the prospective employee and employer.

Basic Law and Operating Practices (Elements 1 & 2)

Elements 1 and 2 of the FCC commercial radiotelephone examination must be successfully completed before issuance of a Third Class operator permit. Each of these elements consists of 20 questions. Each element is graded separately, with a score of 75% required for passing.

ELEMENT 1: BASIC LAW

The following 20 questions are representative of those you will be asked in the Element 1 examination.

2-1. Where and how are FCC licenses and permits obtained?

Applications shall be governed by applicable rules in force on the date when application is filed. The application in the prescribed form and including all required subsidiary forms and documents—properly completed and signed and accompanied by the prescribed fee—shall be submitted to the appropriate office (see Section 1). If the application is for renewal of a license, it may be filed at any time during the final year of the license term or during a one-year period of grace after the date of expiration. During this period, of course, the expired license is not valid. A renewed license issued upon the basis of an application filed during the grace period will be dated currently and will not be backdated to the date of expiration of the original license. A renewal application must be accompanied by the license to be renewed.

2-2. When a licensee qualifies for a higher grade of FCC license or permit, what happens to the lesser grade license?

If the holder of a license qualifies for a higher class in the same group, the license held will be canceled upon the issuance of the new license Similarly, if the holder of a restricted operator permit qualifies for a First or Second Class operator license of the corresponding type, the permit held will be canceled upon issuance of the new license.

2-3. Who may apply for an FCC license?

Commercial licenses are issued only to citizens and other nationals of the United States except, in the case of aliens who hold aircraft pilot certificates issued by the Federal Aviation Administration, the Commission may waive the requirement of United States nationality.

If a license or permit is lost, what action must be taken by the operator?

An operator whose license or permit has been lost, mutilated, or destroyed shall immediately notify the Commission. If the authorization is of the diploma form, a properly executed application for duplicate should be submitted to the office of issue. If the authorization is of the card form (restricted radiotelephone operator permit), a properly executed application for replacement should be submitted to the Federal Communications Commission. Gettysburg. Pa. 17325. In either case the application shall embody a statement of the circumstances involved in the loss, mutilation, or destruction of the original. If the authorization has been lost, the applicant must state that reasonable search has been made for it and, further, that in the event it is found, either the original or the duplicate (or replacement) will be returned for cancellation. If the authorization is of the diploma form, the applicant should also submit documentary evidence of the service that has been obtained under the original authorization or a statement embodying that information.

2-5. **What is the usual license term for radio operators?**

Commercial operator licenses are normally issued for a term of 5 years from the date of issuance.

2-6. **What government agency inspects radio stations in the U.S.?**

The Federal Communications Commission has the authority to inspect all radio installations associated with stations required to be licensed by any federal law or which are subject to the provisions of any treaty or convention binding on the United States. The commission may ascertain whether in construction, installation, and operation they conform to the requirements of the Rules and Regulations of the Commission. the provisions of any law, or the terms of any treaty or convention.

2-7. **When may a license be renewed?**

An application for renewal of license may be filed at any time during the final year of the license term or during a one-year period of grace after the date of expiration of the license sought to be renewed.

2-8. **Who keeps the station logs?**

The licensee or permittee of each standard broadcast station shall maintain *program* and *operating* logs as set forth in Sections 73.112 and 73.113 of the rules. Each log shall be kept by the station employee or contract operator competent to do so and having actual knowledge of the facts required, who, in the case of program and operating logs, shall sign the appropriate log when starting duty and again when going off duty.

2-9. **Who corrects errors in the station logs?**

The corrections should be made by the station employee or contract operator competent to do so and having actual knowledge of the facts required. Where—in any program log. preprinted program log. or program schedule which upon completion is used as a program log—a correction is made before the person keeping the log has gone off duty. such correction (no matter by whom made) shall be initialed by the person keeping the log prior to his signing of the log when going off duty. If corrections or additions are made on the log after it has been so signed, explanation must be made on the log or an attachment to it. dated and signed by either the person who kept the log, the station program director or manager, or an officer of the licensee.

2-10. In general, how are station logs kept and corrected?

The logs shall be kept in an orderly and legible manner, in suitable form, and in such detail that the data required for the particular class of station concerned is readily available. Key letters or abbreviations may be used if proper meaning or explanation is contained elsewhere in the log. Each sheet shall be numbered and dated. Time entries shall be either in local standard or daylight saving time and shall be indicated accordingly. No log or preprinted log or schedule which becomes a log, or portion thereof, shall be erased, obliterated, or willfully destroyed within the period of retention provided by the provisions of the rules. Any necessary correction shall be made only pursuant to Sections 73.112 and 73.113, only by striking out the erroneous portion or by making a corrective explanation on the log or attachment to it as provided in those sections. Additional information, such as that needed for billing purposes or the cuing of automatic equipment, may be entered on the logs. Such additional information is not subject to the restrictions and limitations on the making of corrections and changes in logs.

2-11. Under what conditions may broadcasts be rebroadcast?

No broadcasting station shall rebroadcast the program or any part thereof of another broadcasting station without the express authority of the originating station.

2-12. What messages and signals may not be transmitted?

No licensed radio operator shall transmit: unnecessary, unidentified, or superfluous radio communications or signals; communications containing obscene, indecent, or profane words, language, or meaning; or false or deceptive signals or communications by radio, or any call letter or signal which has not been assigned by proper authority to the radio station he is operating.

2-13. May an operator ever deliberately interfere with any radio communication or signal?

Of course not. The rules say: "No licensed radio operator shall willfully or maliciously interfere with or cause interference to any radio communication or signal."

2-14. What type of communication has top priority in the mobile service?

The order of priority for communications in the mobile service:

1. Distress calls, distress messages, and distress traffic.
2. Communications preceded by the urgency signal.
3. Communications preceded by the safety signal.
4. Communications relating to radio direction finding.
5. Communications relating to the navigation and safe movement of aircraft.
6. Communications relating to the navigation, movements, and needs of ships, and weather observation messages destined for an official meteorological service.
7. Government radiotelegrams: Priorite Nations.
8. Government communications for which priority has been requested.
9. Service communications relating to the wording of the radiocommunications previously exchanged.
10. Government communications other than those shown in 7 and 8 above, and all other communications.

2-15. What are the grounds for suspension of operator licenses?

The FCC may suspend the license of any operator upon proof sufficient to satisfy the Commission that the licensee

1. has violated any provision of any act, treaty, or convention binding on the United States which the Commission is authorized to administer or any regulation made by the Commission under any such act, treaty, or convention; or
2. has failed to carry out a lawful order of the master or person lawfully in charge of the ship or aircraft on which he is employed; or
3. has willfully damaged or permitted radio apparatus or installations to be damaged; or
4. has transmitted superfluous radio communications or signals or communications containing profane or obscene words, language, or meaning, or has knowingly transmitted
   (a) false or deceptive signals or communications or
   (b) a call signal or letter which has not been assigned by proper authority to the station he is operating; or
5. has willfully or maliciously interfered with any other radio communications or signals; or
6. has obtained or attempted to obtain, or has assisted another to obtain or attempt to obtain an operator's license by fraudulent means.

2-16. When may an operator divulge the contents of an intercepted message?

No person receiving or assisting in receiving, or transmitting or assisting in transmitting any interstate or foreign communication by wire or radio shall divulge or publish the existence, contents, substance, purport, effect, or meaning thereof, except through authorized channels of transmission or reception, to any person other than: the addressee, his agent, or attorney; a person employed or authorized to forward such communication to its destination; proper accounting or distributing officers of the various communicating centers over which the communication may be passed; the master of a ship under whom he is serving, a court of competent jurisdiction in response to a subpoena or, on demand, other lawful authority. No person not being authorized by the sender shall intercept any communication and divulge or publish the existence, contents, substance, purport, effect, or meaning of such intercepted communication to any person; no person not being entitled thereto shall receive or assist in receiving any interstate or foreign communication by wire or radio and use the same or any information therein contained for his own benefit or for the benefit of another not entitled thereto; and no person having received such intercepted communication, knowing that such information was so obtained, shall divulge or publish the same or any part thereof, or use the same or any information therein contained for his own benefit or for the benefit of another not entitled thereto. This prohibition shall not apply to the receiving, divulging, publishing, or utilizing the contents of any radio communication broadcast or transmitted by amateurs or others for the use of the general public or relating to ships in distress.

2-17. If a licensee is notified that he has violated an FCC Rule or provision of the Communications Act of 1934, what must he do?

Except in cases of willfulness or those in which public health, interest, or safety requires otherwise, any licensee who appears to have violated any provision of the Communications Act of 1934 or the rules will—before revocation, suspension, or cease-and-desist proceedings are instituted—be served with a written notice calling these facts to his attention and requesting a statement concerning the matter. FCC Form 793 may be used for this purpose.

Within 10 days from receipt of notice or such other period as may be specified, the licensee shall send a written answer, in duplicate, direct to the office of the Commission originating the official notice. If an answer cannot be sent nor an acknowledgment made within such 10-day period by reason of illness or other unavoidable circumstances, acknowledgment and answer shall be made at the earliest practicable date with a satisfactory explanation of the delay.

The answer to each notice shall be complete in itself and shall not be abbreviated by reference to other communications or answers to other notices. In every instance the answer shall contain a statement of action taken to correct the condition or omission complained of and to preclude its recurrence. In addition:

1. If the notice relates to violations that may be due to the physical or electrical characteristics of transmitting apparatus and any new apparatus is to be installed, the answer shall state the date such apparatus was ordered, the name of the manufacturer, and the promised date of delivery. If the installation of such apparatus requires a construction permit, the file number of the application shall be given, or if a file number has not been assigned by the Commission, such identification shall be given as will permit ready identification of the application.

2. If the notice of violation relates to lack of attention to or improper operation of the transmitter, the name and license number of the operator in charge shall be given.

2-18. *If a licensee receives a notice of suspension of his license, what must he do?*

Whenever grounds exist for suspension of an operator license, the Chief of the Field Engineering Bureau may issue an order suspending the operator license. No order of suspension of any operator's license shall take effect until 15 days' notice in writing of the cause for the proposed suspension has been given to the operator licensee, who may make written application to the Commission at any time within the 15 days for a hearing upon such order. The notice to the operator licensee shall not be effective until actually received by him, and from that time he shall have 15 days in which to mail the application. In the event that physical conditions prevent mailing of the application before the expiration of the 15-day period, the application shall then be mailed as soon as possible thereafter, accompanied by a satisfactory explanation of the delay. Upon receipt by the Commission of such application for hearing, the order of suspension shall be designated for hearing by the Chief, Field Engineering Bureau, and the order of suspension shall be held in abeyance until the conclusion of the hearing. Upon the conclusion of the hearing, the Commission may affirm, modify, or revoke the order of suspension. If the license is ordered suspended, the operator shall send his operator license to the office of the Commission in Washington, D.C., on or before the effective date of the order, or if the effective date has passed at the time notice is received, the license shall be sent to the Commission forthwith.

2-19. *What are the penalties provided for violating a provision of the Communications Act of 1934 or a Rule of the FCC?*

Under the Communications Act of 1934, permits any person who willfully and knowingly does or causes or to be done any act, matter, or thing in this Act prohibited or declared to be unlawful; or who willfully and knowingly causes or permits such omission or failure, shall, upon conviction thereof, be punished for such offense (for which no penalty other than a forfeiture is provided in this Act) by a fine of not more than $10,000 or by imprisonment for a term not exceeding one year, or both. Any person, having been once convicted of an offense punishable under this section, who is subsequently convicted of violating any provision of this Act punishable under this section, shall be punished by a fine of not more than $10,000 or by imprisonment for a term not exceeding 2 years, or both.

Any person who willfully and knowingly violates any rule, regulation, restriction, or condition made or imposed by the Commission under authority of this Act; or any rule, regulation, restriction, or condition made or imposed by any international radio or wire communications treaty or convention, or regulations annexed thereto, to which the United States is or may hereafter become a party; shall (in addition to any other penalties provided by law) be punished, upon conviction thereof, by a fine of not more than $500 for each everv day during which the offense occurs.

2-20. *Define "harmful interference."*

Harmful interference: Any emission, radiation, or induction which endangers the functioning of a radionavigation service or of other safety services or seriously degrades, obstructs or repeatedly interrupts a radio communication service operating in accordance with FCC Regulations.

ELEMENT 2: OPERATING PRACTICE

A licensed radio operator should remember that the station he desires to operate should be licensed by the Federal Communications Commission. To prevent interference and give others an opportunity to use the airways, he should avoid unnecessary calls and communications. He should remember that radio signals normally travel outward from the transmitting station in many directions and can be intercepted by unauthorized persons.

2-21. *What should an operator do when he leaves a transmitter unattended?*

While a radio transmitter is in a public place it should at all times be either attended by or supervised by a licensed operator, or the transmitter should be made inaccessible to unauthorized persons.

2-22. *What are the meanings of: Clear, Out, Over, Roger, Words Twice, Repeat, and Break?*

Some radio-operating companies, services, networks, associations, etc. select and adopt standard procedure words and phrases for expediting and clarifying radiotelephone conversations. For example, in some services, "Roger" means "I have received all of your last transmission"; "Wilco" means "Your last message received, understood, and will be complied with"; "Out" or "Clear" means "This conversation is ended, and no response is expected"· "Over" means "My transmission is ended, and I expect a response from you. "Speak slower" and "Say again' are radio phrases whose meanings are obvious.

2-23. *How should a microphone be used?*

A radiotelephone operator should make an effort to train his voice for most effective radio communication. His voice should be loud enough to be distinctly heard by the receiving operator; but it should not be too loud, since it may become distorted and difficult to understand at the receiving station. He should articulate his words and avoid speaking in a monotone. The working distance of the transmitter is affected to some extent by the loudness of the speaker's voice. If the voice is too low, the maximum range cannot be attained; and if the voice is too loud, the distance range may be reduced to zero by the signals becoming distorted beyond intelligibility. In noisy locations the operator sometimes cups his hands over the microphone to exclude extraneous noise. Normally, the microphone is held from 2 to 6 in. from the operator's lips.

2-24. *Why should radio transmitters be off when signals are not being transmitted?*

A radio transmitter should not be on the air except when signals are being transmitted. The operator of a radiotelephone station should not press the push-to-talk button except when he intends to speak into the microphone. Radiation from a transmitter may cause interference even when voice is not transmitted.

2-25 *Why should an operator use well known words and phrases?*

It is important in radiotelephone communications that operators use familiar and well known words and phrases to issure accuracy and save time from undue repetition of words.

2-26. *How is the station's callsign transmitted?*

In making a call by radio the callsign or name of the called station is generally given three times, followed by the call letters of the calling station given three times.

2-27. *Where does an operator find specifications for obstruction marking and lighting (where required) for the antenna towers of a particular radio station?*

If an operator wishes to determine the specifications for obstruction marking and lighting of antenna towers, he should look in Part 17 of the Rules and Regulations of the FCC. If he wishes to determine the specifications for a particular station, he should examine the station authorization issued by the Commission.

2-28. *What should an operator do if the station he is calling does not answer within a reasonable length of time?*

When radio communications at a station are made unreliable or disrupted by static or fading, it is not a good practice for the operator to continuously call other stations in attempting to make contact, because his calls may cause interference to stations that are not experiencing static or fading.

2-29. *When may an operator use his station without regard to certain provisions of his station license?*

The licensee of any station (except amateur, standard broadcast, FM broadcast, noncommercial educational FM broadcast, or television broadcast) may, during a period of emergency in which normal communication facilities are disrupted as a result of hurricane, flood, earthquake, or similar disaster, utilize such station for emergency communication service in communicating in a manner other than that specified in the instrument of authorization, provided: that as soon as possible after the beginning of such emergency use notice be sent to the Commission at Washington, D.C., and to the engineer in charge of the district in which the station is located, stating the nature of the emergency and the use to which the station is being put (2) that the emergency use of station shall be discontinued as soon as substantially normal communication facilities are again available, (3) that the Commission at Washington, D.C., and the engineer in charge shall be notified immediately when such special use of the station in terminated, (4) that in no event shall any station engage in emergency transmission on frequencies other than, or with power in excess of, that specified in the instrument of authorization or as otherwise expressly provided by the Commission or by law, (5) that any emergency communication undertaken under this section shall terminate upon order of the Commission. Further information regarding operation of broadcast stations during periods of emergency is found in Part 73 of the Rules.

2-30. *Who bears the responsibility if an operator permits an unlicensed person to speak over his station?*

When a licensed operator in charge of a radiotelephone station permits another person to use the microphone and talk over the facilities of the station, he should remember that he continues to bear responsibility for the proper operation of the station.

2-31. *What is meant by a "phonetic alphabet" in radiotelephone communications?*

Often in radio telephone communications, a *phonetic alphabet* or word list is useful in identifying letters or words that may sound like other letters or words. For example. *group* may sound like *scoop* or *bridge* may sound like *ridge*. A phonetic alphabet or word list consists of a list of 26 words, each word beginning with a different letter for identifying that particular letter. If the letters in *group* are represented in a phonetic alphabet by George, Roger, Oboe, Uncle, and Peter; the word *group* is transmitted as "*Group*: *G* as in *George*, *r* as in *Roger*, *o* as in *Oboe*, *u* as in *Uncle*, *p* as in *Peter*.

2-32. *How does the licensed operator normally exhibit his authority to operate the station?*

An operator normally exhibits his authority to operate a station by posting a valid operator license or permit at the transmitter control point.

2-33. *What precautions should be observed in testing a station on the air?*

If a radio station is used for occasional calls, it is a good practice to test the station regularly. Regular tests may reveal defects or faults which, if corrected immediately, may prevent delays when communications are necessary. Technical repairs or adjustments to radiotelephone communication stations are made only by or under the immediate supervision and responsibility of operators holding First or Second Class licenses.

Broadcast Endorsement for Third Class Operator License (Element 9)

Recent changes in the Rules have affected the duties of broadcast operators. This section contains information on changes that apply to the Third Class radiotelephone permit endorsed for broadcast station operation. It provides the answers to the Commission's list of study question related to this endorsement. This information is actually excerpted and paraphrased from the Rules and Regulations. It may be used as a general guide; however, the material herein—even though provided by the FCC—cannot be deemed as substituting for the Rules themselves. Examination questions and inquiries made during station inspections will be based on current rules and regulations and practical operating procedures that would be followed by an operator at a broadcast station. This study guide may be used to prepare for examinations, but it should be remembered that questions in the study guide are only indicative of the general areas covered. Specific examination questions and very recent rule changes are not included. Most or all of the terms used in the following discussion should be familiar to you. Terms that may need clarification are covered in the questions and answers that follow the discussion.

LICENSE REQUIRED

Except for a very limited number of standard broadcast stations using critical directional antenna arrays, licensees of AM and FM broadcast stations may employ Third Class operators for routine station operation. If a station licensee elects to use Third Class operators, however, he is subject to additional requirements. For this reason some stations may not want to employ Third Class operators but may continue to employ First Class operators.

EQUIPMENT ADJUSTMENTS

Transmitter operators are responsible for proper operation of the equipment. A First Class operator may repair a transmitter, maintain it, and make major adjustments. A Third Class operator may only make minor adjustments. At AM and FM broadcast stations, a Third Class operator may make adjustments only of external controls necessary to turn the transmitter on and off, to compensate for voltage fluctuations in the primary power supply, and to maintain modulation levels of the transmitter within prescribed limits.

Third Class operators at AM standard broadcast stations may also make adjustments of external controls necessary to carry out routine changes in operating power required by the station authorization and to change between nondirectional and directional or between differing radiation patterns, provided that such changes require only activation of switches and do not involve the manual tuning of the transmitter final amplifier or antenna phasor equipment. The switching equipment shall be so arranged that the failure of any relay in the directional antenna system to activate properly will cause the emissions of the station to terminate.

NORMAL OPERATING POSITION

The normal operating position is to be located so that the transmitter, required monitors, and other required metering equipment are readily accessible and sufficiently close to the operator so that deviation from normal indications of required instruments can be observed in a 360° arc. However, if operation by remote control is authorized, the normal operating position must be placed so that the required instruments *and controls* are readily accessible and located sufficiently close to the operator so that deviations from normal indications of required instruments can be observed in a 360° arc.

OPERATING POWER

Each AM and FM broadcast station is authorized to operate at a specified power level. Operating power must be maintained as near as practicable to this specified power and shall not be more than 105% nor less than 90% of this level. Noncommercial educational FM broadcast stations licensed to operate with transmitter output power of 10W or less may be operated at less than authorized power but with not more than 105% of the authorized power.

At AM broadcast stations power determined by the *direct* method is equal to the product of the antenna resistance and the square of the antenna current. Directional AM stations employ multiple towers. For these stations power (direct method) is equal to the product of the resistance common to all towers (called *common-point resistance*) and the square of the *common-point current* (current common to all towers). Remember the equation—I^2R! At FM broadcast stations power determined by the *direct* method is read directly from the transmission line meter, which must be calibrated twice a year.

Generally, AM broadcast stations must determine the operating power by the direct method. FM broadcast stations may determine the operating power by either method, but most use the indirect method.

For both AM and FM broadcast stations, operating power determined by the *indirect* method is equal to the product of the plate voltage (E_P); the plate current (I_P) of the last radio stage, and an efficiency factor (F):

$$\text{Operating power} = E_P \times I_P \times F$$

When the power of an AM station is determined by the *indirect* method, the calculated value is to be entered in the operating log when required transmitter meter readings are taken.

MODULATION

The percentage of modulation at AM and FM broadcast stations should be maintained at as high a level as possible consistent with good-quality transmission. Generally, the modulation should not be less than 85% on peaks of frequent recurrence. However, it may be less than 85% when necessary to avoid objectionable loudness. At AM standard broadcast stations modulation must not exceed 100% on negative peaks and 125% on any positive peak. At FM broadcast stations modulation must not exceed 100% on either positive or negative peaks.

Each station must have in operation a modulation monitor which the operator uses to determine whether the modulation is at the proper level. This device consists of a meter and peak flasher. The meter reads modulation but is not "fast" enough to indicate peaks. The flasher portion, with its almost instantaneous response time, lights up when modulation exceeds 100%. A flashing condition is a signal to alert the operator that corrective action *must be taken*.

OPEARATING LOG ENTRIES

At AM and FM broadcast stations certain meter readings must be recorded in the operating log at the beginning of operation in each mode and at intervals not exceeding 3 hours. These entries must be the readings observed before making any adjustments. Operating log entries are made by the licensed operator on duty in charge of the transmitter.

At all AM standard broadcast stations, the following entries shall be made in the operating log:

1. Last-stage plate voltage meter reading.
2. Last-stage plate current meter reading.
3. Antenna current or common-point current meter reading.

At AM broadcast stations employing directional antennas, additional operating log entries must include:

1. Antenna base current meter readings.
2. Antenna monitor sample current meter readings.
3. Antenna monitor phase readings

At FM broadcast stations operating with a transmitter power output above 10W, the following entries shall be made in the operating log:

1. Last-stage plate voltage meter reading.
2. Last-stage plate current meter reading.
3. Transmission line meter reading (only at FM stations determining the operating power by the direct method).

At FM stations with SCA, entries are required of:

1. Time subcarrier is turned on and off (excluding interruptions of less than 5 minutes).
2. Time of application and removal of subcarrier modulation.

FM stations with an operating power of 10W or less are only required to log the time the station begins to apply power to the antenna, the time it stops, and entries concerning the daily operation of tower lights.

STATION IDENTIFICATION

Broadcast station identification announcements shall be made at the beginning and ending of each period of operation, and hourly (as close to the hour as feasible) at a natural break in programing. Official station identification shall consist of the station's call letters, immediately followed by the name of the community or communities specified on the license as the station's location.

BROADCAST OF RECORDED MATERIAL

Any taped, filmed, or recorded program material in which *time* is of special significance (or where an attempt is made to create the impression that an event is occurring at the time of the broadcast) shall be identified at the beginning as taped, filmed, or recorded. The language of the announcement shall be clear and in terms commonly understood by the public.

REBROADCAST

The term *rebroadcast* means reception by radio of the programs of a radio station and the simultaneous or subsequent retransmission of such programs by a broadcast station. No broadcast station shall rebroadcast a program or part of a program of another broadcast station without the express authority of the originating station. A copy of the written consent of the licensee originating the program shall be kept by the licensee of the station rebroadcasting the program.

ANTENNA TOWER LIGHTING

Once each day, an operator is required to check for the proper operation of the tower lighting system. Most tower lighting system are turned on and off with an automatic switch controlled by a photocell. Any observed failure or improper functioning of a code or rotating beacon light or top light not corrected in 30 minutes should be reported to the nearest Flight Service Station of the FAA. Notice should also be given to the same FAA office when the repairs have been completed.

EMERGENCY BROADCASTING SYSTEM (EBS)

Each station must have in operation at the control point a monitor receiver for receiving the *emergency action notification* of termination announcements transmitted by a designated control station. During national level emergency conditions certain stations will continue operating. Other stations not participating in the national level emergency plan must discontinue operations for the duration of the national condition.

Each station is required to transmit at least once each week an EBS test transmission announcement and signal. All station operators must be thoroughly familiar with the procedures for transmitting the EBS signals and prepared to take appropriate action in the event of an actual alert. The operator must also be familiar with the purpose and operation of the EBS monitor receiver and procedures to follow upon receipt of an alert or test signal from another station.

POSTING OPERATOR PERMITS

The operator must post his permit or posting statement at the place where he is on duty at the transmitter control point. FCC Form 759 is a posting statement used by operators employed at more than one station. Operators who have applied for renewal of a permit prior to the expiration date, should post a copy of the renewal application in lieu of the permit being renewed. If an operator fails to apply for a renewed permit prior to the expiration date of the permit being renewed, the permit is not valid and may not be used after the date of expiration. The operator may not be employed as a transmitter operator again until he has applied for and received his renewed permit.

STUDY QUESTIONS

3-1. Define the following words or phrases:

Standard broadcast station. The term *standard broadcast station* means a broadcasting station licensed for the transmission of radiotelephone emissions primarily intended to be received by the general public and operated on a channel in the band 535 – 1605 kHz.

Standard broadcast band. The term *standard broadcast band* means the band of frequencies extending from 535 to 1605 kHz.

Standard broadcast channel. This means the band of frequencies occupied by the carrier and two sidebands of a broadcast signal, with the carrier frequency at the center. Channels are designated by their assigned carrier frequencies. The 107 carrier frequencies assigned to standard broadcast stations begin at 540 kHz and are in successive steps of 10 kHz.

FM broadcast station. A station employing frequency modulation in the FM broadcast band and licensed primarily for the transmission of radiotelephone emissions intended to be received by the general public.

FM broadcast band. The band of frequencies extending from 88 to 108 MHz, which includes those assigned to noncommercial educational broadcasting.

Daytime. The term *daytime* means that period of time between local sunrise and local sunset.

Nighttime. The term *nighttime* means that period of time between local sunset and local sunrise.

Broadcast day. This term means that period of time between local sunrise and 12 midnight local standard time.

Emergency Broadcast System (EBS). The Emergency Broadcast System (EBS) is a system of facilities and personnel of nongovernment broadcast stations and other authorized facilities licensed or regulated by the Federal Communications Commission, including approved and authorized integral facilities or systems, arrangements, procedures, and interconnecting facilities, which have been authorized by the Commission to operate in a controlled manner during a grave national crisis or war.

3-2. Make the following transformations:

Kilohertz to hertz
Milliamperes to amperes

The terms *kilo* and *milli* are prefixes meaning *thousand* and *thousandths*, respectively. Thus, kilohertz (1 kHz) equals 1000 hertz, and a milliampere(1 mA) is one thousandth of an ampere.

3-3. What are the readings of meters in Fig. 3-1? (Give numerical values.)

The readings are: (A) 95%, (B) −20 Hz, (C) 1500V, and (D) 350 mA. According to FCC representatives, many applicants answer questions relating to meters incorrectly. Be sure you understand the layout of each meter before answering any questions relating to it. How much value is represented by each meter increment? You *must* learn to interpolate readings in which the meter needle points to some position between increments. This is extremely simple to do and there are no tricks. Just take your time.

3-4. What should an operator do if the remote antenna ammeter becomes defective?

Each standard broadcast station shall be equipped with indicating instruments which conform with the specifications set forth in Sec. 73.39 for measuring the dc plate circuit current and voltage of the last radio-frequency amplifier stage; the radio-frequency base current of each antenna element; and, for stations employing directional antenna systems, the radio-frequency current at the point of common input to the directional antenna. In the event that any one of these indicating instruments becomes defective when no substitute which conforms with the required specifications is available, the station may be operated without the defective instrument, pending its repair or replacement, for a period not in excess of 60 days without further authority of Commission, *provided* that: (1) Appropriate entries shall be made in the maintenance log of the station showing the date and time the meter was removed from and restored to service. (2) If the defective instrument is the antenna current meter of a nondirectional station which does not employ a remote antenna ammeter, or if the defective instrument is the common-point meter of a station which employs a directional antenna and does not employ a remote common-point meter, the operating power shall be determined by the indirect method in accordance with Sec. 73.52 during the entire time the station is operated without the antenna current meter or common-point meter. However, if a remote antenna ammeter or a remote common-point meter is employed and the antenna current meter or common-point meter becomes defective, the remote meter may be used in determining operating power by the direct method, pending the return to service of the regular meter, provided other meters are maintained at same value previously employed.

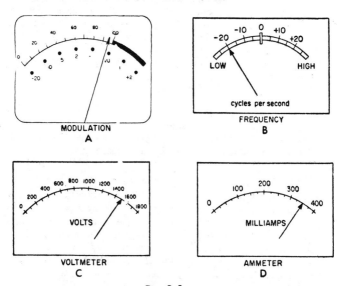

Fig. 3-1.

Remote antenna ammeters and remote common-point meters are not required; therefore, authority to operate without them is not necessary. However, if a remote antenna ammeter or common-point meter is employed and becomes defective, the antenna base currents may be read and logged once daily for each mode of operation, pending the return to service of the regular remote meter.

3-5. *What should an operator do if the remote control devices at a station so equipped malfunction?*

A malfunction of any part of the remote control equipment and associated line circuits resulting in improper control or inaccurate meter readings shall be cause for the immediate cessation of operation by remote control.

3-6 *What is the permissible frequency tolerance of standard broadcast stations and FM stations?*

The operating frequency of each standard broadcast station shall be maintained within 20 Hz of the assigned frequency. The center frequency of each FM broadcast station shall be maintained within 2000 Hz of the assigned center frequency.

3-7. *What are the general requirements relating to logs to be kept by broadcast stations?*

The licensee or permittee of each standard broadcast station shall maintain *program* and *operating* logs as set forth in Sections 73.112 and 73.113 of the rules. Each log shall be kept by the station employee or contract operator competent to do so and having actual knowledge of the facts required, who, in the case of program and operating logs, shall sign the appropriate log when starting duty and again when going off duty. The logs shall be kept in an orderly and legible manner, in suitable form, and in such detail that the data required for the particular class of station concerned is readily available. Key letters or abbreviations may be used if proper meaning or explanation is contained elsewhere in the log. Each sheet shall be numbered and dated. Time entries shall be either in local standard or daylight saving time and shall be indicated accordingly. No log or preprinted log or schedule which becomes a log, or portion thereof, shall be erased, obliterated, or willfully destroyed within the period of retention provided by the provisions of the rules. Any necessary correction shall be made only pursuant to Sections 73.112 and 73.113, only by striking out the erroneous portion or by making a corrective explanation on the log or attachment to its as provided in those sections. Additional information. such as that needed for billing purposes or the cuing of automatic equipment. may be entered on the logs. Such additional information is not subject to the restrictions and limitations on the making of corrections and changes in logs.

3-8. *What entries are made in the program log?*

The following entries shall be made in the program log: (1) for each program—an entry identifying the program by name or title, an entry of the time each program begins and ends, an entry classifying each program as to type (news, religious, entertainment, sports), an entry classifying each program as to source, an entry for each program presenting a political candidate showing the name and political affiliation of such candidate; (2) for commercial matter—an entry identifying the sponsor(s) of the program, other person(s) who paid for the announcement, or the person(s) who furnished materials or services of any kind (such as records, transcriptions, talent, scripts, etc.), an entry showing the total amount of commercial continuity within each commercially sponsored program, an entry showing the total amount of commercial continuity within each commercially sponsored program, an entry showing the duration of each commercial announcement, an entry which shows either the beginning time of each such announcement or which divides the log to show the 15 min. time segment within which the announcement was broadcast, and an entry showing that the appropriate announcements (sponsorship, furnishing material, or services, etc.) have been made; (3) for public service announcements—an entry showing that a public service announcement has been broadcast together with the name of the organization or interest on whose behalf it has been made; (4) for other announcements—an entry of the time that each station identification is made (call letters and licensed location), an entry for each announcement presenting a political candidate, showing the name and political affiliation of such candidate and an entry showing that a mechanical reproduction announcement has been made. The licensee, whether employing manual or automatic logging or the combination thereof, must be able accurately to furnish the Commission with all information required to be logged.

3-9. *According to the Rules and Regulations of the FCC, how long must station logs be retained?*

Logs of standard broadcast stations shall be retained by the licensee or permittee for a period of 2 years; *provided, however,* that logs involving communications incident to a disaster or which include communications incident to or involved in an investigation by the Commission and concerning which the licensee or permittee has been notified shall be retained by the licensee or permittee until he is specifically authorized in writing to destroy them. Logs incident to or involved in any claim or complaint of which the licensee or permittee has notice shall be retained by the licensee or permittee until such claim or complaint has been fully satisfied or until the same has been barred by statute limiting the time for the filing of suits upon such claims. Note: Application forms for licenses and other authorizations require that certain operating and program data be supplied. These application forms should be kept in mind in connection with maintenance of station program and operating records.

3-10. *What information must be given an FCC inspector at any reasonable hour?*

The following shall be made available upon request by an authorized representative of the Commission: (1) program, operating, and maintenance logs; (2) equipment performance measurements required by Sec. 73.47; (3) copy of most recent antenna resistance or common-point impedance measurements submitted to the Commission; (4) copy of most recent field intensity measurements to establish performance of directional antennas.

3-11. *What should an operator do if the modulation monitor becomes defective?*

Each station shall have in operation, either at the transmitter or at the place the transmitter is controlled, a modulation monitor of a type approved by the Commission. In the event that the modulation monitor becomes defective, the station may be operated without the monitor, pending its repair or replacement, for a period not in excess of 60 days without further authority of the Commission, *provided* that: (1) Appropriate entries shall be made in the maintenance log of the station showing the date and time the monitor was removed from and restored to service. (2) The degree of modulation of the station shall be monitored with a cathode-ray oscilloscope or other acceptable means.

3-12. *What should an operator do if the frequency monitor meter becomes defective?*

The licensee of each station shall have in operation, either at the transmitter or at the place where the transmitter is controlled, a frequency monitor of a type approved by the Commission, which shall be independent of the frequency control of the transmitter.

In the event that the frequency monitor becomes defective the station may be operated without the monitor, pending its repair or replacement, for a period not in excess of 60 days without further authority of the Commission, *provided* that: (1) Appropriate entries shall be made in the maintenance log of the station showing the date and time the monitor was removed from and restored to service. (2) The frequency of the station shall be compared with an external frequency source of known accuracy at sufficiently frequent intervals to insure that the frequency is maintained within the tolerance prescribed in Sec. 73.269. An entry shall be made in the station log as to the method used and the results thereof.

3-13. *May the sponsor's name ever be omitted when reading commercials on the air?*

Absolutely not. When a standard broadcast station transmits any matter for which money, service, or other valuable consideration is either directly or indirectly paid or promised to, or charged or received by, such station, the station shall broadcast an announcement that such matter is sponsored, paid for, or furnished, either in whole or in part, and by whom or on whose behalf such consideration was supplied. Where an agent or other person contracts or otherwise makes arrangements with a station on behalf of another and such fact is known to the station, the announcement shall disclose the identity of the person or persons in whose behalf such agent is acting instead of the name of such agent.

3-14. *How often should the tower lights be checked for proper operation?*

The licensee of any radio station which has an antenna structure requiring illumination pursuant to the provisions of the Communications Act of 1934 shall make an observation of the tower lights at least once each 24 hours—either visually or by observing an automatic, properly maintained indicator designed to register any failure of such lights—to insure that all such lights are functioning properly as required. If automatic control devices, designed to turn lights on at night and off at dawn, are not properly functioning, the station is required to burn the lights continuously. Malfunctions that can't be fixed within 30 minutes must be reported immediately to either FAA or the nearest Flight Service Station. Notification must also be given when the situation is corrected.

3-15. What record is kept of tower light operation?

The licensee of any radio station which has an antenna structure requiring illumination shall make the following entries in the station record: (1) the time the tower lights are turned on and off each day if manually controlled; (2) the time the daily check of proper operation of the tower lights was made if automatic alarm system is not provided; (3) in the event of any observed or otherwise known extinguishment or improper functioning of a tower light: (a) nature of such extinguishment or improper functioning, (b) date and time the extinguishment of improper functioning was observed, or otherwise noted, (c) date, time, and nature of the adjustments, repairs, or replacements made, (d) indentification of Flight Service Station (Federal Aviation Administration) notified of the extinguishment or improper functioning of any code or rotation beacon light or top light not corrected within 30 minutes and the date and time such notice was given; (e) date and time notice was given to the Flight Service Station that the required illumination was resumed.

3-16. What should an operator do if the tower lights fail?

The licensee of any radio station which has an antenna structure requiring illumination pursuant to the Communications Act of 1934, shall report immediately by telephone or telegraph to the nearest Flight Service Station or office of the Federal Aviation Administration any observed or otherwise known extinguishment or improper functioning of a code or rotating beacon light or top light not corrected within 30 minutes. Further notification by telephone or telegraph shall be given immediately upon resumption of the required illumination.

3-17. What is an "emergency action condition"?

The emergency action condition is the period of time between the transmission of an emergency action *notification* and the transmission of the emergency action *termination*.

3-18. What equipment must be installed in broadcast stations for reception of an "emergency action notification"?

To insure the effectiveness of the Emergency Action Notification System, all broadcast station licensees must install and operate during their hours of broadcast operation equipment capable of receiving emergency action notifications or terminations transmitted by other radio broadcast stations. This equipment must be maintained in operative condition, including arrangements for human listening watch or automatic alarm devices, and shall have its termination at each transmitter control point. However, where more than one broadcast transmitter is controlled from a common point by the same operator, only one set of equipment is required at that point.

The off-the-air monitoring assignment of each standard, FM, and television broadcast station is specified in the *detailed state Emergency Broadcast System (EBS) operational plan*. Particular attention should be paid to avoiding "closed loops" in monitoring assignments.

Prior to commencing routine operation or originating any emissions under program test, equipment test, experimental, or other authorizations or for any other purpose, licensees or permittees shall first ascertain whether an emergency action condition exists and, if so, shall operate only in accordance with the basic EBS plan and detailed state EBS operational plan.

3-19. How often should EBS test transmissions be sent? During what time period are they sent?

Test transmissions of the Emergency Action Notification System will be conducted by standard, FM, and television broadcast stations once each week on an unscheduled basis.

3-20. During a period of an emergency action condition, what should all nonparticipating stations do?

All broadcast stations are furnished complete with emergency action notification instructions on color-coded cards (yellow, white, red, and blue). Each card specifies the procedure to be followed. Immediately upon receipt of an emergency action notification (yellow card), all standard, commercial FM, noncommercial educational FM broadcast stations with a transmitter output of over 10W and television broadcast stations, including all such stations operating under equipment or program test authority, will proceed as set forth below:

On receipt of the emergency action notification *without* attack warning:

1. Discontinue normal program and follow the detailed transmission procedures set forth on the white card entitled *Broadcast Message, EAN-1*. This white card has been furnished to all licensed broadcast stations for posting in all studios and operating positions.

2. Upon completion of these detailed transmission procedures, all licensed broadcast stations which do not hold a *national defense emergency authorization* shall discontinue operation for the duration of the emergency action condition.

On receipt of the emergency action notification *with* attack warning:

1. Discontinue normal program and follow the detailed transmission procedures set forth on the red card entitled *Broadcast Message, EAN-2*. This red card has been furnished to all licensed broadcast stations for posting in all studios and broadcast operating positions.

2. Upon completion of these detailed transmission procedures, all licensed broadcast stations which do not hold a national defense emergency authorization shall discontinue operation for the duration of the emergency action condition.

A station which normally broadcasts a substantial part of its programing in a language other than English may broadcast the required announcements as well as EBS programing in such foreign language sequentially with the broadcast in English, provided such station has been authorized to do so as part of an approved *detailed state EBS operational plan.*

Noncommercial educational FM broadcast stations with a transmitter power output of 10W or less will, upon receipt of an Emergency Action Notification, interrupt the program in progress and broadcast the appropriate Emergency Action Notification message but without the transmission of the *attention signal*. Such stations will then discontinue operation and maintain radio silence in accordance with the basic EBS plan.

International broadcast stations will cease broadcasting immediately upon receipt of an Emergency Action Notification and will maintain radio silence in accordance with the basic EBS plan.

3-21. *If the tower lights of a station are required to be controlled by a light sensitive device and this device malfunctions, when should the tower lights be on?*

Antenna structures over 150 ft, up to and including 300 ft in height above the ground, shall be lighted as follows: All lights shall burn continuously or shall be controlled by a light sensitive device adjusted so that the lights will be turned on at a north sky light-intensity level of about 35 foot-candles and turned off at a north sky light-intensity level of about 58 foot-candles.

3-22. *What are the requirements relating to the broadcast of phone conversations?*

The parties to the conversation must be informed of the intention to broadcast the conversation. Naturally, this does not apply to station employees who may be presumed to have knowledge that such conversation is being aired.

3-23. *When may the broadcast material of one station be rebroadcast by another?*

Rebroadcasting is only permissible when written permission has been obtained from the originating station. A copy of the consent letter must be retained by the station that rebroadcasts the material.

3-24. *When must an operator license be renewed?*

Operator lecenses must be renewed within 1 year of expiration. The operator has no operating authority between expiration date and receipt of renewal license.

3-25. *How often are station identifications required?*

Station identification is required every hour on the hour, or as close to the hour as feasible during a natural break in programing.

3-26. *Tower 1 of a 3-tower noncritical ditectional array is the reference tower, with an antenna current of 6 amperes. The antenna current of tower 2 is 2.3 amperes, and the antenna current for tower 3 is 2.8 amperes. What is the antenna base current ratio of tower 2?*

The antenna base current ratio of any tower is the measured current of that tower divided by the value of the reference tower. Thus, the antenna base current ratio of tower 2 is $2.3/6 = 0.383$; the antenna base current ratio of tower 3 is $2.8/6 = 0.467$. For problems of this type, remember this phrase, *divided by the reference.*

3.27. *Calculate the power by the direct method of a station with a measured antenna resistance of 40 ohms and a total antenna current of 5 amperes.*

The formula for power is I^2R (The I stands for current *intensity*, the R for *resistance*.) You *must* remember this formula if you're to answer the FCC test questions relating to calculating power by the direct method. The answer in this case is 5^2, or 25, times 40—$25 \times 40 = 1000$ *watts.*

Basic Radiotelephone Theory (Element 3)

4-1. *By what other expression may "difference of potential" be described?*

The most common expression is **voltage**, but the following terms are also used: *IR drop, electromotive force* (or *emf*), *intensity of charge, charge difference, charge pressure, electrical pressure, voltage drop*, and *fall of potential*.

4-2. *By what other expression may an "electric current" be described?*

It may be described as **electron flow** or *electron migration*.

4-3. *What factors determine the amplitude of the emf induced in a conductor which is cutting magnetic lines of force?*

If the lines of force are created by a magnet or a current-bearing conductor (which has a magnetic field), the amplitude of the voltage depends on:

1. The effective **length of the conductor**. If it is a coil, the more turns it has, the higher the induced emf.
2. The **intensity of the magnetic field**. The higher the flux density, the higher the induced emf.
3. The **angle at which the field is cut**. The closer the moving conductor approaches the lines of force at a right angle, the higher the induced emf.
4. The **rate at which the conductor moves** through the magnetic field. The induced emf's amplitude is proportional to the speed of the conductor through the force field.

4-4. *Name four methods by which an electrical potential may be generated.*

An electrical potential may be generated by any of the following means:

Piezoelectricity. By applying a varying physical pressure to certain materials, such as Rochelle salts or quartz, an alternating voltage is produced that has an intensity proportional to the strength of the applied pressure. Crystal microphones are excellent examples of piezoelectric generators. A diaphragm is attached to a quartz crystal in such a manner that movement of the diaphragm applies a pressure to the crystal. Sound pressure causes rapid vibration of the diaphragm, which, in turn, creates an ac voltage from the crystal whose frequency is proportional to the rate of applied vibration.

Chemical Action. Two different metals immersed in a chemical solution that acts more quickly on one of the metals than the other will develop an electrical potential between them as the chemical acts. The intensity of the emf between the two metals depends on the types of metals used. The type of chemical (electrolyte) has little effect on the voltage produced. The common storage battery is an example of voltage generation by chemical action. Chemical action produces a direct, nonalternating voltage.

Mechanical. One of the most important voltage-producing methods, the mechanical generator involves rotating electrical conductors in a magnetic field. The intensity of the voltage output is proportional to the rate at which lines of force are cut. An alternator on an automobile is an example of mechanical voltage generation, as are dynamos that produce the electricity we use in our homes.

Photoelectricity. This source of electrical power is becoming increasingly important as we enter the space age. Photoelectricity is the generation of an electric current by conversion of light. Some elements, such as silicon, react to light by molecular agitation which creates a difference of potential across the material. By placing a sufficient number of such tiny generators in series and parallel, impressive power sources can be constructed. Most space satellites employ this form of voltage generation.

Thermal Action. Two dissimilar metals react differently to applied heat. If one of the two metals builds up an excess of free electrons at a faster rate than the other, a difference of potential will be observed between the two metals. A *thermocouple* is an example of voltage generation by thermal action.

4-5. *If the diameter of a conductor of a given length is doubled, how will the resistance be affected?*

The surface area of a cross section of a conductor determines the resistance of that conductor. When the diameter is doubled, the area is quadrupled; so the **resistance is decreased to one-fourth of its original value.**

4-6. *If the value of resistance to which a constant emf is applied is halved, what will be the resultant proportional power dissipation?*

With applied voltage held constant, power is inversely proportional to resistance ($P = E^2/R$). When resistance decreases, power dissipation *increases* proportionally; when resistance increases, power dissipation *decreases* proportionally. **If resistance is halved, power dissipation is doubled.**

4-7. *What method of connection should be used to obtain the maximum no-load output voltage from a group of similar cells in a storage battery?*

Connecting cells **in series** increases the voltage according to the number of cells so connected, the total voltage being equal to the sum of the voltages of all the series-connected cells. Connecting them in parallel increases the current capability, the total current capability being equal to the sum of the current-delivering capabilities.

4-8. *What is the sum of all voltages around a simple dc series circuit, including the source?*

If the voltage drops are considered *negative* voltages and the source is considered *positive*, **the sum is zero**. The voltage drops are added together and subtracted from the source voltage, and the resultant will always be zero. In short, the sum of the drops must always equal the source voltage.

4-9. *What method of connection should be used to obtain the maximum short-circuit current from a group of similar cells in a storage battery?*

The **parallel** connection should be used. (See discussion of question 4-7.)

4-10. *If the value of a resistance across which a constant emf is applied is doubled, what will be the resultant proportional power dissipation?*

The power dissipation will be **halved**. (See answer to question 4-6.)

4-11. *Name four materials that are good insulators at radio frequencies. Name four materials that are not good insulators at radio frequencies, but that are satisfactory for use at the commercial power frequency (60 Hz).*

For radio frequencies all of the following insulators are effective and are typically used as the **dielectric material for capacitors in rf circuits**: polyester, polystyrene, polypropylene, tantalum, **mica, air, quartz**, and man-made **ceramics**. Materials that are good insulators at power-line frequencies but which tend to act as a resistance rather than an insulator at higher frequencies include the following: **glass, paper, phenolic, cloth, rubber**.

4-12. *Explain the factors that influence the resistance of a conductor.*

The **nature of the material** itself is the prime determinant, because the larger the number of free electrons in the outer orbit of the material's atoms, the better the conductor, and the lower its resistance. The **length** of the conductor, the **diameter** (cross-sectional area), and the **temperature** all influence the resistance. Resistance increases as conductor length is increased but decreases as diameter is increased. Most materials exhibit increased resistance as the temperature increases (carbon is an exception).

4-13. *What effect does the cross-sectional area of a conductor have upon its resistance per unit length?*

The **resistance** per unit length of a conductor **is inversely proportional to the cross-sectional area**. As the cross-sectional area is increased, the resistance is decreased by the same percentage, and vice versa.

4-14. *Name at least four conducting materials in the order of their conductivity.*

The following materials are listed in descending order of conductivity: **silver, copper, gold, aluminum**, beryllium, calcium, magnesium, sodium, thorium, zinc, nickel, iron, platinum, tin, lead, and titanium. If you have trouble remembering the sequence of any four, use the initial letters of the first few to make a memorable phrase, such as: *Southern California's going ape.*

4-15. *What effect does a change in the dielectric constant of a capacitor's insulating material have on the capacitor's value?*

The **value of the capacitor will change proportionally** with the change in dielectric constant.

The dielectric constant is a numerical value that is, in essence, a comparison of a material to air (the value of which is 1.0). In insulating materials the value is generally much higher. The higher the dielectric constant of the dielectric, the greater the capacitance value. The relationship between capacitance, area of a capacitor's plates, distance between plates, and the dielectric constant may be expressed mathematically as

$$C = 0.2246 \ \frac{kA}{d}$$

where C is the capacitance value in picofarads, k is the dielectric constant, A is the area of the plate in square inches, and d is the distance in inches between plates.

4-16. *Explain the effect of increasing the number of plates of a capacitor.*

As can be seen from the formula in the answer to question 4-15, increasing the number of plates *increases* the total capacitance.

4-17. *If the specific inductive capacity of a capacitor's dielectric material were changed from 1 to 2, what would be the resultant change in value?*

The term *specific inductive capacity* refers to the dielectric constant. Since dielectric constant is directly proportional to capacitance, the value of the capacitor would be **doubled.**

4-18. *State the formula for determining the quantity of charge on a capacitor.*

The charge of a capacitor is equal to the charging voltage multiplied by the capacitance, or

$$Q = CE$$

where Q is the charge, in coulombs C is capacitance, in farads; and E is charging potential, in volts.

4-19. *Neglecting the temperature coefficient of resistance and using the same gage of wire and the same applied voltage in each case, what would be the effect upon the field strength of a single-layer solenoid, if you made a small increase in the number of turns?*

The **field strength would** probably **not change** significantly. Increasing the number of turns would tend to increase the field strength, but the resultant increase in the length of the solenoid would have the opposite effect. The two effects would cancel.

When there is a current in a solenoid, the coil is surrounded by a magnetic field like that shown in Fig. 4-1. The intensity of the field at the axis and near the middle of the coil is given by

$$H = \frac{4\pi nI}{10l}$$

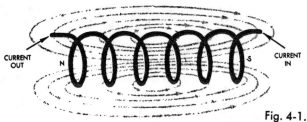

Fig. 4-1.

where H is the intensity in oersteds, n is the number of turns, I is the current, and l is the length of the coil in centimeters. This shows that the strength is proportional to the number of turns per unit length. In fact, the formula for field strength is often written $H = 0.4\ NI$, where $N = n/l$, the number of turns per unit length.

The answer to this depends on whether (and how much) the length of the coil is increased by adding turns. The field strength increases with the number of turns but decreases with the length; it depends on the *ratio* of turns to length. Since the field strength depends on the number of turns per unit length, a small increase in the number of turns will have no effect on the intensity of the field.

When current flows through a solenoid, the coil is surrounded by a magnetic field like that of Fig. 4-1. The intensity of the field at the axis and near the middle of the coil is

$$H = \frac{4\pi NI}{10l}$$

4-20. *How may a magnetic compass be affected when placed within a coil carrying an electric current?*

Since a coil has magnetic poles (north and south), the compass indicator will point toward the north pole. To determine the polarity of the coil without a compass, grasp the coil with the left hand so that the fingers point in the direction of actual electron flow. The thumb will then be pointed in the direction of the north pole of the coil. (See Fig. 4-1.)

4-21. *What factors influence the direction of magnetic lines of force generated by an electromagnet?*

The direction of the magnetic lines of force is determined by the direction of current. If you grasp a conductor with the left hand so that your thumb points in the direction of currents, your fingers will point in the direction of the lines of force.

The lines of force travel clockwise or counterclockwise around a conductor. In Fig.4-2A the small inner circle represents the cross section of a current-carrying conductor whose electrons are traveling directly into the page. The circumferential arrows indicate the direction of magnetic force lines. In Fig. 4-2B the electrons can be considered to be coming from the page; here, the force lines are clockwise, as shown by the concentric circles.

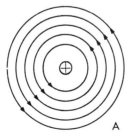
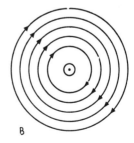

A   B

Fig. 4-2.

4-22. Define the term "permeability."

Permeability is a measure of the ease with which magnetic lines of force pass through a magnetic circuit. The term is roughly comparable to *conductance*, which indicates the ease with which electrical current flows in a conductor.

4-23. What unit is used to express the alternating-current impedance of a circuit?

Impedance is the ac equivalent of dc resistance, and the **ohm** is the unit of measurement.

4-24. What is the basic unit of resistance?

The **ohm** is the basic unit of resistance as well as impedance.

4-25. Explain the meaning of the prefix "pico," or "micromicro."

The latter term is seldom used today, but you're still likely to find questions about it on the exam. The two prefixes mean the same thing: **a millionth part of a millionth part**. It is the reciprocal of *giga* and is equal to 10^{-12}.

4-26. What is the unit of capacitance?

The basic unit of capacitance is the **farad**. The unit is terribly impractical, though, because practical values are usually a very small fraction of one farad. In practice, microfarads (equal to one-millionth farad) and picofarads (equal to one trillionth of a farad) are quite common, though the nanofarad (one billionth of a farad) is becoming more and more fashionable.

4-27. What single-purpose instrument may be used to measure electrical resistance? Electrical current? Electromotive force?

The word *single-purpose* is used to prevent you from taking the easy way out and saying something like volt-ohm-milliammeter (VOM). But the VOM (most of which don't measure power anyway) could hardly be considered a single-purpose instrument. Here's what you'd better be prepared to answer on the exam:

> An **ohmmeter** measures **resistance**.
> A **wattmeter** measures **electrical power**.
> An **ammeter** measures **current**.
> A **voltmeter** measures **electromotive force**.

4-28. Define the term "residual magnetism."

The **tendency of a conductor to remain magnetized** after removal of the energizing force is referred to as *residual magnetism*.

4-29. What is the unit of electrical power?

The basic unit of electrical power is the **watt**.

4-30. What is the unit of conductance?

This should be particularly easy to remember if you can bear in mind that conductance is the reciprocal of resistance (conductance = 1/resistance). The basic unit is the **mho**, which of course is *ohm* spelled backward.

4-31. What is the unit of inductance?

The basic unit of inductance is the *henry*. While the henry is not as unwieldy as the farad, the subunits are still a little more common, particularly at radio frequencies. The subunits are the millihenry, microhenry, and nanohenry.

4-32. *What is the meaning of the prefix "kilo?"*

Kilo means **thousand**. A kilovolt, for example, is equal to 1000V

4-33. *What is the meaning of the prefix "micro"?*

Micro means **millionth**. One microfarad is equal to 0.000001F.

4-34. *What is the meaning of "power factor"?*

Power factor is the **cosine of the phase angle between voltage and current** in a circuit, and is usually expressed as a decimal fraction or a percentage. Since power calculations using Ohm's law do not take reactance into account, power calculations on ac circuits result in an "apparent" power, which must be corrected for by multiplying apparent power by the power factor.

4-35. *What is meant by the prefix "meg" or "mega"?*

Mega means **million**. One megohm is 1,000,000 ohms; one megahertz is 1,000,000 hertz.

4-36. *Define the term "conductance."*

Conductance is the reciprocal of resistance and is used to express a material's ability to support electron flow (current).

4-37. *What instrument is used to measure current?*

The **ammeter** measures current. Meters for measuring smaller currents than one ampere are usually referred to as *milliammeters* and *microammeters*.

4-38. *Define the word "decibel."*

A simple answer to this question won't help you on the FCC exam, because the FCC will not likely ask the question this way. The questions relating to decibels will be designed to find out if you really understand the meaning of the term and how it may be applied to voltage, current, and power.

The decibel gives us a linear means of expressing logarithmic changes in power or level. The international transmission unit is the *bel*, which is equal to 10 decibels. So the first definition of the decibel is "one-tenth part of a bel." The bel is itself equivalent to a 10:1 ratio of power. So the gain in bels is the number of times that 10 is taken as a factor to equal the ratio of output power (of an amplifier or any other device) to input power.

There are some convenient rules of thumb, but if you use them you have to remember what you're measuring. Voltage changes bring about current changes that, in turn, increase power levels, which are themselves the elements actually being compared in decibel values. Doubling any power is the same as increasing the power by 3 decibels (dB). Halving any power value is the same as decreasing the power by 3 dB. Doubling of either voltage or current, though, results in a 6 dB increase—that is because doubling of voltage forces a doubling of current as well, resulting in a quadrupling of power.

Each time a power value is increased by an order of magnitude (factor of 10) the gain is increased by 10 dB. The basic ratios are as follows:

Power Ratio	No. of 10 Factors	No. of Bels	No. of dB
1,000,000 to 1	6	6	60
100,000 to 1	5	5	50
10,000 to 1	4	4	40
1,000 to 1	3	3	30
100 to 1	2	2	20
10 to 1	1	1	10
1 to 1	0	0	0

4-39. What is meant by "ampere-turns"?

One ampere-turn is the **magnetomotive force required to establish** a current flow of **one ampere through one turn of wire** in a magnetic circuit.

1-40. Define the term "inductance."

Inductance is the property of a circuit that causes it to oppose any change in current through it. But while this describes the character of inductance, it does not actually define the term.

Michael Faraday discovered that a voltage may be developed by changing the direction of the flux (lines of force) or the amount of flux that links with a conductor or coil. The phenomenon of his discovery is what we refer to as inductance.

Later experimentation showed that the magnitude of the generated voltage is directly proportional to the rate at which a conductor cuts magnetic lines of force. (This statement is now known as *Faraday's law.*)

The rate at which a conductor cuts the magnetic lines of force depends on the number of turns in the coil, the strength of the magnetic field, and the speed with which the magnetic field or coil is moved. When a wire is moved parallel to the magnetic field, it cuts no lines of force, and no voltage is developed. Cutting across a field at an angle less than 90° will result in a lower voltage than if the wire were moved at the same speed perpendicular to the field.

When a conductor moves at a constant speed across a magnetic field of uniform flux density, one volt is generated for every 100 million lines cut per second. The amount of emf generated this way can be put in the form of a formula:

$$E = \frac{\phi}{t \times 10^8}$$

where E is the voltage in volts generated in the conductor, ϕ is the total flux cut, and t is the time in seconds during which the field cutting takes place.

When the conductor consists of several turns in the form of a coil and when the magnetic field is not uniform or is not cut at a uniform rate, the formula becomes more complex.

The polarity of the induced voltage is always in opposition to the force that produces it. To illustrate this, take a wire coil wound around a simple form such as that shown in Fig. 4-3. Across the coil connect a galvanometer to complete the circuit, so that there will be current flow when a voltage is induced. When the north pole of the magnet is inserted into the center of the coil as shown, an emf is induced. The current will flow in the direction indicated by the arrow labeled i. As far as the

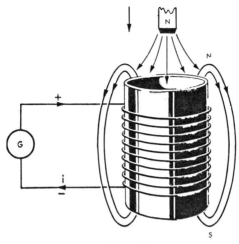

Fig. 4-3

external circuit is concerned, polarity of the induced voltage is as shown, the top lead being positive and the lower being negative. This causes the top end of the coil to appear as a north pole, which opposes the downward direction of the magnet. The induced polarity of the coil must be the same as that of the approaching magnetic pole; otherwise it would be necessary only to start a magnetic pole into the coil and, upon its inducing an opposite pole in the coil, the magnet would be drawn in, inducing additional emf without work. This would be a "perpetual motion" machine and would provide an unlimited source of energy without consuming energy—a condition that is contrary to the law of conservation of energy.

Next, consider a wire moving downward with its length perpendicular to a magnetic field which runs from left to right, as shown in Fig. 4-4. Think of the lines as being distorted as though they were rubber bands and were wrapping themselves around the wire. These lines of force would encircle the wire in a counterclockwise direction. Cutting the lines of force induces a voltage along the wire, so that current flows. If

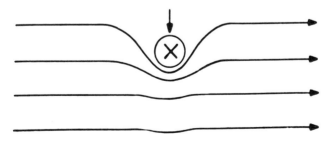

Fig. 4-4.

the circle marked with the X is considered the cross section of a conductor going through the page, current flow would be away from you and down into the page.

4-41. *Define the term "coulomb."*

The coulomb is the basic unit of charge. Charged bodies act on each other with a force of attraction when they are oppositely charged and with a force of repulsion when they are similarly charged. The forces of attraction or repulsion change with the magnitude of the charges and the distance between them. Expressed mathematically, the relationship, known as *Coulomb's law*, is

$$F = \frac{Q_1 Q_2}{d_2}$$

where Q_1 and Q_2 represent the charges and d is the distance between them. One coulomb is equal to the charge of 6.28×10^{18} electrons. It is also the amount of electricity that is transferred by a current of one ampere in one second.

4-42. *State three mathematical forms of Ohm's law.*

$$E = IR \qquad I = E/R \qquad R = E/I$$

If the formulas themselves are difficult for you to remember, try memorizing the diagram in Fig. 4-5. By covering the symbol for the function you need to figure, the other two symbols appear in a format that indicates whether to multiply or divide.

E = IR
R = E/I
I = E/R

Fig. 4-5.

4-43. *If a vacuum tube having a filament rated at 0.25A and 5.0V is to be operated from a 6V battery, what is the value of the necessary series dropping resistor?*

The resistor must drop 1V; the current through the resistor will be 0.25A. We thus have two of the values necessary to calculate the drop per Ohm's law: $E = 1.0, I = 0.25$. In this case E divided by I is 4; so the value of the resistor is 4Ω.

4-44. *If the voltage applied to a circuit is doubled and the resistance of the circuit is increased to three times its original value, what will be the final current?*

The final current value will be two-thirds the initial value. Doubling the voltage doubles the current; increasing the resistance causes a reciprocal change in current.

4-45. *What would be the minimum power dissipation rating of a resistor of 20,000Ω connected across a 500V source?*

From Ohm's law we know that a 20K resistor connected across a 500V source draws 0.025A, or 25 mA. Power is equal to volts times amperes (EI), so we know the resistor will be required to dissipate 12.5W. Most resistors are rated at values of ⅛, ¼, ½, 2, 5, 10, 15, and 20 watts. The nearest standard value above 12.5W is **15W**, which is the minimum value usable in the circuit. To allow for possible changes in resistance and voltage, it is usually wiser to use a resistor that has a wider safety margin. So, while 15W would be the minimum acceptable rating, the 20W resistor would be the best choice.

4-46. *If the resistors of 3, 5, and 15 ohms are connected in parallel, what is the total resistance?*

The value of parallel resistance is equal to the reciprocal of the sum of the individual reciprocal values, or:

$$R_p = \cfrac{1}{\cfrac{1}{R1} + \cfrac{1}{R2} + \cfrac{1}{R3}}$$

The answer is 1⅔Ω. To work the problem, convert the fractions to fifteenths, then add them. The first answer, $^{9}/_{15}$ (or 0.6) is then divided into 1 to give $^{15}/_{9}$, or 1⅔.

4-47. *What is the maximum current-carrying capacity of a resistor marked "5K, 200W"?*

The maximum current allowable would be 282 mA (0.00282A) at full rated power. Current is equal to the square root of power divided by resistance ($I = \sqrt{P/R}$).

4-48. *A milliammeter with a full-scale deflection of 1 mA and a resistance of 25Ω was used to measure an unknown current by shunting the meter with a 4Ω resistor. If a meter indicates 0.4 mA, what would be the actual current value?*

The current in the individual resistances will be inversely proportional to the ratio of resistance values. The ratio of values is 25:4, or 6.25; thus, the value through the shunt will be 6.25 times the value indicated on the meter, or 6.25 × 0.4 = 2.5 mA. The value through the meter is additive with the paralleled value, or 0.4+2.5 = 2.9 mA.

4-49. *What will be the heat dissipation (in watts) of a 20Ω resistor having a current of 0.25A?*

Power dissipation equals current squared times resistance, or I^2R. Current squared, in this case, is 0.0265A; this figure multiplied by 20Ω equals **1.25W**.

4-50. *If two 10W, 500Ω resistors are connected in parallel, what is the dissipation capability of the combination?*

The resistance value has no bearing on the power dissipation rating. If each resistor can dissipate 10W, the total power dissipation capability of the pair is **20W**.

4-51. *What is the formula used to determine total capacitance of three or more capacitors connected in series?*

Interestingly, the value of capacitors in series can be calculated exactly the way resistances in parallel are calculated: The value is equal to the reciprocal of the sum of the individual-value reciprocals, or

$$C = \cfrac{1}{\cfrac{1}{C1} + \cfrac{1}{C2} + \cfrac{1}{C3} + \cfrac{1}{C4} \ldots}$$

4-52. *If capacitors of 1, 3, and 5 μF are connected in parallel, what is the total capacitance?*

The value would be 9 μF. Capacitances in parallel are additive in precisely the same way as resistors in series.

4-53. *What would be the total capacitance of 5, 3, and 7 μF capacitors in series?*

Based on the equation of 4-51, the value would be 1.48 μF. The idea is to convert the fractional values to a common denominator so they may be added. If the values are multiplied together to get a common denominator of 105, the reciprocal values of the capacitance will be 21/105, 35/105, and 15/105. These add to 71/105, or 0.676. The reciprocal of 0.676 is 1.48.

4-54. *In what portion of a capacitor is the charge stored?*

The charge in a capacitor is stored **in the dielectric** between the plates. Charging may be accomplished by connecting the capacitor to a battery or other source of dc voltage. (See Fig. 4-6.) Electrons will be released from one plate of the capacitor and will flow through the external circuit to the other plate. The charge builds up as a result of the deficiency of electrons on one plate and the abundance of electrons on the other. The capacitance value depends on the area of the plates, the distance between them, and the dielectric material.

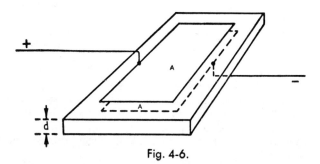

Fig. 4-6.

4-55. *Having available a number of capacitors rated at 2 μF, 400V each, how many would be necessary to obtain a combination rated at 1.5 μF, 1.6 kV?*

Twelve. Capacitors may be placed in series for equal distribution of voltage, but the capacitance of the combination of four 2 μF capacitors in series would be only 0.5 μF. Since paralleling capacitors adds capacitance values, three such series strings would result in a total value of 1.5 μF, 1.6 kV.

When connecting capacitors in series, it is a good idea to place a high-value resistor across each capacitor. As long as all resistors are the same value, the voltage across the capacitors will be evenly distributed (neglecting any excessive leakage).

4-56. *The voltage drop across an individual capacitor of a series string, when the string is placed across a source voltage, is proportional to what factors?*

It is inversely proportional to the number of identical capacitors in the string. If there are two capacitors, one capacitor develops half the total voltage. If there are three, each capacitor develops one third, etc.

4-57. *What factors determine the charge stored in a capacitor?*

Stated as a formula, charge is equal to **capacitance times voltage**. But since several factors determine capacitance, so too must these factors influence the total charge. Similarly, the higher the dielectric constant (k), the greater the stored charge (Q). The charge depends on capacitance, area of plates, distance between plates, dielectric constant, applied voltage, and duration of applied voltage. The equation for charge becomes $Q = 0.2246E \, (kA/d)$, where E is voltage, k is dielectric constant, A is area of plates, and d is the distance between plates.

4-58. *You are given two identical mica capacitors of 0.1 μF. One is charged to a potential of 125V and disconnected from the charging circuit. The charged capacitor is then connected in parallel with the uncharged one. What voltage will appear across the pair?*

The voltage across the two will be approximately half the total voltage of the first capacitor before making the connection. The uncharged capacitor acts to discharge the charged one while it is actually being charged; thus the voltage is equally distributed between the two capacitors. The ultimate charge will be slightly less than 62.5V because the act of charging a capacitor takes a small amount of energy.

4-59. *What is the effect of adding an iron core to an air core inductance?*

When an iron core is inserted into the coil (Fig. 4-7), the inductance of the coil becomes the product of the core's permeability and the original inductance of the air core coil. As a formula

$$L = \mu L_0$$

where L_0 is the inductance of the coil with an air core, and μ is the permeability of the iron core.

4-60. *What would be the effect of a shorted turn in a coil?*

The shorted turn is isolated from the main coil and acts as a transformer secondary winding. Since one turn has almost zero resistance, the induced current in that single shorted winding is quite high. The excessive current through the single turn could generate enough heat to burn through the surrounding insulation, destroying the entire coil.

4-61. *What is the relationship between the number of turns and the inductance of a coil?*

The *inductance varies with the square of the number of turns*. The relationship is expressed in the equation

$$L = \frac{n\phi}{I}$$

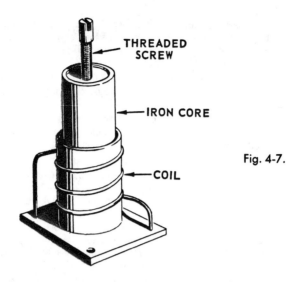

THREADED SCREW

IRON CORE

COIL

Fig. 4-7.

where n is the number of turns, and ϕ is the magnetic flux linking the coil and produced by current I. Multiplying the result by 10^{-10} (0.0000000001) yields inductance in henrys.

4-62. *Define the term "reluctance."*

Reluctance is defined as the **opposition to flux** in a magnetic circuit; it is thoroughly comparable with resistance in a dc circuit. Quantitatively, the basic unit of reluctance, the *rel*, is the reluctance of a magnetic circuit one centimeter long and one centimeter in cross section with a permeability of 1.0. As a mathematical expression, reluctance in rels is length divided by permeability times area or

$$\mathcal{R} = l/\mu A$$

4-63. *State the formula for determining resonant frequency when inductance and capacitance are known.*

Assuming a coil with a normal figure of merit (Q), the formula is

$$f = \frac{1}{2\pi\sqrt{LC}}$$

4-64. *What is the formula for figuring the power in a dc circuit when the voltage and resistance are known?*

The power is equal to voltage squared, divided by resistance or

$$P = E^2/R$$

4-65. *What is the formula for determining power in a dc circuit when current and resistance are known?*

The power is equal to current squared times resistance, or

$$P = I^2R$$

4-66. *What is the formula for determining power in a dc circuit when voltage and current are known?*

Power is voltage multiplied by current, or

$$P = EI$$

4-67. *What is the formula for determining the wavelength when the frequency is known?*

Wavelength is the length of a wave in a field emitted by a radio transmitter. Since radio signals travel at the speed of light, the wavelength can be calculated by dividing the number of waves passing a point in one second into the speed of light (in units per second). As an equation,

$$\lambda = \frac{c}{f}$$

where λ is wavelength, c is the speed of light, and f is frequency.

Wavelength generally is expressed in meters, though it could be expressed in centimeters, inches, feet, yards, or miles. For wavelength in meters, the speed of light in meters per second must be used in the formula. Since the speed of light is 300 million (3×10^8) meters per second (or at least close enough to it so that this number can be used for calculations), the math is greatly simplified.

For example, you can divide 300 million by the frequency in hertz, 300,000 by frequency in kilohertz, or 300 by the frequency in megahertz. In other words, you can simplify the problem by the expedient of removing zeros from 300 million, according to the hertz multiplier.

4-68. *State Ohm's law for ac circuits.*

It may be stated in the same three basic forms as Ohm's law for dc circuits, except that impedance (Z) must be substituted for resistance:

$$E = IZ$$

$$I = \frac{E}{Z}$$

$$Z = \frac{E}{I}$$

In some ac circuits, impedance includes not only resistance but reactance as well, both capacitive and inductive.

4-69. *Draw a simple schematic diagram showing a tuned-plate, tuned-grid (TPTG) oscillator with a series-fed plate, indicating the polarity of all applied voltages.*

Refer to Fig. 4-8. This oscillator has tuned circuits in both grid and plate circuits, and it is advantageous because it may be used equally well at low as well as ultrahigh frequencies. Notice in the figure that the inductance in the plate tank circuit is not inductively coupled to the inductance in the grid circuit. The feedback to sustain oscillation occurs through the interelectrode capacitance of the tube from grid to plate; this is illustrated by a broken line showing the grid-to-plate capacitance (C_{gp}) inherent in the tube.

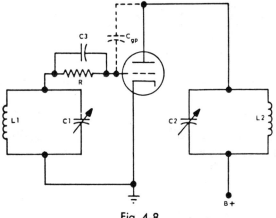

Fig. 4-8.

4-70. *Draw a simple schematic diagram showing a Hartley triode oscillator with a shunt-fed plate, indicating voltage polarities.*

In the shunt-fed Hartley oscillator (Fig. 4-9) direct current does not flow through any part of the tank circuit, and the plate supply voltage is in parallel with the tube and tank circuit. An rf choke keeps radio-frequency signals out of the plate supply, and dc is kept out of the tank circuit by a blocking capacitor.

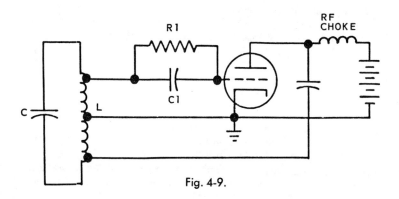

Fig. 4-9.

4-71. *Draw a simple schematic diagram showing a tuned-grid Armstrong triode oscillator with a shunt-fed plate, indicating voltage polarities.*

The Armstrong oscillator is perhaps the oldest of all oscillators. You can recognize it easily by the "tickler" winding it incorporates to introduce feedback. In the circuit pictured in Fig. 4-10, $B+$ voltage is applied through an rf choke to the plate. Varying the number of turns in the tickler winding adjusts the feedback fraction. Questions on the Armstrong oscillator show up on numerous FCC tests in spite of the fact that the vacuum-tube version is virtually obsolete and even the transistor equivalent is rarely seen.

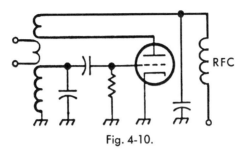

Fig. 4-10.

4-72. *Draw a simple schematic diagram showing a tuned-plate, tuned-grid oscillator (triode) with shunt-fed plate. Indicate voltage polarities.*

The shunt-fed TPTG oscillator looks very similar to the series-fed unit. As shown in Fig. 4-11, the only difference is that the shunt-fed type receives its plate voltage directly from the source (through an rf choke). The tuned circuit that makes up the plate tank connects directly to ground.

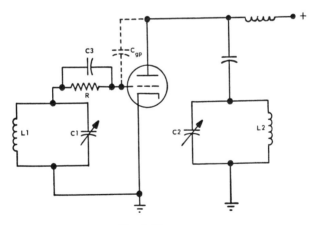

Fig. 4-11.

4-73. *Draw a simple schematic of a crystal-controlled tube-type oscillator indicating polarities of power supply voltage.*

Since a quartz crystal is equivalent to a resonant circuit, it can be used in place of the usual tuned circuit as a frequency-controlling element in an oscillator. The circuit shown in Fig. 4-12 is a common triode oscillator using a quartz crystal.

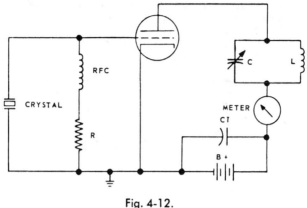

Fig. 4-12.

4-74. *Draw a simple schematic diagram showing a Colpitts oscillator (triode) with shunt-fed plate.*

The Colpitts oscillator is essentially the same as the Hartley, except that a pair of capacitances in series is connected across the tank coil. The capacitive combination of $C1$ and $C2$ in Fig. 4-13 forms a voltage divider that splits the potential across the resonant circuit. The voltages at the ends of the resonant circuit are opposite in polarity with respect to the cathode and in the right phase to sustain oscillation. Total tank capacitance consists of $C1$ and $C2$; the grid-leak bias combination is made up of $C3$ and R_g.

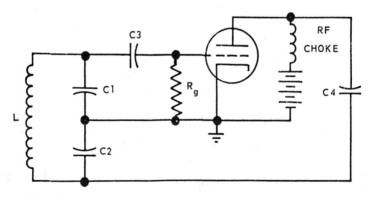

Fig. 4-13.

4-75. *Draw a simple diagram of a tuned-grid Armstrong triode oscillator with a series-fed plate, indicating voltage polarities.*

The series circuit differs from the shunt circuit in plate supply. Note in Fig. 4-14 that $B+$ is supplied to the plate through the tickler winding. And note the bypass capacitor in the $B+$ line.

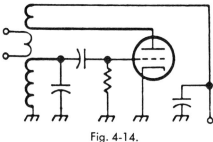

Fig. 4-14.

4-76. *Draw a simple schematic diagram of an electron-coupled oscillator, indicating voltage polarities.*

Actually a modified version of the Hartley, the electron-coupled oscillator (Fig. 4-15) combines the functions of both an oscillator and an amplifier. The control grid's tank circuit, the control and screen grids, and the cathode form a series-fed oscillator with the screen grid serving as the plate. Capacitor C2 places the screen at zero potential (rf) and, like C3, bypasses the plate supply. The output tuned circuit is in the plate circuit, so the only coupling path is the electron stream between grid tank and plate tank (hence the circuit's name).

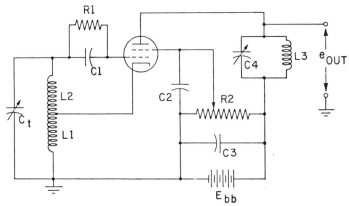

Fig. 4-15.

4-77. *Draw a simple schematic of a pentode crystal oscillator, indicating voltage polarities.*

A pentode oscillator such as the one shown in Fig. 4-16 is a good deal more common than a triode crystal oscillator because it requires far less excitation to drive the tube to full power output. The battery is marked $B+$, and no other polarities are shown. Always remember, the long parallel plates on a schematic battery symbol represent the positive ends of the battery cells.

In the pentode oscillator shown, capacitor $C4$ represents a value that may have to be added to supply the necessary feedback to sustain oscillation. Note that grid-leak bias is supplemented by cathode bias, which itself is developed by resistor R. The dc flowing from cathode to plate develops a voltage positive with respect to ground. Since the lower end of the cathode resistor is effectively connected to the grid by $R1$ and the choke, any voltage developed across R appears between the grid and the cathode. This makes the grid negative with respect to the cathode by an amount equal to the voltage drop across R. Capacitor C bypasses the rf component of plate current around the cathode resistor.

The cathode resistor might well be referred to as the "minimum bias resistor," for bias voltage is developed across it every time plate current flows in the oscillator circuit. Thus the cathode bias is independent of oscillation and prevents excessive tube current if oscillation stops.

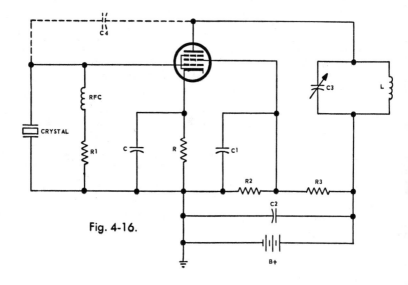

Fig. 4-16.

4-78. *Draw a simple schematic showing a method of coupling a high-impedance loudspeaker to an audio-frequency amplifier tube without the flow of tube plate current throught the speaker windings and without the use of a transformer.*

A high-impedance loudspeaker may be connected to the plate of the tube through a series capacitor. The loudspeaker serves as the tube's load, and the capacitor blocks the plate's high-voltage dc from the loudspeaker voice coil. Since high-impedance speakers are expensive and bulky, it is generally more practical to couple the audio from the tube to the speaker through a transformer. The transformerless connection is shown in Fig. 4-17.

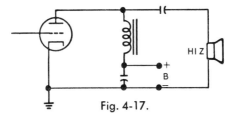

Fig. 4-17.

4-79. *Draw a simple schematic of a triode audio amplifier inductively coupled to a loudspeaker.*

Figure 4-18 shows a triode stage inductively coupled to a loudspeaker. The inductance is used as an impedance-matching device. Because the plate resistance of an audio output tube may range from 1K to more than 20K, while the loudspeaker might be anywhere between 3.2Ω and 16Ω, the transformer has to be used to change the effective impedance of the output circuit. The transformer has a stepdown turns ratio that provides the speaker with a signal of the proper impedance. The output voltage of a transformer varies in direct proportion to the turns ratio. The transformer's primary impedance is usually established at twice the tube's plate resistance (r_p) to give maximum undistorted output. If the speaker is 4Ω, the turns ratio will be about 612:1.

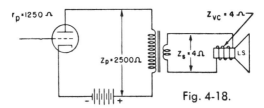

Fig. 4-18.

4-80. *Draw a simple schematic showing a method of resistance coupling between two triodes in an audio amplifier.*

The resistance-coupled amplifier is shown in Fig. 4-19. The components pictured are as follows: $R1$ is the grid leak, $R2$ provides cathode bias, $R3$ is the plate load, $R4$ provides plate decoupling, and $R5$ is the second-stage grid leak. Capacitor $C1$ is for input coupling, $C2$ is the cathode bypass, $C3$ is the plate bypass, and $C4$ is for output coupling.

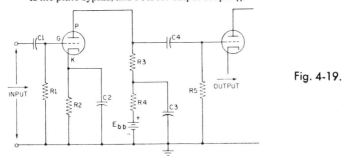

Fig. 4-19.

4-81. *Draw a simple schematic showing a method of transformer coupling between two triode audio amplifiers.*

Transformer coupling in an amplifier has certain advantages over other coupling methods (Fig. 4-20). The voltage amplification may exceed the amplification factor of the tube itself when the transformer has a stepup turns ratio. Direct-current isolation of the grid of the next tube is

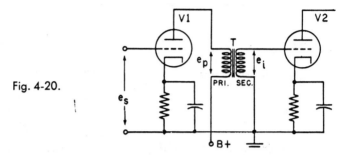

Fig. 4-20.

provided without the need of a blocking capacitor and the voltage drop across the coupling resistor (required in *RC* coupling) is avoided.

The disadvantages can't be overlooked, however. Transformers are bulky and costly. They require greater shielding and impose frequency response limitations not shared by other coupling methods.

2-82. *Draw a simple schematic showing a method of impedance coupling between two vacuum tubes in an audio amplifier.*

Impedance coupling is simply a replacement of the load resistor in a standard *RC*-coupled amplifier with a choke or inductor, as shown in Fig. 4-21. To obtain as much amplification as possible, particularly at lower frequencies, the inductor is made as large as practical. To avoid undesirable magnetic coupling, a closed-shell type of inductor is used. Because of the low dc resistance of the inductor, a small dc voltage is developed across it. Thus the tube will operate at a higher plate voltage.

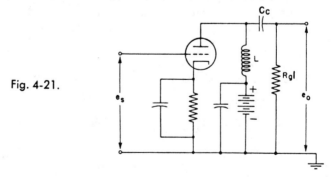

Fig. 4-21.

4-83. *Draw a simple diagram showing a method of coupling the rf output from a transmitter's final stage to an antenna.*

One common coupling method is shown in Fig. 4-22. The antenna-tuning system is made up of antenna-coupling capacitor *C1*, antenna-coupling

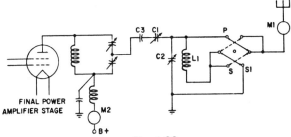

Fig. 4-22.

inductor $L1$, antenna-tuning capacitor $C2$, and antenna feed switch $S1$. The dc-blocking capacitor ($C1$) is connected in series with $L1$ and the antenna is current fed. In position P the antenna is voltage fed.

4-84. *Draw a simple schematic showing a method of coupling between two tetrode vacuum tubes in a tuned rf amplifier.*

Figure 4-23 shows a pair of tetrodes impedance-coupled. Actually, the circuit closely resembles transformer coupling and is referred to as *tuned impedance* coupling.

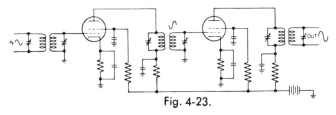

Fig. 4-23.

4-85. *Draw a simple schematic diagram showing a method of coupling between two triodes in an rf amplifier. Show neutralization to prevent oscillations.*

The second half of a 2-stage amplifier is shown in Fig. 4-24. The coupling between stages is exactly the same as that shown in Fig. 4-23. The capacitor between the grid and the bottom of the tank circuit (C_n) provides the necessary neutralization.

A transmitter rf amplifier having a plate tank and grid tank circuit, both tuned to the same frequency, resembles a tuned-plate, tuned-grid

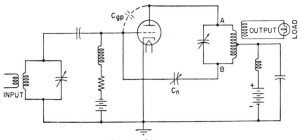

Fig. 4-24.

oscillator. Unless some precaution is taken to prevent it, the amplifier may break into oscillation. If a voltage is fed back from plate to grid in phase with the grid signal, oscillation will occur. If the voltage that is fed back is 180° out of phase, the action is *degenerative*, and oscillations are stopped by virtue of signal cancellation.

Neutralization is a process of balancing the voltage fed back by the interelectrode capacitance of the tube with an equal voltage of opposite polarity. Dividing the plate circuit so that the neutralization voltage is developed across a part of it is called *plate neutralization*. If the voltage of neutralization is developed in the grid circuit, the arrangement is called *grid neutralization*.

In Fig. 4-24 the plate tank coil has a centertapped connection. The voltage between point *A* and ground is 180° out of phase with the voltage from point *B* to ground. Feedback through the plate-to-grid capacitance of the triode produces the voltage across the grid input circuit that is in phase with the grid excitation voltage and, therefore, tends to cause the amplifier to break into oscillations.

4-86. Draw a simple schematic of a diode vacuum-tube detector. Show the diode connected to an audio amplifier.

The diode detector may be either a tube or semiconductor. The vacuum-tube type shown in Fig. 4-25A has been the standard because of its ideal resistance characteristic. The input (rf) tuned circuit can be at any appropriate frequency. The output (e_o) is at a high impedance and can be fed directly into an audio amplifier. Figure 4-25B shows one amplifier stage driving a loudspeaker. The grid of the audio amplifier may be fed directly from the output of the detector, but conventional practice is to couple through a series capacitor to block any dc that might be present on the input line.

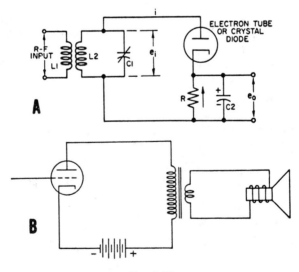

Fig. 4-25.

4-87. *Draw a schematic of a triode connected for plate (power) detection.*

In a plate detector the signal is first amplified in the plate circuit, and then it is detected in the same circuit. A plate detector circuit is shown in Fig. 4-26. The cathode bias resistor ($R1$) is chosen so that the grid bias is

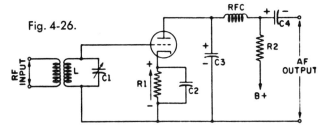

Fig. 4-26.

approximately at cutoff during the time that an input signal of proper strength is applied. Plate current then flows only on the positive swings of grid voltage, during which time average plate current increases. The peak value of the ac input signal is limited to slightly less than the cutoff bias to prevent driving the grid voltage positive on the positive half-cycles of the input signal; thus no grid current flows at any time in the input cycle, and the detector does not load the input tuned circuit ($LC1$).

Cathode bypass capacitor $C2$ is large enough to hold the voltage across $R1$ steady at the lowest audio frequency to be detected in the plate circuit. Capacitor $C3$ is the demodulation capacitor across which the audio component is developed.

4-88. *Draw a simple schematic of a triode connected for grid-leak capacitor detection.*

The grid-leak detector (Fig. 4-27) functions like a diode detector combined with a triode amplifier. It is convenient to consider detection and amplification as two separate functions: In the figure the grid functions as a diode plate. (The subscript d stands for *diode* in the drawing.) The values of C_d and R_d must be chosen so that C_d charges during the positive peaks of the incoming signal and discharges during the negative peaks. The time constant of these two devices should be long with respect to the rf cycle and short with respect to the audio cycle.

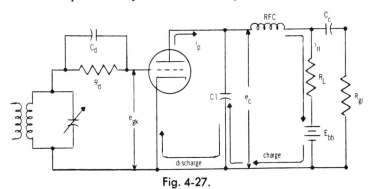

Fig. 4-27.

4-89. Draw a simple schematic of a regenerative detector.

When high sensitivity and selectivity are the most important factors, a regenerative detector may be used. However, the linearity as well as the ability to handle strong signals without overloading is very poor.

A grid-leak detector may be modified to operate as a regenerative detector, as shown in Fig. 4-28. Because an amplified rf component is

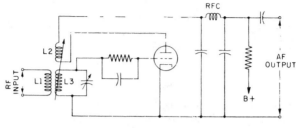

Fig. 4-28.

present in the plate circuit of the grid-leak detector, regeneration may be obtained by connecting a tickler coil (*L2*) in series with the plate circuit so that it is inductively coupled to the grid coil (*L3*).

With an rf signal across *L3*, an rf component of plate current flows through *L2*. Coil *L2* is connected so that the voltage it induces in *L3* is in phase with the incoming signal voltage applied to the grid. Thus, the voltage gain of this stage is increased. It is important that the voltage fed back by the tickler coil be in phase with the incoming signal voltage. Otherwise, the feedback will be degenerative, and the amplification will be reduced. Further, if the coupling between *L2* and *L3* is too great, oscillation will take place. For receiving code signals, oscillation is desirable to produce an audible beat tone; however, it is not desirable for voice or music reception, because of the objectionable squeal from the beat tone. The regenerative detector is the most sensitive triode detector circuit possible when it is operated just below the point of oscillation.

4-90. Draw a simple schematic of an rf multiplier stage and show the distinguishing characteristics.

Figure 4-29A is a schematic of a transistor frequency doubler. A basic electron-tube circuit, operating as a frequency tripler, is illustrated in Fig. 4-29B. The frequency multiplier is operated class C, with the collector (or plate) tank resonant at a multiple of the base (or grid) signal frequency.

When a signal applied to base (or grid) rises above the cutoff value of the amplifier device, there will be a pulse of current (at the same frequency as the input signal) flowing from the emitter (or cathode) to the collector (or plate), energizing the collector (or plate) tank circuit. As the pulses of collector (or plate) current in Fig. 4-29 have appreciable energy at the second and third harmonics, and the resonant frequency of the tank circuit (determined by values of *L* and *C*) is twice (or three times) the input frequency; collector (or plate) current will arrive at the tuned circuit during every second (or third) cycle of output voltage and deliver sufficient energy to the tuned circuit to sustain oscillation (by flywheel effect) during cycles when no current flows.

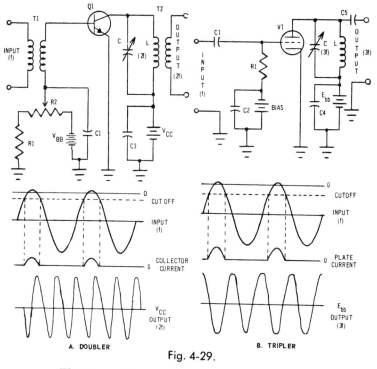

Fig. 4-29.

When the amplifier goes into cutoff, energy supplied to the output tank circuit is sufficient to maintain oscillation between current pulses. The reason the tuned circuit continues to oscillate is that pulses of current always arrive at the same time during every other (or every third) cycle of the doubled (or tripled) frequency, thus energizing the tank circuit at the proper time.

The distinguishing features of the multiplier are the values of L and C, which determine the frequency multiple of the input to which the tank will respond.

4-91. *Draw a simple schematic showing the method of connecting three resistors of equal value so that the total resistance will be two-thirds the resistance of one unit.*

The battery and resistors illustrate the circuit in Fig. 4-30. If each resistor is 3Ω, the total resistance at the battery terminals is two-thirds the resistance of any of the three resistors of identical value. Calculating the

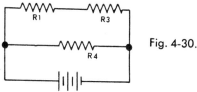

Fig. 4-30.

value is done by first computing the total resistance of the two series resistors and treating the total of the two as a single resistor of twice the value of the parallel unit.

4-92. *Draw a simple schematic showing the method of connecting three resistors of equal value so that the total resistance will be one and one-half times the value of one unit alone.*

This is a series—parallel arrangement, as shown in Fig. 4-31. If all resistors are 3Ω, the total value is 4.5Ω. The parallel resistors amount to 1.5Ω; and this, in series with the 3Ω resistors, results in a total value of 4.5Ω

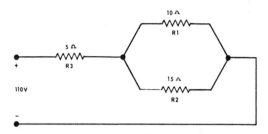

Fig. 4-31.

4-93. *Draw a simple schematic showing the method of connecting three resistors of equal value so that the total resistance will be one-third the value of a single resistor.*

This is a straight parallel arrangement, as shown in Fig. 4-32. The total value of equal parallel resistors is equal to the value of one divided by the number of resistors. If there are three equal resistors in parallel, the total resistance is one-third the value of one resistor.

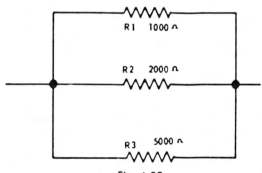

Fig. 4-32.

4-94. *Draw a simple schematic showing the method of connecting three resistors of equal value so that the total resistance will be three times the resistance of a single unit.*

These three resistors would be connected end-to-end in a straight series arrangement, since series resistors are simply additive.

4-95. Draw a diagram of a single-button carbon microphone circuit, including the microphone transformer and source of power.

The single-button carbon microphone (Fig. 4-33) consists of a diaphragm mounted against carbon granules that are contained in a small carbon cup (or button). To produce an output voltage, this microphone is connected in a series circuit containing a battery and the primary winding of a microphone transformer. The pressure of sound waves on the diaphragm, which is coupled to the carbon granules, causes the resistance of the granules to vary; thus, a varying direct current in the primary produces an alternating voltage in the secondary of the transformer. This voltage has essentially the same waveform as that of the sound waves striking the diaphragm. The current through a carbon microphone may be as great as 100 mA, and the resistance may vary from about 50Ω to 100Ω. The voltage developed across the secondary depends upon the turns ratio and the rate of change in primary current. Normal output voltage of a typical circuit is from 3V to 10V peak across the secondary terminals.

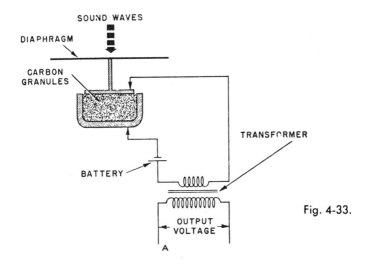

Fig. 4-33.

4-96. What is meant by a "soft" vacuum tube?

A "soft" tube is one that has a leaky seal. The presence of gas is distinguished by a bluish haze under full excitation.

4-97. Describe the electrical characteristics of the pentode, tetrode, and triode.

One of the most important characteristics of the triode (Fig. 4-34A) is the *interelectrode capacitance*. The grid, plate, and cathode form an electrostatic system in which each electrode acts as one plate of a small capacitor. The capacitances are those existing between grid and plate (C_{gp}), between plate and cathode (C_{pk}), and between grid and cathode

75

(C_{gk}). The capacitance between grid and plate is of the most importance. In high-gain rf circuits this capacitance may produce undesired coupling between the input and output circuit. Such undesirable coupling causes instability and erratic operation.

The tetrode is shown in Fig. 4-34B. One of the principal advantages of this 4-element tube is the diminished interelectrode capacitance. This is attributable to the additional electrode (screen grid) between the control grid and the plate. The screen grid has another desirable effect in that it makes plate current practically independent of plate voltage over a specific range of operating parameters. The screen grid is operated at a positive potential with respect to the cathode, so it attracts electrons from the cathode. However, because of the coarse screen construction, most of the electrons drawn toward it pass right through to the plate. Thus, while the screen grid shields the electrons on the cathode side of the screen grid from the plate (preventing an electrostatic effect between the two), it does serve to bolster the passage of electrons in the tube.

One disadvantage of the tetrode is the increased susceptibility to *secondary emission*, the action of electrons being knocked loose from the plate. The presence of the screen grid causes these electrons to be drawn back toward the screen, thus reducing the plate current and limiting the useful plate voltage swing.

The pentode's extra grid serves to check the problem of secondary emission. In this device (Fig. 4-34C) an additional element (suppressor grid) is placed between the screen grid and plate. Since this element is tied internally to the cathode, its low potential shields the screen grid from the electrons bounced off the plate.

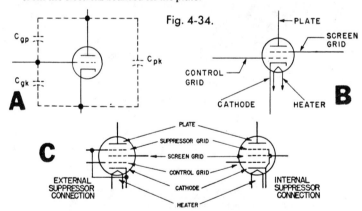

Fig. 4-34.

4-98. *What are the visible indications of a "soft" tube?*

A "soft" tube is often characterized by a bluish haze between its elements when it is under full excitation. Also, plate current may fall off rapidly after excitation.

4-99. *Describe the physical structure of a triode vacuum tube.*

Refer to the text of question 4-97 and Fig. 4-34A.

4-100. *Describe the physical structure of a tetrode.*

See Fig. 4-34B and associated text.

4-101. *Does a pentode normally require neutralization when used as an rf amplifier?*

It does not. Neutralization requirements result from interelectrode capacitances, as noted in the answer to question 4-97. The problem of interelectrode capacitance is largely overcome when one or more elements are inserted between the control grid and plate.

4-102. *What is the meaning of "secondary emission"?*

Secondary emission is the phenomenon in which electrons bombarding the plate cause electrons to be dislodged from the plate. The presence of the screen grid—which is maintained at a potential designed to attract electrons—makes this problem severe in the tetrode. A suppressor grid, at the charge level of the tube's cathode, prevents the problem.

4-103. *What is the meaning of "electron emission"?*

Electron emission is the escape of outer-orbit electrons from individual atoms of any conductor. Such outer electrons can be dislodged and freed in many ways. In the cathode of a tube it is accomplished by heating. Electrons thus released are attracted by the charge of the plate and thus "boil off" the cathode, flow across to the plate, and enter the plate circuit.

4-104. *Describe the characteristics of a tube acting as a class C amplifier.*

A class C amplifier is one in which the **grid bias is appreciably greater (more negative) than** the **cutoff** value. When **no alternating voltage is applied to the grid, plate current is zero**; however, when an ac voltage **is applied to the grid, plate current flows for appreciably less than one-half cycle**. Since current flows for only a small part of an input cycle, the distortion in the class C amplifier is quite high, as shown in the input–output waveform sketch of Fig. 4-35.

A class C amplifier grid usually swings sufficiently positive to allow saturation current to flow through the tube. As a result, the plate output waves contain harmonics, and suitable means must be provided to remove them from the output. Efficiency of a class C amplifier is high.

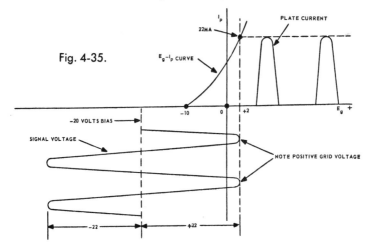

Fig. 4-35.

77

4-105. *During what approximate portion of the excitation voltage cycle does plate current flow when a tube is used as a class C amplifier?*

As shown in Fig. 4-35, plate current flows for about one-third of the input cycle. Current flow is indicated by the $e_G - i_P$ curve. In the example shown, the grid is biased at $-20V$. As the grid goes more negative, the tube remains at cutoff. The cycle returns to zero, then goes more positive. When the grid potential approaches $-10V$ because of the input signal's positive swing overcoming the bias, the tube begins to conduct. It continues to do so until the input signal again drops out of the amplifier's operating curve. In the example shown, the grid is held at about 10V beyond cutoff under no-signal conditions.

4-106. *Describe the characteristics of a tube acting as a class A amplifier.*

An amplifier is considered to be operating class A when the grid bias and alternating grid voltages have such values that **plate current flows** continuously **throughout the cycle** of the applied voltage and never reaches zero. Class A amplifiers are normally biased at about one-half of cutoff value. This establishes an operating point in the central portion of the amplifier's $e_G - i_P$ curve. Figure 4-36 shows the basic class A amplifier along with characteristic waveshapes.

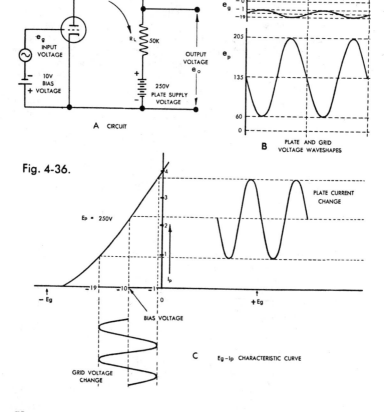

Fig. 4-36.

A CIRCUIT

B PLATE AND GRID VOLTAGE WAVESHAPES

C Eg–Ip CHARACTERISTIC CURVE

Class A amplifiers are characterized by **low efficency** (ratio of total power output to total power input). Practically speaking, the efficiency range is 20% to 25%, though such amplifiers are theoretically capable of attaining efficiency ratios of as high as 50%. Class A amplifiers are typically used where **low distortion** is of importance, such as audio systems and some rf amplifier systems.

4-107. Describe the characteristics of a tube operating as a class B amplifier.

Class B amplifiers are **biased to approximately the tube's cutoff point;** thus **plate current flows only during the positive half-cycle** of the applied signal. **The efficiency is higher and the current consumption is less than with the class A** amplifier, but efficiency is not as high as with the class C amplifier. Power loss in class B amplifiers is low for two reasons: **Plate current does not flow when there is no signal applied** to the grid, which cuts power wastes during no-signal conditions. **Plate current flows only during positive excursions of the incoming wave,** which means the average current will be only 32% of the peak current in the stage.

Figure 4-37A shows the relation between grid voltage and plate current in a tube-type class B amplifier. Note that grid current flows only during the time that the grid is driven positive. Class B amplifiers are used mostly as power amplifiers, and their power output is proportional to the square of the grid excitation voltage. The best bias for class B operation is that which corresponds roughly to the cutoff bias that would be obtained if the main part of the characteristic curves shown in Fig. 4-37B were projected as straight lines. Notice the broken straight line extended from the straight part of the 300V plate voltage curve. The point at which the line strikes the grid voltage line (about +75V) gives the cutoff bias for 300V plate operation. Curves of this type provide a convenient means for determining grid bias for class B operation for different plate voltage conditions.

Distortion occurs in class B amplifiers under much the same conditions as in class A amplifiers. Frequency and phase shift distortion are essentially alike in both. Harmonic distortion in the

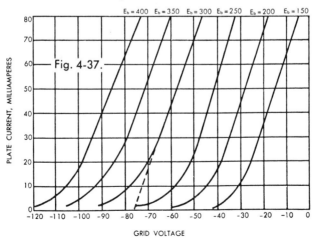

GRID VOLTAGE

output of a class B amplifier operating with the proper load resistance depends on the departure of the operating curve from the linear.

4-108. *During what portion of the excitation voltage cycle does plate current flow in a tube used as a class B amplifier?*

Plate current flows only during the **positive portion** of the excitation signal, since the tube's operating point is established exactly at cutoff.

4-109. *Does a properly operated class A audio amplifier produce serious modification of the input waveform?*

No. Since the operating point of the class A amplifier is established at the center of its linear region, the input signal can swing either plus or minus; the tube conducts at all times. As long as neither cutoff nor saturation is reached, the amplifier's output signal is a replica of the input signal waveform.

4-110. *What is meant by the term "maximum plate dissipation"?*

Dissipation always refers to power. Thus *maximum plate dissipation* refers to the maximum power capable of being handled by the plate element in a vacuum tube, as calculated by multiplying plate current by plate voltage. Maximum plate dissipation is a tube rating expressed in watts.

4-111. *What is meant by a "blocked grid"?*

A blocked grid is one that has no path to ground for the accumulated electrons flowing from cathode to plate. A proper value of grid-leak resistor prevents the blocked-grid situation. A blocked grid results in a voltage buildup in the grid circuit that was unintended in the circuit design; it causes unpredictable and unstable tube operation.

4-112. *What is meant by "load" on a vacuum tube?*

The load is the series resistance in the plate circuit. In Fig. 4-38 the load on the tube is the resistance labeled R_L. The load is the factor that determines the operating conditions of the tube and is the prime means by which amplifier operation can be analyzed. The straight line drawn across the voltage–current curves is called the *load line*. It is the result of plotting the values of plate current and plate voltage in the triode circuit and connecting all of the plotted points by a straight line. One extremity of the load line is the point where the plate current is zero and the voltage drop across the load is zero. The other extreme is the point where the plate current is absolutely unlimited by the tube—that is, the tube acts as a short circuit. Current at this point is limited only by the load and may be calculated using Ohm's law. When the tube is shorted, plate voltage is zero. The slope of the load line is determined by the load itself. The greater the load, the less the slope. The load line and the curves in Fig. 4-38 are based on the triode circuit shown.

4-113. *What circuit and vacuum-tube factors influence the voltage gain of a triode audio amplifier?*

The principal **circuit factors** that must be considered are **the grid-leak resistance and load resistance**. Since gain is the ratio of power input to power output, the grid resistance must be high enough to prevent excessive loading, and the load must be many times higher than the tube's internal plate resistance. **Tube factors are amplification factor** (μ) **and plate resistance** (r_p).

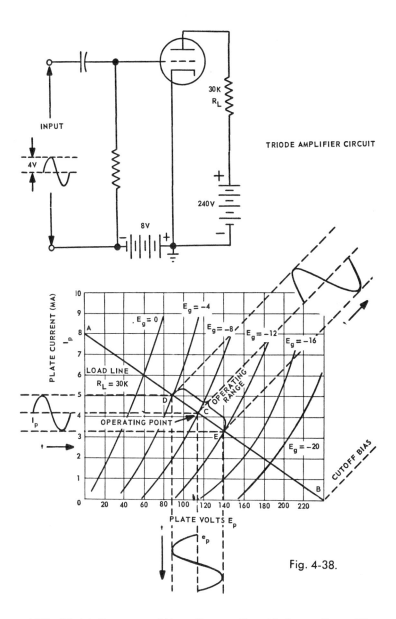

TRIODE AMPLIFIER CIRCUIT

Fig. 4-38.

4-114. *What is the purpose of bias voltage on the grid of an audio amplifier tube?*

The bias voltage **holds the tube at the approximate center of its** *linear* operating range during no-signal conditions. This results in linear response to both positive and negative signal excursions. Look again at

81

the characteristic curve in Fig. 4-36B. The bias is shown to be at −10V under no-signal conditions. When the applied input signal swings positive, the bias drops toward zero and the tube is driven toward its saturation point. When the applied signal voltage swings negative, the amplifier is driven toward its cutoff point. Linear amplification results when the quiescent (no signal) point is about halfway between cutoff and saturation.

4-115. *What is the primary purpose of a screen grid?*

The screen grid's chief purpose is **to minimize a tube's interelectrode capacitance**. The triode's principal drawbacks for high-frequency work result from the capacitance existing between the grid and plate. The screen grid in a tetrode (and pentode), between grid and plate, diminishes this effect.

4-116. *What is the primary purpose of a suppressor grid?*

The suppressor **minimizes** the problems of **secondary emission**. Since the suppressor grid is electrically at the same potential at the cathode, electrons escaping from the plate are shielded from the attraction of the screen grid. The suppressor grid is so named because it suppresses secondary emission.

4-117. *What is meant by "plate saturation"?*

Plate saturation is the point in an amplifier's operating curve where **further increases in grid voltage do not result in appreciable increases in plate current**, regardless of the plate voltage. At this point the plate resistance of the of the tube is essentially zero. In the triode amplifier load line of Fig. 4-38, saturation is indicated at point A on the graph. The opposite end of the line, point B, is the cutoff point. Audio amplifiers are operated in the linear region between the two extremes.

4-118. *What is the most desirable feature of a vacuum tube to be used as a voltage amplifier?*

The single most important factor is **amplification factor** (μ). Since a voltage amplifer is not intended to produce a current gain, power amplification need not be considered. The load of a voltage amplifier should be at the highest resistance possible, so that a large voltage will be developed across it.

4-119. *What is the principal advantage of a tetrode over a triode as an rf amplifier?*

The primary advantage is the fact that the effects of interelectrode capacitance are minimized; and this results in two ancillary features:

1. **Neutralization problems are minimized** because input signals are less likely to be fed back to the input through the tube's internal capacitance.
2. Tetrodes **can be used at higher frequencies** than triodes because a tetrode's interelectrode capacitance is negligible over a greater range.

4-120. *What is the principal advantage of a tetrode as compared with a triode when used in a radio receiver?*

Elimination of the need for **neutralization** is the most important characteristic of the tetrode in receiver circuits. Triodes tend to

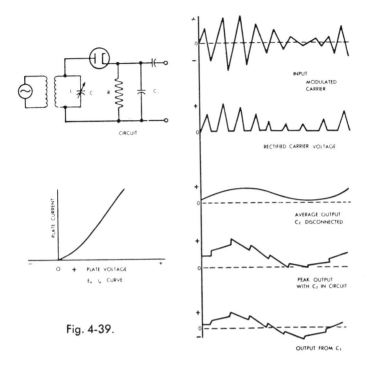

Fig. 4-39.

oscillate because of the regenerative feedback that occurs when the output signal is coupled back to the grid in phase with the input signal. Such coupling causes squeals and whistles that disrupt the desired signal.

4-121. *What is the principal advantage of using a diode detector rather than a grid-leak detector?*

The diode detector has a number of advantages over the grid-leak detector. For purposes of the FCC examination, the most important is **probably the diode detector's immunity to signals of extremely high amplitude.** There is practically no limit to the strength of signals that can be handled by the diode detector, while the grid-leak detector's input signal must not be so high that it causes the average grid voltage to exceed plate current cutoff voltage for the particular tube. A secondary advantage of the diode detector is its selectivity as compared to the grid-leak detector. The grid current requirement of the latter type draws heavily on the preceding tuned circuit, thereby lowering its Q to a point substantially less than the same tuned circuit used to drive a diode detector.

A diode detector circuit with its operating curve and various waveforms is shown in Fig. 4-39. A basic grid-leak detector and representative waveforms are pictured in Fig. 4-40.

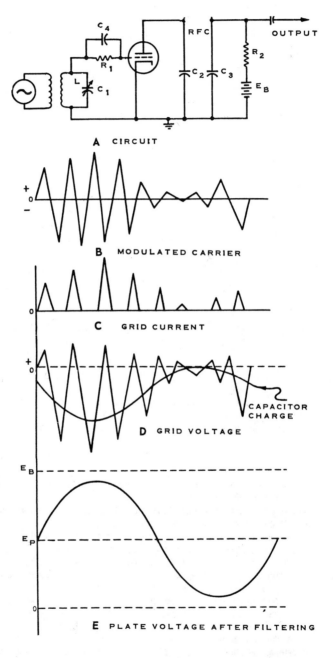

A CIRCUIT

B MODULATED CARRIER

C GRID CURRENT

CAPACITOR
CHARGE

D GRID VOLTAGE

E_B

E_P

E PLATE VOLTAGE AFTER FILTERING

Fig. 4-40.

4-122. *Draw a grid voltage, plate current characteristic curve of a vacuum tube and indicate the operating points for class A, class B, and class C amplification.*

Figure 4-41 shows two curves. The curve for a screen-grid tube can be used to illustrate the grid-plate characteristic for all amplifier classes. The linear portion of this curve extends from about −2V to −7V grid voltage; thus, a class A amplifier's operating point would be established in the center of this range, or at −4.5V. The cutoff point of this curve is shown to be at −15V, so the operating point of the class B amplifier would be established here. Since the class C amplifier conducts only during a small portion of the input signal excursions, the operating point is established well below cutoff; in the graph shown, the class C operating point for the screen grid tube would be about −22V.

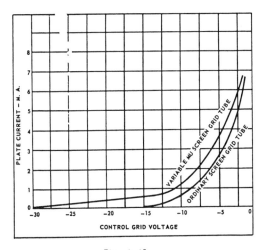

Fig. 4-41.

4-123. *What operating condition determines that a tube is being used as a power detector?*

If a detector is to handle rf carrier voltages having amplitudes greater than one volt, it is called a *power detector*. If the input signal is less than one volt, it is called a *weak-signal detector*. Weak-signal detectors are always of the *square law* type, while a power detector may be either linear or square law. The operating condition that determines whether or not a tube is being used as a power detector is the **input amplitude** of the intended signal.

4-124. *Why is it desirable to use an ac filament supply for tubes?*

It is curious that this question appears on the exam, since there are advantages with dc that outweigh any advantages ac might offer, particularly in mobile or battery-operated equipment. Nonetheless, the FCC would like you to answer this way: An ac supply is desirable because use of ac for filaments will prolong tube life. Unequal emission (and nonuniform "wear") of the cathode results from dc operation, since that portion of the filament most negative with respect to the supply will emit the greatest number of electrons.

Still, the use of ac-operated filaments sometimes results in an unacceptable amount of 60 Hz hum in audio circuits. It is often simpler to convert the ac to a pure dc than to provide the necessary grounding and wire twisting required to eliminate such hum.

4-125. *Why is it advisable to periodically reverse the polarity of the filament supply for high-powered vacuum tubes with dc filaments.*

Since one side of the filament is more negative than the other, electrons will not be emitted uniformly from the surface of the filament. Occasional polarity reversal will considerably increase the tube's useful life by distributing wear equally over the filament.

4-126. *Why is it important to maintain transmitting-tube filaments at recommended voltage levels?*

Excessive filament voltage will greatly reduce tube life. The operation of the tube is designed around a specific cathode temperature, which itself is a measure of the electrons being "boiled off" the cathode. When the heater temperature increases beyond the design optimum, electron emission will increase, and the cathode emitting surface will wear out prematurely. Low filament voltage, on the other hand, will cause low emission and symptoms of aging.

4-127. *When an ac filament supply is used, why is a filament centertap usually provided for the plate and grid return circuits?*

This is a **hum reduction** feature. When all ground returns are connected at the center point of the filament's operating voltage, the filament supply voltage is said to be balanced. Hum is reduced because the signal level attributable to the filament's ac voltage is always close to ground potential. If only one side of the filament were at ground, the level might be excessive during half of each cycle.

4-128. *Explain the operation of a grid-leak detector.*

The grid-leak detector is similar to the diode detector, except that it includes a stage of amplification. Grid-leak detectors use no fixed-bias arrangement in the grid circuit; they depend on the flow of grid current during periods when the grid is driven positive.

In the typical grid-leak detector circuit shown in Fig. 4-42, the grid, cathode, C4, R1, and the tuned circuit form a diode detector circuit. If capacitor C4 and resistor R1 are correctly proportioned, the capacitor charges during the period of current flow and discharges during periods of no current flow. Discharge is through R1 and occurs slowly. Since the capacitor maintains an average charge, it places an average negative value of voltage on the grid with respect to the cathode. The rf voltage at the grid varies around this average value. If the capacitor should discharge slightly, the next positive cycle of the modulated voltage will go higher in the positive direction, recharging the capacitor. As the modulated waveform decreases in amplitude (positive peaks become smalller), the capacitor does not fully recharge with each cycle, and the average (grid bias) reaches a lower value. Thus, the average grid voltage varies in accordance with the variation of the amplitude of the

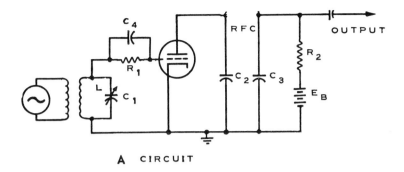

A CIRCUIT

Fig. 4-42.

modulated wave and reproduces the signal voltage. The voltage applied to a grid-leak detector must be low enough to insure that the average grid voltage does not exceed the tube's plate current cutoff.

4-129. *List and explain the characteristics of a square law vacuum-tube detector.*

First, we must define a square law detector: It is a detector that is operated in the nonlinear region of its operating curve, where each doubling of voltage results in a quadrupling of current. In Fig. 4-43 two curves are shown. Curve A is considered ideal because it has two linear regions, one on either side of the operating point (designated P). Overall, of course, the curve is still nonlinear. The square law curve in Fig. 4-43B has almost no linearity. In summary, the principal characteristics of the square law detector are these:

1. An operating curve whose **current varies with the square of the voltage**.
2. **Output contains harmonics of all the input frequencies**. These occur because voltage inputs that have a large amplitude are distorted differently from voltage inputs that have a low amplitude.
3. **Considerable distortion**, caused by the presence of signal harmonics that cannot be filtered out.
4. **Greater output** for a given input than that obtainable with a linear device, since output amplitude varies with the square of the input.

4-130. *Explain the operation of a diode-type detector.*

The diode detector is one of the simplest and most effective detectors and one with nearly an ideal nonlinear resistance characteristic. Notice the curve in Fig. 4-44B. This is the type of curve on which the diode detector shown in Fig. 4-44A operates. The rounded portion of the curve is the region of low plate current and indicates that, for small signals, the output of the detector will follow the square law (see answer to question 4-129). For input signals with large amplitude, however, the output of the detector will be essentially linear in the positive direction from the operating point. This type of detector is classed as a power

87

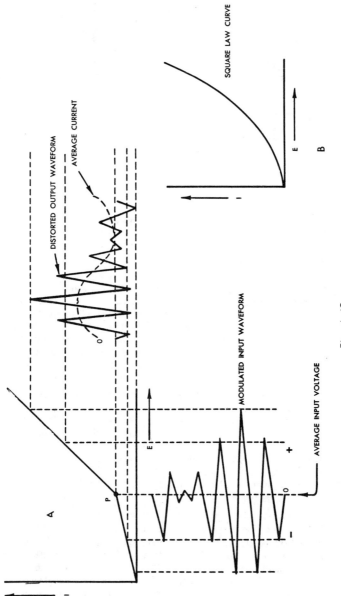

Fig. 4-43.

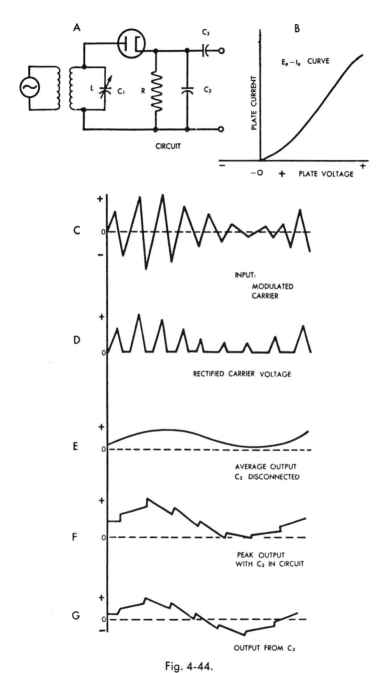

A

C₃

C₁   R   C₂

CIRCUIT

B

Eₚ−Iₚ CURVE

PLATE CURRENT

−   −O   +   PLATE VOLTAGE   +

C

INPUT:
MODULATED
CARRIER

D

RECTIFIED CARRIER VOLTAGE

E

AVERAGE OUTPUT
C₂ DISCONNECTED

F

PEAK OUTPUT
WITH C₂ IN CIRCUIT

G

OUTPUT FROM C₃

Fig. 4-44.

detector since it handles large input amplitudes without much distortion.

The modulated carrier is introduced into the tuned circuit made up of $LC1$, which is designed so that the receiver has a high degree of selectivity. The waveshape of the input to diode plate is shown in Fig. 4-44C. As a diode conducts only during positive half-cycles, the circuit removes all the negative half-cycles and gives the result shown in Fig. 4-44D. The average output is shown in Fig. 4-44E.

Although the average input voltage is zero, the average output voltage across R always varies above zero and has an average voltage of 50% of the capacitor's average charge, times the peak voltage for any positive half-cycle.

The low-pass filter made up of capacitor $C2$ and resistor R removes the rf (carrier frequency), which serves no useful purpose in the receiver. Capacitor $C2$ charges rapidly to the peak voltage through the small resistance of R. The sizes of R and $C2$ normally bring about a relatively short time constant at the audio frequency and a very long time constant at the radio frequency carrying the audio intelligence. The resultant output with $C2$ in the circuit is a varying voltage that follows the peak variation of the modulated carrier (Fig. 4-44F). The dc component produced by the detector circuit is still in the waveshape but may be removed by capacitor $C3$, producing the ac waveshape in Fig. 4-44G. In communications receivers the dc component is often used for providing the agc voltage.

The advantages of a diode detector are:

1. High efficiency. Ninety percent is achievable by proper design.
2. High-power capability. There is no practical limit to the power levels that can be handled.
3. Low distortion. The higher the input amplitude, the lower the distortion.
4. Developed voltage can be used for automatic gain control.

Disadvantages are:

1. Power is absorbed from the input circuit, which lowers the circuit Q and decreases selectivity.
2. No amplification is possible, since the circuit is entirely passive.

4-131. *Explain the operation of "power" or "plate rectification" type of vacuum-tube detector.*

For this discussion refer to the plate detector drawings (in Fig. 4-45). In this type of detector plate current flows only during positive halves of the input signal and a small portion of the negative halves. The grid does not draw current as long as the signal does not drive the grid into the positive region of the characteristic curve. The average plate current shown at Fig. 4-45A by broken lines varies as the modulation varies.

The removal of the rf component from the plate circuit is accomplished by the low-pass filter formed by the rf choke and capacitors $C1$ and $C2$. The variation remaining after removal constitutes the orignal modulation. Because of the amplification factor of the tube, the voltage representing the modulation (which appears across the load resistor) is greater than the input (grid) voltage. All

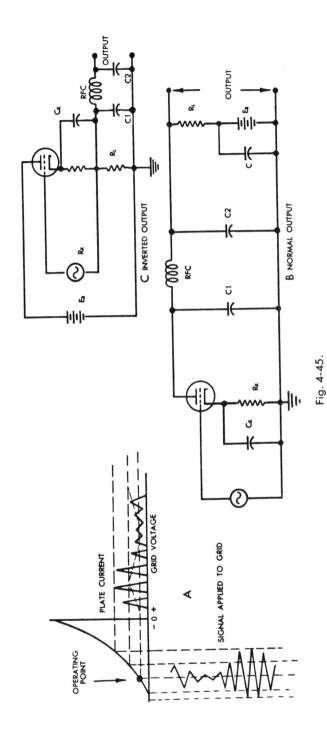

Fig. 4-45.

other ac voltages are effectively placed at ground potential by capacitor C1

When a pulse-modulated signal is applied to the detector, a pulse appears that is positive at the grid and negative in the circuit. In some applications a positive pulse output is desired. This is achieved by changing the circuit so that the load resistor (R_L) is located in the cathode-to-grid circuit instead of the plate circuit. By this arrangement the output has the correct polarity and may be taken across the load resistor. The other ground connections are removed, as you can see by examining the inverted output circuit for pulse-type modulation in Fig. 4-45C.

The advantage of the plate detector is that, since the grid does not draw current, the Q of the input circuit remains the same, and amplification occurs in the circuit. Its disadvantages are higher distortion and lower power handling ability than the diode detector.

4-132. *Is a grid-leak detector more or less sensitive than a power detector?*

The grid-leak detector is more sensitive, since the other type's signal must be at least one volt to qualify it as a power detector.

4-133. *Describe what is meant by a "class A" amplifier.*

A class A amplifier is an amplifier whose **operating point** is established **in the central portion of the grid voltage, plate current curve**. Since this operating point allows an equal amount of signal voltage swing (both positive-going and negative-going), with linear plate current variations, it makes the class A amplifier ideally suited to audio amplification. A unique characteristic of the class A amplifier is the fact that the stage draws current constantly—even during the quiescent (no-signal) state—because of the bias required to hold the operating point at the center of the linear region of the operating curve.

4-134. *What are the characteristics of a class A amplifier?*

Class A amplifiers have a grid bias that holds the tube at an operating point in the center of the operating region, approximately halfway between cutoff and saturation. With a normal input signal, plate current flows during the entire input cycle, and the amplification is essentially linear, as indicated in the curve of Fig. 4-46.

The principal characteristics of the class A amplifier are minimum distortion, low overall power efficiency, and continuous plate current drain.

4-135. *What is the effect of incorrect grid bias in a class A audio amplifier?*

The most noticeable effect is distortion, particularly with large signals. If the bias error is not excessive, low signal levels can still be processed within the linear portion of the $e_G - i_P$ curve, and there will be no measurable distortion. With larger swings of the input, however, the tube can be driven to saturation or cutoff, depending upon whether the bias is excessive or insufficient. With excessive grid bias, input signal peaks drive the tube into cutoff. With insufficient bias, peaks drives the tube into saturation.

3-136. *What factors determine the bias voltage for the grid of a tube?*

The individual tube characteristics (curves) make up one powerful determinant. The class of operation is equally important, for some switching amplifiers are operated very close to saturation (little or no bias), audio amplifiers are operated in the center of the linear portion of the operating curve (moderate grid bias), class B amplifiers are operated near cutoff, and class C amplifiers are operated at a point well below cutoff (heavy negative bias).

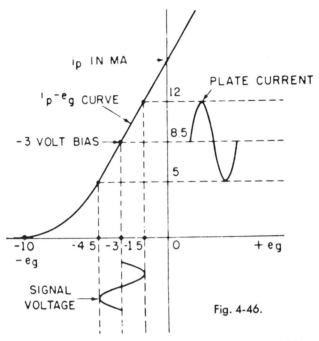

Fig. 4-46.

4-137. *Why are tubes operated as class C amplifiers not suited for audio amplification?*

A tube operated as a class C amplifier would reproduce only a small portion of the applied input signal, and the reproduced output would thus be heavily distorted. (See discussion in answers to preceding questions.)

4-138. *Draw a circuit diagram of a frequency doubler and explain its operation.*

The circuit in Fig. 4-47 is that of a frequency doubler. (In this discussion, whenever *collector* is mentioned, insertion of the word *plate* will make the term applicable to a tube circuit. Similarly, *emitter* and *base* can be replaced with *cathode* and *grid*, respectively.)

The frequency multiplier is operated class C, with the collector tank circuit resonant at twice the base frequency. When the signal applied to the base rises above the cutoff value of the transistor, there will be a pulse of current at the same frequency as the input signal flowing from emitter to collector and energizing the collector circuit. These pulses contain appreciable energy at the second and third harmonics, and the resonant frequency of the tank circuit (determined by values of L and

C) is twice the input frequency. The output tank, being tuned to twice the input frequency, is responsive to the energy at the second harmonic and thus sustains oscillatory action. When the transistor goes into cutoff (approximately two-thirds of each operating cycle), energy delivered to the collector circuit is sufficient to sustain oscillation until the next pulse arrives.

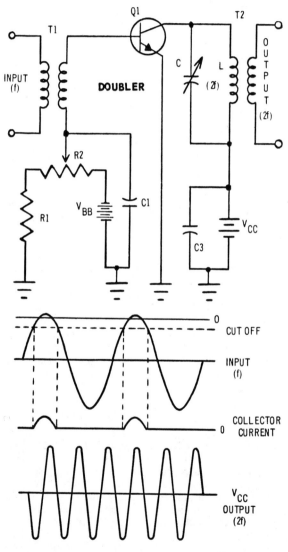

Fig. 4-47.

4-139. For what purpose is a doubler amplifier used?

A doubler amplifier typically is used **to double the frequency of a signal** that has been generated in a preceding transmitter stage. An oscillator might be combined with a doubler or tripler, or a series of such stages, to obtain the desired carrier frequency.

A doubler differs from a conventional rf amplifier in that its output tuned circuit is resonant at twice the frequency of the input tuned circuit.

4-140. Describe what is meant by "link coupling."

Link coupling is a means for transferring rf energy from one circuit to another without physical connection between the two circuits. Normally, a wire loop of a few turns is placed in proximity to a larger coil, often with the turns interleaved. The energy present in the field of the larger coil is inductively transferred to the loop. The loop is itself connected to a second loop at the other end of an rf line, and the second loop is coupled to a coil in the succeeding stage or circuit.

4-141. What factors may cause low plate current in a vacuum-tube amplifier?

This is one of the kinds of questions that give applicants headaches, for there is almost no limit to the reasons for low plate current. However, the following might be considered principal choices:

1. **Low emission** because of the cathode emitting surface (oxide) wearing out.
2. **Low filament voltage.** Low filament voltage causes low emission, hence low plate current.
3. **Low plate voltage.** When plate voltage falls off, plate current decreases proportionately, provided the tube is not operated in its saturation state.
4. **Excessive grid bias.** When the grid is biased excessively, plate current is allowed to flow for a smaller portion of the input cycle; as a consequence, the tube may not be driven to full power before it reaches cutoff.
5. The presence of **secondary emission.**
6. **Insufficient excitation voltage.** This factor may be caused by a whole new Pandora's box of problems, not the least of which are "soft" tubes in a preceding stage, too low a value of grid-leak resistor, or low output from the driver stage.
7. An **open grid circuit.** With rf amplifiers and class B amplifiers, plate current drops to zero; with class A amplifiers, current will drop to the level established by the grid bias.

4-142. Given the following vacuum-tube constants, what would be the value of grid bias: $E_P = 1\,kV$, $I_P = 150\,mA$, $I_G = 10\,mA$, and $R_G = 5K$?

The key parameters here are grid current (I_G) and grid-leak resistance (R_G); the total plate current and plate voltage have no bearing on the bias voltage. Since a current of 10 mA, or 0.01A, flows through the grid-leak resistor—and this resistor is 5000Ω, according to Ohm's law—the grid voltage is $-50V$ ($E = IR$).

4-143. Explain how you would determine the value of cathode bias resistance necessary to provide correct grid bias for any particular amplifier.

95

Ohm's law is used to determine the value. For example, if the desired bias is 10V and the cathode current is 30 mA, then the cathode resistor would be equal to E_G/I_K or 10V divided by 0.03A, which is 333Ω. Notice in Fig. 4-48 that a capacitor is placed across the cathode resistor. The reactance of the capacitor should not be more than 10% of the value of the cathode resistor at the lowest frequency to be amplified.

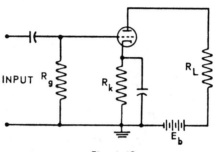

Fig. 4-48.

4-144. *What is the chemical composition of the active material composing the negative plate of a lead—acid storage cell?*

The material is **sponge lead.**

4-145. *What is the chemical composition of the active material composing the negative plate of an Edison cell?*

It is **powdered iron oxide mixed with cadmium.**

4-146. *What is the composition of the positive plate of a lead—acid cell?*

The material is **lead dioxide.**

4-147. *How does a "primary" cell differ from a "secondary" cell?*

A *primary* cell consists of two metals immersed in a solution that produces greater chemical action on one metal than on the other. With a primary cell, the voltage is created when the metals are placed in the solution (electrolyte). Generally speaking, **primary cells cannot be recharged.** A primary cell appears in cross section in Fig. 4-49.

A *secondary* cell must have energy stored in it by charging before it can deliver useful energy. Charging is accomplished by forcing a current to flow in the cell in a direction opposite to the flow during discharge. A common secondary cell contains two lead electrodes (one sponge lead, the other lead dioxide) immersed in a solution of diluted sulfuric acid.

A group of cells placed in a single package together are connected to produce an output greater than any individual cell could deliver; the total group is referred to as a *battery* (Fig. 4-50). The automobile storage battery is a typical cell group, and consists of six series-connected cells (usually).

4-148. *What is the active material composing the positive plate of an Edison cell?*

The positive plate is made of **nickel hydroxide.**

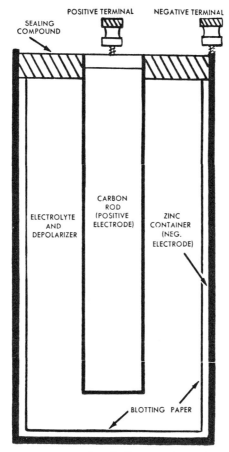

POSITIVE TERMINAL   NEGATIVE TERMINAL

SEALING
COMPOUND

ELECTROLYTE
AND
DEPOLARIZER

CARBON
ROD
(POSITIVE
ELECTRODE)

ZINC
CONTAINER
(NEG.
ELECTRODE)

BLOTTING PAPER

Fig. 4-49.

4-149. *What is the chemical composition of the electrolyte used in an Edison cell?*

It is an **alkaline solution of potassium hydroxide**, with a small amount of lithium hydroxide.

4-150. *What is the chemical composition of the electrolyte of a lead–acid storage cell?*

The electrolyte is a dilute solution of **sulfuric acid**.

4-151. *What is "polarization" of a primary cell and how may its effect be counteracted?*

Polarization is a phenomenon whereby gas buildup on one or both battery electrodes increases the resistance of the cell during discharge. The accumulation of hydrogen bubbles around the positive electrode insulates the electrode from the electrolyte. The effect is counteracted by mixing manganese dioxide with the electrolyte. The oxygen in the manganese dioxide is released during cell gassing so that sufficient amounts of hydrogen and oxygen combine to form water. The formation of water on the positive electrode does not increase resistance, because the water formed is conductive; but the hydrogen bubbles are nonconductive. When polarization occurs, the positive electrode will appear more negative than the negative electrode.

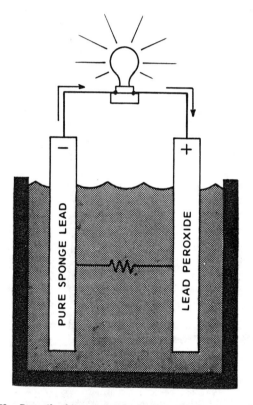

Fig. 4-50.

4-152. *Describe three causes of a decrease in capacity of an Edison cell.*

Current-supplying capacity in the Edison cell can be decreased by **operating the cell at too high a temperature, too low a temperature, or with insufficient load.** Allowing the cell to remain idle for long periods will have the same effect as insufficient load.

4-153. *What is the cause of heat developed within a storage cell during charge or discharge?*

Excessive current—either to charge the cell or to power a load—is the primary cause of heat within the cell. Heat is attributable to the friction of moving electrons.

4-154. *How may a dry cell be tested to determine its condition?*

The terminal voltage of a dry cell should be checked while the cell is under a normal load. The dry cell cannot be tested during no-load conditions, because the open circuit voltage might not drop—regardless of cell condition.

4-155. *What would be the result of discharging a lead–acid battery at an excessively high current rate?*

The battery will tend to **overheat**, thereby accelerating the discharge rate and perhaps damaging the battery permanently. Excessive heating **causes sulfation, plate buckling, and electrolyte boiloff**.

4-156. *What is the approximate fully charged voltage of an Edison cell?*

Under a relatively light load, the closed-circuit voltage of the Edison cell is roughly 1.4V. When the terminal voltage drops to about a volt, the cell is considered to be discharged.

4-157. *A hypothetical 6V storage battery has an internal resistance of 0.1Ω. What current will flow when a 3W lamp of the proper voltage rating is connected?*

Remember, the battery's internal resistance must be taken into consideration, because it becomes part of the circuit, just as the resistor is shown to be part of the battery in Fig. 4-50. The 3W resistor would draw 0.5A from a 6V source, but the source voltage is dropped because of the 0.1Ω resistance. Based on the wattage rating of the lamp, its resistance is 12Ω; thus the series resistance totals 12.0Ω. From Ohm's law, then, current is **6 divided by 12.1, or 0.496A (496 mA)**.

4-158. *What is the approximate fully charged voltage of a lead–acid cell?*

The lead–acid cell's terminal voltage at full charge is approximately 2.1V.

4-159. *Why is a low internal resistance desirable in a storage cell?*

The lower the internal resistance, the higher the voltage delivered to any load, since the internal resistance may be considered as a series resistor in any circuit connected to the battery. As the internal resistance increases, the battery's remaining capacity is reduced; a new battery's internal resistance is extremely low. As the cell ages, the internal resistance increases, which results in a progressively lower closed-circuit terminal voltage, until the cell is useless (discharged).

4-160. *How may the charge in an Edison cell be determined?*

Since the specific gravity of the Edison cell remains essentially the same whether the cell is at full charge or almost spent, a hydrometer (specific-gravity tester) *cannot* be used to determine condition of the battery. The most effective way to determine the condition of this type of battery is to **measure the terminal voltage under normal load**. If the terminal voltage is less than 1.1V, the battery should then be recharged; if it is between 1.25V and 1.4V the battery can be assumed to be fully charged.

4-161. *If the charging current through a battery is maintained at the normal rate but its polarity is reversed, what will be the result?*

Reverse-polarity current can cause cell buckling, overheating, or sulfation—all of which can bring on premature exhaustion or failure.

4-162. *What are the effects of sulfation?*

Sulfation **increases the internal resistance** of the battery, thus **lowering the effective closed-circuit voltage**. It results in **less usable power** from the battery and **reduced ampere-hour capacity**. In extreme cases—particularly where the sulfation is caused by insufficient electrolyte—**plate buckling** can occur, which drastically shortens battery life.

4-163. *How may the state of charge of the lead−acid cell be determined?*

One very effective method is to use a hydrometer to measure the specific gravity of the electrolyte. As a cell discharges, its acidic electrolyte, which has a relatively high specific gravity, is slowly converted to water. Since water is known to have a specific gravity of 1.000 and sulfuric acid a specific gravity of about 1.290, the hydrometer can be calibrated to indicate the state of charge.

When fresh distilled water has just been added to the battery, the hydrometer test cannot be used. In this case it is best to measure the closed-circuit voltage while the battery is powering a load of 15% to 20% of its ampere-hour rating.

4-164. *Why is laminated iron or steel generally used in the construction of the field and armature cores of motors and generators instead of solid metal?*

The use of metal laminations greatly **reduces eddy current losses**. Eddy currents are electrical currents induced in the core of a motor, generator, or transformer by variations in the device's magnetic field. The currents serve no useful purpose but generate heat, which represents wasted energy, or losses. The eddy currents and losses are reduced in a laminated core because the laminations have a relatively small cross-sectional area and hence a relatively large resistance.

4-165. *What is the purpose of commutating poles (interpoles) in a dc motor?*

Commutating poles are placed between the field coils to **counterbalance the effects of field distortion** and **increase speed regulation**. Without them, sparking at the brushes would occur and the motor would be sensitive to load changes.

4-166. *How may the output voltage of a separately excited ac generator, at a constant output frequency, be varied?*

The output voltage may be adjusted by a potentiometer connected in series with the field windings. The field windings carry dc to the generator from a separate voltage source. As the field voltage is decreased (by increasing the series resistance), the alternator's output voltage is reduced.

4-167. *If the field of a shunt-wound dc motor is opened while the motor is running without any load, what would be the probable result?*

The speed of a shunt motor is dependent on the magnetic strength of the field; the higher the field strength, the slower the motor will turn. An open field winding would cut off the field, and the motor speed would increase beyond the design point. Such operation **could damage or destroy the motor**.

4-168. *Name four causes of excessive sparking at the brushes of a dc motor or generator.*

Sparking at the brushes may be attributable to **worn brushes, defective or open interpoles**, a damaged **commutator**, **brushes not seated** properly in their races, **uneven wear** on brushes and commutator so the brushes do not contact the commutator completely during each armature revolution, a **shorted armature winding** (causing "welding") or an **open armature** winding (causing arcing).

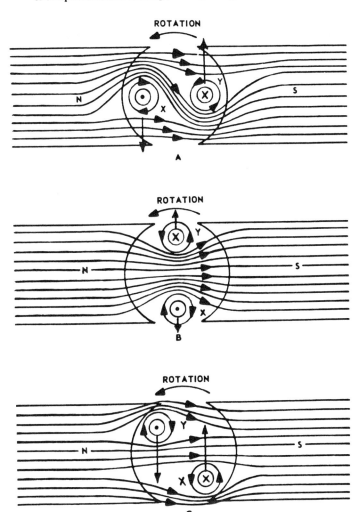

Fig. 4-51.

4-169. *What is the purpose of a commutator on a dc motor? On a dc generator?*

In a dc motor the commutator is used to supply a reversal of current to the motor periodically to miantain a continuous rotating force. **In a dc generator a commutator is used as a rectifier, to supply a pulsating undirectional current.** A dc motor operates because a force is exerted on a current-carrying conductor placed in a magnetic field. Figure 4-51 shows the force acting on a single-turn coil in a magnetic field. Current is flowing out of the left conductor and into the right conductor. The force tends to move the right conductor up and the left conductor down (Fig. 4-51A), producing a turning effect. The rotational force is called *torque*. When the coil reaches the position shown in Fig. 4-51B, the forces tend to spread the coil apart and there is no torque. If the current in the coil reverses at this point and the coil is also carried beyond dead center, forces will be developed as shown in Fig. 4-51C. The torque tends to continue turning the coil in the same direction as before.

4-170 *What is meant by "counter emf" in a dc motor?*

Counter emf is the **voltage induced** in a motor's windings **that opposes the applied voltage.** Figure 4-52 shows a conductor on the armature of a dc motor moving up through a magnetic field. The voltage induced in this conductor by its upward motion through the magnetic field will tend to cause current to flow in the conductor from right to left, thus opposing the current flowing in the wire as a result of the applied voltage. The directions of these currents are shown by the arrows in the figure. Since the counter emf opposes the current entering the armature, it must also oppose the applied voltage. The difference between the applied voltage and the counter emf is the effective voltage in the armature. The armature current, then, is

$$I_a = \frac{E_a - E_c}{R_a}$$

where E_a is the applied voltage, E_c is the counter emf, and R_a is the resistance of the armature. The counter emf can be found by solving

$$E_c = -I_a R_a$$

In keeping with the law of conservation of energy, the counter emf must always be less than the applied voltage.

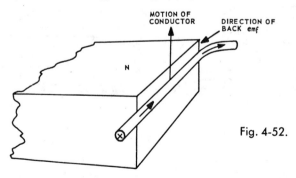

MOTION OF CONDUCTOR

DIRECTION OF BACK emf

N

Fig. 4-52.

4-171. *What determines the speed of a synchronous motor?*

The speed is determined solely by the **frequency of the applied ac and the number of poles**, according to the formula

$$rpm = \frac{30f}{n}$$

The frequency of the applied ac voltage determines the speed where n is the number of poles. Figure 4-53A shows the poles of a synchronous motor field and two of the conductors in the armature. The field is constant, since it is caused by a direct current. The current through the armature is alternating. At the instant shown, the torque on the two conductors tends to move them to the left. The next half-cycle will find the current through the armature reversed, and the torque reversed if the wires remain in the same relative position. If the armature moved far enough so that wire No. 2 were beneath the north pole and wire No. 1 below the south pole, the torque would be in the same direction, keeping the armature turning in the same direction as during the first half-cycle.

If each half-cycle sees the armature conductors move the same distance of one pole, the torque will always be in the same direction, resulting in continuous motion. Thus, the synchronous motor must operate at a constant speed if the frequency is constant. If the average speed differs from the synchronous speed, the average torque becomes zero and the motor will stop.

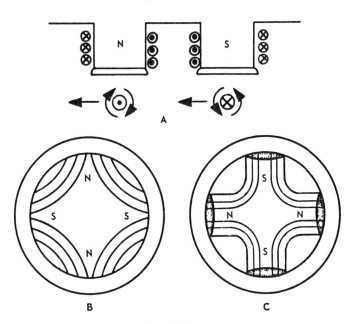

Fig. 4-53.

4-172. *Describe the action and list the main characteristics of a shunt-wound dc motor.*

In a **shunt-wound motor** (or shunt motor) **the armature and the field coils**, which have fairly high resistance, **are connected in parallel across the applied voltage.** When a load is applied to a motor, the speed of the motor immediately tends to decrease. In a shunt motor, since the field coils are connected directly across the source, the flux remains constant. From the formula for counter emf (cemf), you can see that a decrease in speed produces a corresponding decrease in cemf. A decrease in cemf causes an increase in armature current. Since torque depends on armature current as well as field flux, this increase in armature current increases the torque developed by the motor. The cemf decreases and the armature current increases until the developed torque is enough to power the load.

The **speed** of the shunt motor is essentially **dependent on armature current.** When the load on a motor is increased, the armature current increases and tends to prevent the motor from slowing down. Hence, a shunt motor is considered a constant-speed motor. As the armature current increases, the motor speed increases enough to compensate for the speed reduction that would otherwise result from the load.

A rheostat is usually connected in series with the field of a shunt motor. Changing the amount of resistance in series with the field changes the strength of the field. In this way the speed of a shunt motor can be varied. A **decrease in field strength increases motor speed.** In fact, if the field winding opens up while the motor is not under load, it may attain a destructively high speed.

A shunt motor is characterized by fairly **high starting torque** and current. Torque is proportional to the product of the armature current and flux. Since the applied voltage is always across the field coils, the flux is practically the same at all times in a shunt motor. However, the cemf as the motor starts is very low, so the armature current is quite high. This means that the starting torque is equal to or greater than the torque at full load.

4-173. *Describe the action and list the main characteristics of a series motor.*

A *series* motor is so called because the **field coils are connected in series** with the armature. The field coils usually consist of a few turns of low-resistance wire. Since the field and armature are in series, the strength of the field depends on the armature current. For this reason the **torque** of a series motor can be considered ideally **proportional to the square of the armature current.** However, armature reaction and saturation of the iron in the armature keep the torque from increasing as fast as the square of the current.

When the **load on a series motor is increased, the speed of the motor immediately tends to decrease.** The decrease in speed produces a decrease in the counter emf, which allows more armature current to flow. The speed and current continue to change until the developed torque is balanced with the applied torque (load) and any losses.

When the **load on a series motor is decreased, the speed tends to increase** at that instant. An increase in speed results in an increase in the cemf. This increase in cemf produces a decrease in armature current and field strength. As the current and flux decrease, the developed torque and speed decrease. The speed and current continue to adjust until the torques are balanced.

If the **load on a series motor were removed, the speed would continue to increase**, developing more and more cemf, thus cutting down the armature current and the field strength. This increase in speed with decrease in load is shown graphically in Fig. 4-54. The flux becomes so small that the speed of the motor becomes excessive in trying to reach a point where the cemf is equal to the applied voltage. At this point the developed torque would balance the zero torque of no load. With a motor having little residual magnetism in the field structure, the armature can reach such a high speed, if the load is removed, that the armature structure itself flies apart. For this reason most large series motors are directly geared to their loads rather than connected with drive belts.

Series motors have a **widely variable speed, depending on the load**. They have a **very high starting torque** and moderately **high starting current**. Series motors are used where a high starting torque is needed; where the load is constant, so that variations in speed are not produced; or where a change in speed with load is desirable to prevent excessive current with increased torque, as in a traction motor.

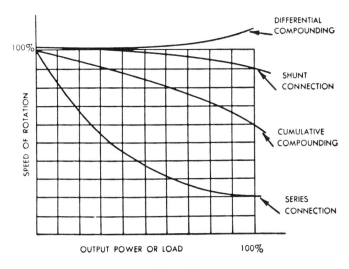

Fig. 4-54.

4-174. *Describe the action and list the main characteristics of a series dc generator.*

The operation of a dc generator is shown in Fig. 4-55 and 4-56. The commutator shown is an elementary one, composed of two cylindrical halves separated by an insulating material. Each cylinder half is connected to the generator coil. At the instant the induced voltage in the

105

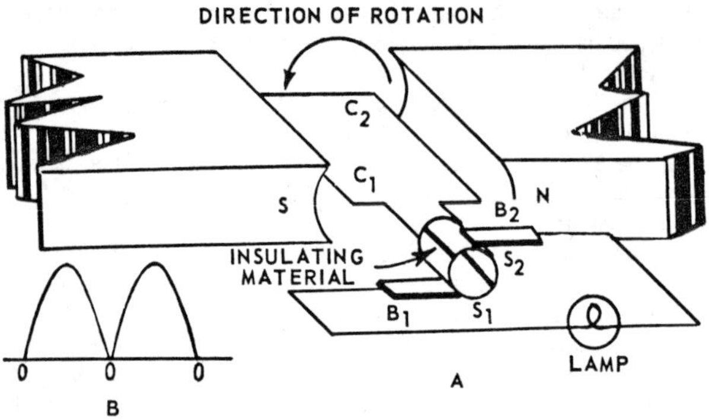

Fig. 4-55.

lamp circuit reaches zero, the brushes cross the insulator, separating the halves.

Induced voltage in the coil at the instant shown in Fig. 55A is such that current flow is from side $C1$ to commutator segment $S1$, where it is picked up by brush $B1$. Current flows through the load to brush $B2$, which is in contact with segment $S2$, and into side $C2$ of the coil.

When the coil reaches the position shown in Fig. 4-56, side 2 is cutting down through the magnetic field. The induced voltage now causes current to flow from side 2 of the coil to $S2$. But brush $B1$ is now in contact with $S2$, and current continues to flow through the load from $B1$ to $B2$ and back through $S1$ to side $C1$ of the coil. Although the induced emf in the coil reversed direction, the brushes were in contact with the opposite ends of the coil, and current in the external circuit continued to flow in the same direction.

Notice that, in both Fig. 4-55 and 4-56, brush $B1$ is always negative and brush $B2$ is always positive. The current in the external circuit varies from zero to a maximum but is always in the same direction (pulsating dc). When more commutator segments are used (more than the two used in our example), the pulsations are closer together and smoothed to a practically pure direct current.

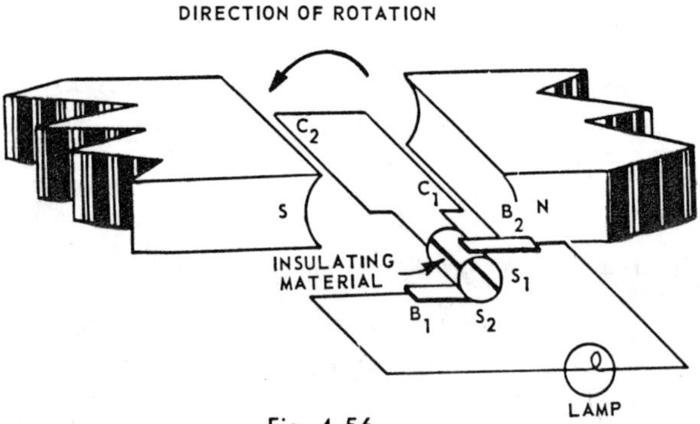

Fig. 4-56.

4-175. *List the main advantages of a full-wave rectifier as compared to a half-wave rectifier.*

The ripple frequency of the pulsating dc output signal is at twice that of the half-wave rectifier. Thus the output voltage is easier to filter. Also, since the transformer supplying the rectifier is used for a full cycle (rather than one-half cycle), both voltage and circuit efficiency are increased with no performance or operational penalty.

4-176. *Why is a transformer not used with direct current?*

An expanding or collapsing current is required to induce voltage in the secondary winding of a transformer. When a dc voltage is first applied to the transformer's primary winding, a short voltage pulse (transient) is induced in the secondary; but since the current source is unchanging (magnetic field not expanding or collapsing), the output drops quickly to zero. When the dc voltage is removed from the transformer, the collapsing field induces another transient in the secondary. For a transformer to supply a constant output voltage, a continuously expanding and collapsing current must be applied. Alternating current, which varies continuously, provides the required variation of the magnetic field in a transformer.

4-177. *What are the primary advantages of a high-vacuum rectifier as compared to the hot cathode type of mercury vapor rectifier?*

A high-vacuum rectifier is advantageous for several reasons (though the mercury tube has certain advantages over the high-vacuum tube, too). The high-vacuum tube **can be operated in any position**, while the mercury tube must be mounted upright. The high-vacuum tube requires **minimal warmup time**, even when new; the mercury tube requires a very long warmup when new, and up to a full minute's warmup in normal service. And **mercury tubes tend to generate rf interference, while high-vacuum tubes do not**. High-vacuum tubes tend to have **higher peak-inverse-voltage ratings** than mercury types.

4-178. *What are the primary characteristics of a gas-filled rectifier tube?*

The gas rectifier has a **cold cathode**; **no filament voltage** is required for electron flow. It will conduct **more current with a lower internal voltage drop** than a comparable high-vacuum rectifier tube, so gas rectifiers are generally more efficient where high power is required. The gas in the tube ionizes when the anode is positive with respect to the cathode; but if the cathode is made positive with respect to the anode, ionization ceases and current will no longer flow.

4-179. *What are the principal advantages of a mercury vapor tube as compared to a high-vacuum (thermionic emission) tube?*

The **voltage drop across the mercury vapor** tube is **constant** and independent of applied voltage or current (about 15V.) Mercury tubes are capable of handling considerably **greater loads** and are **more efficient** for high-power applications. Normally, a mercury tube will **run cooler** than the equivalent high-vacuum tube because of its increased efficiency. **Regulation is easier** with mercury vapor tubes, too, because of their constant *IR* drop.

4-180. *Why is it desirable to have low-resistance filter chokes?*

Chokes offer a high-impedance path for ripple and a low-impedance path for dc. The lower the impedance of the choke to dc, the higher the degree of regulation under load. The lower the resistance of the choke winding, the **less** the **voltage drop** across it and the **more usable voltage delivered to the load.**

4-181. *When filter capacitors are connected in series, high-value resistors are often connected across the individual capacitors. Why?*

The characteristics of electrolytic capacitors vary from one unit to the next, and the leakage is not uniform. Using resistors across electrolytics connected in series **insures that voltage distribution will be equal**; thus, no one capacitor will develop more than its rated dc voltage. The resistor string will also aid in draining off the filter's charge once power is removed, thus reducing the chance for electric shock from a stored charge.

4-182. *What is the primary purpose of a bleeder resistor in a filter system?*

The principal purpose is to drain off the stored charge from filter capacitors after the power supply has been turned off, **for safety** purposes. A secondary purpose is to provide a minimum load when a choke input filter is used, so that output voltage remains constant from no load to full load.

4-183. *Describe the construction and characteristics of a thermocouple type of meter and of a wattmeter.*

The thermocouple is a very simple source of electricity; when the junction between two dissimilar metals is heated, a voltage is generated between the two unheated metal ends. Thermocouples are commonly used with dc meter movements to measure alternating currents and voltages. Figure 4-57A illustrates a typical thermocouple ammeter. The heating element $(a-b)$, through which the current to be measured flows, might be a strip of resistance alloy having a temperature coefficient of resistance of zero (no change in resistance with temperature). It is connected to two large conductive (usually copper) blocks. The hot junction (c) of a thermocouple is hard-soldered or welded to the center of the heater. The cold ends of the thermocouple $(d$ and $e)$ are soldered to the center points of two copper compensating strips that are connected to the leads of the meter movement. These strips are in thermal contact with the copper terminals of the heater (though they are electrically insulated by thin mica strips). Since external temperature changes affect the cold ends of the thermocouple to a different degree than the hot junction, the large copper blocks and copper compensating strips are used to prevent errors.

A vacuum thermocouple has a very small thermal junction in contact with a small heater (through which the measured current flows), all sealed within a small evacuated bulb. This reduces heat dissipation and prevents errors resulting from external variations in temperature or air currents.

The meter scale is calibrated in terms of current in the heater circuit. Since the heater temperature increases with the square of the current (I^2R), the usual permanent magnet, moving-coil movement would require a square-low scale. This would be undesirable in many cases, so a specially designed movement is used with the

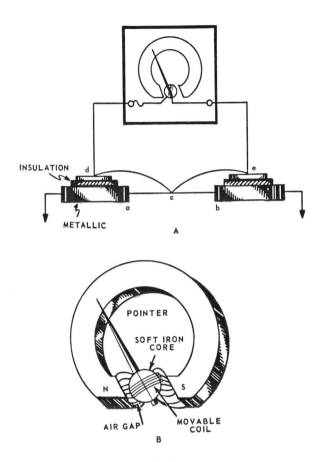

INSULATION

d e

METALLIC

a c b

A

POINTER

SOFT IRON
CORE

N S

AIR GAP

MOVABLE
COIL

B

Fig. 4-57.

thermocouple. Figure 4-57B shows how the air gap is increased so that the flux density through which the coil turns decreases as the coil moves toward the high side of the scale. This decreases the sensitivity as the pointer moves up the scale, and a nearly linear scale is obtained.

Because this instrument depends on the heating effect of the current, it can be used to measure currents that are not sinusoidal. There are practically no capacitive or inductive effects in the heater circuit, so a thermocouple instrument works well in rf measurements.

Meter movements used with thermocouples must be very sensitive, because the output voltage of the thermocouple may be no more than 15 mV or so and the internal resistance 5Ω. The heater circuit is delicate, and its rating is normally limited to very small currents.

By using a small heater wire and a high resistance in series (multiplier), this instrument can be used as a voltmeter.

109

The most common wattmeter is an *electrodynamometer*, in which a pair of fixed coils are used in conjunction with a movable coil with pointer. The fixed coils are made up of a few turns of comparatively large wire. The movable coil, also referred to as the *voltage* or *potential coil*, consists of a large number of turns of fine wire. It is mounted on a shaft carried in jeweled bearings, so that it may pivot freely within the space between the fixed coils. The pointer, attached to the voltage coil, moves over a suitably graduated scale. Flat coil springs hold the needle to a zero position.

As shown in the sketch of Fig. 4-58, the fixed coils (also called *current coils*) are connected in series with the external circuit (load), and the movable coil is connected across the line. When line current flows through the current coil of a wattmeter, a field is set up around the coil. The strength of this field is proportional to the line current and in phase with it. The voltage coil generally has a high-value resistor connected in series with it. This is for making the voltage circuit of the meter as purely resistive as possible. As a result, current in the voltage circuit is practically in phase with line voltage.

The actuating force of a wattmeter is derived from the interaction of the field of its current coils and the field of its voltage coil. The force acting on the movable coil at any instant (tending to turn it) is proportional to the product of the instantaneous values of line current and voltage.

The wattmeter consists of two circuits, either of which will be damaged if too much current is passed through it. This fact is to be especially emphasized because the reading of the instrument does not serve to tell the user that the coils are being overheated. If an ammeter or voltmeter is overloaded, the pointer will indicate beyond the upper limit of its scale; but in the wattmeter, either the current or the voltage circuit may be carrying such an overload that insulation might be burning and yet the pointer may be only partway up the scale. This, of course, is because the position of the pointer depends on the *power*

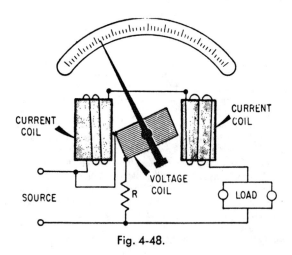

Fig. 4-48.

factor of the circuit as well as on the voltage and current. Thus, a low-power-factor circuit may give a very low reading on the wattmeter even when the current and voltage circuits are loaded to the maximum rated limit. The safe rating is generally given on the face of the instrument.

A wattmeter is normally rated not in watts but in volts and amperes (voltamperes).

4-184. *Describe the construction and operational characteristics of a d'Arsonval meter movement.*

The d'Arsonval meter consists of a coil of many turns of fine wire suspended between the poles of a permanent magnet. The coil is affixed to a pointer, so that coil movement can be indicated by pointer position. An exploded view of the d'Arsonval movement appears in Fig. 4-59. The

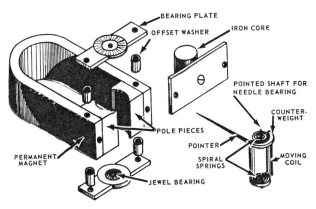

Fig. 4-59.

movement is shown in its assembled configuration in Fig. 4-60. Two phosphor—bronze springs serve as leads to the moving coil and also control the turning. Any tendency of the coil to turn is opposed by these two springs, which are coiled in opposite directions to compensate for temperature changes which might cause one of the two to coil or uncoil.

The coils couple current from the circuit under test to the bobbin coil supported between jeweled pivots (Fig. 4-60). When current flows through the coil, the resulting magnetic field reacts with the field of the permanent magnet and cause the coil to turn, overcoming the opposing forces of the coil springs. The greater the intensity of the current through the coil, the stronger the magnetic field produced; and the stronger the magnetic field, the greater the rotation of the coil. The moving coil stops when the forces applied by the coil springs and magnetic fields are equal. When the test circuit is removed, the springs return the indicator to its zero position.

Since the moving coil can handle only a very small current, the d'Arsonval movement is generally used with a *shunt* when employed as an ammeter and with a high series resistance when used as a voltmeter. Ammeter shunts are low-resistance conductors connected in parallel

111

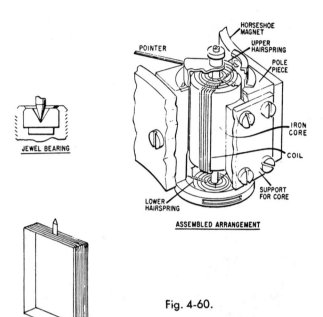

JEWEL BEARING

COIL ON BOBBIN

Fig. 4-60.

with the meter movement so that only a small fraction of the current flows through the moving coil.

The shunt, generally made of manganin, has a very low temperature coefficient, while the copper coil has a much higher coefficient. This means that an increase in temperature will change the proportion of current going through the coil and cause the meter to read low. To prevent this, a *swamping resistor* with zero temperature coefficient and a resistance four or five times that of the coil is connected in series with the coil. A change in coil resistance with temperature has little effect on the overall resistance of the coil circuit.

The d'Arsonval movement offers a number of advantages over other movements. Among these are lower power consumption, high torque-to-weight ratio, linearity of scale and the possibility of a very long (300° or so) scale, and the capability of a wide range of current and voltage measurements. Furthermore, there is no hysteresis error and very little error from stray magnetic fields, and perfect damping can be obtained by the eddy currents induced in the metal bobbin on which the moving coil is wound. The instrument is delicate but extremely rugged compared to other instruments of comparable sensitivity.

4-185. *Describe the construction and characteristics of a repulsion-type ammeter.*

In the repulsion-type ammeter a small strip of soft iron bent into a cylindrical shape is mounted on a spindle as shown in Fig. 4-61. A

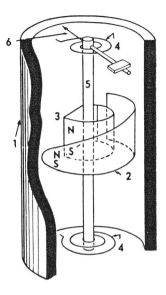

Fig. 4-61.

similar piece, tongue or wedge shaped and with a larger radius, is fixed inside a cylindrical coil. The current being measured flows through this coil and magnetizes both iron strips. The upper edges of the two strips will always have the same polarity (and the lower edges of the two strips will always have polarity opposite to the upper edges) no matter which direction current is flowing. In the figure the upper edges are north poles and the lower edges are south poles.

Since like poles repel, there will always be a force of repulsion between the upper and the lower edges. Because of the shape of the fixed strip, the repulsion causes the movable vane to rotate about its axis. The spiral springs resist the rotation and cause it to be proportional to the torque, which is dependent upon the square of the current in the coil. The pointer connected to the movable vane moves across a scale indicating the amount of current in the coil.

Since the movement of the needle is proportional to the *square* of the current, the distances between the scale markings are not uniform as they are in the *linear scale* shown in Fig. 4-62A. In an instrument in which the turning of the movable part is proportional to the square of the current, when the current is doubled, the pointer moves four times as far; when the current is tripled, the pointer moves nine times as far; and so on. Figure 4-62B shows such a *square law scale*. Notice how difficult it is to read at the left end of the scale.

Errors in repulsion-type ammeters are caused by hysteresis (magnetization and demagnetization) and stray magnetic fields. However, the repulsion-type instrument, also called *iron vane* instrument, is practically the only kind used for commercial instruments.

In Fig. 4-61 the parts are as follows: *1*, cylindrical coil wound with many wire turns; *2*, fixed strip of iron (wedge shaped); *3*, cylinder of

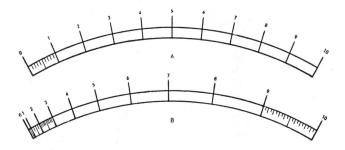

Fig. 4-62.

soft iron sheeting; *4*, spiral springs; *5*, axle on which pointer is mounted; *6*, pointer (which indicates as a result of moving vane).

4-186. *Describe the construction and characteristics of a dynamometer ammeter and voltmeter.*

The dynamometer wattmeter was described in the answer to question 4-183. Figure 4-63A shows the principle of the electrodynamometer ammeter. The fixed coil is split into two electrically continuous parts. The moving coil is mounted between the two fixed coils; it is mounted on a vertical spindle with a hardened steel pivot at each end. The pivots turn in jeweled bearings. Two spiral springs oppose the turning of the coil and conduct the current to the moving coil. As the springs can conduct only a very small current, the movable coil is wound with a fine wire.

Assume, at one instant, the direction of the field of the fixed coils in Fig. 4-63A is from the bottom to the top. At the same time, the current in the moving coil produces a field whose direction is indicated by ϕM (upper ring on sketch). The reaction of the two fields (moving, or ϕM; and fixed, of ϕF) tends to turn the moving coil clockwise so the fields can align themselves and the number of flux linkages can become maximum. The torque developed is proportional to the strength of the two fields and the sine of the angle between the moving and fixed coils. Since the flux in each case is proportional to the current through the coils, the torque is proportional to the product of the two current, or I^2.

Figure 4-63B illustrates the connections for a dynamometer voltmeter. The resistance limits the current through the fixed coils, which are wound with fine wire and connected in series with the moving coil. The current in the dynamometer is proportional to the voltage being measured; therefore, the deflection of the pointer is proportional to the square of the voltage. The scale that must be used is similar to that of Fig. 4-62B.

The dynamometer voltmeter requires about five times as much current as a d'Arsonval dc voltmeter of the same rating. And it uses an appreciable amount of power. Unless the instrument is shielded, stray magnetic fields, wires carrying currents, inductive apparatus, and even iron alone (if brought too near) may cause large errors in the indications.

Figure 4-63C shows the usual connection for an ammeter. With this connection the time constants of the two parallel branches can readily be made equal, so that the division of current between them will be independent of frequency.

The dynamometer-type instrument is not nearly as useful for measuring dc as the d'Arsonval type. It must have a heavier moving system, so the torque−weight ratio is small. Friction tends to cause errors. Since the deflecting torque varies with the square of the current, a nonlinear scale must be used. In addition, dynamometer meters are more expensive than those using permanent magnets. For these reasons dynamometer ammeters and voltmeters are rarely used in dc circuits. The iron vane ammeter is more commonly used in ac circuits than the shunted dynamometer ammeter.

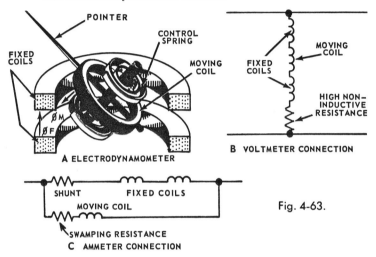

Fig. 4-63.

4-187. *If two voltmeters are connected in series, how would you be able to determine the total drop across both instruments?*

Add the individual readings.

4-188. *What type of meter may be used to measure rf currents?*

A thermocouple ammeter is used in this application. The table in Fig. 4-64 lists the most common measuring instruments for various applications. To get a high score on test questions dealing with measuring instruments, it will pay you to study the chart and learn the relative merits and measuring ranges of these instruments.

4-189. *Why are copper-oxide rectifiers, associated with dc voltmeters for the purpose of measuring ac, not suitable for the measurement of voltages at radio frequencies?*

Instruments using copper-oxide rectifiers are subject to frequency errors that increase in proportion to frequency. This is because the **copper oxide reacts inductively** at very high frequencies.

4-190. *If two ammeters are connected in parallel, how may the total current through the two meters be determined?*

The total current is equal to the sum of the branch currents; thus, to determine the total current when two parallel ammeters are connected, simply add their readings.

INSTRUMENT TYPE	ACCURACY CAPABILITY OF INSTRUMENT	EXPECTED ACCURACY RANGES OF AMMETER	EXPECTED ACCURACY RANGES OF VOLTMETER	ADVANTAGES
Permanent-magnet moving-coil (DC only) (Combined ammeter and voltmeter test set)	From 0.2% to 1%	Up to 500 amps	Up to 750 volts	Most accurate for DC measurements
Moving iron	1% for DC and AC up to 60 cycles per second	0.5 to 10 amps	Above 75 volts	Cheapest
Electrodynamic ammeters and voltmeters	0.3% to 0.5% for DC and AC up to 60 cycles per second	0.5 to 10 amps	Above 75 volts	Measures either DC or AC of low frequency
	1%	Above 10 amps	Above 300 volts (single range) or 600 volts (multirange)	
Hot-wire, (DC and AC up to 100 cps, shunted type. AC up to 1 mc, unshunted)	3.5%	Maximum current less than 3 amps	DC and AC up to 5,000 cps	Calibration same for DC and AC Readings independent of frequency, waveform, or stray magnetic fields
Thermocouple (self-contained)	3.5%, DC and AC up to 1 mc	5 ma to 1 amp	Rarely used	Gives extremely accurate readings at higher frequencies
Rectifier voltmeters and milliammeters	3.5%, 25 to 10,000 cps (Indications affected by waveform)	1 ma to 50 ma for full-scale deflection	Not less than 10 volts for full-scale deflection	For precision measurements

Fig. 4-64.

4-191. *Is the angular scale deflection of a repulsion-type (iron vane) ammeter equal to the square or square root of the current, or merely directly proportional to the current?*

In the basic meter the deflection is proportional to the *square* of the current. Many modern instruments, however, are corrected in such a manner that they read linearly.

4-192. *Does an ac ammeter indicate peak, average, or effective values of current?*

If the ac ammeter is the **rectifier type**, the deflection of the pointer is proportional to the **average** value of the rectified wave. The ratio of the rms value to the average value is 1.11 when the current is a sine wave. Assuming that the current is sinusoidal, the scale must be marked in values of 1.11 times the current actually measured to give rms value. If the ammeter is of a type that will measure alternating current directly—such as the **moving-vane type**—it **will read** directly in values that indicate **effective current**.

4-193. *If two ammeters are connected in series, how may the total current through the two meters be determined?*

Each meter reads the total current, so the value can be determined by reading either one.

4-194. *How may a dc milliammeter, in an emergency, be used to indicate voltage?*

All that is needed to measure dc voltages with a current-measuring meter is to **connect the required values of multiplier resistors in series** with one of the two meter leads. The concept is shown in Fig. 4-65. Here, a 50 μA meter, shunted by a 263Ω resistor, serves as a voltmeter. With the 263Ω shunt, the multiplier resistor values are selected for a ratio of 1000Ω per volt. Thus, in the *5K* position, a 5V input will cause 50 μA of current to flow through the meter. Since the current through the meter is directly proportional to the applied voltage, a reading of 50 μA will mean that 5V is being measured, 30μA will mean that 3V is being measured, etc.

4-195. *Why is a multiplier resistance used with a voltmeter?*

The multipliers **increase the resistance of the dc circuit so that more voltage can be applied to a given voltmeter** and the meter can be used to measure a wider range of voltages. Note in Fig. 4-65 that there is approximately 5K of resistance in the circuit for a 5V signal to deflect the 50 μA meter full scale, and there is approximately one megohm of resistance for the same sensitive meter to read an applied voltage of 100V.

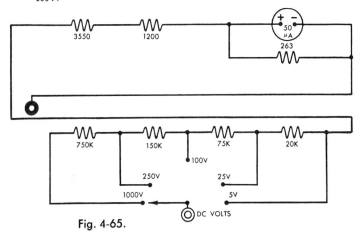

Fig. 4-65.

117

4-196. *What type of indicating instrument is best suited for measuring rf currents?*

The thermocouple instrument is best suited for rf current indications. (See chart of Fig. 4-64.)

4-197. *What is the purpose of a shunt as used with an ammeter?*

A shunt is used to **bypass some of the circuit current around the meter**, effectively reducing its sensitivity. The 263Ω meter shunt shown in Fig. 4-65 effects a 20:1 current bypass. If the shunt were removed from this meter, the sensitivity would be 20,000Ω per volt; with the shunt in place, the sensitivity is 1000Ω per volt.

4-198. *What effects might be caused by a shorted grid capacitor in a 3-circuit regenerative receiver?*

The effect on detection is tantamount to shorting the filter capacitor at the output of a diode detector; **no detection** will take place. Grid bias will be lost and plate current will increase—possibly to a destructive level. The receiver would be inoperative of course.

4-199. *What would be the effect of a shorted coupling capacitor in a conventional RC coupled audio amplifier?*

The dc collector (or plate) voltage of the feeding stage would be allowed to pass through the capacitor to the succeeding stage. At the very least the bias of the succeeding stage would be grossly affected and the amplifier's **operating point would be shifted** out of its linear region. At worst the succeeding transistor (or tube) may be destroyed by excessive collector (or plate) current caused by the bias upset. In some cases the base—emitter junction or grid circuitry of the succeeding stage may be destroyed.

4-200. *What might be the cause of low sensitivity of a 3-circuit regenerative receiver?*

Insufficient or improperly phased feedback would be the most likely cause, assuming the tube or transistor voltages were correct and circuit components were all right.

4-201. *What is the effect of "local action" in a lead—acid storage cell and how may it be compensated?*

Local action is the **current flow that takes place inside a cell when it is not connected into a closed circuit**. Its intensity depends on the internal resistance of the battery or cell; the older the cell, the higher the local action. The effect of local action is to exhaust the battery prematurely and cause sulfation. A trickle charge will counteract the effects.

4-202. *Why should adequate ventilation be provided in a room housing a large group of cells under charge?*

During charging, the chemical action inside a cell will cause a formation of hydrogen, an extremely flammable gas. A well ventilated room will **allow the gas to be dissipated and will minimize the likelihood of explosion**. It should go without saying that fires, lighted cigarettes, or spark-producing equipment should never be used near batteries, especially when they are being charged.

4-203. *When should distilled water be added to a lead—acid storage battery and for what purpose?*

Distilled water should only be added to a battery **when it is in a good state of charge** and only to replenish the electrolyte lost by gassing. The electrolyte used in a lead—acid cell is sulfuric acid, but as the cell is discharged, the acid is converted into water. Recharging converts the water into acid again. The electrolyte level should be just high enough to cover the plates in the individual cells.

4-204. *How may the polarity of the charging source to be used with a storage battery be determined?*

There is almost no limit to the number of ways to determine the polarity of a dc voltage source for charging a battery. One method is to connect one terminal of the storage battery to one terminal of the source and then connect a dc voltmeter between the remaining two terminals. If the meter pegs off the scale to the left, reverse the meter leads. Now, if the voltage indicates more than the voltage of either the battery or the source alone, the positive terminal of the source is connected to the negative terminal of the battery and must be reversed for charging. If the meter indicates less than either the battery or source voltage, it is reading a difference voltage, which means that like terminals are connected. In that case simply remove the meter and attach the remaining electrodes together.

A voltmeter alone is certainly an adequate means of checking. When a dc voltmeter is connected to the source and the meter is deflecting properly, the negative lead of the meter indicates the negative lead of the voltage applied to it, and the positive lead identifies the positive terminal of the applied voltage.

4-205. *Describe the care that should be given a group of storage cells to maintain them in good operating condition.*

These are some of the ways to preserve the capacity of a battery:

1. Never add electrolyte except to replace that lost during spills.
2. Maintain the electrolyte level above the cell plates.
3. Leave sufficient room between the top of the electrolyte level and the battery vent to allow for expansion due to gassing.
4. Make sure the vent is not clogged, so that gases can escape during charge.
5. Do not charge the battery beyond its recommended charge rate. Normally, the charge should be computed according to the ampere-hour capacity of the battery. The ideal charge is 10% of the ampere-hour rating for a period of 15 hours when the cell or battery is fully discharged. This applies a charge equal to 150% of the discharge.
6. Do not discharge the battery at a rate high enough to cause overheating. The maximum discharge rate under normal conditions should be 25% of the ampere-hour rating.
7. Add distilled water rather than tap water or acid when a charged battery is low on electrolyte. Tap water allows mineral deposits to build up on the plates and electrodes of the battery, thus increasing the internal resistance and shortening the battery life. Adding acid electrolyte instead of water can cause sulfation.

119

8. Be sure to keep the top of the battery, particularly the area near the vents, free from foreign matter. Indroducing impurities into the electrolyte will accelerate battery wearout because of plate and electrolyte contamination.

9. Prevent local action by applying a trickle charge when a battery is to stand idle for extended periods. The trickle charge should be sufficient to overcome the effects of local action; so the charge rate will vary according to the internal resistance of the battery. In general, the trickle charge should be at one percent of the ampere-hour rating.

10. Keep the environmental temperature of batteries cool: do not charge batteries when the ambient temperature is more than 100°F. If possible, keep the battery temperature below this level during discharge as well, particularly when the discharge rate is extreme.

4-206. *What may cause the plates of a lead—acid cell to buckle?*

Buckling may be caused by excessive current through the battery, either during charge or discharge. It may also occur when sulfation occurs and when electrolytic deposits build up on one side of an electrode's plates and not the other. The construction of a conventional storage cell is shown in Fig. 4-66. Note that each positive plate is sandwiched between two negative plates. This construction prevents buckling of the positive plates under normal conditions, because it tends to keep the chemical action equal on both sides of each positive plate. When any cell condition causes chemical action to be unbalanced, buckling of plates will be the result.

4-207. *What may cause sulfation of a lead—acid storage cell?*

Sulfation may be caused by local action, particularly in batteries with a fairly high internal resistance. This type of problem can be prevented by making certain the cell is charged fully before allowing it to stand idle for long periods. Another major cause of sulfation is operating the battery with insufficient electrolyte. When the level of the electrolyte drops below the surface of the tops of the plates, sulfation is almost sure to result.

When excessive gassing occurs, sulfation is accelerated, too; to avoid this, be sure to avoid overcharging and overdischarging. Adding electrolyte to a fully charged cell can cause excessive gassing (the result of which is sulfation); this may be avoided by adding electrolyte only when some of the electrolyte in the battery has been lost by spillage. When the battery is fully charged or is about to be charged, distilled water may be added to bring the electrolyte to its proper level.

There are 10 maintenance measures for batteries listed in the answer to question 4-205. Sulfation may be caused by neglecting any of them.

4-208. *What chemical may be used to neutralize a storage cell's acid electrolyte?*

Bicarbonate of soda, or baking soda, effectively neutralizes sulfuric acid.

4-209. *What steps may be taken to prevent corrosion of the lead—acid cell's terminals?*

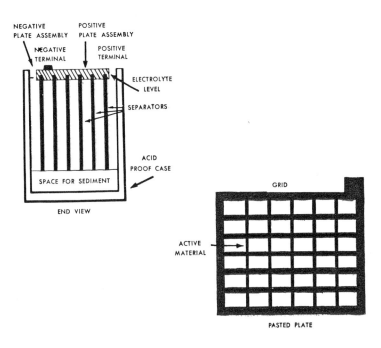

NEGATIVE PLATE ASSEMBLY

POSITIVE PLATE ASSEMBLY

NEGATIVE TERMINAL

POSITIVE TERMINAL

ELECTROLYTE LEVEL

SEPARATORS

ACID PROOF CASE

SPACE FOR SEDIMENT

END VIEW

GRID

ACTIVE MATERIAL

PASTED PLATE

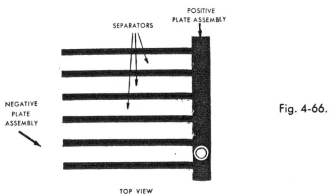

SEPARATORS

POSITIVE PLATE ASSEMBLY

NEGATIVE PLATE ASSEMBLY

TOP VIEW

Fig. 4-66.

Corrosion may be prevented by making good connections and coating the terminals with petroleum jelly or baking soda.

4-210. *Why are bypass capacitors often connected across the brushes of a high-voltage dc generator?*

Sparking of the brushes can cause interference at radio frequencies. The spark pulses are extremely rich in harmonics. A bypass capacitor serves as a **short circuit for rf signals, thus preventing the generation of rf interference.**

4-211. *What may cause the bearings of a motor—generator to overheat?*

The bearings of a motor—generator can overheat when they are operated without lubrication, when the motor—generator shaft is out of round, when the motor is operated at maximum load for excessive periods, when bearings are not seated properly initially, when bearings are showing signs of wearout, when there is excessive friction during any part of an armature cycle, or when the motor's speed is excessive.

4-212. *How may rf interference from sparking brushes be minimized on dc generators?*

The first step is to minimize the sparking by seeing to it that the brushes and commutator are in proper working order. The second step is to install the appropriate value of bypass capacitors from brushes to ground. Additional measures include the installation of series rf chokes and shielding of the generator or equipment in which the interference is observed.

4-213. *Why are high-reactance headphones generally more satisfactory for use with radio receivers than low-reactance types?*

Since high-reactance types more closely match the output characteristics of the tubes with which they are used, they require less excitation energy and offer more efficient operation in the range of audio signals. They do not require impedance transformation or amplification when used with vacuum-tube stages having a high-impedance output.

4-214. *What may cause packing of the carbon granules in a carbon button microphone element?*

The carbon granules may become tightly packed as a result of excessive excitation (input signals too strong), excessive humidity, or an external shock (from dropping etc.). The surest way to determine if the granules have become packed is to compare the output of the microphone with another of similar design. When packing occurs, the output drops considerably, and often distortion occurs as a result of a new resonance. Except in cases where the packing is caused by humidity extremes over long periods, the microphone often can be freed from the condition by rapping it sharply against a hard object.

4-215. *Why should polarity be observed in connecting headphones directly into the plate circuit of a vacuum tube?*

Observance of headphone polarity serves as protection for the headphones by insuring that excitation voltage to the earphone windings is always the same. Reversal of the polarity on the windings could reduce the residual magnetism in the permanent magnet core, thus reducing the sensitivity.

5-216. *What precautions should be observed in the use of a double-button carbon microphone?*

As shown in Fig. 4-67, the double-button microphone is excited by a dc voltage applied to both buttons through an audio transformer. If the excitation voltage is higher on one side or the other, distortion of the audio output will occur. A current-measuring meter placed in series with each lead during the no-signal state will ascertain whether or not the two buttons are balanced. To reduce the no-signal current of one side in order to match the two buttons, a low-value resistor may be used. Also, carbon microphones tend to have mechanical resonance at certain frequencies that cause audio peaks. This is usually a sign of poor design, but its effects can be minimized with selective filtering at the microphone.

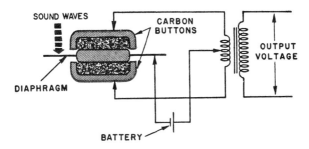

Fig. 4-67.

4-217. *If low-impedance headphones of about 75Ω are to be connected to the output of an audio amplifier (tube type), what procedure will effect the most satisfactory operation?*

A matching transformer should be used so that the output tube receives the proper load under all conditions, and a resistor should be used to shunt the headphone so that it will not be damaged during high-volume settings of the gain control. The ac voltage to the headphone must not exceed the input rating of the phones.

4-218. *What is the effect on the resonant frequency when an inductor is connected in series with an antenna?*

An inductor in series with an antenna serves to lengthen the antenna effectively, thereby lowering the frequency of resonance. (Lengthening an antenna makes it resonant to a longer wave; and the longer the wave, the lower the frequency.)

4-219. *What is the effect on the resonant frequency when adding a capacitor in series with an antenna?*

A capacitor in series with an antenna has the effect of making the antenna electrically shorter, thereby raising its resonant frequency. Lengthening or shortening an antenna will also affect the antenna's *impedance.* As shown in Fig. 4-68, the antenna may be resistive, inductive, or capacitive. A half-wavelength antenna (4-68A) is a resistive load, and antenna longer than one-half wavelength is an inductive load (4-68B), an antenna shorter than one-half wavelength (4-68C) is a capacitive load. Figure 4-68D shows graphically the effects of adding inductance and capacitance in series with an antenna.

4-220. *What is the velocity of propagation of radio-frequency waves in space?*

The speed is very slightly less than 300,000,000 meters per second, but the figure is so close that it is used as the standard for all antenna calculations. Stated as another unit of measure, the speed is 186,000 miles per second.

4-221. *What is the relationship between the electrical and physical length of a Hertzian antenna?*

The physical length of an antenna is nearly 5% less than the electrical length. If an antenna were made of extremely fine wire and isolated

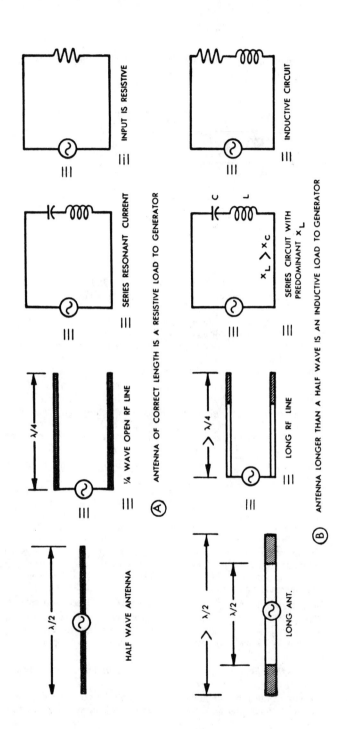

INPUT IS RESISTIVE

INDUCTIVE CIRCUIT

SERIES RESONANT CURRENT

C   L

$x_L > x_c$

SERIES CIRCUIT WITH PREDOMINANT x_L

ANTENNA OF CORRECT LENGTH IS A RESISTIVE LOAD TO GENERATOR

ANTENNA LONGER THAN A HALF WAVE IS AN INDUCTIVE LOAD TO GENERATOR

λ/4

¼ WAVE OPEN RF LINE

Ⓐ

> λ/4

LONG RF LINE

Ⓑ

λ/2

HALF WAVE ANTENNA

> λ/2

λ/2

LONG ANT.

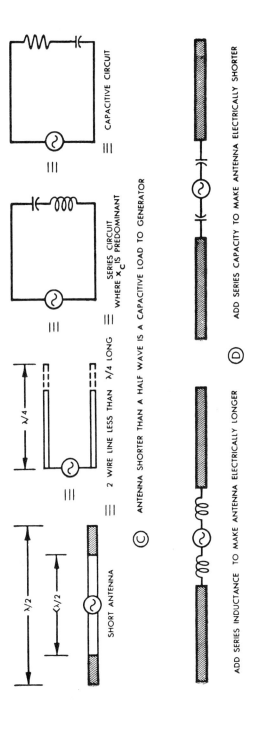

CAPACITIVE CIRCUIT

SERIES CIRCUIT
WHERE x_c IS PREDOMINANT

$\lambda/4$

2 WIRE LINE LESS THAN $\lambda/4$ LONG

© ANTENNA SHORTER THAN A HALF WAVE IS A CAPACITIVE LOAD TO GENERATOR

$\lambda/2$

$<\lambda/2$

SHORT ANTENNA

ADD SERIES INDUCTANCE TO MAKE ANTENNA ELECTRICALLY LONGER

ⓓ ADD SERIES CAPACITY TO MAKE ANTENNA ELECTRICALLY SHORTER

Fig. 4-68.

perfectly in space, its electrical length would correspond to it physical length. In practice, however, an antenna is never totally isolated from the ground or surrounding objects. Therefore, the velocity of the wave along the conductor is always slightly less than the velocity of a wave in free space; so the physical length of the antenna must be correspondingly less (very close to 5%). The physical length (l), in feet, of a half-wave antenna for a given frequency in megahertz is approximately

$$l = \frac{300 \times 3.28 \times 0.952}{2f} = \frac{468}{f}$$

The *300* refers to millions of meters per second, but the zeros aren't necessary, because frequency (f) is to be expressed in millions of hertz. The *3.28* in the equation is the conversion factor from meters to feet, since there are 3.28 ft per meter. The *0.952* is a typical velocity factor for an antenna; it says, in effect, that a wave on the antenna is being propagated at a speed 4.8% slower than a wave in free space.

4-222. *If you desire to operate on a frequency lower than the resonant frequency of an available Marconi antenna, how may this be accomplished?*

The resonant frequency of the Marconi antenna may be lowered by reducing the series capacitance of its input line or adding an appropriate inductance. A Marconi antenna is normally base-fed, and an inductor in series with the antenna is referred to as a *loading coil*.

4-223. *What will be the effect on the frequency if the physical length of a Hertzian antenna is reduced?*

When the physical length of a Hertzian (ungrounded dipole) antenna is reduced, the antenna becomes resonant to shorter waves, i.e. higher frequencies.

4-224. *Which type of antenna has a minimum of directional characteristics in the horizontal plane?*

Vertically mounted Hertzian and Marconi antennas are theoretically omnidirectional in the horizontal plane. The Hertzian is a half-wave dipole; when it is mounted vertically and away from surrounding objects, the radiation pattern is pictured in Fig. 4-69.

The Marconi antenna, a quarter-wavelength vertical radiator, is an "image" antenna; that is, the ground surface on which the radiator is mounted is used to provide an image of what the antenna would be as a half-wave radiator. Figure 4-70 shows this graphically.

4-225. *What factors determine the resonant frequency of any particular antenna?*

Resonant frequency of an antenna is determined by:

- The physical size of the antenna (or its elements, if it is a *beam* type)
- The series inductance or capacitance at the feed point

An antenna of the correct length for the operating frequency acts as a resonant circuit and presents a pure resistance to the excitation circuit. (Refer to Fig. 4-68.) An antenna having other than resonant length displays both resistance and reactance to the excitation circuit. An antenna slightly longer than a half-wavelength, for example, acts as an inductive circuit. A slightly short antenna "looks" capacitive.

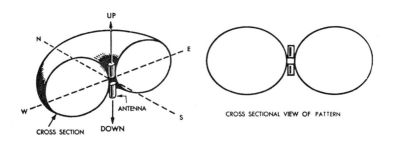

CROSS SECTIONAL VIEW OF PATTERN

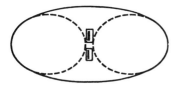

THREE DIMENSIONAL VIEW OF ANTENNA PATTERN

Fig. 4-69.

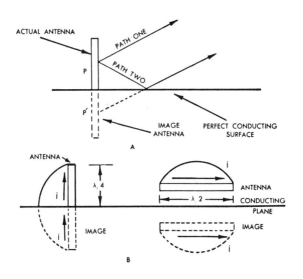

Fig. 4-70.

2-226. *If the resistance and current at the base of a Marconi antenna are known, what formula could be used to determine the power in the antenna?*

The power being fed to the antenna is equal to the square of the current multiplied by the resistance. This neglects any losses in the antenna that might be attributable to radiation resistance and conductor resistance.

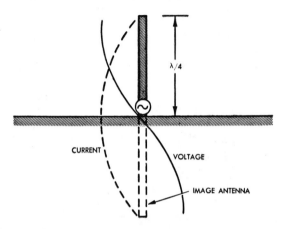

A   THE QUARTER WAVE GROUNDED ANTENNA IS CALLED THE "MARCONI."

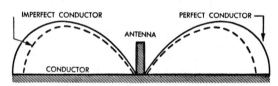

B   VERTICAL FIELD STRENGTH PATTERN

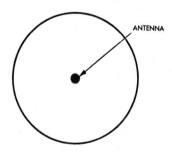

C   HORIZONTAL POLAR DIAGRAM OF MARCONI

Fig. 4-71.

4-227. *Does the resistance of a copper conductor vary with variations in temperature?*

As temperature increases, the resistance of a copper conductor also increases. Decreases in temperature tend to lower the resistance of copper. Copper, like most metals, is said to have a positive temperature coefficient of resistance.

4-228. *What material is best suited for use as an antenna strain insulator that will be exposed to the elements?*

Ceramic is about the best because it offers exceptional dielectric properties and high strength. If the surface is glazed, the material is dust resistant and heat reflectant, which serves to maintain the dielectric strength constant in varying climatic conditions.

4-229. *What material is frequently used for relay contacts, and why?*

Gold-flashed silver is frequently used for relay contacts because it offers a durable contact of extremely high conductivity and does not lose its conductivity with oxidation, as most metals do.

4-230. *Describe the operation of a crystal detector.*

A small piece of germanium, silicon, galena, iron pyrite, quartz, or carborundum is capable of providing the nonlinear diode characteristic required for detection. When a crystal of one of these elements is in direct contact with a sharp-pointed wire, the arrangement offers a different resistance to current from the crystal to the wire than it does from the wire to the crystal. Crystals of modern vintage are encapsulated in tiny containers with axial leads, so that they often appear much like a resistor.

Crystal detectors are excellent for detector applications at ultrahigh radio frequencies. They are typically used as both mixers and detectors, as shown in Fig. 4-72. The characteristics of the crystal diode detector are quite similar to those of the vacuum-tube type (compare the charactistic curves of Figs. 4-39 and 4-72). When used as an rf detector fed directly from an antenna, an *LC* circuit couples the signal from the antenna to the diode. For use in other detector applications, the rf signal may be coupled by other means.

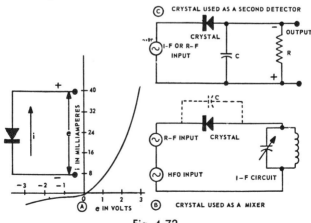

Fig. 4-72.

The detector diode conducts only during positive half-cycles of the input signal; so the diode's output is a rectified version of the modulated input. The positive peaks vary in amplitude according to the audio frequency carried on the rf signal. The average voltage output varies above zero at the audio rate. Thus, this average can be used to provide audio information by simply applying the output through filter a low-pass filter that will remove the rf component. In the sketches the low-pass filter consists of the resistor and capacitor. The *RC* network has a short time constant at the audio frequency but quite a long one at rf. The output, then, is a varying signal that follows the peak variation of the modulated carrier.

4-231. *Why is rosin used instead of acid as soldering flux in radio construction work?*

Unlike acid flux, rosin provides a cleansing action without corrosion and insures an electrically conductive joint free of residue.

4-232. *What is meant by a "harmonic"?*

A harmonic is a multiple of any referenced frequency. However, the first harmonic is regarded as the fundamental frequency being referenced; so the second harmonic is a signal at twice the frequency of the fundamental, the third harmonic is a signal three times the fundamental, and so forth.

4-233. *Why should all exposed metal parts of a transmitter be grounded?*

One ground point electrically tying all exposed metal parts to ground offers adequate protection against shock but very little protection against painful rf burns. To protect against rf burns, each exposed metal ground area should be grounded in the vicinity of the exposed metal. Otherwise, the metal parts could act as an antenna when the transmitter is operating, and they may radiate very high rf voltages at chassis points not physically close to the electrical ground.

4-234. *What is the difference between electrical power and electrical energy?*

Electrical energy is the capacity of an electrical device for doing work; for example, the capacity to heat or physically move something. Electrical power is the rate at which work is done or energy is used. Electrical power is measured in watts or kilowatts. Electrical energy is measured in watts times a unit of time, typically in kilowatt-hours. Energy may be stored, for later use in supplying power.

4-235. *How can the direction of direct current in a conductor be determined?*

Electron flow is from minus to plus, so direction of flow can be determined by observation of the source polarity. If the source is not accessible, the voltage on the conductor can be measured with an appropriate voltmeter or VOM. If no meter is available but current can be monitored, a diode can be placed in series with the conductor. If current flow continues when the cathode is nearest the source, the diode is in the negative lead. If no current flows with the diode is in this position, the diode is in the positive lead.

4-236. *What instrument measures electric power?*

Electric power may be measured directly with a wattmeter.

4-237. *What instrument measures electrical energy?*

Any instrument that measures watts as a function of time may be used to measure energy consumed; typical devices are watt-second meter, watt-hour meter, and kilowatt-hour meter. Kilowatt-hours may be converted into joules (metric system) by multiplying kilowatt-hours by 3,600,000.

4-238. *What is an electron? An ion?*

An electron is a negatively charged particle orbiting around a nucleus in an atom. The nucleus of a helium atom, for example, is made up of a proton and a neutron, as shown in Fig. 4-73. If an atom is thought of as being a solar system, the nucleus is the sun and the electrons are the planets. Electrical effects are due entirely to the action of electrons; when electrons in outer orbits are dislodged and attracted systematically by atoms with a deficiency of electrons, we have electron flow, or current. Figure 4-73 is not to scale, but it serves to illustrate the helium atom. Some materials have many rings of electrons and many electrons in each ring.

Atoms themselves are normally neutral—their charge is evenly divided between the protons and the electrons. When an atom is depleted of some of its electrons or when additional electrons have been added into the atom's outer electron orbit, the atom gains a charge—either positive or negative, depending on whether electrons have been added (negative) or subtracted (positive). A charged atom is called an *ion*.

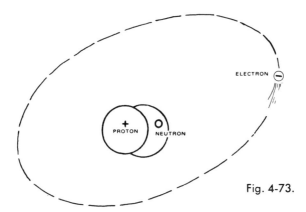

Fig. 4-73.

4-239. *With respect to electrons, what is the difference between conductors and nonconductors?*

A conductor is a material that has a relatively large number of free electrons. A nonconductor has few free electrons. A free electron is one that can be readily dislodged from its orbit in an outer ring.

4-240. *Describe an electrolyte.*

An electrolyte is a conductive liquid or paste that supports current flow by transfer of ions, usually as a result of chemical action between the electrolyte and an electrode.

4-241. *What is an A-battery? A B-battery? A C-battery?*

An *A*-battery is a low-voltage battery used to supply power to the filaments of tubes in portable electronic apparatus. A *B*-battery is used to supply the high-voltage plate potential in portable vacuum-tube equipment; the term *B+* was derived from this designation. A

C-battery, also associated with tube-type equipment, is the low-current voltage source for supplying bias to stages.

4-242. *What are the lowest radio frequencies useful in radio communications?*

The lowest official range of radio frequencies extends from 10 to 30 kHz and is referred to as *VLF*, for very low frequency.

4-243. *What radio frequencies are useful for long-distance communications requiring continuous operation?*

The most useful radio frequencies for reliable communications under all conditions are those frequencies that do not depend on the presence of ionized layers above the earth (ionosphere) for reflection; thus, the low-frequency region, **from 30 to 300 kHz**, would be the most suitable. However, range can be extended by depending on the ionsphere for reflection. The most satisfactory consistent performance from reflected signals can be obtained by communicating in the medium-frequency (MF) range, which extends from 300 to 2000 kHz.

4-244. *What frequencies have substantially straight-line propagation characteristics analogous to those of light waves and unaffected by the ionosphere?*

The radio frequencies that are most analogous to light waves are the ones that provide line-of-sight communications, and they include the upper end of the VHF range and the entire UHF range (which extends from 300 MHz to 3000 MHz). Signals transmitted at frequencies higher than these are dissipated rapidly and so require tremendous amounts of energy for effective propagation over long line-of-sight distances.

4-245. *What effect do sunspots and aurora borealis have on radio communications?*

The sunspots are solar storms that send charged particles of matter into space; these temporarily increase the electron concentration of the ionosphere and form a reflecting conductive layer. The aurora is thought to be a collection of ions trapped in the earth's magnetic field. Both of these phenomena are responsible for reflection of radio signals that otherwise would penetrate the ionosphere and for generation of radio noise. For commercial communications they sometimes present a disruption in routine communications capability.

4-246. *What type of modulation is largely contained in static and lightning discharges?*

Modulation is a misnomer, because *modulation* technically refers to intelligence. However, the pulse-type noises associated with lightning and static are amplitude variations such as are associated with **amplitude modulation**.

4-247. *What types of radio receivers do not respond to static interference?*

Most receivers respond to some extent, but receivers designed to accept phase-modulated and frequency-modulated signals are affected the least, particularly where the receivers are of good design (that is, where they have sufficient limiting action to effectively reject pulses of interference).

4-248. *What crystalline substance is widely used in crystal oscillators?*

The most widely used crystalline substance is quartz, which may be either natural or man-made. Quartz exhibits a characteristic called *piezoelectricity,* whereby an applied mechanical pressure causes generation of a voltage. The quartz is cut in slabs and mounted in holders that sandwich the crystal element between two conductors, as shown in Fig. 4-74. A spring, compressed between the top of the holder and one of the electrodes, maintains a pressure on the crystal. In an oscillator the crystal acts as an *LCR* circuit that is both highly active and extremely stable. Note in the sketch that the electrode plate, shown connected to, but extending out of, the holder, has four contact "feet." This provides an air gap between the electrode plate and the crystal, allowing it to vibrate freely.

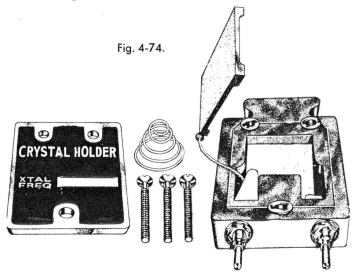

Fig. 4-74.

4-249. *Why is the crystal in some oscillators operated at a constant temperature?*

The resonant frequency of most crystals will change slightly with temperature changes. Since the crystal is the frequency-determining element in many transmitters and receivers, means are provided to maintain the crystal's temperature at a constant value. In most communications transmitters and receivers, the crystal holder is enclosed in a special constant-temperature oven.

4-250. *What is meant by the "negative temperature coefficient" of a crystal when it is used in an oscillator?*

The temperature coefficient of a crystal in an oscillator is the relationship between the frequency shift and the temperature change. If the frequency decreases with a rise in temperature, the crystal is said to have a negative temperature coefficient. If the frequency increases with rises in temperature, the crystal has a positive temperature coefficient. If variations in frequency have little or no effect on resonant frequency of the crystal, it has a zero temperature coefficient. The temperature coefficient is usually given as either a percentage of change or a number of hertz per megahertz of change for each Celsius

133

(centigrade) degree of temperature variation from a specified operating temperature.

4-251. *What is the seventh harmonic of 360 kHz?*

The seventh harmonic of any frequency is a frequency that is seven times the referenced, or fundamental, frequency. Thus, 2520 kHz (2.52 MHz) is the seventh harmonic of 360 kHz.

4-252. *Describe the directional characteristics of the following types of antennas: (1) horizontal Hertz, (2) vertical Hertz, (3) vertical loop, (4) horizontal loop, (5) vertical Marconi.*

1. The horizontal Hertz antenna, also referred to as the *half-wave dipole,* is bidirectional. As shown in the drawing of Fig. 4-75A, the antenna radiates two major horizontal lobes in the plane containing the antenna. The radiation pattern is actually donut shaped. Figure 4-75B shows the pattern "looking into" the end of the antenna.

2. The vertical Hertz antenna radiates a donut pattern that is completely nondirectional in the horizontal plane. Figure 4-75A represents a side view of the antenna and its radiation pattern. Figure 4-75B represents a top view of the antenna and pattern.

3. The vertical loop antenna has a bidirectional radiation pattern in the horizontal plane. The lobes are broadside to the loop and have the appearance of the lobes of a horizontally mounted dipole (Fig. 4-75A).

4. The horizontal loop is virtually nondirectional in the horizontal plane, except that a null will occur in the direction toward the loop's feed point.

5. The vertically mounted Marconi antenna radiates a circular pattern in the horizontal plane (as shown in Fig. 4-75B).

4-253. *What is meant by "efficiency" of a radio device?*

In a radio device efficiency is the ratio of energy applied to energy used. It is normally expressed as a percentage.

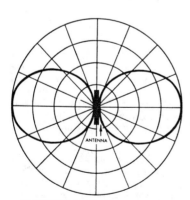

POLAR DIAGRAM FOR HALF-WAVE ANTENNA
IN ANY PLANE CONTAINING THE ANTENNA

A

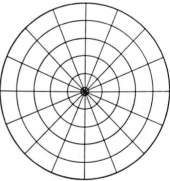

POLAR DIAGRAM FOR HALF-WAVE ANTENNA
IN PLANE PERPENDICULAR TO ANTENNA

B

4-254. *What form of energy is contained in a sound wave?*

A sound wave contains mechanical energy because it causes pressure changes in the medium that conveys the energy.

4-255. *What is meant by the "pitch" of a sound?*

The pitch of a sound is the frequency of the sound waves.

4-256. *How many microfarads are there in one farad? How many picofarads (micromicrofarads) in a microfarad?*

A farad is the basic unit of capacitance. A microfarad is one-millionth of a farad—that is, there are one million microfarads in a farad. The microfarad is a common unit in electronics, particularly at audio frequencies. The picofarad, equal to one-millionth of a microfarad (a trillionth of a farad), is also common in electronics, particularly at radio frequencies. The picofarad at one time was referred to as a *micromicrofarad*.

4-257. *What is the difference between a milliwatt and a kilowatt?*

A milliwatt is one-thousandth of a watt. A kilowatt is 1000 watts. The conversion table of Fig. 4-76 shows the relationship among various values. By substituting the words *volt, ampere,* or *hertz,* the prefixes can apply to these other units of measure, too. The prefix *kilo* always means *thousand, mega* means *million, giga* means *thousands of millions.* Submultiple prefixes are *deci, centi, milli, micro, nano,* and *pico;* and they represent, respectively, the following submultiples: tenths, hundredths, thousandths, millionths, thousandths of millionths, and millionths of millionths.

4-258. *What precaution should be observed when connecting electrolytic capacitors into a circuit?*

Polarities should be observed at all times, and the **voltage** of the circuit must not exceed the working-voltage rating of the electrolytics. When

NUMERICAL MAGNITUDE	NUMBER OF 10 FACTORS	PREFIX	SYMBOL
1 000 000 000 000 =	10^{12}	TERA	T
1 000 000 000 =	10^{9}	GIGA	G
1 000 000 =	10^{6}	MEGA	M
1 000 =	10^{3}	KILO	k
100 =	10^{2}	HECTO	h
10 =	10	DEKA	dk
0.1 =	10^{-1}	DECI	d
0.01 =	10^{-2}	CENTI	c
0.001 =	10^{-3}	MILLI	m
0.000 001 =	10^{-6}	MICRO	u or µ
0.000 000 001 =	10^{-9}	NANO	n
0.000 000 000 001 =	10^{-12}	PICO	p
0.000 000 000 000 001 =	10^{-15}	FEMTO	f
0.000 000 000 000 000 001 =	10^{-18}	ATTO	a

Fig. 4-76.

several electrolytic capacitors are connected in a series circuit, an appropriate high-value resistor must be placed across each capacitor to insure that the total voltage is evenly distributed. A single electrolytic capacitor must never be placed in an ac circuit. If a high-value capacitor is required, a nonpolarized capacitor should be used. (Two electrolytics can be series-connected in a back-to-back arrangement to make a nonpolarized capacitor if their characteristics are the same, their combined capacitance is appropriate, and high-value resistors are used to equalize the distributed voltage.)

4-259. *Show how to connect dry cells in series.*

Figure 4-77A shows how cells are connected in series. When more than one cell is connected in a series arrangement, the cell group is referred to as a *battery*. The total voltage is equal to the sum of the individual cell voltages, and the current capability is equal to the capability of a single cell.

4-260. *Show, by a diagram, how cells may be connected in parallel and in series—parallel.*

The sketch of Fig. 4-77B shows a group of cells connected in parallel. A schematic representation is shown beneath the sketch. The output voltage of parallel-connected cells is the same as the output voltage of a single cell, but the current capability for identical cells is equal to the capacity of one cell multiplied by the number of parallel-connected cells.

Figure 4-77C illustrates a series—parallel connection. The total voltage of such an arrangement is equal to the cell voltage multiplied by the number of cells in each series string. The current is the capacity of a single cell multiplied by the number of strings. The output voltage of the battery shown is 6V. If the capacity of a single cell is 1 ampere-hour, the total capacity of the battery would be 2 ampere-hours.

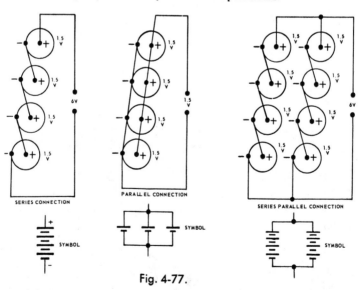

Fig. 4-77.

4-261. *What materials are used for the electrodes of a common dry cell?*

A typical dry cell is pictured in Fig. 4-78. The positive is a carbon rod; the negative terminal, which also serves as the cell container, is made of zinc.

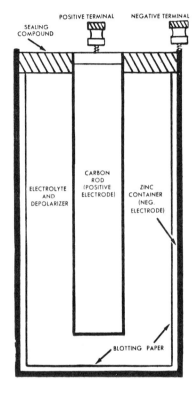

Fig. 4-78.

4-262. *If the period of one complete cycle of a radio wave is one microsecond (one-millionth of a second), what is the frequency and wavelength?*

Since one million such cycles would be propagated in a one-second period, the frequency is one megahertz (1 MHz). The wavelength may be calculated by dividing the velocity of light (velocity of rf propagation) by frequency, or $\lambda = c/f$. The speed of light is 300 million meters per second. Dropping the millions of both speed and frequency, the equation becomes $\lambda = 300/1$, or 300. Thus, the wavelength of a one-megahertz signal is 300 meters.

4-263. *Compare the selectivity and the sensitivity of the following three types of receivers: (1) tuned radio frequency (trf), (2) superregenerative, and (3) superheterodyne.*

Of the three, the superheterodyne is the most selective, and the superregenerative receiver is the least. The sensitivity of superregenerative receivers is comparable to the sensitivity of the superheterodyne. The tuned-rf receiver is an in-between compromise: it is more selective than the superregenerative but lacks the sensitivity of either of the other two types.

4-264. *What type of radio receiver contains i-f transformers?*

An i-f transformer is a transformer that couples an intermediate frequency into a succeeding stage. Only superheterodyne radios employ intermediate frequencies and i-f transformers.

4-265. *What type of receiver is subject to image interference?*

Image interference results when an unintended signal mixes with the local oscillator signal to produce an i-f signal. The image signal frequency is one that is removed from the desired signal frequency by twice the intermediate frequency. If a **superheterodyne receiver** is tuned to 1000 kHz, the local oscillator might be set at 1455 kHz to produce a 455 kHz i-f. A strong signal at 1910 kHz would also produce a 455 kHz i-f signal and would interfere with the desired 1000 kHz signal. The 1910 kHz signal, then, would be an image signal.

4-266. *What type of radio receiver using vacuum tubes does not require an oscillator?*

Two such types are the diode detector receiver, which involves nothing more than a tuned circuit and a rectifier, and the tuned-rf receiver, which is composed of a number of cascaded rf amplifiers feeding a detector stage.

4-267. *Describe the operation of the regenerative receiver.*

The regenerative receiver is a combination oscillator and detector. In a tube-type circuit the rf signal is fed into the grid of an amplifier stage, and the output is taken from the plate. Feedback from plate to grid allows a portion of the output signal to be reapplied with the incoming signal at the grid of the stage to bolster it. The phase of the feedback signal is critical; if the signal is fed back out of phase, cancellation of the rf input signal will occur, and if the signal is fed back in phase but at too high an amplitude, the stage will act as an oscillator.

One typical scheme for feedback is the *tickler winding* approach, whereby the plate circuit is fed in series with the primary of an rf transformer. Variation of the plate current as a result of the input signal causes in-phase variations in the transformer's secondary, which is in the grid circuit. Since the quantity of feedback is critical, a control is normally provided so that feedback can be increased to the point of oscillation, then diminished to an operating level that is just below this threshold.

A superregenerative circuit (Fig. 4-79) is similar in operation to a regenerative type. The important difference is that the superregenerative receiver has a low-level rf voltage (*quench* voltage) introduced in series with the applied plate voltage, as shown in Fig. 4-79. Introduction of the rf signal at this point reduces the criticalness of the regeneration control because it allows the receiver to break into and out of oscillation at regular intervals. As shown in the sketch, the plate is held to a level that is on the threshold of oscillation. Introduction of the quench voltage causes oscillation momentarily on its peaks.

The regenerative receiver is the same as the circuit shown in Fig. 4-79, except for the fact that it does not have the quench voltage source in the plate supply line (shown in the sketch as a circle with a sine wave).

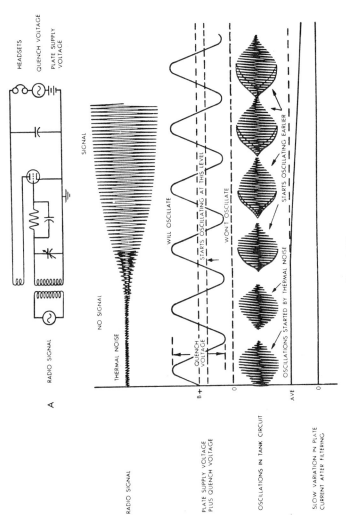

Fig. 4-79.

4-268. *How may a regenerative receiver be adjusted for optimum sensitivity?*

The feedback is adjusted to a level that is just below the threshold of oscillation.

4-269. *What effect does the reception of modulated signals have on the plate current of a grid-leak detector?*

In a grid-leak circuit, the application of a signal **causes grid bias to be applied and plate current to be reduced.**

The grid-leak detector functions like a diode detector combined with a triode amplifier. It is convenient to consider detection and amplification as two descrete functions. In Fig. 4-80A the grid functions as the diode plate. The values of C_D and R_D must be so chosen that C_D charges during the positive peaks of the incoming signal and discharges during the negative peaks. The time constant of $R_D C_D$ should be long with respect to the rf cycle and short with respect to the audio cycle.

An approximate analysis of the waveforms existing in the diode (grid) circuit is shown in Fig. 4-80B. Part 1 shows the input waveform, which is also the waveform in the input tuned circuit. Because rf current (i_g) flows in only one direction in the grid circuit, part 2 (these numerals refer to circled numbers on schematic) shows a rectified current waveform in this circuit. Part 3 shows the waveform developed across C_D. This audio waveform is produced in the same way as the audio waveform in the diode detector (Fig. 4-39); however, the waveform shown in part 3 is not the output voltage. In the grid-leak detector the waveform produced across C_D is combined in series with the rf waveform in the tuned circuit to produce the grid-to-cathode waveform shown in part 4.

An approximate analysis of the waveforms existing in the triode plate circuit is shown in Fig. 4-80C. Part 5 is the plate current waveform, and part 6 is the plate voltage waveform. Capacitor C discharges on the positive half-cycles of grid input voltage (points 1, 3, 4, 7, 9, 11, 12, and so forth). The discharge path is clockwise through the circuit, including the tube and capacitor. The time constant of the discharge path is the product of the effective tube resistance and the capacitance of capacitor C, and this time constant is short because the effective tube resistance is low. The increase in plate current is supplied by the capacitor rather than the $B+$ supply, thus preventing any further increase in current through the rf choke and plate load resistor R_L. Therefore, any further change in plate and capacitor voltage is limited.

Capacitor C charges up as plate voltage rises on the negative half-cycles of rf grid input voltage (Fig. 4-80C)—points 2, 4, 6, 8, 10, 12, 14, and so forth. The charging path is clockwise through the circuit containing the capacitor, rf choke, load resistor, and $B+$ supply. The rise in plate voltage is limited by the capacitor charging current, which flows through the rf choke and R_L. The plate current decrease is approximately equal to the capacitor charging current; thus, the total current through the rf choke and R_L remains nearly constant, and the plate and capacitor voltage rise is checked.

Positive grid swings cause sufficient grid current to flow to produce grid-leak bias. Low plate voltage limits the plate current on no-signal conditions in the absence of grid bias. Thus, the amplitude of the input signal is limited, since with low plate voltage the cutoff bias is low, and that portion of the input signal that drives the grid voltage below cutoff is lost. The waveform of the voltage across capacitor C is shown by the solid line in part 6 of Fig. 4-80C. The plate voltage ripple is removed by the rf choke. Part 7 shows the output voltage waveform. This waveform is the difference between (1) the voltage at the junction of the load resistor and rf choke with respect to the negative terminal of E_{BB} and (2) the voltage across coupling capacitor C_C which, for practical purposes, is a pure dc voltage.

Because the operation of the grid-leak detector depends on a certain amount of grid current flow, a loading effect is produced that lowers the selectivity of the input circuit. However, the sensitivity of the grid-leak detector is moderately high on low-amplitude signals.

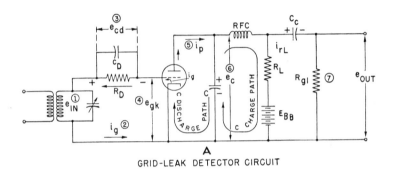

A

GRID-LEAK DETECTOR CIRCUIT

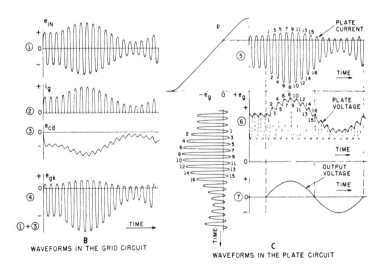

B

WAVEFORMS IN THE GRID CIRCUIT

C

WAVEFORMS IN THE PLATE CIRCUIT

Fig. 4-80.

4-270. *What is meant by "double detection" in a receiver?*

Double detection is a term used (rarely) in reference to superheterodyne receivers. *First detector* is an outmoded name for the mixer, and *second detector* is an outmoded name for the audio detector of a superhet.

4-271. *What is the purpose of wave trap in a radio receiver?*

A wave trap (also referred to as a *suckout trap*) is highly selective filter. It is tuned to the frequency of an undesired signal and placed in the input circuit to a receiver.

In practice, the wave trap is a *bandstop filter*, and it may be either series or parallel resonant. A *series resonant* circuit offers minimum opposition to the resonant frequency. A circuit such as that shown in Fig. 4-81A would effectively short out the frequency to which the series circuit was resonant. All other frequencies would be passed into the receiver. A *parallel resonant* circuit (Fig. 4-81B) offers maximum opposition to the frequency of resonance and low impedance to other frequencies.

A filter made up of both series and parallel resonant circuits, such as that shown in Fig. 4-81C, would be effective in eliminating one sideband of a modulated signal and is frequently used in such applications.

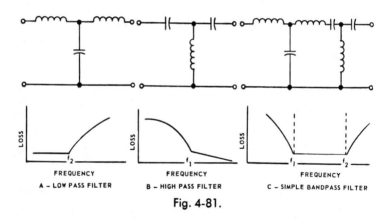

Fig. 4-81.

4-272. *What is the purpose of an oscillator in a receiver operating on a frequency near the i-f of the receiver?*

The local oscillator produces an rf signal that is fed to a mixer along with the incoming rf signal from the antenna. The mixer produces an output that is the difference frequency between the two signals. This difference frequency is the i-f, or intermediate frequency.

4-273. *Explain the purpose and operation of the first detector in a superheterodyne receiver.*

The first detector is more frequently known as a *mixer* these days. Mixer action is illustrated in Fig. 4-82. When the two slightly different

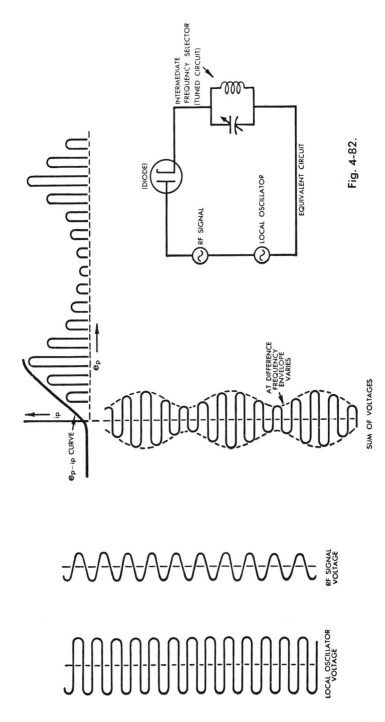

INTERMEDIATE FREQUENCY SELECTOR (TUNED CIRCUIT)

(DIODE)

RF SIGNAL

LOCAL OSCILLATOR

EQUIVALENT CIRCUIT

Fig. 4-82.

ep

ip

ep–ip CURVE

AT DIFFERENCE FREQUENCY ENVELOPE VARIES

SUM OF VOLTAGES

RF SIGNAL VOLTAGE

LOCAL OSCILLATOR VOLTAGE

frequencies are added in a nonlinear device such as a diode, the waveshape representing the combination of the local oscillator and the rf signals contains not only these two frequencies but a frequency equal to their sum and another equal to their difference. Since it is normally the difference frequency that is desired, the tuned circuits in the i-f amplifier select this frequency and the stage amplifies it. The rf signal is modulated, the difference frequency (intermediate frequency) will also be modulated in the same manner.

4-274. *What is a getter in a vacuum tube?*

A getter is a material enclosed in the envelope of a vacuum tube to collect traces of gas remaining after evacuation.

4-275. *What is a space charge in a vacuum tube?*

Space charge might be referred to as *electron spill* since the space charge is a cluster of electrons suspended in space between the cathode and plate of a vacuum tube (Fig. 4-83).

At low plate voltages electrons are emitted by the cathode faster than they can be attracted to the plate. The electrons therefore tend to remain in the space between these two elements and produce a negative charge which exerts a repelling force upon other electrons being emitted from the cathode. At any instant, the number of electrons traveling between the cathode and plate cannot be greater than the

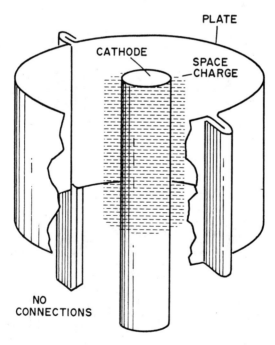

Fig. 4-83.

number required to neutralize the attraction of the plate voltage. All electrons in excess of this number are repelled back to the cathode (unless additional tube elements are introduced to counteract this effect). Thus, plate current is independent of cathode emission as long as the negative space charge exists.

At higher plate voltages the plate attracts more of the electrons emitted from the cathode and reduces the tendency for electrons to remain in the space charge region and repel other electrons. The higher the plate voltage, the greater the proportion of electrons attracted and the smaller the space charge.

4-276. *Explain the operation of a triode tube as an amplifier.*

In the single-stage triode amplifier shown in Fig. 4-84, the signal voltage is applied in series with the grid—cathode circuit and grid bias voltage. The changes in the grid-to-cathode voltage with changes in the signal voltage cause the plate current to change. The plate current changes flow through resistor R_L, which is in series with the plate—cathode circuit and the plate supply. The resistor is called the *plate load* resistor; the voltage developed across it varies with the plate current. Since the load resistor is farly large—approximately five times the internal plate resistance of the vacuum tube—the voltage developed across the resistor by the varying current through it is greater than the signal voltage applied to the grid. Hence, by the action of the amplifier, a small grid voltage change produces a larger voltage change in the plate circuit.

The grid of the amplifier is normally biased so that it remains negative with respect to the cathode regardless of the alternating cycle of the input voltage waves. As long as the grid is negative with respect to the cathode, it does not attract any electrons. When no electrons are attracted by the grid, no current flows in the grid circuit. Under this condition the grid circuit consumes no power. But if the grid becomes positive with respect to the cathode, current flows in the grid circuit and it draws power. In the circuit illustrated, the grid is operated at a negative potential with respect to the cathode, and there is no power lost in the grid circuit.

4-277. *What are the approximate efficiencies of class A, class B, and class C amplifiers?*

Class A amplifiers are typically 20% to 25% efficient. Class B amplifiers are typically 60% to 65% efficient, though they are theoretically capable of efficiencies as high as about 80%. The class C is the most efficient amplifier of them all, with a typical range from 60% to 80%.

4-278. *Does dc grid current normally flow in a class A amplifier employing a single tube?*

A single-stage class A amplifier operates with no grid current.

4-279. *Why must some rf amplifiers be neutralized?*

Neutralization is employed in some rf amplifiers to avoid oscillation. Interelectrode capacitances, such as that typically encountered in triode vacuum tubes, result in positive feedback of signals. Neutralization offsets the capacitance of the feedback paths.

4-280. *Describe how a vacuum tube oscillates in a circuit.*

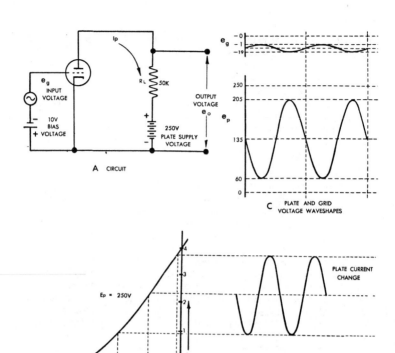

Fig. 4-84.

An oscillator is, in essence, an amplifier. A signal is applied to the grid and appears at the plate in amplified form. When a portion of this signal at the plate is fed back to the grid in phase with the signal already appearing at the grid, the output signal is increased. When the amplitude of the fed-back signal is high enough, regeneration occurs—the signal is amplified, fed back, amplified, fed back, etc. until the tube goes into saturation. When sustained regeneration takes place, the effect is oscillation.

4-281.   *Is the dc bias normally positive or negative in a class A amplifier?*

The dc bias applied to the grid of a class A amplifier is normally negative. Negative bias is necessary to keep the grid from drawing current. The amount of dc bias determines the class of amplifier. A class A amplifier is negatively biased so that the tube operates in the center of its linear region.

4-282. *What is the composition of filaments, heaters, and cathodes in vacuum tubes?*

Filaments, cathodes, and heaters may be constructed of a number of metals, but the most common are *tungsten*, thoriated tungsten, oxide-coated tungsten, and tungsten alloy. The characteristics of the tube depend to a large extent on the composition of the heater or cathode element, as shown in the curves of Fig. 4-85. At high plate voltages the flow of plate current is practically independent of plate voltage but is a function of the cathode temperature. However, at lower values of plate voltage, the plate current is controlled by the voltage between the plate and cathode and is substantially independent of cathode temperature.

The dotted portion of the curves in Fig. 4-85 is representative of tungsten and thoriated-tungsten cathodes, and the solid curves are typical of oxide-coated cathodes. It is unlikely that the plate current in a tube employing an oxide-coated cathode will ever be entirely independent of the plate voltage. Before the plate voltage can be increased sufficiently to produce emission saturation, it is probable that the cathode will be damaged seriously from overheating.

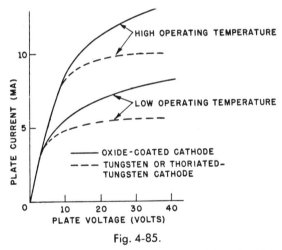

Fig. 4-85.

4-283. *What is the direction of electron flow in the plate and grid circuits of vacuum-tube amplifiers?*

The application of heat frees a large number of electrons from the cathode, and these drift into the surrounding space. The positive charge on the plate attracts these electrons, which flow from the cathode to the plate and into the positive terminal of the voltage source.

If the grid is made positive with respect to the cathode, it will aid in drawing electrons from the space charge, and there will be an increase in the number of electrons reaching the plate. Some of the electrons will be attracted to the grid, which acts as a plate when positive, and grid current will flow. When electrons flow in the grid circuit, they flow from cathode to grid to grounds and back to the cathode.

4-284. *Draw a diagram showing a method of obtaining grid bias for a tube with an indirectly heated cathode by use of a resistance in the cathode circuit.*

Figure 4-86 shows a simple method of obtaining grid bias by insertion of a resistor between the cathode of the tube and ground. The flow of plate current back to the cathode develops an *IR* drop across this resistor, making the cathode more positive than ground. With the grid of the tube connected to ground through either a resistor or the secondary winding of a transformer, no dc voltage can exist between grid and ground as long as no grid current is allowed to flow.

If the voltage developed across the cathode resistor is 10V, the cathode is 10V positive with respect to ground. Stated another way, the ground is 10V negative with respect to the cathode. Since the control grid is at the same dc potential as ground the grid is 10V negative with respect to the cathode. It also follows that unless an alternating voltage with a peak value of more than 10V is applied between grid and cathode, no grid current will flow in the circuit.

A capacitor is usually connected across the cathode resistor to keep the ac components of the cathode current from varying the *IR* drop across the resistor. The ac voltage developed across the cathode resistor by the cathode−plate signal would oppose the input signal were it not for the cathode bypass capacitor.

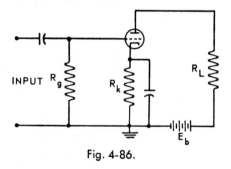

Fig. 4-86.

4-285. *What are causes of downward fluctuation of the antenna current of a plate-modulated transmitter?*

This *downward modulation* is a common condition in AM transmitters where poor voltage regulation, soft tubes, or inadequate impedance matching between the modulator and the final exists. The problem might be caused by any of the following:

1. Final amplifier biased too near amplifier cutoff
2. Rf driver stage not producing enough excitation, as from
   (2) faulty driver tube
   (b) low driver filament voltage
   (b) insufficient coupling between driver and final
   (d) soft driver tube
3. Excessive voltage drops when amplifier is keyed (poor voltage regulation)
4. Soft final amplifier tube or insufficient filament voltage

5. Inadequate impedance matching between the modulator and final amplifier
6. Shorted rf choke in the plate supply lead of the final amplifier.

4-286. *What is the impedance of a solenoid if its resistance is 5Ω and 0.3A flows through the winding when 110V at 60 Hz is applied to the solenoid?*

The Ohm's law formula for impedance is parallel to that for resistance. According to Ohm's law for ac circuits, impedance is equal to voltage divided by current. Thus, 110V divided by 0.3A equals 366.67Ω. The dc resistance of the coil can be ignored. It's a distractor in this question and has no bearing on the calculated impedance value.

4-287. *What is the conductance of a circuit if a 6A current flows when 12V dc is applied to the circuit?*

Conductance is the reciprocal of resistance. Simply determine the resistance and divide into 1. From Ohm's law, $R = E/I$. Here $R = 12/6 = 2A$. The reciprocal of 2 (1 divided by 2)—the conductance—is 0.5 mho.

4-288. *What is the relationship between the effective, or rms, value of an rf current and the heating value?*

The heating value of an rf current is equal to the effective, or rms, current. Practical antennas have heat losses caused by current flowing through the conductors that must be replaced by the rf source. The losses tend to make the input of the antenna resistive, and the resistance is a combination of the following: the ohmic resistance of the antenna and transmission line conductors and the *radiation resistance*. (Radiation resistance is the resistance that would dissipate the same amount of energy in the form of heat as is actually radiated.)

4-289. *What safety precautions should a person observe when making internal adjustments to a television receiver to avoid personal injury?*

If the adjustments are to be made under a condition where voltage to the cathode-ray tube is not required, it is best to make certain no residual voltage exists on exposed terminals. Because of charge storage capability of the large capacitors in various circuits, it is wise to discharge them to ground. Use insulated tools, make certain the chassis is well grounded, and try to keep one hand away from the chassis during all adjustments. If the set is a "hot chassis" type, use an isolation transformer to supply operational power during servicing.

4-290. *With measuring equipment that is widely available, is it possible to measure a frequency of 10 MHz to within one hertz of the exact frequency?*

Widely available frequency meters and frequency counters are capable of making measurements to the accuracy of one part in 10 million. The very best counters have an accuracy of 5 parts in 10^{10}, but counters have an inherent one-count ambiguity. To overcome this, one can measure the **period** of a signal to the great accuracy of one of these counters and convert to frequency; using the formula $f = 1/t$. Thus, 10 MHz could be measured to an accuracy of 0.005 Hz.

4-291. *Do oscillators operating on adjacent frequencies have a tendency to synchronize, or drift apart in frequency?*

149

The stability of the oscillators depends on the degree of coupling between them. If signal cross coupling does occur, there will be a definite tendency for the oscillators to each shift toward the other. Eventually, they will both be operating at the same frequency, provided their tuned circuits are broad enough to allow it.

4-292. *What type of energy is stored in a lead—acid storage battery?*

Chemical energy is stored in a battery cell.

4-293. *What precautions should be observed when using and storing crystal microphones?*

Crystal microphones are extremely sensitive to heat, shock, and overvoltage. Thus, it is wise to use and store microphones of this type in cool places. A crystal microphone should never be used in a portable or mobile application, where ambient temperature excesses could easily damage the crystal element. A crystal microphone should never be used as a speaker, even though it can be, because of the likelihood of damage by overvoltage. A crystal will normally tolerate an overload of only 50% beyond the amount of voltage it will produce. Crystal microphones are inherently shock sensitive and should be employed only in applications where no jarring is likely to be encountered.

4-294. *If a 1500 kHz radio wave is modulated by a 2 kHz sine-wave tone, what frequencies are contained in the modulated wave?*

The modulated wave contains the carrier frequency (1500 kHz), its upper sideband (1502 kHz), and its lower sideband (1598 kHz). Figure 4-87 indicates that the resultant wave with single-tone amplitude modulation consists of three separate waves of constant amplitude. The lower sideband has a frequency equal to the difference between the modulation and carrier frequencies, as shown in Fig. 4-87. The upper sideband has a frequency equal to the sum of the carrier and modulation frequencies, as is shown above the carrier. The carrier and the sidebands are not merely mathematical abstractions; they may be separated from one another by filters and used individually.

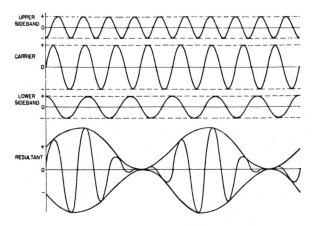

Fig. 4-87.

In an AM wave only the sidebands contain intelligence (modulation); the audio frequency, as such, is not transmitted. Because the modulating frequencies represent the information to be transmitted, as much power as possible should be put into the sidebands. A single-sideband communication system is based on the fact that power not put into the sidebands is power wasted.

4-295. *Why are laminated iron cores used in audio and power transformers?*

Laminated cores are used to minimize eddy current losses.

4-296. *What are cathode rays?*

A cathode ray is a beam of electrons emitted from the cathode of a viewing tube, such as is used for television picture tubes and display tubes for oscilloscopes.

4-297. *Why is a high ratio of capacitance to inductance employed in the grid circuit of some oscillators?*

The ratio of capacitance to inductance is made high deliberately to make the oscillator stable and selective. Particularly where interelectrode capacitance could prove problemsome, the ratio is kept high so that the inherent capacitances of the tube amount to only a small fraction of the total capacitance of the tuned circuit.

At radio frequencies below VHF, the interelectrode capacitances in a vacuum tube have reactances that are so large that they do not cause any serious trouble. However, as frequency increases, the reactance of the capacitances becomes small enough to materially affect the performance of a circuit. A 1 pF capacitor, for example, has a reactance of 159,000Ω at 1 MHz. If this capacitor is the plate-to-grid capacitance and the rf voltage between the electrodes is 500V, there will be an interelectrode capacitance current of 500/519,000, or 0.00315A, or 3.15 mA—an amount that might not seriously disturb circuit operation. On the other hand, at 100 MHz the reactance of this capacitor becomes 1590Ω, and the current is 500/1590, or 315 mA—an amount which certainly would seriously affect circuit performance.

Since interelectrode capacitances are effectively in parallel with the tuned circuit, they affect the frequency at which the tuned circuit resonates. As you can see in Fig. 4-88, the plate-to-cathode capacitance is in parallel with the series combination of the

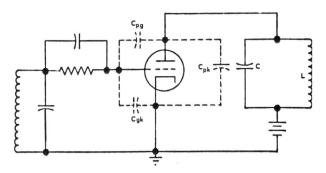

Fig. 4-88.

plate-to-grid and grid-to-cathode capacitance. All these capacitances together form a part of the total capacitance of the tuned circuit.

Interelectrode capacitance limits the frequency by establishing a minimum capacitance below which it is impossible to go. In addition, interelectrode capacitance varies with the applied voltages and loading of the oscillator. This causes frequency instability, particularly when the interelectrode capacitance forms a large part of the tuning-circuit capacitance.

4-298. *What is the purpose of a buffer amplifier stage in a transmitter?*

A buffer amplifier is placed between the oscillator and power amplifier (Fig. 4-89) to isolate the oscillator from the load and thus improve the frequency stability of the transmitter.

If the frequency of the plate tank circuit of the buffer amplifier is the same as that of the oscillator driving it, the stage is a conventional type of amplifier. If the plate tank circuit of the buffer is tuned to the second harmonic (to increase the frequency of the radiated signal) of the driving signal applied to the grid, the stage becomes a frequency doubler, and the output voltage has a frequency equal to twice that of the input. The buffer amplifier may also be a tripler or a quadrupler.

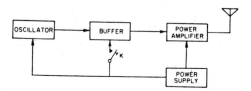

Fig. 4-89.

4-299. *What determines the speed of (1) a synchronous motor, (2) an induction motor, (3) a dc series motor?*

1. The speed of a **synchronous motor depends on the frequency of the applied voltage**; if the frequency is constant, the speed will be constant. The design of a synchronous motor is almost the same as that of an alternator. Figure 4-90A shows the poles of a synchronous motor field and two of the conductors in the armature. The field is constant, since it is due to direct current. The current through the armature is alternating. At the instant shown, the torque of the two conductors tends to move them to the left. Since this is alternating current, the next half-cycle will find the current through the armature reversed, and the torque reversed if the wires remain in the same relative position. If the armature moved far enough so that wire 2 were beneath the end pole and wire 1 below an S-pole, the torque would be in the same direction, keeping the armature turning in the same direction as during the first half-cycle. If each half-cycle sees the armature conductors moved the distance of one pole, the torque will always be in the same direction, resulting in continuous motion. Thus, the synchronous motor must operate at constant speed if the frequency is constant. If the average speed differs from synchronous speed, the average torque actually becomes zero, and the motor must stop.

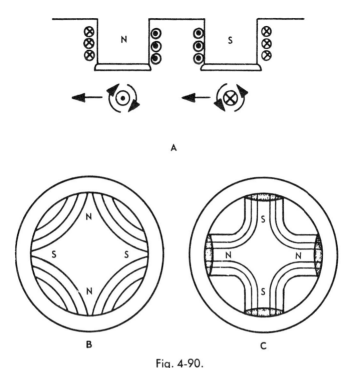

A

B   C

Fig. 4-90.

2. The speed of the rotating field of an **induction motor is equal to the frequency of the applied voltage divided by the number of pole pairs**. If the frequency in hertz is multiplied by 60, the speed will be in revolutions per minute. The actual speed of the motor will be slightly less than the speed of the rotating field, since there must be some relative motion (the difference between motor speed and speed of rotating field) for torque to exist. Figure 4-91 is an illustration of the basic principle of the induction motor. A horseshoe magnet is placed over a disc of metal so that its magnetic field passes through the disc. The disc is mounted so that it can rotate freely and the magnet is rotated clockwise above the disc (Fig. 4-91A). As it moves, the magnetic flux cuts through the disc. This metal disc can be considered to be made up of many conductors side by side. Figure 4-91B is a side view, looking at the edge of the disc below the north pole. Since the results would be the same if the disc were moved counterclockwise (the relative motion between conductor and flux would be the same), the conductors are indicated as moving.

    Eddy currents are induced in the disc by the cutting of the lines of force. They are shown in Fig. 4-91B as coming out of the paper. The lines of force about the conductor are shown in Fig. 4-91C. Remember that these lines of force are due to the induced current in the conductor. The magnetic field on the right side of the conductor

153

in Fig. 4-91C is weakened, while the field to the left is increased. The force acting on the conductor tends to move it to the left. This is the same direction we are moving the magnet above the disc. The disc is rotating in the same direction as the magnet but at a slightly slower rate. It can never rotate as fast as the magnet, because if it were to do so, there would be no relative motion. With no relative motion, there could be no induced voltage and no magnetic field about the disc conductor. There would be, therefore, no reaction between magnetic fields, no torque, and a slowing down of the disc. Once the disc began to slow down, there would be relative motion between the magnet and the disc, resulting in induced currents in the disc with their accompanying magnetic fields. The disc once more would have a force tending to rotate it. The difference of speed between the magnet and the disc is called the *revolutions slip*.

Instead of a disc, a cylinder may be used. Instead of a horseshoe-shaped magnet, four poles may be rotated within the cylinder. The cylinder is more like what would be found in a commercial induction motor and works on the same principle as the disc. Rather than rotating a magnet, a rotating field is used in a practical induction motor. The rotating field is due to polyphase currents in polyphase windings. The rotation of the fields is produced by electrical means.

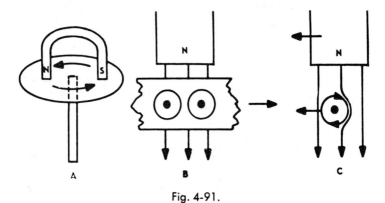

Fig. 4-91.

3. The speed of a **dc series motor is determined largely by the load** on the motor. The formula for the speed of a dc series-type motor is

$$S = k \; \frac{E - I(R_a + R_f)}{\phi}$$

where k is a constant, E the applied voltage, I the armature current, R_a the armature resistance, R_f the resistance of the field coils, and ϕ the flux entering the armature from one pole. (Armature current and flux both vary with load.) **When the load on a series motor is increased, the motor speed tends to decrease**. This decrease in speed produces a decrease in the back emf, which allows more armature current to flow. The numerator of the fraction in the

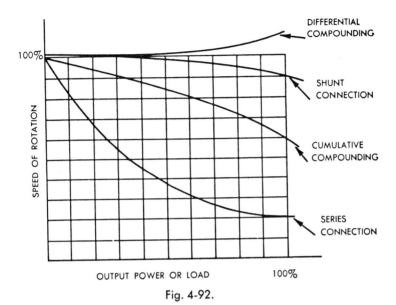

DIFFERENTIAL
COMPOUNDING

SHUNT
CONNECTION

CUMULATIVE
COMPOUNDING

SERIES
CONNECTION

SPEED OF ROTATION

OUTPUT POWER OR LOAD 100%

Fig. 4-92.

formula above becomes slightly smaller. The flux (ϕ) increases with an increase in current. The increase in armature current increases the denominator and decreases the numerator of the fraction in the speed formula, resulting in a drop in the motor speed. The decrease in motor speed brings about an increase in armature current and field strength. The speed and current continue to change until the developed torque is balanced with the applied (load) torque (and any losses).

When the load on a series motor is decreased, the speed tends to increase at that instant. An increase in speed results in an increase in the back or **counter** emf. (Current and flux have not had a chance to change yet.) This increase in counter emf (cemf) produces a decrease in the armature current and field strength. As the current and flux decrease, the developed torque decreases, and the speed also decreases. The speed and current, as before, continue to adjust until the torques are balanced.

4-300. *What is the total resistance of a parallel circuit consisting of a branch of 10 Ω and one of 25 Ω?*

The total resistance is 7.143 Ω, as calculated from the formula for two parallel resistances.

$$R_P = \frac{R1R2}{R1+R2}$$

The quotient of 250 (or 10 $\times$ 25) and 35 (or 10+25) is 7.143.

4-301. *Draw a diagram of a resistive load connected in the plate circuit of a vacuum tube and indicate the direction of electron flow in the load.*

The drawing in Fig. 4-93 is a conventional triode amplifier circuit. The negative side of the battery is connected to chassis ground, and the

155

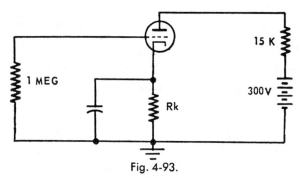

Fig. 4-93.

positive side is connected to a series resistor feeding the plate. Current flow is from the negative side of the battery (chassis ground) up through the cathode. Electrons boil off the cathode and are attracted to the plate. The electrons are attracted from the plate through the series resistor toward the positive terminal of the B-battery.

4-302. *Draw a sine wave of voltage displaced 180° from a sine wave of current.*

The curves in Fig. 4-94 represent sine waves of current and voltage that are 180° apart. Since one complete cycle of any cyclic wave represents 360°, one-half of one cycle is 180°. Thus, each vertical line in the graphical wave picture represents 180°. If either the voltage (E_P) or current (I_P) wave were to be moved either to the left or right by exactly 180° (one square), the two waves would be in phase.

4-303. *Show by a diagram how a voltmeter and ammeter should be connected to measure power in a dc circuit.*

The diagram in Fig. 4-95 shows an actual wattmeter connected in a circuit. As can be seen, the wattmeter contains two coils, one for measuring current and one for measuring voltage. Note that the *potential* coil is *across* the line, while the *current* coil is *in series* with it.

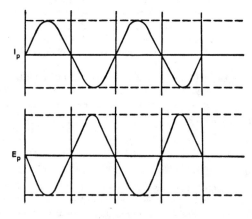

Fig. 4-94.

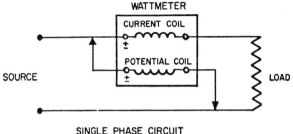

WATTMETER

SINGLE PHASE CIRCUIT

Fig. 4-95.

If an ammeter is substituted for the current coil and a voltmeter for the other coil, dc power can be measured. To determine the power in watts that the load is using, simply multiply indicated current (amperes) by indicated potential (volts). Of course, this will not work with ac unless the load is purely resistive.

4-304. *Indicate by a diagram how the total current in three branches of a parallel circuit can be measured by one ammeter.*

The circle shown in the schematic of Fig. 4-96 represents an ammeter in the line feeding the paralleled resistors. The total current through any circuit can be determined by placing an ammeter in series with either the positive or the negative supply line.

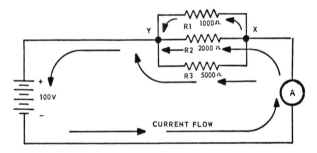

Fig. 4-96.

4-305. *Draw a graph illustrating how the plate current in a vacuum tube varies with the plate voltage when the grid bias remains constant.*

Characteristic curves of this type are called $e_P - i_P$ curves, the subscript letter P referring to the plate of a vacuum tube. These are *static* operating curves as opposed to *dynamic* curves. A static curve is taken under no-signal conditions, and a dynamic curve represents the tube under actual operating conditions. The six curves plotted in Fig. 4-97 represent a triode under six differing conditions of fixed grid bias. Such static curves as this—although obtained under nonoperating conditions—will give a considerable amount of information about the tube's operating capabilities.

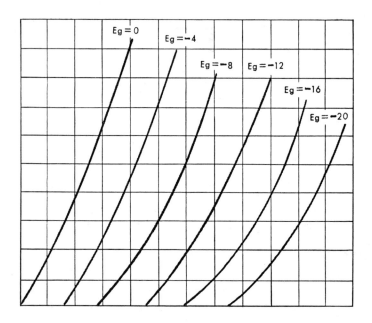

Fig. 4-97.

4-306. *Draw two cycles of an rf wave and indicate one wavelength thereof.*

Refer back to Fig. 4-94 for this one. Since each half-wavelength of the two sine waves is contained within one pair of vertical lines, a wavelength would occupy two full squares (three vertical lines).

4-307. *Explain the purposes and procedures of neutralization in rf amplifiers.*

The purpose of neutralization is **to eliminate unwanted positive feedback** from plate (or collector) to grid (or base). *Unwanted feedback* refers to feedback that is in phase with the stage's input signal and might cause oscillation of the stage.

There are several neutralization systems in common use. Two of these—plate (or collector) neutralization and grid (or base) neutralization—have the advantage of being useful over a wide frequency range. Their names are derived from the part of the circuit in which feedback voltage is developed.

The procedures for neutralization are almost independent of the type of circuit used. First, the plate (or collector) voltage is removed from the stage to be neutralized, so that any signal present in the plate (or collector) circuit is due to interelectrode capacitance coupling. Then the master oscillator and amplifier stages that precede the unneutralized stage are tuned. This will provide a strong signal to the grid (or base) of the unneutralized stage. The next step involves the adjustment of the neutralizing capacitor (C_N) until there is a minimum amount of energy transferred to the plate (or collector) circuit.

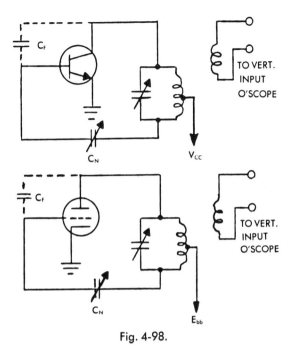

Fig. 4-98.

One method of indicating the null places a pickup coil near the plate (or collector) tank. The coil leads are connected to the vertical input of an oscilloscope, as shown in Fig. 4-98. The neutralizing capacitor (C_N) is then adjusted so that no rf voltage appears on the screen of the oscilloscope when the tank is tuned to resonance. Under these circumstances, the rf current divides equally through C_F and C_N. The resulting rf currents in the tank flow in opposite directions and cancel the tank inductive effect, so that no resonant buildup occurs between the coil and capacitors. A neon glow lamp, a loop of wire attached to the filament connections of a flashlight bulb, or a sensitive rf galvanometer may be used if an oscilloscope is not available.

When there is a millammeter in the amplifier grid (or base) circuit, as in Fig. 4-99, adjustment of C_N may be made by observing the meter as the output tank is tuned through resonance with no plate (or collector) voltage applied. When there is an imbalance between C_F and C_N, the output becomes alternately positive and negative as the tank approaches resonance. On positive swings output current flows. As the tank circuit is tuned to the resonant frequency, some of the current that was input directed now becomes output directed, thereby causing a dip in the input current. However, if C_N in properly adjusted, no dip in the input current occurs as the output tank is tuned through resonance.

In some transmitter circuits it is more convenient to turn off the filament voltage on the amplifier stage instead of removing the plate voltage. If this is done, the process of neutralizing the amplifier is carried out in the same way, except that no current flows in the grid

159

circuit. The absence of rf in the plate tank, as evidence of the correct adjustment of C_N, may be determined by the effect on the exciter stage or on an rf pickup coil and associated indicator.

Once a neutralizing capacitor is adjusted for use with a particular tube or transistor, it will require only occasional checks. However, if the transmitter or tube is replaced, the neutralizing capacitor will require adjustment since the new device could have a slightly different value of C_F.

Some common neutralizing methods are: *input neutralization* (also called *gate*, *grid*, or *base* neutralization, depending on the device used), *output neutralization* (also called *drain*, *plate*, or *collector* neutralization, depending on the device used), *inductive neutralization* (also called *coil* neutralization), and *cross neutralization* (used between tube pairs).

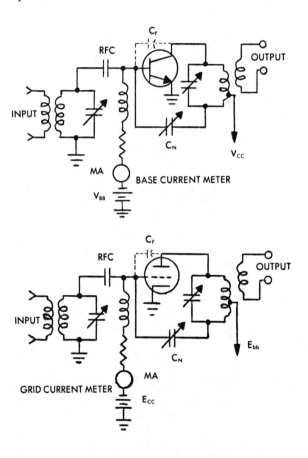

Fig. 4-99.

4-308. *In a circuit consisting of an inductance having a reactance of 100Ω and a resistance of 100Ω, what will be the phase angle of the current with reference to the voltage?*

The phase angle will be precisely 45°. The phase angle, θ, is the angle that applied voltage vector **E** (Fig. 4-100) makes with vector $\mathbf{E_R}$, the voltage across the resistance. The angle may be determined from any of its trigonometric functions, depending on the values known. If the voltage across the resistance is large with respect to that across the inductance, the resultant vector will approach the horizontal, and the phase angle will be very small (approaching zero). If the voltage across the resistance is small in relation to the voltage across the inductance, the resultant vector will approach the vertical, and the phase angle will be large (up to 90°). When the reactive and resistive voltages are equal,

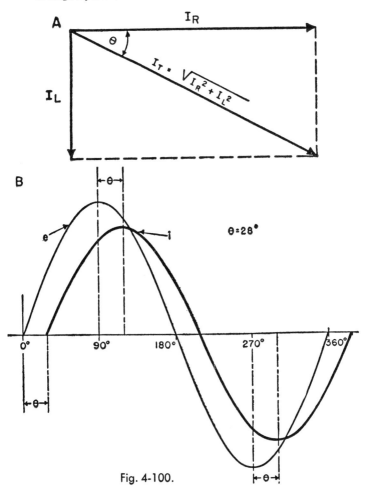

Fig. 4-100.

the vector angle is 45°. The phase angle may also be determined in terms of R and X_L by

$$\theta = \arctan \frac{X_L}{R}$$

Since the reactance and resistance in the question are both 100Ω the tangent is 1.0. Any table of trigonometric functions will show that the angle whose tangent is 1.0 is 45°.

4-309. *What is the effective value of a sine wave in relation to its peak value?*

The effective value is more commonly referred to as the *rms value.* The (effective) value of a sinusoidal voltage or current is 0.707 times the peak value, or equal to the peak (or maximum) value divided by the square root of 2.0 (1.414). The average, effective, and maximum values of a sine wave are shown graphically in Fig. 4-101.

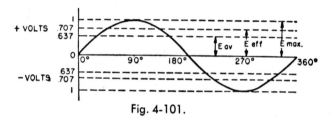

Fig. 4-101.

4-310. *What is the meaning of "phase difference"?*

Phase difference is the difference in time between any point on a cycle and the beginning of that cycle. The beginning of a cycle generally is taken to be the point at which the cycle passes through zero, moving in a positive direction. Such a consideration of phase difference, although seldom used in reference to a single voltage, is of practical importance when two ac voltages or currents are present in the same circuit. The time of a cycle of alternating current or voltage is usually expressed in electrical degrees, with 360° (number of degrees in a complete circle) representing one full cycle. Thus, 90° is one-fourth of a cycle and represents a specific amount of time depending on the frequency. If the voltage considered is the usual 60 Hz ac used in the home, one cycle is completed in one-sixtieth of a second. Then 90°, or one-fourth cycle, actually represents one-fourth of one-sixtieth of one second. That is, $90° = \frac{1}{4} \times \frac{1}{60} = \frac{1}{240}$ seconds. Phase, like time, is expressed in degrees; so a time lag of 90° is a phase difference of 90°.

4-311. *What factors must be known to determine the power factor of an ac circuit?*

The power factor is the ratio of true power to apparent power, and is equal to the cosine of the phase angle between current and voltage, or $\cos \theta$. Since $\cos \theta$ is also the ratio of resistance to impedance, these two factors would be sufficient to determine the power factor. However, Ohm's law can be used to determine power factor, too.

$$pf = \cos \theta = \frac{I^2 R}{EI}$$

The I^2R function is, of course, equal to true power, and EI (or I^2Z) is equal to apparent power. The power factor (cos θ) will be a decimal fraction between 0 and 1.0.

It is important to realize that a power factor close to 1.0 is generally to be desired for all ac circuits using appreciable power. A low power factor means that there is a large discrepancy between the voltage and current in the circuit and the smaller voltage and current actually needed to perform the work desired. The generator source and circuit elements, therefore, would have to be designed to produce and withstand larger values than necessary. As the power factor approaches 1.0, the generator and circuit elements need be only slightly larger than their useful values.

For example, in circuit C of Fig. 4-102, the power factor is

$$pf = \cos \theta = 0.446$$

The current through all elements is 1.34A. The voltage across the inductance, E_L, is equal to IX_L, and the voltage across the capacitance is equal to IX_C. Then:

$$E_L = 1.34 \times 300 = 401\text{V}$$
$$E_C = 1.34 \times 100 = 134\text{V}$$

It is interesting to note also that, at resonance, a special condition in respect to the power factor occurs: Since the reactive elements cancel each other, R is equal to Z, the phase angle is equal to zero degrees, apparent power is equal to true power, and the power factor is equal to 1.0. However, because of resonance, the current in the circuit is maximum; accordingly, the voltages across the reactive elements may be very high—a condition characteristic of circuits of low power factor.

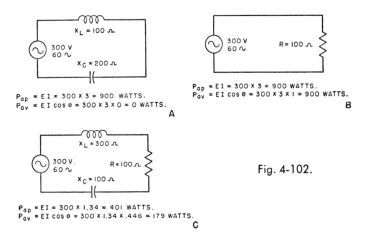

$P_{ap} = EI = 300 \times 3 = 900$ WATTS.
$P_{av} = EI \cos \theta = 300 \times 3 \times 0 = 0$ WATTS.

A

$P_{ap} = EI = 300 \times 3 = 900$ WATTS.
$P_{av} = EI \cos \theta = 300 \times 3 \times 1 = 900$ WATTS.

B

$P_{ap} = EI = 300 \times 1.34 = 401$ WATTS.
$P_{av} = EI \cos \theta = 300 \times 1.34 \times .446 = 179$ WATTS.

C

Fig. 4-102.

4-312. *What are the properties of a series capacitor acting alone in an ac circuit?*

In Fig. 4-103 a sine wave of voltage is applied to a pure capacitance. The variation in charge on the plates of the capacitor also follows the form of the sine wave and is in phase with the voltage, since for any given capacitor the voltage across the capacitor depends directly on the charge (B and C). The current in the circuit also follows the sine wave, but since a capacitor tends to retard voltage change, it is necessary to determine precisely the delay in time between current flow and the building up of voltage—that is, the phase shift between current and voltage.

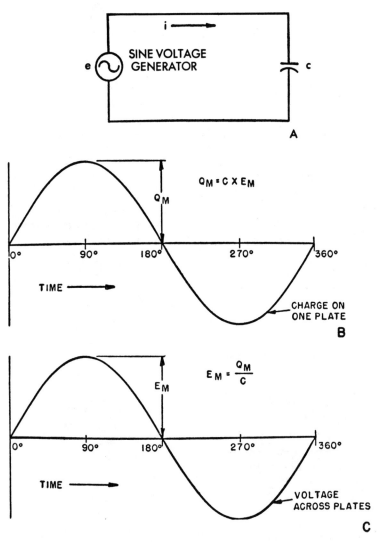

Fig. 4-103.

By definition, current in any circuit is the time rate of change of charge; thus

$$i = \frac{Q}{t}$$

where Q is the charge and t is time.

Current at any instant may be expressed as

$$i = \frac{dq}{dt}$$

where dq is a very small change of charge (in coulombs), dt is the very small change in time (seconds) required for the dq change, and i is the average current during that very small time period. (The time is short enough for i to be considered instantaneous. This expression reveals that dq/dt, the rate of change of charge, is positive when the current is positive; and when one is negative, so is the other.

In Fig. 4-104, sketch A illustrates the sine curves of current and variations in charge for the circuit of Fig. 4-103. At a time corresponding to point a, the current i is positive, $dqdt$ is positive, and therefore the charge is increasing with time. At point b, the current is negative, dq/dt is negative, and the charge is decreasing with time. For some time, then, between points a and b, dq/dt is equal to zero; that is, in going from a positive to a negative value, dq/dt must go through zero. Thus, at point A (180° on the time axis), the curve for charge must flatten out (neither increasing or decreasing) as it passes through its maximum value. In like manner the rest of the curve for charge may be drawn. It may be seen, then, that the charge is zero when the current in the circuit is maximum, and it's maximum when the current is zero. Therefore, the charge on the plate of a capacitor is said to *lag* the current through it by 90°.

Since the building-up and falling-off of charge is the building-up and falling-off of voltage, the voltage across the capacitor lags the current through it by 90°, or the current leads the voltage by 90° (Fig. 4-104B).

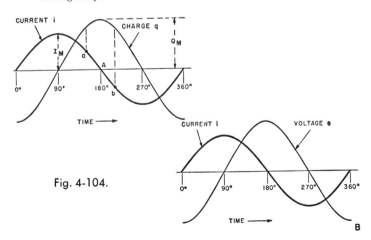

Fig. 4-104.

4-313. *What is the reactance of a 0.005 μF capacitor at a frequency of 1 kHz?*

Capacitive reactance, expressed in ohms, is given by

$$X_C = \frac{1}{2\pi f C}$$

where 2π is 6.28. Here, f is 1000 Hz and C is 0.005×10^{-6}. The reactance is

$$X_C = \frac{1}{6.28 \times 10^3 \times 0.005 \times 10^{-6}}$$

$$= \frac{10^6}{6280 \times 0.005}$$

$$= \frac{1,000,000}{31.4}$$

$$= 31,847\,\Omega$$

4-314. *State the mathematical formula for electromagnetism that is the equivalent of Ohm's law for dc circuit.*

$$\phi = \frac{F}{R}$$

gives the relation between magnetomotive force (F), flux (ϕ), and reluctance (R).

4-315. *What is the voltage and current relationship when inductive reactance predominates in an ac circuit?*

The current in such a circuit will lag the voltage by 90°. Figure 4-105 illustrates the voltage and sine curves for this circuit. At a time corresponding to point a, the voltage (e) is positive, di/dt is less than zero, and current is decreasing with time. For some value of time, then, between points a and b, di/dt is equal to zero (as it goes from a positive to a negative value). Thus, at point A (180°), the curve for current must flatten out (neither increasing nor decreasing) as it passes through its maximum value. In like manner the rest of the current curve in B may be drawn. Thus, the current is zero when the applied voltage is maximum, or maximum when the applied voltage is zero.

4-316. *In a series circuit consisting of a resistance of 6Ω, an inductive reactance of 8Ω, and a capacitive reactance of 16Ω, the applied circuit alternating potential is 300V. What is the voltage drop across the inductance?*

The circuit is shown in Fig. 4-106A. Waveforms and baselines are shown in Fig. 4-106B and C. Since current in a series circuit is the same throughout the circuit, **I** is the reference vector. Voltage $\mathbf{E}_R$ is in phase with **I**, $\mathbf{E}_L$ leads **I** by 90°, and $\mathbf{E}_C$ lags **I** by 90°. So $\mathbf{E}_C$ and $\mathbf{E}_L$ are 180° out of phase, and their vector sum is merely the difference between them. Then, since $\mathbf{E}_C$ is larger than $\mathbf{E}_L$, the resultant reactive voltage is $\mathbf{E}_C - \mathbf{E}_L$, or

$$16\mathbf{I} - 8\mathbf{I} = 8\mathbf{I}$$

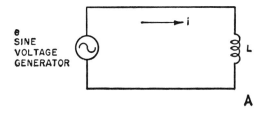

A

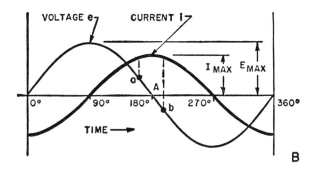

B

Fig. 4-105.

The resultant reactive voltage vector lags **I** by 90° because it has the direction of E_C, the larger vector. Figure 4-106D shows the resultant vector diagram.

From the figure we find that

$$E^2 = (IR)^2 + (IX)^2$$
$$300^2 = 36I^2 + 64I^2 = 100I^2$$

Taking the square root of each side,

$$300 = 10I$$
$$I = 300/10, \text{ or } 30A$$

The voltage drop across the resistance is I times R, or 30 times 6, which is 180V. The voltage across the inductance is I times X_L, or 30 times 8, or 240V. The voltage across the capacitor is I times X_C, or 30 times 16, which is 480V. Because the larger capacitive reactance cancels the inductive reactance, the circuit is capacitive, and so the current leads the applied voltage.

The series *LCR* circuit illustrates the following important points:

1. The current in a series *LCR* circuit either leads or lags the applied voltage, depending on whether the capacitive or inductive reactance is larger.
2. A capacitive voltage drop in a series circuit always subtracts directly from an inductive voltage drop.
3. The voltage across a single reactive element in a series circuit can have a greater effective value than the actual applied voltage.

167

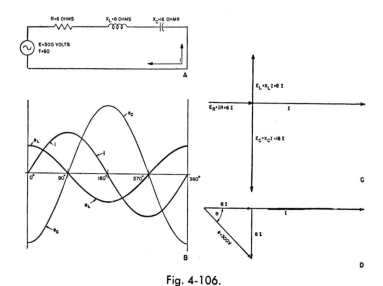

Fig. 4-106.

4-317. *What would be the effect if dc were applied to the primary of a transformer?*

A large secondary voltage would develop because of the sudden change of the primary from no voltage to full voltage. However, the secondary voltage would only last momentarily. It would occur once more when the dc voltage was removed.

A continuous dc voltage should never be applied to a transformer except through a current-limiting resistor, to protect the transformer from possible damage by excessive current. Transformers are designed for ac and pulse signals.

4-318. *If a power transformer having a stepup ratio of 1:5 is placed under load, what will be the approximate ratio of the* primary *to* secondary *current?*

Since there is no power gain in a transformer, there can be no more power out than power in. Neglecting eddy current and hysteresis losses, if the voltage input ratio is 1:5, the current output ratio will be 5:1. In other words, the output current will be decreased by the same proportion as the input voltage is increased.

4-319. *What is the meaning of "skin effect" in conductors of rf energy?*

The **tendency for electrons to flow close to the surface of a conductor** is referred to as *skin effect*. As shown in Fig. 4-107, the center portion of a conductor is surrounded completely by metal, while the surface region has conducting material only on one side of it. This causes the center to have more inductance than the surface. With dc it makes no difference, because inductance is only a factor when ac is flowing. With ac, though, which includes rf, the resulting inductive reactance means that the wire's impedance is quite low on the surface and somewhat higher in the center. Naturally, the effect increases with frequency. The

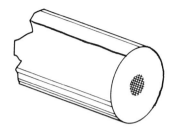

Fig. 4-107.

reduction in effective cross-sectional area causes an increase in resistance.

Skin effect can cause a considerable increase in the resistance in a vacuum-tube circuit and results in a lower Q and increased I^2R losses. To prevent skin effect losses in antennas, the elements are sometimes made quite large in diameter and tubular in shape. Silver plating is used in some critical circuits, since it has a higher conductivity than copper.

4-320. *Neglecting distributed capacitance, what is the reactance of a 5 mH choke at a frequency of 1 MHz?*

The formula for inductive reactance is $X_L = 2\pi fL$. The values for frequency (1,000,000 Hz), inductance (0.005H), and 2π are plugged into the equation as follows:

$$6.28 \times 1,000,000 \times 0.005 = 31,400\Omega$$

4-321. *What is meant by the term "radiation resistance"?*

Radiation resistance is the ratio of total power dissipated to the square of the effective current for a given antenna, or

$$R = P/I^2$$

where R is the radiation resistance, I is the effective value of antenna current at the feed point, and P is the total power radiated from the antenna.

An understanding of the power dissipation in electromagnetic fields produced by an antenna may be obtained by considering the familiar concepts of power and phase angle in an ac circuit, such as a resonant tank circuit. In an ac circuit true power is equal to voltage times current multiplied by the cosine of the phase angles between them. In an ideal tank circuit each reactive component produces a 90° phase shift between current and voltage. Since the cosine of 90° is zero, the power dissipated over a complete cycle is zero.

An antenna may be considered as a tank circuit. Since the magnetic field is directly proportional to antenna current, it may be used to compute the power dissipated. In the induction field the electric and magnetic components are 90° out of phase, as illustrated in Fig. 4-108B. Consequently, no power is dissipated by the *induction* field. Any power delivered to the field during one portion of a cycle must be returned during another portion.

The electric and magnetic components of the *radiation* field are in phase, as illustrated in Fig. 4-108A, and power is therefore dissipated. The power, which is radiated by the antenna to form the familiar

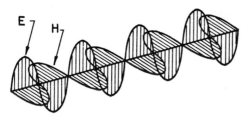

(A) RADIATION FIELD

Fig. 4-108.

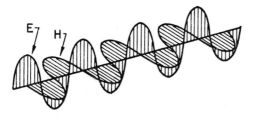

(B) INDUCTION FIELD

radiation patterns, is comparable to the power dissipated by the resistance of a practical tank circuit. The value of resistance that will dissipate the same amount of power that the antenna dissipates is called radiation resistance. Since a relationship exists between the power dissipated by the antenna and the antenna current, radiation resistance is mathematically defined as noted above.

The radiation resistance varies with antenna length, as shown in the graph of Fig. 4-109. For a half-wavelength antenna the radiation resistance measured at the current maximum (center of antenna) is approximately 73Ω. For a quarter-wavelength antenna the radiation resistance measured at its current maximum is approximately 36.6Ω. These are *free space* values, that is, the values of radiation resistance that would exist if the antenna were completely isolated so that its radiation pattern would be unobstructed.

For practical antenna installations the height of the antenna affects radiation resistance. Changes in radiation resistance occur because of ground reflections, which intercept the antenna and alter the amount of antenna current flowing. Depending on their phase, the reflected waves may *increase* antenna current or *decrease* it. The phase of the reflected waves arriving at the antenna, in turn, is a function of antenna height and orientation.

At some antenna heights it is possible for a reflected wave to induce antenna currents in phase with transmitter current, so that total antenna current increases. At other antenna heights, the two currents may be 180° out of phase, so that total antenna current is actually less than if no ground reflection occurred.

With a given input power, if antenna current increases, the effect is as if radiation resistance decreases. Similarly, if the antenna height is

170

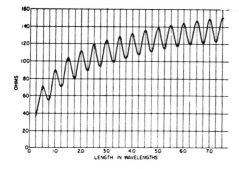

Fig. 4-109.

such that the total antenna current decreases, the radiation resistance is increased. The actual change in radiation resistance of a half-wavelength antenna at various heights above ground is shown in Fig. 4-110. The radiation resistance of the horizontal antenna rises steadily to a maximum value of 90Ω at a height of about 3λ/8 (three-eighths wavelength). Then the radiation resistance falls steadily to 58Ω at a height of about 5λ/8. The resistance then continues to rise and fall around an average value of 73Ω, which is the free-space value. As the height is increased, the amount of variation keeps decreasing, as shown.

The variation in radiation resistance of a vertical antenna is much less than that of a horizontally mounted antenna. The radiation resistance is a maximum value of 100Ω when the center of the antenna is λ/4 above ground. The value falls steadily to a minimum value of 70Ω at a height of λ/2 above ground. The value then rises and falls by several ohms about an average value slightly above the free-space value of a horizontal half-wavelength antenna.

Since antenna current is affected by antenna height, the field intensity produced by a given antenna also changes. In general, as the radiation resistance is reduced, the field intensity increases; whereas an increase in radiation resistance produces a drop in radiated field intensity.

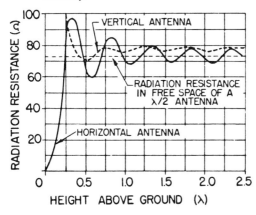

Fig. 4-110.

4-322. *What is the value of the total reactance in a series resonant circuit at the resonant frequency?*

A series circuit is said to be in resonance when the inductive reactance equals the capacitive reactance. In this case the inductive and capacitive voltage drops are equal in magnitude and 180° out of phase, and the vector sum of the two is zero. Thus, for a series resonant circuit, **the reactance is zero at the frequency of resonance.**

A series resonant circuit is shown in Fig. 4-111A. The circuit is connected to an ac voltage source of magnitude E and frequency f. Figure 4-111B shows the initial vector diagram. The voltage drop across the resistance ($\mathbf{IR}$) is drawn in phase with the current. The voltage drop across the inductance is drawn above the zero axis. and the voltage drop across the capacitance is drawn below the axis. Figure 4-111C shows the resultant vectors. and the voltage triangle (with base $\mathbf{E}_R$ and vertical side $\mathbf{E}_L - \mathbf{E}_C$) is illustrated in Fig. 4-111D. The resultant voltage. $\mathbf{E}$. equal to the applied voltage. is the hypotenuse of the right triangle. Then

$$E^2 = I^2R^2 + I^2 (X_L - X_C)^2$$

or

$$E^2 = I^2 [R^2 + (X_L - X_C)^2]$$

Take the square root to find E and I.

$$E = I\sqrt{R^2 + (X_L - X_C)^2}$$

and

$$I = \frac{E}{\sqrt{R^2 + (X_L - X_C)^2}}$$

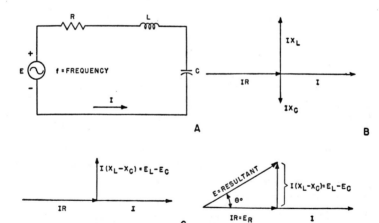

Fig. 4-111.

4-323. *What is the value of the reactance across the terminals of a capacitor in a parallel resonant circuit at the resonant frequency, assuming there is no resistance in either leg of the circuit?*

The reactance at the resonant frequency would be zero. With no resistance in a parallel resonant circuit, current and voltage are in phase, and capacitive and inductive reactances cancel. The impedance, under this condition, would be infinite.

4-324. *Given a series resonant circuit consisting of a resistance of 6.5Ω and equal inductive and capacitive reactances of 175Ω, what is the voltage drop across the resistance, assuming the applied circuit potential is 260V?*

The voltage drop, because of the direct cancellation effect of the inductance and the capacitance, is 260V. To learn why, study the answer to question 4-316.

4-325. *Given a series resonant circuit consisting of a resistance of 6.5Ω and equal inductive and capacitive reactances of 175Ω, what is the voltage drop across the inductance when the applied circuit potential is 260V?*

The voltage drop across the inductance is 7000V, or the product of current (40A) and reactance (175Ω). When X_C and X_L are equal in a series resonant circuit, their effects cancel each other, and impedance is minimum. . .equal only to the series resistance. Since the series resistance is 6.5Ω, the impedance is 6.5Ω. Ohm's law for ac is $I = E/Z$. Here, the current is 260 divided by 6.5, which is 40A.

The reactance multiplied by the current results in a very high voltage; however, when the capacitive and inductive reactances are equal, their individual voltages are 90° out of phase with current and 180° out of phase with each other. Since they are equal and opposite, their net effect is zero. Thus, while the individual voltages are out of phase, the applied line voltage and current are in phase, and the condition is the same as if there were only resistance (and no reactances) in the circuit. This is resonance.

4-326. *Under what conditions will the voltage drop across a parallel tuned circuit be at a maximum?*

When the impedance is highest, the voltage drop across the tuned circuit will be highest. At resonance, an LC parallel tuned circuit offers maximum impedance to the applied voltage, and line current drops to a minimum at this point.

Also, since in any ac circuit I is equal to E/Z, then Z (total impedance of an LCR circuit) is given by

$$Z = \sqrt{R^2 + (X_L - X_C)^2}$$

If the inductive reactance is greater than the capacitive reactance, the inductive voltage drop will be greater than the capacitive voltage drop; their sum will be inductive, and the voltage will lead the current by 90°. If the capacitive reactance is greater than the inductive reactance, the reverse is true, and the voltage will lag the current by 90°. If the inductive and capacitive reactances are equal, however, the sum is zero, and the circuit is said to be resonant.

4-327. *Draw a simple schematic showing a method of coupling a modulator tube to an rf power amplifier tube to produce plate modulation of the amplified rf energy.*

173

One method of accomplishing plate modulation is shown in Fig. 4-112. In this system the audio signal is injected into the plate circuit at a very high plate voltage. The triode class C power amplifier (V1) is tuned to a carrier frequency of 1 MHz. The plate current is 100 mA, and the plate supply potential is 1000V. The grid input driving voltage is produced by the rf oscillator and buffer amplifier.

An audio signal of about 1000V peak, having a sinusoidal waveform and a frequency of 1 kHz, is produced by the af section shown at the right in the figure and appears as an output of the modulation transformer (M). This audio output voltage is in series with the rf voltage across tank circuit LC and plate power supply B+, and it produces a modulation of the 1 MHz rf output voltage.

4-328. *Draw a diagram of a carrier wave modulated 50% by a sinusoidal wave. Indicate on the drawing the dimensions from which the percentage of modulation is determined.*

Figure 4-113 shows examples of modulated AM signals. The top sketch represents a 100% modulated signal. Notice that the section labeled W is of constant amplitude; this is the carrier before it has been modulated. Since the carrier and modulating voltages are of equal amplitude, the carrier appears to increase in amplitude until, at point X, the amplitude of the composite waveshape is twice that of the unmodulated carrier. At Z the amplitude has decreased to zero. After 1½ cycles of the modulating signal, the carrier is again unmodulated and of constant amplitude.

In the envelope drawing of Fig. 4-113B, the modulating voltage ampltiude is only one-half that of the carrier. The composite waveshape does not increase as much as in the first example, nor does the amplitude ever drop to zero.

Figure 4-113C shows an overmodulated carrier. Here, the peak voltage is greater than twice the unmodulated carrier, while the output drops to zero at an earlier point than in example A and remains there for a finite period of time. The envelope in Fig. 4-113C does not resemble the original modulating signal and is thus distorted.

Note these envelope characteristics: A 100% modulated signal consists of envelopes that touch each other even though they drop to zero. An undermodulated signal does not drop to zero. An overmodulated signal consists of envelopes that drop to zero but which are separated by some distance (time).

4-329. *Draw a diagram of a microphone circuit complete with two stages of audio amplification.*

The 2-stage transistor schematic in Fig. 4-114 represents two identical audio stages. They are coupled through a series capacitor and a high-frequency compensation network (broken-line box). The compensation network serves as a filter that provides attenuation of certain frequencies more than others. In the case shown, the network boosts the treble to compensate for deficiencies in the high-end response of the microphone. The microphone supplies the circuit at the far left. The arrows on the right indicate the output leads, which may be fed to another audio stage or to a transformer that drives a speaker. Figure 4-115 shows a complete multistage amplifier system.

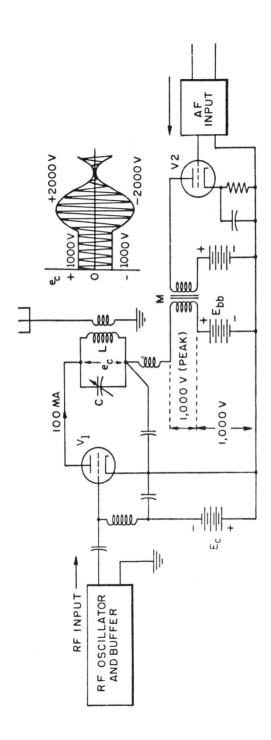

Fig. 4-112.

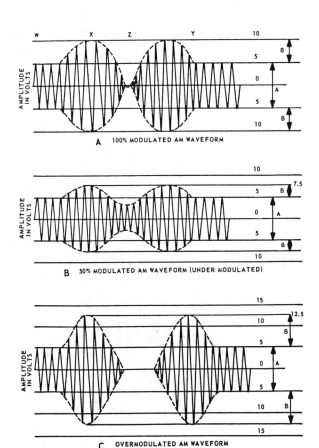

A 100% MODULATED AM WAVEFORM

B 50% MODULATED AM WAVEFORM (UNDER MODULATED)

C OVERMODULATED AM WAVEFORM

A = CARRIER VOLTAGE
B = MODULATING VOLTAGE

Fig. 4-113.

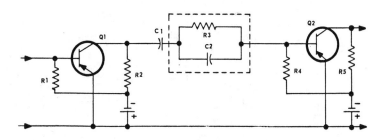

Fig. 4-114.

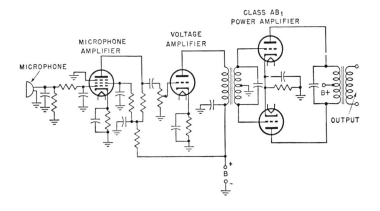

Fig. 4-115.

4-330. *Draw a simple schematic showing a Heising modulation system capable of producing 100% modulation. Indicate power supply polarities where important.*

A Heising system is illustrated in Fig. 4-116. Note that this circuit is quite similar to a conventional plate—screen modulation approach; the only difference is that the Heising circuit employs an iron core choke rather than a modulation transformer.

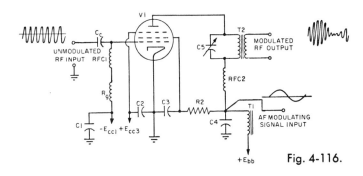

Fig. 4-116.

4-331. *Draw a simple schematic diagram showing a method of suppressor grid modulation of a pentode vacuum tube.*

The schematic is shown in Fig. 4-117.

4-332. *Draw a simple schematic showing a method of coupling a modulator tube to an rf power amplifier tube to produce grid modulation.*

Grid modulation requires less bulky equipment than plate modulation, with consequent savings in space, weight, and input power. The audio

177

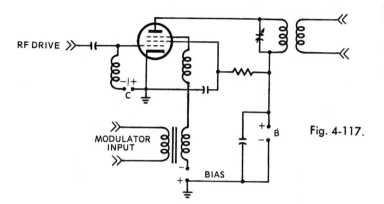

RF DRIVE

MODULATOR INPUT

BIAS

Fig. 4-117.

signal is applied in series with the grid circuit of the rf power amplifier tube. The audio signal varies the grid bias, which, in turn, varies the power output of the rf amplifier. The variaton in power output causes a modulated wave to be radiated. This method is also known as *grid bias modulation.*

A circuit using this type of modulation is shown in Fig. 4-118. The modulator tube supplying the modulation transformer (*M*) must be operated as a class A amplifier. Varying the grid dias of the rf stage does not require a great mount of power. However, it is difficult to achieve any large degree of modulation by this method, and the rf carrier output power is about 25% that of the plate-modulated transmitter; thus, the intelligibility of the signal is decreased.

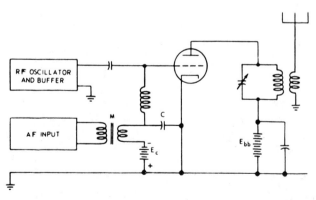

RF OSCILLATOR AND BUFFER

AF INPUT

Fig. 4-118.

4-333. *What is meant by "frequency shift" or "dynamic instability" with reference to a modulated rf emission?*

Frequency shift in an AM transmission is a deviation from the desired carrier frequency as a result of changes in the dc plate current of an rf amplifier. In severe cases—particularly where the AM transmitter is mobile and the plate current is affected by variations that are attributable to insufficient isolation between stages or oscillator instability—frequency shift can be extreme and rapid enough to appear as FM.

4-334. *What is meant by "high-level plate modulation"?*

The term *high level* comes from the fact that with this type of modulation the modulation takes place at a point where the rf power approximates the transmitter output power. Audio is injected into the plate circuit of the *final* rf amplifier at a high level of plate voltage.

4-335. *What is meant by the terms "grid modulation" and plate modulation"?*

With grid modulation plate voltage is constant and modulation is accomplished by varying the bias on the final amplifier at the rate of the applied audio.

With plate modulation (or collector modulation, using transistors), the modulating voltage is impressed on the dc supply voltage to the plate (or collector) of one of the rf amplifiers in the transmitter. The output of the modulated stage is varied by varying the plate (or collector) supply voltage with the modulating signal. When pate modulation of any stage other than the final rf amplifier stage is used. the subsequent stages in the transmitter cannot be operated class C. Class C amplifiers are nonlinear, and therefore cannot give an undistorted output of a fully modulated input signal. Any additional amplification must be done with a linear amplifier—normally with an amplifier operating point established between complete linearity and cutoff, or a combination of classes A and B (referred to as class AB).

4-336. *What is mean by "low-level" modulation?*

The FCC, in its "Code of Federal Regulations," defines low-level modulation as "modulation produced in an earlier stage than the final."

4-337. *Describe the construction and characteristics of a crystal microphone.*

In a crystal microphone (shown in Fig. 4-119), sound impinges on a diaphragm that is either bonded directly onto the surface of a crystal (Fig. 4-119A) or connected to the crystal element through a coupling member (Fig. 4-119B). A metal plate or electrode is attached to the other surface of the crystal. The vibrations of the diaphragm produce a

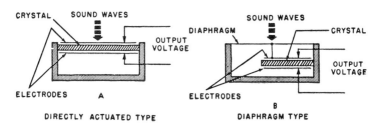

Fig. 4-119.

varying pressure on the surface of the crystal, which creates an alternating voltage across the electrodes.

The crystal microphone is extremely sensitive to high temperature, humidity extremes, and rough handling. It is never used in mobile or rugged-duty applications, but it is an excellent choice for mild environmental conditions when a high-output, fairly high-quality, low-cost microphone is required.

4-338. *Describe the construction and characteristics of a carbon button microphone.*

A single-button carbon microphone is pictured and described in the answer to question 4-95 (Fig. 4-33). A double-button microphone is shown in Fig. 4-67 and described in the answer to question 4-216.

4-339. *What might be the cause of variations in plate current of a class B modulator?*

Variations in average plate current are the result of variations in grid voltage(Fig.4-120). This is a normal operating condition. Sometimes the fluctuating output current of a class B amplifier is unintentionally coupled into the power source, thereby causing irregularities in the dc operating potentials. When this occurs, additional filtering is indicated.

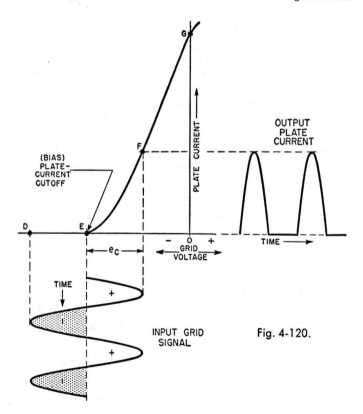

Fig. 4-120.

Most high-power audio amplifiers used as modulators are operated class B, because this is the most efficient method of amplification that still preserves the input waveshape. In general, transformer coupling is used oth in the input and output circuits, and all class B amplifiers tend to have the same basic circuit regardless of size.

4-340. *What is the relationship between the average power output of the modulator and the plate circuit input of the modulated amplifier under 100% sinusoidal plate modulation?*

The modulator supplies one-half of the power that is supplied by the dc plate supply of the modulated stage. If the dc plate power input to the final amplifier is, say, 500V at 200 mA, or 100W, the modulator should supply an audio power of 50W, for a total power of 150W in the final amplifier stage.

4-341. *What would be the effect of a shorted turn in a class B modulation transformer?*

A shorted turn in a class B modulation transformer would result in an increase in the primary current and a consequent decrease in the secondary voltage. Such a condition might cause overheating of the modulator plates and the transformer itself.

4-342. *Why is a high percentage of modulation desirable in an amplitude-modulated rf amplifier?*

One-hundred-percent modulation allows the greatest amount of power in the intelligence component of the resultant modulated waveform. The carrier/frequency power remains unchanged regardless of the modulation percentage.

4-343. *What are some of the possible results of overmodulation?*

If modulation exceeds 100% there is an interval during the audio cycle when the carrier is interrupted. In Fig. 4-121 the modulation is shown in excess of 100%. The amplitude of the resting carrier is E_R, and the peak-to peak modulating voltage is E_A. Since the peak-to-peak amplitude of the carrier cannot be less than zero, the carrier is cut off completely for all negative values of E_A greater than E_R. This results in a distorted signal.

Stated another way, if the modulating voltage is increased beyond the amount required to produce 100% modulation, the negative peak of the modulating signal becomes larger in amplitude than the dc plate supply voltage to the final rf power amplifier. This causes the final plate voltage to be negative for a short time near the negative peak of the modulating signal. For the duration of this negative plate voltage, no rf energy is developed across the plate tank circuit and the rf output voltage remains at zero for this period of time, as shown.

A careful examination of the modulation envelope shown in Fig. 4-122A shows that the negative peak of the modulating signal has effectively been clipped. When detected (demodulated) in the receiver, the signal would have an appearance somewhat similar to a square wave. to the ear, the signal would sound severely distorted (although this would depend largely on the degree of overmodulation).

If a radio receiver tuned to a frequency near but somewhat outside the channel on which the transmitter is operating, overmodulation is

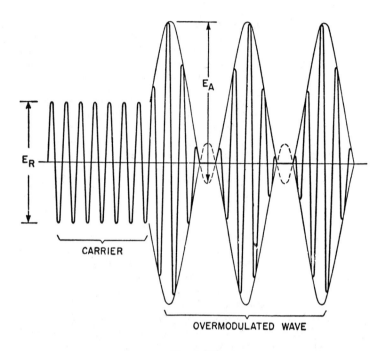

Fig. 4-121.

found to generate unwanted sideband frequences (called *splatter*) which appear a considerable ways above and below the desired channel. These spurious signals, shown in Fig. 4-122B, can cause interference to other stations operating on adjacent channels. Overmodulation and its concomitant distortion and interference are to be avoided.

Besides the above problems, overmodulation also causes abnormally large voltages and currents to exist at various points within the transmitter. Where sufficient overload protection by circuit breakers, fuses, etc. is not provided, these excessive voltages can cause arcing between transformer windings and between the plates of capacitors, permanently destroying the dielectric material. Excessive currents can cause overheating of tubes and other components.

Although it is desirable to operate a transmitter at 100% modulation to inject a maximum amount of energy into the sidebands, this ideal condition is seldom possible when a carrier is modulated by voice or music signals. The reason for this is the great and rapid fluctuations in amplitude that these signals normally contain. When the modulator is properly adjusted, the loudest parts of the transmission will produce 100% modulation. The quieter portions of the signal produce lesser degrees of modulation.

Compresser amplifiers are frequently employed to compress the dynamic (amplitude) range of the voice so that 100% modulation is obtainable even during periods of low-level audio inputs.

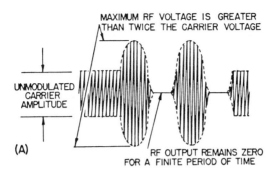

MAXIMUM RF VOLTAGE IS GREATER THAN TWICE THE CARRIER VOLTAGE

UNMODULATED CARRIER AMPLITUDE

(A)

RF OUTPUT REMAINS ZERO FOR A FINITE PERIOD OF TIME

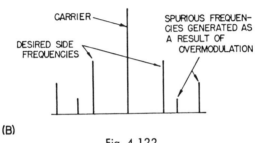

CARRIER

DESIRED SIDE FREQUENCIES

SPURIOUS FREQUEN-CIES GENERATED AS A RESULT OF OVERMODULATION

(B)

Fig. 4-122.

4-344. *What might cause frequency modulation in an amplitude-modulated transmitter?*

Poor regulation in the oscillator voltage supply is probably the most common cause, particularly when the early transmitter stages are operated from the same voltage supply as the final rf amplifier and modulator. Variations in the power supply load during modulation often result in similar variations in the voltage supplied to the oscillator and multipliers. When this occurs, the result is a rapid deviation of the carrier from its intended frequency.

4-345. *What percentage of rf power (current and voltage) increase should be expected between unmodulated conditions and 100% sinusoidal modulation?*

The power of a 100% modulated rf signal is 150% of the level of the same signal when unmodulated. Antenna power is equal to voltage times current; when both voltage and current are increased by 22.5% the resultant power increase is 50%.

4-346. *What might be the cause of a decrease in antenna current of a high-level-modulated AM radiotelephone transmitter when modulation is applied?*

This condition, commonly experienced by radio amateurs, is referred to as *downward modulation*. It may be caused by a number of problems, including:

● Inadequate regulation on a power supply used to provide voltages to all transmitter stages

- Insufficient rf drive to the final amplifier
- Soft tube in the final amplifier stage
- Inability of the final rf amplifier to handle peak currents of twice the normal unmodulated value (which may be attributable to a wide variety of problems, including poor design)
- Modulation transformer problems, including arcing because of excessive voltage or rf leakage

4-347. *Why is it necessary to use an oscillator-type detector for detecting an unmodulated carrier?*

An oscillator is required to supply a signal against which the incoming unmodulated signal is "beat" (heterodyned). This action is required to make the unmodulated signal audible. The resultant audio signal will be the difference frequency between the frequency of the incoming signal and the frequency of the local oscillator.

4-348. *What is the purpose of shielding in a multistage radio receiver?*

Multistage receivers employ oscillators and rf amplifiers as well as detection and mixing circuits. Without shielding, many of the frequencies present in a circuit or stage can be coupled to other stages, where unintended mixing and coupling can take place, resulting in the generation of spurious signals. Shielding serves to isolate the various stages from one another, and prevents radiation of local signals.

4-349. *Explain what circuit conditions are necessary in a regenerative receiver for maximum response to a modulated signal?*

The detector—amplifier should employ positive feedback, and the amount of feedback must be controlled to such an extent that the stage is just below the threshold of oscillation.

4-350. *What feedback conditions must be satisfied in a regenerative detector for the most stable operation of the detector circuit in an oscillating condition?*

The feedback must be regenerative (positive), and the tickler winding should be tightly coupled to the input tank circuit to maintain a stable state of oscillation (used for detecting CW signals).

4-351. *What are the advantages to be obtained from adding a tuned-radio-frequency amplifier stage ahead of the first detector (converter) stage of a superheterodyne receiver?*

Besides amplifying the rf signal and allowing selection of the desired station from the many that may be present, such an rf stage ahead of the converter has two other important functions:

1. It isolates the local oscillator from the antenna system, thus preventing radiation of part of the local oscillator signal.
2. It minimizes the likelihood of images which would occur if the converter were connected directly to the antenna. Such images might otherwise be received, because the converter (mixer stage) produces the intermediate frequency by heterodyning two signals whose frequency difference equals the intermediate frequency. Thus, any strong signal that might enter the converter directly from the antenna would heterodyne with the local oscillator, causing images equal to the sum and difference between the local oscillator's and incoming signal's frequency.

4-352. *What feedback conditions must be satisfied in a regenerative detector to obtain sustained oscillations?*

The feedback must be regenerative, and the feedback should be increased well beyond the point at which oscillation begins. If a grid-leak detector is modified to serve as the receiver, no additional oscillator is required to receive CW signals. In this case, a *tertiary* (third) winding on the input transformer is used to couple the plate's variation back to the grid of the tube in phase with the incoming signal.

4-353. *How is automatic volume control achieved in a radio receiver?*

Automatic volume control, or avc, amounts to applying degenerative feedback in a controlled manner to maintain a relatively constant output amplitude of received signals. A diode detector's output consists of a dc voltage that varies at an audio rate representing the rate of the incoming modulation. The stronger the signal at the antenna of the receiver, the higher this dc voltage. An avc circuit is a circuit that accepts this signal (after filtering) and changes it to a level suitable for application to preceding stages so as to cause attenuation in these earlier stages.

The schematic diagram of a simple avc circuit used in conjunction with a series diode detector is shown in Fig. 4-123. Components $T1$, $CR1$, $C1$, and $R1$ constitute a normal series diode detector. The avc network is composed of $R1$ and $C2$. In normal operation of the detector circuit with the potential shown $CR1$ conducts. Conduction of the diode will cause a charging current (shown by dotted line) to flow through the avc capacitor ($C2$) and avc resistor ($R2$). This charging current will cause $C2$ to assume the polarity shown. Resistor $R2$ and capacitor $C2$ form a voltage divider causing the voltage across $C2$ to be only a portion of the voltage present across output resistor $R1$.

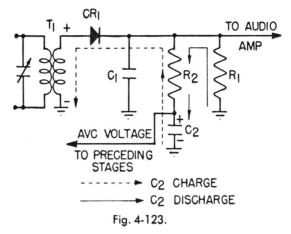

Fig. 4-123.

When the potential across $T1$ reverse-biases the diode and charging current ceases to flow, $C2$ will begin to discharge. However, the discharge time constant of $C2$, $R2$, and $R1$ is chosen to be longer than the

185

lowest audio frequency present in the output of the detector. Consequently, $C2$ will not discharge appreciably between peaks of the modulating signal, and the voltage across $C2$ will be a dc voltage. The voltage across $C2$ is proportional to the average carrier signal. Thus, if the signal strength should vary, the average of the carrier signal will vary. This will cause $C2$ to either increase or decrease its charge, depending on whether the signal strength increased or decreased.

Since the charge of the avc capacitor responds only to changes in the *average* signal level, instantaneous variations in the signal will not affect the avc voltage.

The term *avc* is used interchangeably with *agc* (automatic gain control).

4-354. *If a superheterodyne radio is tuned to a desired signal at 1000 kHz and its conversion oscillator is operating at 1300 kHz, what would be the frequency of an incoming signal that could cause image reception?*

An image can be caused from another signal separated the same distance above the local oscillator as the desired signal is below the local oscillator. In the case noted, the desired signal is 300 kHz below the oscillator frequency. If another signal, 300 kHz above the oscillator frequency, were picked up, mixing would occur. The frequency of incoming signal that could cause an image here is 1600 kHz.

4-356. *If a tube in the only rf stage of your receiver burned out, how could temporary repairs or modifications be made to permit operation of the receiver if no spare tube is available?*

The signal at the grid of the rf amplifier may be coupled directly into the first detector stage of the receiver. The possible penalties would be reduced selectivity, reception of images, and lower sensitivity.

4-356. *What are the characteristics of plate detection?*

With plate detection, the rf signal is amplified and detected in the plate circuit of a triode. Operation of the circuit (Fig. 4-124) is similar to that of a class B amplifier. Although cathode bias, provided by R_K, cannot bias a tube to plate current cutoff, operation at the lower end of the dynamic characteristic is possible.

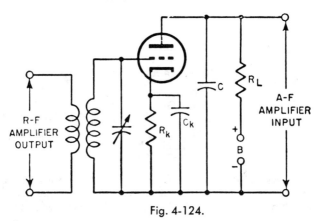

Fig. 4-124.

Normal plate current flows during the positive half-cycles of the input signal voltage. However, most of the negative half-cycles are cut off. Hence detection has occurred. The average value of the plate current varies in accordance with the audio-frequency variations. Capacitor C acts as an rf filter.

4-357.   *What is the purpose of an rf choke?*

An rf choke is placed in a circuit to prevent the passage of radio-frequency energy. The choke offers a high impedance to rf but passes dc.

4-358.   *What would be the effect upon a radio receiver if the vacuum-tube plate potential were reversed in polarity.*

The radio receiver would be completely inoperative. A vacuum-tube receiver is based on the principle of electron flow from the cathode to the positive plate element. If the plate elements were made negative, no electron flow would take place in any tube circuit.

4-359.   *Draw a simple schematic showing a method of coupling a single electron tube employed as an rf amplifier to a Hertz antenna.*

The one-tube amplifier is shown in Fig. 4-125. The two leads marked *to antenna* connect directly to the arrows shown on the dipole. A Hertz antenna is any half-wavelength ($\lambda/2$) antenna or any antenna that is a multiple of half wavelengths long. It is distinguished by the fact that neither of its two input leads must be grounded.

The rf amplifier circuit is a tetrode (notice the absence of neutralization). Capacitor $C7$ is simply a bypass capacitor that permits grounding the rotor of $C6$ to rf. This is occasionally desirable even though it requires a fairly high-voltage capacitor.

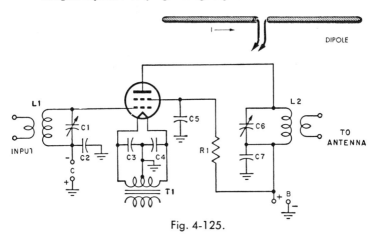

Fig. 4-125.

4-360.   *Draw a simple schematic showing a link-coupling system between a tuned-plate, tuned-grid oscillator and a neutralized one-tube amplifier.*

The circuit is shown in Fig. 4-126. The plate tank circuit in the TPTG oscillator is carrying $B+$ voltage, while the tank circuit in the grid stage of the single-tube rf amplifier is carrying a negative voltage for biasing the final stage. Coupling is by means of a low-impedance line connecting a few turns around the output coil of the oscillator tank to a few turns around the rf amplifier's input tank.

The plate tank circuit of the final rf amplifier is composed of C6 (a variable is used to obtain the out-of-phase voltage that is fed back through capacitor C7 to provide the required neutralization. The output tank circuit may be coupled to an antenna by a second link coil around L2.

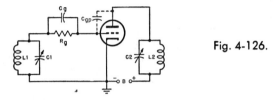

Fig. 4-126.

4-361. *Draw a simple schematic of a neutralized push-pull rf amplifier stage coupled to a Marconi antenna.*

The push-pull amplifier shown in Fig. 4-127 employs cross neutralization. The input tank circuit supplies equal and opposite voltages to the grids of the two triodes. The rf choke provides a means of inserting grid bias from a fixed bias supply. The plate tank circuit is made with a split-stator capacitor (C2) and recombines the output from the two triodes. Since opposite sides of any tank circuit are 180° out of phase with each other, neutralizing voltages may be obtained simply by feeding back some of the energy at these points to the opposite grids. This is accomplished by capacitors C3 and C4 in Fig. 4-127.

The antenna in this circuit is fed by link coupling, with L2 as the link. The bottom lead of the coil connects to the ground radiating surface (car body, etc.) at a point near where the top lead of the coil connects to the quarter-wave vertical radiator. In most instances a coaxial line will be used between the output circuit and antenna.

A *Marconi antenna* is a quarter-wavelength grounded antenna.

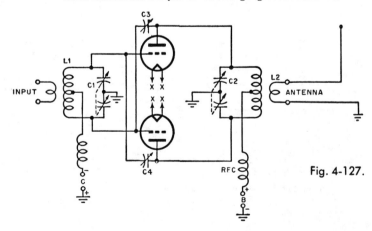

Fig. 4-127.

4-362. *Draw a simple system of neutralizing the grid—plate capacitance of a single electron tube employed as an rf amplifier.*

The class C amplifier pictured in Fig. 4-128 has a neutralizing capacitor (C_N) connected from the bottom end of the tank coil to the grid. The capacitor is adjustable so that the amount of feedback can be varied in accordance with the individual requirements of various tubes. The capacitor shown in broken lines represents the interelectrode capacitance of the tube. The feedback capacitance of C_N is adjusted to the point where the interelectrode capacitance is precisely canceled. The neutralizing capacitor could not be connected to the other side of the tank coil, because cancellation of the interelectrode capacitance depends on feeding back a signal that is 180° out of phase with the signal existing on the grid. There would be no such phase reversal if the capacitor were connected at any other point than the one shown.

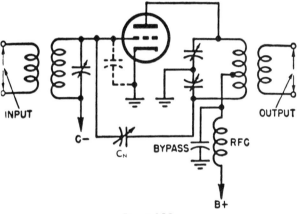

Fig. 4-128.

4-363. *Draw a simple schematic showing the proper method of obtaining dc screen grid voltage from the plate supply in a modulated pentode class C amplifier.*

In Fig. 4-129 resistor $R3$ provides the proper $B+$ voltage drop from the plate source for supplying the pentode's screen. Capacitor $C3$ is an rf bypass that maintains the rf ground at the screen grid. The rf choke and capacitor $C4$ isolate the output circuit from the power supply.

4-364. *Discuss the reasons for using a buffer amplifier in a transmitter.*

A buffer amplifier is introduced between the oscillator and power amplifier of a transmitter to isolate the two stages from each other. One of the characteristics of class C amplifiers is the consumption of power in the input circuit, which is by the grid voltage going positive and drawing current during part of the operating cycle. This power, called *excitation power*, must be supplied by the preceding rf stage.

For the power amplifier to operate efficiently, the required minimum power must be supplied. The actual excitation amount is

189

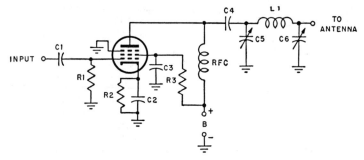

Fig. 4-129.

determined by the type of tube and the dc voltage applied to it. The stages before the final amplifier must be able to supply the required excitation without overloading. Because the frequency of an oscillator depends to some extent on the load impressed upon it, it is undesirable from the standpoint of frequency stability to attempt to supply excitation energy directly from the oscillator.

Another consideration is the modulation impressed on a carrier wave in the power amplifier. In this case a varying amount of drive is demanded by the power amplifier as the modulation changes. This changing load also can seriously affect the frequency stabilization of the oscillator if the oscillator is used to drive a modulated amplifier directly. The buffer amplifier is usually operated class A, so that it will not affect the oscillator. In this condition no power is drawn in its grid circuit. For class A service the efficiency is low, and tubes of fairly high ratings must be used in buffer circuits for high-power final amplifiers.

In broadcast service many buffer stages are used to build up the low-level output from the oscillator to a value sufficient to provide excitation to the rf power amplifier. In general, the buffer must supply from 5% to 20% as much power as the final amplifier will produce.

The buffer amplifier must supply this drive and have considerable reserve power, so that its output does not vary with changing load. This is termed *good regulation*. Since the efficiency of the class A buffer is low, its plate dissipation can be as great as one-half that of the tube used as the final rf power amplifier. Excitation requirements increase as the frequency of operation is increased. That is because losses in the input circuit are greater at higher frequencies. In the oscillator—buffer circuit shown in Fig. 4-130, a triode is used as a low-power crystal-controlled oscillator. Its output is coupled through a resistance—capacitance network to the buffer amplifier grid, which is self-biased for class A operation by the resistor and capacitor in its cathode circuit. The buffer amplifier is a pentode. The plate of the buffer is connected to the $B+$ of the power supply through a parallel resonant circuit tuned to the crystal frequency. The output of the buffer amplifier is coupled to the following stage in the transmitter by the link coil coupled to the resonant output circuit.

In a practical transmitter, buffer amplifiers are used between the oscillator and frequency multiplier, and between the oscillator and frequency multiplier, and power amplifier stage.

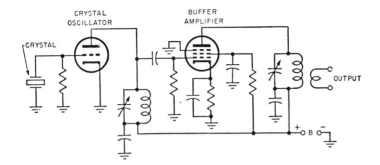

Fig. 4-130.

4-365. *What are the characteristics of a frequency doubler stage?*

Crystals used in transmitters to generate the carrier are available only in the range of frequencies between about 100 kHz and 30 MHz. High-stability crystals are available only in the lower part of this range, between 100 kHz and 10 MHz or so. Therefore, some means must be used to raise the frequency of the crystal if it is desired that the final carrier be of a higher frequency with high stability. For this purpose a special type of amplifier, called a *frequency multiplier*, is used. This circuit always operates class C. One of the characteristics of this type of operation is an output rich in harmonics. Such a circuit is shown in Fig. 4-131. The total circuit, which consists of two one-tube doubler stages, gives a total frequency multiplication of four.

In the circuit shown, the electrical connections of each stage are nearly the same as those of the class C amplifier. The difference lies in the frequency to which the parallel resonant circuits are tuned. The **output of the plate circuit in each stage is tuned to twice the frequency** of the input circuit. If desired, greater multiplication may occur in each stage. When it is tuned to twice the frequency of the input circuit, the stage is called a *doubler*; three times the frequency, a *tripler*; four times the frequency, a *quadrupler*. In general, a multiplication of more than four is seldom used.

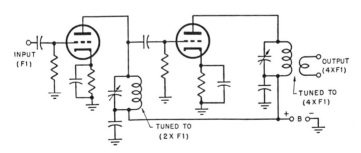

Fig. 4-131.

191

Class C operation produces pulses of current in the plate circuit considerably shorter than a half-cycle of input. These pulses shock-excite the tuned circuit to oscillation at its resonant frequency. Its resonant frequency can be any whole number times the frequency of the input wave. When the pulses are at exactly one-half, one-third, or one-fourth the frequency to which the output circuit is tuned, they reinforce its current swing every second, third, or fourth cycle (depending on multiplication factor).

Consequently, the pulses will help to sustain the oscillation in the tuned circuit. To do this most efficiently, **the pulses must be made short and sharp by biasing the tube even farther beyond cutoff than is common for a normal class C power amplifier and by using a larger** amount of excitation. The voltage and current relations in the grid, plate, and tank circuits are illustrated in Fig. 4-132, which also shows the steep pulses of plate current and resultant current in a tank output circuit tuned to twice the input frequency (a doubler).

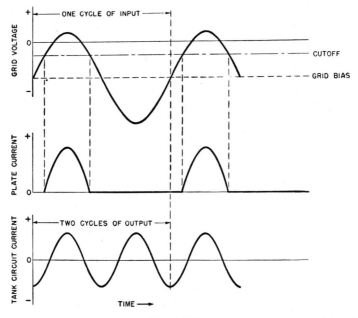

Fig. 4-132.

Since the input and output circuits of frequency multipliers are tuned to frequencies that differ by a large amount, there is little danger of undesirable feedback and oscillation taking place through the grid-to-plate capacitance. Therefore, no neutralization is normally required. The operating condition with high negative grid bias and a large grid voltage swing to obtain steep pulses of plate current means that the frequency multiplier requires more excitation than the same tube operated as an ordinary class C amplifier.

The efficiency is lower than that of the corresponding class C amplifier. A doubler runs at less than 50% plate efficiency. The tripler and quadrupler operate at efficiencies even lower than this; the more the frequency spread between input and output, the lower the efficiency, all other factors being equal. It is not practical to multiply more than four times, because the efficiency drops off too much. As the multiplication increases, the grid bias must be made greater and the grid voltage swing correspondingly larger.

In a frequency multiplier the Q of the tank must be higher than the Q of an ordinary amplifier, so that the multiplier action will be more efficient. Then there will not be too much loss of amplitude of oscillation between pulses of plate current.

4-366. *What are the advantages of a master oscillator and power amplifier (MOPA) type of transmitter as compared with a simple oscillator transmitter?*

This question is a bit vague, but it probably means: "Why is it better to have a separate and isolated oscillator rather than an oscillator that connects directly to the final amplifier?" The trouble with using a simple oscillator for a transmitter or connecting an oscillator directly to a final amplifier is that changes in the load conditions on the oscillator (which could easily occur in either of these cases) could cause intolerable frequency instability. An oscillator performs best when the supply voltages are well regulated and the loading on the output circuit is constant.

4-367. *What are the differences between Colpitts and Hartley oscillators?*

The Hartley and Colpitts oscillators are the two basic types of split-tank oscillators. **The Hartley is a split-inductance type and the Colpitts is a split-capacitance type.** Both are shown in Fig. 4-133.

In the Hartley, one tank circuit is made to serve both as plate and grid circuit. The grid is coupled to one end of the tank, and the plate is coupled to the other end. The cathode is connected to a point on the inductor. This provides an inductive voltage divider between the grid and the plate circuits, as shown in Fig. 4-133A. The voltage across $L1$ is between the grid and cathode, thereby applying a signal to the grid. The amplified voltage at the plate appears across $L2$. This provides the necessary feedback to sustain oscillation.

The Colpitts oscillator also uses a split tank. The capacitance of the tank circuit, provided by $C1$ and $C2$, is divided between the grid and plate circuits, as shown in Fig. 1-33B. Capacitors $C1$ and $C2$ form a capacitive voltage divider in which $C1$ provides the grid signal and $C2$ provides feedback from the plate. By adjusting $C1$ and $C2$ it is possible to control the frequency and amount of feedback. If you have trouble remembering which circuit has a split *inductance* and which has a split *capacitance* let the C in Colpitts be your reminder.

4-368. *What is the primary purpose of a grid leak in a vacuum-tube transmitter?*

In a frequency multiplier a grid leak is a convenient means of providing the high bias required without the requirement for external voltage sources. There are several methods other than a grid leak for obtaining self-bias, but a grid leak offers the advantage of preventing *blocking* (isolation of the grid from dc ground) as well.

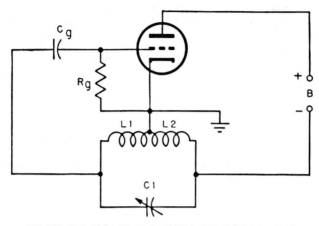

HARTLEY (SPLIT-INDUCTANCE) OSCILLATOR

A

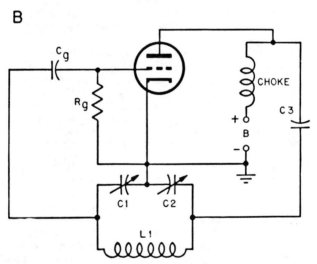

COLPITTS (SPLIT-CAPACITANCE) OSCILLATOR

Fig. 4-133.

4-369. *By what means is feedback coupling obtained in a tuned-plate, tuned-grid oscillator circuit?*

The TPTG oscillator on the interelectrode capacitance of the tube for feedback. The circuit in Fig. 4-126 shows this grid-to-plate capacitance (C_{pg}) as a broken-line drawing of a capacitor connected between these two elements of the triode.

4-370. *What may be the result of parasitic oscillation?*

Parasitic oscillations are undesirable because they cause generation and **transmission of spurious signals** and impair the efficiency of an amplifier.

4-371. *How may the production of harmonic energy by a vacuum-tube rf amplifier be minimized?*

Harmonic energy can be minimized **by reducing excitation power** to no more than is required for proper operation, keeping grid bias no greater than that required, using low-impedance (link) coupling between stages, keeping the ratio of inductance to capacitance in the tank circuit low, and using low-pass filters between stages. In particular, a low-pass filter in the feed circuit (between the final tank and transmission line) is desirable, as this will tend to prevent radiation of any harmonic energy that is inadvertently generated in any of the transmitter stages.

4-372. *Define "parasitic oscillation."*

Parasitic oscillation is oscillation in an amplifier at any frequency other than that at which the stage is designed to operate. It often results from stray capacitances and inductances resonating to produce frequencies in the VHF and UHF range.

4-373. *What is the purpose of a Faraday screen between the final tank inductance of a transmitter and the antenna inductance?*

A Faraday screen (or shield) is inserted between the inductances of the transmitter and the antenna to **prevent electrostatic coupling** of harmonic energy from the transmitter to the antenna. The screen is usually in the form of a number of parallel wires connected to a common conductor at one end. The construction of the screen is such that it has little effect on magnetic coupling. Thus, the two inductances interact so that the intended signal is coupled to the antenna properly; however, in the same way a screen grid prevents electrostatic coupling of high-frequency energy, the Faraday screen (which is usually grounded) prevents capacitive interaction between the coils. The higher the frequency, the more effective the screen.

4-374. *How may the distortion effects caused by class B operation of an rf amplifier be minimized?*

Waveforms of the various classes of amplifier are shown in Fig. 4-134. A class A amplifier allows an undistorted version of the input signal, because the output signal represents but a small portion of the applied input waveform. The class B amplifier, however, allows an undistorted output of half the input waveform. Thus, if two class B stages are operated in a **push-pull arrangement**, with each stage amplifying a different half of the total input waveform, the output can be an undistorted version of the total input wave. When the output of the "push" section is coupled with the output of the "pull" section, the composite wave is an amplified replica of the wave applied at the input.

4-375. *What is the effect of carrier shift in a plate-modulated class C amplifier?*

Carrier shift is the name for a condition that results in a change in an AM carrier's average amplitude when modulation is applied. Under

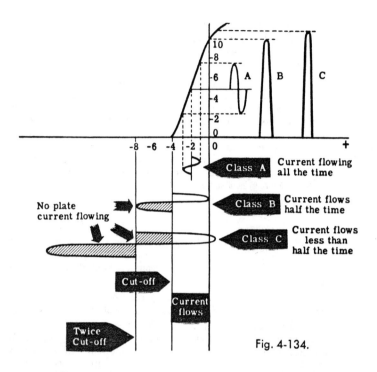

Fig. 4-134.

normal conditions the average amplitude of an AM signal will remain constant, whether the carrier is being modulated or not. An increase in the carrier's average amplitude is referred to as *positive carrier shift*; a decrease is called *negative carrier shift*.

The effect of carrier shift depends on whether the shift is positive or negative. A positive shift results in **signal distortion, spurious radiation, and "splattering."** A negative shift results in **weak or "mushy" sound (distortion), antenna resonance instability (with concomitant spurious radiation)**, and, depending on the cause, some frequency shifting.

Positive carrier shift is the result of an excessive audio signal applied to the plate of the final amplifier, parasitic oscillation, poor neutralization, and improper coupling or shielding between rf stages (or between the final stage and the antenna). Negative carrier shift is the result of a bad audio—rf balance (insufficient audio for the carrier), which might be caused by a number of factors—mismatches, faulty tubes or transistors, lossy modulation transformers, etc.

4-376. *What are some indications of a defective transmitting tube?*

If an rf tube is gassy ("soft"), a bluish haze can often be observed between the tube's electrodes. If the tube is "flat" (has low cathode emission), plate current will drop from its normal value. Often such a drop is accompanied by downward modulation. Another indication is the requirement for increasingly greater excitation power to maintain a given output level.

4-377. *What would be a possible indication that a vacuum tube in a transmitter has subnormal cathode emission?*

There are a number of possible indications that a tube's emission has dropped. One is a lower value of plate current than that normally displayed. Positive carrier shift might be another indication. Low emission is almost always accompanied by plate current drops during voice peaks if the tube is operated at its normal maximum-output point.

4-378. *What are possible causes of negative carrier shift in a linear rf amplifier?*

The most common cause of negative carrier shift in a linear rf amplifier is improper bias. Other causes are excessive drive from the exciter stage, improper tuning of the linear's input or the exciter's output (resulting in an improper resistive load for the exciter), and off-resonance operation of the linear amplifier.

4-379. *In a modulated class C rf amplifier, what is the effect of insufficient rf excitation (drive)?*

When there is insufficient drive to the final amplifier of a plate-modulated transmitter, the plate current will decrease on input audio peaks. Other indications are distortion (mushy audio) and carrier shift.

4-380. *What is the purpose of a "dummy" antenna?*

A dummy antenna (dummy load) is a resistive (noninductive) device, such as a carbon resistor, capable of dissipating the transmitter's output power without overheating. The dummy antenna offers a resistive load to the transmitter that is the same value as the antenna's impedance. The purpose is **to allow the transmitter to be tuned and peaked on the frequency of operation without radiating a signal** (which might cause interference to other stations). After the dummy load has been used to tune the transmitter's tank and rf stages, it is removed and the antenna is connected in its place. When the impedance of the load is the same value as the characteristic impedance of the antenna, no retuning will be required.

4-381. *In a class C rf amplifier stage of a transmitter, if plate current continues to flow and rf energy is still present in the antenna circuit after grid excitation is removed, what defect is indicated?*

The defect indicated is that **oscillation is taking place in the final amplifier**, resulting in spurious radiation. The problem could be attributable to parasitics or poor neutralization. If adjustment of the neutralization capacitor does not remove the rf, some method of parasitic suppression is probably called for. A check of the frequency of the undesired signal will determine whether the problem is indeed a parasitic. There are a considerable number of possible measures to eliminate parasitic oscillations, including installation of a simple choke in the plate lead, changing the value of existing chokes in the grid leak, and replacing bypass capacitors (usually on the screen pin of a pentode).

4-382. *If the transmitter filament voltmeter should cease to operate, how may the approximate filament voltage be found by adjustment of a rheostat in the filament circuit?*

Since an insufficient voltage on the filament results in a faint glow and a cold tube, while an excessive voltage results in a brighter, whitish glow, the proper approximate voltage may be determined by observing the filament while adjusting the rheostat. A properly driven filament will normally glow a bright orange. Since a very small change in filament voltage results in a considerable change in plate current, the setting of the filament voltage can be considerably refined by adjusting the rheostat while monitoring plate current with the transmitter in operation. If the normal, in-resonance value of the plate current is known, the filament can be adjusted until the plate current meter reads this normal value at resonance.

4-383. *What are some causes of overheating vacuum-tube plates?*

Vacuum-tube plates get excessively hot **when plate voltage is increased beyond the rated value**. Plate current increases proportionately with plate voltage, so plate power dissipation increases as the square of voltage increases. Radio-frequency amplifiers overheat **when the final plate tank circuit is out of resonance**; even a slight maladjustment of the tank capacitor can result in very large plate currents. Final amplifiers in transmitters often overheat **as a result of multiple resonances**; this is normally attributable to heavy parasitic oscillation, where the tank may be tuned to the resonant frequency of the amplifier while a spurious signal is being processed out of resonance. **Self-oscillation** (due to lack of neutralization) causes overheating, as does **improper biasing**, where the tube is made to conduct for a greater-than-normal percentage of its operating cycle. Still another cause of overheating in an rf output stage is an **impedance mismatch with the antenna**.

4-384. *Should the plate current of a modulated class C amplifier stage vary, or remain constant under modulation conditions? Why?*

The plate current of a plate-modulated class C amplifier should remain constant during modulation. It consists of rf pulses, but the *average* value remains constant, since the positive excursions from the unmodulated level are balanced by equal-amplitude negative excursions.

If a panel meter should change in the average value of plate current during modulation peaks, a distortion of the output signal is indicated and is a sign of a transmitter fault.

4-385. *What is the effect of a swinging antenna upon the output of a simple oscillator, if the oscillator is connected directly to the antenna?*

An antenna is one plate of a capacitor. The other plate might be the earth beneath the antenna, or nearby objects. As an antenna moves, the effective capacitance changes, as does the antenna's effective resistance and input impedance. The frequency of an oscillator depends to a great extent on the plate load. Since the moving antenna changes the load in the oscillator's plate circuit, the frequency of the oscillator shits accordingly.

4-386. *What factors permit high conduction in a mercury vapor rectifier using a heated cathode?*

Since the voltage drop across the rectifier does not increase with increasing load, considerable current can be drawn through the rectifier without a commensurate increases in voltage drop. A mercury vapor tube with a heated cathode is characterized during operation by high current as a result of ionization caused by heating the mercury. The voltage drop across a mercury vapor tube is a constant 15V.

4-387. *List the principal advantages of a mercury vapor tube over a high-vacuum rectifier.*

Mercury vapor tubes may be of either of two types: One has an oxide-coated filament heated by alternating current, and the other uses a pool of mercury as a cathode.

Mercury vapor rectifiers with filaments are **able to pass much higher currents** than high-vacuum rectifiers because of the ionization of the mercury vapor: The mercury ions make it unnecessary to rely on the electrons produced by the filament alone. The filament is used merely to start the ionization. The heat from the filament vaporizes the small amount of liquid mercury incorporated in the tube's envelope. The tube has a very high efficiency in power rectification because of its low voltage drop. The plate efficiency of a large mercury vapor rectifier easily approaches 99%. Moreover, the tube's voltage drop does not vary with a changing load; therefore, the **voltage regulation is better** than that obtained with a high-vacuum rectifier tube.

Arc tubes (often called *mercury pool rectifiers*) use a pool of mercury as the cathode. An example is the 5554 rectifier. This tube is capable of supplying 75A of direct current continuously. The initial ionization is provided by an arc started between a subsidiary electrode, called the *ignitor*, and the cathode itself. The ionization results in greatly increased current. Since the ignitor must be used to start the arc, the tube can be controlled by small pulses of current to the ignitor, and thus hundreds of amperes can be controlled by only a small amount of current.

Since the mercury vapor tubes do not depend on very hot filaments, they tend to **run cooler** than their high-vacuum counterparts.

4-388. *What effect does the resistance of a filter choke have on the regulation of the power supply in which it is used?*

When a load is placed on a power supply, the terminal voltage tends to decrease. A circuit has poor regulation if a large voltage drop occurs in the terminal voltage when a load is applied. The difference between the no-load voltage and the full-load voltage is caused by the flow of load current through the internal resistance of the power supply. The IR drop caused by the load current within the supply circuit is subtracted from the voltage available for the load at the output terminals. A perfect power supply would have zero internal resistance, and the percentage of regulation error would be zero. Such a supply would provide the same voltage under full load that it does when no load is connected across the output terminals. Thus, the resistance of a filter choke does have a great deal to do with the regulation of a power supply: **the lower the filter's resistance, the better the regulation** of the supply, all other things being equal.

4-389. *Describe the theory of current conduction and rectification by means of a diode rectifier tube using a cold cathode.*

Cold cathode tubes rarely are used as rectifiers, because of their high voltage drop, although a variation of the cold cathode tube was once

199

used (before semiconductors) as a rectifier in vehicular equipment because of the problems involved in obtaining heater power.

The principle of operation is based on the heating of the cathode under ionic bombardment in the region of the curve between F and G of Fig. 4-135. The many varieties of arc, glow, and other gas tubes all operate on some portion of the complete curve shown. (See also answer to question 4-387.)

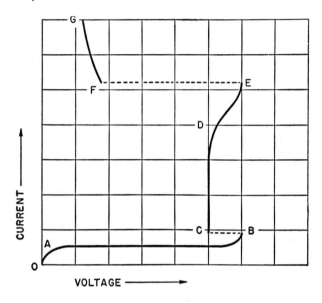

Fig. 4-135.

4-390. *Describe the effects of substituting a resistor for the inductor in a pi-type filter circuit.*

In many cases where cost and size are a factor, the inductance of a pi-type filter can be replaced with a resistor. The value of resistance used, however, will be a compromise between good filtering and high dc output. A low-value resistance can be used to maintain a high output voltage, but the ripple remains high. A high value resistor means reduced ripple but a large voltage drop.

4-391. *What might be the result of starting an electric motor too slowly, using a hand starter?*

The armature resistance of many motors is extremely low, from 0.05Ω to 0.5Ω. Since no counter emf exists until the armature begins to turn at an appreciable speed, a hand starter should either incorporate a series resistance or a means of rapid acceleration. Otherwise, the high current through the armature's low resistance could produce **overheating in the armature winding, causing melting of the conductors**. When speed builds up, of course, the counter emf opposes the applied voltage, and armature current is thus reduced.

4-392. *State the principal advantage of a third-brush generator for a radio power supply in automobiles.*

An ordinary generator has two brushes diametrically opposite one another on the commutator. Adding a third brush between the other two allows a certain degree of output regulation despite changing speed of the generator. The shunt field winding is connected from one of the regular brushes to the third brush; by adjusting the position of this third brush, the shunt field current can be controlled. The advantage of the third-brush generator is the fact that a convenient (though generally not altogether satisfactory) method of regulation is made possible without the requirement for externally connected voltage regulation devices. Third-brush generators are seldom seen any more.

4-393. *What should be used to clean the commutator of a motor or generator?*

If the dirt does not consist of grease or oil, a dry, lint-free cloth is best for cleaning the commutator. Carbon tetrachloride, trichloroethylene, alcohol, and naphtha are all good cleaning agents if the commutator is greasy. Dry the commutator thoroughly by wiping with a lint-free cloth before reinstallation in the generator housing.

4-394. *List three causes of sparking at the commutator* **of a dc motor**.

Sparking often occurs between the brushes and the commutator when the brushes are worn unevenly (usually indicating a need for replacement). **Uneven wear on the commutator** itself will also cause sparking because the brush will not make constant contact over the commutator segment's surface. **Conductive impurities** such as metal filings will cause sparking because they act as a short circuit between the commutator segments. Most sparking problems will occur because of uneven contact, however. Causes for this condition include **worn brushes, improperly seated brushes, snagged brush springs, damaged commutator segments**, and the like. Other causes include **shorted armature windings, open armature windings, and excessive load** on the brushes (which are designed to pass a maximum rated amount of current).

4-395. *Why is it sometimes necessary to use a starting resistance when starting a dc motor?*

The internal resistance of the armature is extremely low—sometimes not much more than a few hundredths of an ohm. This very low resistance can pass a large current unless a counter emf is built up to oppose it. Some motors have a rheostat in the armature winding to reduce the resistance during starting. Once the motor is operating, the resistance may be decreased. (See also answer to question 4-391.)

4-396. *List the comparative advantages and disadvantages of dynamotor and transformer—rectifier supplies.*

The dynamotor may be operated independent from an ac supply. In mobile applications **the dynamotor may be connected directly to the terminals of a battery. The efficiency of the dynamotor, however, is extremely low**—on the order of 43% or so; thus, a great deal of power is required to operate such a unit. The **dynamotor often proves to be the source of rf interference**, too; the contacts make and break at an extremely high rate and generate electrical impulses that can prove difficult to filter. On the other hand, **dynamotors can sustain large current drains over long periods without overheating**, so long as the battery supply is capable of delivering the required power. The **dynamotor is characterized by a high-pitched whine, which can prove annoying and, in military and police applications, sometimes hazardous.**

On the positive side of the ledger, **the output of a dynamotor is a relatively ripple-free dc** that does not itself require filtering other than with ordinary bypass capacitors.

A transformer−rectifier operating at a frequency of 60 Hz requires a conventional power line source, so its portable applications are limited. There are **transformer−rectifier combinations** capable of operating at extremely high frequencies, but all such combinations **do require a source of ac power**, whether it be the power line, a vibrator supply, or a pair of switching transistors. A **low-frequency combination requires considerable filtering to remove the ripple content** and smooth the output to a usable dc for most receivers and transmitters. A **high-frequency combination requires little filtering but may be the cause of inductively coupled whine** (an audio signal at the switching rate) in the radio circuits it is powering. A **low-frequency transformer−rectifier requires a transformer with a considerable core mass—which means more cost, more weight, and more space. A high-frequency combination means a smaller transformer, less filtering, less weight, and less space.** At one time the rectifiers were a major space consideration, too. Today, however, the space consumed by rectifiers—regardless of the circuit in which they are used—is negligible.

A **transformer−rectifier combination is extremely efficient.** A vibrator, transformer, and rectifier combination (assuming solid-state rectifiers are used) can convert battery voltage to $B+$ voltage with a total conversion efficiency of up to about 70%. A solid-state switching circuit in concert with a transformer−rectifier circuit can change battery voltage to $B+$ with a conversion efficiency of up to around 88%. Some switching circuits, which employ two transformers rather than one, can operate with conversion efficiencies as high as 98%.

The **dynamotor has a relatively low reliability because it is a mechanical device with a moving assembly. The transformer−rectifier has a high reliability because it has no moving parts.** When the transformer−rectifier is used with a vibrator supply, the reliability decreases considerably, because the vibrator is a mechanical make−break device. However, **when a transformer−rectifier is used with a solid-state switching system to supply the necessary ac, the reliability can be quite high.**

The **disadvantages of the dynamotor today outweigh the advantages.** And since the advent of inexpensive transistors capable of switching at extremely high rates (the higher the rate, the cheaper the transformer), the dynamotor has all but disappeared from the communications scene.

4-397   *If the reluctance of an iron core choke is increased by increasing the air gap of the magnetic path, in what other way does this affect the properties of a choke?*

Increasing the air gap of an iron core choke **decreases the flux density and the magnetomotive force of the choke.** As a result, a light load through such a choke may not cause core saturation, and the voltage delivered to the load will be higher than desired. Heavy loads may cause choke action, however, dropping the supply voltage to the load substantially. **A widened air gap in an iron core filter choke means poor regulation with varying loads.**

Swinging chokes have a reduced air gap to take advantage of the increased flux density. At full loads the choke saturates and delivers a higher voltage to the load than would otherwise be available. At light loads a swinging choke's inductance is quite high, which serves to hold down the voltage delivered to the load.

4-398. *What is the effect on a filter choke of a large value of dc flow?*

During the period when the rectifiers are conducting, the choke opposes the current buildup; when the rectifiers are not conducting (as the input voltage returns toward zero), the stored energy in the choke supplies current to the load. As long as the current exceeds a minimum value (depending on the inductance of the choke), **the regulation of the output voltage remains fairly high.** With low-current loads, an ordinary filter choke functions in much the same manner as an electrolytic filter capacitor.

4-399. *What are the characteristics of a capacitor input filter in a power supply as opposed to a choke input filter?*

The capacitor input filter is capable of supplying a higher dc voltage (with a given input potential) under fairly light loads. Since the input capacitor can charge to almost peak input voltage, a properly designed capacitive input filter will provide a **high output voltage** in comparison to a choke input filter.

Capacitor input filters are typically used in applications where current drain is to be relatively small. As shown in Fig. 4-136, when a

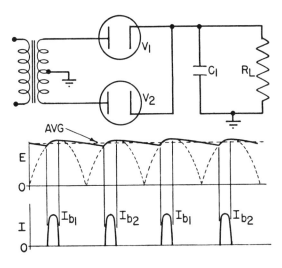

Fig. 4-136.

pair of vacuum-tube rectifiers are used in full-wave rectification, output voltage E remains at an almost constant average level when the load resistance (R_L) is not too low. Plate current (I_b) of the rectifiers increases as R_L decreases; the peak plate current of the tubes must be lower than the peak-current rating of the rectifiers.

The capacitor input filter is also characterized by **poor regulation**. The full-load voltage, when the load resistance is very low, drops significantly (Fig. 4-137). In comparison with the choke input filter, the capacitor input type will exhibit **a greater change in output voltage from no-load to full-load condition**.

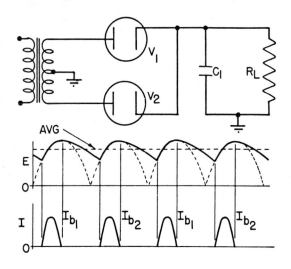

Fig. 4-137.

4-400. *What is the principal function of a filter in a power supply?*

The principal function of a filter in a power supply is to produce a dc voltage that is sufficiently smooth to avoid undesirable coupling of any ac components into an electronic circuit. If the pulsating dc voltage that is present at the output of a rectifier system were directly applied to a vacuum tube, the pulsations would cause improper operation of the tube.

4-401. *What are the characteristics of a choke input system as compared with a capacitor input filter in a power supply?*

Compared to capacitive input filter, the choke input filter will have the following characteristics:

1. **Lower output voltage.** In a full-wave circuit the direct-current output cannot exceed the average value of the input.
2. **Higher current output.** This is due to the lower peak current and higher average current of the rectifier, as illustrated in the waveform in Fig. 4-138.

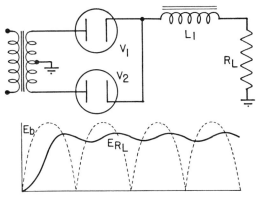

Fig. 4-138.

3. **Better regulation.** There is less change from no-load to full-load conditions. Figure 4-139 shows the effect of load on the terminal voltage of both kinds of filters.

4-402. *What is the percentage regulation of a power supply with a no-load voltage output of 126.5V and a full-load voltage output of 115V?*

The formula for percentage of regulation is:

$$\text{Regulation} = \frac{E_{NL} - E_{FL}}{E_{FL}} \times 100\%$$

where E_{NL} is the no-load voltage and E_{FL} is the full-load voltage. When the no-load voltage is 126.5V and the full-load voltage is 115V, the regulation is given by

$$\text{Regulation} = \frac{126.5 - 115}{115} \times 100 = 0.1 \times 100 = 10\%$$

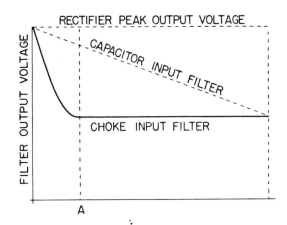

Fig. 4-139.

4-403. *What is the definition of "voltage regulation," as applied to power supplies?*

Voltage regulation is the variation of a referenced dc voltage under changing load conditions. A negligible voltage change in a $B+$ line during high- and low-current drains is referred to as *good regulation*. A power supply whose output drops significantly when a load is applied is said to have *poor regulation*. For this reason the term *percentage of regulation* is actually a misnomer, for it refers not to the percentage of regulation at all but to the percentage of *error* in regulation. If it actually did express a percentage of regulation, a high figure—such as 98% or 99%—would be desirable.

4-404. *May two capacitors with 500V ratings, one an electrolytic and the other a paper type, be successfully used in series across a potential of 1000V?*

They can be used in series, but the electrolytic must be connected with consideration to its marked polarity, and equal resistances should be placed across the capacitors to properly distribute the voltages.

4-405. *What is the principal function of a swinging choke in a filter system?*

A swinging choke has a reduced air gap, which decreases its reluctance. It offers **better power supply regulation** than ordinary chokes; since its inductance increases with light loads and decreases with heavy loads, the output is more uniformly regulated over a broad range of changing load conditions.

4-406. *What is the purpose of a bleeder resistor as used in connection with power supplies?*

The bleeder resistors "bleeds off" the dc voltage from the electrolytic capacitors in the power supply when the power to the supply is turned off. Also, a bleeder resistor, when used with a choke input filter, provides a constant minimum load on the filter, thus improving regulation.

4-407. *What does a blue haze in the space between the filament and plate of a high-vacuum rectifier tube indicate?*

A blue haze between the elements of any tube (other than gas-filled tubes, which does not include the high-vacuum rectifier), indicates **the presence of gas**. One of the requirements of a high-vacuum tube is that it must remain practically free of internal gases during operation. Every precaution is taken during manufacture to pump all the air from the tube. When a tube is not fully evacuated, because of a defect in manufacture or deterioration during use, the flow of current through such a tube is erratic and quite unpredictable, and the tube must be replaced.

4-408. *If a high-vacuum rectifier in a high-voltage power supply should suddenly show severe internal sparking and then fail to operate, what elements of the rectifier should be checked for possible failure before installing a new rectifier tube?*

Sparking in a high-vacuum rectifier is a symptom of excessive current and is often indicative of a short circuit. Before replacing the tube, **the filter capacitors should be checked**, as should the $B+$ supply line feeding the load. Occasionally, bleeder resistors change value and draw excessive current, but this is rare. The first step should be to remove the load from the $B+$ line at the power supply. The next step should be to determine the total resistance of the $B+$ line to ground, with the rectifier tubes out of the circuit. If a dead short is still indicated, the problem is most likely a shorted electrolytic, which is most often caused by applying voltages in excess of the electrolytic capacitors' rated maximum working voltage.

4-409. *If the plate (or plates) of a rectifier tube suddenly becomes red hot, what might be the cause?*

A red-hot plate indicates **excessive current**. The most frequent cause oi excessive plate current is too low a resistance between $B+$ and ground. The short could be anywhere between the cathode of the rectifiers and the output terminal of the disconnected $B+$ supply. If the condition persists after the $B+$ line has been lifted from the cathode, the condition is probably attributable to a shorted rectifier filament winding in the high voltage transformer.

4-410. *Draw a simple schematic diagram of a crystal-controlled oscillator, indicating the circuit elements necessary to identify this form of oscillatory circuit.*

Certain types of crystals, such as quartz and tourmaline, have the natural ability to generate small ac voltages when a mechanical force is applied. Conversely, when an ac voltage is applied, such crystals vibrate at a rapid and very stable rate. These properties permit a crystal to be substituted for a tuned tank circuit of an oscillator. The TPTG oscillator, for example, can have its grid tank replaced by a crystal slab held between a pair of conductive plates.

In Fig. 4-140 such a circuit is shown. The circuit action is the same for both the tank and crystal. The crystal, however, has two great advantages: It can be cut with great precision to resonate within a very small percentage of a given frequency, and it possesses a far higher circuit Q than an LC network.

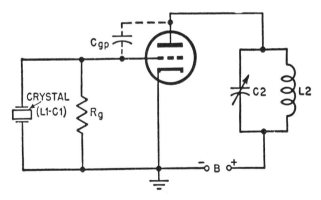

Fig. 4-140.

4-111. *Draw a simple schematic of a dynatron-type oscillator, indicating the circuit elements necessary to identify this form of oscillatory circuit.*

The dynatron oscillator, also referred to as a *negative resistance* oscillator, is shown in Fig. 4-141. Unlike other oscillator circuits using vacuum tubes, the dynatron oscillator does not depend on feedback to the grid to sustain oscillatory action. A negative resistance exists in a circuit if an increase in voltage across the circuit is accompanied by a decrease in current through it. An increase in plate voltage of a tetrode is accompanied by a decrease in plate current over part of the $e_P - i_P$ characteristic.

The circuit of a dynatron oscillator is shown in Fig. 4-141A. Plate current starts to flow when the tube warms up. At point b (sketch B), plate current (i_p) starts to decrease because of secondary emission at the plate. The plate current decrease from point b to point c is accompanied by a decrease in the voltage drop across the plate load impedance (parallel LC tank) and an increase in plate voltage (e_p).

At point c, when secondary emission ceases, plate current in the tube stops decreasing and starts to increase. The increasing voltage across the plate load impedance is accompanied by a decreasing plate voltage. At point b the load impedance again starts to fall as plate voltage rises, and the cycle repeats.

The vectors (sketch C) indicate the phase relationships between plate voltage, plate current, inductor current (i_L), and capacitor current (i_C). As with other oscillator circuits, the frequency of operation depends on the values of L and C in the plate tank circuit:

$$\left(f = \frac{1}{2\pi\sqrt{LC}}\right.$$

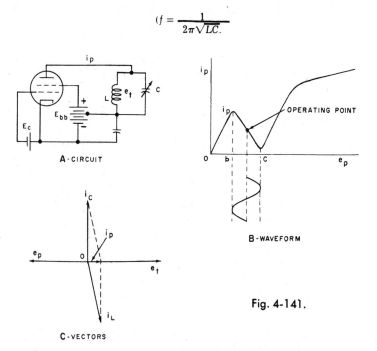

A - CIRCUIT

B - WAVEFORM

C - VECTORS

Fig. 4-141.

4-412. What does the expression "positive temperature coefficient" mean, as applied to a quartz crystal?

Crystals tend to change frequency as the temperature changes. Moreover, the resonant frequency of a crystal is specified at a predetermined temperature of operation. If the frequency of operation of a crystal decreases when it is operated at temperatures higher than the stated operating point, it is said to have a negative temperature coefficient. If the **frequency of the crystal increases when the operating temperature increases,** the crystal is said to have a positive temperature coefficient.

4-413. Draw a simple schematic of a crystal-controlled vacuum-tube oscillator using a pentode. Indicate power supply polarity where necessary.

The electron-coupled oscillator pictured in Fig. 4-142 uses a pentode vacuum tube. The chassis ground points shown are common with the $B+$ common-ground return. As shown, $B+$ is applied to the Hartley oscillator portion of this circuit through the plate tank circuit. The voltage divider supplies the proper voltage for the screen grid.

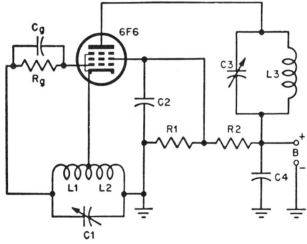

Fig. 4-142.

4-414. What will result if a dc potential is applied between the two parallel surfaces of a quartz crystal?

A crystal is normally supplied with ac, which permits the crystal to warp in two directions. One polarity causes a "positive" bending of the crystal, and the polarity reversal causes a "negative" bending. A dc voltage causes a distortion in one direction only, the proportion of which is dependent on the value of the dc voltage. Like the results of applying dc voltages to a loudspeaker or microphone, if the voltage is high enough, it could **cause permanent damage**—even to the extent of cracking the crystal element.

4-415. *What does the expression "low temperature coefficient" mean, as applied to a quartz crystal?*

A crystal that has a low temperature coefficient is a crystal that will exhibit **very little frequency shift with temperature changes**. A high temperature coefficient means a large amount of frequency shift with temperature changes.

4-416. *What is the function of a quartz crystal in a radio transmitter?*

When placed in an electrical circuit, a crystal acts like a very high-Q series resonant circuit. The electrical circuits associated with a crystal can be represented by an equivalent circuit (Fig. 4-143) composed of a resistance, inductance, and capacitance between the metal plates (C1) of the crystal holder. When the crystal is not vibrating, the circuit acts only as this capacitance. The series combination of L, C, and R represents the electrical equivalent of the vibrating crystal's characteristics. **Since a quartz crystal is equivalent to a resonant circuit, it can be used in place of the usual tuned circuit in the oscillator section of a transmitter.** The high Q of the crystal provides a stability that cannot be matched with ordinary LC components.

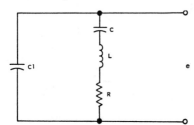

Fig. 4-143.

4-417. *What may be the result if a high degree of coupling exists between the plate and grid circuits of a crystal-controlled oscillator?*

If a high degree of coupling exists between the plate and grid circuits of a crystal-controlled oscillator, an **excessive excitation voltage** may be applied to the crystal. This can cause strenuous vibration in an active crystal, which can shatter the crystal in its holder. For this reason triodes are seldom used in oscillator circuits. (Triodes have a fairly high interelectrode capacitance.) Normally, pentodes or tetrodes are used. With them a comparatively high output power can be obtained with only a small amount of excitation voltage.

4-418. *What is the purpose of maintaining the temperature of a quartz crystal as constant as possible?*

All crystals have at least some degree of thermal sensitivity, referred to as their *temperature coefficient*. This means that all crystals exhibit some drift with temperature changes. Some crystals shift upward in frequency (positive temperature coefficient), and some crystals shift lower in frequency (negative temperature coefficient). All other factors being equal (component values, voltages, etc.), crystals will remain quite stable if they are held to a constant temperature.

Modern two-way radios are equipped with elaborate but tiny *crystal ovens*, which are miniature enclosed heaters that are used to hold the crystal. The ovens are thermostatically controlled, so that they maintain a constant temperature, within a few degrees, at all times.

4-419. *Why is a separate source of plate power desirable for a crystal oscillator stage in a radio transmitter?*

A separate $B+$ supply is often used for the crystal oscillator's plate circuit, **so that the tube's operation will be independent of the loads represented by other circuits within the transmitter.** Unless plate voltages are well regulated, they can drop at the source when high current demands are imposed on them. An oscillator's frequency shifts when its plate voltage changes. It is not uncommon for an AM transmitter to produce a frequency-modulated signal when the same power source is used to provide plate $B+$ for the final amplifier, modulator, and oscillator. In such a case the modulator draws maximum current on voice peaks, and the transmitter's total power output increases significantly. When this power drain causes a drop in the plate voltage of an AM transmitter, undesired frequency modulation is the result.

4-420. *What are the principal advantages of crystal control over tuned-circuit oscillators?*

The crystal's most important advantage over LC networks is its **stability.** It is found, in practice, that the ratio of L to C of the equivalent circuit is extremely large compared with that of a conventional tank circuit. This gives two corollary advantages: The **Q is extremely high,** and the **selectivity is extremely sharp.** Secondary advantages are **simplicity** (since a single crystal replaces at least a capacitor across a series resonant LCR circuit) and **space economy.**

4-421. *What is the approximate range of temperature coefficients encountered with X-cut crystals (quartz)?*

The X and Y cuts have very high temperature coefficients, as shown in Fig. 4-144. The approximate range of temperature coefficients to be encountered with X-cut crystals is **−10 to −25 parts per million per degree (Celsius).** The crystals used in electrical circuits are thin sheets cut from natural or man-made quartz and ground to the proper thickness for the desired resonant frequency. The thinner the crystal, the higher the resonant frequency. The *cut* of the crystal means the definite way in which the usable crystal slab is cut from the "mother" crystal. Crystals are cut at various angles with respect to the X, Y, or Z axis. The X, Y, and AT cuts are illustrated in Fig. 4-145. In the X and Y cuts, the face of the usable crystal is cut parallel to the Z-axis. The AT, BT, CT, DT, ET, FT, and GT cuts are special types that are cut with the face of the crystal at an angle to the Z axis.

4-422. *Is it necessary or desirable that the surfaces of a quartz crystal be clean? If so, what cleaning agents may be used which will not adversely affect the operation of the crystal?*

It is extremely desirable that the crystal slab be clean. Minute particles of dirt or other contaminants can change the frequency of operation or prevent the crystal from oscillating altogether. Even the mark of a pencil will raise the frequency of a crystal. **The cleaning agent should be nonabrasive,** since the thickness of the crystal determines its

Type Cut	Frequency Range	Temperature Coefficient	Remarks and/or Characteristics
X	100 kc to 1100 kc	Negative values 10 to 25 parts per million per degrees C	Complicated spectrum Low activity Obsolete cut
Y	Up to 10 mc	20 to 100 parts per million per degrees C	Discontinuities in frequency with temperature changes Obsolete cut
AT	500 kc to 10 mc	Zero, 40 to 50 C	High activity, extensively used
BT	500 kc to 10 mc	Zero, 20 to 30 C	High activity, extensively used
CT	50 kc to 500 kc	Zero, 20 to 30 C	Extensively used cuts Avoids use of large quartz plates for low frequencies These two cuts are directly related to AT & BT cuts, however, they are physically smaller for these low frequencies
DT	50 kc to 500 kc	Zero, 20 to 40 C	
ET	100 kc to 1 mc	Zero, 70 to 80 C	Harmonic types Crystal produces output voltages at 3rd, 4th, 5th, 6th, and 7th harmonics of fundamental vibration
FT	100 kc to 1 mc	Zero, 70 to 80 C	
GT	100 kc	Zero, 10 to 100 C	Excellent secondary standard of frequency Excellent temperature-versus-frequency characteristics Operates best at 100 kc

Fig. 4-144.

frequency. A crystal slab cleaned with a household scouring compound will resonate at a lower frequency than it would without such cleansing. Greaseless chemicals such as **carbon tetrachloride or alcohol are good cleansing agents.** However, once a crystal has been cleaned, the fingers must not come into contact with it, because of the likelihood of leaving oil deposits on the crystal surface.

4-423. *Upon what characteristic of an electron tube does the dynatron oscillator depend?*

When the plate voltage of a tetrode does not exceed that of the screen, it exhibits a characteristic known as **negative resistance**, whereby any increases in voltage across the circuit is accompanied by a decrease in

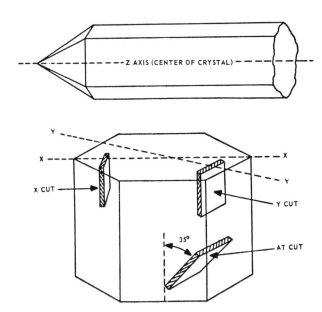

Fig. 4-145.

current through it. This is the characteristic upon which the operation of the dynatron oscillator is based.

4-424. *What is a multivibrator and what are its uses?*

A multivibrator is a class of oscillator circuit used to generate waveforms of specific shapes. A multivibrator is triggered by a voltage or current pulse; when so triggered, it produces one cycle of its design waveshape. A *free-running multivibrator* is a type that produces an unending train of pulses when triggered. A *one-shot*, or *flip-flop*, produces a single pulse. Multivibrators are **used to generate waveforms in signal generators, pulses in counters, and clocked control signals in logic circuits. They are used extensively in timing applications as well as in computation systems.**

4-425. *If a frequency meter having an overall error proportional to the frequency is accurate to 10 Hz when set at 600 kHz, what is its error in hertz when set at 1110 kHz?*

Ten parts per 600 kHz is one part per 60,000 Hz. Dividing 1 by 60,000 yields 0.00001667. Multiply this result by 1,110,000 Hz to determine total error. By manipulating zeros to make the equation manageable,

$$111 \times 0.1667 = 18.5 \text{ Hz}$$

4-426. *What precautions should be taken before using a heterodyne frequency meter?*

There are two important precautions to be observed when using a heterodyne frequency meter. First, make certain the instrument has had **a sufficient warmup time** to preclude the possibility of drift.

Second, calibrate the instrument against a standard such as WWV. Since the heterodyne meter depends on beating the signal from the device under test against an internal frequency standard, it is absolutely imperative that the internal standard be precisely on the frequency indicated. This can best be accomplished by checking the heterodyne meter's frequency against the primary standard (WWV) as close to the frequency of the test unit as possible.

4-427. *What is the meaning of the term "zero beat" as applied to frequency-measuring equipment?*

When two signals are detected by a nonlinear circuit, they combine to produce a new signal whose frequency is equal to their difference. When the signals are quite close, the difference frequency is in the audio range. The lower the difference frequency, the lower the pitch of the note (called a *beat* note). **When the two signals are of precisely the same frequency, the output signal disappears.** At this point **the signals are said to be zero beat.**

A heterodyne frequency meter works on this principle. The heterodyne frequency meter may be used as a secondary frequency standard. The frequency of the unit under test is adjusted until the beat note drops to a lower and lower value. At zero beat the unit under test is supplying a signal of the frequency indicated by the frequency meter.

4-428. *What precautions should be observed when using an absorption-type wavemeter to measure the frequency of a self-excited oscillator? Explain your reasons.*

The *absorption wavemeter* is frequently called an *absorption-type frequency meter* by the FCC. Questions on this instrument may refer to it by either of its names, so it will pay to remember both.

The absorption wavemeter is shown in Fig. 4-146 in its simplest form. It consists of a tuned circuit with a variable tuning element and a load (ammeter or lamp). The meter absorbs its power from the circuit under test when the test circuit is tuned to the resonant frequency of the wavemeter, at which maximum reading or lamp brilliance is obtained. **The most important precaution to be observed with this instrument is to maintain a very loose coupling between the test circuit and wavemeter.**

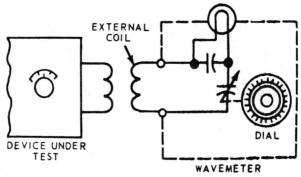

Fig. 4-146.

Tight coupling causes interaction between the two tanks and excessively lowers the Q of the test circuit. Loose coupling minimizes the interaction and prevents the wavemeter from broadening the resonant frequency of the test circuit, thus increasing the accuracy of the reading.

The fixed capacitor in the wavemeter, connected across the terminals of the indicating lamp (Fig 4-146), has a much higher capacitance than the variable capacitor. This large capacitance permits a voltage to be developed at resonance to light the lamp and, provided the coupling between the two tank circuits is loose enough, it has neglible effect on the resonant circuit because of its low reactance.

4-429. *If the first speech amplifier tube of a radiotelephone transmitter were overexcited but the percentage modulation capabilities of the transmitter were not exceeded, what would be the effect upon the output of the transmitter?*

The result of overexcitation of a speech amplifier tube is **audio distortion**. The audio signal drawn from the speech amplifier and fed to the modulator would be clipped at the top and bottom of the audio waveform. This clipped signal would be accurately reproduced by the modulator and impressed on the carrier. Thus, the audio detected from the signal would bear the same distortion.

4-430. *What is the purpose of a preamplifier?*

A preamplifier is a low-level af or rf voltage amplifier. The use of a preamplifier in radio reception **improves sensitivity and image rejection**.

4-431. *What are the advantages of using two tubes in push-pull as opposed to using the same tubes in parallel in an audio amplifier?*

For a single tube or transistor or a number of tubes or transistors in parallel to reproduce a complete cycle of an input signal, the amplifier stage must be operated in the center of its linear range. This dictates the use of class A amplification in such a circuit. (A class A state, remember, is the only type of stage capable of conducting fully over 360° of the input signal.) Unfortunately, the class A amplifier is quite inefficient.

A class B amplifier is reasonably efficient. However, a class B amplifier is capable of reproducing only half of the complete input cycle. One way out is to employ two tubes or transistors operating class B—one to reproduce only the first half-cycle of the input signal and the other to reproduce the second. Such an arrangement is referred to as push-pull. (Push-pull operation can also be used for amplifiers in classes A and AB.)

The resultant characteristic of class B push-pull operation is shown in Fig. 4-147. Note that the bias is not quite at cutoff. If the exact cutoff point were used, the output waveform would be distorted because of the nonlinearity near cutoff in the characteristic curve. The efficiency of push-pull class B amplifiers may be as high as 65%. Class A amplifiers operating push-pull approach only 30% to 35% efficiency. Class AB push-pull amplifiers reach efficiencies as high as 55%.

Push-pull circuits are frequently used in audio amplifiers and in some rf amplifiers.

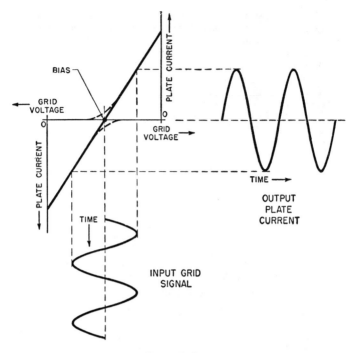

Fig. 4-147.

4-432. *List four causes of distortion in a class A audio amplifier.*

Four common causes of distortion in class A audio amplifiers are:

1. **Excessively high level of the input signal** drives the amplifier beyond the linear portion of its characteristic curve. When this occurs, positive-going input signals drive the amplifier into saturation, and negative-going signals cause the plate current to cut off.

2. **Improperly biased amplifier stages**. The amplifier must be biased so that its operating point is established in the center of its linear region. If the bias is too positive, the tube or npn transistor will saturate on positive-going signals even though it reproduces well on negative-going signals. If the bias is too negative, the plate (or collector of an npn transistor) current will cut off prematurely on negative half-cycles of the input signal even though the positive half-cycles are reproduced properly.

3. **Impedance mismatch** between the amplifier stage and its load. Maintaining the proper operating point depends on keeping the amplifier stage matched to the load. Biases are established, based on specific input and output values of impedance. When the impedance changes, so does the operating point.

4. **Nonlinearity** of the output characteristic. This type of problem is indicative of a faulty tube or transistor in the amplifier stage.

4-433. *How may the generation of even harmonics in an rf amplifier stage be minimized?*

Generation of even harmonics can be minimized by use of **a push-pull circuit**. Once generated, harmonics must be suppressed by filters.

4-434. *What tests will determine if an rf power amplifier is properly neutralized?*

The following method can be used to determine a need for neutralization:

1. Connect the stage to a dummy load through a sensitive in-line wattmeter, swr meter, or other sensitive device capable of indicating the presence of rf energy.
2. Remove the tube serving as an exciter to the stage in question.
3. Key the stage (apply power that would normally be applied during transmitter operation).
4. If any rf is indicated on the meter, the stage requires neutralization. If the stage has a neutralizing capacitor, adjust it for minimum output under this condition.

4-435. *Why is the plate circuit efficiency of an rf amplifier tube operating class C higher than that of the same tube operating class B? If the statement is false, explain your reasons for such a conclusion.*

The statement is not false. Look for a moment at the dynamic characteristic of a class C amplifier (Fig. 4-148). Note that the stage is

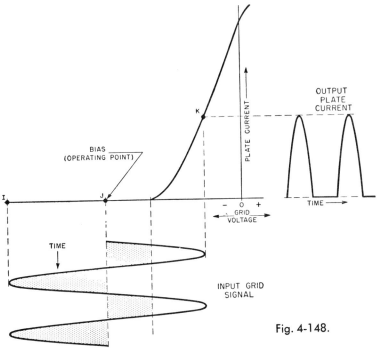

Fig. 4-148.

217

biased well below cutoff. This means that, **for the complete negative half-cycle and a fair portion of the positive half-cycle of the input signal, the amplifier is not drawing current.** Hence heat is generated (power wasted) for a relatively small part of the input cycle. **This allows efficiencies as high as 80%.** A class B amplifier conducts current and generates heat for a full 50% of the input cycle and can thus attain efficiencies no higher than about 50% to 60%.

4-436. *Why does a class B audio amplifier require considerably greater driving power than a class A amplifier?*

A class B amplifier needs more drive than a class A stage to take advantage of its capability as an efficient power amplifier. Examine the characteristic curve shown in Fig. 4-149. The input signal for a class A amplifier must not exhibit too great a voltage swing in either the positive or negative direction, or the input signal will drive the amplifier out of its linear operating region. In the example illustrated, the input signal swings only about a volt above and below the −2V point (grid voltage). The −2V bias point establishes the middle of the amplifier's linear region.

A class B amplifier is biased at cutoff, as shown (−4V). Thus, when the input signal goes even more negative than the −4V bias, the amplifier is not conducting at all. It will not even begin to conduct until

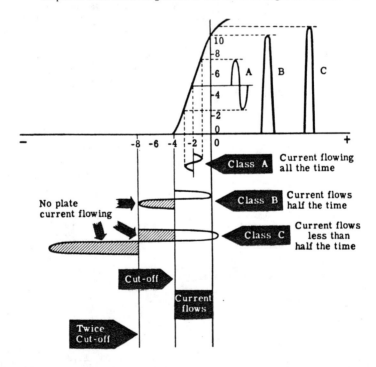

Fig. 4-149.

after the input signal reaches its maximum negative peak and returns to the zero point (−4V at the grid). The tube begins to conduct, and the positive-going input signal reaches its peak at a point at the upper limit of the tube's linear region, just below saturation.

The class B amplifier requires an input signal that takes the amplifier almost to the point of saturation. The class C amplifier requires an input signal that takes the tube all the way into its saturation region on positive-going peaks.

In the figure the three input signals are drawn to scale, so that the classes might be more easily compared with regard to their input—output characteristics.

4-37. *Discuss the input requirements for a class B audio amplifier's grid circuit.*

The input requirements are shown graphically in the combination drawing of Fig. 149, and basic information in regard to the operation is presented in the answer to the previous question. The important consideration here is that the amplifier is biased at the tube's cutoff point. If the class B amplifier is to be used in a push-pull circuit, however, the stage is biased just above cutoff, and a phase-splitting arrangement is used to feed the two grids 180° out of phase.

4-438. *When a signal is impressed on the grid of a properly adjusted and operated class A stage, what change in the average value of plate current will take place?*

The average value of plate current in a class A audio amplifier **will remain unchanged**. If the dynamic operating curve (refer again to Fig. 4-149) were perfectly linear, the increase in plate current on the positive alternation of the input signal and the decrease in current on the negative alternation would be perfectly balanced. The average then would be the same, with or without a signal. Some plate current flows during the no-signal state because of the manner in which the tube is biased. But every increase of plate current is precisely matched by an accompanying decrease, so average current does not vary.

4-439. *If the capacitance of a coupling capacitor in an RC-coupled audio amplifier is increased, what effect may be noted?*

The capacitive reactance is reduced at the low-frequency end of the response bandwidth, with the result that the low-frequency response is improved.

4-440. *Why does a tube with a screen grid normally require no neutralization when used as a radio-frequency amplifier?*

The screen grid is placed at rf ground potential and, since it is between the plate and grid, it shields the input from the output.

4-441. *What instruments or devices may be used to adjust and determine that an amplifier stage is properly neutralized?*

There are a large number of instruments and devices to determine the presence of unwanted signals from self-oscillation of an amplifier, including neon lamps and flashlight bulbs. Meters in the grid and plate stages of the final amplifier, however, provide a more certain approach. Other instruments include field strength meters, rf wattmeters, vswr meters and bridge circuits, and sensitive communications receivers. (Refer to the answer to question 4-434 to see how the neutralization checks can be performed.)

4-442. *What is meant by the term "unity coupling"?*

Unity coupling is **the theoretical maximum coefficient of coupling between two coils.** In an electrical circuit a change of current is always accompanied by a change in the magnetic field surrounding the circuit. If the current is increasing, the field is expanding; that is, the intensity at any particular point is increasing. On the other hand, if the current is decreasing, the field is collapsing, or decreasing in intensity. When a coil is placed within the magnetic field of another coil in which collapsing or expanding lines of force cut the turns of the second coil, a voltage will be induced in the second coil. The value of the voltage will depend on, among other things, the degree of coupling between the coils. Even though two coils may be close together, not all of the flux produced by coil *1* links coil 2. The proportion that does link coil 2 is indicated by the symbol k and called the *coefficient of coupling,* which is always less than unity.

4-443. *Draw a diagram illustrating capacitive coupling between two tuned rf circuits.*

Capacitive coupling may be something of a misnomer. More common terms for rf coupling using a capacitor are *tuned RCL* and *impedance coupling.* The arrangement is illustrated in the broken-line box of Fig. 4-150. Capacitor C1 tunes L1 to resonance. At resonance a large voltage

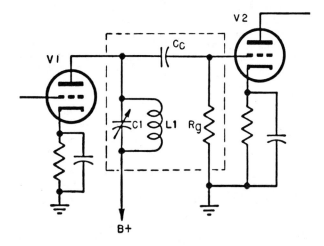

Fig. 4-150.

appearing across the parallel resonant circuit is transferred to the grid of *V*2 through coupling capacitor C_C. This capacitor has a small reactance at the resonant frequency and permits a maximum transfer of energy.

4-444. *Draw a diagram illustrating inductive coupling between two tuned rf circuits.*

Inductive coupling, also referred to as *transformer* coupling, is pictured in Fig. 4-151. The method shown is called *double-tuned inductive coupling*, because both inductances in the coupling network may be tuned with the parallel capacitances. In practice, only one of the two inductances need have a variable capacitor across it. In such a case the arrangement would be called *single tuned* inductive coupling.

In the circuit shown coil L1 is the primary and coil L2 the secondary. Capacitor C1 tunes L1 to resonance at the signal frequency. A large signal voltage is produced across the high impedance of the parallel resonant circuit formed by L1 and C1. The large circulating tank current in the primary creates a magnetic field which induces a voltage in the secondary (L2).

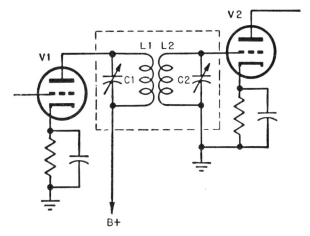

Fig. 4-151.

4-445. *Draw a diagram illustrating direct, or Loftin-White, coupling between two stages of audio-frequency amplification.*

A direct-coupled amplifier is one that can amplify dc and very low-frequency voltages and currents. In vacuum-tube circuits its distinguishing feature is that the plate of one stage is coupled directly to the grid of the next stage without the use of a capacitor or transformer. In Fig. 4-152 the plate of V1 is coupled to the grid of V2. For convenience, a voltage divider made up of series resistors may be used to supply the necessary dc operating voltages for the amplifier, as shown. The B+ voltage is impressed across voltage divider resistor R_D which is tapped at various points. The capacitor shunting the series divider (C_D) is used to bypass any ac variations of voltage that might otherwise appear across R_D.

4-446. *List four classes of stations that may be operated by a person holding a radiotelephone Second Class license.*

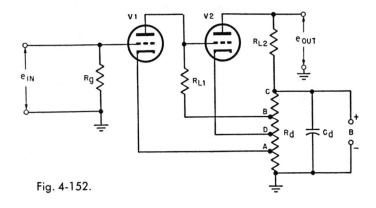

Fig. 4-152.

The Second Class licensee may operate, maintain, and repair **two-way radios in the marine, industrial, land transportation, public safety, citizens, and business radio classes**. He is allowed to *operate commercial broadcast stations* (including AM , FM, and TV) and all other class of stations not requiring special additional skills .

4-447. *May the holder of a Second Class operator license adjust and service or supervise the adjustment and servicing of any class of police radio station?*

Yes. As mentioned above. he may service any station in the public safety radio service. which includes police radio.

4-448. *List three classes of stations that may not be serviced or adjusted by the holder of a radiotelephone Second Class operator license.*

Three classes that cannot be serviced by such a licensee are the following broadcast facilites: AM. FM. and TV.

4-449. *Is it necessary that the original operator license be posted at an aeronautical station? An aircraft station? An airport station? A broadcast station? A ship station?*

Operator licenses must be posted at all stations in the aviation service. except in the case of mobile units. which require either the license or a verification card (Form 758) on the operator's person while he is on duty. At broadcast stations the original operator license or FCC Form 759 must be posed at the place of duty. On ship stations the original license must be posted or an FCC Form 758 verification card must be carried by the operator.

If an operator is required to post his radio operator license at more than one station. he may post the original license or permit at one station and post *verified statements,* Form 759. at all other stations. Verification cards or statements may be obtained by filing a properly completed application (Form 756). The license (or permit and applicable fee must accompany the request for verification. In lieu of the license or permit. the operator must exhibit a signed copy of the application that has been submitted by him until action is taken on the request.

4-450. *What is a verification card? Under what circumstances may it be used?*

Operators holding a radio operator license of the diploma form (other than restricted) may obtain a verification card (Form 758-F), which is an FCC form that attests to the operator's authority as a license holder. The card may be carried on the person of the operator in lieu of the license when operating a station at which the posting of an operator license is not required. When such verification cards are used, the original license or permit must be readily accessible for inspection by an authorized government representative.

4-451. *If a ship telephone station is assigned the frequency of 2738 kHz and the maximum frequency tolerance of error is 0.02%, what are the highest and lowest frequencies within the tolerance limits?*

Since 0.02% means 0.02 part per hundred, it may be replaced with a numerical decimal: 0.0002. By multiplying 0.0002 times the frequency, the error (0.54760 kHz, or 547.60 Hz) is obtained. Thus, the minimum frequency within the tolerance limits would be the basic frequency minus the error, or 2737.4524 kHz. The maximum frequency within the tolerance limits would be the basic frequency plus the possible error, or 2738.5476 kHz.

4-452. *If an aircraft station is assigned the frequency of 3117.50 kHz and the maximum tolerance is 0.01%, what are the lowest and highest frequencies within the tolerance limits?*

The calculation is accomplished as described in the preceding answer. The lower limit would be 3117.18825 kHz, and the upper limit would be 3117.81175 kHz.

4-453. *If a heterodyne frequency meter having a calibrated range of 1000 to 5000 kHz is used to measure the frequency of a 500 kHz transmitter by measuring the second harmonic of the transmitter, and if the indicated measurement is 1008 kHz, what is the actual frequency of the transmitter output?*

The frequency of 1008 kHz is the second harmonic of 504 kHz. Thus, the measured transmitter operating frequency is 504 kHz.

4-454. *Define the following types of emission: A0, A1, A2, A3, A4, and A5.*

A0—Continuous, unmodulated pure carrier
A2—Continuous-wave telegraphy by carrier keying
A3—Amplitude-modulated telephony
A4—Facsimile (amplitude-modulated)
A5—Amplitude-modulated television

4-455. *In the adjustment of a radio transmitter, what precautions should be observed?*

If the transmitter is to be tuned, it should first be connected to a dummy load of the same resistive value as the antenna. When the stages are tuned, such functions as modulation percentage, frequency, and power input to the final stage should be checked. Before reconnecting the transmitter to an antenna, the frequency of operation should be monitored with a receiver to be certain it is not in use.

4-456. *Explain the relationship between the signal frequency, the oscillator frequency, and the image frequency in a superheterodyne radio receiver.*

The signal frequency is the frequency on which the desired station is operating. The oscillator frequency is that generated by the local oscillator in the receiver.

If the mixer stage were connected directly to an antenna, unwanted signals (called *images*) might be received. The image frequency is equal to the station frequency plus (or minus) twice the intermediate frequency.

The image frequency is higher than the station frequency if the local oscillator "tracks" (operates) above the station frequency (Fig. 4-153A). The image frequency is lower than the station frequency if the local oscillator tracks below the station frequency (Fig. 4-153B). The latter arrangement is generally used for the higher frequency bands and the former for the lower frequency bands.

If a superheterodyne radio having an i-f of 455 kHz is tuned to receive a station frequency of 1500 kHz (Fig. 4-153A) and the local oscillator has a frequency of 1955 kHz, the output of the i-f amplifier may contain two signals—one from the 1500 kHz station and the other from an image station at 2410 kHz (1500 + twice 455 = 2410 kHz). The same receiver tuned near the low end of the band to a 590 kHz station has a local oscillator frequency of 1045 kHz. The output of the i-f amplifier contains the station signal (1045 − 590 = 455 kHz) and an image signal of 1500 kHz (1500 − 1045 = 455 kHz).

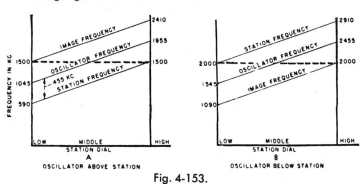

Fig. 4-153.

It may also be possible for *any* two signals having sufficient strength and separated by the intermediate frequency to heterodyne and produce unwanted signals in the speaker. The selectivity of the preselector (rf stages preceding the mixer) tends to reduce the strength of the images and other unwanted signals. However, there is a practical limit to the degree of selectivity obtainable in the preselector, because the rf stage must have a much wider bandwidth than the bandwidth of the desired signals.

The ratio of the amplitude of the desired signal to that of the image is called the *image rejection ratio*. It is an important specification of a receiver.

4-457. *What means are used to prevent interaction between the stages of an audio-frequency amplifier?*

Interaction between stages of audio amplifiers is prevented by the use of properly designed coupling networks between stages and the use of resistive *decoupling* (filter) *networks* in the plate leads of the individual stages.

4-458. *For what period of time must a log containing distress entries be retained?*

Logs with distress entries must be retained until (1) the FCC notifies the license holder that destruction of the records is permissible, (2) the statute of limitations prevents any legal proceedings from occurring based on the content of the material in the log, or (3) all claims resulting from the distress have been fully satisfied.

4-459. *What effect, if any, does modulation have on the amplitude of the antenna current of a frequency-modulated transmitter?*

The antenna current will remain the same in amplitude, though it will vary with respect to frequency and phase with modulation.

4-460. *How would loss of rf excitation affect a class C amplifier when using grid-leak bias only?*

If grid-leak bias only were used, loss of excitation would remove the bias and place the grid at the same potential as the cathode. The plate current would rise drastically in such an amplifier, and destruction of the tube probably would occur.

4-461. *What is the purpose of a centertap connection on a filament transformer?*

A centertap on the filament transformer allows a central ground return point that cuts the amplitude of 60 Hz hum components by 50%.

4-462. *What would be the result of a short circuit of the plate rf choke coil in an rf amplifier?*

The plate rf choke provides a dc path for the $B+$ and serves as a high-impedance plate load for the rf. If the choke shorts, $B+$ is still applied to the plate of the amplifier, but the load is no longer matched to the amplifier. One result is that the rf is allowed to feed back into the power supply and be coupled to other stages through the dc lines, and another is that the plate current will exceed its safe limit, destroying the tube.

4-463. *What are the advantages of push-pull operation compared to single-ended operation of amplifiers?*

Push-pull operation has a number of advantages, but the most significant are these:

- Less distortion
- Greater power output with a given amount of drive
- Higher plate efficiency
- Greater variation of input signal without saturation

Push-pull operation is examined in the table of Fig. 4-154. Note how this type of operation compares with single-ended operation for each amplifier class (except C, where push-pull operation is inapplicable). This table summarizes the operation points, distortion, power output, and plate efficiency of the basic amplifier classes.

Class	Location of operating point on dynamic characteristic	Relative distortion	Relative power output	Approximate percentage of plate efficiency
A single-tube	On linear portion	Low	Low	Under 20%
A push-pull		Very low	Moderate	20 to 30%
AB single-tube	Between linear portion and plate-current cut-off	Moderate	Moderate	40%
AB push-pull		Low	High	50 to 55%
B single-tube	At vicinity of cut-off	High	High	40 to 60%
B push-pull		Low	Very high	60 to 65%
C single-tube	About 1½ to 4 times plate-current cut-off	Very high	Very high	60 to 80%

Fig. 4-154.

4-464. *What is the ratio of modulator power output to modulated-amplifier plate power input for a 100% modulated AM transmitter?*

The audio power should be equal to one-half the dc input power to the final rf amplifier stage; thus, the ratio is 1:2.

4-465. *Describe the construction and characteristics of a beam power tube, a thyratron, and a battery-charger rectifier tube.*

Beam Power Tube. The beam power tube has the advantages of both the tetrode and pentode, and it is capable of handling relatively high levels of electrical power in the output stages of receivers and amplifiers and in different parts of transmitters. The power-handling capacity stems from the concentration of the plate current electrons into beams, or sheets. In the usual type of electron tube, the plate current electrons advance in a predetermined direction but without being confined into beams.

The external appearance of the beam power tube is like that of other receiving-type tetrodes and pentodes. They are slightly larger because they are called upon to handle somewhat more power.

The construction details of a beam power tube are shown in Fig. 4-155. Although it is not evident, the control grid and screen grid "windings" are of the same pitch (spacing), and the wires of these electrodes are in line with each other relative to the paths of the plate current electrons. (Refer to Fig. 4-156.)

Sketch A of Fig. 4-156 illustrates how the screen and control grid wires in the ordinary tetrode determine the electron paths. The wires are out of alignment; therefore, electrons that pass through the control grid are partially deflected through their paths, and many strike the screen wires. This produces a screen current and thus limits the value of plate current.

In sketch B the results are different. Because of the arrangement of the control and screen grids, the screen intercepts fewer electrons; therefore, the relative screen current is less in the beam power tube than in the ordinary tetrode or pentode. In turn, more electrons reach the plate, thereby making the plate current considerably higher.

The cumulative effect of the arrangement in sketch B is a tube in which the plate and control grid are electrically isolated. The plate

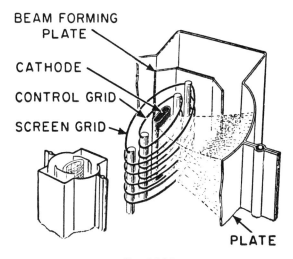

BEAM FORMING PLATE

CATHODE

CONTROL GRID

SCREEN GRID

PLATE

Fig. 4-155.

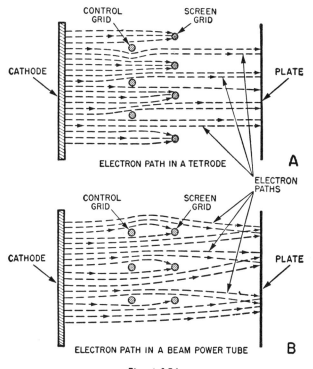

CONTROL GRID

SCREEN GRID

CATHODE

PLATE

ELECTRON PATH IN A TETRODE

A

ELECTRON PATHS

CONTROL GRID

SCREEN GRID

CATHODE

PLATE

ELECTRON PATH IN A BEAM POWER TUBE

B

Fig. 4-156.

current is high, the plate resistance is relatively low, and a substantial amount of electrical power can be handled with reduced distortion.

The beam-forming plates further influence the movement of the plate current electrons from the time they pass the screen electrode and strike the plate. The beam electrodes are connected internally to the cathode and consequently are at the same potential as the cathode. Because of this potential of the beam-forming plates, the equivalent of a space charge is developed in the space between the screen and plate. The effect is as if a conducting surface (broken lines joining ends of the beam-forming plates in Fig. 4-157) existed in the screen—plate space. This is identified as the *virtual cathode*. The presence of this electric plane repels secondary electrons liberated by the plate and prevents them from moving to the screen. Figure 4-157 represents a beam power tube as seen from the top of the envelope.

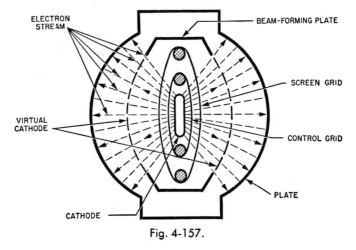

Fig. 4-157.

In some tubes the effect of a virtual cathode is achieved by the use of a third grid in place of the beam-forming plates; the results are identical. Figure 4-158A symbolizes the beam power tube with the beam-forming plates, and sketch B symbolizes the version in which a grid replaces the beam-forming plate. There is no difference between the symbol shown in sketch B and that of the ordinary pentode.

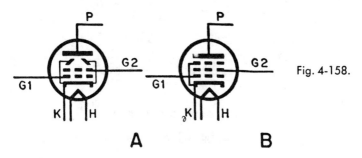

Fig. 4-158.

For comparison Fig. 4-159 shows the plate current, plate voltage characteristics of a beam power tube and a conventional pentode. Note the rapid rise in plate current for the beam power tube, as shown by the solid line. The more gradual rise for pentode, shown by the broken line, indicates power-handling ability with minimum distortion. The solid curve shows that the zone in which the plate current is primarily a function of the plate voltage is much more limited for a beam power tube (the plate current becomes substantially independent of palte voltage at much lower values of pate potential). This characteristic enables the beam power tube to handle greater signal power at lower values of plate voltage than an ordinary pentode. In addition the beam power tube produces less distortion that the ordinary pentode while accommodating an increased grid swing and plate current change.

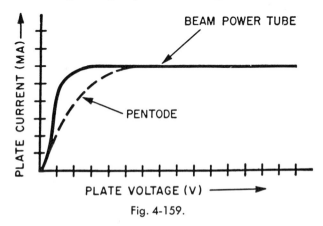

Fig. 4-159.

Thyratron Tube. A thyratron is a gas-filled tube. If a grid is placed between the cathode and plate of a gas tube, the voltage at which breakdown occurs (firing potential) can be controlled by the voltage on the grid. (Breakdown is the abrupt increase in cathode—plate conductivity that takes place as a result of ionization of the gas by electron collision.) The entire plate surface in this tube usually is shielded by the grid, which is placed close to the plate. In a grid-controlled gas discharge tube, the plate supply voltage exceeds the plate—cathode breakdown voltage, and the grid is held either zero or negative with relation to the cathode.

A Thyatron is a gas-filled triode or tetrode (Fig. 4-160). The grid in this tube functions somewhat the same as that of an ordinary tube, but

THYRATRON

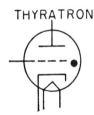

Fig. 4-160.

the resultant control action is entirely different. When ionization (breakdown) occurs, the internal resistance of the tube drops to a small value and a large current flows immediately.

The ionization potential depends upon both the plate and grid voltages. The grid control characteristics of a typical thyratron are shown in Fig. 4-161. At a given plate voltage—for example, 800V—the bias would have to be reduced from −10V to −8V before the tube would begin to conduct. Likewise, at a plate voltage of 300V, the tube would begin to conduct at a grid potential of about −4V. When conduction starts, the grid loses control over the plate current and is no longer effective as a control element. To stop plate current, the plate voltage must be reduced below the breakdown potential. The grid operates in this manner because, when conduction starts, positive ions are formed by collisions and some of them are attracted to the grid. A positive ion sheath is formed around the grid, thus destroying its effectiveness as a control element. Other positive ions move toward the cathode and neutralize the space charge. These two actions account for the fact that, once plate current starts, the grid loses control and the current rises rapidly to a large value.

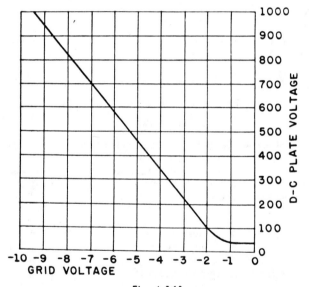

Fig. 4-161.

Battery Charger Rectifier Tube. High-current, low-voltage rectifier tubes have all but passed out of existence since the development of modern solid-state silicon rectifiers. However, some textbooks and the FCC do still refer to special tubes capable of handling large amounts of power at low voltages. These are known as *arc tubes* because of the manner in which they are fired. One such tube, mercury pool rectifier type 5554, uses a pool of mercury as the cathode. This tube can supply high currents (75A) on a continuous-duty basis.

The initial ionization is provided by an arc started between a subsidiary electrode, called an *ignitor*, and the cathode. The ionization results in greatly increased current. Since the ignitor must be used to start the arc, the tube can be controlled by small pulses of current to the ignitor, and thus hundreds of amperes may be controlled by very small amounts of current.

4-466. *What kind of vacuum tube responds to filament reactivation, and how is reactivation accomplished?*

Vacuum tubes with thoriated-tungsten filaments can be reactivated under some conditions, particularly where impurities in the thorium coating reduce the emission over a period of time when the filaments were not operated at their proper temperature.

Thoriated-tungsten filaments are manufactured by adding thorium to a tungsten filament. The thorium coating behaves as a profuse emitter of electrons and gradually evaporates during use. As it "boils off," it is replenished from inside the tungsten filament wire. At the same time, a gradual evaporation of the wire occurs; consequently, it becomes thinner with time. Eventually, one part of the filament becomes too fine to carry the current, and the wire burns in two at that spot. However, if the filament was operated at lower-than-normal voltages, it can be reactivated by applying very high filament voltages for brief periods. The high voltage causes the temperature of the filament to increase to the point where a fresh thorium supply is brought to the surface.

4-467. *How much energy is consumed in 20 hours by a radio receiver rated at 60W?*

Energy may be measured in *watt-hours*, which is watts multiplied by hours (so long as the power drain is continuous). One watt-hour is the equivalent of one watt of power used over the period of one hour. The radio receiver's total energy consumption would be 1200 watt-hours.

4-468. *How does the value of resistance in the grid leak of a regenerative detector affect the sensitivity of the detector?*

The value of the grid-leak resistance must be such that, when the resistor is paralleled with its mating capacitance, the time constant of the pair of components is long with respect to the rf signal and short with respect to the audio cycle. With the proper value of resistance and capacitance in the series grid lead, the regenerative detector (which normally is based on a grid-leak detector) is the most sensitive of the various vacuum-type detector circuits.

4-469. *Compare the design and operating characteristics of class A, class B, class AB, and class C amplifiers.*

Class A Operation. The class A amplifier is so biased that plate current flows constantly. In Fig. 4-162 point B is the operating point and is determined by the bias voltage E_{CC}. The grid signal voltage varies on both sides of the operating point. The output (plate current) waveform is obtained in the figure by extending dotted lines from various points of the input (grid voltage) signal to the dynamic characteristic curve. Note that the plate current waveform is practically undistorted—that is, it closely resembles the input. Minimum distortion takes place, because operation occurs along the linear portion of the curve. In

231

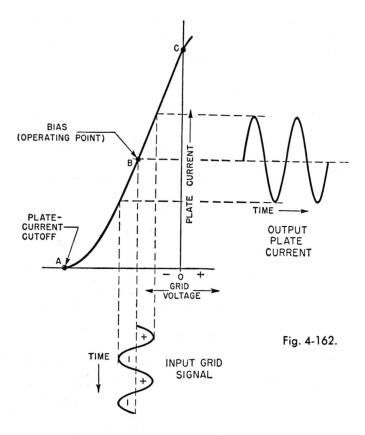

BIAS
(OPERATING POINT)

PLATE-
CURRENT
CUTOFF

B

A

PLATE CURRENT

− O +
GRID
VOLTAGE

C

TIME ⟶

OUTPUT
PLATE
CURRENT

Fig. 4-162.

TIME

INPUT GRID
SIGNAL

addition, the peak-to-peak amplitude of the input grid signal is comparatively small. This prevents it from extending into the nonlinear portions of the curve.

It may seem desirable to have the grid signal extend along the entire length of the characteristic curve from point A to point C. This produces a plate current waveform of maximum amplitude, which in turn produces maximum amplification. However, distortion results because the dynamic characteristic is not perfectly linear along this entire length. This is true of any tube or transistor. In most cases of class A operation, a distortionless output is preferred to large amplification.

If the positive half of the grid signal goes beyond point C, the control grid becomes positive in respect to the cathode, and grid current flows. Part of the input grid signal is lost, or clipped, and the positive half of the plate current waveform is distorted. Similarly, if the negative half of the input grid signal goes beyond point A, plate current stops flowing (the stage cuts off), and the negative half of the plate current waveform is clipped. Distortion results once again, of course, because the output signal does not resemble the input signal over the entire cycle.

From this analysis the following conclusions can be made concerning distortion in class A operation. **The more linear the dynamic characteristic of a tube or transistor, the less distortion it introduces.** Grid signal voltages should extend only into the most linear portion of the dynamic characteristic. **Class A amplifiers generally are biased to about one-half their cutoff value.** Finally, increasing the load produces a more linear dynamic characteristic. If the load is increased excessively, however, a great deal of power is lost. Therefore, some intermediate value of load is selected. In this way a minimum amount of distortion is obtained with a reasonable amount of power output.

The question often arises whether triodes or pentodes should be used for class A operation when vacuum tubes are used. The advantages of using triodes is that their dynamic transfer characteristics usually are more linear and therefore produce less distortion. Pentodes have the advantage of producing a greater power output for a given power input.

Classes of amplifiers are often compared with each other in terms of plate efficiency. *Plate efficiency* is defined as the ratio of ac power output that is developed across the load to the dc power supplied to the plate. **In class A amplifiers the plate efficiency is about 20% or less.** This low efficiency is due to the high average value of plate current and consequent high plate dissipation.

Class B Operation. A class B amplifier is one that is biased at or near cutoff (Fig. 4-163). **Plate current flows during the positive halves of the input grid signal and stops flowing during the negative half-cycles.**

Operating point E equals the bias voltage (E_{CC}), which is established at the point where the amplifier is not conducting. Any positive swings from this point will cause the amplifier to conduct, and any negative swings will keep the amplifier cut off. Plate current starts to flow when the instantaneous value of grid voltage (e_C) rises above the plate current cutoff point. Plate current continues to flow during the positive half of the input grid signal (the unshaded portion of the input grid signal. During the shaded portion of the input signal, the plate current is zero. The shaded portion indicates the part of the input grid signal that has been clipped. Clipping results in severe distortion of the output waveform. Note that the waveform swing of the **grid signal extends into the nonlinear portion of the dynamic characteristic**—that is, from the cutoff point to point F. This also causes distortion.

If the amplitude of the grid signal is increased so that it extends beyond point F, the amplitude of the plate waveform is increased, resulting in a greater power output. If the positive peak of the grid signal extends beyond point G, grid current flows, causing the positive peak of the plate current waveform to be clipped. Therefore, distortion is increased.

A single tube that operates as a class B amplifier produces a great deal of distortion. Therefore, it is undesirable to use this type of stage in audio amplifiers, where fidelity of reproduction is necessary. However, two tubes operating in a push-pull configuration often are used in audio amplifiers. A push-pull amplifier produces twice the output of a single tube; in addition, the output waveform contains a minimum of distortion.

233

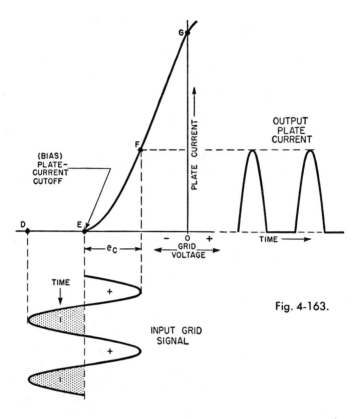

Fig. 4-163.

A single-tube class B amplifier delivers a greater amount of power than a single-tube class A amplifier. This is, in part, because of the greater voltage swing that is permissible in class B operation. **In a class B push-pull amplifier, the power output is about five times as great as in a single-tube class A amplifier using the same tube type.**

The **plate efficiency of a class B amplifier is about 40% to 60%**—about double that obtained in a class A amplifier. **The high plate efficiency permits the use of small power supplies for the dc operating potentials.** Sometimes the fluctuating output current of a class B amplifier is unintentionally coupled into the power source, causing irregularities in the dc operating potentials. When this happens, additional filter circuits are needed.

Class AB Operation. An amplifier that operates in the region between class A and class B is called a *class AB* amplifier. **In a class AB amplifier, the plate current flows for more than one-half cycle but less than the entire cycle of input grid signal.** Class AB operation may be subdivided into classes AB_1 and AB_2. The subscript numeral *1* indicates that grid current does not flow during any part of the input cycle. The subscript numeral *2* indicates that grid current does flow during some portion of the input cycle.

Class AB_1 operation is shown in sketch A of Fig. 4-164. The operating point (H) is located between plate current cutoff and the linear portion of the dynamic characteristic. The positive peak of the grid signal extends into the linear region of the dynamic characteristic. To prevent the flow of grid current, the positive peak of the grid signal extends beyond the cutoff point. The shaded areas of the input grid signal indicate those portions of the input signal that are cut off. The plate current waveform is distorted by the clipping action of the negative peaks.

Class AB_2 operation is illustrated in sketch B of Fig. 4-164, with the same operating point (H) as shown in sketch A. In class AB_2 operation the peak value of grid signal exceeds the fixed bias of the tube. The positive peaks of input grid signal extend into the positive region of grid voltage. This causes grid current to flow. Just as in class AB_1 operation, **the negative input peaks make the grid go beyond the cutoff point**.

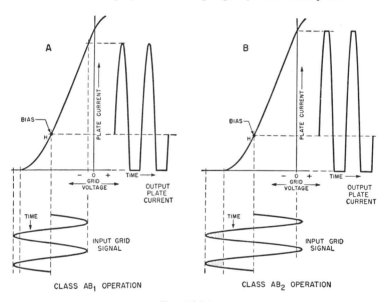

Fig. 4-164.

Clipping is much greater in class AB_2 operation than in AB_1. However, because of the greater grid voltage swing in class AB_2 operation, a greater output exists. The plate efficiency in AB_1 operation is somewhat greater than in AB_2. **Compared with class A, class AB operation produces more distortion, more power output, and a greater plate efficiency.**

Class C Operation. A class C amplifier is one whose operating point is located well below (more negative than) the plate current cutoff point, so that plate current flows for appreciably less than one-half cycle. Class C operation is shown in Fig. 4-165. The operating point for the input grid signal shown is point J. The voltage for this point is about

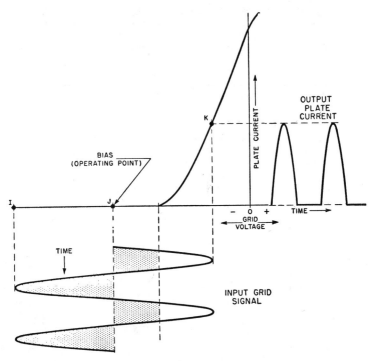

Fig. 4-165.

1.5 times the cutoff value. **The operating point for class C operation usually is made from 1.5 to 4 times cutoff.** The positive peak of the input grid signal extends to point K on the dynamic characteristic, and the negative peak extends to point I. The shaded areas indicate the portions of the input signal that are cut off. The output waveform represents a small part of the positive peaks of input grid signal.

If the positive peak of the grid signal extends beyond point L on the dynamic characteristic curve and into the positive region, grid current flows. The result is an output waveform that is greater in amplitude; however, it contains more distortion, since its positive peaks are clipped. **In a class C amplifier the large grid signal swing produces a greater power output as compared to classes A, B, and AB.**

Class C amplifiers generally are used as rf amplifiers, where **a large power output** and **a high plate efficiency** are often desired. The **plate efficiency of a class C amplifier is usually 60% to 80%.** The **high distortion** of a class C stage is overcome by the flywheel effect of tuned circuits.

4-470. *Why is it inadvisable to bias class B push-pull audio-frequency amplifiers right at plate current cutoff?*

If exact cutoff bias were used, **distortion** would occur, as shown in the characteristic curve of Fig. 4-166. Here the resultant dynamic

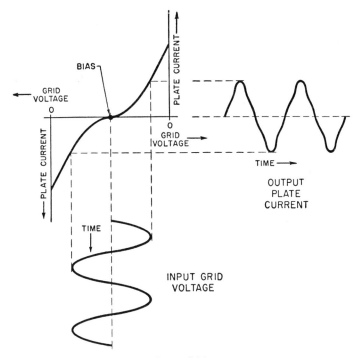

Fig. 4-166.

characteristic has an S-shape that causes severe distortion of the plate current waveform. The bias point ties the individual dynamic curves together. Thus, **when each amplifier is biased slightly above cutoff, the total dynamic characteristic is linear, and the output waveform is an amplified mirror image of the input waveform.**

4-471. *What may cause downward and upward fluctuation of the antenna current of an AM transmitter when the transmitter is modulated?*

Downward fluctuations of the antenna current may be caused by a number of transmitter anomalies, as described in the answer to question 4-285. **Upward fluctuations in antenna current might be caused by excessive modulation applied to the plate** of the final amplifier or related condition, such as the final amplifier being tuned to lower power output than normal while full modulation is applied. It may also be caused by the presence of **spurious signals,** as from **parasitics** or **self-oscillation (improperly neutralized stage).**

4-472. *Explain how grid bias voltage is developed by the grid leak in an oscillator.*

Grid bias is developed in a number of oscillator types by grid-leak action. The tuned-grid oscillator shown in Fig. 4-167 illustrates but one example. In this method of biasing, resistor R_G is connected in parallel with C_G. The charge path for the grid-leak capacitor is from cathode to

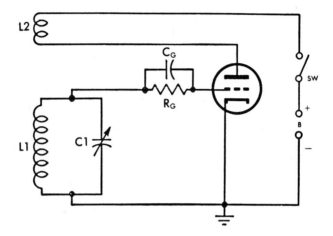

Fig. 4-167.

grid toward the input tuned circuit. The discharge path is clockwise through the grid-leak resistor, R_G. The operation is illustrated in greater detail in Fig. 4-168. The bias voltage for the oscillator tube is provided by the voltage drop across the grid-leak resistor that occurs as a result of the discharging of the grid-leak capacitor. The total instantaneous grid voltage (e_G) equals bias voltage (E_{CC}) plus grid signal voltage (e_g).

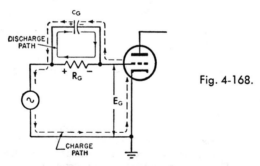

Fig. 4-168.

During the positive half of the circuit oscillation, the grid becomes positive with respect to the cathode. The grid draws current and charges C_G to the peak value of E_G, so that the plate of the capacitor connected to the grid becomes negative. During the negative half-cycles, the grid becomes negative with respect to the cathode and R_G carries the discharge current of the grid capacitor. The discharge of the capacitor through R_G produces a pulsating dc voltage whose average value is the negative bias voltage of the oscillator.

4-473. *Explain why rf chokes are sometimes placed in the power leads between a motor—generator power supply and a high-powered radio transmitter.*

A motor–generator lead can carry an rf current developed by the spinning armature. If this is introduced into the transmitter, it can add to the output signal from the transmitter, resulting in erratic operation of the transmitter, spurious signals, and signal distortion. Similarly, the trasmitter's signal can be coupled back down the primary power leads and coupled to other stages in the transmitter, resulting in rf feedback, the symptoms of which are similar. One method of preventing coupling of radio signals is to use rf chokes in series with the power leads; **rf chokes trap out rf signals but allow dc to pass.**

4-474. *What effect does inductive reactance in an ac circuit have on the power factor of the circuit?*

The presence of inductive reactance **tends to lower the power factor.** Ideally, when the power factor is unity (or as close to unity as possible), the circuit impedance is equal to the resistance, and **true** power is the same as **apparent** power. A high inductive reactance, however, keeps the ratio of resistance to impedance from being 1:1. The result is a low power factor and, consequently, a true power that varies considerably from apparent power.

4-475. *In what circuits of a radio station are 3-phase circuits sometimes employed?*

Three-phase power is sometimes used for the high-voltage power supply circuits in transmitters, because this allows use of smaller rectifiers and less filtering than would be required with single-phase circuits.

4-476. *Explain the operation of a vacuum-tube rectifier power supply and filter.*

The schematic of a typical full-wave rectifier circuit using a twin diode is illustrated in Fig. 4-169. Since a directly heated rectifier tube is used, the load resistance is connected between the filament-type cathode and the centertap of the high-voltage secondary. To simplify the wiring, the metal chassis is used to complete the connection between the bottom of the load resistance and the secondary centertap. This is shown schematically by grounding each of these two points. An additional

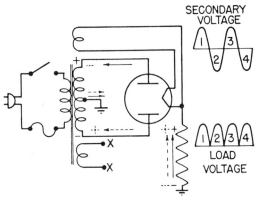

Fig. 4-169.

secondary winding on the power transformer supplies heater voltage to other tubes that may be contained in the equipment.

The operation of this full-wave rectifier circuit is as follows. (The individual alternations of the total secondary voltage have been numbered for identification.) During positive alternation *1*, the top end of the secondary is positive with respect to ground, and the bottom end of the secondary is negative with respect to ground. Only the upper diode has the necessary positive plate voltage required for conduction. Current will flow from ground, up through the load resistor to the cathode, from the cathode to the upper diode plate, down through the top half of the transformer secondary to the centertap, and back to the bottom of the load resistor by way of the metal chassis. This current develops a pulse of voltage across the load resistor that makes the top of the resistor positive with respect to ground.

The waveform across the resistor is shown by the load-voltage alternation marked *1* in the diagram. Upon completion of the positive alternation, the polarities across the secondary winding reverse. This makes the plate of the top diode negative, causing the top diode to cut off. The bottom diode plate becomes positive, and conduction occurs over the path marked by the dotted arrows.

The important fact to note about the circuit arrangement is that current flows through the load resistance in the same direction for both positive and negative alternations of the applied sine wave.

When the output waveform from the full-wave rectifier is examined, it is seen to consist of two pulses of current or voltage for each cycle of input voltage. The *ripple frequency* at the output of a full-wave rectifier is therefore twice the line frequency. The high ripple frequency at the output of a full-wave rectifier is a distinct advantage. As a result of this higher pulse frequency, the output more closely approximates pure dc and is easier to filter.

The output voltage is not normally usable without being filtered because of the high ripple content. The filtering method may be inductive, capacitive, or a combination of inductive and capacitive. Figure 4-170 illustrates one simple combination type, called an *L*-filter.

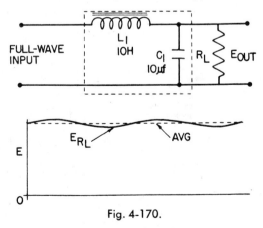

Fig. 4-170.

The inductor, L, is directly in series with the rectifier. Therefore, the filter is classified as a choke-input type. Since the inductor is in series with the rectifier and transformer winding, the reactance of the coil affects the charge time of the capacitor. The charge time of $C1$ is longer than it would be if the same capacitor were used in a circuit with no inductor (a simple capacitance filter). This action of the input choke allows a continuous flow of current from the rectifiers. Because of the uniform flow of current the L-type filter has applications where high currents are incurred. Figure 4-170 shows the output (solid line) of an L-type filter imposed on a theoretically perfect (broken line) dc voltage.

4-477. *What are the merits of an FM communications system compared to an AM type?*

The FM communications sytem has a large number of advantages over the AM system of comparable power output, not the least of which are:

1. Superior signal-to-noise ratio.
2. Lower usable signal level.
3. Received signal does not deteriorate gradually with distance between transmitter and receiver.
4. Carrier power does not depend on audio power.
5. Freedom from noise interference (on receiving) because most noises are impulse-type interference whose basic component is AM rather than FM.
6. The fully modulated FM signal can be increased with an add-on class C power amplifier of high efficiency, while a fully modulated AM transmitter signal must be increased with an add-on linear (usually class AB) amplifier of low efficiency.
7. Interference between signals is rare because of FM's *capture effect*, whereby the stronger of two competing signals "captures" the receiver, so that the receiver "hears" only one signal.

4-478. *What is meant by horizontal and vertical "polarization" of a radio wave?*

The radiated energy from an omnidirectional antenna is in the form of an expanding sphere. A small section of this sphere is called a *wavefront*; it is perpendicular to the direction of travel of the energy. All energy on this surface is in phase. Usually all points on the wavefront are at equal distances from the antenna. The farther from the antenna, the less spherical the wave appears. At a considerable distance the wavefront can be considered as a plane surface at right angles to the direction of propagation.

The radiation field is made up of magnetic and electric lines of force, which are always at right angles to each other. The direction of polarization of most electromagnetic fields is considered to be the direction of the electric vector. That is, if the lines of force are horizontal, the wave is said to be horizontally polarized (Fig. 171A); and if the electric lines are vertical, the wave is said to be vertically polarized. As the electric field is parallel to the axis of the antenna (dipole, in this reference), the antenna is in the plane of polarization. The horizontally placed antenna in Fig. 4-171 produces a horizontally polarized wave, and a vertically placed antenna produces a vertically polarized wave.

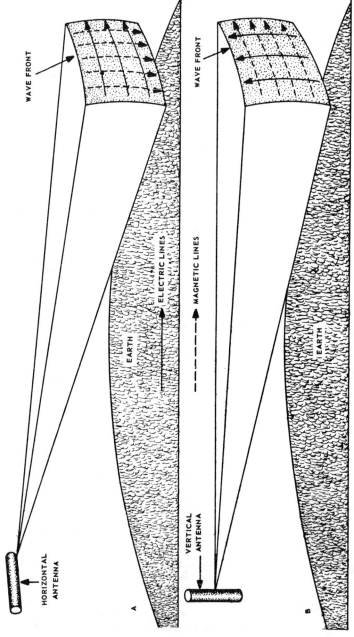

WAVE FRONT

WAVE FRONT

ELECTRIC LINES

MAGNETIC LINES

EARTH

EARTH

HORIZONTAL
ANTENNA

VERTICAL
ANTENNA

A

B

Fig. 4-171.

For maximum absorption of energy from the electromagnetic fields, it is necessary that a receiving dipole be located in the plane of polarization. This places the conductor at right angles to the magnetic lines of force that are moving through the antenna and parallel to the electric lines.

In general, the polarization of a wave does not change over short distances. Therefore, transmitting and receiving antennas are oriented alike, especially if a short distance separates them. Over long distances the polarization tends to change. The change is usually small at low frequencies, but at high frequencies the change is quite marked.

4-479. *Draw a block diagram of an FM receiver and explain its principle of operation.*

Frequency-modulation receivers are supplied with rf signals that vary in frequency (and phase), according to the information transmitted. The amount of the variation, or *deviation*, from the center frequency at a given instant depends on the amplitude of the impressed audio signal. The function of the receiver (Fig. 4-172) is the same as the function of an AM superheterodyne receiver. That is, the amplitude of the incoming rf signals is increased in the rf stages; then the frequency is reduced in the mixer stage to the intermediate frequency and amplified in the i-f amplifier section; finally, the amplitude is clipped in the limiter stage and the modulation component is reproduced by the detector, or *discriminator*, as it is called in an FM receiver.

There are a few major differences between AM and FM receivers. The greatest difference is in the method of detection. Also, the tuned circuits of the FM receiver have a wider bandpass, and the last i-f stage is especially adapted for limiting the amplitude of the incoming signal. However, in both systems, the audio amplifiers and reproducers are similar. The rf amplifier, or *preselector*, performs essentially the same function in the FM receiver as it does in the AM receiver; that is, it increases the sensitivity of the receiver.

The frequency converter (mixer) employed in the FM receiver functions much the same as the one employed in the AM superheterodyne receiver. However, additional problems are involved. For example, at FM broadcast frequencies, the stability of the local oscillator becomes a major problem. There is a tendency for the local oscillator to become synchronized with the incoming signal and thus to lose the i-f output entirely. The tendency is more pronounced in the FM band because the station and oscillator frequencies are relatively close together.

The i-f amplifier in an FM receiver is usually tuned to a center frequency of 8–10 MHz. It generally employs double-tuned transformers having equal primary and secondary inductances. The bandpass is from 150 to 250 kHz. The last one or two i-f stages function as a limiter.

The gain of each wideband i-f stage is considerably less than that of the narrowband AM i-f amplifier. Therefore, an FM receiver employs more i-f stages than a corresponding AM receiver.

A low value of intermediate frequency is undesirable, because drift in the local oscillator might force the set to operate outside the i-f range. Also, it would be pointless to have the intermediate frequency lower

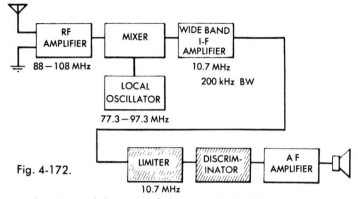

Fig. 4-172.

than the total frequency of deviation (bandwidth) of any one FM station. In the choice of optimum i-f value, such factors as image response, response to signals at the same frequency as the i-f, response to beat signals produced by two stations separated in frequency by the i-f value, and response to harmonic frequencies must be considered.

The *limiter* in an FM receiver removes amplitude variations and passes on to the discriminator an FM signal of constant amplitude. As the FM signal leaves the transmitting antenna, it is varying in frequency according to an audio modulating signal but it has essentially a constant amplitude. As the signal travels between the transmitting and receiving antennas, however, natural and man-made noises or static disturbances are combined with it to produce variations in the amplitude of the modulating signal. Other variations are caused by fading of the signals as might be caused by movement of a vehicle carrying the transmitter or receiver. Still other amplitude variations are introduced within the receiver itself because of a lack of uniform response of the tuned circuits. All of these undesirable variations in the amplitude of the FM signal are amplified as the signal passes through the successive stages of the receiver up to the input of the limiter. This condition in which both frequency modulation (desired) and amplitude modulation (undesired) are present at the same time, is shown in Fig. 4-173A.

The character of the signal after leaving the limiter should be as indicated in Fig. 4-173B, in which all amplitude variations have been removed, leaving a signal that varies only in frequency.

The *discriminator* interprets the frequency variations of the frequency-modulated rf energy in terms of the audio signal—the operation is analogous to detection in an AM receiver.

In FM transmission the intelligence to be transmitted causes a variation in the instantaneous frequency of the carrier above or below the *center frequency*. The detecting device must therefore be so constructed that its output will vary linearly according to the instantaneous frequency of the incoming signal. Since the detecting device must be insensitive to amplitude variations produced by interference or receiver nonlinearities, a limiter must precede the discriminator.

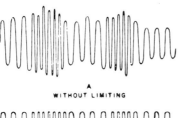

A
WITHOUT LIMITING

Fig. 4-173.

B
WITH LIMITING

Several types of FM detectors have been developed and are in use, but perhaps the most common types are the *Foster-Seely discriminator* and the *ratio detector*. The discriminator requires a limiter, which, in turn, requires considerable amplification ahead of its input. A ratio detector eliminates the need for a limiter and, in addition, one or more i-f amplifier stages can be eliminated.

4-480. *Draw block diagrams of frequency- and phase-modulated transmitters and discuss the characteristics of each.*

There are two basic approaches to FM. One is variation of the actual carrier frequency at an audio rate, and the other is variation of the phase angle of the carrier wave. For a "true" FM system, as used in most broadcast stations, the oscillator frequency is varied with a *reactance modulator*, as shown in the block diagram of Fig. 4-174. A block diagram of the phase-modulated approach to FM is shown in Fig. 4-175.

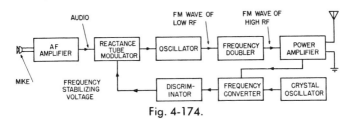

Fig. 4-174.

Reactance Modulator Approach. In the reactance system of frequency modulation, a reactance modulator tube (or transistor) is connected in parallel with the oscillator tank; this device functions as a capacitor whose capacitance is varied in accordance with an audio signal. **The frequency of the oscillator, which is set at some submultiple of the desired center frequency of the carrier, is thus changed, and the resulting FM signal is passed through a frequency multiplier to increase the carrier frequency and the deviation frequency.**

The theory of operation of a reactance modulator circuit may be understood with the aid of Fig. 4-176. The reactance modulator, $V1$, is effectively in shunt with the oscillator tank, LC, and the phase shift

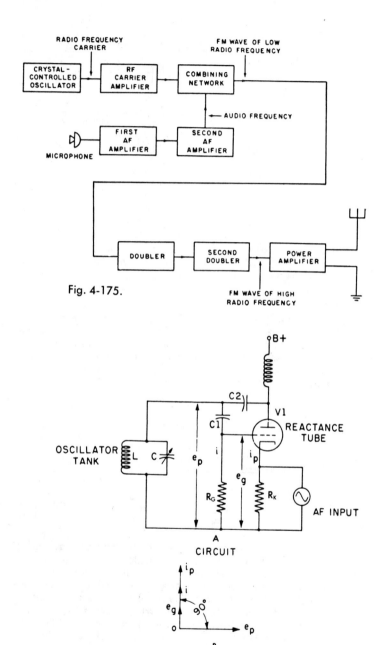

Fig. 4-175.

A

CIRCUIT

B

VECTOR DIAGRAM

Fig. 4-176.

circuit, R_G-$C1$. The reactance of the capacitor is large compared with the value of the resistor; and the current (i) in this circuit leads the voltage (e_p) across the circuit by approximately 90°. The voltage e_p is the alternating component of the plate-to-ground voltage appearing simultaneously across the reactance tube, phase shift circuit, and oscillator tank.

The coupling capacitor ($C2$) has a relatively low reactance to the ac component that passes through it; it blocks the dc plate voltage from the phase shift circuit and tank. The reactance tube receives its ac grid input voltage (e_g) across R_G. This voltage is the IR drop across R_G and is in phase with plate current (i_p).

Because e_g is in phase with both i and i_p, and e_g leads e_p by approximately 90°, both i and i_p lead e_p by approximately 90°. These relations are shown in the vector diagram of Fig. 4-176B. Both i and i_p are supplied by the oscillator tank circuit; and because both are leading currents with respect to the tank voltage (e_p), they act like the current in tank capacitor C. Therefore, the effect of these currents on the frequency of the tank is the same as though additional capacitance was connected in parallel with it.

Consider now the effect of introducing an audio signal across the cathode resistor (R_K). With zero audio voltage, rf plate current is a succession of rapid pulses of constant amplitude, and the oscillator tank operates at a constant frequency, called the *resting, quiescent,* or *center* frequency. When the audio voltage rises with the polarity that swings the cathode negative with respect to the grid, the pulses of plate current gradually increase in amplitude. This leading rf plate current is drawn through the oscillator tank and is equivalent to an increasing value of tank capacitance. Thus, the oscillator frequency is lowered. Conversely, when the audio signal swings the grid of the reactance tube negative with respect to the cathode, the rf plate current pulses gradually decrease in amplitude and the oscillator frequency increases.

The *frequency* of the audio signal determines the number of times per second that the oscillator tank frequency changes. On the other hand, the *amplitude* of the audio signal determines the extent of the oscillatory frequency change—that is, the deviation frequency. Thus, the reactance modulator, with its audio signal input, produces an FM output.

Phase Modulator Approach. All modulating processes are based on changing the rf carrier wave in some respect. The variation normally is dierectly proportional to the instantaneous value of the modulating voltage. When the instantaneous frequency of the carrier is varied in direct relation to the modulating wave, the result is frequency modulation. If the instantaneous phase of the carrier is varied by an electrical angle directly proportional to the instantaneous modulating voltage, phase modulation is obtained. Virtually all communications-type FM systems employ this phase-angle modulation approach. Varying the carrier frequency also changes the instantaneous phase relation of the carrier frequency to its own fixed unmodulated state. Likewise, varying the carrier phase changes the carrier frequency.

The carrier variation occurs at a rate of change equal to the frequency of the modulating wave. For example, a 1000 Hz tone changes

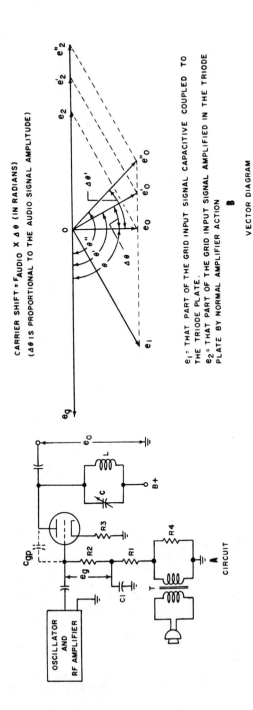

CARRIER SHIFT = $F_{AUDIO} \times \Delta\theta$ (IN RADIANS)

($\Delta\theta$ IS PROPORTIONAL TO THE AUDIO SIGNAL AMPLITUDE)

e_1 = THAT PART OF THE GRID INPUT SIGNAL CAPACITIVE COUPLED TO THE TRIODE PLATE.

e_2 = THAT PART OF THE GRID INPUT SIGNAL AMPLIFIED IN THE TRIODE PLATE BY NORMAL AMPLIFIER ACTION

B

VECTOR DIAGRAM

OSCILLATOR AND RF AMPLIFIER

A

CIRCUIT

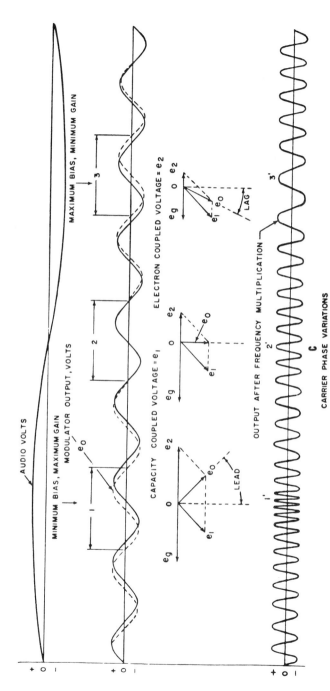

AUDIO VOLTS

MINIMUM BIAS, MAXIMUM GAIN

MAXIMUM BIAS, MINIMUM GAIN

MODULATOR OUTPUT, VOLTS

CAPACITY COUPLED VOLTAGE = e_1

ELECTRON COUPLED VOLTAGE = e_2

LEAD

LAG

OUTPUT AFTER FREQUENCY MULTIPLICATION

C

CARRIER PHASE VARIATIONS

Fig. 4-177.

the carrier frequency (and phase) ± 75 kHz at the rate of 1000 times per second in a broadcast FM system at maximum modulation (deviation).

A typical PM system is shown in the block diagram of Fig. 4-175. Note the contrast between reactance- and phase-modulated FM systems: **In the reactance modulation approach, the oscillator frequency itself is varied at an audio rate; in phase-modulation, the oscillator frequency is constant and does not change. In this latter arrangement the audio signal is applied to the rf carrier by means of a combining network. The output of the combining network is fed into a series of class C amplifiers, the plate circuits of which are tuned to a multiple of the oscillator frequency. The output of the last multiplier (if a chain is incorporated) is fed to a power amplifier that couples the FM signal to the antenna.** (Note that, with FM, fully modulated signals can be processed through class C amplifier stages, but, with AM fully modulated signals must be processed through linear amplifiers, the efficiency of which is considerably lower than that of the class C amplifier.)

A diagram of the combining network in which the phase shift is accomplished is shown in Fig. 4-177A. The rf and audio voltages are applied across the grid voltage divider, which consists of $R2$, $R1$, and $R4$. The triode plate load is a broadly tuned LC tank. The rf signal of constant frequency and amplitude appears across $R2$ as grid voltage e_g. As the instantaneous value of the audio signal varies through each audio cycle, the triode bias is increased and decreased at the modulation rate because of the audio voltage that appears across resistors $R4$ and $R1$. Consequently, the triode gain is varied in accordance with the audio signal.

Now consider how this varying gain is translated into phase shift. The instantaneous plate load voltage (e_o1, shown in Fig. 4-177B, is the resultant of two rf voltages in the triode plate circuit. These two rf voltages are (1) the portion of the grid input signal that is coupled to the plate circuit by means of the grid—plate capacitance of the triode (e_1), and (2) the grid input signal amplified in the triode plate by normal amplifier action (e_2).

The resultant of vectors e_1 and e_2 is indicated in the vector diagram as e_o. In the same diagram, e_g is the grid input rf signal. The triode amplifier voltage (e_2) is relatively low because of inverse feedback obtained by omitting the usual cathode bypass capacitor across $R3$. Voltage e_1 leads e_g and is of less amplitude than e_g because the interelectrode capacitive reactance acts in series with the plate load and causes a leading current to flow through it. The plate load is resonant at the oscillator frequency and acts as a pure resistance. Thus, e_1 across the load is in phase with the leading current through the load and leads e_g by some angle less than 90°—depending on the magnitude of the interelectrode capacitive reactance and the plate load resistance.

At the time the audio frequency swings the triode bias to the maximum, the triode gain is minimum, and e_2 is relatively small. For this condition, e_o leads e_g by angle θ. The amplified voltage (e_2') represents the condition existing when the audio signal swings the triode bias to a minimum, and the tube gain is higher than before. Therefore, voltage e_o' is larger and combines with e_1 to produce the resultant plate load voltage (e_o'), which leads e_g by angle ($\theta + \Delta\theta$). The resultant voltage (e'_0) undergoes a change in phase angle ($\Delta\theta$) with respect to e_g in accordance with the change in triode bias, gain, and instantaneous values.

The difference in the angles θ and θ' ($\Delta\theta$) is the change in the phase shift angle of e_b and is a factor governing carrier swing. When voltage variations e_0 e'_0, and so forth are applied to a tuned circuit, a smooth wave having both positive and negative alternations is formed as the result of the flywheel effect in a tank circuit. This wave has the same varying time interval between positive peaks as the applied voltage variations, and therefore its frequency is shifted in accordance with the audio modulation signal during the time the phase angle is changing.

The variation in phase of the carrier output voltage with audio modulation is illustrated in Fig. 4-177C. As the audio signal voltage varies the gain of the modulating stage from maximum to minimum, the carrier output voltage is shifted in phase from leading to lagging the zero-signal position.

On the positive half of the audio cycle, e_b is advanced in phase ahead of the zero-signal position. The angle of lead is equivalent to a slight increase in frequency of e_b and a corresponding decrease in the time for each carrier cycle, as indicated at 1 and compared with the time at 2.

On the negative half-cycle of the audio signal, the carrier voltage lags in phase behind the zero-signal position. The lag is equivalent to a slight decrease in frequency of e_b and a corresponding increase in the time for each carrier cycle, as indicated at 3 and compared with the time at 2.

The phase-modulated carrier is fed through several frequency multiplier stages, and the output waveform then contains many more cycles, as shown in the lower curve of the figure. Frequency multiplication increases the carrier frequency and the changes in the carrier as the result of modulation. Thus, the frequency is increased to a higher value in the vicinity of 1' and decreased to a correspondingly lower value at 3', compared with the no-signal value at 2'.

In a phase modulation system the carrier shift is proportional to the product of the audio frequency and the phase shift angle. It is therefore necessary to introduce an action that will prevent a signal that changes in audio frequency but remains at constant amplitude from influencing carrier swing. Only the amplitude of the modulating signal and not its instantaneous frequency should influence the extent of the frequency swing (deviation) of the carrier. This action may be accomplished by introducing a preemphasis circuit such as the one composed of $R1$ and $C1$ in Fig. 4-177A.

When the audio signal of constant amplitude is decreased from a high frequency to a lower frequency, the audio voltage across $C1$ is increased in amplitude. Therefore, the tube bias swing and the change in the tube gain cause the normal amplifier component of output voltage to be increased from e'_2 to e'_2 (Fig. 177B). Carrier shift is proportional to the product of the audio frequency and the phase shift angle ($\Delta\theta$), as indicated in Fig. 4-177B. Then an increase in the phase shift angle from $\Delta\theta$ to $\Delta\theta'$ compensates for the decrease in audio frequency. Thus, the product of audio frequency and $\Delta\theta$ remains constant, and the carrier swing is now independent of the audio frequency. The output FM signal from the phase-modulated transmitter is therefore similar to that of a reactance-tube-modulated FM transmitter. Hence, an FM receiver performs equally well regardless of which approach is used in the transmitter.

Summary and Comparison. Phase modulation may be called *indirect FM.* With this modulation approach, the modulating signal is passed through some type of correction network before reaching the modulator. A 90° phase shift in the phase-modulated signal makes it possible to distinguish from *direct FM.* The two methods are shown graphically in Fig. 4-178. The output of the modulator (fed by a crystal oscillator) is applied through frequency multipliers to a final amplifier when phase modulation is employed.

In the *direct FM* transmitter, the output of the speech amplifier is usually connected directly to the modulator stage, which supplies an equivalent reactance to the oscillator stage. This causes the frequency of the oscillator to vary with the modulating signal. The FM output of the oscillator then is fed to frequency multipliers, which are used to bring the carrier and deviation frequencies up to the desired values. A power amplifier (usually class C) is used in exactly the same manner as with the phase-modulated (indirect FM) method.

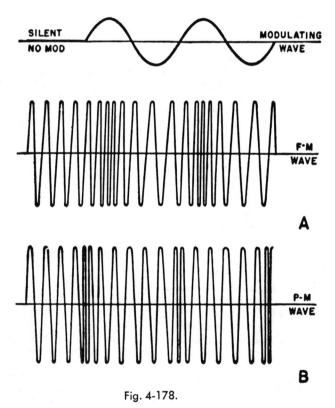

Fig. 4-178.

4-481. *In an FM transmitter, what is the meaning of "modulation index"? Of "deviation ratio"? What values of deviation ratio are used in a frequency modulation system?*

Modulation Index. In an FM system the frequency of the modulating voltage determines the number of times per second that the frequency shifts between the deviation limits. The higher the frequency of the modulating signal, the greater the number of times per second that the frequency varies between the deviation limits set by the peak amplitude of the modulating signal. The ratio between the maximum frequency deviation and the maximum frequency of the modulation signal is called the *modulation index*. Expressed as a mathematical formula

$$M_f \frac{\Delta f}{f_m}$$

where M_f is the modulation index, Δf is the frequency deviation, and f_m is the maximum frequency of the modulating signal.

The percentage of modulation of an FM signal cannot be determined in the same manner as an AM signal, because 100% modulation would mean that the entire carrier varies in frequency from zero to twice the carrier frequency. Percentage of modulation in an FM transmission is defined as the percentage of *maximum deviation*, which varies for different services. Thus, for an FM transmitter with a maximum deviation of 75 kHz, 100% modulation occurs when the transmitter deviates the full 75 kHz. When the deviation falls to 37.5 kHz, the transmitter is being modulated only 50%. Such a definition is flexible, of course, and depends on the maximum deviation of the equipment used.

Deviation Ratio. If the frequency of the modulating signal is held constant, the bandwidth will depend directly upon the amplitude of the modulating signal. On the other hand, if the amplitude is held constant, the lower audio frequencies will produce more sidebands. For commercial high-fidelity broadcasting, the maximum **frequency deviation** of the carrier is limited by the Federal Communications Commission to 75 kHz on either side of the carrier frequency; 15 kHz is the highest **modulation frequency** in use. The ratio between these two maximum limits is called the *deviation ratio*, which can be precisely the same thing as *modulation index*. When the highest audio frequency to be transmitted is used in the formula along with a deviation frequency that represents 100% modulation of the transmitter, the modulation index and the deviation ratio are the same.

Values of Deviation Ratio. Since the modulation index deals with instantaneous functions, it does not directly tell us much. Deviation ratio, though, deals with maximum values of the transmitted FM wave. The modulation index can be used to set standard values of deviation ratio that can be tolerated in an FM communication system, since the modulation index does determine the bandwidth of a transmitting station.

In general, the higher the modulation index, the more sidebands will appear adjacent to the carrier. The calculation of the actual number of sidebands and their relative amplitude requires the use of

Modulation index $M_f = \dfrac{\Delta f}{f_m}$	Number of effective side-band pairs	Effective bandwidth
.5	2	$4f_\Delta$
1	3	$6f_\Delta$
2	4	$8f_\Delta$
3	6	$12f_\Delta$
4	7	$14f_\Delta$
5	8	$16f_\Delta$
6	9	$18f_\Delta$
7	11	$22f_\Delta$
8	12	$24f_\Delta$
9	13	$26f_\Delta$
10	14	$28f_\Delta$
11	15	$30f_\Delta$
12	16	$32f_\Delta$
13	17	$34f_\Delta$
14	18	$36f_\Delta$
15	19	$38f_\Delta$
16	20	$40f_\Delta$
17	21	$42f_\Delta$
18	23	$46f_\Delta$
19	24	$48f_\Delta$
20	25	$50f_\Delta$
21	26	$52f_\Delta$
22	27	$54f_\Delta$
23	28	$56f_\Delta$
24	29	$58f_\Delta$
25	30	$60f_\Delta$

Fig. 4-179.

highly complex Bessel functions. In Fig. 4-179 a table based on Bessel functions lists the number of effective sidebands obtained from some of the common values of the modulation index. The table also shows the effective bandwidth for each listed modulation index. Figure 4-180 shows graphically the relationship between bandwidth and modulation index.

The effective sidebands must be at least as far from the carrier as the frequency deviation limits. Because of this, it is necessary to provide a channel or bandwidth that will handle the highest effective sideband component, plus a *guard band* that will absorb any sidebands that extend beyond these limits. Since the modulating signal cannot always be specified and can vary over wide limits, it is easier to assign the channel in terms of deviation limits and then to set aside some additional frequency space for guard bands on either side of the deviation limits.

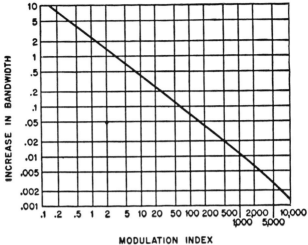

MODULATION INDEX

Fig. 4-180.

The guard bands insure a minimum amount of interference to stations operating on adjacent frequencies. The center carrier frequency of a particular station may vary from the assigned value and cause interference to stations on adjacent channels. and the guard bands also help to prevent this.

In a communications system it is easy to see how the deviation ratio can be used to determine bandwidth requirements. and why the FCC establishes standards governing: (1) deviation frequency maximums. (2) frequency spacing between channels. and (3) limitations on maximum audio frequency that may be transmitted. Since the maximum permissible deviation on most FM two-way-radio channels is ±5 kHz and the maximum audio frequency to be transmited is 3 kHz. the deviation ratio is 5/3 or 1.667.

4-482. *Why is narrowband rather than wideband FM used in modern radio communications systems?*

Narrowband FM **requires less bandwidth** than wideband. The old standard was 15 kHz frequency deviation. and channels were allocated at intervals of 50 kHz. Increased demands for channels within the existing bands necessitated some method for getting more stations into a given spectrum. The FCC. in an attempt to make more efficient use of radio spectrum. split the channels by spacing them at 25 kHz intervals. To do this without interference. the bandwidth restrictions were changed as well. Today's maximum deviation frequency is ±5 kHz.

When FM transmitter deviation is limited to ±5 kHz and the corresponding receiver bandwidth is also set at ±5 kHz. the communication capability is comparable to that of the old 15 kHz standard. The bandwidth reduction has compromised the signal-to-noise ratio somewhat. but the effective increase in overall signal strength as a result of the narrower bandwidth tends to compensate for it.

4-483. *What is the purpose of a squelch circuit in a radio communications receiver?*

The squelch circuit keeps the speaker in a receiver silent unless a usable signal appears on the channel. Without the squelch, ordinary receiver noises and objectionable hiss would be heard at all times. In good communications receivers the squelch circuit is noise-actuated. The presence of any usable signal defeats the squelch circuit for the time the signal is present.

4-484. *Discuss methods by which interference to radio reception may be reduced.*

Interference can take many forms. Automotive devices such as generators, ignitions, electrical accessories, etc. cause problems in vehicles; and machines, appliances, power lines, and the like are trouble sources at fixed locations. Interference can also be caused by harmonic and spurious radiation from other transmitters, oscillator signals from nearby receiving equipment, intermodulation from two signals mixing at some nonlinear element, and from other stations operating either on the same channel or adjacent frequencies.

There are two basic approaches to minimizing interference: The first is to take measures at the source of the interference, and the second is to exercise preventive measures at the receiver. When interference is reduced by doing something at the source of the radiation, that is sometimes called *active* elimination of interference. When steps are taken at the receiver, it is called *passive* elimination of interference.

Active Approaches. When rf interference is attributable to man-made sources, several standard measures are often adopted to reduce the problem. **Bypass capacitors** across suspect circuits; **rf chokes** in series with dc power lines; and additional, **heavier ground cables** all help to reduce radiation from vehicular sources. **Shielding** is also a powerful weapon, but more often than not it becomes impractical either because of the size of the offending device or the basic construction requirements of the device.

When the source of the interference is another transmitter, it is best to determine the exact nature of the problem. **Parasitic chokes can be used to suppress parasitic radiation**, as can rerouted leads and the addition of new ground points in the transmitter (when the offending transmitter's chassis is doing the radiating). **If the problem is attributable to a self-oscillating stage, the problem can often be cured by neutralization.**

An extremely effective deterrent to harmonic radiation is **the low-pass filter**, which should be installed in the transmitter's transmission line. A low-pass filter will tend to suppress radiation of all signals beyond those for which the transmitter was designed.

Passive Approaches. If the interference is caused by other stations operating on adjacent frequencies or even the same frequency, the use of a **directional antenna** might prove extremely beneficial. Not only does a directional antenna reduce the receiver's sensitivity to stations other than those in the path of its beam, it adds considerable gain to signals lying within the beam.

In vehicular receivers, ignition noise and other pulse-type problems can be minimized by effective grounding of the receiver and, possibly, shielding the lines bringing power to the unit.

4-485. *Draw a diagram of an ohmmeter and explain its principle of operation.*

Ohmmeters possess a number of features not found in ammeters and voltmeters. An ohmmeter must supply its own power. Usually this is supplied with a battery of known voltage. In an ohmmeter there two resistors—one fixed and one variable. The fixed resistor (marked R in Fig. 4-181) is of such a value that when points A and B are shorted the meter will read full scale. The variable resistor is connected in parallel with the meter and is called the *zero adjustment*. It serves to compensate for the gradually declining voltage of the internal battery. Usually the adjustment is made with a small control knob on the face of the meter's enclosure.

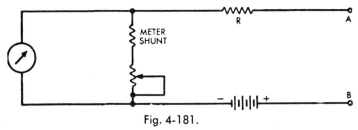

Fig. 4-181.

If zero resistance is connected between points A and B, the meter pointer will deflect full scale. If a resistance equal to R is connected between these points, the deflection will be half-scale. And if a resistance equal to $2R$ is connected, the deflection will be one-third scale. The difference in deflection indicates that the upper end of the scale reads low resistance.

The scales on ohmmeters (Fig. 4-182) are not linear but are similar to a scale of reciprocals. At the lower end (high-resistance end), the calibrations are crowded, making accurate readings difficult. The center of the scale is most accurate, because the scale error increases at the high end (error on most meters is based on a certain percentage of full-scale reading). A typical ohmmeter has more than one range. Additional ranges are made possible by the use of various values of R and battery voltages. On some meters there is a special range for reading very low resistances. This is made possible by connecting the unknown resistance in parallel with a known resistance. Readings of resistance in this case appear on a special scale called *low ohms*. On this scale, zero is at the left.

The ohmmeter is not as accurate a measuring device as the ammeter and the voltmeter, because of the circuit associated with it. Therefore, do not expect to read resistance with greater than 5% to 10% accuracy—even with meters boasting a full-scale accuracy of better than 3%. While there are instruments that read the resistance of an element with very great accuracy, they usually involve some sort of bridge network and are much more complex to use.

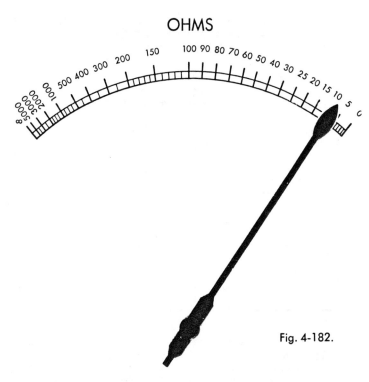

OHMS

Fig. 4-182.

4-486. *Discuss Lecher wires, their properties, and their use.*

Lecher line is a 2-wire rf line which is one-quarter to several wavelengths long. Such a device is used for either investigating standing-wave phenomena, accurately measuring wavelengths, or conveying rf energy from a generator to an antenna. In the Lecher line of Fig. 4-183A wires run parallel for about one wavelength. With this line you can determine several facts by experimentation. For example, when the frequency of a transmitter is unknown, you can use a Lecher line to measure the wavelength of the transmitted frequency. And, since the velocity at which energy travels on a line of this type is about 97.5% of the velocity in free space (300 million meters per second), you can compute the frequency by the formula

$$f = \frac{300 \times 10^6 \times 0.975}{2d}$$

where d is the distance between two minimum or maximum standing-wave points, and f is the frequency in hertz.

Generally, a sliding shorting bar is a part of a Lecher line. As the sliding bar moves toward the generator, the standing waves move with it. Results are read by a pickup coil with an indicating meter which is placed near the excitation coil of the Lecher line.

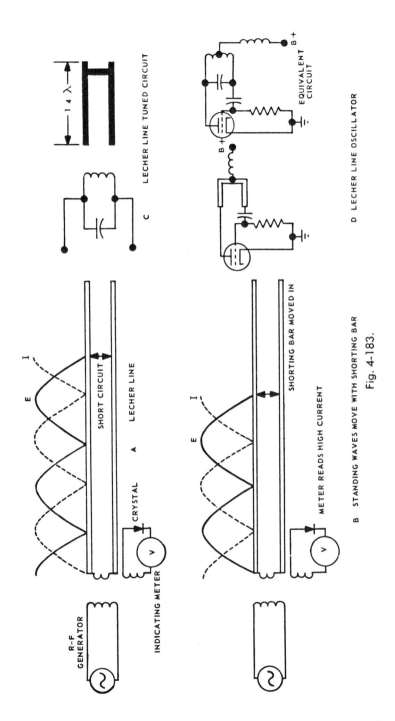

A   LECHER LINE

B   STANDING WAVES MOVE WITH SHORTING BAR

C   LECHER LINE TUNED CIRCUIT

D   LECHER LINE OSCILLATOR

Fig. 4-183.

Figure 4-183 illustrates the use of the shorting bar and pickup coil in determining current minimums and maximums. The standing current waves in Fig. 4-183A show that the standing wave of current is minimum at the location of the excitation coil. Thus, very little current flows through it, and the small magnetic field resulting induces little voltage in the meter circuit. The meter will indicate a current minimum. In Fig. 4-183B, which shows the shorting bar moved, the current is maximum at the excitation coil, and the meter pickup coil is excited by the strong magnetic field about the excitation coil. The high current on the meter shows the presence of a current maximum.

A Lecher line one-quarter wavelength ($\lambda/4$) long displays the characteristics of a parallel resonant circuit. For this reason a quarter-wave Lecher line is often used as a tuned circuit in an ultrahigh-frequency oscillator. At 211 MHz, $\lambda/4$ is only about 14 in., which is small enough for practical use, as is shown in Fig. 4-183C. (Note the typical Lecher-line oscillator in sketch D.) A Lecher line oscillator is impractical at lower frequencies. For example, at a frequency of 1 MHz, a quarter-wavelength line is 250 ft long. Obviously, this is too long for the ordinary transmitter operating at these frequencies.

4-487. *If a 0−1 mA dc milliammeter is to be converted into a voltmeter with a full-scale calibration of 100V, what value of resistance should be connected in series with the meter?*

A simple application of Ohm's law is all that's necessary here; resistance required is equal to voltage divided by current. The voltage of 100V, divided by the current of 0.001A (1 mA), yields 100,000Ω, or 100K.

4-488. *What are waveguides? Cavity resonators?*

A waveguide is an enclosed metallic tube used for transmission of rf energy at microwave frequencies. Cavity resonators are metal chambers for storing rf energy and are analogous to LC tank circuits. Their Q is generally much higher than that of conventional LC circuits. The following paragraphs outline the applications and construction details of both waveguides and cavities.

Waveguides. Fundamentally, there are two methods of transferring electromagnetic energy: by current through a pair of wires and by guiding the movement of complete electromagnetic fields. At first glance the two methods may appear to be unrelated. However, by considering 2-wire lines as elements which guide electromagnetic fields, the current flowing through the conductors may be considered to be the result of moving fields.

At microwave frequencies a 2-wire transmission line is a poor means of transferring rf energy because it does not confine electromagnetic fields in a direction perpendicular to the plane which contains the wires. This results in energy escaping by radiation, as illustrated in Fig. 4-184B. Electromagnetic fields may be completely confined when one conductor is extended around the other to form a coaxial cable. Figure 4-184C illustrates this. Electromagnetic fields that move in space are confined largely to the area between the earth and the ionosphere, as shown in Fig. 4-184A. While the change in the dielectric constant of the ionosphere is sufficient to reflect most

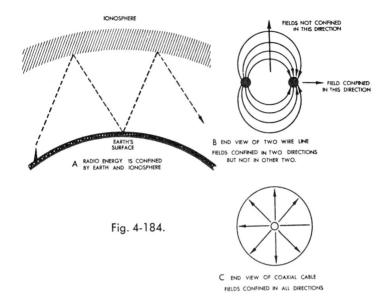

Fig. 4-184.

A RADIO ENERGY IS CONFINED BY EARTH AND IONOSPHERE

B END VIEW OF TWO WIRE LINE
FIELDS CONFINED IN TWO DIRECTIONS BUT NOT IN OTHER TWO.

C END VIEW OF COAXIAL CABLE
FIELDS CONFINED IN ALL DIRECTIONS

electromagnetic fields that strike it, extremely high-frequency radiation that strikes it perpendicularly is not reflected.

Energy in the form of electromagnetic fields may be transferred very efficiently through a line that does not have a center conductor. The type of line used for this purpose is a waveguide. The field configuration in a waveguide is different from that in a coaxial cable because of the missing conductor. Waveguides may be rectangular, circular, or elliptical in cross section.

Electromagnetic energy can be transferred in a line that does not have a center conductor, provided the configuration of the fields is changed to compensate for the missing conductor. The area remaining—which might be considered a pipe—is the actual waveguide.

Metallic walls are not necessary to guide electromagnetic fields in a waveguide, for the fields will be reflected whenever they encounter any kind of a substance which has a different dielectric constant from the substance in which they are traveling. For example, fields can be made to travel through a ceramic rod with little loss of energy. When they encounter the air at the surface of the rod, they are reflected back into the rod.

The three types of losses in rf lines are copper losses, dielectric losses, and radiation losses. Briefly, these losses are described as follows: *Copper loss* is an I^2R loss. It becomes appreciable whenever skin effect reduces the conducting area of the lines. *Dielectric losses* are losses caused by the heating of the insulation between the conductors. *Radiation losses* are losses by energy escaping from rf lines in the form of radiation. Let us consider waveguides from the standpoint of these losses.

261

Copper losses are small in waveguides. Since a 2-wire line consists of a pair of small conductors, the surface area of each is likewise small. Although the surface area of the outer conductor of a coaxial cable is large, the inner conductor is small and produces considerable copper losses. On the other hand, a waveguide has a large surface area, as it does not have a center conductor. Therefore, whenever current flows, the copper losses in the waveguide are less than those in other types of lines.

Dielectric loss of energy is eliminated in a waveguide, since there is no center conductor requiring a solid dielectric support. One of the major reasons for signal attenuation in a coaxial line is the leakage in the dielectric used to support the inner conductor. Because the dielectric material has some resistance, a part of the energy transmitted down the line is absorbed by the insulator.

Radiation losses are less in a waveguide than in a 2-wire line. In a waveguide the fields are contained wholly within the guide itself, just as in a coaxial line. Therefore, only a negligible amount of energy is radiated.

An exact mathematical analysis of the way in which fields exist in a waveguide is quite complicated. But it is possible to obtain an understanding of many of the properties of a waveguide by using the following simple analogy, which shows both how the fields are able to exist in a waveguide and how you can handle them.

To understand the action of a waveguide, assume that the device has the form of a 2-wire line. In this condition there must be some means of supporting the two wires. Further, the support must be a nonconductor, so that no power will be lost by radiation leakage. An efficient way for both insulating and supporting the 2-wire line is shown in Fig. 4-185A. This line is spaced, insulated, and supported by porcelain standoff insulators. At communications frequencies, the absorption of power by the dielectric material (insulators) causes them to act like a low resistance and capacitance.

The equivalent electrical circuit at higher frequencies is shown in Fig. 4-185B. For frequencies of 3000 MHz (3 GHz) and up, a better insulator than porcelain must be used. A superior high-frequency insulator for this purpose is a quarter-wave section of rf line, called a *metallic insulator* (Fig. 4-185C). As there are no dielectric losses in a quarter-wave section of rf line, the impedance at the open end (the junction of the 2-wire line) is very high.

A metallic insulator can be placed anywhere along a 2-wire line. Figure 4-186A shows several on each side of a 2-wire line. A point to note in this line is that the supports are $\lambda/4$ at only one frequency; this limits the high efficiency of the 2-wire line to one frequency only.

The use of several insulators results in the improved conductivity of a 2-wire line when the sections are connected together. This connection is made between the two adjacent insulators through a switch, as shown in Fig. 186B When the switch is open, both quarter-wave sections are excited by the main line. In this condition there will be standing waves on the quarter-wave sections.

When the switch is connected to the same place on each section, the relative phase relationship of the voltages at the connection will be the

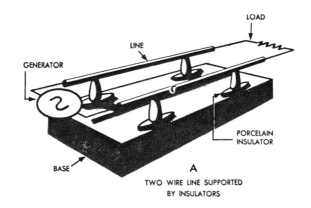

GENERATOR

LINE

LOAD

PORCELAIN
INSULATOR

BASE

A

TWO WIRE LINE SUPPORTED
BY INSULATORS

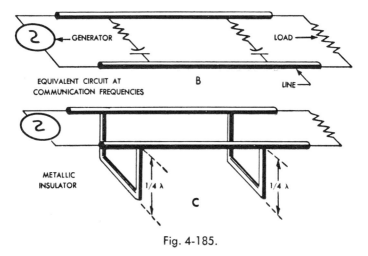

GENERATOR

LOAD

LINE

EQUIVALENT CIRCUIT AT
COMMUNICATION FREQUENCIES

B

METALLIC
INSULATOR

1/4 λ

1/4 λ

C

Fig. 4-185.

same for each section. In this condition the No. 1 section will be excited first by the generator. When the switch is closed, the No. 2 section will be partly excited by the No. 1 section through the switch connection. In this manner, less energy from the main line is required to excite the No. 2 section. The parallel paths shown cause less resistance to exist along a given length of line, and rf energy is transferred with less copper loss.

When more and more quarter-wave sections are added to the line until each section makes contact with the next, the result is a rectangular box in which the line is at the center (Fig. 4-186C). The line itself is actually part of the wall of the box. The rectangular box thus formed is a waveguide. Figure 4-187 illustrates some of the waveguide sections manufactured for specific applications. Special flexible waveguide sections have been developed to be used where the standard fixed-curvature sections cannot be used.

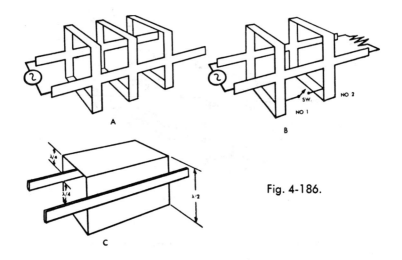

Fig. 4-186.

Cavity Resonators. In ordinary radio work the conventional low-frequency resonant circuit consists of a coil and capacitor that are connected either in series or parallel, as shown in Fig. 188A. To increase the resonant frequency, it is necessary to decrease either the capacitance or inductance, or both. However, a frequency is reached where the inductance is a half-turn coil and the capacitance consists of nothing more than the stray capacitance of the coil (Fig. 4-188B). In this circuit the current-handling capacity and the breakdown voltage for the spacing would be quite low.

The current-carrying ability of a resonant circuit may be increased by adding half-turn loops in parallel. This does not change the resonant frequency appreciably, because it adds capacitance in parallel, which lowers the frequency, and inductance in parallel, which raises the frequency. So the effects of one cancel the effects of the other; the frequency remains about the same.

In Fig. 4-188C several half-turn loops are added in parallel. Sketch D shows several parallel quarter-wave Lecher lines, which are resonant when they are near $\lambda/4$. When more and more loops are added in parallel, the assembly eventually becomes a closed resonant box as

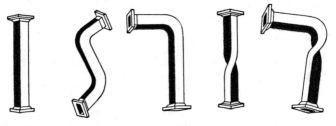

Fig. 4-187.

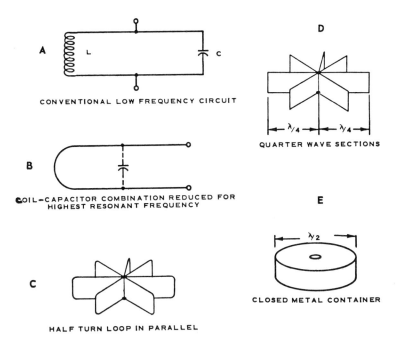

A **CONVENTIONAL LOW FREQUENCY CIRCUIT**

L

C

B **COIL–CAPACITOR COMBINATION REDUCED FOR HIGHEST RESONANT FREQUENCY**

C **HALF TURN LOOP IN PARALLEL**

D **QUARTER WAVE SECTIONS**

$\lambda/4$ — $\lambda/4$

E **CLOSED METAL CONTAINER**

$\lambda/2$

Fig. 4-188.

shown in sketch E. This box, called a *resonant cavity*, is λ/4 in radius, or λ/2 in diameter.

A resonant cavity displays the same resonant characteristics as a tuned circuit composed of a coil and a capacitor. In it there are a large number of current paths. This means that the resistance of the box to current is very low and that the Q of the resonant circuit is very high. While it is difficult to attain a Q of several hundred in a coil of wire, it is fairly easy to construct a resonant cavity with a Q of many thousands. Although a cavity is as efficient at low frequencies as it is at high frequencies, the large size required at low frequencies makes it prohibitive for most applications.

For example, at 1 MHz, a resonant cavity would be a cylinder about 500 ft in diameter! When the frequency is in the vicinity of 10 GHz, the diameter is only 0.6 in.; this makes the cavity smaller than a conventional tuned circuit. Therefore, equipment that operates at a frequency of 3 GHz or above usually uses resonant cavities as resonant circuits.

If there were no losses in the cavity, the waves would bounce back and forth between the end walls indefinitely. However, just as in any resonant circuit, some energy is lost during each cycle. Usually a source of microwave energy feeds the cavity continuously so as to overcome the losses.

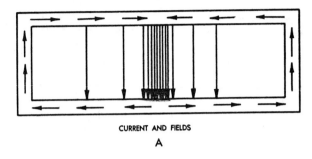

CURRENT AND FIELDS

A

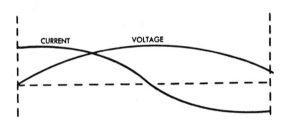

CURRENT   VOLTAGE

VOLTAGE AND CURRENT DISTRIBUTION
ACROSS WIDTH

B

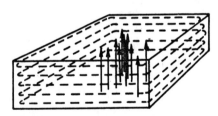

FIELDS IN CYLINDRICAL CAVITY

C

SQUARE CAVITY OR HALF WAVE LENGTH
SECTION OF WAVEGUIDE

D

Fig. 4-189.

A resonant cavity may be compared to a waveguide, since its operation is best described in terms of the fields rather than in terms of the currents and voltages present. As in waveguides, the different field configurations in cavities are called modes. In Fig. 4-189, which shows the *dominant mode* of the cylindrical cavity, note that in A the voltage is represented by E-lines between the top and the bottom of the cavity. The current flows in a thin layer on the surface of the cavity because of

266

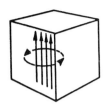

CUBE (Q = 28,000)

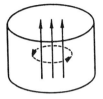

CYLINDER (Q = 31,000)

SPHERE (Q = 26,000)

DOUGHNUT-SHAPED

CYLINDRICAL RING (Q = 26,000)

SECTION OF WAVEGUIDE

Fig. 4-190.

skin effect. The strength of the current is indicated by graduated arrows.

The magnetic field is strong where the current is high. The strongest H-field is at the vertical walls of the cylinder, and the field diminishes toward the center, where the current is zero. This is due to the standing waves on the quarter-wave sections. The E-field is maximum at the center and decreases to zero at the edge, where the vertical wall is a short circuit to the voltage. The curves of E-field and H-field density are shown in Fig. 4-189B. Sketches C and D of that figure show two types of cavities with their fields.

The modes in a cavity are identified by the same numbering system that is used with waveguides, except that a third subscript is used to indicate the number of patterns of the transverse field along the axis of the cavity (perpendicular to the transverse field).

Cavities may have various physical shapes, for any chamber enclosed in conducting walls resonates at several frequencies and produces a number of modes. Note in Fig. 4-190 examples of several types of cavity resonators (or, simply, cavities). The Q of each cavity is indicated. Of those shown, the cylindrical cavity is useful in wavemeters and frequency-measuring devices. The cylindrical ring type is used in superhigh-frequency oscillators as the frequency-determining element. The section of waveguide that is shown is used in some radar systems as a mixing chamber for combining signals from two sources.

4-489. *What is the purpose of a "diversity antenna" receiving system?*

A *diversity antenna* receiving system consists of a receiver and a number of antennas placed a wavelength or two apart. The receiver has a number of rf inputs—one for each antenna—but one common audio stage. Another type of diversity reception system uses several receivers and antennas, with the audio stages of all receivers tied together. The various antennas, with their wide spacing, helps **to reduce the effects of fading.** The greater the number of antennas and rf sections used, the smaller the effects of fading.

A radio wave may be refracted many times between the transmitter and receiver locations, as shown in Fig. 4-191. In this example the radio wave strikes the earth at location *A* and is reflected back to the ionosphere; there it is refracted and returned to earth a second time. Frequently, a sky wave has sufficient energy to be refracted and reflected several times and still be usable, greatly increasing the range of transmission. Because of this so-called

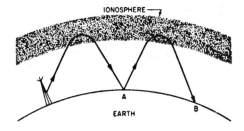

Fig. 4-191.

multiple-hop transmission, transoceanic and around-the-world communications is possible with moderate power (without the use of space satellites).

Fading is a term used to describe variations in signal strength that occur at a receiver during the time a signal is being received. Fading may occur at any point where both the ground wave and the sky wave are received, as shown in Fig. 4-192A. The two waves may arrive out of phase, thus producing cancellation of the usable signal. This type of fading is encountered in long-range communications over bodies of water, where ground wave propagation extends for relatively long distances.

In areas where sky wave propagation is prevalent, fading may be caused by two sky waves traveling different distances and thereby arriving at the same point out of phase, as shown in Fig. 4-192B. Such a condition may be caused by a portion of the transmitted wave being refracted by the *E*-layer while another portion of the wave is refracted by the *F*-layer. A complete cancellation of the signal would occur if the two waves were to arrive 180° out of phase with equal amplitudes. Usually one signal is weaker than the other, and therefore a useful signal (the difference between the two out-of-phase signals) is obtained.

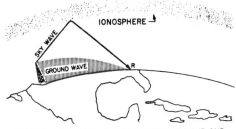

A. FADING CAUSED BY ARRIVAL OF GROUND WAVE AND SKY WAVE AT THE SAME POINT (R) OUT OF PHASE

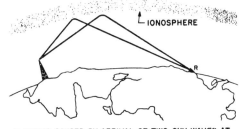

B. FADING CAUSED BY ARRIVAL OF TWO SKY WAVES AT THE SAME POINT (R) OUT OF PHASE

Fig. 4-192.

Variations in absorption and the length of the path in the ionosphere are also responsible for fading. Occasionally, sudden disturbances in the ionosphere cause complete absorption of all sky wave radiation.

Receivers located near the outer edge of the skip zone (where signals are returned from the ionosphere) are subjected to fading as the sky wave alternately strikes and skips over the area. This type of fading sometimes causes the received signal strength to fall to zero.

One method used to help reduce the effects of this fading is to place two or more receiving antennas a wavelength or two apart, each antenna feeding its own receiver (or a different front end of a common receiver) with all receiver audio outputs combined. This process is known as *diversity reception*.

4-490. *Why are insulators sometimes placed in antenna guy wires?*

Insulators are sometimes used to break a long guy wire into smaller segments. Such a practice is extremely beneficial when the guy wire might otherwise act as a resonant line, radiating energy at some harmonic of the actual antenna signal. Similarly, when the guy wire connects to the supporting structure at a place that allows a high degree

269

of coupling between the guy wire and the antenna, the effects of theguy wire can be minimized if its effective length is changed by the insertion of insulators at strategic points along the wire.

4-491. *A relay with a coil resistance of 500Ω is designed to operate when 0.2A (200 mA) flows through the coil. What value of resistance must be connected in series with the coil if operation is to be made from a 110V direct-current line?*

The use of Ohm's law will tell us what resistance value must be used in series with the 500Ω relay coil to allow 200 mA of current to flow. We have two values already—total voltage (110V dc) and total circuit current (0.2A). Since R is equal to E divided by I, we know that the total circuit resistance, including the resistance of the relay coil, is 550Ω. Since the relay coil itself accounts for 500Ω of the required 550Ω, our series resistor must supply the balance of resistance, or 50Ω.

4-492. *What value of resistance should be connected in series with a 6V battery that is to be charged at a 3A rate from a 115V direct-current line?*

The resistor must drop 109V and pass a current of 3A. From Ohm's law, 109 divided by 3 (or E/I) equals 36.33Ω. Thus, the dropping resistor must be about 36Ω.

4-493. *What may cause self-oscillation in an audio amplifier?*

Self-oscillation in an audio amplifier may be caused by interstage coupling of audio signals through circuits other than the coupling circuits designed for the job. Often an amplified signal will feed back to an earlier stage through the power source wiring or badly positioned chassis components. Microphonic (vibration sensitive) tubes provide another source of self-oscillation. The problem can be eliminated with nonmicrophonic tubes, careful layout and shielding, effective bypassing of power leads, and the use of decoupling filters in multistage audio amplifiers.

4-494. *Why are pairs of wires carrying ac heater currents in audio amplifiers twisted together?*

Twisting the two wires together prevents coupling of the 60 Hz component into adjacent circuits. It causes the magnetic fields of the two wires to cancel.

4-495. *Draw a block diagram of a tuned-radio-frequency (trf) receiver.*

The *trf* receiver consists of one or more rf stages, a detector stage, one or more audio amplification stages, a speaker, and the necessary power supply. The block diagram of such a receiver is shown in Fig. 4-193. The waveforms that appear in the respective sections of the receiver are shown below the block diagram.

The amplitude of the AM signal at the input of the receiver is relatively small because it has been attenuated in the space between the transmitter and receiver. It is composed of the carrier frequency and modulation. The rf amplifier stages amplify the waveform, but they do not change its basic shape if the circuits are operating properly. The detector rectifies and removes the rf component of the signal. The output of the detector is a weak signal made up only of the modulation component (envelope) of the incoming signal. The rf amplifier stages

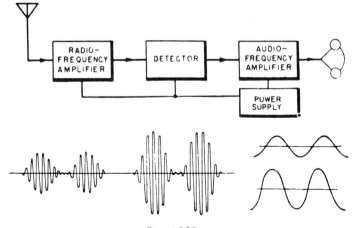

Fig. 4-193.

following the detector increase the amplitude of the af signal to a value sufficient to operate a loudspeaker (or, as shown, earphones).

4-496. *What would be the effects of connecting 110V at 25 Hz to the primary of a transformer rated at 110V, 60 Hz?*

Overheating would be the immediate result. Before long the primary winding would burn through. Low-frequency transformers require considerably greater core masses than higher frequency transformers. The core mass and primary winding resistance (length) of a transformer designed to operate with a 60 Hz input would be inadequate for the slow-changing input voltage of 25 Hz. Inductive reactance is proportional to frequency ($X_L = 2\pi fL$); so a much lower frequency means a much higher current.

4-497. *Draw a diagram of a one-tube audio oscillator using an iron core choke.*

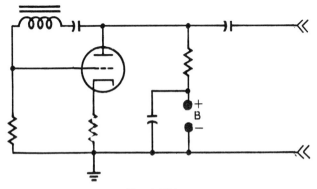

Fig. 4-194.

271

Whenever a portion of the output of an audio amplifier is fed back into the grid circuit in phase, oscillations will start. They will continue as long as in-phase voltage is applied to the grid circuit by the output circuit. This is accomplished in the oscillator circuit of Fig. 4-194 by the use of an iron core choke. Feedback of this kind is called *regenerative* (or *positive*) feedback since it is in phase with the grid voltage.

4-498. *Show by a diagram how a 2-wire rf transmission line may be connected to feed a Hertz antenna.*

Any ungrounded antenna that is one-half wavelength long, or any even or odd multiple thereof, is a Hertz antenna. Hertz antennas showing two different methods of connecting the feedline, together with the equivalent resonant circuits, are shown in Fig. 4-195. For a half-wave dipole, the effective current is maximum at the center and minimum at the ends, while the effective voltage is minimum at the center and maximum at the ends. The voltage and current relationships are similar to those of the simple dipoles shown in the drawings.

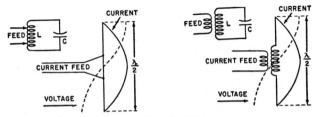

Fig. 4-195.

4-499. *Draw a diagram of a synchronous vibrator power supply and a nonsynchronous vibrator power supply.*

The two typical power supply systems using vibrators are shown in Fig. 4-196. In sketch A a nonsynchronous supply is shown. This type of power supply requires a separate rectifier and filter. Both cold cathode gas-filled tubes and vacuum-tube rectifiers were once used with these vibrator circuits. Recently these rectifiers were replaced with semiconductors. (Of course, the vibrator itself was replaced eventually by a pair of switching transistors.)

Operation of the nonsynchronous vibrator supply can be easily understood by referring to Fig. 4-197. When the battery switch is closed, current flows through the lower half of the primary, the electromagnet, and back to the battery, producing an expanding magnetic field. As the armature (mounted on a flexible reed) is drawn down, the electromagnet is temporarily short-circuited through contact *1*, and it loses its magnetism. The armature is released, permitting the reed to swing back and make contact with terminal *2*. Current now flows through the upper half of the primary and back to the battery. At the same time this is occurring, the magnetic field of the primary, previously established by the current in the lower half winding, is collapsing. The effect of the simultaneous expansion of one field and collapsing of the other is to increase the magnitude of the induced voltage in the secondary.

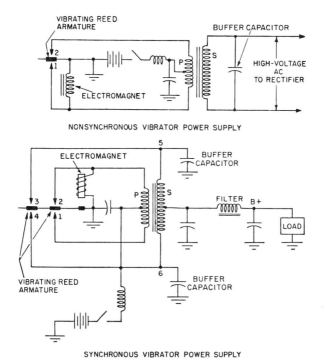

NONSYNCHRONOUS VIBRATOR POWER SUPPLY

SYNCHRONOUS VIBRATOR POWER SUPPLY

Fig. 4-196.

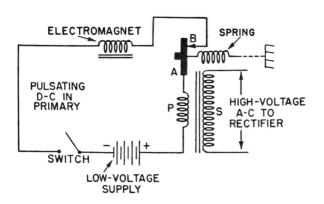

Fig. 4-197.

The synchronous vibrator shown in Fig. 1-196B does not require a rectifier tube (or semiconductor circuit). In this type of vibrator two additional contacts connected to the ends of the secondary windings are synchronized with the contacts in the primary circuit so that rectification takes place.

Contacts 3 and 4 perform the function of rectification. Insofar as the primary is concerned, the action is similar to that of the nonsynchronous vibrator. If, at a given instant, point 5 is negative and the armature is touching points 2 and 3, electrons will flow from point 5 to 3, to ground, and return to the centertap on the secondary by way of the load. A half-cycle later, point 6 is negative and the armature is touching points 4 and 1. Electrons then flow from point 6 through 4 to ground, and return to the centertap of the secondary via the load. Thus, current always flows through the load in the same direction.

4-500. *In accordance with FCC Rules and Regulations, what is the primary standard for rf measurements of radio stations in the various services?*

The adopted frequency standard in the United States is the *primary standard* as transmitted by U.S. Government radio stations WWV, WWVH, and WWVB.

4-501. *What is meant by "carrier frequency" and "carrier wave"?*

In a frequency-stabilized system, **a carrier wave is the sinusoidal component of a modulated wave whose frequency is independent of the modulating wave; or the output of a transmitter when the modulating wave is made zero; or a wave generated at a point in a transmitting system and subsequently modulated by the signal; or a wave generated locally at the receiving terminal which, when combined with the sidebands in a suitable detector, produces the modulating wave.** (The definitions as given above are quoted from FCC Rules and Regulations, Part 2.1.)

Carrier frequency refers **to the number of cycles per second (hertz) the transmitter generating the carrier wave is producing for the purpose of carrying the intended modulation.** Carrier frequency is normally thousands (and sometimes millions) of times greater than modulating frequency and may be converted to wavelength. To convert carrier frequency to wavelength in meters, divide 300 by the frequency in megahertz.

4-502. *Define the following: land station; base station; mobile station; experimental station; domestic fixed service; public correspondence; facsimile; fixed service; industrial radio services; industrial, scientific, and medical equipment; land transportation radio services; public safety radio services; and citizens radio service.*

These definitions are copied verbatim from the Rules and Regulations:

Land station. A station in the mobile services not intended for mobile operations while in motion.

Base station. A land station in the land mobile service carrying on a service with land mobile stations.

Mobile stations. A station in the mobile service intended to be used while in motion or during halts at unspecified points.

Experimental station. A station utilizing Hertzian waves in experiments with a view to the development of science or technique. This definition does not include amateur stations.

Domestic fixed service. A fixed service intended for the transmission of information between points, all of which lie within the 48 [contiguous] states and the District of Columbia, except for the domestic haul of international traffic.

Public correspondence. Any telecommunication which the offices and stations, by reason of their being at the disposal of the public, must accept for transmission.

Facsimile. A system of telecommunication for the transmission of fixed images with a view to their reception in a permanent form.

Fixed service. A service of radiocommunication between specified fixed points.

Inductrial radio service. Any service of radio communication essential to, operated by, and for the sole use of, those enterprises which for purposes of safety or other necessity require radio communication in order to function efficiently, the radio transmitting facilities of which are defined as fixed, land, or mobile stations.

Industrial, scientific, and medical equipment. Devices which use Hertzian waves for industrial, scientific, medical, or any other purposes including the transfer of energy by radio and which are neither used nor intended to be used for radio communication.

Land transportation radio service. Any service of radio communication operated by and for the sole use of certain inland transportation carriers, the radio transmitting facilities of which are defined as fixed, land, or mobiles stations.

Public safety radio services. Any services of radio communication essential to either the discharge of nonfederal-governmental functions relating to public safety responsibilities or the alleviation of an emergency endangering life or property, the radio transmitting facilities of which are defined as fixed, land, or mobile stations.

Citizens radio service. A radio communication service of fixed, land, or mobile stations, or combinations thereof, intended for use by citizens of the United States for private or personal radio communication (including radio signaling, control of objects by radio, and other purposes).

4-503. *What are the frequency ranges included in the following frequency subdivisions: MF (medium frequency), HF (high frequency), VHF (very high frequency), UHF (ultrahigh frequency) and SHF (superhigh frequency)?*

Abbreviation	Frequency band	Frequency range
VLF	Very low frequency	below 30 kHz
LF	Low frequency	30 – 300 kHz
MF	Medium frequency	300 – 3000 kHz
HF	High frequency	3000 – 30,000 kHz
VHF	Very high frequency	30 – 300 MHz
UHF	Ultrahigh frequency	300 – 3000 MHz
SHF	Superhigh frequency	3000 – 30,000 MHz
EHF	Extremely high frequency	30 – 300 GHz

4-504. Identify the following types of emission:
F0. F1. F2. F3. F4, and P0.

The prefix *F* denotes that the transmitter is normally using frequency modulation. Bearing this in mind, the following definitions may be used:

F0 Absence of any modulation.

F1 Telegraphy without the use of audio frequency (frequency shift keying).

F2 Telegraphy by the keying of a modulating audio frequency or audio frequencies or by the keying of the modulated emission (special case: an unkeyed emission modulated by audio frequency).

F3 Telephony.

F4 Facsimile.

P0 Absence of any modulation intended to carry information, when the transmitter is normally used for pulse-type emissions.

4-505. What are the requirements for posting of operator license for (a) the operator performing duties other than or in addition to service or miantenance at two or more stations and (b) the operator performing service or maintenance duties at one or more stations?

R & R Part 2, Sec. 13.74

Posting requirements for operator. (a) Performing duties other than, or in addition to, service or maintenance, at two or more stations. The holder of any class of radio operator license or permit of the diploma form (as distinguished from the card form) who performs any radio operating duties, as contrasted with but not necessarily exclusive of service or maintenance duties, at two or more stations at which posting of his license or permit and shall post at one such station his operator license or permit is required shall post at all other such stations a duly issued verified statement (Form 759). *(b) Performing service or maintenance duties at one or more stations.* The holder of a radiotelephone or radiotelegraph First or Second Class radio operator license who performs, or supervises, and is responsible for service or maintenance work on any transmitter of any station for which a station license is required, shall post his license at the transmitter involved whenever the transmitter is in actual operation while service or maintenance work is being performed: Provided, that in lieu of posting his license, he may have on his person either his license or a verification card (Form 758-F); and provided further, that if he performs operating duties in addition to service or maintenance duties he shall, in lieu of complying with the foregoing provisions of this paragraph, comply with the posting requirements applicable to persons performing such operating duties, as set forth in paragraph (a) of this section, and in the Rules and Regulations applicable to each service

4-506. If service or maintenance logs are required to be kept at a radio station, what entries are required to be entered in the log?

R & R Part 2. Sec. 13.75

Record of service and maintenance duties performed. In every case where a station log or service maintenance records are required to be kept and where service or maintenance duties are performed which may affect the proper operation of a station, the responsible operator shall sign and date an entry in the log of the station concerned, or in the station maintenance records if no log is required, giving:

(a) pertinent details of all service and maintenance work performed by him or under his supervision;

(b) his name and address; and

(b) The class, serial number and expiration date of his license;

Provided, that the responsible operator shall not be subject to requirements of paragraphs (b) and (c) of this section in relation to a station, or stations of one licensee at a single location, at which he is regularly employed as an operator on a full-time basis and at which his license is properly posted.

4-507.   *In communication services such as the public safety radio services, (a) what percentage of modulation is normally required when amplitude modulation is used for radiotelephony and (b) what maximum frequency deviation arising from modulation is permitted when phase or frequency modulation is used for radiotelephony?*

R & R Part 2, Sec. 10.105

Modulation requirements. (a) When amplitude modulation is used for telephony, the modulation percentage shall be sufficient to provide efficient communication and shall be normally maintained above 70 percent on peaks, but shall not exceed 100 percent on negative peaks.

(b) When phase or frequency modulation is used for telephony, the deviation arising from modulation shall not exceed plus or minus 15 kHz form the unmodulated carrier.

(c) Each transmitter first authorized or installed after july 1, 1950, shall be provided with a device which will automatically prevent modulation in excess of that specified in paragraphs (a) and (b) of this section which may be caused by greater than normal audio level: Provided, however, that this requirement shall not be applicable to transmitters authorized to operate as mobile stations with a maximum plate power input to the final radio frequency stage of 3 watts or less.

4-508.   *In communication services such as the public safety radio services, how often should (a) transmitter frequencies be measured, (b) transmitter power be measured, and (c) percentage of modulation be measured? What entries relative to technical measurements are required to be entered in station records?*

R & R Part 2, Sec. 10.108

Transmitter measurements. (a) The licensee of each station shall employ a suitable procedure to determine that the carrier frequency of each transmitter authorized to operate with a plate input power to the final radio-frequency stage in excess of 3 watts is maintained within the tolerance prescribed in this part. This determination shall be made, and the results thereof entered in the station records, in accordance with the following:

(1) When the transmitter is initially installed;

(2) When any change is made in the transmitter which may affect the carrier frequency or the stability thereof;

(3) At intervals not to exceed 6 months, for transmitters employing crystal-controlled oscillators;

(4) At intervals not to exceed one month, for transmitters not employing crystal-controlled oscillators;

(b) The licensee of each station shall employ a suitable procedure to determine that the plate power input to the final radio-frequency stage of each base station or fixed station transmitter authorized to operate with a plate input power to the final radio-frequency stage in excess of 3 watts does not exceed the maximum figure specified on the current station authorization. When the transmitter is so constructed that a direct measurement of plate current in the final radio-frequency stage is not practicable, the plate input power may be determined from a measurement of the cathode current in the final radio-frequency stage. When the plate input to the final radio-frequency stage is determined from a measurement of the cathode current, the required entry shall indicate clearly the quantities that were measured, the measured values thereof, and the method of determining the plate power input from the measured values. This determination shall be made, and the results thereof entered in the station records, in accordance with the following:

(1) When the transmitter is initially installed;

(2) When any change is made in the transmitter which may increase the transmitter power input;

(3) At intervals not to exceed 6 months.

(c) The licensee of each station shall employ a suitable procedure to determine that the modulation of each transmitter authorized to operate with a plate input power to the final radio-frequency stage in excess of 3 watts does not exceed the limits specified in this part. This determination shall be made and the results thereof entered in the station records, in accordance with the following:

(1) When the transmitter is initially installed;

(2) When any change is made in the transmitter which may affect the modulation characteristics;

(3) At intervals not to exceed 6 months.

(d) The determinations required by paragraphs (a), (b) and (c) of this section may, at the option of the licensee, be made by any qualified engineering measurement service, in which case, the required record entries shall show the name and address of the engineering measurement service as well as the name of the person making the measurements.

(e) In the case of mobile transmitters, the determinations required by paragraphs (a) and (c) of this section may be made at a test or service bench; provided the measurements are made under load conditions equivalent to actual operating conditions, and provided further that after installation the transmitter is given a routine check to determine that it is capable of being satisfactorily received by an appropriate receiver.

4-509. *Describe the physical structure of two transistor types and explain how they operate as an amplifier.*

Bipolar Transistors. One of the easiest ways to understand the bipolar transistor is to use equivalent circuits using components we are more familiar with, like resistors and batteries. There is usually some flaw in analogous circuits, though; otherwise, we could do away with the devices we are trying to explain and settle instead for the common components we use for the explanations. Take the simple circuit of battery and resistors shown in Fig. 4-198, for example. Even though these components will not amplify a signal, the circuit will help you to understand what a bipolar transistor does when it is properly connected into a circuit and the proper voltages are applied.

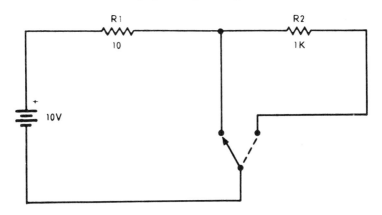

Fig. 4-198.

With the switch in position *1*, a current of one ampere will flow from the battery through resistor *R1*. When the switch is placed in position 2, the current drops because of the increased resistance provided by *R2*. But just suppose that there were some way to maintain the original on ampere of current from the battery when the switch is placed in position 2. Since the resistance of *R2* is 100 times greater than that of *R1*, that one single ampere of current would cause the resistors to dissipate 100 times the power of *R1* alone.

The resistors, of course, cannot perform this power amplification feat; but the bipolar transistor can, which is why the words *transfer resistor* were combined into the word *transistor* in the first place.

The transistor is an intrinsic (pure) semiconductor material that has been doped with impurities. If it is an *npn* transistor, the center of the material is doped with a positive material, and the two ends are doped with a negative material. Thus, there are two junctions—one junction between the center section and the left end, and the other between the center section and the right end. The bipolar transistor gets its identifying name from these two junctions (*bi* meaning *two* and *polar* referring to *junction polarities*). The construction of an *npn* bipolar transistor is shown in Fig. 4-199.

In an *npn* transistor the emitter injects free electrons into the positive-type (*p*-type) base region, where they are attracted across the collector junction by the positive potential applied to the collector.

In summary, the bipolar transistor is a valve that controls the flow of current carriers through the semiconductor crystal material of which it is made. As the current carriers pass through the transistor, they are controlled as easily as if the same current carriers were passing through an electron tube. The transistor's ability to control current carriers and their associated voltages makes it potentially the most useful single element in modern electronics.

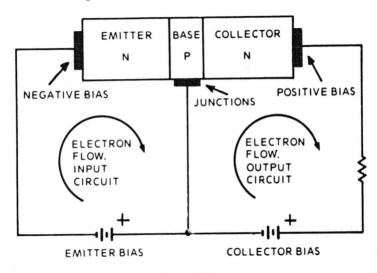

Fig. 4-199.

Field-Effect Transistors. The field-effect transistor, or FET, as it is more commonly known, still is occasionally referred to as a *unipolar transistor*, in contrast to the *bi*polar transistor described earlier. Where a conventional bipolar junction transistor depends on the flow of charge carriers (donors, or electrons, and acceptors, or holes), a field-effect device operates with the flow of but one type—either electrons or holes.

It is not difficult to understand the field-effect transistor if you think of it as an ordinary piece of wire whose conductivity can be altered in response to an electric field. In this analogy the source and drain elements represent the two ends of the wire, and the gate element is the means by which the variations in the electric field are introduced.

The wire itself, in our analogy, is a good conductor only because it is made of a material that has an excess of free electrons in its basic atomic structure. If the resistivity of the wire itself could be changed, the effect would be the same as placing a resistor in the line. Suppose, for instance, that you had some method of gradually turning a highly conductive silver wire into a silk thread. It is easy to see that, at one extreme (silver), the wire's resistance would be virtually zero. The resistance would gradually increase as the wire's characteristics took on those of the silk thread. As silk, of course, the resistance of the line would be infinitely high, and no amount of applied voltage could induce current to flow. The basic reason for this change in resistivity (or conductivity, depending on your viewpoint) is the difference in the wire material's number of available free electrons. If there were some way to *deplete* the wire of its free electrons, there would be none left to dislodge and cause to migrate. And the result would be no current flow. On the other hand, if there were some means to increase the number of free electrons in the wire's material, conductivity would be *enhanced*. This is where the *field effect* comes in. When an intrinsic semiconductor material is doped either with a donor impurity or an acceptor impurity, the material becomes potentially a good conductor. (Donor impurities make the semiconductor an n-type material; acceptor impurities make it a p-type.)

The most important point is that the availability of charge carriers within a semiconductor can be enhanced or depleted by an electric field created within the semiconductor. The field and how it works can be best understood by observing the very simplified cross-sectional view of the FET in Fig. 4-200. In this particular FET the conductive element is a narrow channel created by doping the semiconductor with n-type impurities. The n-type semiconductor is surrounded by a p-type sleeve, which forms the gate electrode.

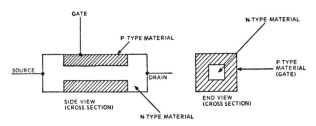

Fig. 4-200.

When the source and gate are shorted together and a positive voltage is applied to the drain, the FET becomes nothing more than a reverse-biased pn junction that prevents current from flowing in the gate connection. But what also happens is that the n-channel within the p-material's circumference is subject to the pn junction's field. At high drain-to-source voltages, this field depletes the channel of almost all of its free electrons, which prevents the flow of current along the channel. That is why the part of the channel lying within the gate's control area is sometimes referred to as the *depletion region*.

Owing to the short circuit at the source end (between source and gate), the field is negligible here. But it is extremely strong at the far end of the channel (between gate and drain). As the voltage is reduced and the electric field decreases, the *n*-channel becomes conductive again, and current flows freely from drain to source.

Amplification results when a load resistor is placed in the output (drain) circuit and a modulated gate voltage is applied, as shown in Fig. 4-201. The input signal varies the conductivity of the depletion region and effectively controls the current supplied by the source. Current through the load resistance produces an output voltage that is proportional to the input but significantly larger.

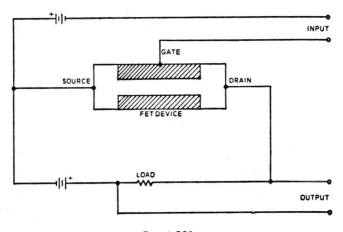

Fig. 4-201.

4-510. *Draw a simple schematic diagram of a 2-stage audio amplifier using transistors.*

The 2-stage audio amplifier shown in Fig. 4-202 is a direct-coupled amplifier with built-in compensation for an inferior microphone.

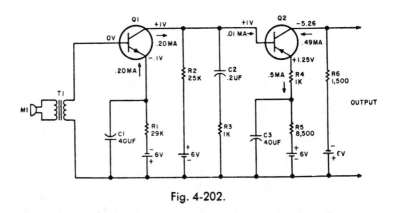

Fig. 4-202.

By direct-coupling transistor $Q1$'s output to the input of $Q2$, use of a coupling capacitor is avoided. Coupling capacitors, like transformers, tend to attenuate the low frequencies.

Transformer $T1$ couples the output of the microphone ($M1$) to the base of transistor $Q1$, which is the first amplifier. Resistor $R1$ is the *emitter swamping* resistor (overcomes variations in resistance of base−emitter junction): capacitor $C1$ is the bypass for $R1$. Collector load resistor $R2$ develops the output signal. Capacitor $C2$ and resistor $R3$ constitute a low-pass filter. The signal is amplified again by transistor $Q2$. Resistor $R4$ produces negative feedback. Resistor $R5$ is the swamping resistor of the second audio amplification stage. Capacitor $C3$ bypasses the ac signal around resistor $R5$. Collector load resistor $R6$ develops the output signal.

4-511. *Describe briefly the construction and purpose of a waveguide. What precautions should be observed in the installation and maintenance of a waveguide to insure proper operation?*

A waveguide is the microwave-frequency equivalent of a transmission line. It consists of metal **conduit so constructed that effective direction of contained microwaves is achieved, and such waves can be transferred from one point to another with very little loss.** It is extremely important **to position the waveguide so that it will not be dented or punctured.** A dent in a waveguide creates an impedance mismatch comparable to the mismatch in a coaxial line resulting from crimping. Another important physical consideration is the actual joining of the waveguide sections. **All joints should be soldered or brazed completely, with no unsoldered or open areas around the joint.** Unsoldered areas can develop oxides that build up a resistivity different from that of the main body of the waveguide, which would result in nonuniform characteristics that cause excessive losses through increased radiation resistance.

4-512. *Describe the physical structure of a multianode magnetron and explain how it operates.*

Since the exact theory of cylindrical multianode magnetrons is more difficult to understand than that of the plane form, the plane form is discussed first.

Plane-Form Magnetrons. To understand the operation of the plane-form magnetron, consider a magnetron oscillator that is composed of a continuous planar cathode and a segmented anode of which the alternate sections are connected to the opposite sides of its tank circuit. In Fig. 4-203, which shows this magnetron, note that the alternating electric field is sketched in the space between the cathode and anode at the instant when alternate anode segments are at their maximum positive and negative values.

Important considerations in the operation of this magnetron are: (1) which electrons tend to sustain oscillations, (2) which electrons tend to absorb energy, and (3) the probable electron paths. In this connection, consider an electron in a uniform electric field directed as shown in *region 1* in Fig. 4-203. The direction of the resultant field is obtained by adding the ac and dc fields that correlate at this point. (The dc field, which is not shown, is directed downward.) The approximate direction of the electric field and the path of the electron are shown in Fig. 4-204A.

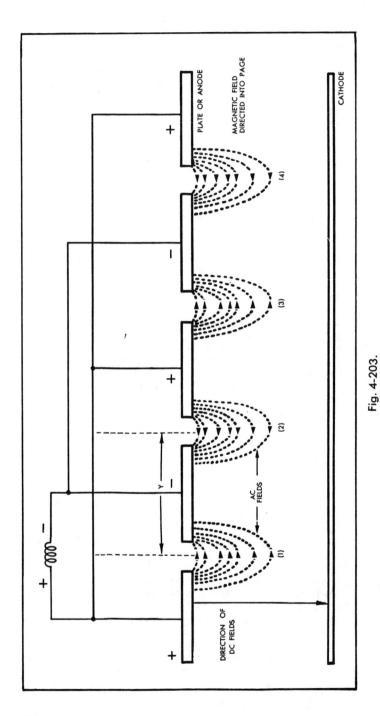

Fig. 4-203.

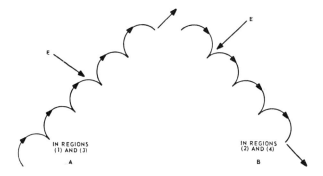

Fig. 4-204.

As shown in this figure, the electron makes cycloidal paths. Since the general progression of a cycloid is always at right angles to the resultant electric field, these cycloids progress upward and to the right with the magnetic field directed into the page. But an electron in a uniform field whose direction is the same as the resultant shown for region 2 in Fig. 4-203 would progress downward and to the right as shown in Fig. 4-204B. The direction of the uniform electric field is also indicated.

Since the electron of diagram A moves, on the average, from cathode to anode, it must absorb energy from the source of the steady field. This same electron, however, tends to deliver energy to the alternating field, since it moves in a direction that is opposed by the field of the tank circuit. Because the average velocity (v) of an electron does not change as it progresses toward the anode, it is a very efficient means for converting energy from the dc sources into energy of oscillation for the tank circuit. By the same reasoning, the electron in region 2 of Fig. 4-302 tends to absorb energy from the alternating field and to transfer it to the steady field.

Whenever oscillation is to be maintained, the electron following the path in sketch A must be made to continue its path to the anode (plate). The other electrons—the ones that absorb energy—must be removed from the field quickly. An electron following the path in sketch B, starting from the cathode with a small velocity, will strike the cathode before completing its first loop. Had the fields of regions 1 and 2 been static, the electron of sketch A would tend to turn downward as it approached region 2. Since the fields are alternating, this will not necessarily be the case. In fact, if the left-to-right velocity of the electron of sketch B is such that it arrives in region 2 in exactly one-half cycle, it will encounter there exactly the same kind of field that it encountered in region 1 one-half cycle earlier.

Thus, if this electron, shown in the magnetron in Fig. 4-302, continues to progress distance Y from left to right during each half-cycle, it will go all the way to the anode, following a path similar to that of an electron in sketch A of Fig. 4-204. This condition is necessary for oscillation. Oscillation is sustained since the electron of sketch A contributes energy to the tank circuit for a much longer time than the electron of sketch B takes energy away from the tank circuit.

Multianode Magnetron. The cylindrical (or cavity) magnetron is analogous to the planar magnetron rolled up into a circle. The number of segments (anodes) that may be used in it varies widely. As many as 32 have been tried on certain occasions. Here, for simplicity, the discussion considers a magnetron with six segments. Figure 4-205A shows the circuit of a 6-anode magnetron and the approximate ac field between the segments. Figure 4-205B is its equivalent circuit.

To qualitatively understand the performance of the multianode magnetron, consider the sketch in Fig. 4-205A. Since the ac field is much narrower near the cathode than near the anode in the cylindrical magnetron (shown in Fig. 4-205A), the linear distance (the distance that the electron must progress around the cathode per anode segment) is less near the cathode than near the anode. If the theory of the plane magnetron is to be applicable to the cylindrical unit, it will be necessary to choose an effective, or average, value of Y. This value is one-sixth of the circumference of the circle halfway between the cathode and anode. These assumptions about Y and the electric field lead to the same resonance condition as before.

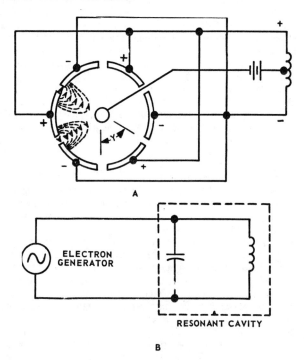

Fig. 4-205.

In developing the discussion of cylindrical multianode magnetrons, it is desirable to see how some simpler systems of several resonant cavities work. The *buncher* and *catcher* cavities of a nonreflex klystron and a single velocity-modulated electron beam are examples. The theory of buncher and catcher cavities is beyond the scope of this study guide.

Figure 4-206 depicts a 2-cavity system consisting of two resonant cavities tuned to the same resonant frequency, with an electron beam passing through both sets of cavity grids. Assume that the first cavity is excited at its resonant frequency through the coaxial input line and that the electron beam is velocity-modulated. With a properly adjusted system and the correct electron velocity and modulation level, the beam should be bunched at the grids of the second cavity. This being true, oscillations will occur in the second cavity when a large signal is present. The phase of the second-cavity oscillations must be such that the bunched electrons are decelerated as they pass through the cavity grids. In the deceleration of the electron beam, energy is given to the cavity.

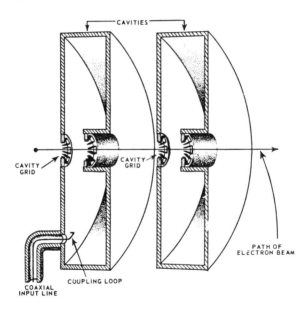

Fig. 4-206.

At any other phase, oscillation will be unaffected by the electron beam if bunched electrons pass through the cavity grids when both are at the same potential. And oscillation at any other phase will transfer energy from the cavity to the beam if the bunched electrons pass through the cavity grids at an accelerated rate. Therefore, the electron beam has the capability of transferring energy from one cavity to another.

287

If the second cavity is moved toward the first, the electron beam then is "underbunched" at the grids of the second cavity; that is, bunching is not complete. As there is only partial bunching, electron flow is not smooth, but the second cavity is able to absorb energy from the beam. By absorbing energy, the phase of oscillation (frequency) in the second cavity automatically adjusts itself to slow the greatest possible number of electrons. The remaining electrons are accelerated as they pass the cavity grids when the second grid is more positive than the first grid. The second cavity actually slows down over half the electrons that pass through its grid and accelerates less than half the electrons. This reduces the average velocity of the electrons and adds to the velocity modulation of the beam.

In a cavity system that has more than two cavities, it is possible for each cavity, from the second cavity on, to absorb energy from the beam and improve the velocity modulation of the beam for the next cavity. A small portion of the energy comes from the source that feeds the first cavity; most of the energy comes from the electron beam source. Each cavity reduces the average velocity of the electrons in the beam. The system is very sensitive to adjustment, as the energy absorbed by each cavity is dependent upon the relation of the spacing between cavities and the bunching distance.

Let us take a multicavity system, with all six cavities tuned to the same frequency, and arrange it as shown in Fig. 4-207. Assume that a beam of electrons is influenced so that the beam travels in a closed loop. This loop passes through the associated grids of each cavity. Any irregularity or roughness in the electron beam will cause one or more of the cavities to ring (or oscillate). This modulates the beam, and energy

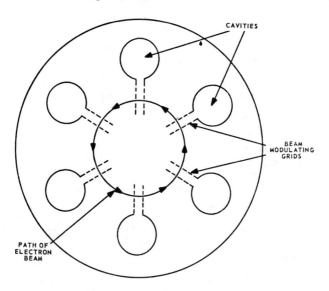

Fig. 4-207.

is delivered to all cavities. **The velocity of the electron beam is the source of the microwave energy, and the transfer of energy is a result of the reduction of the average electron velocity. As long as there is a continuous supply of accelerated electrons, while slow electrons are removed from the system a certain amount of energy will be transferred from the electron beam to all of the cavities. This rf energy is in the form of electric and magnetic fields.** The cavity magnetron operates the same way.

Figure 4-207 illustrates one of the more common magnetron anodes, a hole-and-slot type. Although six cavities are shown, magnetrons with other numbers and shapes of cavities are not uncommon. Other types of magnetron anodes are shown in Fig. 4-208. Sketch A shows a slot anode, B a vane anode, and C a rising-sun anode. The choice of one anode type over another is based largely on design specifications, as all types behave the same way.

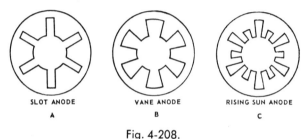

SLOT ANODE   VANE ANODE   RISING SUN ANODE

A   B   C

Fig. 4-208.

Summary. By using multiple anodes (or a segmented anode), you can make the electrons work against an alternating electric field that is crosswise to the steady field. In this way it is possible to get the electrons to go all the way to the anode without much increase in kinetic energy. This results in high power and high efficiency.

Calculation shows that there are more electrons that give energy to the tank circuit than electrons that remove energy from the tank circuit. Further, it shows that, on the average, each of the former electrons gives more energy to the tank circuit than each of the latter takes away.

Magnetrons in use at present have a wavelength range from about 50 centimeters down to less than 1 centimeter.

Efficiencies of present-day magnetrons, at moderate power, have values from 30% to 40% and, at powers greater than 200 kW, from 50% to 60%.

The actual tuned circuit will resonate at several different frequencies, each of which corresponds to a distinct phase difference between anodes (or anode segments).

Magnetrons are readily adaptable to pulsed modulation.

4-513. *Describe the physical structure of a klystron tube and explain how it operates as an oscillator.*

The klystron shown in Fig. 4-209 can operate as an amplifier or oscillator over a relatively small tunable range. It depends on the changes introduced in the velocity of a stream of electrons, using the

289

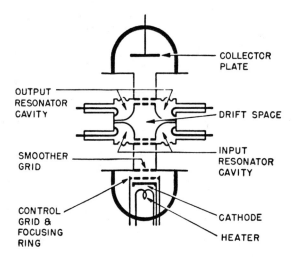

COLLECTOR PLATE

OUTPUT RESONATOR CAVITY

DRIFT SPACE

SMOOTHER GRID

INPUT RESONATOR CAVITY

CONTROL GRID & FOCUSING RING

CATHODE

HEATER

Fig. 4-209.

transit time between two points to produce an alternating current. In this sense the tube is similar to a magnetron, since both are velocity-modulated. In use as an oscillator, the power delivered to the resonant cavity is used in the input resonator.

The cathode emits a stream of electrons that is smoothed out to uniform velocity by the *smoother* grid. An rf field is applied to the grids of the input cavity resonator. This imposes a varying velocity on the stream, retarding or speeding it up. In the drift space the electrons that have been speeded up will overtake those that have been slowed down on an earlier cycle. This produces a still stronger pulsation in the electron stream as it passes through the grids of the output cavity resonator. The latter takes power from the stream if it is tuned to the frequency of the pulsation. Therefore, amplification takes place between the input and output resonator cavities. The tube can be used as an oscillator if some power from the output is coupled back to the input in the proper phase.

Small tubes called *reflex klystrons* have been designed solely for use as local oscillators in microwave superheterodyne receivers. They use a single cavity resonator, the electron stream passing through it twice—once in a forward direction and then (reflected) back through the cavity again. They can be tuned over a wide range of frequencies but have limited power output. These are the klystrons most frequently used in microwave equipment.

Both the klystron and magnetron make use of electron streams or beams to operate at microwave frequencies. They transfer energy to cavity resonators through these electron streams. The cavity resonator is a device with an inherently high ratio of reactance to resistance. In other words, it is equivalent to a tuned circuit with a very high Q. At a resonant frequency of 10 GHz, a Q of 5000 is common.

The advantages of the klystron as compared with the magnetron are many. First, physical considerations are simplified. In the magnetron the cathode and anodes are included in the frequency-determining system can be designed independently of the rf section to handle the desired power. Cooling methods are simplified, since most of the heat is generated in the collector and can be dissipated by a cooling system without consideration of the rf portion of the tube. Figure 4-210 illustrates a 3-cavity klystron.

From the standpoint of electrical performance, the klystron again excels. The magnetron is a power oscillator and is the frequency-determining element of most complex radar systems. But its frequency stability is dependent on the combination of a magnetic and an electric field, either of which is subject to variations over short periods of time.

The disadvantages of the klystron are chiefly the circuit complexities of the transmitter. A series of amplifiers are inserted between the frequency-determining oscillators and the power amplifier klystron. These stages must be individulally tuned when the operating frequency is chosen or changed. Most of these stages are pulsed, and synchronizing problems arise. Power supply requirements are also increased. The bulk of the equipment required in a microwave station using a high-power klystron limits the mobility of such a system, and the microwave installation employing klystrons is either a fixed station or one of limited mobility. Regardless of the disadvantages, the klystron system's complexity and bulk are justified in that they insure consistent performance that excels that possible with magnetrons.

4-514. *Describe three methods for reducing the rf harmonic emission of a radio-telephone transmitter.*

Methods of reducing harmonic interference include:

1. Proper tuning of the driver stage. Excessive rf drive to the final rf amplifier is an invitation to harmonic generation. The final tank should be driven with no more excitation power than that required to produce full power output.
2. Installation of a low-pass filter in the transmission line attenuates signals above the intended transmission frequency and allows signals of longer wavelengths to pass.

3. Use of adequate shielding in the output tank circuit. A Faraday screen works well in suppressing harmonic radiation because it prevents coupling by any means other than the inductive coupling used to transfer the required signal from the tank to the antenna.

4-515. *A ship radiotelephone transmitter operates on 2738 kHz. At a certain distance for the transmitter, the 2738 kHz signal has a measured field of 147 mV/m (millivolts per meter). The second-harmonic field at the same point is measured at 405 μV/m (microvolts per meter). To the nearest whole unit, in decibels, how much has the harmonic emission been attenuated below the 2738 kHz fundamental?*

First, convert the fields to the same units of measurement—to microvolts. The fundamental measures 147,000 μV and the harmonic measures 405 μV. There are a couple of handy rules of thumb when

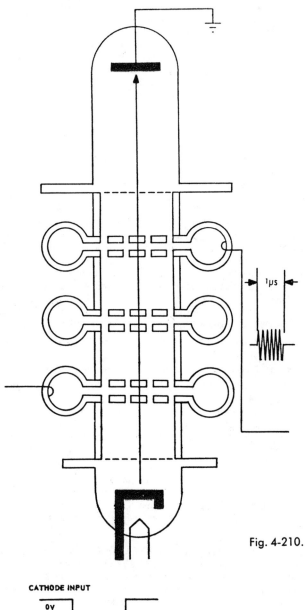

Fig. 4-210.

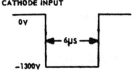

working with decibels, but they are a bit different for voltage than for power. When determining decibels for power, add 10 dB for every order-of-magnitude (tenfold) increase; when determining decibel levels for voltage or current, add 20 dB for every order-of-magnitude increase. For power, add 3 dB for every doubling of power; for voltage or current, add 6 dB for every doubling (and subtract 6 dB for every halving of value).

Since 147,000 μV divided by 405 μV is about 363, we know that the fundamental signal is 363 times stronger than the second-harmonic signal. One way to attack the problem is to assign a value of 1.0 for the harmonic signal and a value of 363 for the fundamental. When the value of 1.0 changes to 10, the voltage increase is 20 dB; when it changes to 100, the voltage increase is twice 20 dB, or 40 dB. You can double the value of 100 and add 6 dB more; so 200:1 = 46 dB. Doubling it again would increase the signal 6 dB more; hence we know the answer to be less than 52 dB and more than 46 dB. We know the signal attenuation is in the neighborhood of 50 dB. By using logarithms it is found to be 51.2. Since the FCC uses multiple-choice questions, the less formal method used here will be accurate enough for the exam.

A convenient means for double-checking your answer is to double the basic unit until you arrive at a value that is an order of magnitude smaller than the ultimate signal. In this case the ultimate signal is 363 (since the other signal is assigned a value of 1.0). So you can double the 1.0 (add 6 dB) and get 2, double that (add 6 dB more) and get 8, double 8, (6 dB more) and get 16, double 16 (6 dB more) and get 32. This is the nearest we can come to an order of magnitude below 363. Now add all the 6 dB increases; since there are five 6 dB increases, the total is 30 dB. Now increase the 32 value by an order of magnitude to add 20 more decibels. The result shows that a 320 value would yield a decibel figure of exactly 50 dB. Since 320 is below 363, we know that the decibel figure we want is slightly in excess of 50 dB (51.2 dB).

4-516. *Draw a block diagram of a superheterodyne receiver capable of receiving amplitude-modulated signals and indicate the frequencies present in the various stages when the receiver is tuned to 2450 kHz. What is the frequency of a station that might cause image interference to the receiver when tuned to 2450 kHz?*

Figure 4-211 shows the block diagram. The rf amplifier is tuned to the frequency of the station (2450 kHz). This amplifier feeds its signal into the mixer, which also accepts a 2855 kHz signal from the local oscillator. The output of the mixer is the difference between the two signals, or 455 kHz. The detector separates the audio component from the 455 kHz signal, and passes the resultant to the audio (af) amplifier.

If a superheterodyne receiver having an intermediate frequency of 455 kHz is tuned to receive a station frequency of 2450 kHz, and the local oscillator has a frequency of 2905 kHz, the output of the i-f amplifier may contain two interfering signals—one from the 2450 kHz staiton and the other from an image station of 3360 kHz (2450 + 2 × 455 = 3360 kHz). The same receiver tuned to receiver a 1540 kHz station has a local oscillator frequency of 1995 kHz. The output of the i-f amplifier contains the station signal (1995-1540 = 455 kHz) and an image signal (2450 − 1995 = 455 kHz). Thus, the 2450 kHz signal is an image heard simultaneously with the 1540 kHz signal.

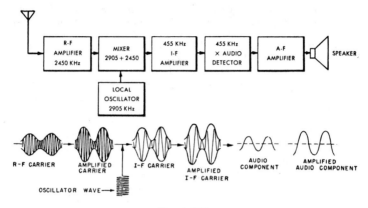

Fig. 4-211.

4-517. *Show, by a diagram, how to connect a wave trap in the antenna circuit of a radio receiver to attenuate an interfering signal.*

Wave traps, sometimes used in the antenna circuits of radio receivers, are forms of band elimination filters. The two general types of wave traps are the parallel-tuned filter and the series-tuned filter. These traps are used to prevent interference—for example, from a nearby station that is strong enough to be heard over the entire frequency band of the receiver. The trap reduces the signal strength from the unwanted station so that it will not be heard except when the receiver is tuned to that station.

The parallel circuit, in series with the antenna in Fig. 4-212A, is tuned to resonance at the frequency of the undesired signal.

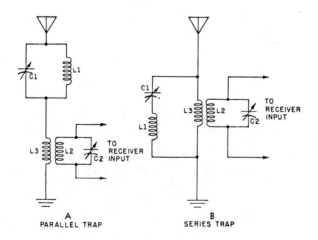

Fig. 4-212.

The parallel wave trap presents a high impedance to currents of this unwanted frequency and allows currents of other frequencies to enter the receiver with only slight attenuation.

The series circuit, connected as shown in sketch B of Fig. 4-212, is tuned to resonance at the frequency of the undesired signal. The impedance of the series circuit (C1L1) at resonance is low. Hence, these unwanted frequencies will be bypassed to ground around the receiver input transformer primary (L3). The desired frequencies will be essentially unaffected because either L or C acts as a high impedance when not in resonance.

The sketches show how the filters are connected to the receiver.

Supplement to Element 3

The FCC has published a supplemental set of questions for updating those appearing in the preceding section. In the supplemental list the FCC departs from the practice of simply posing questions in a random fashion; instead, questions are organized by subject. It should be emphasized that these supplementary questions today account for the great majority of the questions that will actually be asked on the FCC exam. Thus, you should study this section thoroughly in preparing for the exam.

ALTERNATING & DIRECT CURRENT

5-1. *What is the relationship between impedance and admittance? Between resistance and conductance?*

Admittance is the reciprocal of impedance; conductance is the reciprocal of resistance. In ac circuits, admittance is comparable to dc conductance, and **impedance is comparable to dc resistance.** Admittance and conductance are both expressed in mhos (*mho* is *ohm* spelled backwards). Conductance in mhos may be obtained by dividing unity by the resistance value in ohms, and admittance may be obtained by dividing unity by impedance in ohms. Conductance is the conductivity of the conductor's material, multiplied by the cross-sectional area and divided by the length.

5-2. *Draw a circuit composed of a 12V battery with three resistors (10Ω, 120Ω, and 300Ω) arranged in a pi network. Then answer the following questions: (1) What is the total current as well as the current through each resistor? (2) What is the voltage across each resistor? (3) What power is dissipated in each resistor, and what is the total power dissipated by the entire circuit?*

The circuit is shown in Fig. 5-1. It should be emphasized that a *pi network* of resistors refers strictly to the physical configuration (the resistors in the circuit resemble the Greek letter π), so the battery might be connected anywhere. In the circuit shown, the battery is connected across the 300Ω resistor. The circled letter *A* represents an ammeter that can measure the total circuit current.

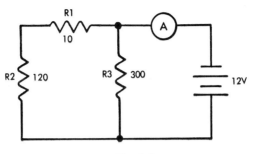

Fig. 5-1.

1. The total circuit current is 132.3 mA. The current through the two series resistors (R1 and R2) is 92.3 mA, and the current through R3 is 40 mA.
2. The voltage drop across R3 is the full 12V potential supplied by the battery, the voltage drop across R1 is 923 mV (0.923V), and the drop across R2 is 11.077V. Note that the total of drops in any series circuit always equals the supply voltage (in accordance with Kirchhoff's law).
3. The total power dissipated is 1.5877W, which can be obtained by any of three methods: multiplying total resistance by the square of total current, multiplying total voltage by total current, or dividing the square of total voltage by total resistance. The individual quantities of power dissipated must add up to the calculated total value, 1.5877W. In the circuit shown, resistor R1 dissipates 0.0852W (85.2 mW), resistor R2 dissipates 1.0225W, and resistor R3 dissipates 0.4800W (480.0 mW).

5-3. *Draw a circuit composed of a voltage source of 100V at 1000 Hz, in series with a 12.73 mH coil and an 80Ω resistor. If the voltage drop across each component is 70.7V and the total current is 884 mA, what is the inductive reactance of the circuit? The impedance? Explain the phase relationships of the circuit.*

The circuit of Fig. 5-2A is the one asked for. There is an ammeter connected in series with the circuit elements to allow measurement of total circuit current. Voltmeters are connected in parallel with the individual components to measure resistor voltage (E_R) and inductor voltage (E_L). A voltmeter is also connected in parallel with the whole series circuit to allow measurement of the total voltage (E).

In the analysis of any problem, the first step in a logical procedure is the listing of all the known facts. From the circuit and meter readings of Fig. 5-2A, the following facts are known:

$E = 100$V	$E_L = 70.7$V
$f = 1000$ Hz	$E_R = 70.7$V
$R = 80$Ω	$I = 884$ mA
$L = 12.73$ mH	

The only quantities of importance as yet undetermined are the inductive reactance, circuit impedance, and circuit phase angle.

From the information available, inductive reactance can be found by an application of Ohm's law, $I = E \, X$. Transposing, $X = E \, I$. Since the total current in a series circuit is also the coil current, $X_L = 70.7/0.884$, or 80Ω. Inductive reactance could also be found by application of the standard equation $X_L = 2\pi f L$.

For determination of phase angle (θ), note that $\tan \theta = X \, R$; that is, $\theta = $ arc tan $X_L \, R$, or arc tan $80/80$. The angle whose tangent is unity is $45°$; hence $\theta = 45°$.

By Ohm's law for ac circuits, impedance (Z) is equal to total voltage divided by total current. In this case $Z = 100/0.884$, or 113. The total impedance could also be determined by trigonometry.

The vector diagram (Fig. 5-2B) illustrates the voltage, current, and phase relationships of the circuit. Current, being a common quantity, is graphed in the standard reference position. Resistor voltage is seen to be in phase with **L**, while the inductor voltage is leading **I** by $90°$. The total voltage—which is the same as the source voltage—is the vector sum of the component voltages and ($\sqrt{70.7^2 + 70.7^2}$) is leading the total current by $45°$

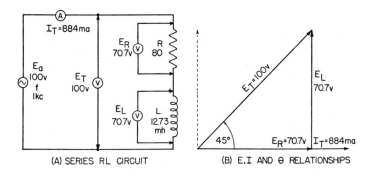

(A) SERIES RL CIRCUIT   (B) E, I AND θ RELATIONSHIPS

Fig. 5-2.

5-4. *What is the relationship between wire size and resistance of the wire?*

The longer the wire, the higher its resistance; the larger the diameter, the lower the resistance.

In the diagram of Fig. 5-3, the letter l is the length of a conductor parallel to the direction of current through the conductor, and A is the cross-sectional area of the conductor perpendicular to the direction of current. The resistance of the specimen may be found from the formula $R = \rho \, (l/A)$, where the ρ is the resistivity (a constant depending on the material of the specimen), l is the length of the specimen parallel to electron flow, and A is the cross-sectional area.

In the equation $R = \rho \, (l/A)$, letting l equal one centimeter (1 cm) and A be equal to a centimeter squared, we see that R is equal to ρ. Therefore, the resistivity of any material is the resistance of a cube of the material one square centimeter on each side (Fig. 5-4).

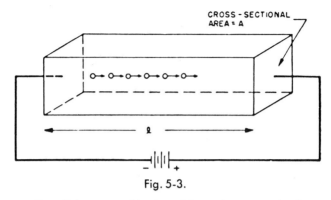

Fig. 5-3.

Since R is expressed in ohms. l in centimeters. and A is square centimeters. from the initial equation we see that ρ has the dimensions of

$$\frac{\text{resistance} \times \text{area}}{\text{length}} = \frac{\text{ohms} \times \text{square centimeters}}{\text{centimeters}} = \text{ohm-centimeters}$$

However. it is customary to speak of ρ as the resistance of one cubic centimeter of the material.

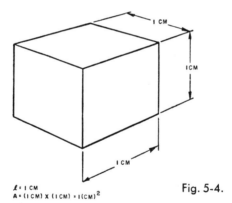

$l = 1$ CM
$A = (1 \text{ CM}) \times (1 \text{ CM}) = 1(\text{CM})^2$

Fig. 5-4.

Obviously, the more free electrons a conductor has, the greater will be the current for any given value of applied voltage. Thus, the greater the number of free electrons a conductor has, the lower will be its resistance. Since the drift velocity of the electrons depends on the number of collisions with other electrons and molecules, then the greater the length of the conductor, the greater will be the number of collisions and, consequently, the smaller the drift velocity. However, the current is proportional to the drift velocity, and therefore its value will be decreased with an increase in the length of conductor.

Also, the greater the cross-sectional area of a conductor, the smaller the number of collisions due to the decreased density of electrons and molecules. Thus, the greater the cross-sectional area, the lower the resistance. And so we know that resistance varies directly with the length and inversely with the area of the conductor.

5-5. *Why is impedance matching between electrical devices an important factor? It is always to be desired? Can it always be attained in practice?*

In the transfer of power from electrical sources to their load, the impedance of the load must equal or match the internal impedance of the source for maximum transfer of power. The simple dc circuit and table of Fig. 5-5 will illustrate this principle. A 10V battery with an internal resistance R_B of 1Ω feeds an external circuit of variable resistance R_0. When R_0 is 4Ω, the total resistance of the circuit is 5Ω (R_B+R_0), the current in the circuit is 2A, and the voltage drop across the load (E) is 8V. Then the power absorbed by the load is E_L times I, or 16W. The power dissipated in the battery as heat is E_B multiplied by I, or 4W. When R_0 s 3Ω, total resistance is 4Ω, I is 2.5A, and E_L is 7.5V. The power absorbed by the load is 18.75W and by the battery, 6.25W. When R_0 is 2Ω, total resistance is 3Ω, I is 3.33A, and E_L is 6.67V. The power absorbed by the load is 20W, and by the battery, 10W. When R_0 is 1Ω, total resistance is 2Ω, I is 5A, and E_L is 5V. The power absorbed by the load is 25W, and by the battery, 25W. When R_0 is less than 1Ω, power falls off in the load as indicated in the table. Thus, the greatest power is

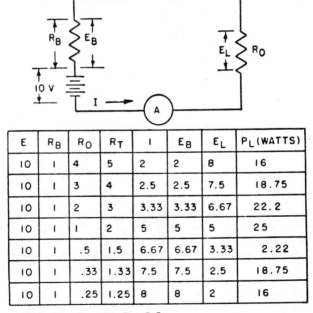

E	R_B	R_O	R_T	I	E_B	E_L	P_L(WATTS)
10	1	4	5	2	2	8	16
10	1	3	4	2.5	2.5	7.5	18.75
10	1	2	3	3.33	3.33	6.67	22.2
10	1	1	2	5	5	5	25
10	1	.5	1.5	6.67	6.67	3.33	2.22
10	1	.33	1.33	7.5	7.5	2.5	18.75
10	1	.25	1.25	8	8	2	16

Fig. 5-5.

delivered to the load when the impedance of the load is equal to the internal impedance of the source.

To answer the FCC question, then: **Impedance matching between electrical devices is an important factor because it governs the percentage of total power delivered to the load**. It is always to be desired if circuit efficiency is a criterion of circuit performance. Unfortunately, it **cannot always be achieved** in practice, because impedance is frequency dependent. A 4Ω speaker in an audio circuit, for example, will only be precisely matched to the amplifier at one frequency.

5-6. *A loudspeaker with an impedance of 4Ω is working in a plate circuit which has an impedance of 4000Ω. What is the impedance ratio of an output transformer to match the plate circuit to the speaker? What is the turns ratio of the transformer?*

The ratio of impedances across a transformer varies as the square of the turns ratio; conversely, the **turns ratio is equal to the square root of the impedance ratio**. The impedance ratio of the transformer in question is 4000/4, or 1000/1, or simply 1000. The **turns ratio would then be about 32 to 1**, or simply 32 ($\sqrt{1000} = 31.62$).

5-7. *Compare some properties of electrostatic and electromagnetic fields.*

The properties of electrostatic and electromagnetic fields are compared in the table below.

Electrostatic Fields

When a charged body is brought into close proximity with another charged body, there is a force that causes the bodies to repel or attract one another. If the charged bodies possess the same sign of charge, the force will be one of repulsion; if they possess opposite signs of charge, they will attract each other.

Charged bodies develop an electrostatic field such as illustrated in Fig. 5-6. The field consists of lines of force, as illustrated by the arrows in the sketch.

The force between charges is described by Coulomb's law: The force existing between two charged bodies is directly proportional to the product of the charges and inversely proportional to the square of the distance separating them.

The electric field associated with a pair of charged bodies is capable of storing energy. The energy stored in a common capacitor is contained within the electrostatic field.

Electromagnetic Fields

When a magnet is is brought into close proximity with another magnet, there is a force that causes the magnets to attract or repel one another. If the two magnets are positioned so that they are end to end, with like poles proximal to each other, the force will be one of repulsion; if the adjacent poles are opposite in polarity, the magnets will attract each other.

Magnetized bodies develop a magnetic field such as that illustrated in Fig. 5-7. The fields consists of lines of force, as illustrated by the filings pictured.

The force between magnetic poles varies directly as the product of the strength of the poles and inversely as the square of the distance between them.

The magnetic field associated with an electromagnet, or current-carrying conductor, is capable of storing energy. The energy stored in a common inductor is contained within the electromagnetic field.

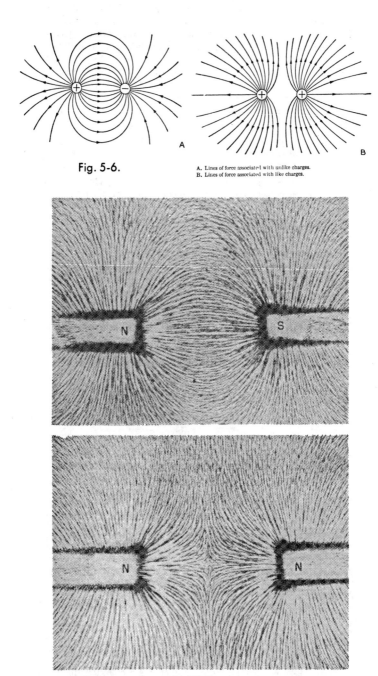

Fig. 5-6.

A. Lines of force associated with unlike charges.
B. Lines of force associated with like charges.

Fig. 5-7.

5-8. *In what ways are interstage connecting leads susceptible to electromagnetic fields?*

Component leads, like interstage wiring, tend to pick up, by induction or capacitance, signals at the frequency of the adjacent electromagnetic field. This stray signal pickup is almost always undesirable and can be eliminated by several methods, including: (1) judicious placement of signal leads, particularly in stages where amplifier stages are to follow, (2) shielding high-impedance audio leads (which tend to be more susceptible to stray fields than other leads), (3) shielding sections that are likely to be the source of electromagnetic signals, and (4) twisting together wires carrying ac.

5-9. *Define the term* **reluctance.**

Reluctance is the opposition a material offers to magnetic lines of force. Mathematically, reluctance is $\mathcal{R} = l/(\mu A)$, where $\mathcal{R}$ is the symbol for reluctance, l is the length of the core in centimeters, μ is the permeability of the core material, and A is the area in square centimeters.

It can be seen from the above equation that reluctance is a direct function of the length of the core and an inverse function of the cross-sectional area and permeability of the material used. For example, if a core with a low reluctance is desired, it should be physically large in cross-sectional area and made of material with a high permeability.

5-10. *In what way does an inductance affect the voltage—current phase relationship of a circuit? Why is the phase of a circuit important?*

The current lags the applied voltage in an inductive circuit by an angle of 90° and leads the induced voltage (counter emf) by an angle of 90°. The induced voltage is always of opposite polarity to the applied voltage.

Any change in current through a coil causes a corresponding change in the magnetic flux around the coil. If the current change is sinusoidal, the induced voltage will also have the form of a sine wave. **Because the current changes at its maximum rate when passing through its zero value (at 0°, 180°, and 360°), the flux change is also greatest at those times.** Figure 5-8 shows an inductive circuit (sketch A) and three sine waves (sketch B) representing current (I), voltage (E), and counter emf (induced voltage). Notice that the counter emf is at its peak at zero current.

Lenz' law states that counter emf always opposes a change in current. When the current is rising in a positive direction at 0°, the counter emf is of opposite polarity to the applied voltage and opposes the rise in current. When the current is falling toward its zero value at 180°, the polarity of the counter emf is such as to keep the current from falling. Thus, the counter emf can be seen to lag the current by 90°. The dc resistance of the coil is small, and the principal opposition to the current through the coil is the counter emf. The applied voltage is slightly larger than the induced voltage.

Knowing the phase relations of a circuit is extremely important in radio and electronics. **Knowledge and control of phase allow precise control of amplification, oscillation, and other functions.** Oscillators

303

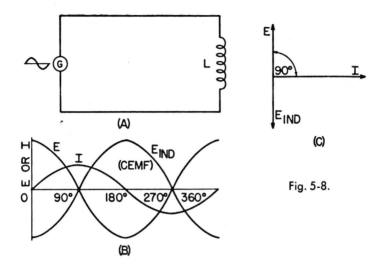

(A)

(C)

(B)

Fig. 5-8.

require in-phase feedback of the output signal to the input circuit to bring about oscillation. Distortion in audio amplifiers is controlled and limited by the use of out-of-phase signal feedback. Interelectrode capacitances are canceled by feeding back out-of-phase signals that are equal in magnitude and opposite in polarity to the unwanted and inadvertently coupled signals. Semiconductors are made to handle much larger currents than their device ratings simply because they can be made to switch circuits as the circuit currents and voltages pass through zero. Antennas are fed at current-maximum points, so that maximum transfer of energy is made from the transmission line to the antenna and little signal is lost by radiation from the line. Without knowledge and control of phase relationships in practical electronic circuits, our exploitation of electrical phenomena would be considerably limited and restricted.

5-11. *Draw two cycles of a sine wave on a graph of amplitude versus time. Assume a frequency of 5 MHz.*

1. *What would be the wavelength of one cycle in meters and centimeters?*
2. *How many degrees does one cycle represents?*
3. *How much time would it take for the wave to rotate 45°, 90°, and 280°?*
4. *If there were a second harmonic of this frequency, how many cycles thereof would be represented on this graph?*
5. *On the same graph draw two cycles of another sine wave leading the first by 45°.*
6. *What would be the velocity of this wave or any other electromagnetic wave in free space?*

Figure 5-9 is a drawing of two cycles of a 5 MHz sine wave plotted on a horizontal time axis and a vertical amplitude axis.

1. **Wavelength in meters** may be determined by dividing the speed of light (in millions of meters) by the sine-wave frequency (in

304

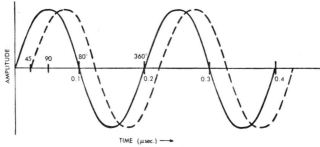

Fig. 5-9.

megahertz), or $\lambda = c \, f$. The speed of light is 300 million meters per second, and the sine-wave frequency is 5 MHz. The wavelength, then, is 300/5, or 60 m. Since there are 100 cm for each meter, the wavelength in centimeters would be

$$60 \times 100, \text{ or } 6000 \text{ cm}.$$

2. **One cycle always represents 360°**, on this graph or any other.

3. Since there are 5 million cycles in each second, we know that the duration of a single cycle (360°) is one five-millionth of one second, or $^1/_5$ microsecond, or 0.2 microsecond (μsec). It would take 0.0025 μsec for the wave to vary over 45°. We know this because we know that 45° represents one-eighth of a full 360° cycle. Thus, the time for 45° is $^1/_8 \times 0.2 \, \mu$sec. A 90° rotation is one-fourth of the full 360° value of 0.2 μsec, or 0.05 $-$ ec. A rotation of 280° represents a time of $280/360 \times 0.2 \, \mu$sec, or 0.15555 μsec.

4. If there were a **second harmonic** of this frequency, there **would be four cycles on the graph** instead of two. The second harmonic of any frequency is twice the frequency of the referenced signal. The second harmonic of 5 MHz is 10 MHz.

5. In the graph the solid wave leads the broken-line wave by 45°.

6. **The velocity of any electromagnetic wave in free space is almost 300 million meters per second.** Stated in more familiar terms, the speed of light is 186,000 miles per second.

5-12. *Explain how to determine the sum of two equal vector quantities having the same reference point but whose directions are 90° apart, 0° apart, and 180° apart? How does this pertain to electrical currents or voltages?*

To illustrate the application of vectors, two sine waves ($E1$ and $E2$) are shown in Fig. 5-10; sine wave $E2$ is phased to lag sine wav $E1$ by 90°.

In constructing the vector diagram, one of the sine waves is chosen as a reference, and a vector representing this wave is constructed in

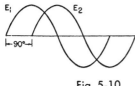

Fig. 5-10.

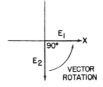

305

standard position on the X-axis. Once the vector representing E1 has been placed on the diagram, a second vector can be drawn to represent E2. This vector must be place on the diagram so as to show E2 lagging 90° behind E1.

Since the vectors rotate in a counterclockwise direction, vector **E2** is drawn pointing downward along the Y-axis. The complete vector diagram appears as though a high-speed photograph were taken just as reference vector **E1** arrived at the X-axis. Vector **E2** then appears to be trailing along 90° behind **E1**.

It is frequently necessary to add out-of-phase voltages or currents in the process of solving ac circuit problems. The vector lends itself well to such solutions and is a valuable timesaving tool.

In Fig. 5-11 two vectors ($\mathbf{E}_a$ and $\mathbf{E}_b$) are to be added together. These vectors are shown in sketch A as they would normally appear on a vector diagram. To obtain the sum of these two vector quantities, the tail of the second vector ($\mathbf{E}_b$) is placed at the head of the first vector ($\mathbf{E}_a$), as shown in sketch B. This must be done without changing the direction or the magnitude of either vector. A third vector is then drawn from the tail of the first vector to the arrowhead of the second vector. This third vector is called the *resultant* and is the sum of the two originally plotted vector quantities.

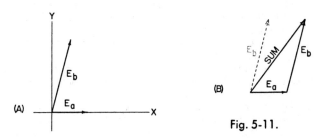

Fig. 5-11.

Using this procedure, any number of vectors can be added. Each vector is placed, in turn, with its tail at the arrowhead of the previous vector. The sum is always found by drawing a vector from the tail of the first vector to the head of the last vector.

A simplified procedure for adding two vectors consists of constructing a parallelogram in which the vectors form two adjacent sides. In Fig. 5-12 the resultant is to be obtained for the two vectors shown. A parallelogram is developed by constructing line CD parallel to OE, and a line ED parallel to vector **OC** (Fig. 5-12B). A vector is now drawn from O to D. This third vector, **OD**, is then the sum of the two original vectors.

If this method is compared to that used in Fig. 5-11, the end result of the two methods is seen to be identical. In using the parallelogram method, however, the vectors must be added in pairs. Three vectors cannot be added simultaneously. In adding more than two vectors by the parallelogram method, two of the vectors are added, and then their resultant is added to a third vector. This process is continued until all the vectors have been added and a final resultant obtained.

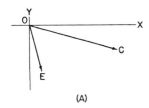 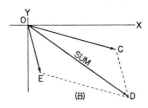

Fig. 5-12.

5-13. *Explain how the values of resistance and capacitance in an RC network affect its time constant.*

The time constant (in seconds) of an *RC* network is equal to the product of capacitance (in farads) and resistance (in ohms). Thus, the higher the value of either quantity, the longer the time constant. The growth and decay of output voltages in an *RC* network follows an *exponential* rather than linear curve, as shown in the universal *RC* time constant chart of Fig. 5-13. The percentages in the chart are referenced to the total supply voltage. In other words, it takes one time constant for a capacitor in an *RC* network to charge to a value that represents 63.2% of the applied supply voltage. Yet, it takes more than five such time constants for the capacitor to attain a charge that is equal to the full voltage. The descending curve shown in the figure represents decay time for an *RC* network.

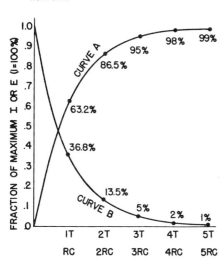

Fig. 5-13.

5-14. *Explain how the values of resistance and inductance in an RL network affect its time constant.*

The time constant (in seconds) of an *RL* network is equal to the inductance (in henrys) divided by the circuit resistance (in ohms).

307

Thus, the higher the value of inductance, the longer the period. Conversely, the higher the value of resistance, the shorter the time constant. The growth and decay curves for an *RL* network are exponential, as with *RC* networks. The universal time constant chart in Fig. 5-14 shows the relative time it takes to develop various percentages of output voltages. It also shows the voltage decay curve as a mirror image of the voltage rise curve.

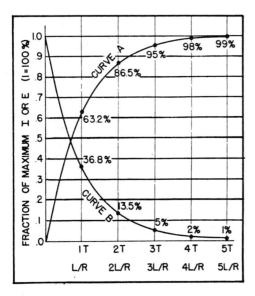

Fig. 5-14.

5-15. *Explain the theory of molecular alignment as it affects magnetic properties of materials.*

One of the simplest theories of magnetism is that a piece of iron or steel consists of millions of tiny elementary magnets. These tiny magnets, which are so small that they cannot be seen even with a very powerful microscope, may consist of atoms or molecules so aligned as to form iron or steel crystals. Before a piece of iron or steel has been magnetized, these tiny magnets may be thought of as being jumbled, with no definite order of crystal orientation, as shown in the sketch of Fig. 5-15A. If the north pole of a magnet is drawn over the bar, it attracts the south poles of the tiny magnets and turns them so that they will align themselves in a given direction (Fig. 5-15B). This definite alignment of molecular magnets will give the bar a definite north pole at one end and a south pole at the other end.

5-16. *Explain how inductance produces transformer action.*

When a conductor is placed within a magnetic field of a circuit in which the expanding or collapsing lines of force cut the conductor, a voltage will be induced in it. In this connection, consider coils *1* and *2* of Fig. 5-16 placed side by side. Assume that battery **B** is connected to coil *1* and

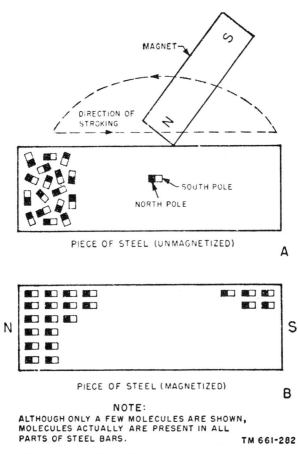

MAGNET

S

N

DIRECTION OF STROKING

SOUTH POLE

NORTH POLE

PIECE OF STEEL (UNMAGNETIZED)

A

N

S

PIECE OF STEEL (MAGNETIZED)

B

NOTE:
ALTHOUGH ONLY A FEW MOLECULES ARE SHOWN,
MOLECULES ACTUALLY ARE PRESENT IN ALL
PARTS OF STEEL BARS.

TM 661-282

A. Bar showing jumbled condition of tiny magnets before magnetization.
B. Bar showing orderly alinement after magnetization.

Fig. 5-15.

galvanometer G (an instrument for indicating the amount and direction of current flow) is connected to coil 2. As long as the current flowing in coil *1* is steady, the magnetic field likewise will be steady, and there will be no voltage induced in coil 2. However, if you change variable resistance R, there will be a change in the current in coil *1*. As a result, the flux through coil 2 will change, and the galvanometer will show a momentary deflection. The action in which a change in current in one coil induces a voltage in another coil is called *mutual induction*.

If, in a short period of time, the current in coil *1* in Fig. 5-16 changes and causes a change in the flux linking coil 2, the voltage induced in coil 2 is an emf of mutual induction. Its average value may be obtained mathematically.

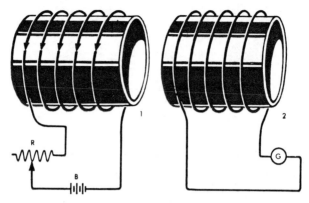

Fig. 5-16.

Even though coils *1* and *2* are close together, not all of the flux produced by coil *1* links coil *2*. The proportion that does link coil *2* is indicated by the symbol *k*, called the *coefficient of coupling*, which is always less than unity.

The flux in coil *1* may be assumed to be proportional to the current in that coil. The change in flux, then, is proportional to the change in current. **The inductance of a coil of many turns is much greater than the inductance of a coil of a single turn, since the induced voltage is dependent not only on the change in flux but on the number of turns through which the flux passes.** Inserting an iron core in a coil greatly increases the inductance; however, the increase is not constant over a wide range of current.

When two coils are placed close together, the relation between the mutual inductance (M) of two coils and their individual inductances ($L1$ and $L2$) is

$$M = k\sqrt{L1\,L2}$$

The transfer of energy from one circuit to another through mutual induction is referred to as *transformer action*.

5-17. *How should electrolytic capacitors be connected in a circuit in relation to polarity? Which type of low-leakage capacitor is used most often in transmitters?*

The positive plate of an electrolytic capacitor typically consists of aluminum foil covered with an extremely thin film of oxide formed by an electrochemical process. The thin oxide film acts as the dielectric of the capacitor. A thin strip of paper or gauze, impregnated with the electrolyte, contacts the oxide. The electrolyte serves as the negative plate of the electrolytic capacitor. A second strip of aluminum foil is placed against the electrolyte to provide electrical contact to the negative electrode. When the three layers are in place, they are rolled up into a cylinder as shown in Fig. 5-17.

The principal disadvantages of **electrolytic capacitors are** that they **are polarity sensitive and have a low leakage resistance.** Should the positive plate be accidentally connected to the negative terminal of the

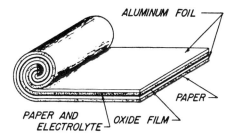

Fig. 5-17.

source, the thin oxide-film dielectric will dissolve and the capacitor will become a conductor (the plates will become shorted). Since electrolytics are polarity sensitive, **their use is ordinarily restricted to dc** circuits or circuits where a small ac voltage is superimposed on a dc voltage.

For **transmitter applications oil capacitors** are quite common where high capacitance values are required along with low leakage and imperviousness to high voltages. Oil-filled capacitors are normally nothing more than paper capacitors that are immersed in oil. The oil-impregnated paper has a high dielectric constant, which lends itself well to the production of capacitors with a high value. Many capacitors use oil with another dielectric material to prevent arcing between the plates. If an arc should occur between the plates of an oil-filed capacitor, the oil will tend to reseal the hole caused by the arc. These types of capacitors are often referred to as *self-healing* types.

5-18. *A certain power company charges 7 cents per kilowatt—hour. How much would it cost to operate three 120V lamps connected in parallel, each with an internal resistance of 100Ω for 24 hours?*

The current each lamp draws is equal to the supply voltage divided by the resistance, in accordance with Ohm's law. If the supply voltage is 120V and the resistance of each lamp while burning is 100Ω, the current drain per lamp is 1.2A. Total power consumed by each lamp is equal to the product of current squared and resistance, or I^2R, which is $1.2 \times 1.2 \times 100 = 144W$. Three such lamps, then, consume three times the individual power of 144W, or 432W. The total work expended to produce 432W for 24 hours is 432×24, or 10.368 watt-hours. Converting watt-hours to kilowatt-hours is simply a matter of dividing by 1000 or substituting a decimal point for the comma in the above number: 10.368 kilowatt-hours. If the cost of operation is 7 cents per kilowatt-hour, the total cost of operating the three lamps for 24 hours is 0.07×10.368, or $0.726—above 73 cents.

5-19. *The output of an amplifier stage having a voltage gain of 30 dB is 25V. What is the input voltage level?*

Each time the voltage is doubled, there is a voltage gain of 6 dB. Since 30 dB represents five such 6 dB increases, or voltage doublings, the 25V figure is the result of five voltage doublings. Hence, the input voltage may be obtained by halving the 25V figure five times. Halving 25V results in a value of 12.5V; twice, 6.25V; three times, 3.125; four times, 1.5625V; and five times, 0.78125V. The input value, then, is 781.25 mV.

With voltage, an order-of-magnitude (tenfold) increase is equal to 20 dB. In other words, increasing the input level from 0.78125V to 7.8125V would be a 20 dB increase. Increasing the level to 78.125V would be a total level jump of 40 dB. Close approximations of gain can be made without reference to logarithm tables if the "doubling" and "orders of magnitude" rules for power and voltage changes are kept in mind.

5-20. *What is the impedance of a parallel circuit composed of a pure inductance and a pure capacitance at resonance? Of a series circuit at resonance?*

In an ideal parallel resonant circuit, the line current is zero. Since impedance is equal to applied voltage divided by circuit current, which is zero, the impedance must approach infinity.

In a series resonant circuit, the impedance is equal to the resistance. If there is pure capacitance and pure inductance with no resistive elements, the resistance can be assumed to be zero (or near zero), and the impedance is likewise close to zero.

5-21. *What is the Q of a circuit? How is it affected by the circuit resistance? How does the Q of a circuit affect bandwidth?*

During the time the magnetic field is being established in an inductor, the ratio of the energy stored to the energy lost is referred to as the ratio of *quality*, or Q. Sometimes the term is referred to as a coil's *figure of merit*. **The Q of the inductor is equal to the ratio of the** *inductive reactance* **to the** *effective resistance in series with it*, **and it approaches a high value as R approaches a low value.** Thus, the more efficient the coil, the lower the losses in it and the higher the Q.

In terms of the impedance triangle in Fig. 5-18, Q is equal to the tangent of the phase angle between the hypotenuse (Z) and base (R). As phase angle approaches 90° tan θ approaches infinity, and the coil losses approach zero.

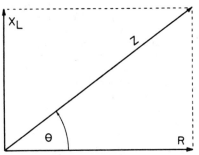

Fig. 5-18.

The Q of a coil does not vary extensively within the operating limits of a circuit. It would seem, from the equation $Q = X_L/R$, that since inductive reactance is a direct function of frequency, Q also must be a direct function of frequency. Such is not the case, however. It is true that as frequency increases, the inductive reactance increases; but as frequency increases, the effective resistance of the coil also increases. Since Q is an inverse function of the effective resistance, the net effect of a frequency increase is to leave Q relatively unchanged.

The higher the Q, the sharper the bandwidth. If the circuit Q is low, the amplification at resonance is relatively small and the circuit does not discriminate sharply between the resonant frequency and the frequencies on either side of resonance, as is shown by the lower curve in Fig. 5-19. The range of frequencies included between the two frequencies at which the current drops to 70% of its value at resonance is the *bandwidth for 70% response*. When the current is 70% of maximum, the power is one-half of maximum. Hence, the bandwidth is often referred to as the *half-power bandwidth*.

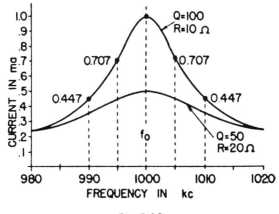

Fig. 5-19.

Frequencies beyond the 70% or half-power point are considered to produce no usable output. The series resonant circuit is seen to have two half-power points—one above resonance and one below. The two points are designated *upper cutoff frequency* and *lower cutoff frequency*. in Fig. 5-20 these points are labeled $f1$ and $f2$. The range of frequencies between theses two points comprises the bandwidth. Figure 5-20 illustrates the bandwidths for high- and low-Q series resonant circuits. The bandwidths (B) may be determined by the equation $B = f_0/Q$, or center frequency divided by circuit Q. Bandwidth may also be determined by subtracting the lower cutoff frequency from the upper cutoff frequency, or $B = f2 - f1$.

The terms *bandwidth*, *bandpass*, and *selectivity* may also be applied to parallel resonant circuits, because the shape of the resonant curve that describes the impedance variations with respect to frequency has the same general structure as the curve used for series

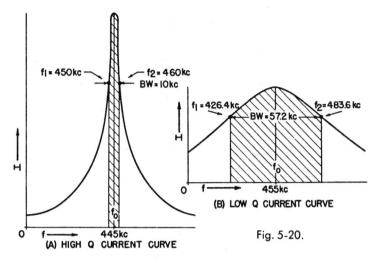

f₁ = 450kc — f₂ = 460kc
BW = 10kc

f₁ = 426.4kc   BW = 57.2 kc   f₂ = 483.6 kc

f₀

O   f ⟶   455kc
(B) LOW Q CURRENT CURVE

O   f ⟶   445kc
(A) HIGH Q CURRENT CURVE

Fig. 5-20.

resonant curves. Curves of a high-Q and a low-Q circuit are shown in Fig. 5-21. Notice that in the high-Q circuit, the selectivity is good. The low-Q curve shows a wider bandwidth, hence poor selectivity. A comparison pertaining to the overall merit of each curve cannot be made, because each curve has its advantages and disadvantages when applied to a particular cirucit.

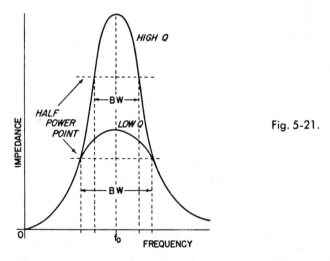

Fig. 5-21.

5-22. *Draw a circuit diagram of a low-pass filter composed of a constant-k and an m-derived section.*

A constant-k filter is a conventional RC filter in which the R has been replaced with an L element. An m-derived filter is one in which one of the C or L elements is converted to a tuned circuit. The term m is a

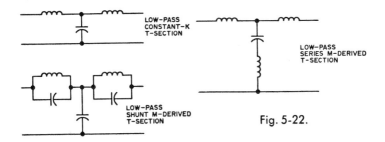

Fig. 5-22.

variable used in the design of the filter and refers to the ratio between the filter's cutoff frequency and the resonant frequency of the tuned circuit.

Figure 5-22 shows constant-k paralle-resonant m-derived, and series resonant m-derived filter networks. If a capacitor is placed across either of the two inductances in the top left filter shown, the low-pass filter becomes a combination m-derived (with tuned circuit) and constant-k (series L, shunted C) network.

If both inductors are shunted with a capacitance, the filter becomes an m-derived filter, as shown in the lower left sketch. It takes a complete series L, parallel C, parallel L to make a constant-k section.

5-23. *In general, why are filters used? Why are bandstop, high-pass, and low-pass filters used? Draw schematic diagrams of the most commonly used filters.*

Filters are used to control the frequencies to be transferred from one circuit to another, much as filtration paper is used to control the amount of impurities circulating in an automobile's engine oil. A bandstop filter, also referred to as a *band rejection* filter, is shown in Fig. 5-23A. Here, the resonant band of frequencies find the series resonant circuits (S and S') to be a low-impedance path and the parallel resonant circuit (P) a high-impedance path; thus, the resonant band of frequencies is rejected, or shunted to ground. All other frequencies find S and S' high-impedance paths and P a low-impedance path; accordingly, they pass from input to output with little opposition. In B the resonant-band frequencies find the parallel resonant circuit (P and P') high-impedance paths and the series resonant circuit (S) a low-impedance path. Thus, the resonant band of frequencies is passed from input to output with little opposition, while all other frequencies find P and P' low-impedance paths and S a high-impedance path. Accordingly, frequencies other than those desired are rejected.

Figure 5-24 shows the basic low-pass and high-pass filters. In sketch A high frequencies at the input meet a relatively high inductive reactance in L and a low capacitive reactance in C. So high frequencies are stopped by L and short-circuited by C, and low frequencies meet little opposition in L and high opposition in C. This is a low-pass filter, typically used in the rf output circuit of transmitters to prevent the transfer of harmonics and spurious frequencies.

Sketch B of Fig. 5-24 shows the basic high-pass filter. The theory of operation is basically the same as for the low-pass filter, except that the

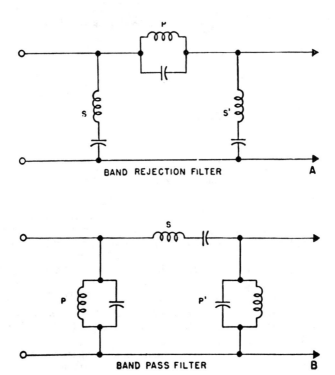

BAND REJECTION FILTER A

BAND PASS FILTER B

Fig. 5-23.

filter offers little opposition to frequencies above the design frequency and high opposition to frequencies below the design frequency. High-pass filters are used in such places as television receivers to prevent the passage into the TV set of frequencies below the television band. Amateur and other radio services might otherwise cause interference to these receivers, since such services may be operating on frequencies close to but below the lowest desired television frequency.

The schematics shown in Fig. 5-25 illustrate practical low-pass and high-pass filters.

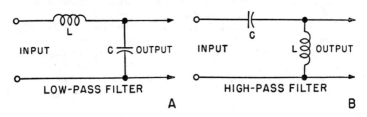

LOW-PASS FILTER A

HIGH-PASS FILTER B

Fig. 5-24.

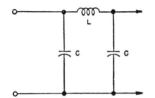

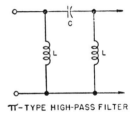

Fig. 5-25.

π-TYPE LOW-PASS FILTER

π-TYPE HIGH-PASS FILTER

5-24. *In an iron-core transformer, what is the relationship between the transformer turns ratio and primary-to-secondary current ratio: between turns ratio and primary-to-secondary voltage ratio, assuming no losses within the transformer itself?*

The primary-to-secondary current ratio is equal to the reciprocal of the turns ratio. Since *total power in* is equal to *total power out* (neglecting losses), the primary-to-secondary voltage ratio must be equal to the turns ratio itself.

5-25. *What prevents high currents from flowing in the primary of an unloaded transformer?*

The ability of a transformer to transfer energy from its primary to its secondary through flux linkage depends on inductive coupling or high mutual inductance. This means that the inductance of each winding should be as great as possible. If the transformer were ideal (the windings showing infinite inductance), the inductive reactance of the primary would also be infinite for any ac frequency. At the usual 60 Hz power-line frequency, however, the inductance of the primary must be large to generate an appreciable reactance. Thus, if the iron core of a 60 Hz transformer were removed, the inductive reactance would fall and the primary circuit would show a high current even with no load on the secondary.

This initial *magnetization current* in the primary of a transformer under no load should be kept as low as possible, since it represents a loss. The greater the inductance, the greater the reactance and the less magnetization current needed to set up the required flux linkage.

5-26. *How is power lost in an iron-core transformer? In an air-core transformer?*

An ideal transformer would be 100% efficient: that is, the ratio of power output compared to power input would be 1:1. Practical iron core transformers are not, however. 100% efficient: but, when carefully designed, they will show an efficiency that ranges from 95% to about 98%. This high efficiency is possible in a transformer because of the careful attention devoted to minimizing the effective losses due to flux leakage, hysteresis, eddy currents, flux saturation of the core, copper losses of the coil windings, and losses from distributed capacitances.

The inductance of an air-core winding on a transformer is inherently lower than the inductance of a comparable winding of an iron core. Thus, the I^2R losses in the primary of such a transformer are higher. Since flux leakage is also inherently higher with air-core windings, less energy is coupled from the primary to the secondary of

317

such transformers. The current in the primary and secondary of transformers must flow through the dc resistance of the wire itself. A certain amount of power is lost through heat—particularly with air-core transformers—since this represents a true I^2R loss. However, transformers carrying appreciable amounts of power use wire of large cross section to cut down heat losses, which tend to increase the resistance of wires in general and, where an iron core is used, lower the permeability of the core material.

Since a high percentage of flux linkage (low flux leakage) at power-line frequencies requires a large inductance, some compromise between size of core and number of windings must be made. A huge core and small windings for a given inductance would show little copper loss; but the transformer would be heavy and awkward, and core loss would be considerable.

On the other hand, a small core reduces core loss, but it increases copper loss because of the increased number of turns. For most applications the dc resistance of the wire may be ignored if the ratio of inductive reactance to resistance is 10:1 or greater. Skin effect (the tendency of alternating current to travel near the surface of a conductor) also raises the resistance of the wire, but this effect, although present at all frequencies, is generally considered negligible at normal power-line frequencies.

5-27. *Explain the operation of a* **break contact** *relay and a* **make contact** *relay.*

A *break contact* relay is also frequently called a *normally closed* relay, because, in its *off* state, its contacts are closed. In a relay a small electromagnet is so connected to a switch that, when the electromagnet is energized, the switch changes states; and, when it is deenergized, the switch returns to its original position. The wiper arm of the switch is mechanically connected to an armature of the electromagnet. In a normally closed relay, energization of the solenoid creates a strong magnet that pulls the armature against the solenoid's core, thus opening the contacts. Removing the applied voltage from the solenoid causes the coil to lose its magnetic strength, and the armature, attached to a spring, returns to its original position against its mating contact.

A *make contact* relay is similarly built. Again, the armature is mechanically linked to the wiper arm of the switch, but a spring applies tension on the armature to keep the wiper arm from contacting its mating terminal. Application of voltage to the solenoid creates a strong magnetic field that overcomes the spring tension and pulls the armature against its mating contact. Removal of voltage from the solenoid removes the magnetic field, and the spring once again pulls the armature away from the electrical contact. The circuit of a simple relay of this type is shown in Fig. 5-26.

5-28. *State the value and tolerance of a resistor that is color-coded as follows: red, black, orange, and gold.*

The resistor in question would have a value of $20,000\Omega$ (20K) and a tolerance (possible error) of 5%. The color bands on a resistor are read from left to right. Hold the resistor horizontally so the color band closest to the resistor end is to your left. The first band is the first digit of the value, the second band is the second digit, and the third band tells the

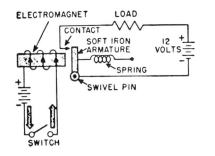

ELECTROMAGNET   LOAD
CONTACT
SOFT IRON   12 +
ARMATURE   VOLTS
SPRING
SWIVEL PIN
SWITCH

Fig. 5-26.

number of zeros to add to the first two digits. The fourth band gives the
tolerance. The first band in the referenced resistor is red, which
represents the digit 2. The second band is black, which stands for 0. The
third band, orange, tells us that three zeros follow the first two digits. So
we have, from left to right, the digits 2, 0, and 000, which gives us
20,000Ω.

RESISTOR COLOR CODES

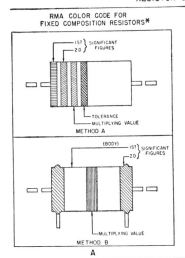

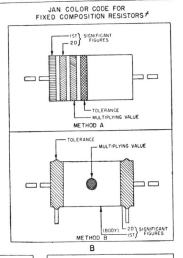

COLOR	SIGNIFICANT FIGURE	MULTIPLYING VALUE	TOLERANCE (%)
BLACK	0	1	
BROWN	1	10	
RED	2	100	
ORANGE	3	1,000	
YELLOW	4	10,000	
GREEN	5	100,000	
BLUE	6	1,000,000	
VIOLET	7	10,000,000	
GRAY	8	100,000,000	
WHITE	9	1,000,000,000	
GOLD	—	0.1	± 5
SILVER	—	0.01	± 10
NO COLOR	—	—	± 20

NOTES

✱ INSULATED FIXED COMPOSITION RESISTORS
WITH AXIAL LEADS ARE DESIGNATED BY
A NATURAL TAN BACKGROUND COLOR
NON-INSULATED FIXED COMPOSITION RESIS-
TORS WITH AXIAL LEADS ARE DESIG-
NATED BY A BLACK BACKGROUND.

✔ RESISTORS WITH AXIAL LEADS ARE IN-
SULATED. RESISTORS WITH RADIAL LEADS
ARE NON-INSULATED.

RMA RADIO MANUFACTURERS ASSOCIATION

JAN JOINT ARMY–NAVY

THESE COLOR CODES GIVE ALL RESISTANCE
VALUES IN OHMS.

Fig. 5-27.

The tolerance band (if any) is usually silver or gold. Silver identifies the tolerance as 10%. Gold is 5%. No tolerance band at all means the resistor's tolerance is ±20%. The color codes for resistors are shown in Fig. 5-27. The coding system shown at the left is that adopted by the Electronic Industries Association (EIA); the system at the right is the older Joint Army/Navy (JAN) system. Unless you plan to work with military surplus equipment, you'd do well to remember the EIA system only.

5-29. *Using the EIA standard 6-dot color system, what would be the value and tolerance of a capacitor whose first-row colors are (left to right) white, red, and green, and whose second-row colors are green, silver, and red?*

The value of this capacitor would be 2500 pF. The tolerance would be ±5%. The EIA 6-dot capacitor color-coding system involves the reading of two rows of three dots each. As shown in Fig. 5-28, the top row of dots is marked with arrowheads to enable easy orientation by the reader. The capacitor is held so that the arrows are on the top row and point to the right. The upper left dot identifies the capacitor type. The second and third colors of the top row identify the first and second numbers of the value. The lower right number (second row) identifies the multiplier, and the dot in the lower center position is the tolerance of error. The final dot (lower left) identifies the class of capacitor or any other special characteristics, such as temperature coefficient or methods of testing.

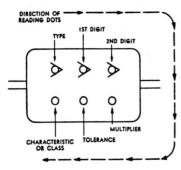

Fig. 5-28.

TYPE	COLOR	1ST DIGIT	2ND DIGIT	MULTIPLIER	TOLERANCE (PERCENT)	CHARACTERISTIC OR CLASS
JAN, MICA	BLACK	0	0	1.0		APPLIES TO
	BROWN	1	1	10	± 1	TEMPERATURE
	RED	2	2	100	± 2	COEFFICIENT
	ORANGE	3	3	1,000	± 3	OR METHODS
	YELLOW	4	4	10,000	± 4	OF TESTING
	GREEN	5	5	100,000	± 5	
	BLUE	6	6	1,000,000	± 6	
	VIOLET	7	7	10,000,000	± 7	
	GRAY	8	8	100,000,000	± 8	
EIA, MICA	WHITE	9	9	1,000,000,000	± 9	
	GOLD			.1		
MOLDED PAPER	SILVER			.01	±10	
	BODY				±20	

5-30. *List three precautions that should be taken in soldering electrical connections to insure a permanent junction.*

The cardinal rule is to **keep the joint immobile** until the solder solidifies and cools. Two other good rules are: **Use no more solder than necessary** to secure the joint, and use sufficient heat to cause the solder to flow freely over the joint and terminal. Following these rules, however, means that other rules must be adhered to as well. If the iron is blackened, for example, it will be difficult to get solder to flow freely. Thus, a good rule to follow is to **keep the soldering iron's tip clean and shiny.** If the soldering iron does not develop enough heat, the solder will not flow freely over the joint, and consequently a good connection is impossible. So another rule is to **make certain the iron has enough power to deliver sufficient heat to cause the solder to flow freely over the joint.** Large metal surfaces require higher heating powers than simple wire-to-terminal connections or PC-board soldering. Hence, a high-wattage iron or gun is required to secure a large-conductor cable to the ground cable of a car battery, or a bus wire to a metal chassis.

Many newcomers to electronics do their first few soldering jobs by touching solder to the iron rather than to the work. As a consequence, the solder solidifies without making good contact to the joint. Another rule, then, is: **Heat the joint and apply solder to the joint only**—*do not* apply solder to the iron or tool.

ELECTRON TUBES

5-31. *Discuss the characteristics and a common use of each of the following electron-tube types: diode, triode, tetrode, pentode, beam power, remote cutoff, duo-triode, cold cathode, and thyratron.*

Diode. In truth, the FCC question is out of date, for there simply are no common applications of vacuum-tube diodes these days. However, until fairly recently, tube-type diodes were commonly used in FM receivers as limiters, in AM and FM receivers as detectors, and in power supplies as rectifiers.

The simple diode tube contains a heated cathode a cold plate. The plate of the tube collects electrons emitted by the cathode when the plate is supplied with a high positive dc voltage with respect to the cathode. One version of the tube-type diode is shown in Fig. 5-29A, with its two elements labeled *plate* and *filament*. As shown in the symbol beneath the drawing, this type of diode possesses a directly heated cathode, or *filament*. Another version is shown in sketch B; in this type of diode the filament serves only as a heater.

A diode acts in the manner of a check valve in a water pipe. The behavior of a diode can be observed after connecting the plate and cathode in series with a battery and milliammeter, as shown in Fig. 5-30. The cathode is brought up to normal temperature by applying the rated voltage across the heater terminals. If the battery is connected so that the plate is positive with respect to the cathode, as shown in A, the meter will indicate a current. This phenomenon, the emission of electrons from hot bodies, was first observed by Thomas Edison in 1883 and is known as the *Edison effect*. When the battery is reconnected as shown in B, so that the plate is negative with respect to the cathode, the meter will indicate no plate current.

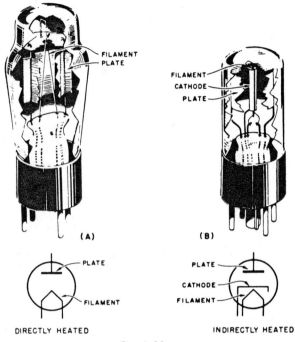

Fig. 5-29.

The principle characteristics of the diode are these:

1. When a diode is properly connected into a circuit with proper voltages, electrons "boil off" the cathode and are attracted to the plate. Since electrons flow from cathode to plate and not from plate to cathode, the diode is a valve that allows a flow in one direction only. This feature made the vacuum-tube diode extremely valuable as a rectifier in the years before the semiconductor diode was introduced.

2. The diode has only two elements (hence the name)—a cathode (or filament) and a plate (or anode).

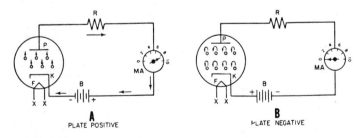

Fig. 5-30.

3. The diode cannot amplify because it has no tube element between the cathode and plate with which to introduce signal voltages to control the electron flow.
4. Diodes have a point of sharp transition between the conducting and nonconducting states, a factor that gives them a nonlinear characteristic, which allows demodulation (detection) of modulated rf signals.

Triode. The triode, or 3-element tube, is similar in construction to the diode, except that a grid of fine-mesh wire is added between the cathode and plate. The addition of the grid gives the tube its most useful function—the ability to amplify. It is common practice to make the grid in the form of a spiral of circular or elliptical cross section, with the cathode at the center. Other arrangements may be used, provided the essential requirement (of being able to control the flow of plate current with the potential applied to the grid) is met.

The space between the grid wires is sufficient to allow the flow of electrons from cathode to plate, yet it is small enough and close enough to the cathode to effectively control the quantity of electrons that are allowed to flow.

The construction features of a typical triode are shown in Fig. 5-31. Electrical connections to the grid and plate are made through the base pins and support wires. The cathode sleeve is insulated from the filament and is connected by means of a short lead to one of the base pins. The grid is placed much closer to the cathode than to the plate.

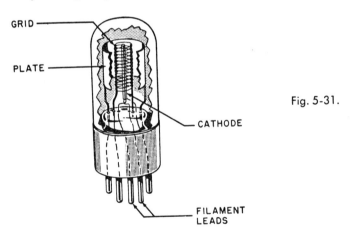

GRID

PLATE

CATHODE

Fig. 5-31.

FILAMENT
LEADS

While plate current in a diode depends only on plate voltage and cathode temperature, plate current in a triode depends on these factors as well as on voltage on the grid with respect to the cathode. A very small change in grid voltage causes a relatively large change in plate current.

The principal use of triodes is as amplifiers. Triodes can be used to amplify audio signals as well as radio-frequency signals. When a triode is used to amplify rf signals, certain precautions must be observed to minimize the coupling that takes place between the elements inside the tube.

The characteristics of triodes involve the relation between grid and plate voltages and the resulting plate current with cathode temperature held constant. Since grid and plate voltages and plate current are functions that may vary from one tube to another and between identical tubes under various use conditions, they are classed as *variable characteristics* or *parameters*.

Characteristic curves—graphs showing predictable performance of tubes based on specifid values of tube parameters—show static characteristics. *Static characteristics* is defined as the relation between a pair of variables, such as electrode voltage and current in a specified operating circuit when all direct electrode supply voltages are constant. The static characteristics of a triode provide an understanding of how the tube operates.

The voltage amplification of a tube is known as the *amplification factor*, designated by the Greek letter μ. This is the ratio of the change in plate voltage to the change in grid voltage required to produce the same change in plate current. A typical *transfer characteristic* curve for a triode is shown in Fig. 5-32. The grid voltage is adjusted to operate the tube at point A on the curve while the plate voltage is 200V.

Next, the value of grid voltage is changed to -4V, thus giving Δe_g a value of 2V (the delta means the voltage has undergone a *change of*

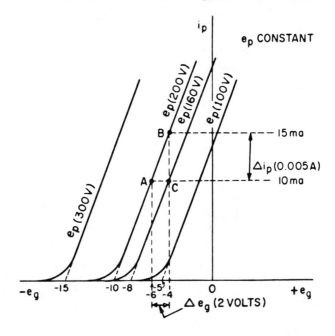

Fig. 5-32.

2V). The plate current now increases to 15 mA from point A to point B, as shown. It can be seen that a small change in grid voltage has produced a significant change in plate current (5 mA). Triodes have amplification factors (μ) ranging from 3 to about 100.

The second important characteristic of the triode is the *ac plate resistance*, designated r_p. It is the ratio, for a constant grid voltage, of a plate voltage change to the resulting plate current change. It is expressed in ohms. Three plate characteristic curves for a triode are shown in Fig. 5-33. The middle curve is arbitrarily chosen and the grid bias of $-2V$ held constant as the plate voltage is adjusted to operate the tube at point A. The plate voltage is increased 20V, so that the tube now operates at point B. The ratio of this increase in plate voltage to the increase in plate current that it produces is a measure of the *dynamic*, or *ac*, plate resistance. Thus, plate resistance is equal to Δe_p divided by Δi_p (with grid voltage held constants). In the case shown, this is $20/0.002$, or $10,000\Omega$.

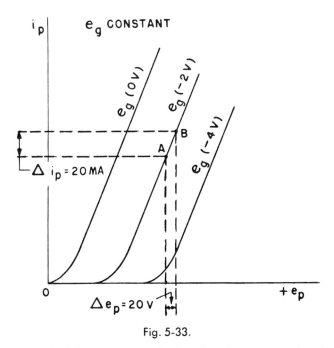

Fig. 5-33.

A third characteristic used in describing the properties of triodes is the grid-to-plate *transconductance*, designated g_m. It is defined as the ratio of a change in plate current to the corresponding change in grid voltage with the plate voltage held constant. It is usually expressed in micromhos. (The mho is the unit of conductance and is the reciprocal of the ohm, or $1/R$.)

Tetrode. The relatively large values of interelectrode capacitances of the triode, paticularly the plate-to-grid capacitance, imposes a serious limitation on the tube as an amplifier at high frequencies. To reduce the plate-to-grid capacitance, a second grid, referred to as a *screen* grid, is inserted between the grid and plate of the tube, as shown in Fig. 5-34.

Because the screen grid is shunted by a screen bypass capacitor having a low reactance at the signal frequency, it acts as a shield between the plate and control grid. It effectively reduces the interelectrode capacitance coupling between the plate and control grid circuits. The screen is supplied with a potential somewhat less positive than the plate. The positive voltage on the screen grid accelerates the electrons moving from the cathode to the plate. Some of these electrons strike the screen and produce a screen current. The larger portion of them, however, pass through the open mesh screen grid to the plate.

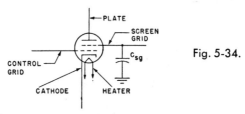

Fig. 5-34.

Because of the presence of the screen grid, a variation in the plate voltage has little effect on the flow of plate current. The control grid, on the other hand, retains its control as in the triode. The tetrode has high plate resistance and a high amplification factor in comparison to the triode. The high amplification factor is brought about by the close proximity of the control grid to the cathode and the electrical isolation of the plate from the control grid. The transconductance of tetrodes is also relatively high when compared with that of triodes.

A typical family of plate characteristic curves of a tetrode is shown in Fig. 5-35A. The negative slope of the characteristic at plate voltages lower than the screen voltage (90V) is the result of secondary emission from the plate. This condition results from the fact that, with the screen voltage fixed, the velocity with which the electrons strike the plate increases with plate voltage. When the electrons strike the plate with sufficient force, other loosely held electrons are knocked out of the plate material into the space between the plate and the screen. Because the screen is at a higher positive potential than the plate, the secondary electrons are attracted to the screen. The flow of these electrons to the screen is in the opposite direction to the normal flow from cathode to plate, and the plate current is decreased. This reduction in plate current continues until the potential of the plate approaches the screen grid potential. Any further increase in plate voltage causes the secondary electrons to be pulled back to the plate, and the plate current again increases.

The action in the region where plate current decreases as plate voltage increases is called *negative resistance*. This action is opposite to that encountered in a normal resistor. When the tetrode is used as an amplifier, plate voltage should not fall below the screen voltage. If plate voltage does fall below that of the screen, plate current will fail to follow the grid signal waveform, and the output signal is clipped, as shown in Fig. 5-35B. This distortion may be eliminated by reducing the amplitude of the grid signal or increasing the $B+$ supply voltage. However, the relatively large screen current and the effects of secondary emission from the plate limit the usefulness of the tetrode as an rf voltage amplifier. Still, the tube has been successfully used in rf amplification applications, both for transmitting and receiving.

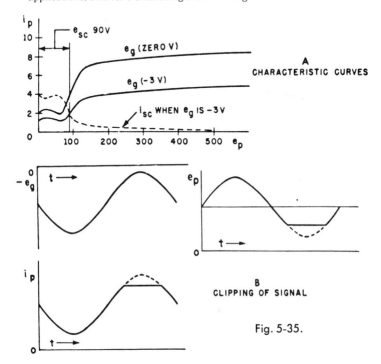

Fig. 5-35.

Pentode. A pentode has, as the name implies, five elements. The secondary-emission problem of the tetrode is overcome with the addition of another grid element between the screen grid and plate. This element, referred to as the *suppressor* grid, is typically at the same potential as the tube's cathode, so the effects of the screen's high potential are negated. Figure 5-36 is a schematic diagram of the pentode.

In the pentode the suppressor grid serves to repel, or suppress, secondary electrons from the plate. It also serves to slow down the primary electrons from the cathode as they approach the suppressor. This action does not interfere with the flow of electrons from cathode to plate but serves to prevent any interchange of secondary electrons between screen and plate. The suppressor thus eliminates the negative resistance effect that appears in a tetrode in the region where plate voltage falls below that of the screen. Thus, plate current rises

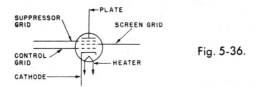

Fig. 5-36.

smoothly from zero up to its saturation point as plate voltage is increased uniformly with grid voltage held constant. Typical pentode plate characteristic curves are shown in Fig. 5-37. The amplification factor of pentodes is very high in comparison with triodes and tetrodes.

In the rf pentode the chief purpose of the screen grid is to eliminate the effects of interelectrode capacitance coupling between control grid and plate circuits. In the power pentode. at audio frequencies. the screen permits the output signal to be relatively large without regeneration occurring as it does in the triode. Plate current is substantially independent of plate voltage in the power pentode. since the screen voltage is the principal factor influencing plate current. With the addition of the suppressor. the allowable output voltage variation is larger than that of the tetrode. and the distortion effects shown in the tetrode. of Fig. 5-35B are eliminated. Thus. an audio-frequency power pentode has an allowable output signal variation in which the plate voltage can fall a large amount below that of the screen on the positive half-cycle of input signal without clipping the plate signal current. And the ratio of output power to grid driving voltage is relatively large.

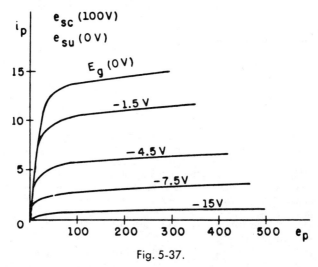

Fig. 5-37.

Pentodes have traditionally been used extensively in applications where high amplification requirements are involved.

Beam Power. The beam power tube has the advantages of both the tetrode and the pentode. This tube is capable of handling relatively high

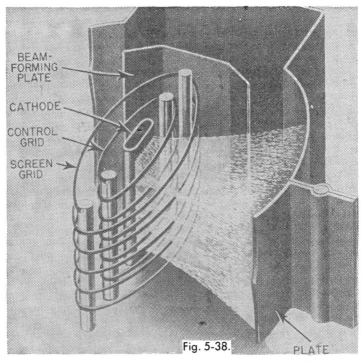

BEAM-
FORMING
PLATE

CATHODE

CONTROL
GRID

SCREEN
GRID

Fig. 5-38.

PLATE

levels of electrical power for application in the output stages of receivers and amplifiers and in different portions of transmitters. The power-handling capability stems from concentration of the plate-current electrons into *beams*, or sheets of moving charges (Fig. 5-38). In the usual types of electron tube, the plate-current electrons advance in a predetermined direction but without being confined into beams.

The external appearance of these tubes is like that of other standard receiving-type tetrodes or pentodes; they are slightly larger in dimension because they are called upon to handle somewhat more power, but they have no distinctive external identifying features.

Sketch A of Fig. 5-39 shows how the screen-grid wires and control-grid wires in the ordinary tetrode determine the electron paths. The wires are out of alignment; therefore, electrons that pass through the control-grid wires are partially deflected from their paths and many strike the screen wires. This produces a screen current and thus limits the value of plate current.

In sketch B the results are different. Because of this arrangement of the control and screen grids, the screen intercepts fewer electrons; therefore, the relative screen current is less in the beam power tube than in the conventional tetrode or pentode. In turn, more electrons reach the plate, thereby making the plate current higher.

The cumulative effect of the arrangement in sketch B is a tube in which the plate and the control grid are electrically isolated; the plate

329

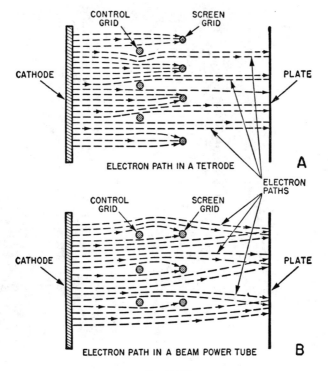

ELECTRON PATH IN A TETRODE **A**

ELECTRON PATH IN A BEAM POWER TUBE **B**

Fig. 5-39.

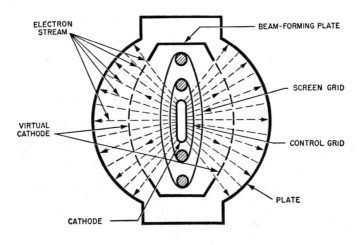

Fig. 5-40.

current is high, the plate resistance is relatively low, and a substantial amount of electrical power can be handled with reduced distortion.

The beam-forming plates (Fig. 5-40) further influence the movement of the plate-current electrons from the time they pass the screen electrode and strike the plate. The beam electrodes are connected internally to the cathode, and consequently they are at the same potential as the latter.

Because of this potential of the beam-forming plates, an effect equivalent to a space charge is developed in the space between the screen and the plate. The effect is as if a surface (broken lines joining the ends of the beam-forming plates in Fig. 5-40) existed in the screen-plate space. This is identified as the "virtual cathode." The presence of this electric plane repels secondary electrons liberated by the plate and prevents them from moving to the screen. Figure 5-40 represents a beam power tube as seen from the top of the envelope.

In some tubes, the effect of a virtual cathode is achieved by the use of the third grid in the place of the beam-forming plates. The results are identical in both versions. In order to satisfy two types of construction, two references are made to the symbol of the pentode (Fig. 5-41). Sketch A symbolizes the beam power tube with the beam-forming plates and sketch B symbolizes the version in which a grid replaces the

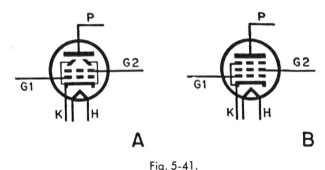

Fig. 5-41.

beam-forming plate. There is no difference between the symbol shown in B and the ordinary pentode.

For comparison, Fig. 5-42 shows the plate current vs plate voltage characteristics of a beam power tube and a conventional pentode. Note the rapid rise in plate current for the beam power tube, as shown by the solid line. The more gradual rise for the normal pentode shown by the broken line is an important detail relative to power-handling ability with minimum distortion. The solid-line curve shows that the zone in which the plate current is merely a function of the plate voltage is much more limited; the plate current becomes substantially independent of plate voltage at much lower values of plate potential. This characteristic enables the beam power tube to handle greater amounts of electrical power at lower values of plate voltage than in the ordinary pentode. In addition, the beam power tube produces less distortion than the ordinary pentode while accommodating an increased grid swing and plate-current change.

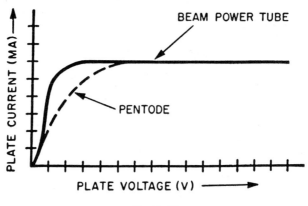

Fig. 5-42.

Remote Cutoff Tube. The amplification constant, or *mu* (μ), of an electron tube is a function of the geometry of the tube—that is, of the shape and organization of the electrodes. Slight variations in its value may occur under different operating voltages, but for practical purposes, it is considered to remain substantially constant. This accounts for the fact that each vacuum tube bears a single μ rating, which is assumed to be fixed.

The amplification constant of a tube expresses the relationship between plate current cutoff and negative grid voltage when a fixed value of plate voltage is applied. High-mu tubes such as tetrodes and pentodes (especially the latter) reach plate current cutoff at relatively low values of negative grid voltage. Low-mu tubes allow the application of much higher negative grid voltages before cutoff is reached.

Such plate current, grid voltage relationships and the fixed μ stem from the kind of control grid used in most of the tubes discussed previously—that is, a grid in which the wires are uniformly spaced throughout the length of the tube structure. Application of a voltage to the control grid results in the same effect on the plate current electrons all along the control grid wires.

The fixed-mu property poses a problem when high-mu tubes are used in communications systems. Frequently large-amplitude signals are encountered, and they must be controlled in the equipment to produce the desired intelligence with a minimum of distortion. To accomplish this, special kinds of tetrodes and pentodes are used. These are known as *variable mu* or *remote cutoff* tubes, and they differ from ordinary tubes in the construction of the control grids. In these tubes the grid wires are unequally spaced. Turns are closer together at the top and bottom of the winding and wider apart at the center. This form of control grid construction, shown in the metal 6SK7 pentode (Fig. 5-43A), produces a tube that does not have a constant μ; instead μ changes with the value of grid voltage applied to the control grid.

At low values of bias the grid operates in a normal manner. As the control grid is made more negative, the effect of the closely spaced grid wires becomes greater and the electron flow from the space charge in

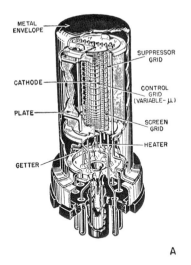

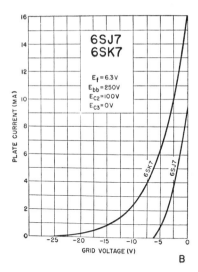

METAL
ENVELOPE

SUPPRESSOR
GRID

CATHODE

CONTROL
GRID
(VARIABLE- μ)

PLATE

SCREEN
GRID

HEATER

GETTER

6SJ7
6SK7

$E_f = 6.3V$
$E_{bb} = 250V$
$E_{C2} = 100V$
$E_{C3} = 0V$

PLATE CURRENT (MA)

6SK7   6SJ7

GRID VOLTAGE (V)

A   B

Fig. 5-43.

this region is cut off completely. The center of the grid structure also displays a greater effect but still allows electrons to advance to the screen and plate. The overall reduction in plate current is therefore gradual.

Eventually, with sufficient negative voltage on the grid, all parts of the grid electrode winding act to cut off the plate current; but the negative grid voltage required to attain this is perhaps three to four times as much as for the conventional tube operated at like screen and plate voltages.

The transfer characteristic of a remote cutoff pentode is shown in Fig. 5-43B. A curve for a standard pentode (6SJ7) is shown for comparison.

Remote cutoff tubes are used in locations in communications equipment where high bias voltages may be necessary to provide control of the signal level.

Duo-Triode. The term *duo* means that two tubes are incorporated within the same glass envelope. Thus, in the duo-triode or *twin triode* there are two triodes in one envelope. There are a large number multiunit tubes. The symbols for the most common of these types are shown in the alphabetically designated sketches of Fig. 5-44.

A multiunit tube has the advantage of being more compact and considerably more economical than a pair of tubes each having the capability of one of the tubes in a combined pair. Duo-diodes and duo-triodes are the most common combined-pair tubes. Frequently a single, common cathode is used to supply electrons to both sets of elements in a multielement tube. Occasionally an electrode of one set of elements is connected internally to an electrode of another set of elements

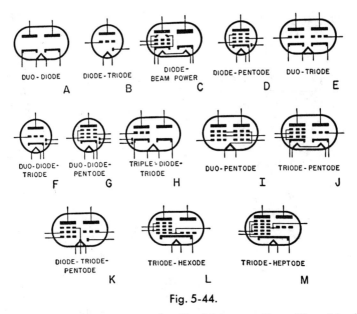

Fig. 5-44.

There are many types of multiunit tubes, used for a wide variety of purposes. The tube symbolized in A can be used as a full-wave rectifier, an FM discriminator, or a combination detector and avc rectifier. The diode—triode in sketch B can be used as a diode detector and a triode amplifier. The duo-triode shown in E is used as a push-pull amplifier, two amplifiers in cascade, or as a special type of wave generator, to name but a few of the more conventional applications.

The table in Fig. 5-45 lists typical examples of multipurpose tubes to be found in older receiving-type equipment. The letters in the first column refer to the symbols used in Fig. 5-44.

Examples of Multipurpose Tubes in Receiving Equipment

Symbol desig-nation	Multipurpose tube	Examples of tube types	Symbol desig-nation	Multipurpose tube	Examples of tube types
A	Duo-diode	5U4, 5V4, 5Y3, 6AL5, 6X5, 12AL5	F	Duo-diode-triode	1H5, 6AQ7, 6SQ7, 6V7, 7K7, 7X7, 12SQ7
B	Diode-triode	1H5, 1LH4	G	Duo-diode-pentode	1F6, 7R7, 14E7, 14R7
C	Diode-beam power	70L7, 117L7, 117N7, 117P7	H	Triple-diode-triode	6S8, 6T8, 12S8
D	Diode-pentode	1N6, 1T6, 6SF7, 12A7, 12SF7	I	Duo-pentode	1E7
			J	Triode-pentode	6AD7, 6P7, 25B8
E	Duo-triode	1J6, 6J6, 6N7, 6NS7, 6SL7, 12AT7, 12AU7	K	Diode-triode-pentode	3A8
			L	Triode-hexode	6K8, 12K8
			M	Triode-heptode	7J7, 7S7, 14J7

Fig. 5-45.

Cold Cathode Tube. A gas-filled tube in which two electrodes are inserted is called a *gas diode*. The electrode to which the positive potential is applied is called the plate, and the other is called the

334

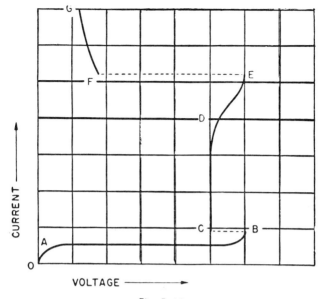

Fig. 5-46.

cathode, as in ordinary vacuum tubes. The cathode in a gas diode can be an electrode like the plate, or it can be a thermionic emitter. The former is known as a *cold cathode*, and the latter as a *hot cathode*.

Cold cathode tubes are used for many purposes; among these are voltage regulation, rectification, oscillation, circuit protection, and light production (as for neon signs).

Referring to Fig. 5-46, the small change of voltage from *d* to *E* is used in a voltage regulator circuit. In the simple circuit shown in Fig. 5-47, the black dot within the envelope signifies that the tube is filled with gas. The resistance R is high enough to limit the tube current to the constant-voltage range when the load current is low. When the load current increases, the voltage drop across R increases and reduces the

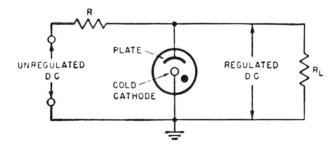

Fig. 5-47.

tube voltage. A small reduction of tube voltage in this range, the "normal" region of the glow discharge, results in a large decrease in tube current, which decreases the voltage drop across R. Therefore small variations of load current cause compensating variations in tube current, and the voltage across the tube remains essentially constant. A typical tube used in this circuit is the OV3−VR150.

Cold cathode tubes rarely are used as rectifiers because of their high voltage drop, although a variation of the cold cathode tube is used where filament power for a heater−cathode rectifier is difficult to obtain. An example of a cold cathode rectifier was once used in vehicular equipment (it has since been replaced by semiconductors). The principle of operation is based on the heating of the cathode under ionic bombardment in the region of the curve between F and G (Fig. 5-46).

If a cold-cathode gas diode is connected as shown in Fig. 5-48A, the resulting circuit is known as a *relaxation oscillator*. With a dc input, capacitor C charges through the high resistance of R. The voltage across the capacitor rises as the capacitor charges. When the capacitor voltage becomes equal to the breakdown voltage, the glow tube fires, and the capacitor discharges through the tube. The capacitor discharges very quickly to a voltage equal to the extinction voltage of the tube. This is the voltage at which the tube ceases to conduct. Consequently, the capacitor begins to charge again. The output voltage is a sawtooth. Several capacitor charge−discharge cycles generate the waveform shown in Fig. 5-48B.

Thyratron. If a grid is placed between the cathode and plate of a gas tube, the voltage at which breakdown occurs can be controlled by the voltage on the grid. The entire plate surface in this tube usually is shielded by the grid before breakdown. The grid is placed close to the plate to prevent discharge between the two. If such a discharge does take place, it is only in the unimportant dark-current range. In a grid-controlled gas-discharge tube, the plate supply voltage exceeds the plate-to-cathode breakdown voltage and the grid is held either zero or negative with respect to the cathode. Under these conditions, breakdown does not take place.

If the grid voltage is raised, breakdown occurs between the grid and the cathode. This ionizes all the gas in the tube, and the discharge continues with plate−cathode current flow. Resistance in series with the grid limits its current on breakdown to a safe value. After breakdown, the grid can no longer control the discharge. If it is made negative with respect to the cathode, positive ions surround the grid wires, and electrons are repelled from them. The discharge, then, is shielded completely from the grid. To reestablish grid control, the plate voltage must be reduced to the extinction potential of the cathode−plate discharge.

This principle of grid control can be applied to almost any gas-discharge tube. It is used with cold-cathode, hot-cathode, and arc tubes. All of these types are given the generic name of *thyratron*. Where a hot-cathode tube is used, as in the 2D21 or 884, the grid acts primarily as a shield between the plate and the cathode, preventing electrons emitted by the cathode from ionizing the gas between the electrodes. By

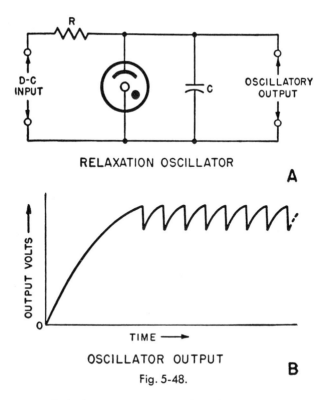

RELAXATION OSCILLATOR

A

OSCILLATOR OUTPUT

B

Fig. 5-48.

proper electrode arrangement. a positive voltage on the grid is needed to start the discharge.

The effectiveness of grid control is indicated by the grid control characteristic curve for the 884 in Fig. 5-49. The curve shows the relationship between the plate voltage which must be applied with a given grid voltage to cause the tube to conduct. If the grid is below −30V, no amount of plate voltage can fire the tube. If the grid is above −30V, conduction begins within a few microseconds after the proper plate voltage is applied. depending on the gas used.

5-32. *Compare tetrodes to triodes in reference to high plate current and interelectrode capacitance.*

The interelectrode capacitance of the triode limits its usefulness at radio frequencies because of excessive signal feedback at these higher frequencies. The tetrode. with a screen grid separating the control grid from the plate. possesses a much lower value of capacitance between these electrodes: so the tetrode may be used at much higher frequencies than the triode. without tedious and critical neutralization (This is not to say that a tetrode stage is never neutralized. To the contrary. many rf circuits require neutralization. Neutralization. however. is less critical. less frequently necessary. and easier to accomplish in a tetrode circuit than in a triode circuit.)

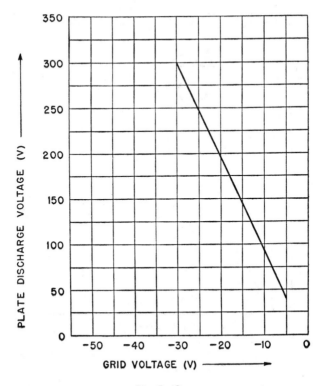

Fig. 5-49.

The behavior of the tetrode under various conditions can be analyzed from its characteristic curves (Fig. 5-50). The now-obsolete UY-224 tetrode was used to obtain the curves illustrated, because this tube exhibits certain properties of fundamental interest that later types of tetrodes do not show as well.

Figure 5-50 shows curves for only one control grid and screen grid voltage setting. The control grid voltage is held constant at $-1.5V$, and screen grid voltage is held constant at $+75V$. The filament voltage is 2.5Vdc.

Referring to Fig. 5-50, current (Y-axis) for the stipulated changes in plate voltage (X-axis), it can be seen that great changes occur in the curves for plate current and screen grid currents below a certain value of plate voltage; that is, from E_{bb} values of zero to about 90V. It is in this region that great interest lies, although the operating range of the two curves, when used for amplifier design, would be substantially above the 90V value. The plate and screen grid curves are added in Fig. 5-50 to show that changes in plate voltage do not appreciably affect the total current through the tetrode.

The previous statement—that the plate current is not affected too much by changes in plate voltage in a tetrode—appears to be

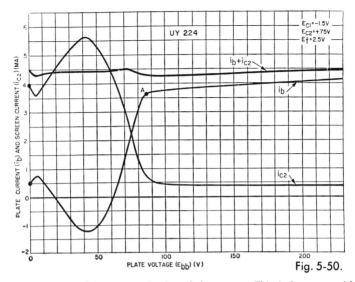

Fig. 5-50.

contradicted in an examination of the curves. This is because, with voltage applied to the plate and +75V to the screen, an electrostatic field exists between the screen and the cathode, and not between the cathode and plate (cathode is at zero potential). This field attrácts electrons to the screen grid and a small screen current (4 mA) flows in the external screen circuit. Some electrons do reach the plate, however, as evidenced by the flow of a very small plate current (0.5 mA) at zero plate voltage.

Raising the plate voltage from zero to +2V causes an increase in plate curent and a decrease in screen current. This is indicated by the uward slope in the plate-current characteristic and the downward slope of the screen-current characteristic. Notice that as the plate voltage is increased to +5V and slightly higher, the plate-current curve slopes downward and continues so for an appreciable distance. This appears to be the contrary of what should happen. By ordinary tube behavior, the plate current should increase rather than decrease as the plate voltage increases. The decrease is caused by the phenomenon of *secondary emission*.

Secondary emission occurs when electrons from the space charge strike the plate with sufficient force to dislodge electrons from the plate material itself. These dislodged electrons are known as secondary electrons. With the screen voltage fixed, the velocity with which the space-charge electrons (primary electrons) arrive at the plate inceases as the plate voltage increases. At low plate voltages, secondary electrons dislodged from the plate under primary-electron bombardment are attracted to the higher-potential screen. The movement of these secondary electrons is in the direction opposite to the regular flow of electrons from cathode to plate. The result of this duo-directional current flow is that the current in the plate circuit decreases as more and more secondary electrons are dislodged from the plate.

5-33. Are there any advantages or disadvantages of filament-type vacuum tubes as compared with tubes having indirectly heated cathodes?

The chief advantage of an indirectly heated cathode is the fact that the cathode surface heats evenly, so that electron flow is uniform over the cathode surface. The advantage tends to disappear when a filament-type tube is powered by ac, except that either one end or the other of the filament produces more electron "boiloff" than the center of the filament during any alternation. When such a filament is connected to ac, the filament end nearest the negative terminal will produce more electrons during the half-cycle when the filament is so polarized; when polarity reverses, the opposite end is more negative, so it will produce more electrons. Over a complete cycle the emission averages out at the ends, but it is still greater at the ends than at the center.

Even though use of ac does tend to make the electron emission more uniform than it would be if the tube were powered from a dc source, the use of ac can, and frequently does, contribute to hum in the amplifier stage in which the tube is connected. The filament will tend to impart to the grid a signal that is the frequency of the applied filament voltage, particularly where the filament leads are separated from each other in such way that stray signals can be coupled into the 2-wire line. Twisting the filament line helps a great deal by keeping both leads exposed to the same fields and keeping the two leads spaced uniformly from each other. The chassis is a good shield, and most amplifier circuits that use tubes powered by ac filament voltages use leads that are twisted and routed along the metal chassis. But these measures don't always work.

There is no hum problem with dc-operated filaments, of course; but dc tends to hasten tube wear because the filament terminal connected to the more negative side of the power line will give up more electrons than the other terminal, resulting in premature wear on that end.

The obvious solution would be to use indirectly heated filaments (cathodes) for uniform distribution of electrons over the surface of the plate. While this does not help the problem of hum and won't make the tubes last longer when they're connected to dc, it will give consistent service for the life of the tube.

One other advantage of cathode-type tubes is the fact that the cathode is isolated from the filament. Thus, the cathode may be connected to ground or any other signal element in complete independence from the power requirements of the tube itself.

Of course, an indirectly heated cathode requires a bit more power than a directly heated type, simply because the heater has to generate enough heat to cause thermionic emission from an adjacent surface. Also, as might be expected, the directly heated filament comes to the required temperature in a shorter time than the indirectly heated cathode. Because of this one significant advantage, tube-type equipment that was manufactured to serve in applications where instant usability was required almost always was designed around the directly heated vacuum tube.

In general, the indirectly heated vacuum tube was the more popular type during its time, and this popularity was probably based on the uniformity of temperature of the cathode of this type of tube when powered by ac filament voltage. This uniformity of emission temperature makes the "indirect" tube a more stable all-around performer.

5-34. *Draw a simple circuit diagram of each of the following and describe operation (show a signal source and include coupling and bypass capacitors, power supply connections, and plate load):*

- *Audio-frequency grounded-cathode triode amplifier with cathode resistor biasing for class A operation*
- *Audio-frequency grounded-cathode pentode amplifier with battery biasing for class A operation*
- *Radio-frequency grounded-grid triode amplifier with LC tank plate load for class B operation*
- *Audio-frequency cathode-follower type of triode amplifier*
- *Audio-frequency push-pull pentode amplifier with transformer coupling to a loudspeaker*

Triode Audio Amplifier with Cathode Bias Resistor. The most common method of obtaining bias in class A amplifier tubes is to incorporate a series resistor in the cathode circuit, as shown in the circuit diagram of Fig. 5-51. In this circuit the bias voltage is developed across the cathode resistor. Under quiescent conditions (the no-signal state), plate current flows continuously from cathode to plate and back to the cathode through its series resistor. Since the plate current flows from chassis ground to the cathode through the resistor, the chassis is negative with respect to the cathode.

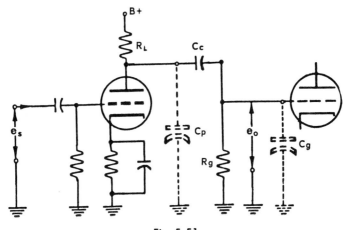

Fig. 5-51.

In the figure the signal source is shown by the symbol e_s. The output signal is designated e_o (as it appears at the grid of the succeeding stage).

Assume that the voltage drop across the cathode resistor is 5V. This makes the cathode 5V positive with respect to the grid (or the grid 5V negative with respect to the cathode). The grid resistor is part of the coupling network for the input signal (e_s). If the input signal is

341

sinusoidal, the plate current will vary sinusoidally about an average dc value. The varying plate current flows through the cathode resistor. Since the required bias is a fixed voltage (5V), the ac component of plate current through the cathode resistor must be removed. This is accomplished by the bypass capacitor across the cathode resistor. The capacitor acts as a short circuit to the alternating current. The value of the capacitor is large, so that its capacitive reactance is small compared with the resistance of the cathode resistor at the frequency of operation (within the audible range). The value for audio applications would be in the general range of 0 to 50 μF. The value of the cathode resistor is usually from 250Ω to 3000Ω.

Since the amplifier is to be biased for class A operation, the operating point (quiescent values of plate current versus grid voltage) must be established at the center of the tube characteristic's linear region. With an increase in the amount of negative bias, less plate current will flow; with a decrease in bias, more plate current will flow. The cathode resistor maintains a constant negative grid potential of 5V. Let us assume that when no input signal is applied to the amplifier, this 5V negative bias causes 5 mA of current to flow from cathode to plate.

The input signal is an ac waveform that rises and falls about a fixed reference point. When the signal is applied to the grid, the reference point becomes the negative 5V bias on the grid; that is, when the signal stops, the bias is at precisely 5V. As the signal goes positive, the grid bias drops below the -5V level (goes more positive); as the signal goes negative, the grid bias is increased beyond the -5V level.

The plate current, then, is a direct function of grid bias. When the grid goes slightly more negative, plate current drops considerably but in direct proportion to the negative-going grid signal. For a one-volt variation in grid voltage, the plate current may vary by, say, 10 mA.

The proportional variation in output current is passed through a resistor in the plate lead, called the *load resistor* (R_L). In accordance with Ohm's law, the voltage drop across a resistor changes according to the current applied to the resistor. The changing voltage here, brought about by the changing current, is the signal that is applied to the next stage. However, since this voltage is dc, it cannot be applied directly to the next stage without upsetting the next stage's biasing. The coupling capacitor (C_C) is used to pass the amplified signal while blocking the high dc potential.

The variations produced in the plate current of a vacuum tube when a signal voltage is applied to the control grid are exactly the same as would be produced in a generator developing a voltage and having an internal resistance equal to the plate resistance of the tube. Thus, the RC-coupled amplifier shown in Fig. 5-51 can be represented by the equivalent circuit shown in Fig. 5-52. The minus sign on the equivalent generator voltage is used only to indicate that the voltage is of opposite polarity to the signal voltage. This indicates the fact that there is a 180° phase shift between the grid and plate signal voltages in a grounded-cathode vacuum tube.

Note that the cathode and bypass capacitor and biasing resistor are omitted in the equivalent circuit. This omission is permissible; first, becaus the capacitor is of such size that it places the cathode at ground potential for ac and, second, because the biasing resistor is considered

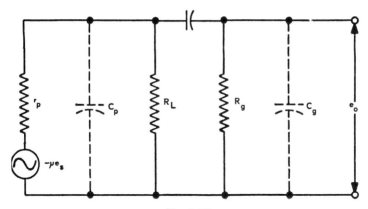

Fig. 5-52.

part of the plate load. All the circuit constants shown in the equivalent circuit are those that affect any ordinary triode amplifier. In fact. depending upon the frequency. some of the constants shown may be omitted. Thus. for example. in the midfrequency band (200 to 10,000 Hz) the electrode capacitances C_c and C may be omitted in equivalent circuits because their impedances are so large that they act as open circuits.

Grounded-Cathode Audio Amplifier with Battery Biasing. The circuit diagram shown in Fig. 5-53 is for a single-triode class A amplifier that obtains all its operating voltages, including grid bias, from batteries. The bias battery, in series with the signal source, is 8V, which sets the operating point for the tube. The phase and character of the input signal is described by the sine wave labeled e_c. The varying plate current in the output is labeled i_b. The plate load resistor signal is labeled e_{RL}. The output signal, 180° out of phase with the input, is labeled $e_{b\ out}$.

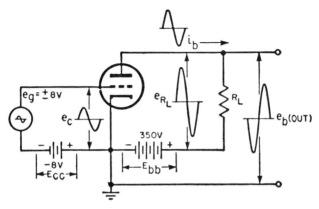

Fig. 5-53.

Assume that the triode shown in the figure is a 6J5 tube with operating voltages as illustrated ($-8V$ grid bias and 350V plate supply potential). Under no-signal conditions, the plate current is 5.2 mA, and plate voltage is 220V. The load resistor is 25K. The voltage drop across the load resistor under no-signal conditions is the supply voltage minus the plate voltge, $350V - 220V$, or 130V. The various voltages and currents appearing in the triode circuit are shown graphically in Fig. 5-54. The waveshapes shown are obtained in the following manner: Points A, $A1$, $A2$, $A3$, and $A4$, connected by a vertical dotted line, represent conditions which occur at quiescence, or with no signal. The signal voltage (in graph A) is zero at point A, and the total grid voltage

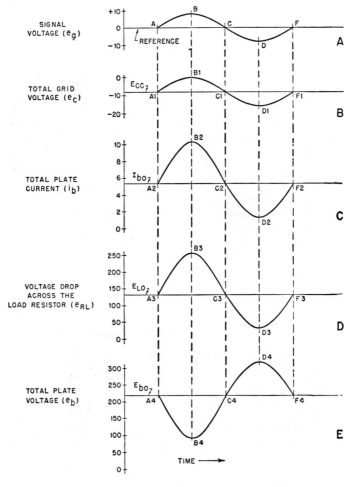

Fig. 5-54.

(in B) equals −8V at point *A1*. which is the value of bias. At the same time, the total plate current. in graph C. equals 5.2 mA at point *A2*. The dc voltage drop across the load resistor (referred to in the graph as E_{Lo}) in D. equals 130V at point *A3*. The total plate voltage. in graph E. is equal to 220V at point *A4*.

When the grid signal voltage reaches its most positive value at point *B*. the total grid voltage (e_c) is zero volts at point *B1*. The maximum signal voltage on the grid causes the plate current to rise to a maximum value of 10.1 mA at point *B2*. This maximum current ⌐auses the voltage drop across the load resistor to be a maximum value of 252V at point *B3*. The load resistor R_L. plate resistance r_p. and plate supply E_{bb} comprise a series circuit. The voltage drops across R_L and r_p equal the supply source voltage. If the voltage drop across R_L increases. the voltage drop across r_p must decrease. The output voltage from plate to cathode is the voltage drop across r_p. Since the voltage drop across R_L is at a maximum at point *B3*. voltage is at a minimum. This is shown at point *B4*. which equals 98V.

With no signal. the same conditions prevail at points *C*. *C1*. *C2*. *C3* and *C4* as at points *A*. *A1*. *A2*. *A3*. and *A4*. When e_g reaches its most negative value. at point *D*. total grid voltage is −16V at point *B1*. This minimum input voltage causes total plate current to be a minimum (1.3 mA at point *D3*). In turn. the minimum plate current causes the voltage across the load resistor e_{RL} to be a minimum value of 33V at point *D3*. Since the voltage across R_L is a minimum. the voltage drop across r_p is a maximum and total plate voltage e_b is a maximum (317V at *D4*). Points *F*. *F1*. *F2*. *F3*. and *F4* occur at no-signal and have the same numerical values at the corresponding points *C*. *C1*. *C2*. *C3*. and *C4*.

From the foregoing analysis it is noted that the waveshapes shown in graphs A. B. C. and D are in phase with each other but are 180° out of phase with waveshape E.

Consequently. the following conclusion can be made: The signal on the control grid of an electron tube is always in phase with the plate current but is 180° out of phase with the output plate voltage. This statement holds true for all types of electron tubes. whether they are triodes. tetrodes. or pentodes.

Class B Grounded-Grid RF Triode Amplifier with LC Tank Plate Load. In the grounded-grid amplifier (Fig. 5-55) the signal is applied between the cathode and ground. the grid is grounded. and the output is taken across a load between plate and ground—in this case. the LC tank plate load.

The grounded-grid circuit permits a triode to be operated at high frequencies without the need for neutralization. Therefore. one of the most objectionable drawbacks of a triode rf power amplifier is overcome. In this circuit the grid is grounded through an rf bypass capacitor and serves as a shield between the input and output circuits. thus preventing feedback of energy and resultant oscillation. It also has the advantage of very low output capacitance. since the only capacitance across the output added by the tube is that between grid and plate (Fig. 5-55). In tubes designed especially for this purpose. the capacitance is made very low. and larger values of inductance may be used in the plate circuit at relatively high frequencies. This results in higher efficiency.

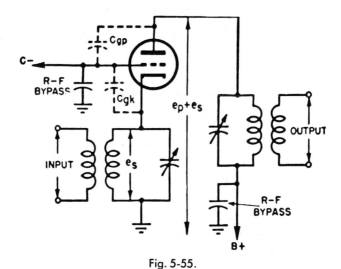

Fig. 5-55.

Another characteristic of the grounded-grid amplifier is that both the driver stage (which supplies the input) and the amplifier stage itself supply the plate load circuit. The driver stage produces an rf voltage across the input terminals. An rf voltage also is produced across the plate and cathode elements of the tube. These voltages are 180° out of phase in respect to the cathode, and therefore the rf output voltage from plate to ground is the sum of the two out-of-phase voltages.

The plate current generally is 180° out of phase with the plate voltage; this means that the signal current flowing in the cathode circuit must be the same as the plate current. The cathode can now have a low impedance, and the plate circuit can have a high impedance. Therefore, the tube acts as a device to transfer the space current from a low impedance to a high impedance. The output power is proportional to the square of the current multiplied by the resistance; therefore, the input (cathode power) is low, the output (plate power) is high, and the tube acts as a power amplifier. The gain of the amplifier is proportional to the ratio of output impedance to input impedance.

Because the input impedance can be made small, the bandwidth in the input circuit can be very great. Since the output capacitance is that from plate to grid, the inductance in the plate circuit can be made large for a given resonant frequency. So the selectivity of the output circuit can also be made broad.

Being a class B amplifier, the tube is biased for operation at plate current cutoff; thus, the tube conducts during approximately 50% of its total input signal period.

To summarize, the grounded-grid circuit permits the use of a triode (with its lower noise figure) and does not require neutralization. However, the voltage gain of the amplifier is not as great as that of the grounded-cathode circuit, because the input impedance is very low. The tuned circuit has little voltage stepup to overcome tube noise, and the overall noise performance tends to suffer somewhat. The low-impedance input circuit permits the attainment of wide bandwidth and a reasonable noise figure without sacrificing too much voltage gain in the input circuit. The gain of the grounded-grid amplifier may not be great enough to override the noise produced by some converter tubes; thus, it is common practice to find two grounded-grid amplifiers in cascade. The added complications arising from this necessity and the need for special tubes limit its use. The tubes themselves must have very low effective plate-to-cathode capacitance if the shielding effect of the grounded grid is to be realized.

Audio-Frequency Cathode Follower. A cathode follower is a single-stage degenerative amplifier in which the output is taken from across the cathode resistor, as shown in Fig. 5-56. This circuit is essentially a means for matching a high-impedance circuit to a low-impedance circuit without discriminating against any ac frequency. Its voltage output is always less than the input voltage, but it is capable of power amplification. Two of the advantages of the cathode and emitter followers are **low input capacitance and distortion-free output.**

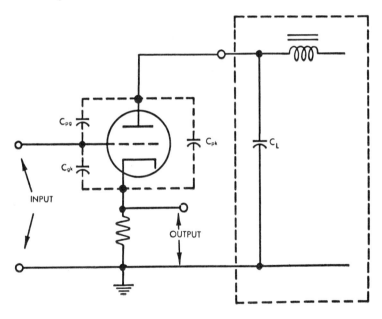

Fig. 5-56.

Serious losses result from the high input capacitance of triodes in general. This is because the resistive load causes a leading current in the grid circuit, and the plate-to-grid capacitance adds to the normal grid-to-cathode capacitance to produce a large capacitance (usually the filter capacitor in the power supply). Nonetheless, as in the triode, the capacitance C_{pg} still must charge when a voltage is applied to it. However, the current in the grid circuit does not lead, because the capacitive load in the cathode follower causes the charging current to shift so that it is exactly in phase with the original grid voltage. Since adding in-phase current is the same as lowering the resistance in the grid circuit, the impedance reflected in the grid circuit is purely resistive, and its effect on all frequencies is the same; that is, there is no frequency attenuation. The input capacitance of a cathode follower is given by $C_{in} = C_{gk} + C_{pg}(1 - A)$.

The cathode follower introduces very little amplitude distortion into the output. It is a **degenerative circuit in which negative feedback is always produced by an unbypassed cathode resistor, and its output is taken from across the cathode resistor and not from the plate**.

The input impedance in a cathode follower is quite high. Since cathode followers are operated with the grid negative with respect to the cathode, a high-amplitude voltage can be applied between the grid and ground without causing grid current to flow. This is due to the degenerative action of the cathode resistor and the high input impedance during the positive input signal. **Because of its high input impedance, the cathode follower has negligible loading effect on the circuit that drives it**.

The cathode follower circuit is shown in its complete form in Fig. 5-57, along with a constant-voltage equivalent circuit. In the diagram this input signal is identified as E_s, the grid-to-cathode voltage as e_g, and the output signal voltage as e_o.

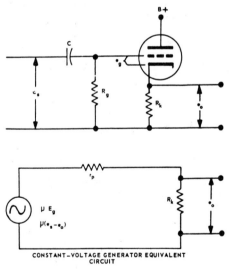

CONSTANT-VOLTAGE GENERATOR EQUIVALENT CIRCUIT

Fig. 5-57.

The size of the cathode resistor is an important design consideration in that it largely determines the output impedance—a factor of special concern in impedance-matching applications. Because of the broad matching capabilities of cathode followers, many audio and radio circuits incorporate input circuits using these amplifiers. Figure 5-58 illustrates a practical twin-triode amplifier incorporating a cathode follower and a conventional amplifier; this circuit is commonly used as the input stage in FM repeaters.

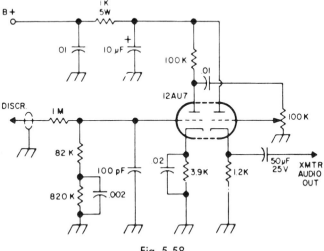

Fig. 5-58.

The left side of the tube (a twin triode 12AU7) is a conventional grounded-cathode circuit. The signal from the preceding audio stage (the discriminator) is fed into the grid of the conventional amplifier. The output of this stage is coupled from the plate circuit through a blocking capacitor to the grid of the cathode follower. The low-impedance output signal is taken from the top of the 1.2K cathode resistor for coupling into the transmitter's input circuit. Note the high value of coupling capacitor in the output; this is made necessary by the low impedance. As the impedance drops, the values of the capacitors must be increased for any given value of signal to be passed to the next stage.

Figure 5-59 shows a 2-transistor stage that serves as an equivalent to the cathode follower; the transistor version is referred to as an *emitter follower*. (This schematic is from the U.S. Navy's **Handbook of Preferred Circuits.**) The amplifier shown provides 12 dB of gain.

Class B Push-Pull Pentode with Transformer Coupling to Speaker. The diagram in Fig. 5-60 shows a push-pull amplifier using beam power pentodes. The circuit is essentially the same as if it were a triode type, except that provisions are made for screen grid voltages. The screen voltage is usually the same as the plate voltage.

Referring to a manufacturer's tube manual, a comparison between the 6V6 class A single-ended and 6V6 class B push-pull amplifiers can be made. With a plate voltage of 250V, the single-ended power output is about 4.5W. For the same plate voltage the push-pull power output is

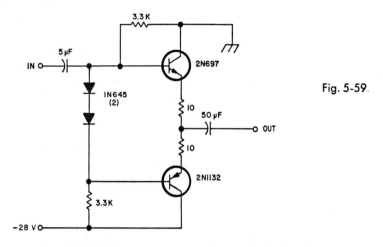

Fig. 5-59.

about 10W. This larger output power is a result of using a larger input signal, made possible by push-pull operation. The upper tube in the push-pull pair may be operated at the lower end of the linear portion of the dynamic curve, and the lower tube is operated in the same manner, with curve reversed. A positive-going signal can go much further positive without distortion and a negative-going signal can go much further negative without distortion, since each tube has its own dynamic characteristic over which to amplify class B signals.

The single-ended stage is biased for class A, while the push-pull stage may be operated class B.

In the circuit shown, the input signal is transformer-coupled to the push-pull pair. The centertap on the input transformer serves to keep the polarities of the two tubes properly opposed. The two output waveforms are applied to an output transformer that is similarly centertapped. The upper tube supplies positive half-cycles to the transformer, and the lower tube supplies negative half-cycles. The output of the transformer, whose impedance matches the speaker, is a composite of the positive and negative half-cycles; this composite is a replica of the original input waveform.

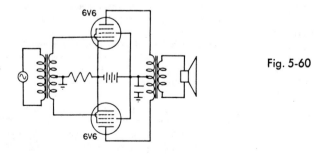

Fig. 5-60

5-35. What kind of vacuum tube responds to filament reactivation, and how is reactivation accomplished?

The filaments of tubes with *thoriated tungsten* filaments are often capable of reactivation. Thoriated-tungsten filaments are manufactured by mixing thorium with tungsten. The thorium coating behaves as a profuse emitter of electrons and gradually evaporates during use. As it boils off, however, it is replenished from inside the tungsten filament wire. If emission falls off when the wire itself is still in good shape, the thorium coating may be replenished by heating the filaments to about 4000°C for several minutes, then dropping the operating temperature to about 2000°C for up to one-half hour. Filaments of this type are normally operated at about 1900°C. At this point the filaments glow bright yellow.

Other filament types that have been successfully reactivated by high-temperature operating periods include the oxide-coated types with barium or strontium as the oxide material; however, the normal operating temperature of these tubes is considerably less than that of filaments of thoriated tungsten, and the consequent reactivation temperature is proportionately less as well.

5-36. Draw a rough graph of plate current versus grid voltage for various plate voltages on a typical triode amplifier.

> *1. How would output current vary with input voltage in class A amplifier operation? Class AB operation? Class B operation? Class C operation?*
> *2. Does the amplitude of the input signal determine the class of operation?*
> *3. What is meant by "current-cutoff" bias voltage?*
> *4. What is meant by plate-current saturation?*
> *5. What is the relationship between distortion in the output current waveform and:*
>   - *class of operation?*
>   - *the portion of the transfer curve over which the signal is operating?*
>   - *amplitude of input signal?*
> *6. What occurs in the grid circuit when the grid is driven positive? Would this have any effect on biasing?*
> *7. In what way is the output current related to the output voltage?*

Each curve in Fig. 5-61 is identified by a specific value of applied plate voltage, and is therefore the resultant of the stated plate voltage and changes in the grid voltage. The curve is formed by noting the plate current as the control-grid voltage is increased in the negative direction, beginning at zero volts. These points are joined and form a curve. The −18V bias limit is set by that range of plate voltages (100 to 300V) considered within the performance capabilities of the tube.

A number of facts immediately become evident. There is a close similarity between the general contours of the characteristic curves. Each has a linear and a nonlinear part. Moreover, each plate-current curve has a cutoff point (on the X-axis), and it is seen that as the plate voltage increases, the value of negative bias required to cut off the plate current also increases. For example, −6.5V causes cutoff when the

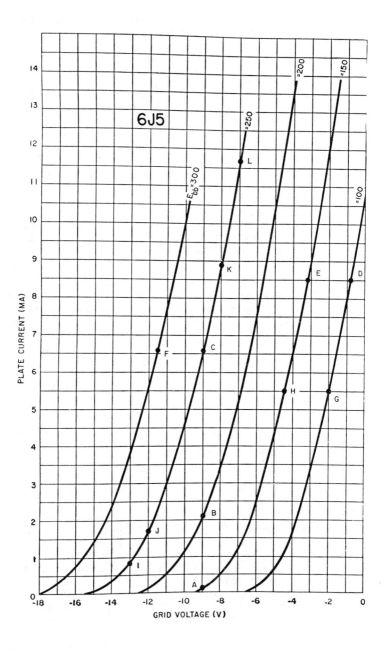

Fig. 5-61.

plate voltage is 100V, whereas −12.6V is required when the plate voltage is 200V, and −15.5V cuts off the plate current when the plate voltage is 250V.

The grid family also discloses an increase in plate current for an increase in plate voltage when the bias voltage is held constant. For example, a −9V bias (point A) results in 0.1 mA plate current with 150V applied to the plate, a 2.1 mA (point B) plate current at 200V on the plate, and a 6.55 mA (point C) plate current with 250V applied to the plate.

The amount of grid voltage required to offset a change in plate current when the plate voltage is changed can be determined from the grid family: these curves indicate the required increase or decrease in bias so that plate current can be held constant when the plate voltage is changed. For example, point D on the 100V plate voltage curve corresponds to 8.5 mA with a negative bias of 0.8V. If the plate voltage is increased to 150V, and the plate current must be held at 8.5 mA (point E), the grid bias must be increased to −3.2V. This indicates that an increase of 50V in plate voltage is offset by an increase of 3.2−0.8, or 2.4V bias. In similar fashion, points C and F, each representing 50V increases in plate voltage, require an increase of 2.5V in negative grid voltage in order that the change in plate voltage be offset and the plate current remain constant at 6.55 mA.

The curves work in the reverse direction as well. They indicate the change in plate voltage required to offset a change in negative grid bias for constant plate currents. For example, assume a starting point (G) representing 100V on the plate and −2V on the grid, and 5.5 mA of plate current. If the bias is increased to −4.4V, what is the new value of plate voltage which will result in the same plate current of 5.5 mA? A vertical projection from the −4.4V bias point intersects the 5.5 mA current projection along the 150V plate-voltage curve (point H). This leads to the conclusion that a 4.4−2, or 2.4V, increase in negative grid bias demands a 50V increase in plate voltage to hold the plate current constant.

Still more information is available from the grid family. This is seen between points I−J and K−L along the 250V characteristic. It shows that the change in plate current corresponding to a fixed change in bias voltage (grid voltage) is a function of the operation region on the plate-current curve. Consider a 1V change, between −12 and −13V (I−J) on the curve of $E_{bb} = 250V$. The plate-current change is 0.84 mA, going from 0.86 to 1.7 mA. The same 1V grid-voltage change higher up on the curve, from −7 to −8V (K−L), results in a change of 2.8 mA going from 11.7 to 8.9 mA.

Examination of the plate-current curve where $E_{bb} = 300V$ discloses even a greater change in plate current for 1V changes in grid voltages. The opposite is true if $E_{bb} = 200V$. This can be seen if the points (−7 to −8) are plotted on the plate-current curve of $E_{bb} = 200V$. A change of 1.8 mA takes place from 3.5 to 5.3 mA. This value is 1V less than the previous value obtained at 2.8 mA when E_{bb} was equal to 250V. This leads to the generalization that **the higher the plate voltage applied to any one type of electron tube, the greater is the change in plate current for a given change in grid voltage.**

With the information above, the FCC subquestions may be answered as follows.

1. **In all classes of amplifier operation, the output current varies in direct proportion to input voltage as long as the input signal is swinging positive below 0V.** In class A operation, the plate current follows the input signal completely, increasing when the grid signal goes positive, decreasing when the grid signal goes negative. In class B operation, the output current follows the grid voltage during positive half-cycles, but current is cut off completely during negative half cycles. In class C operation, since the tube is biased well below plate-current cutoff, plate current flows only during the latter two-thirds or so of its positive swing, so the tube is not drawing current at all during the greater portion of each input cycle. Class AB operation is quite similar to class B, except that the tube is biased so that its operating point is slightly above cutoff; actually, the operating point is often midway between the center of the linear region and cutoff.

2. **The amplitude of the input signal does not in itself determine the class of operation; however, the input-signal amplitude can alter the class.** For example, when a tube or transistor amplifier stage is biased to operate class AB, and a very small input signal is applied to the grid, the tube will conduct during the complete input cycle and the tube can be said to be operating class A. As long as the input signal keeps the tube operating within its linear region, the amplifier is operating class A regardless of the biasing point.

3. **The current-cutoff bias voltage is the amount of negative grid bias required to cause plate current to stop flowing at a particular value of applied plate voltage. As the grid voltage goes more and more negative, plate current decreases.** At some point, called *plate-current cutoff*, the plate current will drop to zero. The value of the grid potential at this point is called *current cutoff bias voltage*.

4. **Saturation occurs when plate current ceases to increase despite changes in grid voltage.** As grid voltage approaches zero (from some negative value), plate current increases in a linear relationship. Close to zero grid voltage, though, the plate current increase does not follow the same constant rising characteristic as it did at the negative value. At zero and slightly above zero, the plate current changes are negligible. This point is referred to as *saturation*.

5. **There is a direct relationship between distortion and class of operation.** Class A operation is the only class that results in distortion-free operation, because it is the only class where the output waveform religiously follows the input waveform. In cases where two class B amplifiers are operated push-pull, the total effect is the same as class A. Distortion occurs when the output waveform ceases to change in accordance with the changes of the input waveform. Since classes B, AB, and C are amplifiers that are not conducting during the total input cycle, they cannot produce a distortion-free signal.

The portion of the transfer characteristic where the tube is biased to operate during quiescence is also a determining factor with respect to total distortion. If the transfer characteristic is linear—that is, if there is a straight-line relationship between grid voltage and plate current over the entire range of input voltages—and the tube is biased so that its no-signal current drain is plotted at the center of this linear region, the output signal will be undistorted as long as the input voltage does not go beyond the limits established by plate-current cutoff and saturation (class A operation). When a class A amplifier is improperly biased—so that the no-signal operating point is above or below the center point on this transfer line—signal excesses will result in distortion. If the class A amplifier is biased too high on the characteristic curve *positive* swings of the input signal will *clip*. If the class A amplifier is biased too low on the line, *negative* swings of the input signal will cause the output signal to clip.

The amplitude of the input signal is important in maintaining any given class of operation. A class C amplifier, for example, requires a very high-amplitude signal in order to bring the grid voltage up to the level required to make the amplifier conduct. If the driving signal is of insufficient amplitude, the tube many never be made to conduct at all. At best, it will be made to conduct for an insufficient period of the total signal's cycle. An insufficient input signal will have no distortion-producing effects on a class A amplifier, however, since the tube is conducting 100% of the time anyway; any change in grid voltage, however small, will be reflected in the output signal. A class B stage (and a class AB stage) that is being supplied with a signal of insufficient amplitude will often produce a full waveform replica of the input. In such cases, the amplifier's efficiency suffers considerably, and the gain is inadequate for use in the amplifier's intended application.

6. **If the grid of an amplifier is driven positive** (that is, if the grid has a positive potential with respect to the cathode, **the grid circuit will draw current**. A current drain in the grid circuit is objectionable in most amplifier circuits because such drain represents a power loss and does not contribute to amplifier performance. The result of such power consumption is deterioration in amplifier operating efficiency. Similarly, a current drain in the grid circuit causes a change in biasing under most amplifier biasing arrangements. Any resistors in the grid circuit will be affected by current flow according to Ohm's law, which states that the voltage drop across a resistor will be equal to the current divided by the resistance.

7. **An increase in output current causes a proportionate drop in plate voltage**; thus, the output voltage of a grounded-cathode amplifier is precisely out of phase with the input voltage; and the plate-current waveform is equal and opposite to the plate-voltage waveform.

5-37. *What is meant by* **amplification factor** *(mu or μ) or a triode? Under what conditions would the amplifier gain approach the value of μ?*

By definition the amplification factor is the **ratio between a small change in plate voltage and a small change in grid voltage that results in the same change in plate current.** It is an indication of the effectiveness of the control grid voltage relative to the plate voltage in controlling the plate current. Expressed as a formula, the amplification factor is

$$\mu = \frac{\Delta e_b}{\Delta e_g}$$

The amplification factor is represented by the Greek letter μ. The Greek letter Δ represents *a small change in*... It is a pure number, without any reference to units. For example, if a tube is said to have a μ of 100, it means that the grid voltage change required to produce a certain change in plate current is 100 times less than the plate voltage changes required to bring about the same change in plate current. In other words, the grid voltage is 100 times more effective than the plate voltage in its influence upon the space charge and, consequently, upon the plate current. To illustrate, suppose that a plate current change of 1 mA is produced by a plate voltage change of 10V, and a grid voltage change of 0.1V produces a 1 mA change in plate current. Then μ is 10/0.1, or 100; and the amplification factor, of course, is 100. Emphasis is placed upon the fact that it is the *change* in plate voltage and the *change* in grid voltage that are important and *not* the individual values of plate and grid voltage.

Developing the amplification factor of a triode from the plate family of curves is a relatively simple process. Simply select a grid voltage value that is about halfway between the usable limits of the grid voltage range shown on the graph of the tube's plate curves. Referring to Fig. 5-62, −8V is a satisfactory grid voltage. Locate a reference point about halfway down the straight portion of the plate current curve for that grid voltage. This is point A. A horizontal projection parallel to the

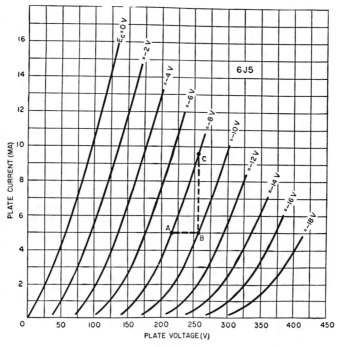

Fig. 5-62.

plate voltage axis shows point *A* as being equal to 5 mA. A vertical projection (downward to the plate voltage scale) shows *A* to be equal to 216V. Point *A*, then, corresponds to a grid voltage of −8V, a plate current of 5 mA, and a plate voltage of 216V.

Now project point *A* along the *X*-axis to an adjacent grid bias curve. The direction of this projection is optional. In this instance it is toward the higher value of negative grid bias. This is point *B*, where the grid voltage is −10V. A vertical projection dropped to the plate voltage axis intersects the 257V point. Point *B* can therefore be described as follows: grid voltage, −10V; plate current, 5 mA; plate voltage, 257V.

The next step is to project the higher plate voltage point on the −8V curve; this results in point *C*. Point *C* corresponds to a grid voltage of −9V, a plate current of 9.6 mA, and a plate voltage of 257V. The information needed to calculate μ has been obtained. With 216V on the plate (point *A*) to 257V on the plate (point *C*), a change in plate current from 5 to 9.6 mA takes place. With 257V on the plate, a change in grid voltage from −10V (point *B*) to −8V (point *C*) causes a change in plate current from 5 to 9.6 mA. Therefore, the equation is

$$\frac{257 - 216}{10 - 8} = \frac{41}{2} = 20.5$$

The value of μ is realized with very high plate load resistance values when the load impedance in the plate circuit is many times the value of the tube's plate resistance.

5-38. *What is meant by "plate resistance" of a vacuum tube? How may its value be determined graphically?*

Plate resistance is another vacuum-tube constant. **It describes the internal resistance of the tube, or the opposition experienced by the electrons in advancing from the cathode to the plate.** This constant is expressed in either of two ways—the dc resistance or the ac resistance. The dc resistance is the internal opposition to current flow when steady values of voltage are applied to the tube electrodes; it is determined by the simple application of Ohm's law at any point on the plate current characteristic. The voltage is the dc plate voltage, symbolized E_{bb}, E_b, or E_p. The current is the steady value of plate current (I_b or I_p). Plate resistance (dc) is identified by the symbol R_p.

Referring to the plate family of curves shown in Fig. 5-63, point *M* is an arbitrary point corresponding to a plate voltage of $E_{bb} = 250$V, grid potential of $E_{cc} = -8$V, and plate current of $I_b = 8.9$ mA. Applying Ohm's law, the plate resistance is

$$R_p = 250/0.0089 = 28,000\Omega$$

For any value of plate voltage the dc resistance is determined by applying Ohm's law, where the numerator is the steady voltage at the plate, and the denominator is the corresponding steady plate current. Point *N* in Fig. 5-63 therefore corresponds to a dc resistance of 37,500Ω, since $E_{bb} = 225$V and $I_b = 6$ mA. Point *O* corresponds to dc resistance of 65K. The various triangles in Fig. 5-63 can be neglected in establishing the dc plate resistance; they are needed for finding the ac plate resistance.

Finding the ac plate resistance from the plate family in Fig. 5-63 is somewhat more involved. The initial point *Q* on the −10V curve •

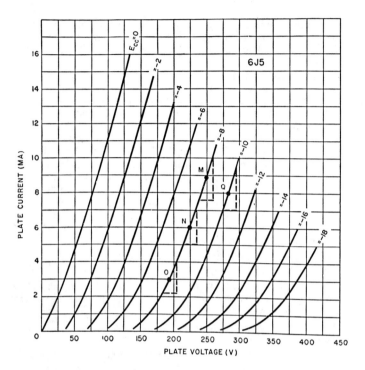

Fig. 5-63.

corresponds to a plate voltage of 265V and a plate current of 8 mA. The dc resistance at point Q, using Ohm's law, is 331K. For ac resistance determination the plate voltage is varied above and below point Q. The operating range is shown by the small triangle drawn about Q. The total change in plate voltage is 20V, with the upper plate voltage limit at 295V and the lower limit at 275V. The variations in plate voltage are arbitrary. The intersections with the appropriate grid voltage curve are determined by projecting voltage lines upward from the plate voltage axis until they intersect the grid voltage curve.

The change in plate current Δi_b, is determined by projecting the points of intersection between the −10V grid voltage curve and the 295V and 275V plate voltage lines, (toward the left) to the plate-current axis. The upper and lower plate-current values are 9.4 and 7 mA. Consequently, the equation for the ac plate resistance at the initial point Q is

$$R_p = \frac{\Delta e_b}{\Delta i_b} = \frac{295 - 275}{0.0094 - 0.007} = \frac{20}{0.0024} = 8333\Omega$$

A comparison of the operating points discloses that the higher the applied plate voltage, the lower the ac plate resistance. Likewise, a change of the negative grid voltage in the positive direction causes a lower plate resistance. This is indicated by a comparison of operating points M, N, O, and Q. In practice, one operating point is given, and the suitability of the tube is determined by the constants prevailing under the single set of conditions. As has been shown, each tube is capable of operation over a number of operating voltages, but only one of these is selected as being typical.

To succinctly answer the second portion of the FCC question, then, **the value of plate resistance depends on the values of plate current and plate voltage at a given operating point.**

5-39. *What is meant by the "voltage gain" of a vacuum-tube amplifier? How does it achieve this gain?*

If the input and output voltages of a vacuum-tube stage are measured, the voltage gain of the tube under its existing operating conditions can be computed. The voltage gain is the output voltage divided by the input voltage (e_o/e_i). If the ac input voltage to a stage is 5V and the output voltage is 100V, the voltage gain is 100/5, or 20. High gain is achieved by keeping the plate load resistance of the tube as high as possible without excessively reducing the dc voltage applied to the plate of the tube. As the value of the plate load resistor is increased, a larger signal voltage appears across it. As a result, the size of the output voltage from the tube is increased and the stage has a larger amplification. There is a practical limit to the value of the plate load resistor, though. If it is too large, it produces a large dc voltage drop, which reduces the voltage applied to the plate of the amplifier and the resultant plate current, so that the tube output is reduced. Typical values for the plate load resistor range from about 25K to 500K.

5-40. *Draw a rough graph of plate current versus plate supply voltage for several different bias voltages on a typical triode vacuum tube. Explain, in a general way, how the value of the plate load resistance affects the portion of the curve over which the tube is operating. How is this related to distortion? Operation over which portion of the curve produces the least distortion?*

The effect of the load applied to a triode (and other electron tubes) can be predicted. This usually is accomplished by adding to the static family of plate characteristic curves a graphical representation of the load known as the *load line*. This shows the distribution of the output of plate voltage supply between the load and the internal resistance of the tube under different conditions of plate current.

For convenience, the plate family of characteristic curves is used for the dynamic charactristics. From it is developed the final transfer characteristic curve which correlates the plate-current/grid-voltage relationship with the load present in the circuit. This curve is called the *dynamic transfer characteristic*. It is to be noted, however, that equal information can be obtained from the dynamic plate characteristic and from the dynamic transfer characteristic.

Figure 5-64, showing a typical static plate family of curves, is a conventional graph plotted at several values of grid bias. However, a load line has been added; the load line is the diagonal $X-Y$ trace labeled R_L. The load line corresponds to a load (R_L) of 25K. The selection of 25K as a load resistor is arbitrary.

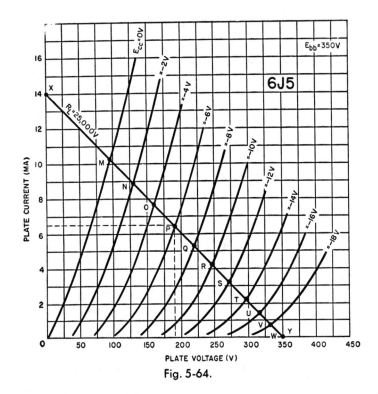

Fig. 5-64.

The load line has no fixed association with tube constants or characteristics. It is simply a means of developing information concerning the behavior of any tube that is used with a certain load. The load may be correct, or it may not be right for the tube. This information appears on the graph when the effects of the load are studied by means of the load line.

The full length of the load line represents one extreme condition—namely, a voltage drop across R_L equal to the full plate supply voltage. This means that the plate voltage e_b equals zero and the plate current equals the full plate supply voltage divided by the load resistor. This figure establishes one terminal of the load line: 14 mA on the plate current axis (point X). The other terminal of the load line corresponds to the other extreme condition; that is, zero plate current and the full supply voltage of 350V on the plate of the tube. This is point Y on the plate voltage axis.

Further reference to Fig. 5-64 discloses that the load line intersects the plate current curves at different points. To establish the distribution of voltages between the tube and load, an operating point must be selected. Assume that the grid voltage chosen for examination is $-6V$. The load line crosses the plate current curve for this bias at point P. A horizontal line drawn to the plate current scale shows that the corresponding plate current is 6.35 mA. A vertical line dropped from point P to the plate voltage axis intersects it at 190V. Therefore, point P can be described as $E_{cc} = -6V$ (grid voltage), $E_{bb} = 190V$ (plate voltage), and $i_b = 6.35$ mA.

The horizontal projection to the plate voltage axis indicates the division of plate supply voltage across the load and internal resistance of the tube. The point of intersection between the horizontal projection to the plate voltage scale and the axis indicates the voltage at the plate (190V). The difference between this value and the total plate supply voltage is the voltage dropped across the load, or $350 - 190 = 160V$. To verify this, the voltage drop across the load resistor (output voltage, e_r) can be computed as follows:

$$e_{RL} = i_b R_L = 0.00635 \times 25,000 = 160V$$

The voltage on the plate and the voltage dropped across the load, for various values of grid voltage, can be determined in similar fashion. For example, point M, corresponding to zero voltage on the control grid, or $E_{cc} = 0$, can be described as

$$E_{cc} = 0V$$
$$i_b = 10.1 \text{ mA}$$
$$e_b = 97V$$
$$E_{RL} = 253V$$
$$E_{bb} = 350$$

Since $E_{cc} = -6V$ is the operating point and $e_{cc} = 0V$ is one extreme, the other extreme can be 6V in the other direction, or $e_{cc} = -12V$. This is point S and can be described as

$$e_c = -12V$$
$$i_b = 3.1 \text{ mA}$$
$$e_b = 272V$$
$$E_{RL} = 78V$$
$$E_{bb} = 350V$$

The three points of intersection, M, P, and S, establish a number of operating factors. For instance, $E_{cc} = -6V$ was selected as the reference operating point. Then an extreme condition, $e_{cc} = 0V$, was selected as one limit of change in grid voltage. The second limit of change in grid voltage was set as $e_{cc} = -12V$. How have these changes affected the plate circuit?

The higher the plate voltage, the higher the value of negative grid bias required to cut off the tube; nonetheless, at some maximum plate voltage value, there will be a determinable negative grid voltage that will cause the tube to cut off, or stop conducting. The lower right terminal of the load line, then, is plotted at the point where applied plate voltage is maximum and current is zero. At the other extreme, there is a point at which plate current will be at its maximum—a point where further decreases in negative grid voltage will not result in additional plate current flow, and where plate voltage will actually drop to zero. At this point, the factor that determines plate current is the plate load resistance. The maximum supply voltage divided by the plate load resistance will yield the total plate current at this extreme. The load line is plotted from this maximum current point to the no-current, maximum-voltage point, as shown

In design of amplifier circuits it is best to choose a load resistor that results in the least possible slope (low plate current at saturation).

Since the slope of the load line is a function of plate voltage divided by load resistance, it follows that the higher the load resistance, the lower the total plate current at saturation and the more horizontal the load line.

Reducing the slope of the load line (by increasing the value of the plate load resistor) serves to improve the symmetry of the signal produced by the amplifier stage. An improvement in the symmetry of a signal is a reduction in signal distortion. To see why it is important to reduce the slope of the load line, examine the circuit and plate curves of Fig. 5-65. With a 30K plate load resistor and a fixed 8V bias on the grid, a signal that varies the grid voltage between −4 and −12V results in a symmetrical change in plate current of plus and minus about 0.9 mA (from 4.1 to 5 mA, and from 4.1 to 3.2 mA). It also results in a symmetrical deviation of plate voltage across the load resistor (88V to 114V and from 114V to 140V) of ±26V. Thus, the signal produced under these conditions will be undistorted and predictable.

But suppose we had selected a 20K plate load resistor rather than 30K load. In this case the plate current maximum would be 12 mA, and the load line would be at about 45°. If you apply such a load line to the graph shown, you will see that plate current at quiescence will be approximately 5.3 mA. At maximum negative signal swings, the current drops to exactly 4 mA, for a total change of 1.3 mA. At maximum positive signal swings, the current increases to 6.7 mA for a total change of 1.4 mA. Thus, the current sine wave is not symmetrical, and the output is distorted. Similarly, the resting output plate voltage is 126V, and the total plate voltage variation is from 100V to 152V, for a total voltage swing of ±26V as a result of a grid voltage swing of ±4V.

In summary, a higher value of plate load resistor in the circuit shown gives an output voltage variation of about 26V and an output current variation of about 0.9 mA. The lower value of plate load resistor results in the same basic variation of plate voltage (yet higher values are required) and an output current variation of about 1.3 mA. It is easy to see that the higher operating voltages and increased current requirement for the lower value of load resistor also tends to lower the efficiency of the amplifier tube without resulting in increased gain.

To answer the second portion of the FCC question, **the least distortion will be observed when the tube is operated over the lower part of the curve. The lower on the curve the load line is drawn, the more linear will be the operation of the amplifier and the more symmetrical the waveshape.**

5-41. *A triode grounded-cathode amplifier has a mu (μ) of 30, a plate impedance of 5K, a load impedance of 10K, plate voltage of 300V, plate current of 10 mA, and cathode bias. The amplifier is operated class A.*

1. *What is the stage gain of this amplifier?*
2. *What is the cutoff bias voltage?*
3. *Assuming the bias voltage is one-half value of cutoff bias, what value of cathode resistor would be used to produce the required bias?*
4. *What size capacitor should be used to sufficintly bypass the cathode resistor if the lowest approximate frequency desired is 500 Hz.?*

362

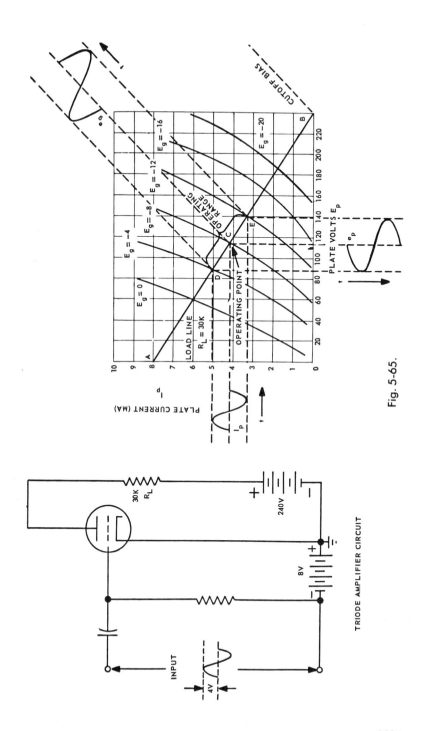

Fig. 5-65.

TRIODE AMPLIFIER CIRCUIT

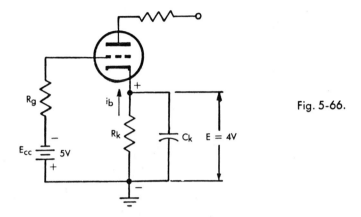

Fig. 5-66.

The triode amplifier circuit is pictured in Fig. 5-66. Refer to this drawing as you look over the answers to each part of the FCC question.

1. The stage gain of this amplifier is 20. Stage gain is independent of plate current and voltage, and is a function of the plate and load resistances and the individual tube's amplification factor, or μ. The equation for calculation of a stage's gain is

$$G_v = \frac{\mu R_L}{R_L + R_p}$$

where μ is amplification factor and the other symbols represent the resistances of the plate and load. With a μ of 30, a load resistance of 10K, and a plate impedance of 5K, the equation becomes

$$G_v = \frac{30 \times 10,000}{10,000 + 5,000} = \frac{3000,000}{15,000} = \frac{300}{15} = 20$$

2. The stage's cutoff bias is equal to the plate voltage divided by the amplification factor, or E_{bb}/μ. The plate voltage is 300V and the amplification factor is 30; so the cutoff bias value is -10V.

3. The grid of the triode amplifier is biased at -5V during the no-signal state. To maintain this 5V bias, the cathode resistor must keep the grid 5V negative with respect to the cathode. Given a plate current of 10 mA and a cathode resistor drop of 5V, the value of the resistor may be determined from Ohm's law. (The 10 mA of plate current flows through the cathode resistor, across the space charge, and out through the plate circuit.) Since E is 5V and I is 0.01A (10 mA), the cathode resistor value is 500Ω (i.e., $5/0.01 = 500\Omega$).

4. The value of the cathode bypass capacitor must be such that its reactance is small compared with the resistance of the cathode resistor at 500 Hz (in this case). A practical value for audio applications would be in the range from 10 to 50 μF. Since there is no set rule for what constitutes "small" when compared with the cathode resistor value, some design specialists like to stay with an arbitrary

percentage of the cathode resistance, such as 10%. If we say that the capacitive reactance at 500 Hz must not exceed 50Ω (10% of 500Ω), we can apply the formula

$$C = \frac{1}{2\pi f X_c}$$

to find the smallest value of capacitance. The capacitance works out to be about $6.3\ \mu F$. A $10\ \mu F$ capacitor will be fine.

5-42. *Why is the efficiency of an amplifier operated class C higher than one operated class A or class B?*

A class C amplifier is operated so far beyond plate current cutoff that the tube only conducts during a small portion of the input signal's operating cycle—sometimes only 25%. Heat dissipation is low and efficiency is high, since the tube has a relaxation period during each cycle in which to cool somewhat.

5-43. *The following are excerpts from a tube manual rating of a beam pentode. Explain the significance of each item:*

Grid-to-plate capacitance .... *1.1 pF*
Input capacitance .... *2.2 pF*
Output capacitance .... *8.5 pF*
Heater · ·ltage *6.3V*
Max dc plate voltage *700V*
Max peak positive-pulse voltage .... *7 kV*
Max negative pulse plate voltage .... *1.5 kV*
Max screen grid voltage *175V*
Max peak negative-control grid voltage *200V*
Max plate dissipation *20W*
Max screen grid dissipation *30W*
Max dc cathode current .... *200 mA*
Max peak cathode current .... *700 mA*
Max control grid circuit resistance *470K*

Grid-to-Plate Capacitance. This important vacuum-tube specification gives valuable information with regard to the inherent coupling between the two key tube elements—the control grid and plate. The value of this interelectrode capacitance helps you to know the frequency limitations on the tube without neutralization. The lower value here, the higher the signal frequency can be without neutralization. The specification is based on a measurement made with the screen and suppressor grids connected to the cathode element.

Input Capacitance. It would be hard to imagine a tube whose grid-to-plate capacitance was 1.1 pF having a total input capacitance of only 2.2 pF. This number is supposed to be the total sum of all the capacitances relative to the control grid; that is, it is the sum of these capacitances: control-grid-to-plate, control-grid-to-suppressor-grid (and cathode, when no internal connection between the two is provided), and control-g.id-to-screen-grid. The specified value is important because the values of capacitance on the control grid are additive to the capacitances in this part of the circuit, and will form part of any resonant circuit connected between these electrodes. A more realistic value for the total capacitance of a beam power pentode would be 15 or 20 pF.

Output Capacitance. The output capacitance is the sum of all capacitances associated with the plate, which include plate-to-grid, plate-to-suppressor, plate-to-screen, and plate-to-cathode. The importance of the specification lies in the fact that all these capacitance values are additive in nature and must be considered when a resonant network is part of the plate circuit.

Heater Voltage. The heater voltage specified is a voltage on which all tube performance ratings are based. Since most tubes will behave quite differently under different heater temperatures, it is important to adhere to this specified value when the tube is employed as an amplifier. Heater voltage ratings affect such important parameters of performance as tube life, maximum plate current, and total output power.

Max DC Plate Voltage. As implied by the specification, this value is the highest permissible dc operating voltage the tube can tolerate under maximum-load conditions.

Max Peak Positive Pulse Voltage. In many applications an amplifier tube will be subjected to pulse voltages far above maximum steady value that can be applied safely under normal operating conditions. This specification permits the user to assess a tube's qualifications for such applications as the *horizontal output* of a television receiver, where extremely high pulse voltages are applied to the plate for brief (microseconds) periods. Exceeding the design values here could result in destruction of the tube, serious internal arcing, or erratic performance.

Max Negative Pulse Plate Voltage. In inductive plate loads high negative voltages often develop for brief "flash" periods as the opposing emf builds across the load. This specification establishes the maximum flash voltage value that can be tolerated without tube deterioration.

Maximum Screen Grid Voltage. Since the screen voltage is a determining factor with respect to the plate current capabilities of tetrodes and pentodes, this specification becomes one of particular importance. The value given represents the maximum working voltage that can be applied to the screen grid.

Max Peak Negative Control Grid Voltage. This specification describes the maximum safe value of negative voltage that can be applied to the tube without internal arcing. The value shown indicates that levels below 200V can be handled without deleterious effects.

Max Plate Dissipation. This specification describes the maximum power the plate can safely dissipate under a normal, sustained-load operation. The value may be exceeded when the tube is cooled by some external means (unless the specification is based on operation while the tube is being cooled, as with many rf power amplifiers).

Max Screen Grid Dissipation. The screen, being positioned opposite the control grid and in line with the cathode, is capable of dissipating power in the same manner as a plate, and many circuits involve use of the screen grid as a plate element. Nonetheless the value listed (30W) is very likely a misprint, since it is unrealistic to rate the screen grid at a greater dissipation value than the plate. A more likely figure would be some value between 10% and 15% of the plate dissipation capability.

Max DC Cathode Current. The cathode supplies the current required in the plate circuit. The value specified here is the maximum current the cathode can deliver without premature burnout or weakening of the heater—cathode material. This current rating is *not* the maximum current a directly heated cathode can draw from its low-voltage supply; that value would be considerably higher (perhaps 10 times as much).

Max Peak Cathode Current. Beyond the normal steady value specified above, the cathode of many types of amplifiers is called upon to deliver very large surge currents. Understandably, the surge capability of a cathode is considerably higher than the normal dc constant-drain capability. The value given under this specification describes the maximum safe value of any high-current pulse. Exceeding the value even briefly may cause serious tube deterioration.

Max Control Grid Circuit Resistance. This specification describes the maximum grid-to-ground resistance of the tube's control grid and must not be exceeded in design of the circuit in which the tube will be used. Higher values than that listed could result in cancellation of the grid bias, with the result that excessive voltage is applied to the grid, thereby destroying the tube or prohibiting normal operation.

5-44. *Name at least three abnormal conditions that would tend to shorten the life of a vacuum tube. Also name one or more probable causes of each condition.*

Excessive heater voltage, excessive power dissipation (plate), excessive dc operating voltage, operating the filaments from a dc supply, operating out of resonance, and improper bias are typical operating conditions that tend to degrade a tube's performance and result in premature failure. Causes are as follows:

Excessive Heater Voltage. In mobile equipment improper adjustment of the car's voltage regulator results in excessive heater voltage. High line voltage is a common cause of this condition in ac equipment. The condition results in rapid deterioration of the filament or cathode.

Excessive Power Dissipation. Each tube designed for "power" applications has a rated dissipation, which can be exceeded only to the detriment of the tube. Excessive plate voltage on the tube will result in a commensurate increase in plate current, the combination of which must be delivered to the load or dissipated by the tube. Excessive dissipation can also be caused by improper load impedance or an out-of-resonance condition in an output rf circuit.

Excessive DC Operating Voltage. This condition may be caused by improper design of the tube's power supply; excessive line voltage; too low a value of plate load resistor; and, in mobile equipment, operation of the equipment when the voltage regulator in the automobile is adjusted for too high a voltage output. In the latter case the excesses can be quite severe. The supply voltage should be about 12.6V (to a maximum of around 14.3V or so). Considering the turns ratio of stepup transformers, it is not surprising that this condition has probably been responsible for the demise of more tubes than all the other faults combined. A transformer designed to produce 480V from a 12V source will produce 640V when supplied with a source of only 16V. Tubes are no longer used in mobile equipment, but transistorized equipment is also very intolerant of excessive supply voltages.

Filament Operation from a DC Supply. Prolonged operation of a tube's filaments from a dc voltage supply will cause deterioration of one side of the heater before the other. Since one end of the heater winding is negative with respect to the other, it will release more electrons than the other end. This is why many economy-minded experimenters reverse the dc heater leads of their expensive power amplifiers from time to time.

Operating Off Resonance. This condition is common with rf power amplifiers operated class C. When the output circuit is in resonance, the plate current is at its minimum value. If any out-of-resonance condition occurs—such as any change in the plate load, change in the antenna, or a change in the setting of the capacitor in the final plate tank circuit—it will cause the plate current to rise steeply, exceeding the maximum rated value of the tube.

Improper Bias. This is particularly problematical with class C and class B amplifiers, which are designed to operate only during part of the input cycle. When a class C amplifier's operating point is moved closer to the tube's plate current cutoff point (as can happen with component value changes or certain other such causes), the tube is made to conduct for longer periods of each cycle. The maximum rating for a particular class of operation are not necessarily applicable when the tube is operated under other classes.

5-45. *Name at least three circuit factors (not including tube types and component values) in a one-stage amplifier circuit that should be considered at VHF but that would not be of particular concern at lower frequencies.*

Three important considerations are (1) lead length, (2) capacitor dielectric material, and (3) positioning of ground points.

Lead Length. The lengths of leads is an important consideration at the higher frequencies; the higher the frequency, the more important this becomes. A 6 in. length of wire becomes a quarter-wave whip at UHF and a serious radiating element in the VHF region. Long leads used in VHF circuits inevitably result in unwanted coupling through stray capacitances, excessive radiation, parasitic oscillation because of unwanted feedback, and a host of other anomalies that can be avoided by use of short, direct wire routes.

Capacitor Dielectric Material. A piece of paper is an excellent dielectric for capacitors used with low-frequency signals. But a piece of paper does have a certain resistive value. As the frequency goes up, the insulating ability of paper diminishes until, at VHF, paper tends to be a resistance rather than a capacitance. At VHF such dielectric materials as mica or Mylar should be used.

Positioning of Ground Points. The nature of rf is such that an electrical ground is not necessarily an rf ground. Even though all grounds in a circuit stage are connected to the same chassis, there may be rf potential differences between the points. When this condition occurs, such problems as parasitic oscillation, spurious radiation, and erratic tuning are common. At VHF it's wise to be judicious in the grounding procedure; if possible, connect all the grounds of any given stage to a common chassis point.

5-46. *What is a* **lighthouse** *triode? An* **acorn** *tube? These tubes were designed for operation in what frequency range?*

UHF tubes are especially constructed for operation at higher frequencies, where it is necessary to reduce interelectrode capacitances and to cut down transit time (the time electrons require to travel from the cathode to the plate). This is done by making the electrodes quite small and spacing them very closely together. Because of these construction features, the power-handling ability of this type of tube is somewhat less than that of tubes used at lower frequencies.

In UHF tubes there is frequently no tube base. Connections to the electrodes are made through pins that protrude through the envelope in a way that keeps the leads short and minimizes capacitance between them. Three special types of UHF tubes—*acorn, doorknob,* and *lighthouse* tubes—are so named because of their shapes and sizes. Acorn and doorknob tubes are available as diodes, triodes, and pentodes. The lighthouse tube is designed to fit directly into the end of a concentric tubing used to form the tank circuit in UHF systems. By directly connecting the tube in this manner, losses due to connecting wires are eliminated. Figure 5-67 shows two acorn tubes; the tube shown at the top is a typical acorn triode, and the lower sketch shows a pentode. Note the

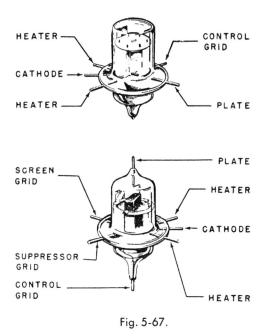

Fig. 5-67.

positioning of the control grid and plate pins of the pentode. Figure 5-68 illustrates the construction of a typical lighthouse tube. In sketch A the tube itself is shown; in B the construction details are given. Although the illustrated tube has heater and cathode pins, many lighthouse tubes do not. The 3CX100A5 (a "souped up" version of the popular 2C39) is one example of a pinless lighthouse tube. With its ceramic base and silver elements, the tube is capable of delivering up to 100W of rf at 500 MHz without external cooling.

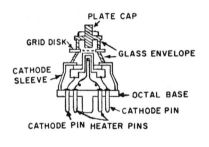

PLATE CAP

GRID DISK

GLASS ENVELOPE

CATHODE SLEEVE

OCTAL BASE

CATHODE PIN

CATHODE PIN HEATER PINS

Fig. 5-68.

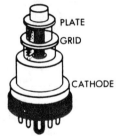

PLATE

GRID

CATHODE

LIGHTHOUSE TUBE

5-47. *Why are special tubes sometimes required at UHF and above?*

As the operating frequency is increased. capacitive reactance between electrodes in a vacuum tube decreases. At frequencies higher than 100 MHz, the interelectrode capacitance of an ordinary vacuum tube bypasses radio frequencies very effectively. Also, the electron transit time is about one nanosecond (one-thousandth of a microsecond). Although this may seem an insignificant amount of time, it approaches and sometimes equals the time of a cycle within the tube, thus causing an undesirable phase shift.

A small number of ordinary vacuum tubes can be operated at frequencies higher than 100 MHz under certain critical operating conditions. The most suitable tubes of this type are triodes having low interelectrode capacitances, close spacing of the electrodes to reduce the transit time, a high amplification factor, and a fairly low plate resistance. Since some of these requirements are conflicting, tubes that strike a happy medium are generally selected. The operation of certain ordinary vacuum tubes at extremely high plate voltages is sometimes permitted in radar circuits to reduce the electron transit time.

The amount of interelectrode capacitance, the effect of electron transit time, and other objectionable features of ordinary vacuum tubes are minimized considerably in the construction of special tubes for use at UHF. The UHF tubes have very small electrodes placed close together and often have no socket base. By reduction in all physical dimensions of a tube by the same scale, the interelectrode capacitances are decreased without affecting the transconductance or amplification factor. Transit time likewise is reduced, as is the power-handling capacity of a tube of small dimensions.

5-48. *Draw a diagram of each of the following power supply circuits. Explain the operation of each, including the relative input and output voltage amplitudes, waveshapes, and current waveforms.*

- *Vacuum-tube full-wave rectifier with a capacitive input pi-section filter.*
- *Vacuum-tube full-wave rectifier with choke input filter.*
- *Silicon diode doubler with a resistive load.*
- *Nonsynchronous vibrator power supply with silicon diode bridge circuit and capacitive input pi-section filter.*
- *Synchronous vibrator power supply with capacitive-input pi-section filter.*

Tube-Type Full-Wave Supply and Capacitive Input Pi Section. The drawing of Fig. 5-69 shows a complete power supply, from the stepup transformer to the output line. Each section is labeled and described according to its function. Immediately below the diagram sections are waveforms that represent the output voltage of each section. As shown, the transformer section of the supply is driven from the 115V primary power line. The transformer is shown with two windings—one for the rectifier's filaments and the other for the high voltage. The rectifier stage allows current to pass in one direction only. The pi-section filter is named because of its shape; notice the resemblance between the filter and the Greek letter π. (The regulator and voltage divider sections, though not required by the FCC question, are presented to allow a better understanding of power supply circuits.)

Note that each section is applicable to virtually any power supply. For example, the transformer section can be used for any of the various power supply configurations; and the filter, a capacitive input type, is applicable to all power supply circuits, be they half-wave or full-wave. The explanations of the circuit functions shown in the drawing are applicable to all other illustrated power supply types except as noted.

Figure 5-70 illustrates the basic power supply circuits. It should be noted that the diode symbol—the arrow with a perpendicular line crossing the point—may be used for diodes of either vacuum-tube, silicon, or selenium construction. Thus, the supplies pictured are applicable to either silicon diode or vacuum-tube circuits.

Tube-Type Full-Wave Supply with Choke Input Filter. The diagram for this supply is precisely the same as that shown in Fig. 5-69, except that the left 10 μF capacitor is removed from the filter section. Use of a choke input filter results in a slight reduction of total supply voltage output but better regulation when a regulator section is not incorporated into the supply.

A capacitor input filter with no load produces a terminal voltage that is nearly equal to the peak value of the applied ac. As the load is increased, however, the terminal voltage falls, because the current drawn by the load prevents the capacitor from retaining its full charge. As shown in Fig. 5-71, the output voltage of a capacitor input filter depends substantially on the drain of the load. As long as the load is quite light or constant, the output voltage is relatively stable; variations in load, though, cause variations in the output voltage. The **capacitor input filter is thus said to have relatively poor regulation.**

As illustrated in Fig. 5-71, the choke input filter's output voltage is relatively constant as long as the load is above a certain minimum value. Since the output voltage remains essentially the same over a wide range of current drains, the **choke input filter is said to have good regulation.**)

Silicon Diode Doubler Circuit with Resistive Load. The basic doubler circuit is shown in Fig. 5-70D. A resistive load is provided by connecting a resistor across each of the capacitors in the output line.

The waveform of a power supply with a highly resistive load is shown in the lower portion of Fig. 5-72. By contrast, note the waveform of the dc voltage output of the supply shown in Fig. 5-73. As indicated, a highly resistive load offers better regulation when a capacitor input filter system is used, regardless of whether the supply is a doubler, conventional full-wave type, or bridge.

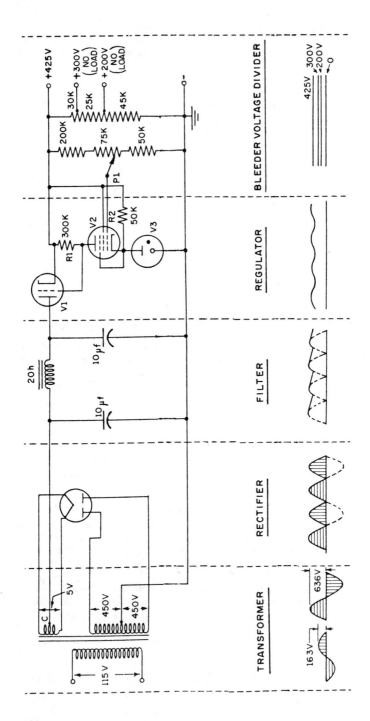

Low voltage is stepped up by the transformer from 115 volts to 900 volts. Center tap provides a dividing point so that 450 volts are applied to each section of the 5U4G rectifier. The ends of the transformer alternately become positive and negative.

Center tap C on heater winding is used to force plate current to divide equally in each filament lead. If there is no center tap, a voltage divider of two equal 50 ohm resistors may be put across the secondary to produce the same effect.

Alternately positive and negative voltage is applied to the plates of the rectifier.

The two plates conduct alternately as each plate is made positive in turn by the transformer. Pulses of current flow from the filament line to each plate in turn. The plates alternately become positive and negative with the applied a. c., but the filament line will show a one-directional flow.

Capacitors charge when the rectifier conducts, and they discharge through the bleeder resistor when the tube is not conducting.

Choke builds up a magnetic field when the tube draws current. The field collapses as current decreases, tending to keep a constant current flowing in the same direction through the bleeder resistor and the load.

Capacitor input (illustrated) gives higher voltage output with low current loads.

Choke input gives steadier output with less ripple under load conditions.

If the load draws more current or if the a-c input voltage falls, the terminal voltage of the power supply falls.

Resistor R1, tube V2, and gas-tube V3 are in series across the rectifier terminals. V3 holds the cathode of V2 at a constant positive potential with respect to ground, and setting of P1 determines bias on V2.

A fall in terminal voltage causes more negative bias on V2, less current through V2, hence, less current through R1. Less IR drop across R1 causes less negative bias on V1. V1, then acts as a lower value resistor, and terminal voltage decrease is checked.

As a bleeder, the resistor is for safety to discharge the capacitors when power is removed.

As a load resistor, it acts as a stabilizer to protect the voltage regulator at no load, and to improve the regulation.

A voltage divider meets the requirements of a load resistor and a bleeder, but in addition has taps placed at intervals for voltage at less than the maximum.

It is usually grounded at the lower end but may be grounded at any higher point to get a negative output.

Fig. 5-69.

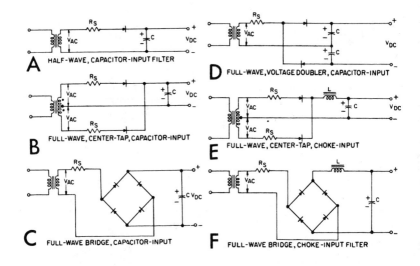

A — HALF-WAVE, CAPACITOR-INPUT FILTER

B — FULL-WAVE, CENTER-TAP, CAPACITOR-INPUT

C — FULL-WAVE BRIDGE, CAPACITOR-INPUT

D — FULL-WAVE, VOLTAGE DOUBLER, CAPACITOR-INPUT

E — FULL-WAVE, CENTER-TAP, CHOKE-INPUT

F — FULL-WAVE BRIDGE, CHOKE-INPUT FILTER

Fig. 5-70.

Fig. 5-71.

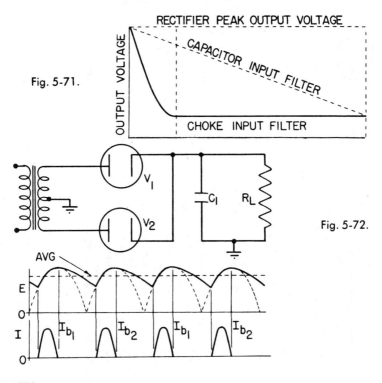

Fig. 5-72.

374

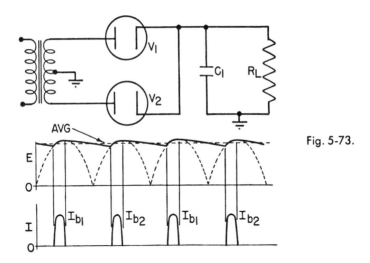

Fig. 5-73.

Nonsynchronous Vibrator Supply with Diode Bridge and Pi Filter. The basic nonsynchronous vibrator supply is shown in Fig. 5-74. The two output lines (identified by the arrows) may be connected to any of the diode rectifier circuits illustrated in Fig. 5-70 in place of the transformer pictured. Thus, to show a nonsynchronous vibrator bridge circuit, the vibrator supply's output lines would be connected in place of the transformer shown in Fig. 5-70C. The capacitor (C, in Fig. 4-70C) represents the first leg of the pi-section filter (which is illustrated in complete form in Fig. 5-69).

It is important to emphasize that power supplies are, by their nature, modular. That is, the vibrator-transformer section can be replaced with a line-transformer section. Any of the rectifier circuits may be connected to the transformer, and any of the filters may be used with the various rectifier circuits.

Synchronous Vibrator Supply with Pi-Section Filter. No rectifier is necessary with the synchronous vibrator supply (Fig. 5-75). As shown, a second pair of vibrator contacts are synchronized with the transformer-driving pair. Since the second set of contacts provides a

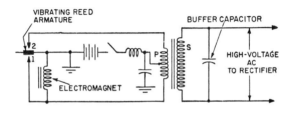

Fig. 6-74.

375

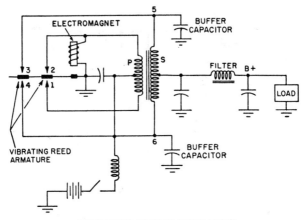

SYNCHRONOUS VIBRATOR POWER SUPPLY

Fig. 5-75.

ground that alternates about the output line at the same rate as the input, the rectification is purely mechanical, but it is effective. As shown, the output is passed through a pi-section filter.

5-49. *What advantage has a bridge circuit over a conventional full-wave rectifier?*

The output voltage of a diode bridge is almost twice the output voltage from a conventional full-wave rectifier circuit. This increase in voltage may be illustrated by comparing the two basic types of rectifiers shown in Figs. 5-76 and 5-77. Figure 5-76 shows a tube-type full-wave circuit, and Fig. 5-77 shows a tube-type full-wave bridge. For the comparison we will assume that the transformers used in the two supplies are identical. (Note that the centertap is not used in the bridge circuit.)

The peak voltage developed between points A and B (transformer secondary) is assumed to be 1000V. In the full-wave circuit of Fig. 5-76, the peak voltage from the centertap (C) to either point A or B is 500V. Because only $V1$ or $V2$ is conducting at any instant, the maximum voltage that can be rectified at any instant is 500V. Therefore, the maximum voltage that can be developed across the load resistor (R) is 500V, less the small voltage drop across the tube that is conducting. (The same explanation holds whether the diode rectifiers are silicon (solid state), selenium (metal), or vacuum-tube; the only difference is the amount of voltage dropped across the rectifier while it is conducting.)

In the bridge circuit of Fig. 5-77, however, the maximum voltage that can be rectified is the full voltage of the secondary of the transformer or, in this case, 1000V. Therefore, the voltage that can be developed across the load resistor is 1000V less the voltage drop across the rectifiers that are conducting. Thus, the full-wave bridge circuit produces a higher output voltage than the conventional full-wave rectifier does with the same transformer.

A second advantage of the bridge circuit is that the peak inverse voltage across a tube is only half the peak inverse voltage impressed on

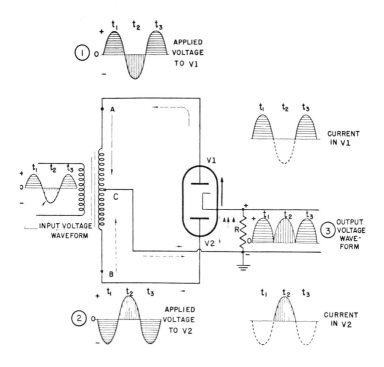

Fig. 5-76.

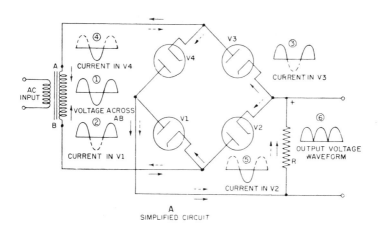

Fig. 5-77.

a rectifier in a conventional full-wave rectifier that is designed for the same output voltage. For example, if the two circuits are to produce the same output voltage (1000V); the transformer secondary in the full-wave rectifier has a 2000V peak developed across it, while that for the bridge rectifier has only a 1000V peak. In this example, when $V1$ in Fig. 5-76 is not conducting, its plate is made negative relative to its cathode by a maximum voltage of 2000V. The same is true for $V2$. This negative voltage is called the *peak inverse voltage* (PIV), and if it is greater than the maximum PIV rating of the tube, breakdown within the tube will occur. Semiconductors, like tubes, have maximum PIV ratings that cannot be exceeded without destroying the device. So, for a given output voltage, it is safer to use a bridge circuit than a conventional full-wave circuit—particularly where the diodes are operating within the marginal limits of their PIV ratings.

5-50. *What are swinging chokes and where are they normally used?*

Swinging chokes, so called because of their varying inductance with changing load, are **inductive filters that provide a very high inductance with light loads and a very low inductance with heavy loads.** They are used in power supplies for loads that vary a great deal, because of their advantage in providing better regulation over a wide range of loads. **Typical uses are in supplies for transmitters, modulators, and other such circuits where a changing** $B+$ voltage might cause degradation in the operation of the load.

5-51. *Show a method of obtaining two voltages from a single supply.*

The simplest way of providing multiple voltages from a single power supply is through the use of divider resistors, as shown in the final modular section in the power supply drawing of Fig. 5-69. In this type of voltage-splitting system, the bleeder resistor in the power supply consists of several series resistors shunted across the load. The values are so chosen that any desired voltage may be obtained.

Another system, which is high'y suitable for applications where a centertapped primary power transformer is used with a full-wave bridge circuit, involves nothing more than using the centertap on the transformer to supply a voltage that is one-half the value of the bridge output. For transmitters, this type of arrangement is particularly suitable, because it allows a considerable change in output power by the simple expedient of providing a means of switching between the bridge output and the centertap. Switching from the bridge output to the transformer centertap cuts the voltage in half, which results in a current drop of 50% as well, and the total power reduction is 75%. In other words, doubling of supply voltage can result in a power increase of four times.

5-52. *What are the characteristics of a capacitor input filter system as compared with a choke input filter system. What is the effect upon a filter choke of a large value of direct current?*

Capacitor Input Filter. A caacitor input filter with no load produces a terminal voltage almost equal to the peak of the applied ac voltage. As the load increases, the terminal voltage drops because the current drawn by the load prevents the capacitor from retaining its charge. This type of filter is undesirable for applications that require a large current, because the peak current that must flow in the diodes to charge the input capacitor may damage the diodes. Since the output voltage falls as the output current is increased, this type of filter has relatively poor regulation, as shown in Fig. 5-71. It may be used, however, where the load is light or very constant.

Choke Input Filter. The regulation of choke input filters may be better understood by considering a specific type of filter—the L-type. At no load, the output voltage of the choke input filter is nearly equal to the peak voltage of the applied ac, as with the capacitor input filter (see Fig. 5-71). This high voltage can be obtained because, with no load current being drawn, the capacitor can be charged to the peak voltage. However, if only a small load current is drawn, the output voltage falls sharply to some lower value. As the load current increases beyond the value indicated by point A in the illustration, there is very little change in voltage except that which takes place in the dc resistance of the choke coil. Since the voltage at the output of a choke input filter changes very little over a wide range of load, a choke input filter has good regulation.

The use of a choke input filter prevents load current from building up or dropping quickly. If the inductance is made large enough, the current becomes nearly constant. The inductance prevents the current from ever reaching the peak value that would be reached without the inductance, so the output voltage never eaches the peak value of the applied ac. A large value of current keeps the filter's output voltage down, but the voltage remains quite constant, even with current decreases and increases.

5-53. *Would varying the value of a bleeder resistor in a power supply have any effect on the ripple voltage?*

The value of the resistor does indeed influence the ripple voltage. The bleeder resistor should be selected so as to draw at least 10% of the total load in order for the change in power supply current to be less for a given change in load and thus reduce the magnitude of the variation in output voltage.

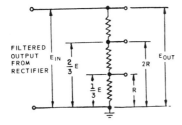

Fig. 5-78.

A bleeder resistor may serve as both a load resistor and voltage divider. Figure 5-78 shows a bleeder composed of three equal-value resistors. This arrangement provides three output voltages. As long as no load current is drawn from any terminal (except the top), the voltages across the resistors will divide in proportion to the resistance of each, as shown.

5-54. *What effect does the amount of current required by the load have upon the voltage regulation of the power supply? Why is voltage regulation an important factor?*

The output voltage developed by any source of power tends to decrease when current is drawn from the source. **Without regulation, the amount of voltage decrease is large when a heavy load current is drawn.** Voltage regulation is important in many electronic circuits because it offers stability and performance predictability. **In such circuits as transmitters and receivers, variations in output voltage cause severe and often unacceptable changes in frequency.**

5-55. *What is meant by "peak inverse voltage" as applied to a diode, and how can it be computed for a full-wave supply?*

Peak inverse voltage is the peak negative voltage applied to the anode of a rectifying device in a power supply during the portion of the cycle when the rectifier is nonconducting. The dc output voltage and peak inverse voltage vary with the type of circuit. In general, however, the peak inverse voltage is equal to or twice the peak value of the dc output voltage of the power supply. One of the principal ratings of a diode is its PIV rating. This rating describes the maximum peak reverse voltage the device can tolerate without being destroyed.

There is no magic universal figure for computation of peak inverse voltage. The peak inverse voltages applied to diodes in various rectifier circuits will vary according to the type of circuit. In a half-wave rectifier the peak inverse voltage is equal to the *full peak value* of the transformer secondary voltage with a resistive or inductive load, or 1.414 times the rms voltage. With a capacitor input filter, the factor is 2.83 instead of 1.414. In a full-wave or bridge rectifier circuit, the peak inverse voltage applied to any diode at any one time is equal to the transformer secondary's peak value (1.414 × rms) regardless of filter type.

5-56. *Discuss the relative merits and limitations (as used in power supplies) of the following types of rectifiers: mercury vapor diode, high-vacuum diode, copper-oxide rectifier, silicon rectifier, selenium rectifier.*

Mercury-Vapor Diode. Mercury-vapor tubes are inherently high-current devices because of the current-carrying capability of the ionized gas in the envelope. The ions make it unnecessary to rely on filament heat alone as an electron source. The very low voltage drop across the tube makes it highly efficient in rectifier service—in practice, the efficiency can approach 90%. Another advantage of the mercury-vapor tube is the fact that the voltage drop is constant—that is, it does not vary with the load as does the high-vacuum rectifier tube. This means a substantial improvement in overall regulation by comparison with other tube-type diodes. Compare the mercury-vapor rectifier with the other diode types listed in the characteristic table of Fig. 5-79.

Virtually obsolete today, mercury-vapor rectifiers were once extensively used as power rectifiers in transmitter supplies. Transmitters tend to require large amounts of current at moderately high voltages, and they exhibit a great deal more stability of performance when the voltage is relatively constant. The

CHARACTERISTIC	MERCURY VAPOR	HIGH VACUUM	COPPER OXIDE	SILICON	SELENIUM
Efficiency	High	Low	Fair	High	Fair to Good
Regulation	Good	Poor		Good	
Current Capability	High	Low	High	High	High
Warmup Time	Long	Short	None	None	None
Ruggedness	Low	Low	High	High	High
Voltage Handling	Moderate	High	Low	Moderate	Low
Stability	Moderate	Good	Poor	Good	Fair
Size	Large	Large	Moderate	Small	Large
Filament Current	Low	High	None	None	None
Heat Generation	Moderate	High	Moderate	Low	Moderate
RF Interference	Yes	No	No	No	No

Fig. 5-79.

mercury-vapor tube offers good service in this capacity. The chief disadvantage is the warmup requirement. The filament must be allowed to heat the mercury pool until it vaporizes—before high voltage is applied to the tube.

High-Vacuum Diode. Until quite recently, this tube has been the workhorse of the diodes for electronics applications. High-vacuum rectifiers have traditionally been used in power supplies for receivers, transmitters, and audio equipment—and also as limiters, detectors, and clippers for radio systems.

As a power rectifier, the high-vacuum tube offers a high peak-inverse-voltage capability, and has enjoyed a reputation for withstanding considerable abuse in terms of excessive voltage without serious degradation of performance. A serious limitation is the tube's large voltage drop, which manifests itself as a percentage of the total voltage applied. Thus, the tube's regulation ability is quite poor.

Copper-Oxide Device. In the copper-oxide rectifier, shown in Fig. 5-80, the oxide is formed on the copper disc before the rectifier unit is assembled. In this type of rectifier the electrons flow more readily from the copper to the oxide than from the oxide to the copper. External electrical connections may be made by connecting terminal lugs between the left pressure plate and the copper, and between the right pressure plate and the lead washer.

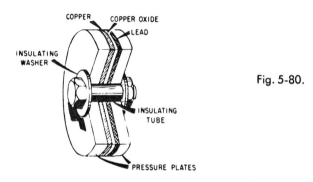

Fig. 5-80.

For the rectifier to function properly, the oxide coating must be quite thin. Thus, each individual unit can withstand only a low inverse voltage. Rectifiers designed for moderate- and high-power applications must consist of many of these individual units mounted in series on a single support. The lead washer enables uniform pressure to be applied to the units so that the internal resistance may be reduced. When the units are connected in series, they normally present a high resistance to the current; the resultant heat developed in the resistance must be removed if the unit is to operate satisfactorily. The useful life of a unit is extended by keeping the temperature low, i.e., below 140°F. The efficiency of this type of rectifier is generally between 60% and 70%—which is low by today's standards.

The disadvantages with respect to total voltage and current-handling capability are manifold. Thus, devices of this type have traditionally had restricted usefulness. A typical application of the copper-oxide device has been as a rectifier in measuring instruments. Today the silicon rectifier is used almost exclusively.

Selenium Device. Selenium rectifiers function in much the same manner as copper-oxide rectifiers. A selenium rectifier is shown in Fig. 5-81. Such a rectifier is made up of an iron disc that is coated with a thin layer of selenium. In this type of rectifier the electrons flow more easily from the selenium to the iron than from the iron to the selenium. This device may be operated at a somewhat higher temperature than a copper-oxide rectifier of similar rating. The efficiency is between 65% and 85%, depending on the circuit and loading.

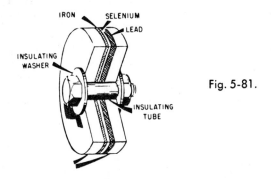

Fig. 5-81.

Selenium rectifiers develop considerable heat when used in high-current applications and are thus usually constructed in the form of a heat dissipator; that is, the rectifier units are placed in series but are separated by a thin air space, which allows optimum radiation of dissipated heat. Traditional applications for selenium "stacks" have been as rectifiers for tube filaments, battery chargers, and automotive alternators. Like the copper-oxide rectifier, the selenium device has all but disappeared from service. To learn why, examine the capabilities and limitations of the rectifiers shown in Fig. 5-79. As can be seen, the advantages of the silicon diode are virtually overwhelming in every category where power output is a requirement.

5-57. *Explain the action of a voltage regulator tube.*

The voltage regulator (VR) tube has been pretty well obsoleted by the zener, or breakdown, diode—which offers all the advantages of the tube-type device in addition to high current-handling capability, virtually no overvoltage requirements, no power consumption, and extremely small size. Nonetheless, questions on the VR tube are likely to appear in the exam because it takes a long time for the FCC exams to catch up to the state of the art.

In a voltage regulator tube the flow of current takes place through a fairly dense gas. When an electron collides with a gas molecule, the energy imparted by the impact can cause the molecule to release an electron. This molecule is known as an *ion*. A gas or vapor containing no ions is an almost perfect insulator. If two electrodes are placed in such a gas, no current flows between them. However, gases always have some residual ionization due to cosmic rays, radioactive materials in the walls of the container, and the action of light itself. If a potential is applied between two electrodes in such a gas, the ions migrate between them, giving the effect of a current. This current is called the *dark current*, because no visible light is associated with it. It is usually about 1 μA.

If the voltage on the electrodes is increased, the current begins to rise. At some specific value, called the *threshold current*, the current suddenly begins to rise without any increase in applied voltage. If there is sufficient resistance in the external circuit to prevent the current from rising quickly, the voltage drops suddenly to a lower value and breakdown occurs. This abrupt change takes place as the result of the ionization of the gas by electron collision. The electrons released by the ionized gas join a stream of electrons and can liberate other electrons. The process is cumulative. The breakdown voltage at which this change takes place is determined by the type of gas, the materials used for the electrodes, their size and spacing, and other factors.

Once ionization takes place, the current can rise to 50 mA or more with little change in the applied voltage. If the voltage is raised still further, the current becomes higher and the electrode acting as the cathode becomes heated by the bombardment of the ions that strike it. If it gets hot enough, it emits electrons by thermionic emission. This emission reduces the voltage drop in the tube, causing a further increase in current and greater emission and ionization. The cumulative action results in a sudden decrease in voltage drop across the tube, and the current rises to the extremely high value of several amperes. Unless the tube is designed specifically to operate under this condition, it can be destroyed by the heavy current. The mechanism just described is the basic process for the formation of an arc, and tubes which operate at these high currents are called *arc tubes*. In the region up to 50 mA, the tube usually is small and is called a *glow tube*, from the soft-colored light it produces. The familiar neon sign is such a glow tube.

In Fig. 5-82 the dark current region is shown from *A* to *B*. The breakdown voltage point is at *B*. The drop in voltage and the sudden rise in current (threshold current) with little change in voltage are shown between *C* and *D*. The current continues to rise until an arc takes place

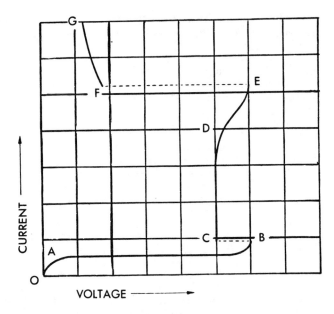

Fig. 5-82.

at E, with a sudden drop in voltage and a great increase in current in the arc from F to G. The many varieties of arc, glow, and other gas tubes all operate on some portion of the compete curve.

The small change of voltage from D to E is the area used when a gas tube operates as a voltage regulator. In the simple circuit shown in Fig. 5-83, the black dot within the envelope signifies that the tube is filled with gas. The resistance (R) is high enough to limit the tube current to the constant-voltage range when the load current is low. When the load current increases, the voltage drop across R increases and reduces the tube voltage. A small reduction of tube voltage in this range, called the *normal region* of the glow discharge, results in a large increase in tube current, which decreases the voltage drop across R. Therefore, small

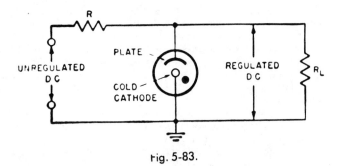

Fig. 5-83.

variations of load current cause compensating variations in tube current, and the voltage across the tube remains essentially constant.

5-58. *If the plate, or plates, of a rectifier tube suddenly became red hot, what might be the cause and how could remedies be effected?*

Examine the circuit diagram of Fig. 5-84. Electron flow follows the path from ground to the cathode of the rectifier through the load resistance (R_L). Electrons boil off the cathode and are attracted to the anode of the tube by virtue of its high potential. From the anode the electrons flow through the transformer secondary, and the path is complete. The load resistance determines the current through the tube when the circuit is functioning normally; if the tube is not functioning normally, the problem can be anywhere between the ground side of the load and the cathode of the tube. If a short circuit exists in the plate circuit of the tube (to ground), the transformer bears the brunt of the current surge and the plates will not overheat.

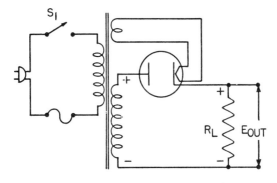

Fig. 5-84.

If the cathode line (+) is placed at or near ground potential (as by a leaky or shorted filter capacitor, a shorted rectifier filament winding, or a short circuit in the load itself), the excessive current resulting from such a condition is forced through the diode. When the current exceeds the rated value of the tube, the anodes will begin to glow. If the condition is allowed to remain unchecked, the tube will soon be destroyed.

To ascertain whether the excessive current can be attributed to the load, supply, or tube, we begin by lifting appropriate leads. Start by disconnecting the load from the power supply; if the condition remains, the problem is in the supply. The next logical step is to disconnect the $B+$ lead from the cathode of the diode. If the conduction remains, the problem is either in the tube itself or the filament and cathode circuits. If the condition disappears (most likely), the problem is a low-resistance ground path in the $B+$ line of the power supply. A shorted or high-leakage electrolytic capacitor is the principal culprit under most circumstances, but occasionally a filter choke winding will short to the case.

5-59. *If a high-vacuum type of high-voltage rectifier tube should suddenly show severe internal sparking and then fail to operate, what elements of the rectifier — filter system should be checked for possible failure before installing a new rectifier tube?*

Internal sparking of a rectifier can occur when an excessive current drain is placed upon the tube, when the rectifier's peak-inverse-voltage rating is exceeded, and when short circuits occur within the tube. A wise move would be to check the resistance to ground of the cathode circuit, as measured at the tube socket. The resistance should be that of the bleeder plus the leakage resistance of the electrolytics. The next step would be to measure the value of the alternating voltate on the secondary of the transformer. If the transformer voltage is excessive, check the primary for possible excessive line voltage. If all functions appear normal, the trouble is probably attributable to a diode whose PIV rating has deteriorated because of gas accumulation within the envelope of the tube.

INDICATING INSTRUMENTS

5-60. *Make a sketch showing the construction of a d'Arsonval meter movement and label the various parts. Draw a circuit diagram of a vacuum-tube voltmeter (VTVM).*

D'Arsonval Movement. The principle of the d'Arsonval movement is clearly shown in the sketch of Fig. 5-85A. In the diagram only one turn of wire is shown, though in practice the coil consists of many turns of very fine wire, each turn adding more effective length to the coil. The coil is usually wound on an aluminum frame or bobbin to which the pointer is attached. Oppositely wound hairsprings are also attached to the bobbin, one at either end. The circuit to the coil is completed through the hairsprings. In addition to serving as conductors, the hairsprings serve as the restoring force that returns the pointer to the zero position when no current flows.

In the movement, the deflecting force is proportional to the current flowing in the coil. The deflecting force tends to rotate the coil against the restraining force of the hairspring. The angle of deflection, then, is porportional to the deflecting force. When the deflecting force and the restraining force are equal, the coil and pointer cease to move further.

The deflecting force is proportional to the current in the coil, the angle of rotation is proportional to the deflecting force, and the angle of rotation is proportional to the current through the coil. When current ceases in the coil, there is no longer a force to oppose the restraining force of the hairspring, and the pointer returns to its resting position. Figure 5-85B is a detailed view of the d'Arsonval movement in which the various parts have been labeled.

Vacuum-Tube Voltmeter. Needless to say, the vacuum-tube voltmeter has all but vanished from the inventory of modern test equipment; it has been replaced by high-impedance meters employing field-effect transistors rather than tubes. The . question about vacuum-tube voltmeters may occur on the exam, however, regardless of the VTVM's antiquity; so it will pay to know the working of this device. In the ac version of the VTVM, the ac voltage to be measured is

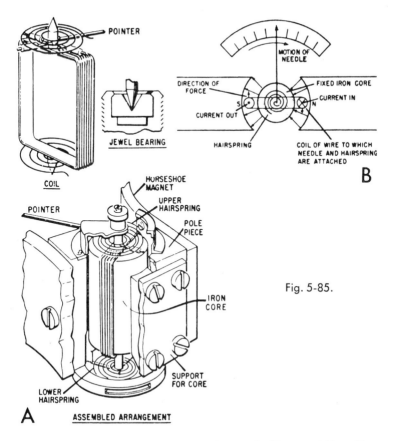

POINTER

JEWEL BEARING

COIL

MOTION OF
NEEDLE

DIRECTION OF
FORCE

CURRENT OUT

HAIRSPRING

FIXED IRON CORE

CURRENT IN

COIL OF WIRE TO WHICH
NEEDLE AND HAIRSPRING
ARE ATTACHED

B

HORSESHOE
MAGNET

POINTER

UPPER
HAIRSPRING

POLE
PIECE

IRON
CORE

SUPPORT
FOR CORE

LOWER
HAIRSPRING

A   ASSEMBLED ARRANGEMENT

Fig. 5-85.

applied to the ac probe (Fig. 5-86A). It is rectified by *V1* and filtered by the *RC* network in the probe.

The meter circuit is a balanced bridge network. When the input voltage between the probe and ground is zero, the bridge is balanced and the voltages across the two arms containing the plate load resistors of *V2* are equal. Thus, the dc meter indicates zero. If a voltage is applied between the probe and ground, the bridge becomes unbalanced and current flows through the meter. The meter is calibrated in rms volts. The input impedance is very high. At the lower frequencies the input capacitance is negligible; but, as the frequency increases, the input capacitance introduces an additional load on the circuit under test and causes an error in the meter reading.

Diode *V1* causes a contact potential to be established across the voltage divider network connected to the grid of V2A. This voltage would unbalance the bridge. Therefore, a similar contact potential is introduced across the grid of *V2B* from *V3* and its associated voltage divider to balance the bridge before the ac voltage to be measured is applied to the diode probe.

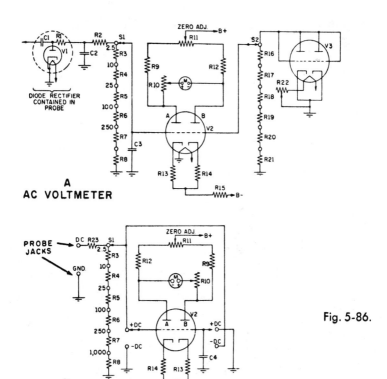

A
AC VOLTMETER

B
DC VOLTMETER

Fig. 5-86.

The dc electron-tube voltmeter circuit is shown in Fig. 5-86B. The dc voltage to be measured is applied between the dc input terminal and ground. The dc input voltage is therefore applied through *R23* to the divider network feeding the grid of *V2A*. The grid of *V2B* is grounded. The meter is connected across a normally balanced bridge so that the application of the dc voltage unbalances the bridge and causes the meter to deflect. The calibration is in dc volts. Bias is obtained for *2A* and *B* through the voltage drop across *R13, R14,* and *R15.* The cathodes are positive with respect to *B−* by an amount equal to the bias. Thus, the grids are correspondingly negative with respect to the cathodes.

In Fig. 5-86B no diode is used in the probe; so no contact potential is established, and *V3* (with its associated voltage divider network) is omitted from the circuit.

Wattmeter. Electric power is measured by means of a wattmeter. This instrument is of the electrodynamometer type. It consists of a pair of fixed current coils and a movable potential coil, as shown in Fig. 5-87. The fixed coils are made up of a few turns of comparatively large-conductor wire. The potential coil consists of many turns of fine wire; it is mounted on a shaft, carried in jeweled bearings, so that it

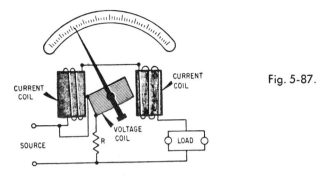

Fig. 5-87.

may turn inside the stationary coils. The movable coil carries a pointer which moves over a suitably graduated scale. Flat coil springs hold the pointer to a zero position.

The current coil (stationary) of the wattmeter is connected in series with the circuit (load), and the potential coil (movable) is connected across the line.

When line current flows through the current coil of a wattmeter, a field is set up around the coil. The strength of this field is proportional to the line current and in phase with it. The potential coil of the wattmeter generally has a high-resistance resistor connected in series with it. This is for the purpose of making the potential-coil circuit of the meter as purely resistive as possible. As a result, current in the potential circuit is practically in phase with line voltage. Therefore, when voltage is impressed on the potential circuit, current is proportional to and in phase with the line voltage.

The actuating force of a wattmeter is derived from the interaction of the field of its current coils and the field of its potential coil. The force acting on the movable coil at any instant (tending to turn it) is proportional to the product of the instantaneous values of line current and voltage.

The wattmeter consists of two circuits, either of which will be damaged if too much current is passed through them. This fact is to be especially emphasized in the case of wattmeters, because the reading of the instrument does not serve to tell the user that the coils are being overheated. If an ammeter or voltmeter is overloaded, the pointer will be indicating beyond the upper limit of its full-scale range. In the wattmeter, though, both the current and voltage circuits may be carrying such an overload that their insulation is burning and yet the pointer may be only part of the way up the scale. This is because the position of the pointer depends upon the power factor of the circuit as well as upon the voltage and current. Thus, a low-power-factor circuit will give a very low reading on the wattmeter even when the current and potential circuits are loaded to the maximum safe limit. This safe rating is generally given on the face of the instrument.

A wattmeter is always distinctly rated, not in watts but in voltage and amperes. Figure 5-88 shows the proper way to connect a wattmeter into a circuit. Note that this figure illustrates the wattmeter from a circuit viewpoint.

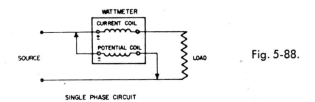

Fig. 5-88.

SINGLE PHASE CIRCUIT

5-61. *Show by a diagram how a voltmeter and ammeter should be connected to measure power in a dc circuit.*

Figure 5-89A shows the manner of power measurement with two individual instruments. The ammeter is connected in series with the load, and the voltmeter is connected across the voltage source (shown in the drawing as the battery). To use this method for measuring power, the reading of one instrument must be multiplied by the reading of the other. (Power in watts is equal to the product of potential in volts and current in amperes.) Figure 5-89B shows the circuit for a 3Ω load drawing 3A from a 12V source. The power consumed is $4 \times 12 = 48W$.

5-62. *If a 0–1 mA dc milliammeter is to be converted into a voltmeter with a full-scale calibration of 100V, what value of resistance should be connected in series with the milliammeter?*

This is easily determined from Ohm's law. We want 1 mA of current to flow (to deflect the meter full scale) when 100V dc is applied. The needed resistance is equal to 100V divided by 0.001A; thus, the value of the resistor would be 100,000Ω (100K).

5-63. *A 1 mA meter having a resistance of 25Ω was used to measure an unknown current by shunting the meter with a 4Ω resistor; it then read 0.4 mA. What was the value of the unknown current?*

There is a formula for calculating the value of the unknown current, but there are logical ways to remember how to determine such values, and the logical processes tend to be easier to remember than the formulas. The first logical step is to remove the decimal points from the values temporarily; thus, 0.4 mA may be thought of as 4 mA (the decimal point can be inserted in the solution). If 4 mA flows through the 25Ω resistance, we know that a considerably larger current will flow through the smaller (4 Ω) resistance. Since 25Ω is 6.25 larger than 4, we know that 6.25 times as much current will flow through the 4Ω resistor. If 4 mA flows through the 25Ω resistance, then 6.25 × 4, or 25 mA, flows through the 4Ω resistor. Since the resistors are paralleled, the currents are additive. Thus, the currents of 25 and 4 mA combine to make a total current of 29 mA. Replacing the decimal point gives a total current for the unknown of 2.9 mA.

5-64. *An rf vacuum-tube voltmeter is available to locate resonance of a tunable primary tank circuit of an rf transformer. If the instrument is measuring the voltage across the tuned secondary, how would resonance of the primary be indicated?*

The VTVM will display a peak reading when the transformer is tuned to resonance. Since the impedance is at maximum at resonance, the voltage

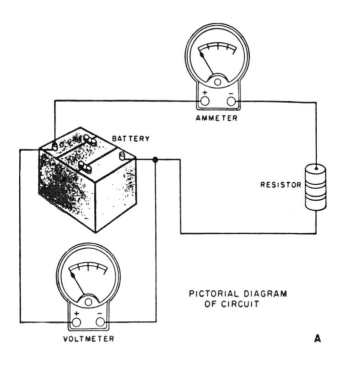

AMMETER

BATTERY

RESISTOR

PICTORIAL DIAGRAM
OF CIRCUIT

VOLTMETER

A

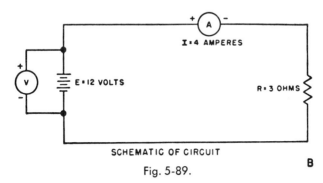

+ (A) −

I = 4 AMPERES

+

(V)

E = 12 VOLTS

R = 3 OHMS

−

SCHEMATIC OF CIRCUIT

B

Fig. 5-89.

is highest as well. With a transformer of fairly high Q, the peak should be sharp enough to identify the resonant point with precision.

5-65. *Define the following and describe a practical situation in which they might be used:*

- *Rms voltage*
- *Peak current*
- *Average current*
- *Power*
- *Energy*

RMS Voltage. The term *rms* means *root mean square* and is applied to alternating voltages as a means of comparison with an equivalent dc voltage value. In ac, then, rms is the voltage required to deliver the same *effective* potential to a load as a *dc* source supplying the same power. As the use of ac gained popularity, it became increasingly apparent that some common basis was needed on which ac and dc could be compared. A 100W light bulb, for example, should work just as well on 120V ac as it does on 120V dc. However, a sine wave of voltage having a peak value of 120V would not supply the lamp with as much power as a steady source of 120V dc.

Since the power dissipated by the lamp is a result of current through the lamp, the problem resolves to one of finding a *mean* alternating-current ampere that is equivalent to a steady ampere of direct current. Figure 5-90 shows a comparison between the various values that are used to indicate the value of a sine wave of voltage. As shown, the effective, or rms, value of the wave—which is the dc equivalent—is 70% (0.707) of the peak value.

Peak Current. One of the most frequently measured characteristics of a sine wave is its amplitude. The amount of alternating current or voltage present in a circuit can be measured in various ways. In one method the maximum amplitude of either the positive or negative alternation is measured. The value of current or voltage obtained is called the *peak* voltage or current. To measure the peak value of current or voltage, an oscilloscope or special meter (peak reading) must be used. The peak value of a sine wave is illustrated in Fig. 5-90; notice that the value is 100 when the average value is 63.7 and the rms value is 70.7.

Measurements of peak current are often made on antennas, transmission lines, audio circuits, and rf amplifiers.

Average Current. The average value of a complete cycle of a sine wave is zero, since the positive alternation is identical to the negative alternation. In certain types of circuits, however, it is necessary to compute the average value of one alternation. This can be accomplished by adding together a series of instantaneous values of the wave between 0° and 180° and then dividing the sum by the number of instantaneous values used. Such a computation would show one alternation of a sine wave to have an average value equal to 0.637 of the peak value, as shown in the comparison sine wave of Fig. 5-90.

Average values of current and voltage are useful in calculating the unfiltered output voltages and currents of rectifiers. The dc output of an unfiltered rectifier is equal to the average value of the applied voltage alternations.

Power. A value of power is a means for measuring the rate at which work is accomplished, and it may be calculated in purely resistive circuits by multiplying a load's current by its source voltage. If the source voltage is unknown, power may be calculated by multiplying the square of the current drain by the resistance of the laod. Power is an extremely common measurement in electronics, for it offers the principal means for measuring circuit efficiencies, circuit performance capability, and requirements of a source to adequately drive a load. The watt is the unit of electrical power, and is equal to work done at the rate of 1 joule of work per second. Typical practical applications where power measurements are made include rf output strength, measurement of

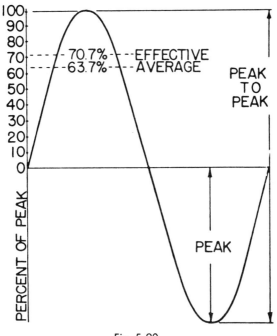

Fig. 5-90.

audio output volume, and an almost unlimited number of other functions, both ac and dc.

Energy. The term *energy* represents the ability to perform work electrically. In other words, a certain amount of energy must be available in order for a source to be able to deliver a certain amount of power to a load. Energy, then, is the capacity to perform work, the basic unit of which is the joule. Practical uses for the term occur in studies related to nuclear physics and in computing the value of laser discharges.

5-66. *Describe how horizontal and vertical deflection takes place in a cathode-ray oscilloscope. Include a discussion of the waveforms involved.*

Figure 5-91 shows the basic construction of a cathode-ray tube (crt) that employs electrostatic deflection. The lower deflection plates are vertically mounted and control the horizontal, or side-to-side, deflection of the electron beam that passes between the plates. The upper deflection plates are mounted horizontally and control the deflection of the electron beam vertically.

When a stream of electrons is propelled into the electrostatic field between two opposed plates, the beam is influenced by the field to such an extent that its line of travel is modified. In Fig. 5-92 the vector **V1** represents the initial velocity of the electron beam as it leaves the electron gun near the base of the cathode-ray tube. The electrostatic field acting on the electron beam results in an acceleration in the direction of the field, causing the electrons to travel in a parabolic path curved

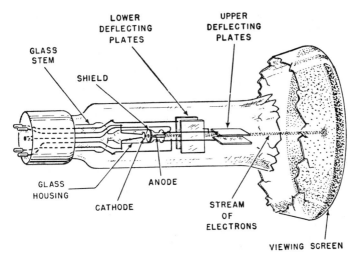

Fig. 5-91.

toward the positive plate. The vector **V2** represents the velocity towards this plate acquired by the electrons at any instant. The resultant velocity is seen to be the vector sum **V3** of the velocities **V1** and **V2**. If the direction of the electrostatic field is reversed, the deflection will be toward the lower plate.

Plates that are horizontally mounted produce a *vertical* deflection, and vice versa. Thus, the horizontally mounted plates are known as *vertical deflection plates* and the vertically mounted plates are called *horizontal deflection plates*. Both sets of plates are mounted in the neck of the tube, just beyond the *accelerating anode*. They usually are constructed as part of the electron gun to simplify manufacturing. Frequently they are flared to permit wide angles of deflection without having the electron beam strike the edges of the plate. Standard practice is to designate the pair of plates nearest the screen as *D1* and *D2*, and use these as the horizontal deflection plates. The other set is referred to as *D3* and *D4*.

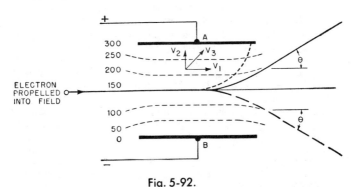

Fig. 5-92.

Waveform. A *linear trace* is the pattern produced by a spot which moves at a uniform velocity (the spot referred to is the place on the face of the tube where the electron beam strikes the phosphors). This spot travels equal distances in equal periods of time. A spot that moves across a 5 in. screen in such a way that it covers a constant distance of 1 in. for every second of elapsed time is said to be moving at a *uniform velocity*. The trace produced by the spot is a linear trace. The linear trace is important because it affords a simple method of making time measurements on the screen of a crt. If it is known that the spot is located at the extreme left of a 5 in. screen at a certain time and that it moves horizontally across the screen at a uniform velocity of 1 in./sec, it is evident that when the spot is at the exact center of the screen, a time interval of 2.5 sec has elapsed. When the spot has moved four-fifths of the entire distance across the screen, a time interval of 4 sec has elapsed. A *time base* has thus been produced. This time base may be traced in any direction, but the common practice is to trace it horizontally. The linear trace also is useful when using a crt to produce a graph of some variable quantity plotted against time.

To produce a linear trace that can be used as a time base, certain requirements must be met. In the case of the electrostatic cathode-ray tube, a gradually rising and rapidly falling sawtooth voltage is required. The amount of deflection is directly proportional to the difference of potential between the deflection plates. In an electromagnetic tube the amount of deflection is directly proportional to the current through the deflection coil. Therefore, a gradually rising and rapidly falling sawtooth current is needed.

Figure 5-93 shows the appearance of the sawtooth required to produce a linear trace. As shown, the trace time is represented by the gradually increasing voltage, and the retrace time (the time required to move the spot from the right side of the screen back to the left to begin the next trace) is represented by the steep drop of the sawtooth wave.

OSCILLATORS

5-67. *Draw circuit diagrams of each of the following types of oscillators. Include any commonly associated components and explain the principles of operation of each.*

- *Armstrong*
- *Tuned plate, tuned grid (LC and crystal)*
- *Hartley (series- and shunt-fed)*
- *Colpitts*
- *Electron-coupled*
- *Multivibrator*
- *Pierce (crystal-controlled)*

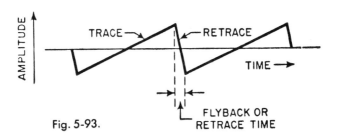

Fig. 5-93.

395

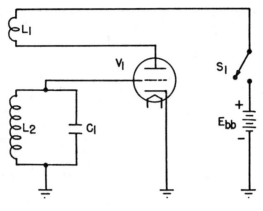

Fig. 5-94.

Armstrong. The simplest of all the oscillators is the Armstrong. The vacuum-tube Armstrong circuit is shown in Fig. 5-94 and the transistor equivalent is shown in Fig. 5-95. In the tube circuit, L2-C1 forms the tank circuit, which determines the resonant frequency, and L1 is the feedback coil (often referred to as a tickler). In both the tube and the transistor circuit, the bias voltages have been omitted for simplicity.

Oscillations begin in the circuit when the bias conditions of the amplifier tube or transistor are normal and power is applied. The amplitude of current flow in the circuit will increase, causing an expanding magnetic field around the tank circuit. This induces a voltage in the tank coil and charges the tank capacitor. The charge of the tank capacitor causes output current to increase by increasing the potential on the tube's grid (or collector, in the common-base transistor Armstrong

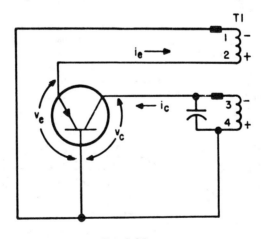

Fig. 5-95.

oscillator). This regeneration continues until the nonlinear characteristics of the amplifying device cause a difference in the rate of change of the output current.

When the induced voltage of the tank coil falls below the charge of the capacitor, the tank capacitor begins to discharge. The discharge of this capacitor causes the input potential to decrease, thereby decreasing output current. When the tank capacitor is completely discharged, the field of the tank coil collapses and charges the capacitor with the opposite polarity. Partway through this portion of the cycle of operation, the input potential will become sufficiently negative to cut the amplifier's conduction off. When the field of the tank coil is completely collapsed, the capacitor will begin to discharge. As the tank voltage becomes nearer the bias point, the input potential will approach the point where the amplifier comes out of cutoff (this oscillator is biased for class C operation). As the amplifier begins to conduct, regenerative feedback occurs and replaces the lost energy. Oscillations can now continue until dc power is removed from the circuit.

Tuned-Plate, Tuned-Grid. In the TPTG oscillator, the grid circuit (L1-C1, Fig. 5-96) is tuned to the resonant frequency desired. When the first surge of current starts this circuit oscillating, the oscillations appear at the grid and are amplified in the plate circuit. The plate circuit

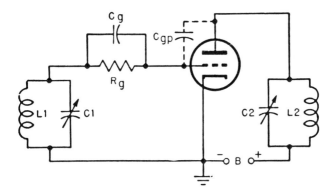

Fig. 5-96.

consists of L2-C2. The feedback path in the TPTG oscillator occurs through the plate-to-grid capacitance of the triode. Energy is coupled from the plate circuit to the grid circuit. If L2-C2 is tuned to the same frequency as L1-C1, the phase of the feedback is not proper to sustain oscillations; for this reason, the plate circuit is made inductive at the frequency of oscillation of the grid circuit to make the feedback regenerative. This is done by tuning the plate circuit to a slightly higher frequency.

In the TPTG oscillator circuit shown in Fig. 5-97, the grid tank has been replaced with a crystal (which itself serves the function of a

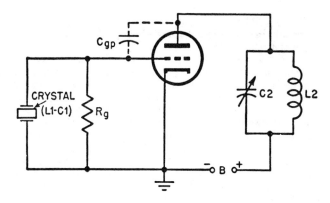

Fig. 5-97.

complete, highly stable tank circuit consisting of a capacitance, an inductance, and a resistance.

Series-Fed Hartley. The principal identifying characteristic of the Hartley oscillator is the split tank coil, half of which feeds the input of the tube or transistor, and the other half of which feeds the output circuit. Figure 5-98 shows the basic series-fed vacuum-tube circuit, and 5-99 shows the transistor version.

In this oscillator, one tank circuit is actually made to serve as both grid and plate resonant circuits. The grid (Fig. 5-98) is coupled to one end of the tank and the plate is connected to the other end. The cathode is attached to a point on the inductor. This divides the coil between the grid and the plate circuits in the form of an inductive voltage divider, as shown. The voltage across L1 is between the grid and cathode, thereby

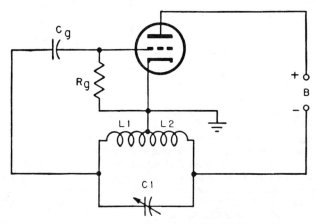

HARTLEY (SPLIT- INDUCTANCE) OSCILLATOR

Fig. 5-98.

applying a signal to the grid. The amplified voltage at the plate appears across L2. This provides the necessary feedback.

In the Hartley, the dc plate current must pass through inductor L2 before it can return to the cathode. The disadvantage in this arrangement is that the plate supply is placed at a high ac potential with respect to the cathode. Also, the supply has a large distributed capacitance to ground, and this capacitance is shunted across the tank coil (L2).

In the transistor version of the series-fed Hartley, shown in Fig. 5-99, resistors R_B and R_F provide the necessary bias for the base—emitter circuit. Collector bias is obtained through transformer winiding 1-2.

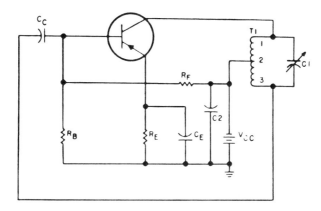

Fig. 5-99.

Capacitor C_E provides an ac bypass around the emitter swamping resistor (R_E). The feedback is obtained from the induced voltage winding 2-3 coupled through capacitor C_C to the base of the transistor. Capacitor $C2$ places terminal 2 of the tank coil at ac ground potential.

Shunt-Fed Hartley. The disadvantages of the series-fed circuit (discussed above) can be overcome by keeping the dc plate supply (tube circuit) and the oscillating plate current separate. This is accomplished in the shunt-fed Hartley (Fig. 5-100). The plate current oscillations are coupled to the split-inductance tank by means of capacitor $C2$. The capacitor prevents the dc plate current from returning to the cathode through the tank. The plate current, therefore, can return only through the choke in series with the B+ source. This choke prevents any oscillations from appearing in the supply because its reactance is very large.

The transistor version of the shunt-fed Hartley is pictured schematically in Fig. 5-101. Resistors R_B, R_C, and R_F provide the necessary bias conditions for the circuit. The frequency-determining network consists of the series combination of windings 1-2 and 2-3 in parallel with capacitor $C1$. Since this capacitor is variable, the circuit may be tuned through a wide range of frequencies. Capacitor $C2$ is a dc blocking capacitor. Capacitor C_E provides an ac bypass around emitter swamping resistor R_E.

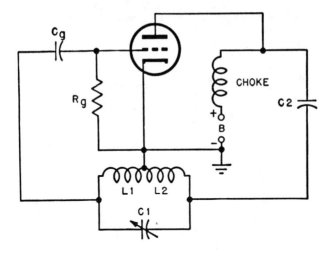

Fig. 5-100.

The coil functions as an autotransformer to provide the regenerative feedback signal. The feedback is obtained from the induced voltage in winding 2-3 coupled through capacitor C_C to the base of the transistor. By shunt-feeding the collector through resistor R_C, direct current flow through the tank coil is avoided.

Colpitts. The Colpitts, like the Hartley, is a split-tank oscillator; the difference is that the Hartley incorporates a split inductance, whereby the Colpitts uses a split capacitance in the tank circuit. The capacitance of the tank circuit in the Colpitts (see Fig. 5-102) is provided by capacitors C1 and C2, which form a capacitive voltage divider between the grid and

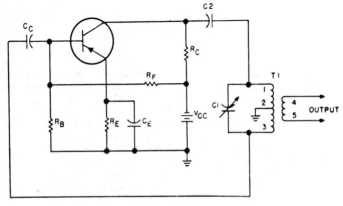

Fig. 5-101.

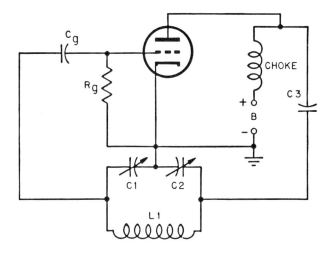

Fig. 5-102.

plate circuits. By adjusting C1 and C2, it is possible to control the frequency and amount of positive feedback.

Figure 5-103 illustrates the transistor Colpitts oscillator circuit. Regenerative feedback is obtained from the tank circuit and applied to the emitter of the transistor. Base bias is provided by resistors R_B and R_F. Resistor R_E develops the emitter input signal and also acts as the emitter swamping resistor. The tuned circuit consists of capacitors C1 and C2 in parallel with inductor winding 1-2. Capacitors C1 and C2 form the voltage divider. The voltage developed across C2 is the feedback voltage. The manner of operation is the same as with the tube circuit.

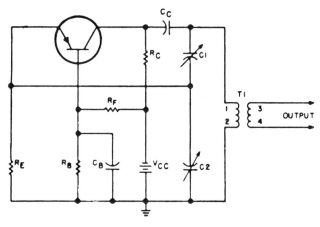

Fig. 5-103

Electron-Coupled. By using a multielectrode tube, the oscillator and buffer stages of a transmitter can be replaced by a single circuit that performs both functions. Such a circuit is called an *electron-coupled oscillator*. Figure 5-104 is a typical circuit arrangement using a pentode.

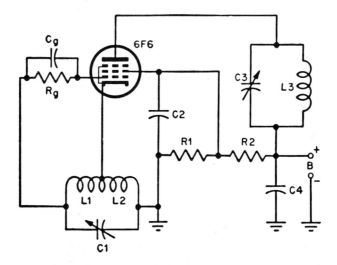

Fig. 5-104.

In this circuit, the cathode, the control grid, and the screen grid perform the function of the triode in the Hartley oscillator. The cathode of the pentode taps the split-inductance tank consisting of $L1$, $L2$, and $C1$. The control grid is coupled to one end of the tank, and the screen grid takes the place of the triode plate. The screen voltage is taken from the voltage divider, consisting of $R1$ and $R2$ across the B+ supply. This part of the circuit can be compared to the Hartley oscillator previously described.

The signal appearing at the grid causes the current through the tube to oscillate. In the ordinary Hartley, this current is collected at the plate, where one portion of it is used for feedback and the rest for output. In the electron-coupled oscillator, however, the screen grid collects only that portion of the current needed for feedback. The output portion of the current passes through the screen grid to the pentode plate, where it is collected and passed through the output tank circuit consisting of $C3$ and $L3$. Capacitors $C2$ and $C4$ serve to bypass oscillations around the power supply.

The only connection between the oscillator and the output circuit is the electron stream itself. This serves to isolate the oscillator from the load. The electron-coupled oscillator, therefore, has all the advantages of a separate oscillator and buffer.

Multivibrator. One of the simplest oscillators that can be used as a frequency divider is the synchronized multivibrator (Fig. 5-105). There are many varieties of multivibrator circuits, but essentially they are all

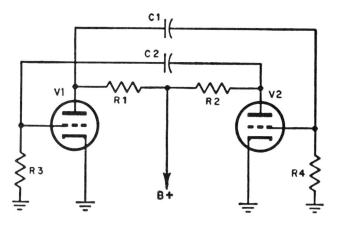

Fig. 5-105.

modifications of a 2-stage resistance-coupled amplifier circuit with the output fed back to the input circuit. When the grid voltage of a vacuum tube is made more positive, the plate voltage decreases. This decrease in plate voltage is coupled into the grid of one tube, causing a decrease of grid voltage. This results in an increase in plate voltage, which is applied to the grid of a second tube; and the cycle reverses. The variations possible consist in using direct coupling, cathode coupling, or mixed types of coupling between the two tubes.

A small amount of voltage applied to the grid circuit can be used to trigger oscillation. Any voltage that is an integral multiple of a natural frequency of the oscillator provides this triggering action. The frequency can be much higher than the actual frequency of operation of the oscillator. The output from one multivibrator controlled in this manner can be 10 times less in frequency than the controlling voltage. The output of this multivibrator can be connected to another multivibrator that also divides by a like amount, providing division by 100. In this way the high frequency of the crystal oscillator and the master oscillator in an FM system can be reduced to a frequency that falls in the audio range.

The basic transistor version of the multivibrator is shown in Fig. 5-106. This is a 2-stage RC-coupled common-emitter amplifier, with the output of the first stage coupled to the input of the second stage and the output of the second stage coupled to the input of the first stage. Since the signal in the collector circuit of a common-emitter amplifier is reversed in phase with respect to the input of that stage, a portion of the output of each stage is fed to the other stage in phase with the signal on the base electrode. This regenerative feedback with amplification is required for oscillation. Bias and stabilization are established identically for both transistors.

Pierce. The Pierce oscillator, also frequently known as the *ultraaudion*, is shown in its vacuum-tube form in Fig. 5-107. This is considered to be the simplest of the tube-type crystal oscillators, for all that is required are a few resistors and capacitors. As with the Colpitts

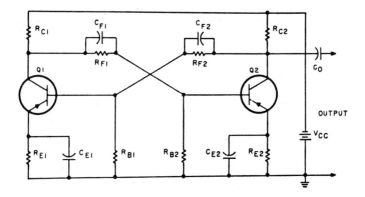

Fig. 5-106.

oscillator, oscillation occurs because of the feedback provided by the voltage divider formed by the grid—plate and grid—cathode capacitances.

The transistor version of the Pierce oscillator is shown in Fig. 5-108. If the crystal were to be replaced by its equivalent *LCR* circuit, the functioning of the circuit would become analogous to that of the Colpitts oscillator. The circuit of Fig. 5-108 shows the common-base configuration, with the feedback supplied from collector to emitter through capacitor $C1$. Resistors R_B, R_C, and R_F provide the proper bias and feedback conditions for the circuit. The emitter resistor is the swamping resistor (R_E). Capacitors $C1$ and C_E form a voltage divider connected across the output. Capacitor $C2$ is an ac bypass around base-biasing resistor R_E. Since no phase shift occurs in this configuration, the feedback signal must be connected so that the voltage across the emitter capacitor will be returned to the emitter with no phase shift occurring. The oscillating frequency of this circuit is determined not only by the crystal but by parallel capacitance of $C1$ and C_E. These are normally made large to

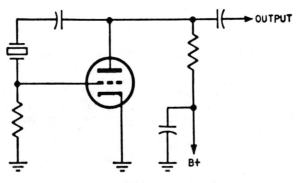

Fig. 5-107.

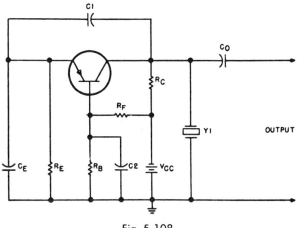

Fig. 5-108.

swamp both the input and output capacitances of the transistor and make the oscillations comparatively independent of changes in transistor parameters.

Since the parallel capacitance of $C1$ and C_E affects the oscillator frequency, the operation of the crystal is in the inductive region of the impedance-versus-frequency characteristic between the series and parallel resonant frequencies.

5-68. *Why should excessive feedback be avoided in a crystal oscillator?*

Increasing the feedback increases the amplitude of the vibrations of the crystal. When feedback rises beyond the maximum tolerable limits of the crystal, the thin wafer will fracture or scorch. Often the only evidence of a fractured crystal is a circuit that will not oscillate. A scorched crystal loses its sensitivity and stability, and often oscillates on some frequency other than that for which it was cut.

5-69. *What is meant by "parasitic oscillations"? How may they be detected and prevented?*

Parasitic oscillations are signals generated within an rf amplifier other than by design. Not all combinations of input and output circuits in a transmitter can be used together successfully, since some of them tend to permit the amplifier stage to oscillate at frequencies that are relatively unrelated to the frequency to which it is tuned. These oscillations are undesirable because they cause the transmission of spurious signals, thus impairing the efficiency of the rf amplifier and causing needless interference to radio reception.

The most noticeable features of parasitic oscillation in an amplifier are **erratic tuning** and the **radiation of spurious signals**. When an rf amplifier is operating properly, the dc plate current dips sharply as the tank circuit is tuned through resonance. This plate current dip also corresponds to maximum power output and (usually) maximum grid current into the final amplifier. If a tetrode is operating normally, the plate current change may not be too great, but the screen current dip will

405

still be significant. With parasitic oscillation, the **plate current may not dip** at all, the minimum may not correspond to maximum power output, **several dips may appear in the tuning range**, or **grid current to the final amplifier will not coincide with the dip in the plate current** reading of the final amplifier.

Since the symptoms presented by a stage that is not properly neutralized are somewhat similar, it is difficult to tell the effects of the two conditions apart unless neutralization is checked first.

All parasitics are attributable to the development of resonant circuits in connection with the tube elements in such a way as to permit enough feedback as to sustain oscillation. They may occur at either high or low frequencies. Parasitic oscillations occurring at much lower than the operating frequency usually are caused by the resonant condition of an rf choke in the circuit, since the rf chokes are the only inductors with sufficient inductance to resonate with various circuit capacitances at low frequencies. High-frequency parasitics can be traced to a much wider variety of causes. Among these are spurious high-frequency resonant conditions in tank circuit inductances, resonant circuits built up in lead inductances, and stray capacitances and resonant conditions built up in bypass and blocking capacitors. Moreover, the parasitic circuit need not involve the final amplifier alone. The driver stage is frequently an important part of the parasitic feedback circuit that permits oscillation.

A recurrent type of high-frequency oscillation is caused by a form of tuned-plate, tuned-grid oscillator in a simple single-ended amplifier like that of Fig. 5-109. The parasitic path is shown in heavy lines. At relatively high frequencies the tank circuit inductance acts like an rf choke, and the

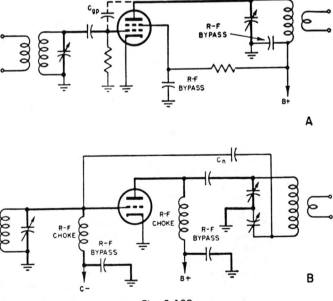

Fig. 5-109.

capacitors and their leads form the equivalent of parallel resonant circuits. The shielding effect of the screen grid in a tetrode is not sufficient at extremely high frequencies. Therefore, energy can feed back to the grid circuit from the plate at high frequencies if both of the parasitic resonant circuits are almost the same in frequency. The difficulty can be cured by inserting a parallel inductance and resistance in the grid or plate lead. This detunes one of the parasitic circuits sufficiently to prevent oscillation. (Usually the process is no more complex than wrapping a few turns of 16-gage solid wire around a carbon resistor so that both the resistance and the inductance are paralleled.)

Another method is to insert a small resistance in series with circuit leads to introduce sufficient loss to stop oscillation. A third alternative is to incorporate a tuned parallel resonant trap that actually inserts a very high impedance in the parasitic frequency path. In addition to the trap, it is common to find small high-frequency capacitors connected from plate and control grid to cathode. These capacitors effectively short the parasitics to ground.

Certain circuit combinations have been found to be particularly troublesome. For example, rf chokes rarely are used in both the grid and the plate circuits of a triode, since they cause a low-frequency tuned-plate, tuned-grid oscillation (Fig. 109B). Hence, shunt-fed circuits are avoided wherever possible. In high-gain screen grid amplifiers, the choice of the screen bypass capacitor becomes very important. The substitution of a different type when servicing a unit often leads to serious instability. Similarly, the choice of cathode and filament bypass capacitors is also a critical matter. When replacing any of these components in a transmitter, use the exact duplicate of the discarded component and pay careful attention to lead dress and parts placement.

5-70. *What determines the fundamental frequency of a quartz crystal?*

The frequency of a crystal is determined by the **thickness of the crystal wafer**. The thicker the wafer, the lower the frequency. Other factors affecting the frequency of the crystal include the **actual physical height and width of the wafer, the capacitance between the crystal and its holder, and the "grain" axis of the crystal material**. A crystal may be cut from many of several angles, as described earlier.

5-71. *What are the characteristics and possible uses of an overtone crystal? A third-mode crystal?*

An overtone crystal is a crystal constructed so as to oscillate at some frequency that is very close to an odd harmonic of the crystal wafer's resonant frequency. **A third-mode crystal, more often called a third overtone crystal, is one that is specifically constructed to oscillate on the third harmonic of the fundamental crystal frequency.** Oscillators that use overtone crystals are referred to as *overtone oscillators*, in contrast to the more conventional *harmonic oscillators*.

The output of any harmonic oscillator contains signal components at frequencies other than the fundamental. Unless these frequencies are separated from the mixer (for example) of a receiver by a sufficient number of tuned circuits, serious difficulties with spurious responses and images can arise. These disadvantages can be overcome with special circuits that use overtone crystals. Another advantage of the overtone oscillator, of course, is that **the number of frequency multiplier stages** can be reduced substantially because the oscillator's output is higher in frequency than the harmonic oscillator. Yet another advantage, though less obvious, is economy; a third-overtone crystal oscillating at 50 MHz is considerably less expensive than a crystal whose resonant frequency is 50 MHz.

The oscillating frequencies of overtone crystals are the mechanical harmonics. Special types of circuits must be employed for using these crystals. Probably the chief advantage in an overtone oscillator lies in the fact that there is negligible output at frequencies other than the design frequency.

All of the overtone oscillator circuits shown in Fig. 5-110 incorporate some form of frequency-selective feedback unlike that used in a conventional harmonic crystal oscillator. An additional resonant circuit is used to feed back energy at the frequency of the desired overtone, so that oscillation takes place only at the desired frequency. The frequency-selective feedback must be adjusted carefully, so that oscillation is caused by the crystal only and not by the feedback circuit.

In Fig. 5-110A a simple Pierce oscillator is modified so that the frequency of feedback is controlled by the tuned circuit formed by $L1$ and $C1$. The amount of feedback is varied by changing the tap on $L1$. A second version of the same oscillator is shown in sketch B, where the amplitude of the feedback is controlled by the coupling between $L1$ and $L2$. These circuits are especially suitable for operation of the crystal on the third overtone, where the frequency of feedback is not particularly critical. Power output of the fifth overtone is poor, and the feedback adjustment becomes fairly critical when ordinary crystals are used.

The overtone oscillator shown in sketch C is capable of extremely stable operation, although it works only with crystals designed for overtone service. Feedback is controlled by the position of the cathode tap on $L1$ and the setting of the desired overtone. Therefore, the capacitance of the crystal and its holder is also a part of the resonant circuit, which is similar to that of the Hartley oscillator. This circuit has good output, especially at higher overtones; and the plate circuit can be tuned to a harmonic of the overtone, producing even further frequency multiplication.

An overtone oscillator that uses a high-gain pentode is shown in sketch D. Feedback is obtained by magnetic coupling. The crystal actually is resonated slightly above the desired overtone. This makes the entire grid circuit equivalent to a high-impedance parallel resonant tank, which easily picks up a regenerative signal from the plate circuit and produces oscillation. At very high overtones the capacitance of the grid circuit is sufficient to resonate with the inductance in the plate circuit. This circuit is capable of producing moderate amounts of output on extremely high overtones. Operation on the 29th overtone has been achieved. This represents an important saving of frequency multiplier stages as well as freedom from spurious responses attributable to the subharmonics of doublers and triplers.

The circuit shown in sketch E is somewhat different from the others shown. The input and the output circuits of the triode are tuned to the same frequency, although the grid is much more broadly resonant than the plate. This is because of the high ratio of inductance to grid–cathode capacitance. The crystal holder capacitance is resonated in the cathode

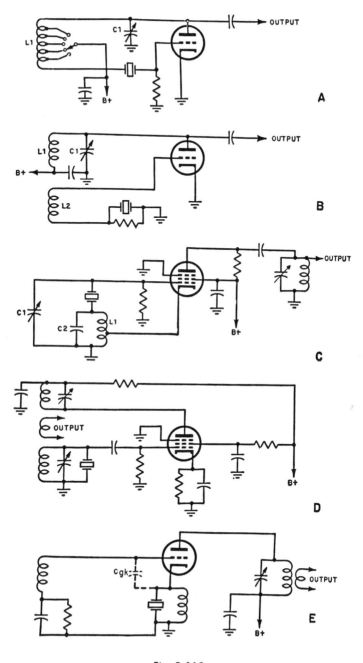

Fig. 5-110.

circuit with an inductor at the desired overtone frequency. The only frequency at which oscillation can take place is that at which the crystal goes through series resonance, producing a low impedance from cathode to ground. To prevent self-oscillation between grid and plate circuits, the inductance in the cathode circuit must be carefully adjusted.

5-72. *Explain some of the factors involved in the stability of an oscillator (both LC and crystal controlled).*

The stability of an oscillator depends on many factors, including:

1. The Q of the oscillator tank circuit
2. Regulation of the circuit supply voltages
3. Stability of the oscillator's ambient temperature
4. Susceptibility of the oscillator to the effects of stray capacitances
5. Susceptibility of the oscillator components to environmental conditions

The Q of the tank circuit is highest when a crystal is used rather than an LC circuit, and this is why crystal oscillators are inherently more stable than their LC counterparts. Supply voltage stability is also an important factor; as a rule, oscillators are supplied from some source that is independent of the voltages used for supplying other portions of receivers and transmitters. When $B+$ voltage for a transmitter is also used to supply the oscillator, the oscillator's voltage will vary according to the transmitter's loading—and a varying oscillator voltage means a varying oscillator output frequency.

Temperature is an extremely important factor, regardless of whether the oscillator uses an LC circuit or a crystal. Many modern transmitters and receivers incorporate oscillators with a crystal in a temperature-controlled oven. The oven keeps the temperature of the crystal relatively constant, thus preventing drift.

Since stray capacitances actually form part of an oscillator's resonant circuit, some form of compensation for these is usually incorporated into high-quality oscillator circuits. For the most part this means keeping the ratio of capacitance to inductance fairly high. The stray capacitances still exist, but with a high enough $C:L$ ratio, the strays form but a small percentage of the total circuit capacitance and thus have a negligible effect on frequency.

Environmental conditions have proved considerably important in the performance of an oscillator. In the early days of mobile operation, designers found that ordinary construction techniques just weren't good enough to maintain the stability of an oscillator used in a vehicle. Temperature extremes, vibration, and varying humidity all play important roles in oscillator stability. Some AM transmitter used in vehicles have actually proved to generate FM because of vibrating components in the oscillator circuit.

Some component types are inherently more stable than others. In high-quality oscillator circuits, high-stability *NPO* (zero coefficient) capacitors and low-temperature-coefficient components are used exclusively. Occasionally, positive-coefficient components are used with negative-coefficient components so as to strike a balance with temperature changes. In such cases the coefficients are chosen so as to precisely balance one another.

AUDIO AMPLIFIERS

5-73. Draw simple schematic diagrams illustrating the following types of coupling between audio amplifier stages and between a stage and a load.

- *Triode vacuum tube inductively coupled to a loudspeaker*
- *Resistance coupling between two pentodes*
- *Impedance coupling between two triodes*
- *A method of coupling a high-impedance loudspeaker to an audio amplifier without flow of plate current through the speaker windings (without use of a transformer)*

Inductively Coupled Triode. The simplest of the vacuum-tube amplifiers is the triode stage connected to a speaker. As shown in Fig. 5-111, the B+ voltage for the plate of the triode is fed through the winding of the output transformer. The fluctuation in the plate current induces voltage variations in the transformer, whose secondary offers a low-impedance output suitable for driving a loudspeaker directly. The impedance of the transformer primary is high to match the requirements of the plate circuit.

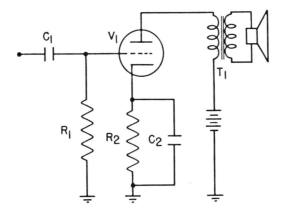

Fig. 5-111.

Resistance-Coupled Pentodes. In the circuit of Fig. 5-112, the coupling network is shown enclosed in a broken-line box. Note that a capacitor (C_C) provides the actual coupling, but the resistors form the impedance loads. This coupling method is more often referred to as *RC* rather than resistance coupling. The *RC* coupling network includes a plate load resistor for the driving stage, a grid resistor for the stage being driven, and a coupling capacitor that allows ac to pass from one stage to another while blocking the passage of any dc (which would upset the bias of the succeeding stage).

Impedance-Coupled Triodes. If a coil is substituted for the load resistor in an *RC* coupling network, an *RLC* coupling network is obtained—this method is also referred to as *impedance coupling*.

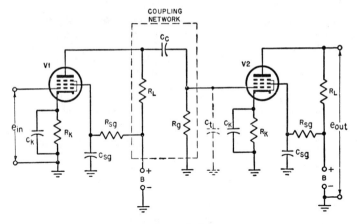

Fig. 5-112.

The impedance-coupled amplifier shown in Fig. 5-113 is similar to a conventional resistance-coupled amplifier except that an inductor is substituted for the plate load resistor. This coil has a certain impedance value Z_L, which is made up of the inductive reactance and the resistance of the coil. The input signal e_{in} is amplified by stage $V1$ and coupled to $V2$ through the impedance coupling network shown within the broken-line box. The output appears from plate to ground.

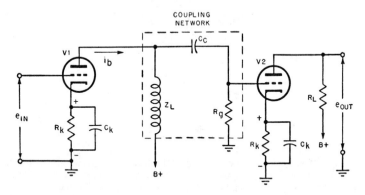

Fig. 5-113.

Transformerless Coupling to Speaker. The efficiency of this approach is anything but optimum and the frequency response is limited, so it has seldom been seen in actual circuits until the advent of the transistor. Figure 5-114 shows the concept: The plate voltage to the audio amplifier is fed to the plate through an audio choke which serves to isolate the power supply from the amplifier. The variation in dc voltage that occurs at the plate side of the inductor as a result of the inductor's reactance to

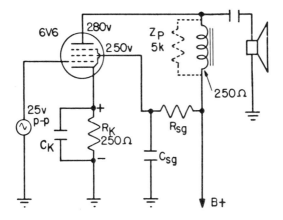

Fig. 5-114.

the load voltage is coupled to the speaker through a capacitor of exceptionally high value.

In order to keep the value requirement of the capacitor as low as possible, the speaker impedance should be as high as practicable. As the speaker impedance decreases the value of the capacitor must be increased in order to pass audio frequencies. The capacitor, of course, must be used in order to prevent direct current from being passed to the speaker windings.

5-74. *What would probably be the effect on the output amplitude and waveform if the cathode resistor bypass capacitor in an audio stage were removed?*

The bypass capacitor places the cathode at gound potential with respect to audio passing through the stage. The ac (audio) component must be removed from the cathode stage if the bias on the amplifier is to remain constant. Removing the bypass capacitor would cause the audio ac voltage to appear across the cathode resistor, thus causing a varying bias on the amplifier. Without a fixed bias point, an amplifier would tend not to be capable of operating in the center of its linear region. However, since current through an unbypassed cathode resistor develops a voltage that varies at the same rate as the plate voltage, negative signal feedback is introduced. Negative feedback tends to **cancel any distortion added by the stage, while reducing the amplitude** drastically; while the operating point will tend to drift, the amplitude of the signal will be low enough to keep it within the linear region.

5-75. *Why do vacuum tubes produce random noise?*

The noise produced by high-gain audio amplifier stages is attributable to high-temperature electron "boiloff." As electrons free themselves from the structure of the cathode, the friction within the cathode is a source of minute broad-spectrum *thermal noise*, which can be amplified and regenerated along with the audio signal itself. Another cause is *shot effect*, a random variation in the quantity and velocity of emitted electrons. These conditions are inherent in thermionic tubes. To

413

overcome them, amplifiers employ negative feedback (which reduces the amplifier gain) and use a number of amplifier stages. This tends to keep the signal-to-noise ratio high enough so that random noises will not be objectionable.

5-76. *How would saturation of an output transformer create distortion?*

When the secondary of an audio output transformer faithfully follows the variations in voltage across the input windings, the output signal is a replica of the input. However, when a transformer is saturated, the input-voltage increases do not result in a proportional increase in the secondary voltage. During this condition the secondary voltage rises to a specific level and remains there until the state of saturation is removed. If the secondary voltage were to be observed on an oscilloscope, the signal would appear to be clipped during saturation. Such a signal would sound quite distorted.

5-77. *Why is noise often produced when an audio signal is distorted?*

Noise is produced when, because of distortion, the output signal contains frequencies that were not present in the input, particularly where the frequencies that occur in the output waveform are within the audio spectrum. Noise is also produced when an amplifier reproduces some frequencies more than others (frequency distortion); this is particularly true when the amplifier reproduces high frequencies at higher amplitudes. Of course, many circuit defects that cause distortion can also cause noise; gas in a tube and faulty electrode contacts are examples. Circuit defects that cause instability and distortion can also cause self-oscillation.

5-78. *What are the factors that determine the correct bias voltage for the grid of a vacuum tube?*

In an audio amplifier the bias is chosen so that the tube operates as closely as possible to the center of its linear transfer characteristic. The bias point must be chosen so that no amount of input signal will cause the grid circuit to draw current. In a class B amplifier such as the type used in push-pull audio amplifiers, each tube must be made to operate (during the no-signal state) near cutoff, which is at the lower limit of the tube's linear region.

A positive control-grid voltage results in the presence of grid current between the grid and cathode through the system external to the tube. This condition cannot be avoided, because the grid wires intercept electrons that are advancing toward the grid on their way to the plate. The positively charged grid attracts electrons into itself. Disregarding for the moment any applications that permit grid current to flow, the presence of grid current is normally undesirable. It represents the needless consumption of power and other unwanted effects.

The signal voltage normally applied to a control grid is alternating; at least it is a voltage that varies in amplitude and, perhaps, in polarity relative to the cathode. During the time that it is negative with respect to the cathode, freedom from grid current is obvious. But when it is positive, grid current is present unless some means is provided to keep the control grid at a negative potential during the positive portion of the input signal. The purpose of the negative grid bias is to establish this operating condition. Bias may be defined as the dc voltage between the grid and the

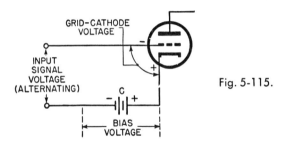

Fig. 5-115.

cathode. It is represented by battery C in Fig. 5-115. The total voltage existing between grid and cathode is the signal voltage plus the bias voltage.

The association between the signal and the grid bias is illustrated in Fig. 5-116. Curve A represents an input ac signal of 5V peak. It varies between 5V positive and 5V negative. To keep the control grid negative during the entire positive alternation of the input signal, the grid bias must equal if not exceed the peak value of the signal. Thus, the control grid bias is arbitrarily set at −6V, as in curve B. Since the grid is negative with respect to the zero-voltage reference level, it is shown below the reference voltage line.

The resultant of the signal and bias voltages at the control grid, instant by instant, is shown as curve C in the same illustration. Curve C is the addition of curves A and B. The fixed bias voltage sets up the initial voltage relationship between the control grid and cathode. This is the no-signal condition (as in curve B). It is represented by 1 to 2 and 8 to 9 in curve A, and $1'$ to $2'$ and $8'$ to $9'$ in curve C. The times from 1 to 2 and 8 to 9 in curve A represent the period of zero signal voltage, during which time the full −6V of grid bias is active on the control grid, as shown in times $1'$ to $2'$ and $8'$ to $9'$ in curve C.

As the signal voltage starts rising in the positive direction (from 2 to 3),it bucks the fixed negative bias, and the control grid becomes less and less negative until, at the peak of the positive alternation of the signal voltage (point 3), the control grid is one volt negative with respect to the cathode, as shown by $3'$ in curve C. As the signal voltage decreases in positive amplitude (from 3 to 4 in curve A), more and more of the bias voltage becomes predominant, until point 4 is reached, which again corresponds to zero signal voltage. The control grid again becomes 6V negative with respect to the cathode, as shown by point $4'$ on curve C. Examining the action during the positive half-cycle of the applied signal voltage, points $2'$ to $4'$ in curve C, it is evident that a 0.5V change in signal voltage in the positive direction has taken place at the control grid, but the grid electrode remains negative throughout the half-cycle.

During the negative alternation of the signal voltage (points 4 to 6), the signal and the fixed negative bias voltages add. The result is a change in voltage at the grid from −6V ($4'$ in curve C) to maximum negative voltage of −11V ($5'$), and then a return to −6V ($6'$) again. The control grid remains negative with respect to the cathode by an amount equal to the sum of the instantaneous signal voltage and the fixed grid bias.

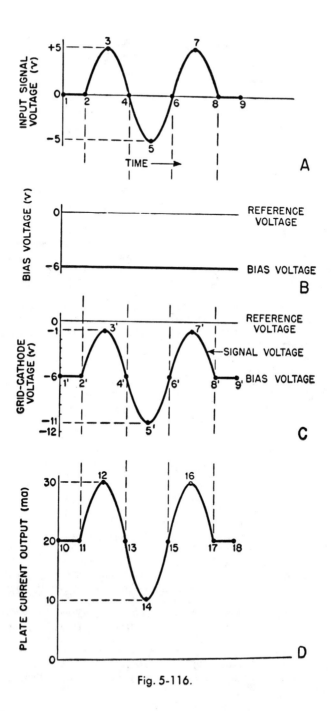

Fig. 5-116.

5-79. *Draw schematics illustrating the following types of grid biasing and explain their operation: battery, cathode resistor, power supply, voltage divider.*

Battery. Bias is the dc voltage applied between grid and cathode of a vacuum tube. A battery (C) that supplies this bias is shown in Fig. 5-115. As shown, the battery's positive terminal is connected to the cathode, so a negative voltage is applied to the grid. The voltage that appears from grid to ground is equal to the bias voltage plus the instantaneous value of the signal voltage. In a fixed-bias arrangement such as that shown, the bias is independent of the input grid signal.

Cathode Resistor. In this circuit (Fig. 1-117) the bias voltage is developed across cathode resistor R_k. Under no-signal conditions, plate current (i_b) flows continuously from cathode to plate, then back to the cathode again through resistor R_k. Since plate current flows from point A to point B, point A is negative with respect to point B. Assume that the voltage drop across R_k is 5V as shown, this makes the cathode 5V positive with respect to the grid (or the grid 5V negative with respect to the cathode).

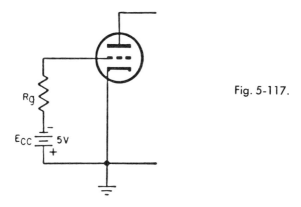

Fig. 5-117.

Resistor R_g is part of the coupling network for the input grid signal. If a sine wave is impressed across R_g, it causes the plate current to vary sinusoidally about an average dc value. The varying plate current flows through cathode resistor R_k. Since the required bias is a fixed voltage, the ac component of plate current through resistor R_k must be removed. This is accomplished by capacitor C_k. The value of this capacitor is large so that its capacitive reactance is small compared with the resistance of R_k at the frequency of the input grid signal. This low value of capacitive reactance effectively short-circuits (bypasses) the ac voltage component around the cathode resistor. The result is that the voltage drop across the cathode resistor does not vary and the bias voltage remains fixed at -5V.

Power Supply. The principle of operation of a fixed-bias arrangement using a separate power is shown in Fig. 5-118. A filtered negative voltage is applied to the grid through a series grid resistor

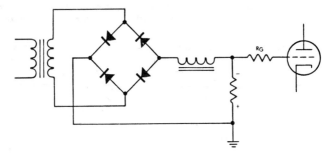

Fig. 5-118.

(R_G). Note that the cathodes of the two joining diodes in the bridge circuit are connected to ground, and the negative voltage is taken from the anode junction.

Voltage Divider. A voltage divider used to supply bias to a tube is shown in Fig. 5-119. As electrons flow down through $R1$ and $R2$, the top of $R1$ becomes negative with respect to the bottom, or ground. The power supply output voltage is 300V, and one-sixtieth of the total

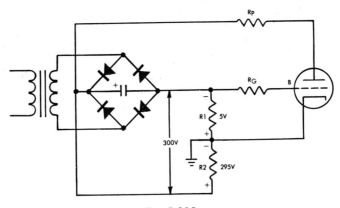

Fig. 5-119.

resistance of $R1$-$R2$ is in $R1$. Hence one-sixtieth of 300V, or 5V, is dropped across $R1$, supplying the required bias. The current direction and relatively large size of divider resistor $R2$ are such that $+295V$ is available at its bottom to supply the plate potential.

5-80. Is grid-leak biasing practical in audio amplifier stages that use tubes?

Grid-leak biasing is not practical in audio applications. It is used in class C rf amplifiers in which only the peaks of the input signal appear in the output. In audio amplifiers the entire input signal must be faithfully reproduced in the output. What is more, grid-leak-biased stages (class C) cannot be used to amplify modulated rf signals; since intolerable distortion would result. Grid-leak biasing and audio signals are not compatible.

5-81. Draw a diagram showing a method of obtaining grid bias for a filament-type vacuum tube by use of resistance in the plate circuit of the tube.

There are several ways to obtain grid bias by using resistors in the plate circuit, but none of them are too practical, because obtaining bias through other schemes is so much simpler. The circuit of Fig. 5-120 is one possible arrangement. The output of the full-wave supply is dropped across a divider consisting of a resistor (high value) and a zener diode (or simply *zener*) whose breakdown voltage is the bias required. As shown, the anode of the zener is kept below ground potential. The zener can be replaced by a resistor, but the operating point is considerably more stable with the zener than with a resistor.

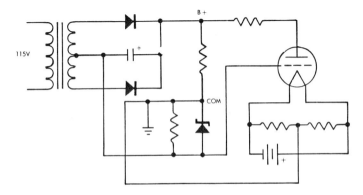

Fig. 5-120.

5-82. Draw circuit diagrams and explain the operation (including input and output phase relationships, approximate practical voltage gain, approximate stage efficiency, uses, advantages, and limitations) of each of the following types of audio circuits:

- *Class A amplifier with cathode resistor biasing*
- *Cathode follower amplifier*
- *At least two types of phase inverters for feeding push-pull amplifiers*
- *Cascaded class A stages with a form of current feedback*
- *Two class A amplifiers operated in parallel*
- *Class A push-pull amplifier.*

Cathode-Biased Class A Amplifier. A cathode-biased class A amplifier is shown in Fig. 5-121. Note that input and output signal polarities (phase relationships) are shown in the accompanying waveforms. This is a conventional amplifier for use in audio circuits; characteristically, its input and output impedances are high. The stage is not very efficient because it requires current during 100% of the signal's cycle. A significant advantage, however, is the circuit's freedom from distortion. Also, the stage requires very little drive and provides excellent gain.

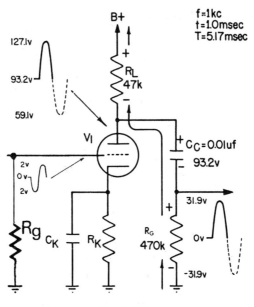

Fig. 5-121.

At the beginning of the positive alternation, the conditions in the plate circuit of the tube are identical to those that exist under no-signal conditions. That is, the plate-to-ground voltage is 93.2V, and coupling capacitor C_C is charged to 93.2V. No voltage appears across grid-leak resistor R_G.

During the first 90° of the plate signal, the plate-to-ground voltage rises rapidly to 127.1V. Since the voltage from plate to ground is 127.1V and the voltage across C_C is only 93.2V, C_C will attempt to charge an additional 33.9V. The charge path for C_C is designated by the arrows in Fig. 5-121. Electrons leave the negative terminal of E_{BB} (ground) and flow up through R_G, C_C, and R_L to the positive terminal of E_{BB} (B+), and then through E_{BB}, completing the circuit. Note that, in charging, the displacement current of C_C must flow through R_L and R_G.

Since the series resistance is large, the time constant for charge is long compared to the period of the sine wave being amplified. The charge time constant of the coupling capacitor is 5.17 msec. A 1 kHz sine wave has a period of 1 msec; therefore, the first 90° of the plate signal requires 0.25 msec. In this brief time (5% of one time constant), the capacitor can only begin to charge to the new value of plate voltage. This short period limits the charging of the capacitor during the first 90° of the signal to about 6% of the available increase of 339V, or to an actual increase of about 2V.

In brief, the single-ended class A stage shown in Fig. 5-121 has these characteristics:

1. It is a phase inverter; that is, the output is always a mirror image of the input.

2. The voltage gain is quite high—considerably better than grounded-grid and grounded-plate circuits.
3. The approximate stage efficiency is 20% or less.
4. Circuits of this type once were accepted as standards for audio amplification, and can be found in obsolete stereo systems, tape recorders, and radios. The phase-inversion phenomenon has also made the circuit useful in applications where a polarity reversal of the input signal is desirable.

Cathode Follower Amplifier. The cathode follower circuit is shown in Fig. 5-122. Until the advent of the transistor, the cathode follower was one of the most useful and common of the basic audio circuits.

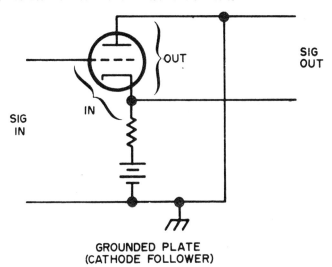

GROUNDED PLATE
(CATHODE FOLLOWER)

Fig. 5-122.

To achieve uniform response over a wide frequency range, an amplifier should have a low effective input capacitance and a low effective load impedance. The overall response may also be improved by the use of degenerative feedback. The cathode follower possesses these qualities and, in addition, it may be used to match the impedance of one circuit to that of another.

The cathode follower is a single-stage class A degenerative amplifier, the output of which appears across the unbypassed cathode resistor. The high input impedance (no grid current) and the low output impedance make it especially useful for matching a high-impedance source to a low-impedance load. Thus, the cathode follower might be used between a pulse-generating stage and a transmission line whose effective shunt capacitance might be great enough to cause objectionable effects. More power, of course, can be delivered when the source is matched to the load. For example, a conventional amplifier having high output impedance would supply less power to a low-impedance coaxial line than would a cathode follower having an output impedance that corresponds to the load impedance.

The advantages obtained by the use of a cathode follower can be had only at the price of a voltage gain that is less than unity. However, the circuit is capable of producing power gain.

A conventional cathode follower is shown along with its characteristics in Fig 5-123A. Under no-signal condition a certain amount of plate current flows through R_K, and this flow establishes the normal bias. When a positive-going signal is applied to the grid, the plate current increases. This increase causes a rise in the voltage drop across R_K, giving the cathode a higher positive potential with respect to ground than it had under the no-signal condition. When a negative-going signal is applied to the grid, the opposite effect occurs. Thus, the output polarity follows the polarity of the signal voltage applied between grid and ground.

Since R_K is not bypassed, degeneration occurs both on the positive half-cycle (when plate current through R_K increases the bias) and on the negative half-cycle (when plate current through R_K decreases the bias). During the positive half-cycle, the increase in bias subtracts from the input signal and reduces the amplitude of the grid-to-cathode voltage. Also, during the negative half-cycle, the bias adds to the input signal and the accompanying decrease in bias again reduces the amplitude of the grid-to-cathode voltage. Thus, in both half-cycles, the peak value of the ac component of plate current is decreased and the output voltage is correspondingly reduced below the value it would have had if degeneration were not present.

Voltage gain in the cathode follower is less than unity. To present the theory of operation of a representative cathode follower, the i_P-e_P characteristi curves for a triode amplifier are used in Fig. 5-123C.

The triode is biased for class A operation. The no-signal plate current is 0.008A, the no-signal plate voltage is 200V, and the grid bias is $-4V$ (point A of Fig. 5-123C). Since the bias of $-4V$ is developed across the cathode resistor, R_K, and there is no plate load resistor, the plate supply voltage is $200 + 4 = 204V$. The cathode resistance is 500Ω. The input signal has a sinusoidal waveform and a peak value of 6.12V. At time t_1 the plate current increases to the peak positive value. The equivalent circuit (Fig. 5-123B) is similar to the equivalent circuit for a conventional triode amplifier, with some modifications. All dc voltage are eliminated; only the ac components are shown. The circuit contains a voltage acting in series with the plate resistance and cathode resistor R_K. The output voltage is equal to the $i_P R_K$ voltage across the cathode load resistor.

To summarize the features and characteristics of the cathode follower, these points are presented:

1. **The input impedance of the cathode follower is high and the output impedance is quite low.**
2. The **distortion of cathode followers is extremely low**—probably the lowest of all the amplifier types.
3. The **input and output waveforms are of the same polarity**; that is, **no phase reversal takes place** as with the common-cathode circuit.
4. For practical purposes the **voltage gain is less than unity** (though the stage does exhibit a power gain).
5. Cathode followers have been replaced in recent years by the emitter follower and source follower, two semiconductor circuits that exhibit the same basic advantages as the cathode follower; but the

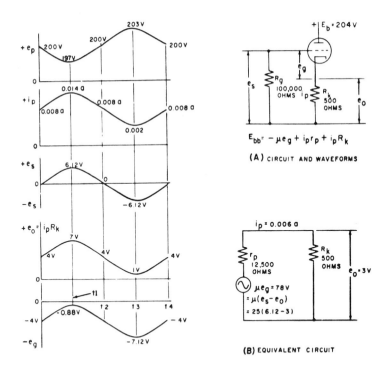

(A) CIRCUIT AND WAVEFORMS

$$E_{bb} = -\mu e_g + i_p r_p + i_p R_k$$

(B) EQUIVALENT CIRCUIT

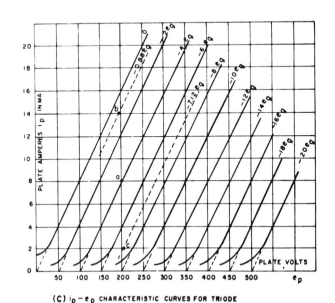

(C) $i_p - e_p$ CHARACTERISTIC CURVES FOR TRIODE

Fig. 5-123.

cathode follower, until recently, has been the **standard audio input stage where signal source impedances tend to vary**. Tape recorders, for example, are often used with microphones of varying impedances; to insure that good a impedance match takes place, good recorders have traditionally incorporated a cathode follower input stage.

Phase Inverters for Push-Pull Stages A phase inverter is a circuit that produces an output voltage of opposite polarity to the input voltage without distorting the waveform. Literally, the commonly accepted term *phase inverter* is something of a misnomer, since phase inversion involves a time lag, and there is no appreciable time lag with conventional phase inverter circuits. In reality, the circuit should be called a *polarity inverter*, which is more accurate.

Most push-pull circuits use inverters called *paraphase amplifiers*, which not only reverse the polarity but offer amplification of input signals as well. Paraphase amplifiers produce two outputs of equal amplitude but opposite polarity. There are two basic types of vacuum-tube paraphase amplifier circuits—the single-tube version and the 2-tube version.

With a single-tube paraphase amplifier (Fig. 5-124), the output is taken from both the cathode and plate of the tube. The cathode load resistor and plate load resistor develop the two output voltages. These resistors are equal, and since the same current flows through them both, equal voltages appear across them. The two voltages, though, are opposite in polarity, since the output is taken from the ositive end of the cathode load resistor and from the negative end of the plate load resistor.

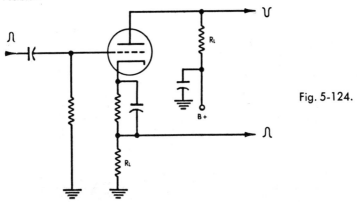

Fig. 5-124.

The 2-tube paraphase amplifier consists of one tube that acts as a conventional amplifier and a second that inverts the output of the first tube.

Figure 5-125 shows the circuit diagram of a typical 2-tube paraphase amplifier. The first tube amplifies the input waveform shown at its grid and impresses the mplified output across the voltage divider consisting of $R1$ and $R2$. Resistor $R2$ is of such value that the varying voltage across it has the same amplitude as the voltage on the grid of $V1$. The voltage across $R2$ is impressed on the grid of $V2$, the phase inverter, where it is amplified. Since the plate resistors ($R5$ for $V1$, $R4$ for $V2$) are equal, the outputs of the two tubes are equal. The

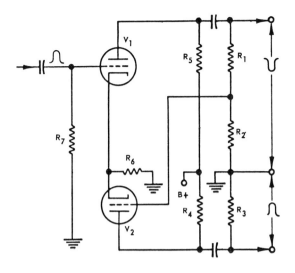

Fig. 5-125.

phase inverter inverts the polarity of the voltage applied to its grid, making it opposite to the signal output of $V1$. Note, in this connection, that the waveform in the output of $V2$ is in phase with the grid voltage to $V1$. Phase inversion has occurred in $V1$ and again in $V2$, thus shifting the phase of this voltage back to its original polarity.

Typical uses of phase inverters and subsequent push-pull amplifiers are in audio circuits where an efficiency beyond that of a conventional class A amplifier is required. Another common application is in radar circuits. For example, sweep voltages are usually applied to the deflection plates in electrostatic cathode-ray tubes in push-pull, since this type of operation reduces the defocusing effects resulting from applying sweep voltages to only one of the pair of deflection plates.

Cascaded Class A Stages with Current Feedback. Current feedback can be obtained in several ways. One arrangement used to obtain negative feedback is illustrated in Fig. 5-126A. In this circuit a feedback voltage is developed across the unbypassed cathode resistor as a result of the plate current flowing through it. Current flow through an unbypassed cathode resistor develops a voltage that varies at the same rate as the plate voltage. Since resistor R_K is located between the cathode and the grid of the tube, any voltage developed across it is in series with the input signal of the tube. The phase relation is correct for phase degeneration to occur. (Phase degeneration is signal cancellation or partial signal cancellation by out-of-phase feedback.)

When a positive signal appears on the grid of the tube, the plate current increases and the voltage drop across R_K also increases. A voltage rise across the cathode resistor makes the grid more negative with respect to the cathode, the reverse of the action by the signa voltage. This arrangement is very useful in canceling distortion in the output signal caused by nonlinearity in the transfer curve of the amplifier. Since plate voltage changes in a tube do not follow the grid

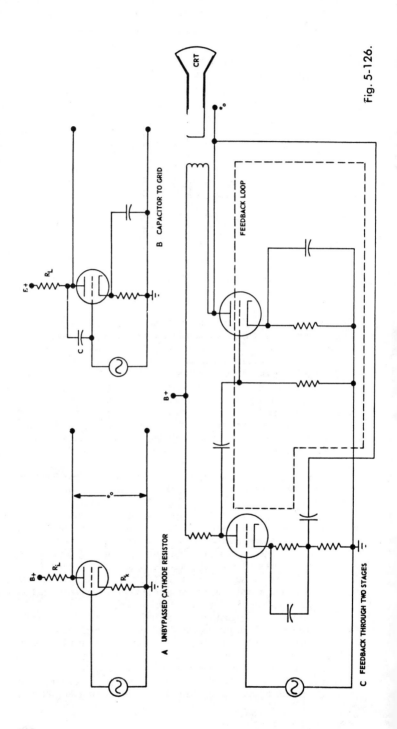

A UNBYPASSED CATHODE RESISTOR

B CAPACITOR TO GRID

C FEEDBACK THROUGH TWO STAGES

FEEDBACK LOOP

CRT

Fig. 5-126.

426

voltage changes exactly, there is some distortion in the output waveform. However, degeneration introduces a portion of the distorted output back into the input in reverse, thus counterbalancing the conditions causing the original distortion.

Feedback can also be obtained by connecting a capacitor from the plate to the grid of the tube, as shown in Fig. 5-126B. Here plate voltage changes produced by plate current variations are opposite in polarity to the original grid voltage changes. The capacitor introduces a small part of the plate voltage change back into the grid circuit; thus, the plate change reflects the distortion in the plate current change in reverse, virtually canceling the distortion originally introduced into the output by the amplifier itself.

Figure 5-126C shows cascaded class A stages using feedback from one stage to another. Not ony is such a circuit useful for counteracting the effects of distortion introduced by the tubes, but it can be used to cancel out-of-phase relationships caused by certain circuit components as well. For example, it compensates for any changes in the inductive reactance of the deflection coil in the circuit. When current flows through this coil, its reactance changes, and this causes a change in the plate voltage of the tube. This change in voltage moves around the feedback loop and counteracts the inductance change. This makes the plate voltage normal and insures an undistorted output voltage.

In some circuits, reactance elements introduce positive feedback into the input, and the circuit oscillates. This is desirable in oscillators but not in amplifiers. Therefore, some type of feedback arrangement similar to that in the 2-tube feedback amplifier must be used to introduce a negative feedback into the input to cancel the effects of the regenerative feedback.

Parallel Class A Amplifiers. The parallel class A amplifier consists of two tubes whose elements are connected directly together; that is, the two grids are tied together, the plates are tied together, and the cathodes are tied together. This arrangement is seldom used, because it offers no significant advantages over single-ended operation and cannot compete with push-pull operation for efficiency. Parallel class A amplifiers have an efficiency that rarely exceeds 25%, a voltage gain comparable to that of a single-ended class A amplifier, and a current gain that is twice that of the single-ended stage. Push-pull operation, on the other hand, offers an efficiency bonus and voltage gain considerably higher than parallel amplifiers.

Class A Push-Pull Amplifier. A push-pull amplifier consists of two tubes whose grid and plate signals are 180° out of phase. Push-pull amplifiers are often used in audio-frequency circuits because of the inherent advantages they offer: less distortion with a greater power output and higher plate efficiency (as high as 30%).

A push-pull triode amplifier circuit is shown in Fig. 5-127. The upper and lower sections of the circuit are similar. Triodes $V1$ and $V2$ are the same type of tube and have similar characteristics. The two grid signals (e_{g1} and e_{g2}) have the same amplitude and frequency but are 180° out of phase with each other. A single bias battery and a single plate supply battery are used to supply both tubes with their proper dc operating potentials. Transformer T acts as a load for the circuit. The

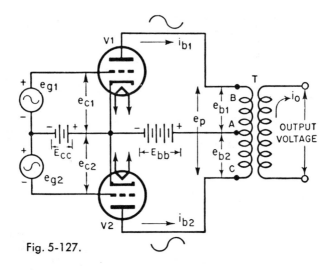

Fig. 5-127.

primary of the transformer is centertapped (point A), so that the output voltages (e_{P1} and e_{P2}) are equal in magnitude. Plate currents i_{P1} and i_{P2} are also equal in amplitude.

The symbols for the various voltages and currents are similar to those used in a simple triode single-ended amplifier stage and represent IEEE notation. The instantaneous voltage across the entire primary is e_P. The instantaneous current in the secondary is i_o.

With no input signals applied to the push-pull circuit, the secondary current is zero. Since steady dc plate current induces no voltage into the secondary, the secondary current is zero. The dc plate current of $V1$ flows from cathode to plate, through the upper half of the primary winding (from point B to point A), and back to the cathode. The dc plate current of $V2$ flows from cathode to plate, through the lower half of the primary winding (from point C to A), and back to the cathode. Points **B** and C are equally negative with respect to point A since the magnitudes of the plate currents are equal. Thus, the total magnetizing force is zero, and dc saturation of the core does not result.

When the sine-wave signals are applied to the respective grids, sine-wave plate currents flow in the primary of the transformer. Current i_{P1} is 180° out of phase with current i_{P2}, since the two grid signals are 180° out of phase with each other. During the positive swing of i_{P1}, point B on the primary becomes more negative with respect to point A. At the same time, the fall in i_{P2} causes point C to become less negative with respect to point A. At the same time, the fall in i_{P2} cause point C to become less negative with respect to point A by an equal amount. Therefore, the voltage across the entire primary is twice the value of either e_{P1} or e_{p2}. In other words, e_P is equal to e_{P1} plus e_{P2}. A half-cycle later, all the polarities reverse. Here again, the voltage across the primary is equal to e_{P1} plus e_{P2}. The relationship of e_P in terms of e_{P1} and e_{P2} holds true for all instantaneous values of plate

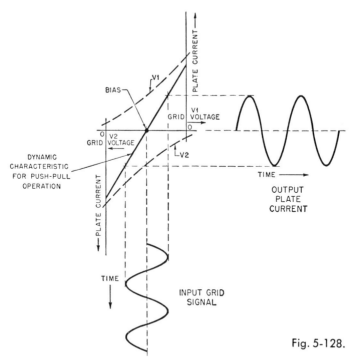

Fig. 5-128.

current. Transformer T couples the output of the push-pull amplifier to another circuit.

There are two common methods of obtaining a 180° phase reversal of the input grid signals. The first is the transformer method; the other is the paraphase amplifier.

The dynamic characteristics for two tubes operating in push-pull are constructed from the individual dynamic characteristics of both tubes. Figure 5-128 shows a dynamic characteristic of two tubes operating in class A push-pull. It is obtained in the following manner. The dotted curve labeled $V1$ is the dynamic characteristic of one tube, and $V2$ is the characteristic of the other. These characteristics are identical; and, because the plate currents of both tubes are 180° out of phase, they are placed 180° out of phase with each other, so that their horizontal axes are common. They are then lined up so that the bias voltage of one tube meets the same bias voltage of the other tube. For example, if E_{CC} equals -5V, this value of voltage occurs at the same place on both grid voltage axes. The resultant dynamic characteristic is obtained by algebraically adding the instantaneous values of plate current for different values of grid signal voltage.

5-83. *Show with circuit diagrams two methods of using single-ended stages to drive a push-pull output stage.*

The first method is shown in Fig. 5-129. The signal is coupled out of the single-ended stage and into the primary of a transformer. The

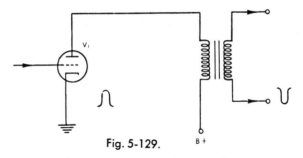

Fig. 5-129.

transformer serves to invert the polarity of the signal; thus, a centertap on the secondary side of the transformer will allow the output signal to be split and applied in reverse polarities to each input of the push-pull stage. The second method is shown in Fig. 5-124. This circuit is the phase inverter described in the answer to a previous question.

5-84. *Draw circuit diagrams and explain the operation of two commonly used tone control circuits and explain their operation.*

Two control circuits are presented in Fig. 5-130. The circuit shown in sketch A is a tone control for bass signals and that at B is the equivalent circuit for treble signals. Note that one circuit is the complement of the other in component placement. The first circuit (for bass signals) uses a high-pass filter network to pass high frequencies while shunting lower frequencies through an attenuator. Conversely, the circuit in B uses a low-pass filter so that low frequencies are passed to the amplifier stage directly while the high-frequency signal components are shunted to an attenuator.

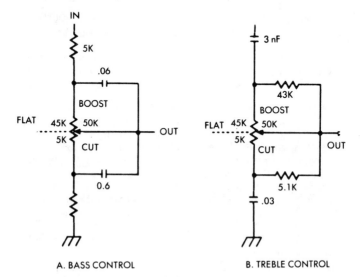

Fig. 5-130.

Examining the bass control circuit as a separate item, you can see the control concept of the passive circuit. In the center position a 5K resistance appears from the wiper arm toward the ground side of the potentiometer, and a 45K resitance appears on the other side (for a total value of 50K across the control). At 50 Hz, the reactance of the capacitor on the hot side is made equal to the 45K portion of the control, and the reactance of the cold-side capacitor is equal to the 5K portion. As the frequency increases, the hot-side capacitor couples more signal to the output, while the cold-side capacitor shunts more signal to ground through its series resistor. This results in a flat response over the amplifier's frequency range, with an insertion loss of 20 dB.

When the wiper arm of the bass control is in the *boost* position, the cold-side capacitor—with a reactance of 10% of the control at 50 Hz—effectively shunts the control out of the circuit. This makes the series resistor (on the hot side of the line) and the cold-side capacitor the components that are dominant in shaping the frequency response characteristic. The full *bass boost* position will supply an output voltage at 50 Hz that is about 20 dB greater than the *flat* position. A 100% boost represents zero attenuation in the tone control of the lower frequencies. The output volume will decrease at about 6 dB per octave until the point where the reactance of the cold-side capacitor is not a factor, at which point the amplitude will be determined by the ratio of the resistors on either side of the bass control. In the *minimum* position (full bass cut), the output level at 50 Hz is determined by the ratio of the capacitive reactance of the hot-side capacitor to the series resistor on the ground side of the potentiometer, which should be about 40 dB below the level indicated by the input voltage.

As frequency increases, the reactance of the hot-side capacitor decreases until it is equal to the resistance of the ground-side series resistor, which again makes the output level a function of the ratio of the hot-side series resistor to the cold-ide series resistor.

Except for the potentiometer, the circuit of the treble control is the inverse of the bass control. That is, where the bass control uses resistances, the treble control uses capacitances; and the treble circuit employs resistances where the bass circuit uses capacitors. At frequencies below 2 kHz the reactances of the two "feeder" capacitors form a 10:1 divider, resulting in a 20 dB insertion loss. Above 2 kHz the two reactances are small relative to the parallel resistive divider combination of the control, which provides a 10:1 voltage division to maintain the 20 dB insertion loss over the high-frequency region. In all, the result is an insertion loss of 20 dB over the entire audio range.

At full boost the hot-side capacitor has a reactance that is roughly equal to the total resistance of the potentiometer at a frequency slightly greater than 2 kHz, so half the input voltage appears at the control output.

By placing a resistor from the wiper to the ground side of the control with a value equal to the center-position resistance (5K), the ratio of the capacitive reactance to this resistor causes a boost starting at 2 kHz.

In the *cut* position (control turned counterclockwise from center), the hot-side resistor in parallel with the hot-side capacitor and the control itself are the response-determining components. From 2 kHz on up, the reactance of the cold-side capacitor decreases until, at about 20 kHz, there is a 20 dB amplitude reduction.

5-85. *Name some causes of hum and self-oscillation in audio amplifiers and the methods of reducing it.*

Hum may be caused by line voltage ac pickup through the filament or grid leads of a vacuum tube. Self-oscillation is usually attributable to unwanted feedback of signal components from an amplifier to its input or to the input of some prior stage.

Hum may be reduced by **using shorter leads** for the tube's electrodes, providing more effective **shielding** for high-impedance lines such as the grid lead, providing more effective **filtering** for the power supply, and by **twisting the filament leads** together. Self-oscillation may be reduced or eliminated by **neutralizing** the positive feedback. This may be accomplished in several ways. One method for removing self-oscillation is to **decouple the audio circuits** from the power supply lines. Another is to **use negative feedback** to cancel the positive feedback causing self-oscillation.

5-86. *What factors should be taken into consideration when ordering a class A audio output transformer? A class B audio output transformer feeding a speaker of known ohmic value?*

Class A Output Transformer. The considerations are output-power-handling capacity, frequency response, impedance of the primary and secondary windings, and the availability of taps.

The first consideration, of course, is impedance of the input and output windings. The input impedance of the transformer (primary winding) should be high if the transformer is to be used with a vacuum-tube amplifier and relatively low if the transformer is to be used in a transistor circuit. A single-ended stage will have a different characteristic impedance than a push-pull output stage. If the transformer is to be used for high-fidelity reproduction, a broad frequency response chracteristic will be required, as well as a higher-than-normal power-handling ability. The presence of taps is ordinarily a desirable transformer characteristic, for it allows a variety of circuit arrangements as well as a multiplicity of impedance-matching options.

Class B Audio Transformer. A class B audio output transformer is one that must be used with a push-pull driving stage, since a single-ended class B amplifier would produce a signal too distorted for audio use. Class B amplification is frequently used in push-pull audio output circuits because of the higher efficiency it affords as compared to class A operation. The transformer to be used in the output stage of a class B push-pull amplifier must be capable of handling the rather high $B+$ voltage supplied to the plates of the tubes used as final audio amplifiers. Normally the dc plate voltage used for the tubes is supplied through the primary winding of the output transformer, as shown in Fig. 5-131. Thus, in addition to the impedance considerations, power-handling capacity, and frequency response, an important consideration for the class B output transformer is the maximum voltage that can be applied without fear of arcing within the transformer's primary winding.

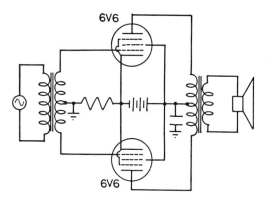

Fig. 5-131.

5-87. *Draw a diagram of a double-button carbon microphone circuit, including the microphone transformer and source of power.*

In a double-button microphone there is a push-pull action. Any movement of the diaphragm increases the pressure in one button while decreasing the pressure in the other.

In the circuit shown in Fig. 5-132A, the microphone button is placed in series with a battery. Any current flowing in the microphone circuit will also flow through the primary of the transformer. With no movement of the diaphragm, there will be no change in the resistance of the button. Under these conditions the dc flowing through the button will be constant, and the resulting magnetic field about the primary of the transformer will not fluctuate. There will be no voltage induced in the secondary of the transformer.

When the diaphragm is compressed, the resistance of the button will decrease and the current through the circuit will increase. The field that was stationary about the primary will now expand and cut the secondary windings; voltage will now be induced in the secondary of the transformer. If the pressure on the diaphragm is reduced, the resistance of the carbon pile increases and circuit current decreases. The voltage induced in the transformer secondary will now reverse polarity. If the diaphragm is moved at an audio rate, the voltage induced in the secondary of the transformer will also vary at an audio rate. Therefore, the amount of voltage induced in the secondary is dependent on the pressure applied to the microphone diaphragm. The frequency of the output voltage is dependent on the frequency of the input. The frequency limit of the microphone is governed by the ability of the carbon granules to change their density rapidly.

When the double-button microphone is used (Fig. 5-132B), the amount of possible distortion realized through the constant shuffling of the carbon granules is reduced. The push-pull effect realized by the use of the double-button microphone and the centertapped transformer tends to cancel the even harmonics.

433

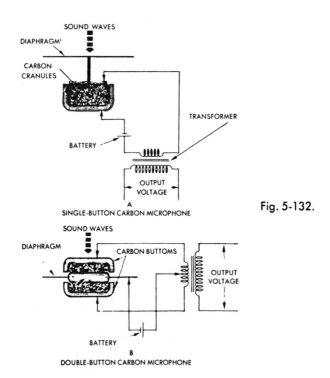

SOUND WAVES

DIAPHRAGM'

CARBON
CRANULES

TRANSFORMER

BATTERY

OUTPUT
VOLTAGE

A
SINGLE-BUTTON CARBON MICROPHONE

Fig. 5-132.

SOUND WAVES

DIAPHRAGM

CARBON BUTTOMS

OUTPUT
VOLTAGE

BATTERY

B
DOUBLE-BUTTON CARBON MICROPHONE

5-88. *Describe the construction and operation of a crystal microphone.*

When pressure is applied to certain crystals, a voltage is generated. This is known as the *piezoelectric* (pee-*ay*-zoe-electric) *effect.* The crystal microphone uses this effect. There are two basic types of crystal microphones—the *directly actuated* and the *diaphragm actuated* type. In the directly actuated type the sound acts directly on the crystal.

When a quartz crystal is subjected to a varying mechanical pressure, the crystal produces a minute alternating voltage that can be measured with ordinary test equipment. Since the electrical energy emitted by the crystal is proportional to the mechanical energy required to drive it, the crystal is indeed an energy converter—or *transducer.* Typical uses for the crystal transducer are in microphones and phonograph cartridges.

A thin diaphragm is employed for microphone transducers. The sounds cause the diaphragm to vibrate, and the vibrations are coupled mechanically to the crystal. Low-frequency sounds, like bass drums and the low keys on the piano, make the crystal vibrate relatively slowly. High-pitched sounds, like brushes against a cymbal and tinkling bells, cause the crystal to vibrate very rapidly. The rate of vibrations, in fact, is directly proportional to the frequency of the sound source.

The crystal responds to vibrations by producing a voltage that reverses polarity in exact correspondence with the physical movement. Low-frequency sounds produce voltages that alternate slowly, and high-pitched sounds produce output voltages that alternate rapidly. The electrical signals generated by the crystal can be used to drive a high-impedance amplifier directly.

A directly actuated microphone transducer is shown in Fig. 5-133. As shown, this type of crystal microphone couples sound vibrations directly to the crystal element. Electrical contact is made to the crystal

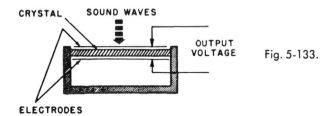

Fig. 5-133.

by the thin metal foil on each side of the element. When this type of crystal is activated directly by the pressure waves of the voice, the device is not efficient. When the sound waves strike the surface, the force is dissipated over the entire surface of the crystal. To obtain higher efficiency, a diaphragm is used. A diaphragm-actuated type is shown in Fig. 5-134. In this arrangement all of the force of the diaphragm is exerted on a small area of the crystal. Therefore, as the diaphragm moves back and forth, the voltage produced by the crystal varies at the same rate. Since the diaphragm is mechanically connected to the crystal element, there will be considerable stress placed on the crystal. The output of the diaphragm-actuated type of crystal mike is higher than that of the directly actuated type.

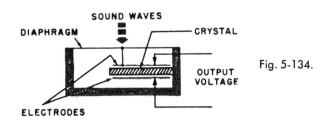

Fig. 5-134.

The frequency response of crystal mike is not too uniform. This is because of the inertia of the crystal itself. However, for noncritical applications, crystal mikes are widely used. Because of its high impedance, the crystal microphone may be directly connected to the input of the grid circuit of a speech amplifier, as mentioned earlier. The output of the crystal microphone is on the order of −55 dBm, although this figure tends to vary from manufacturer to manufacturer, depending on quality of microphone and other factors. The diaphragm type has a frequency response of 80 to about 6000 Hz. The type of crystal most widely used is Rochelle salt, because its sensitivity is somewhat higher than that of natural quartz.

5-89. *What precautions should be observed when using and storing crystal microphones?*

The disadvantages of the crystal microphone are its sensitivity to temperature extremes, humidity changes, and rough handling. When using and storing crystal mikes, it is extremely important to keep them in an environment that is relatively cool. A mere 120°F can destroy a crystal microphone. Thus, it is foolhardy to use or recommend a crystal microphone for mobile applications.

RADIO-FREQUENCY AMPLIFIERS

5-90. *What are the advantages of using a resistor in series with the cathode of a class C rf amplifier tube to provide bias?*

Some biasing arrangements, such as grid-leak biasing, depend on the presence of an excitation signal to develop the proper bias voltage for the class C amplifier. In such cases, if the oscillator of the transmitter or some stage between the oscillator and final amplifier were to cease functioning, bias would be removed from the final amplifier. With zero bias, a transmitter final amplifier tube would draw a great deal of current, causing subsequent destruction of the tube.

The bias afforded by the cathode resistor is designed to be sufficient to protect the tube in the event of an inadvertent signal loss. The value of the grid bias chosen determines the amount of time that plate current will flow duing each input signal cycle. With a high value of bias, transmitter efficiency will be high but the output power increases substantially. With no bias at all, of course, the stage's output soars and the tube burns out.

5-91. *What is the difference between rf voltage amplifiers and rf power amplifiers in regard to applied bias? What type of tube is generally employed in rf voltage amplifiers?*

An rf voltage amplifier is a stage that is designed to increase the voltage level of the input, whereas a power amplifier is a stage that is designed to increase the power level of the input. **Voltage amplifiers are typically designed for class A or class B operation; power amplifiers are designed for class AB, B, or C. Thus power amplifiers are generally biased considerably below the stage's cutoff point** (so the tube does not conduct except during 30% to 50% of the input cycle), while a **voltage amplifier is biased at a point fairly well centered on the linear transfer characteristic** (so the tube will conduct during all or a large part of the input signal swing).

Because of a triode's interelectrode capacitance, which tends to feed back signal portions capacitively at high frequencies, such tubes are rarely used as rf voltage amplifiers. When triodes are used, they often must be neutralized to counterbalance these feedback effects. Tetrodes introduce the problem of secondary emission, so their use is not as common as pentodes. **The pentode offers the easiest solution with respect to capacitances and secondary emission, because it has a screen grid to reduce the interelectrode capacitance and a suppressor grid to reduce the secondary emission.**

The two principal types of amplifiers are voltage amplifiers and current amplifiers. A voltage amplifier produces a relatively large voltage and small current at its output; a power amplifier produces a relatively large current and small voltage at its output. The load resistor for a voltage amplifier is large (10K or more) compared with the plate resistance of the tube. The larger the value of load resistance, the larger the voltage drop across it and the less the current through it. The amplitude of the input grid signal is small, so that a large voltage and small current are obtained.

Power amplifiers are often referred to as *current amplifiers*. In a power amplifier the value of load resistance usually is much smaller than in a voltage amplifier (under 10K), so that its plate current remains quite large. The small value of load resistance produces a small voltage drop across it. The amplitude of the input grid signal to a power amplifier is made large, so that its output plate current is large.

Schematically there is no way of distinguishing between voltage and power amplifiers, except by the values of their individual loads. In typical applications a voltage amplifier feeds its output to a power amplifier (in a transmitter circuit).

Generally, power amplifiers are operated under class C conditions, where efficiency is highest (as is distortion). In rf applications, when tuned circuits are used in the output, class B and C amplifiers can be used without much regard to distortion. The reason for this is the so-called *flywheel effect* of tuned circuits. Even though the stage conducts only during a portion of the input signal's cycle, there is little distortion of the output signal, since the tank supplies the missing portions.

5-92. *Draw schematic diagrams of the following circuits and give some possible reasons for their use.*

- *Link coupling between a final rf stage and an antenna (including a low-pass filter)*
- *Capacitor coupling between an oscillator stage and a buffer amplifier*
- *A method of coupling a final stage to a quarter-wave Marconi antenna other then link or transmission line*

Link Coupling with Low-Pass Filter. The circuit in Fig. 5-135A is the push-pull counterpart of the simple resonant tank. A split-stator capacitor is used, and the rotor is grounded for rf through a bypass capacitor. Plate voltage is series-fed to the center of the inductor through an rf choke. To reduce the voltage across each half of the tuning capacitor, the plate voltage is sometimes connected to the rotor. The shock hazard introduced by this practice can be avoided by grounding the rotor of the tuning capacitor directly and applying the plate voltage through an rf choke.

The signal is coupled into the link inductively. The low-pass filter (shown in Fig. 5-135B) shunts the higher frequencies to ground and allows the lower frequencies to be passed on to the antenna. Component values in the filter are selected so as to provide minimum attenuation of frequencies near the signal frequency but a great deal of attenuation for frequencies above this reference. High frequencies in the link (which is connected directly to the low-pass filter in practice) meet a relatively high inductive reactance in the coil of the filter (L) and a low capacitive reactance in C. Low frequencies meet little opposition in L and high opposition in C.

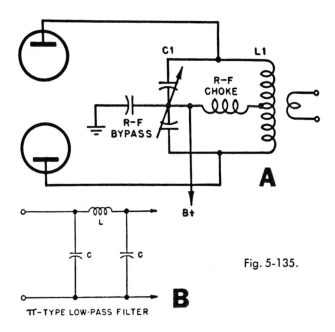

C1

L1

R-F CHOKE

R-F BYPASS

A

B+

L

C   C

B

π-TYPE LOW-PASS FILTER

Fig. 5-135.

Oscillator-to-Buffer Coupling. One of the characteristics of class C amplifiers is the consumption of power in the input circuit caused by the grid voltage going positive with respect to the cathode and drawing current during part of the operating cycle. This power, called *excitation power*, must be supplied by the preceding stage in the transmitter. For the power amplifier to operate efficiently, a certain minimum amount of excitation is required. This is determined by the type of tube and the dc voltage applied to it. The stages before the power amplifier must be able to supply this excitation without overloading. Because the frequency of an oscillator depends to some extent on the load impressed upon it, it is undesirable from the standpoint of frequency stabilization to attempt to supply excitation power directly from the oscillator. Another consideration is the modulation impressed on a carrier wave in the power amplifier. In this case a varying amount of excitation is demanded by the power amplifier as the modulation changes. This changing load also can seriously affect the frequency stabilization of the oscillator if the oscillator is used to drive such a modulated amplifier directly.

Therefore, a buffer amplifier is introduced between the oscillator and the power amplifier **to isolate the two stages from each other**. The buffer amplifier usually is operated class A so that it will not affect the oscillator. In this condition no power is drawn in its grid circuit. For class A service the efficiency is low, and tubes of fairly high ratings must be used in buffer circuits for high-power final amplifier stages. In broadcast service many buffer stages are used to build up the low-level output from the oscillator to a value sufficient to provide excitation to the power amplifier. **In general, the buffer must supply from 5% to 20% as much power as the final amplifier will produce.**

The buffer amplifier must supply this excitation and have considerable reserve power, so that **its output does not vary with changing load**. This is termed *good regulation*. Since the efficiency of a class A buffer is low, its plate dissipation can be as much as half that of the tube used as the final rf power amplifier. Excitation requirements increase as the frequency of operation is increased. This is because losses in the input circuit are greater at higher frequencies.

Because the power level at which the oscillator operates usually is low, the buffer for the oscillator tube generally is of a similar power rating operated class A, as shown in Fig. 5-136. In the circuit shown, a receiving-type triode is used as a low-power, crystal-controlled oscillator. Its output is coupled through an *RC* network to the buffer

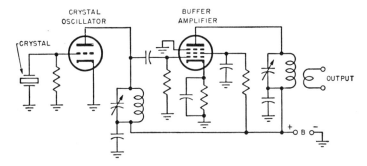

Fig. 5-136.

. amplifier grid, which is self-biased for class A operation by the resistor and capacitor in its cathode circuit. The *RC* coupling is also commonly called capacitive coupling by virtue of the single capacitor used to bridge the two circuits.

The buffer amplifier is a small receiving-type pentode. The plate of the buffer is connected to the *B+* of the power supply through a parallel resonant circuit tuned to the crystal frequency. The output of the buffer amplifier is coupled to the following stage in the transmitter by the transformer action of the link coil coupled to the resonant output circuit. In the practical transmitter, buffer amplifiers are used between the oscillator and frequency multiplier, and also between the frequency multiplier and power amplifier.

Antenna Coupling With No Transmission Line. In portable transmitters it is common to find the antenna connected directly to the tank circuit of the transmitter, with no intervening transmission line. Because the impedance of a quarter-wave (Marconi) antenna changes considerably in the proximity of nearby conductive objects, it must be matched directly to the power amplifier by means of a tank circuit that can compensate for a wide range of possible impedances. Three basic circuits, adaptable to single-ended and push-pull tank circuits alike,

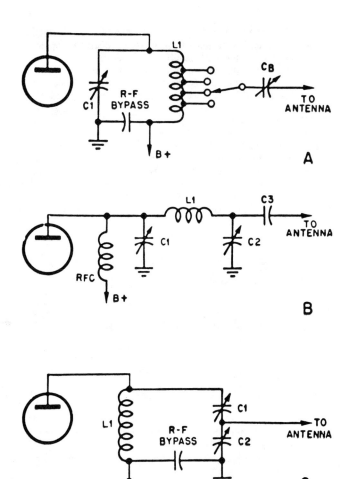

Fig. 5-137.

which provide this variable impedance matching, are shown in Fig. 5-137. A series-fed, parallel resonant, single-ended tank with grounded tuning capacitor rotor and bypassed inductor is illustrated in sketch A. Instead of coupling the antenna inductively to the tank, it is tapped directly to the coil through a blocking capacitor. Since the lower end of the tuned circuit is grounded effectively, the impedance to ground at that point must be zero. As the tap is moved up on the coil, the impedance rises until it reaches the ultimate value of the tank circuit impedance. In a practical transmitter the coil is tapped at intervals, and a rotary switch is used to select the tap that gives the proper value of coupling. Because the dc plate current in the amplifier stage increases with increased loading, the tap can be set at the point that gives the required direct current in the stage when the tuned circuit is resonating. If the blocking capacitor between the tap and antenna is made variable, a further adjustment between separate taps can be obtained.

One of the most frequently encountered variable matching networks for the output of an rf amplifier is the circuit in sketch B. The plate voltage fed through the rf choke is prevented from reaching the antenna by blocking capacitor C3. The simple pi network of C1, L, and C2 is capable of matching a wide range of impedances and operates as a voltage divider. The combination of L1 and C2 forms a divider circuit, which develops higher or lower voltages at the output terminal. Capacitor C1 then tunes the combination of C2 and L1 to resonance at the operating frequency. Depending on the relative values of C1 and C2, a voltage much lower than the ac plate voltage can be developed. Consequently, this circuit can match an extremely wide range of impedances. In addition to matching purely resistive loads, the circuit also can compensate for a certain amount of reactance. This is important when using short antennas, which introduce considerable capacitive reactance.

A variation of the pi network in which one of the capacitors is not grounded is shown in sketch C. Capacitors C1 and C2 themselves form the impedance-matching voltage divider. The circuit cannot match as wide a range of impedances as the pi network can, and it is further limited because the rotor of C1 must be carefully insulated. The response of these circuits to harmonics of the fundamental frequency is poor, which is a desirable feature. The pi network does not discriminate against signals below operating frequencies; this makes it undesirable to use if the amplifier is driven directly by a frequency multiplier.

5-93. *Draw a schematic diagram of a grounded-grid rf amplifier and discuss its merits.*

The grounded-grid circuit, shown in Fig. 5-138, **permits use of the triode, with its lower noise figure, and does not require neutralization.** However, the voltage gain of the amplifier is not as great as that of the

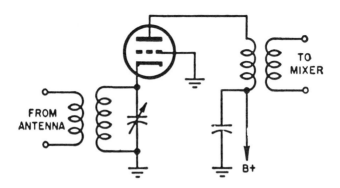

Fig. 5-138.

441

grounded-cathode circuit because the input impedance is very low. The **low-impedance input circuit permits the attainment of wide bandwidth and a reasonable noise figure without sacrificing too much voltage gain in the input circuit.** The gain of the grounded-grid amplifier may not be great enough to override the noise produced by some converter tubes; therefore, it is common practice to find two grounded-grid rf amplifiers in cascade. The added complications arising from this necessity and the need for special tubes limit its use. The tubes themselves must have very low effective plate-to-cathode capacitance if the shielding effect of the grounded grid is to realized

5-94. *Draw a circuit diagram of a push-pull (triode) final power amplifier, with transmission line feed to a shunt-fed quarter-wave antenna, and indicate a method of plate neutralization.*

In the circuit of Fig. 5-139 the neutralization of each half of the push-pull stage is accomplished with an individual capacitance (C_N). Note that the capacitors are cross-connected; that is, the grid of one circuit is fed the out-of-phase signal from the cathode of the other. This push-pull amplifier has an output capacitance equal to the plate—cathode capacitance of each tube in series plus twice the grid—plate capacitance. This extra capacitance is added by the neutralizing circuit. It limits the operating frequency of the amplifier, because the output capacitance is a major factor in determining the plate tank constants at very high frequencies.

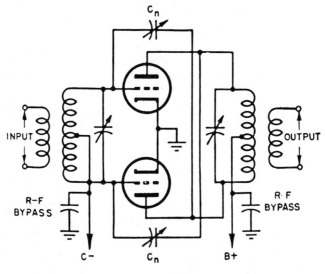

Fig. 5-139.

Shunt feeding the illustrated circuit to an antenna is a simple process. Of the two output lines, the lower one connects to the shield of a coaxial cable, and the upper one connects to the center conductor of the transmission line. The shield is also grounded to the transmitter chassis. At the antenna end the shield attaches to the car body, ground plane, or other metallic reflecting surface, while the center conductor connects to the quarter-wave radiator directly.

5-95. *Draw a circuit diagram of a "push-push" frequency multiplier and explain its principle of operation.*

When the plate tank of the push-push frequency multiplier circuit of Fig. 5-140 is tuned to twice the frequency of the input, the circuit acts as a very efficient doubler. Its operation can be considered similar to that of a full-wave rectifier. The grid of each tube is biased at cutoff or thereabouts, so that plate current flows in each tube on succeeding half-cycles. When the signal input across the secondary of transformer T makes the grid of $V1$ positive with respect to its cathode, the tube conducts. At the same time, the signal applied to the grid of $V2$ is negative, and so $V2$ remains cut off during this period. On the next half-cycle of input voltage, $V2$ conducts and $V1$ is cut off. The plates of $V1$ and $V2$ are connected in parallel; therefore, two pulses excite the tank circuit for each cycle of input voltage.

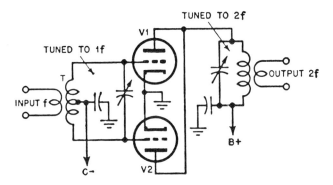

Fig. 5-140.

The pulses drive the tank at a frequency that is twice the frequency of the input signal. The output can be compared to the ripple present in the output of the unfiltered full-wave rectifier circuit. Because of its simplicity, this circuit was widely used in FM and AM transmitters. If compactness is also a consideration in design, the circuit can serve also as combination doubler and power amplifier because of its relatively high efficiency and low output of undesirable harmonics.

5-96. *Push-pull frequency multipliers produce what order of harmonics, even, or odd?*

Push-pull frequency multipliers are used for producing odd-order harmonics. As mentioned in the answer to the preceding question, the *push-push* circuit is excellent for doubling, which also makes the circuit suitable for producing other even-order multiples of the input frequency.

5-97. *Describe some factors in connection with the following items, which should be considered at VHF and above but would not be of particular concern at medium frequencies or below.*

- *Wire diameter and lead length*
- *Wiring configuration (placement and bending)*
- *Coaxial cables and transmission lines*
- *Capacitor types*

Wire Diameter and Lead Length. At VHF it is important to think in terms of wavelengths rather than inches. Since higher frequencies mean shorter wavelengths, it is easy to see how a lead could actually serve as a resonant line, even to the extent of radiating a signal as an antenna would. The diameter of any given conductor must be kept as large as possible to accommodate the current passing though it, but it must also be small enough to prevent the buildup of capacitances between the lead itself and adjacent circuits. With respect to lead length, a good general rule at VHF is to always use the shortest lead length required to get from one point to another and avoid routing the leads near other parts of the circuit to as great an extent as may be considered practical.

Wiring Configuration. As mentioned above, leads should be dressed as far away from other components and other leads as possible, to prevent inadvertent signal coupling via the capacitance of the leads themselves, but not to such an extent that lead length is compromised. Bends in leads should be avoided if possible; whenever a bend in a lead must be made, it is important to keep the angle of the bend as gentle as possible in order to prevent the bend from acting as a coil. In many UHF circuits, inductors themselves take the form of straight lengths of wire. A sharp bend in a lead at higher frequencies could exhibit a characteristic inductance that could seriously affect the performance of a circuit or cause radiation of signals that should be contained within the circuit.

Coaxial Cables and Transmission Lines. A given length of coaxial cable (or other form of transmission line) will exhibit a characteristic loss that rises with frequency—the higher the frequency, the greater the loss. It is extremely important when connecting transmission lines to antennas to keep the line as short as possible without bending. It is equally important to be certain that the line is well matched at both the input and output ends. While signal losses of coaxial cables cannot be avoided, they can be minimized. Another way of keeping losses down is to use the largest diameter cable possible, while avoiding coaxial cables that use dielectrics exhibiting appreciable losses at higher frequencies.

Capacitor Types. Some dielectrics are insulators at low frequencies but conductors at higher frequencies. Paper capacitors, for example, while ideal for the dielectric material in a capacitor used at power-line frequencies, are less than worthless at VHF. Good capacitor dielectrics for VHF include Mylar, air, and some ceramics.

TRANSMITTERS

5-98. *Discuss the following items with respect to their harmonic attenuation properties as possibly used in a transmitter or receiver: link coupling, tuned circuits, degree of coupling, bias voltage, decoupling circuits, shielding.*

Link Coupling. Because of the control in degree of coupling (tightness or looseness), link coupling provides an effective means for transferring a signal from one circuit to another with a minimum of harmonic radiation. Link coupling requires the use of two tuned circuits—one, for example, in the plate circuit of the driver tube and the other in the grid circuit or the amplifier. A low-impedance rf transmission line having a coil of one or two turns at each end is used to couple the plate and grid tanks.

The coupling links, or loops, are coupled to each tuned circuit at its "cold" end (point of zero rf potential). Circuits that are "cold" near one end are called *unbalanced* circuits. Link coupling systems normally are used where the two stages to be coupled are separated by a considerable distance. One side of the link is grounded whenever harmonic attenuation is important as well as when capacitive coupling is to be avoided. The circuit arrangement is illustrated in Fig. 5-141.

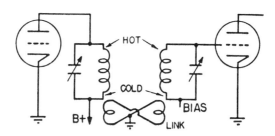

Fig. 5-141.

Link coupling is a very versatile interstage coupling system. It is used in transmitters when the equipment is sufficiently large to permit the coupled coils to be so positioned that there is no stray capacitive coupling between them. Link circuits are designed to have low impedance, so that rf power losses are low. Coupling between the links and their associated tuned circuits can be varied without complex mechanical problems. These adjustments provide a means of obtaining very loose coupling between stages, which means that harmonic generation can be minimized.

Tuned Circuits. There are several methods of coupling signals from one stage to another in a transmitter, but some of these are inherently better than others when it comes to attenuation of harmonic radiation.

One of the most desirable coupling methods using tuned circuits is a type called *untuned-secondary transformer coupling*. This approach discriminates against harmonics of the operating frequency. Figure 5-142 illustrates a tuned circuit connected in this configuration. Two coils, labeled L1 and L2, comprise an air-core transformer. Air-core transformers are used almost exclusively in transmitters because of the operating frequencies involved. At high frequencies the chief difficulty with iron-core transformers is eddy current losses, which are

445

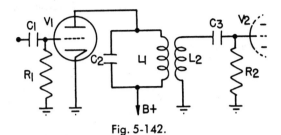

Fig. 5-142.

proportional to the square of the frequency and the square of the thickness of the laminations in the core.

A characteristic of a parallel resonant tuned circuit is that it offers maximum impedance to the resonant frequency, causing plate current to be minimum; thus, the line current is minimum but the tank current is maximum.

Degree of Coupling. It is important to optimize the coupling of one rf stage to another, so that the overall efficiency of the transmitter will be as high as possible. However, as coupling is increased, circuit selectivity suffers. And as the selectivity drops, the chances of harmonic radiation increase. A circuit whose selectivity has been compromised by excessive coupling is said to be *overcoupled*. On the other hand, if the coupling is too loose, insufficient energy will be transferred from one stage to the next. Note the drop in secondary voltage of loose coupling as compared to other degrees of coupling in Fig. 5-143.

As the coefficient of coupling is increased, the reflected impedance— which is resistive at the resonant frequency—continues to increase until, eventually, a value of coupling is reached where the reflected resistance equals the equivalent resistance of the primary. This is called *critical coupling*. At this point there is maximum transfer

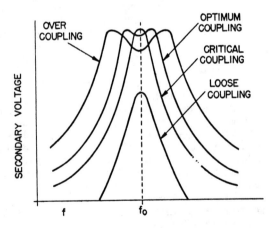

Fig. 5-143.

of energy from the primary to secondary. A critically coupled circuit tends to be unstable, since the slightest change in the spacing between coils has considerable effect on the degree of coupling. Ideally, the proper coupling between transmitter stages is the stable curve labeled *optimum coupling*. Under normal conditions this allows ample transfer of energy without creating a steep selectivity curve that is easily detuned.

Bias Voltage. A class C amplifier is biased below the rf amplifier's cutoff point. But just how far below? In general, the further below cutoff that the tube or transistor is biased, the more efficient the amplifier—but the more distortion will be present. And as distortion increases, so does the inadvertent radiation of harmonic energy. The bias of a class C amplifier must take into consideration these factors. In addition, class C amplifiers that are biased well below cutoff—say, at four times the cutoff voltage—must be driven with an extremely potent excitation signal; and this fact, in itself, results in the increased likelihood of harmonic generation and radiation.

Decoupling Circuits. A decoupling circuit is a network used in a multistage amplifier to negate the effects of in-phase signal feedback. Thus, any distortion (harmonic-producing signal) that is introduced between the input and the final output stage may be canceled using decoupling circuits. In transmitters where decoupling is not incorporated, $B+$ lines and other common leads can carry a portion of the transmitter signal from one of the advanced stages back to an earlier stage; and if the feedback is positive (in phase with the intended signal), the coupled signal will add to the signal already present. If the signal has any characteristics that were not present in the original signal (distortion), such characteristics will be exaggerated by repeated feedback, and the ultimate result is generation of a waveform that is rich in harmonics. The decoupling circuit is used to prevent all this.

Shielding. The need for shielding in a radio transmitter is self-evident. Shielding—that is, inserting a grounded screen between stages that should not be coupled or that contain high-radiation circuits within such screened enclosures—prevents capacitive coupling of a signal from one stage to another. Similarly, shielding contains rf fields that might otherwise radiate before being coupled properly to the antenna.

5-99. *Define "transmitter intermodulation"; give a possible cause, its effects, and steps that could be taken to reduce it.*

When two different frequencies, $f1$ and $f2$, are detected by some nonlinear element, the result is intermodulation—or generation of a signal that is a combination of $f1$ or any of its harmonics with $f2$ or any of its harmonics (i.e., $f1 \pm f2$, $f1 \pm 2f2$, $2f1 \pm f2$, $f1 \pm 3f2$, etc.). Transmitter intermodulation typically occurs when the nonlinear element is the grid circuit of the final amplifier of one of the transmitters involved.

The source of an intermod problem may be difficult to spot, because there are no easy methods by which an operator can determine whether the intermod is a transmitter or a receiver problem, and there is no direct method for determining which of two transmitters is radiating the interfering signal other than to examine the areas where the intermod is occurring. If the signal occurs in but one or two receivers and not in others tuned to the same frequency in the same area, the problem is probably due to a mixing action in the receiver itself.

When the frequencies of the two transmitters are widely separated, the problem can be easily overcome by installation of a *suckout filter* in the offending transmitter's transmission line. (The filter, of course, would be tuned to the frequency of the second transmitter.) Other methods include use of directional antennas on one or both transmitters to minimize radiation in the plane between the two, physically moving one of the transmitter sites, and reduction of transmitter power by either or both stations. Intermodulation distortion can also occur within a single transmitter in any nonlinear circuit. This form of intermodulation may be caused by defective components, improper bias, excessive drive, etc.

5-100. *State a probable cause of and method of reducing transmitter spurious emissions other than harmonics.*

Spurious emissions are signals generated within the transmitter that are not intended to be processed or radiated by the transmitter circuits. Such emissions, of course, include harmonics; but they also include parasitic oscillations, and signals caused by inadvertent positive feedback in the various stages and by intermodulation. A complete discussion of neutralization techniques and tests, and parasitic oscillation remedies has already been given. (See index.)

AMPLITUDE MODULATION

5-101. *If a carrier is amplitude-modulated, what causes the sideband frequencies?*

When an rf carrier is modulated by a single audio modulating frequency, two additional frequencies are produced. One of these frequencies is the sum of the rf carrier and the audio frequency. The other is the difference between the rf carrier and the audio frequency. When the modulating signal is complex, each frequency component of the modulating signal produces a sum and difference frequency with the rf carrier. The sum frequencies are known as the *upper sideband*; and the difference frequencies are known as the *lower sideband*. The location of the various frequencies in the case of a single modulating frequency is shown in Fig. 5-144.

The "space" that a carrier and its associated sidebands occupy in the frequency spectrum is called the *bandwidth*. The bandwidth is equal to twice the highest modulating frequency. In Fig. 5-144 the bandwidth is equal to 2×5 kHz (10 kHz). A tank circuit tuned to the carrier frequency is used as the impedance across which is developed the resultant AM waveform. The half-power points of the response curve for the tuned circuits must enclose the bandwidth of the resultant signal to be transmitted. The audio modulation frequency lies outside of the response curve and therefore will not be developed as part of the resultant waveform. The result of a single-tone amplitude modulation is simply the algebraic combination of the two sidebands and the carrier frequency, as shown in Fig. 5-145.

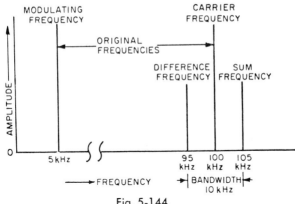

Fig. 5-144.

5-102. *What determines the bandwidth of emission for an AM transmission?*

The bandwidth of an AM wave is a function of the frequencies contained in the modulating signal. For example, when a 100 kHz carrier is modulated by a 5 kHz audio tone, sideband frequencies are created at 95 and 105 kHz. Thus, the total bandwidth of the transmitted signal, in this case, would be 10 kHz (twice the frequency of the applied modulating signal).

Musical instruments produce complex sound waves containing a great number of frequencies. For each modulating frequency there is an instantaneous pair of sidebands above and below the carrier. Hence, it is possible to have a large number of sidebands; and the highest and lowest sidebands will be determined by the highest frequency represented by the modulating signal. To transmit a musical passage with a fairly high degree of fidelity, frequencies up to 15 kHz must be included in the signal. This would require a bandwidth of at least 30 kHz to prevent attenuation of higher order harmonic frequencies.

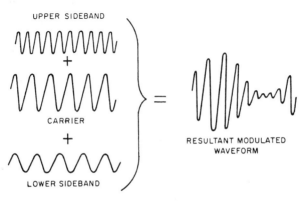

Fig. 5-145.

Radio stations in the AM broadcast band must be spaced far enough apart to preclude interference between adjacent stations. The FCC maintains a spacing between stations of 10 kHz and restricts the modulating frequency to a maximum of 5 kHz.

5-103. *Why does exceeding 100% modulation in an AM transmitter cause excessive bandwidth of emission?*

It is first important to understand that some waveforms are more efficient harmonic generators than others. Square waves, in particular, are very effective in creating harmonic signals. An overmodulated AM signal produces a modulation envelope that is clipped off at the negative half-cycle. This clipped waveform resembles a square wave and is rich in harmonics of the modulating signal. Since the harmonic of a signal is a multiple of the fundamental signal, it stands to reason that an overmodulated signal produces sidebands over a broader range of frequencies than a 100%-modulated rf carrier.

5-104. *Draw a simplified circuit diagram of the final stages (modulator, modulated amplifier, etc.) of a type of low-level plate-modulated transmitter using a pentode tube in the modulated stage. Explain the principles of operation. Repeat, using a tetrode to provide high-level plate modulation.*

The FCC defines high-level modulation as modulation produced in the plate circuit of the last radio stage of the system and low-level modulation **as modulation produced in an earlier stage than the final.** A low-level plate-modulation system is one where some stage before the final is plate-modulated; thus, since the signal fed to the final amplifier is to be fully modulated, the final amplifier must have linear amplification capability. The diagram is thus divided into three

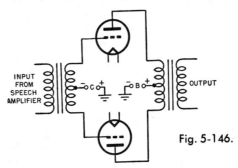

Fig. 5-146.

discrete parts: the modulator (Fig. 5-146), the modulated stage (Fig. 5-147), and the final rf amplifier (Fig. 5-148).

Most high-level modulators are operated class B, because this is the most efficient method of amplification that preserves the waveform of the input signal. Figure 5-146 shows a typical class B push-pull amplifier that is used in modulator service. In a class B amplifier the grids of the two tubes are biased at or near cutoff, and plate current flows only when a signal is actually present. Therefore, with a speech waveform that is highly irregular, a wide variation of current is drawn by the stage. Power supplied for class B stages must have excellent regulation to avoid distortion that might otherwise result.)

The modulation transformer (secondary is labeled *output*) of Fig. 5-146 is reproduced as T1 in Fig. 5-147, the diagram of the modulated pentode stage.

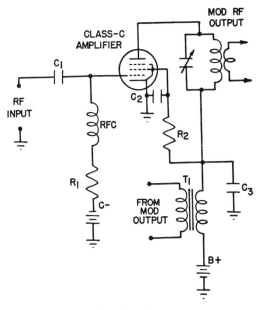

Fig. 5-147.

When triode tubes are used in the plate-modulated stage of a transmitter, carefully adjusted neutralization circuits must be employed. These circuits (and the critical adjustments they demand) can be avoided by using tubes that have screen grids.

The plate current of a screen grid tube is almost independent of plate voltage; however, plate current is very dependent on screen grid voltage. Thus, the modulating voltage may be applied to the screen and plate circuits simultaneously, as shown in the circuit of Fig. 5-147. Notice that the audio modulating voltage across the secondary of the modulation transformer (T1) is in series with the dc supply voltage to both the plate and screen circuits.

To prevent screen degeneration at the carrier frequency, capacitor C2 is connected between the screen grid and cathode; the value of this capacitor is chosen so that its reactance approaches a short circuit at radio frequencies but an open circuit at audio modulation frequencies. Capacitor C3 serves a purpose similar to that of C2. This capacitor must prevent rf from developing across the secondary of T1, while having little effect on the audio voltages present across the secondary of *T1*.

The two arrow-tipped lines (modulated rf output) of Fig. 5-147 are applied to the input of the final stage. This final inductor is reproduced in Fig. 5-148 as *L1*, the input tank circuit.

The input tank circuit, consisting of *L1* and *C1*, provides drive for the final amplifier. Since a fully modulated signal is supplied to the final, this rf amplifier cannot be operated class C. Class C operation would severely distort the audio present on the carrier. Thus, the final must be operated class B or some combination between B and A (such as AB).

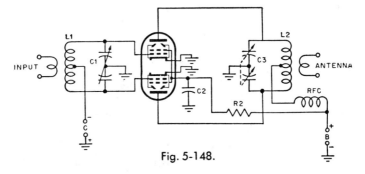

Fig. 5-148.

In the final linear amplifier, grid bias is furnished from a fixed supply. In the tube itself the screens of both sections are connected, and one capacitor (*C2*) serves as a bypass for both. Resistor *R2* provides screen voltage by dropping the plate voltage because of the current that passes through it. The output tank circuit is self-explanatory. The rf choke permits the feeding of plate voltage to both halves of the tube.

5-105. *How does a linear power amplifier differ from other types?*

A linear amplifier is one in which the stage is biased at some point along the linear part of the transfer characteristic. A class A amplifier, used for audio amplification, is biased at the precise center of the linear part of the transfer characteristic. A class B amplifier is biased at the lower limit of this curve. Amplifiers intended for amplification of modulated rf signals are typically biased at some point between class A (midpoint) and class B (cutoff). The class for linear amplification of rf signals has been designated class AB.

In a class A amplifier the plate current flows during the entire cycle of input grid signal; in a class B amplifier the plate current flows during the positive half-cycle of input grid signal. Therefore, in a class AB amplifier, plate current flows for more than one-half but lss than the entire cycle of input grid signal. Class AB operation may be subdivided into classes AB_1 and AB_2. The subscript numeral *1* indicates that the grid current *does not* flow during any part of the input grid signal's cyclic swing. The subscript 2 indicates that grid current *does* flow during some portion of the input cycle.

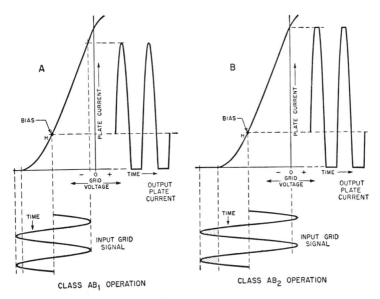

Fig. 5-149.

Class AB₁ operation is shown in Fig. 5-149A. The operating point is located between plate current cutoff and the linear portion of the dynamic characteristic. The positive peak of the grid signal extends into the linear region of the dynamic transfer curve. To prevent the flow of grid current, the positive peak of the grid signal cannot exceed the fixed bias. The negative peak of the grid signal extends beyond plate current cutoff. The shaded areas of the input grid signal indicate those portions of the input signal that are cut off. The output plate current waveform is distorted by the clipping action of the negative peaks. Class A₂ operation is illustrated in Fig. 5-149B, with the same operating point (H) shown in A. In this class of operation the peak value of grid signal exceeds the fixed bias of the tube. The positive peaks of the input grid signal extend into the positive region of grid voltage. This caused grid current to flow. Just as in class AB₁ operation, the negative grid signal peaks go beyond the plate current cutoff point.

Clipping is much greater in class AB₂ operation than in class AB₁. However, because of the greater grid voltage swing in class AB₂, a greater output exists. The plate efficiency in class AB₁ operation is somewhat greater than in class AB₂. Compared with class A, class AB operation produces more distortion, more power output, and a greater plate efficiency.

5-106.   *Draw a simple schematic showing a method of coupling a modulated tube to a radio-frequency power amplifier tube to produce grid modulation of the amplified rf energy. Compare some advantages or disadvantages of this system of modulation with those of plate modulation.*

In the grid-modulated amplifier of Fig. 5-150, the voltage for modulation is introduced by a small transformer in series with the lead to the grid bias supply. The modulator is the push-pull stage.

A disadvantage of plate modulation is the large amount of power required for the modulator stage—a full 50% of the power supplied to the final rf amplifier. Grid modulation is less efficient, produces more distortion, is more difficult to maintain at a modulation level of 100%, and requires the final amplifier to supply all of the power in the output signal. Grid modulation has a major advantage, though, in one area—cost. **Grid modulation does not require much power from the modulator,** which serves to greatly reduce the expenses of transformers (both modulation and power supply).

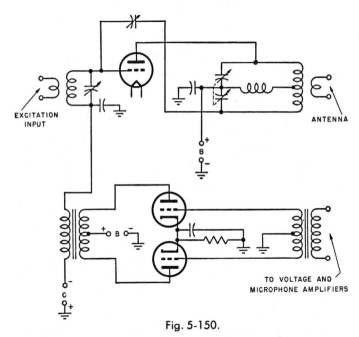

Fig. 5-150.

5-107. *What is the relationship between the amount of power in the sidebands and the intelligibility of the signal at the receiver?*

The greater the amount of power in the sidebands, the more intelligible the signal at the receiver. Unfortunately, it is impossible at 100% modulation to get more power into the sidebands than an amount equal to 50% of the unmodulated carrier. Sideband power decreases as modulation percentage decreases. Total rf power decreases and the signal distorts when modulation percentage is increased beyond the 100% point.

5-108.   Draw a block diagram of an AM transmitter.

An AM transmitter can be divided into two major sections, according to the frequencies at which the sections operate. One section is called the *rf unit* and is the section of the transmitter used to generate the rf carrier wave. As illustrated in the block diagram of Fig. 5-151, the carrier originates in the oscillator stage, where it is generated as a constant-amplitude, constant-frequency sine wave. The carrier must then pass through one or more stages of amplification before it attains the high power required to propagate the signal properly. With the exception of the last stage, the amplifiers between the oscillator and antenna are called *intermediate power amplifiers*. The last stage, which connects to the antenna, is called the *final power amplifier*, or just the *final*.

The second section of the transmitter contains the audio circuitry. This section takes the minute signal from the microphone and increases its amplitude an amount necessary to fully modulate the carrier. The last audio stage applies its signal to the carrier and is called the *modulator*.

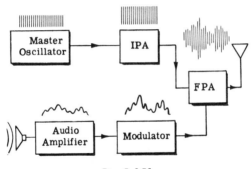

Fig. 5-151.

5-109.   Explain   the   principles   involved   in   a   single-sideband, suppressed-carrier (SSSC) emission. How does its bandwidth of emission and required power compare with that of full carrier and sidebands (conventional AM signal)?

A conventional AM emission consists of a radio-frequency carrier and a pair of sidebands—one above and the other below the carrier. The intelligence is represented by the frequency difference between the carrier and either of the two sidebands. Since the intelligence in one sideband is a duplicate of the intelligence in the other, only one sideband is actually required for communication; the other may be eliminated by selective filtering. Eliminating one sideband reduces the spectrum of the emission and makes more efficient use of the transmitter's available power.

Single-sideband transmitters are rated in terms of *peak envelope power (p.e.p.)*, which is the average power of the transmitter divided by the fraction of each second that an output is actually produced. For comparable operation the carrier power of an AM station must be

455

twice the p.e.p. of a single-sideband station. However, this figure may be misleading in that the single-sideband (SSB) transmitter's operation is based on a duty cycle of 0. (*Duty cycle* is the fraction of each second that a device is actually producing an output.)

The SSB signal is essentially an AM signal whose carrier and one sideband have been removed. To receive the signal successfully, a reference signal must be generated that is close enough to the sideband signal to allow detection by the process of heterodyning. That is, a local oscillator in the receiver generates a signal on the same frequency as the SSB transmitter's removed carrier. The sideband signal will then deviate from this reference by a frequency proportional to the audio modulation.

5-110. *Draw a block diagram of an SSSC transmitter. Explain the function of each stage.*

A functional block diagram of a basic SSB transmitter is shown in Fig. 5-152. The audio amplifier is of conventional design. Audio filtering is not required, because the highly selective filtering that takes place in the SSB generator attenuates the unnecessary frequencies below 300 Hz and above 3 kHz; i.e., those frequencies falling outside the audio communication spectrum. (A voice signal is used only as a convenience for explanation; the input signal may be any desired intelligence signal and may cover all or any part of the frequency range between 100 and 6000 Hz.) The upper limit of the input audio signal is determined by the channel bandwidth and upper cutoff frequency of the filter in the sideband generator. The lower limit of the input audio signal is determined by the lower cutoff frequency of the filter in the SSB generator.

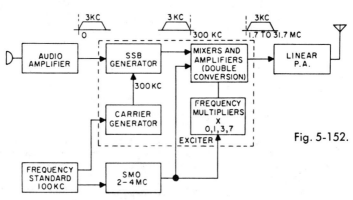

Fig. 5-152.

The SSB generator produces the SSB signal at an intermediate frequency (i-f). To produce the SSB signal, a double-sideband (DSB) signal is generated and passed through a highly selective filter to reject one of the sidebands. The SSB signal is generated at a fixed intermediate frequency because highly selective circuits are required. The filter requirements for the filter method of SSB signal generation are met by either crystal or mechanical filters.

The generated SSB signal at a fixed i-f is passed through mixers and amplifiers, where it is converted to the transmitted radio frequency. Two-stage conversion is shown, with the second conversion frequency being a multiple of the first conversion frequency. The frequency conversions required to generate the radio frequency produce sum and difference frequencies as well as higher order mixing products inherent in mixing circuits. However, the undesired difference frequency or the undesired sum frequency, along with the higher-order mixing products, is attenuated by interstage tuned circuits.

Because an SSB system without a pilot carrier demands an extremely stable frequency system, the frequency standard and stabilized master oscillator (SMO) are extremely important. The standard frequency is obtained from a crystal oscillator, with the crystal housed in an oven. Since the stability of the crystal frequency depends directly on the stability of the oven temperature, stable thermal control of the oven is necessary. This thermal control of the oven is obtained by using heat-sensitive semiconductors in a bridge network. Any vaiation in the oven temperature is corrected by an imbalance in the control bridge. The carrier generator provides the i-f carrier used to produce the fixed i-f SSB signal, and the SMO provides the necessary conversion frequencies to produce the rf SSB signal. The frequencies developed in these units are derived from (or phase-locked to) the single standard frequency, so that the stability of the standard frequency prevails throughout the SSB system. Choice of the fixed i-f and conversion frequencies to obtain the rf is an important design consideration. Optimum operating frequencies of the various circuits must be considered as well as the control of undesirable mixing products. The use of harmonically related conversion frequencies in the mixer permits a very broad frequency range to be covered with a single 2—4 MHz oscillator—a very practical range for obtaining high oscillator stability. Use of the 300 kHz fixed i-f is the optimum operating condition for the filter required in the SSB generator.

The SSB exciter output drives a linear power amplifier to produce the high-power rf signal. A linear power amplifier is required for SSB transmission because it is essential that the plate output rf signal be a replica of the grid input signal. Any nonlinear operation (distortion) of the power amplifier will result in an intermodulation (mixing) between the frequencies of the input signal. This will produce not only undesirable distortion within the desired channel but will also produce intermodulation outputs in adjacent channels.

To add additional channels to the SSB system requires only additional circuits in the SSB generator. One method is to use the upper sideband of one signal and the lower sideband of the other signal. Figure 5-153 shows the circuit for producing these two channels and the location of each channel with respect to the carrier frequency. With this method a twin sideband is transmitted and the signal in the lower sideband is inverted.

5-111. *Explain briefly how an SSSC emission is detected.*

To see the relationship of the parts in a single-sideband receiver, observe the block diagram in Fig. 5-154. Basically, the receiver is

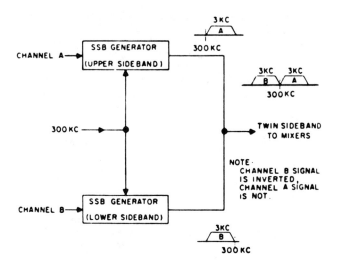

Fig. 5-153.

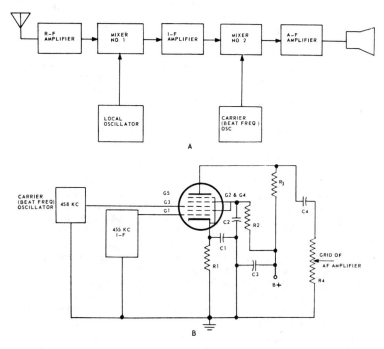

Fig. 5-154.

similar to an ordinary AM superheterodyne; that is, it has rf and i-f amplifiers, a mixer, a detector, and audio amplifiers. However, to permit satisfactory SSB reception, an additional mixer (demodulator) and oscillator must replace the conventional diode audio detector.

As shown before, the carrier frequency was suppressed at the transmitter; thus, for a sideband to be received properly, a carrier must be inserted by the receiver. The receiver illustrated in Fig. 5-154 inserts a carrier frequency immediately preceding the detector, although the carrier frequency may be inserted at any point in the receiver before the detector.

When the SSSC signal is received at the antenna, it is immediately amplified by the rf amplifier and applied to the first mixer. By mixing the output of the local oscillator with the input signal (heterodyning), a difference frequency (i-f) is obtained. The i-f is then amplified by one or more stages. Of course, this is dependent upon the type of receiver. Up to this point an AM superheterodyne receiver is exactly the same. Ordinarily the signal would now be applied to the detector for demodulation of the intelligence.

Since the sideband frequency is the only frequency present, the carrier must now be inserted. This is accomplished by the second mixer (demodulator) and carrier generator. This latter stage is a variable-frequency oscillator that can be adjusted to simulate the carrier frequency that was suppressed at the transmitter. Now the original intelligence can be recovered by the second mixer. In the case of the audio intelligence, the output of the second mixer is applied to a stage of audio amplification and then to the speaker.

The second mixer is identical to the first mixer except for the frequencies at the input and output. Consider an SSB signal of 2 MHz to be transmitted. This signal is generated by combining a carrier of 1997 kHz with an audio frequency of 3 kHz in a balanced modulator and selecting the upper sideband, or 1997 kHZ $+3$ kHz $=2000$ kHz $=2$ MHz. When the receiver is tuned to this frequency, the 2 MHz signal is converted to a 455 kHz signal, amplified, and applied to the second mixer. When the carrier oscillator is adjusted to 458 kHz, a 3 kHz signal ($458-455$ kHz) is produced in the output of the mixer.

Tuning the sideband receiver is somewhat more difficult than tuning a regular AM receiver. The carrier (beat frequency) oscillator must be precisely adjusted to simulate the carrier frequency at all times. Any tendency to drift will cause the output intelligence to be distorted.

5-112. *Draw a block diagram of a single-conversion AM superheterodyne receiver. Assume an incident signal and explain briefly what occurs in each stage.*

The block diagram of a typical superheterodyne receiver appears in Fig. 5-155. Immediately below the corresponding sections of the receiver are shown the waveforms of the signal being processed at each point. The rf signal from the antenna passes first through the rf amplifier, where the amplitude, or level, of the signal is increased. A locally generated unmodulated rf signal of constant amplitude is then mixed with the carrier frequency in the mixer stage. The heterodyning (mixing) of these two frequencies produces an

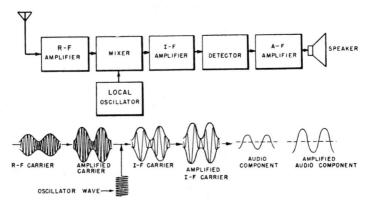

Fig. 5-155.

intermediate-frequency signal that contains all of the modulation characteristics of the original signal. The intermediate frequency is equal to the difference in frequency between the station being tuned and the local oscillator. The intermediate frequency is then amplified in one or more stages (i-f amplifiers) and fed to a conventional detector for recovery of the audio. The detected signal is amplified in the audio-frequency section and then fed to a loudspeaker.

5-113.   *Draw a circuit diagram of an AM second detector and af amplifier (in one envelope), showing avc circuitry. Also show coupling to (and identification of) all adjacent stages. Then explain the principles of operation and state some conditions under which readings of avc voltage would be helpful in troubleshooting a rceiver. Show how this circuit would be modified to give davc (delayed avc).*

Figure 5-156 shows an avc circuit used with a duo-diode—triode in a conventional diode detector circuit. The two diode plates are connected together to form a half-wave rectifier in the rf portion of the circuit. The output of the diode detector is fed to the grid of the triode section, which acts as a class A voltage amplifier.

Low-voltage bias is obtained by using the contact potential developed across R3, which results from the dissimilar elements in the grid and cathode. A disadvantage of ordinary automatic volume control is that even the weakest signals produce some avc bias, which could result in no usable receiver output or a reduction in overall receiver sensitivity. This reduction occurs because a slight increase in the avc signal will cause a decrease in rf amplifier gain, thereby attenuating very weak rf signals. As shown, the avc circuit is fed from the last i-f stage and drives the second af amplifier. Troubles in the rf amplification stages can be traced by checking the avc voltage on incoming signals; the stronger the signal, the higher the avc voltage should be. Also, when a signal that should be strong is received poorly, a quick check of the avc voltage will give an immediate indication as to whether or not the avc circuit is excessively attenuating incoming signals. When the avc circuit itself is not functioning properly, there

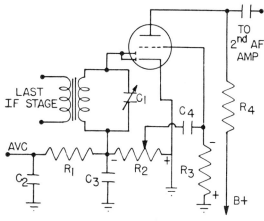

Fig. 5-156.

will be little or no avc voltage variation, regardless of the strength of the incoming signal.

The main disadvantage of automatic volume control (the unwanted attenuation of weak signals) may be overcome by use of delayed avc (davc), as shown in Fig. 5-157. Note that the circuit is quite similar to the ordinary avc circuit pictured in Fig. 156; however, the plates of the duo-diode have been separated and an electrolytic

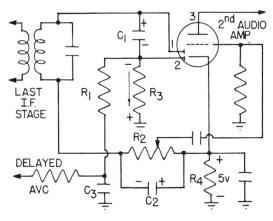

Fig. 5-157.

capacitor has been placed across the volume control potentiometer (R2). In this example a bias of 5V on the davc diode's plate 2 prevents it from conducting until the signal exceeds 5V. The signal across the secondary of the i-f transformer is coupled to plate 2 of the second diode by capacitor C1. Until the signal exceeds 5V, no charge is

461

acquired by the avc capacitor (C3); no additional bias is applied to the grids of the i-f amplifier, preselector, or converter tubes; and their gain is maximum on weak signals. The 5V bias applied to the davc diode's plate 2 is developed across cathode resistor R4 by the current flowing through the triode section of the tube. The triode section serves as a class A voltage amplifier driven by the audio voltage developed across diode load resistor R2.

When the signal across the secondary of the i-f transformer exceeds the 5V bias value across R4, the avc diode (plate 2) conducts on alternate half-cycles and C3 acquires a charge. The voltage developed across C3 constitutes the davc voltage. It is supplied to the grids of the various stages ahead of the second detector, in series with the cathode bias developed by the individual tubes.

5-114. *Draw a bfo circuit diagram and explain its use in detection.*

The beat-frequency oscillator (bfo) is necessary when continuous-wave (cw) signals are to be received, because these signals are not modulated with an audio component. In superheterodyne receivers, the incoming cw signal is converted to the intermediate frequency at the first detector as a single-frequency signal with no sideband components. The i-f signal is heterodyned (with a separate tunable oscillator, the bfo) at the second detector to produce an af output. In the circuit shown in Fig. 5-158, the Hartley oscillator is coupled to the plate of the second detector by capacitor C3.

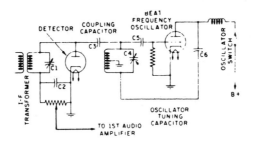

Fig. 5-158.

If the intermediate frequency is 455 kHz and the bfo is tuned to 456 or 454 kHz, the difference frequency of 1 kHz is heard in the output. Generally, the on—off switch for the bfo and the capacitor tuning control are located on the front panel of the receiver.

The bfo should be shielded to prevent its output from being radiated and combined with desired signals ahead of the second detector. If avc voltage is to be used, it should be obtained from a separate diode isolated from the second detector. One way is to couple the output of an i-f amplifier (ahead of the second detector) to the avc diode; otherwise, the output of the bfo would be rectified by the second detector and would develop an avc voltage even during conditions of no input signal.

5-115. Explain, step by step, how to align an AM receiver, using the following instruments; also, explain briefly what is occuring in each step:

1. *Signal generator and loudspeaker*
2. *Signal generator and oscilloscope*
3. *Signal generator and vacuum-tube voltmeter (or other high-impedance voltmeter)*

A brief review of the operation of a typical AM superheterodyne receiver (Fig. 5-159) is offered to clarify the requirements for alignment. Incoming signals strike the antenna and set up magnetic fields around the rf amplifier (TC1). The tuned circuit (TC1) selects the desired rf signal and prevents other signals from reaching the next stage. The selected signal then is amplified in the rf stage and proceeds to the mixer. The tuned circuit in the mixer stage provides

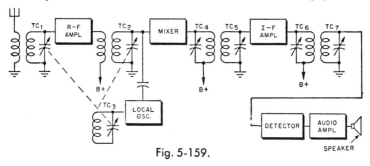

Fig. 5-159.

greater selectivity, allows the desired rf signal to pass, and keeps out any other signals that may have been passed by the rf stage. Tuned circuits TC1 and TC2 therefore are always tuned to the frequency of the incoming signal. The tuned circuit of the oscillator stage (TC3) is tuned to a definite frequency above or below the incoming frequency; and its output is fed to the mixer, where it mixes with the incoming signal to produce new frequencies. These include the desired intermediate (or difference) frequency. For example, if the incoming signal is 1000 kHz and the oscillator frequency is 1456 kHz, the two signals will mix and produce an i-f of 456 kHz. No matter what the frequency of the i-f circuits, the oscillator circuit is tuned so that it will produce the same i-f. Many other frequencies appear at the plate of the mixer stage, but only the i-f passes through to the next stage, because TC4 and TC5 in the plate circuit of the mixer and grid circuit of the i-f amplifier are tuned to the i-f. Tuned circuits TC6 and TC7, in the plate circuit of the i-f amplifier and input circuit to the detector, are also tuned to this frequency. At the detector the audio signal is separated from the i-f and passed through an audio amplifier to the speaker voice coil, which changes the electrical signals to sound.

The purpose of aligning an AM superheterodyne receiver is to tune the rf circuits to the desired rf range of the receiver, tune the local oscillator so that it tracks with the rf circuits through the band, and tune the i-f circuits to the fixed i-f. Tuned circuits *TC1 and TC2* always must be tuned to the same frequency, and *TC*3 must be tuned to a frequency different from these two circuits by the exact amount of the i-f. The i-f transformers—*TC*4, *TC*5, *TC*6, and *TC*7—are tuned to the desired frequency.

A dummy antenna (Fig. 5-160) may be used to match the impedance of the signal generator to the impedance of the receiver. It is placed between the "hot" lead of the signal generator and the receiver antenna terminal, and it should have the same electrical characteristics as the actual antenna for which it is being substituted. The dummy antenna to be used usually is specified in the appropriate receiver instruction manual.

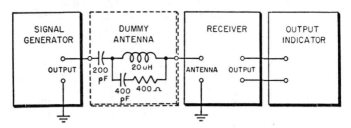

Fig. 5-160.

In alignment the output indicator is read for a maximum value of output. If a signal generator is available and no output indicator is on hand, the speaker itself may be monitored for maximum output; however, this does not allow the alignment precision that an indicating instrument would, because of the ear's relative insensitivity to small changes in level.

An indicating instrument may be connected at places other than across the output. One method is to connect the indicator to the plate of the power output tube. At this point the audio signal has maximum voltage amplitude; and, when circuits are badly misaligned, the output indicator here will provide the most sensitive indication.

Instruments used as output indicators during alignment show relative values of amplitude. The most popular instruments for this purpose are ac VOMs, EVMs (electronic voltmeters), and oscilloscopes. An *output meter* is one of several types of ac voltmeter connected in series with a capacitor to block incoming dc voltage. Such a meter (standard equipment on many of the better VOMs available today) is used when an indication is to be taken at a point where both ac and dc are present, such as the plate of the power output stage. Although ac meters respond to either ac or dc, only the ac signal coming through the receiver is important for alignment purposes. Therefore, when a meter is used at the power amplifier plate, it should be an output meter rather than a conventional ac voltmeter. At the receiver output, where only ac is present, either an ac voltmeter or an output meter can be used.

An oscilloscope gives a visual indication on the face of a cathode-ray tube of any ac voltage waveform applied to the vertical input. Because there is an internal coupling capacitor, the scope leads can be placed at a point where there is only ac or where there may be both ac and dc. The scope can be used as an output meter, an ac voltmeter, or a distortion meter. When it is used as an output indicator, the horizontal gain control can be set to zero. The output of the receiver then will show up as a vertical line increasing in amplitude as the output increases. The trace is observed for maximum height without attempting an exact measurement. The scope also can measure the exact amplitude of the ac signal by first feeding a known voltage to the input and observing its exact height. The signal to be measured then is fed to the input and its amplitude is compared with that of the known voltage. The vertical-amplitude control of the scope is not to be varied when the unknown signal is fed to the input. The scope can measure peak voltages, not only of sine waves, but of irregular waveforms that are almost impossible to measure accurately with any other instrument.

AM receivers can be aligned visually by using a signal generator and oscilloscope. Visual alignment, however, is somewhat more difficult; and it is not necessarily more accurate than the basic alignment described above, which uses an output indicator.

5-116. *What would be the advantages and disadvantages of using a bandpass switch on a receiver?*

A bandpass switch allows the selectivity of the receiver to be varied according to the requirements of the user. A very narrow bandpass increases the selectivity of the receiver considerably, thereby minimizing problems from adjacent-channel interference. But the narrower the bandpass, the more distortion in the received audio signal. In an AM receiver the bandwidth is a function of frequency response. When the bandwidth of the signal is reduced, the higher frequency components of the received signal are removed. This contributes to the overall distortion of the signal and, in many cases, results in very low intelligibilty. When no adjacent signals are present, the bandpass of the receiver can be broadened with a selectable-bandpass switch, thereby increasing the overall intelligibility and quality of the signal.

5-117. *Explain "sensitivity" and "selectivity" of a receiver. Why are these important quantities? In what typical units are they usually expressed?*

Sensitivity. The sensitivity of a receiver is its signal-responding capability. The more sensitive a receiver is, the better that receiver will "hear" very weak signals. Since sensitivity is compromised when noise is received along with the signals, a receiver's sensitivity is usually accompanied by a figure that expresses the receiver's noise immunity. Sensitivity is normally expressed in microvolts, while noise immunity is expressed in decibels. A good communications-type AM receiver might have a sensitivity of 0.5 μV with a ratio of *signal-plus-noise to noise* of 10 dB.

Selectivity. A receiver's selectivity figure is an expression that describes its vulnerability to interference from signals other than those on the desired frequency. A nonselective receiver, such as one of the regenerative types, may have an extremely good sensitivity value, but this is of little help if the receiver is not capable of rejecting signals appearing on frequencies adjacent to the frequency of interest. By the same token, a receiver that is relatively insensitive could prove far more usable than a sensitive receiver if it has a markedly superior selectivity figure, particularly when used in an area where incoming signals are especially strong and closely spaced in frequency. Selectivity is often expressed in hertz or kilohertz; the numerical value itself usually refers to the bandpass of the receiver, from a signal's lower half-power point to its upper half-power point.

FREQUENCY MODULATION

5-118. *Discuss the following in reference to frequency modulation:*

- *The production of sidebands*
- *The relationship between the number of sidebands and the modulating frequency*
- *The relationship between the number of sidebands and the amplitude of the modulating voltage*
- *The relationship between percentage of modulation and the number of sidebands*
- *The relationship between the spacing of the sidebands and the modulating frequency*
- *The relationship between the number of sidebands and the bandwidth of emission*
- *The criteria for determining bandwidth of emission*
- *Reasons for preemphasis*

Production of Sidebands In an FM wave the amplitude of the modulating signal determines the departure of the instantaneous frequency from the center, or carrier, frequency. The instantaneous frequency can be made to deviate as much as desired from the carrier frequency by changing the amplitude of the modulating signal. It is possible to obtain a frequency deviation many times the frequency of the modulating signal itself. In practical equipment this deviation frequency may be as high as several hundred kilohertz, even though the modulation frequency is but a few kilohertz. Therefore, the sidebands generated by FM are not restricted to the sum and difference between the highest modulating frequency and the carrier, as in AM. Whereas in AM only two sidebands, spaced equally on both sides of the carrier frequency, are generated, in FM many sidebands are generated, depending both in number and amplitude on the modulation index.

Number of Sidebands vs Modulating Frequency. The first pair of sidebands in an FM signal are those of the carrier frequency plus and minus the modulating frequency; a pair of sidebands will appear also at each multiple of the modulating frequency. As a result, an FM signal occupies a greater bandwidth than an AM signal. For example, if a carrier of 1 MHz is frequency-modulated by an audio signal of 10 kHz, several sidebands will be spaced equally on either side of the carrier frequency—at 990 and 1010kHz, 980 and 1020kHz, 970 and 1030 kHz, and so on. The total number present of significant amplitude (more than 1% of the amplitude of the unmodulated carrier) depends on the modulation index. With a high modulation index, more sidebands are of appreciable amplitude, and the bandwidth is correspondingly greater.

Number of Sidebands vs Modulation Amplitude. The FM wave consists of a center frequency and a number of sideband pairs, which, for a given audio frequency and amplitude, are constant. However, the resultant wave varies in frequency but is constant in amplitude. This resultant wave is the algebraic sum of the components that form it, and the center frequency will vary in amplitude with the modulation. When the transmitted signal is unmodulated, there is a certain constant amount of power in the carrier signal. When modulation is applied, power is taken from the carrier and forced into the sidebands; therefore, the carrier amplitude (center-frequency component) is reduced. The maximum power (Fig. 5-161) is carried in the fourth sideband, which is 4×15, or 60 kHz, away from the carrier frequency.

The carrier frequency changes in amplitude with modulation, whereas in AM the power for the sidebands is supplied by the modulator and is not drawn away from the carrier. Since no information is in the carrier, reducing its amplitude increases the efficiency of operation in terms of power consumed. For some value of modulation index and modulating frequency, carrier amplitude falls to zero and all the power is contained in the sidebands.

Number of Sidebands vs Percentage of Modulation. Percentage of modulation in FM is defined as the percentage of mximum deviation incorporated in a transmitter for a particular type of service. For an FM transmitter with a maximum deviation of 75 kHz, 100% modulation occurs when the transmitter deviates the full 75 kHz. When the deviation level falls to 37.5 kHz, the transmitter is being

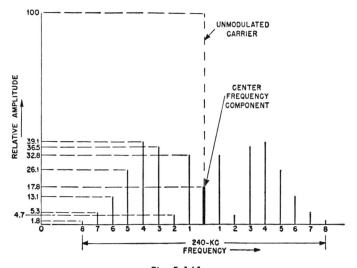

Fig. 5-161.

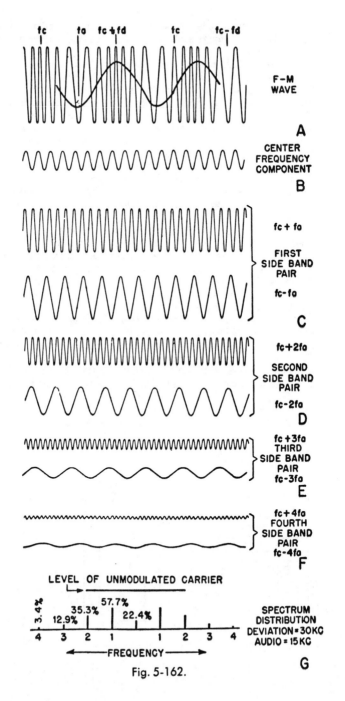

Fig. 5-162.

modulated only 50%.

The relationship between the amplitudes of the sidebands and an audio modulating frequency for a modulation index of 2 is shown in Fig. 5-162. The deviation is 30 kHz, with a modulating frequency of 15 kHz. The modulated carrier wave, which is the resultant of the algebraic sum of the carrier and the sidebands, is shown in A with the modulating frequency superimposed upon it. At the positive peaks of the modulation cycle, the instantaneous frequency of the wave is $f_c + f_d$, the frequency peak deviation; whereas, at the negative peaks, the frequency is $f_c - f_d$. The peak-to-peak deviation is therefore $2 f_d$. If the carrier frequency is 100 MHz with a frequency deviation of 30 kHz, then the lower deviation limit is 99.97 MHz; and the upper one is 100.03 MHz. There are four sideband pairs whose amplitudes exceed the 1% level, and some of these are greater in amplitude than the center frequency. These are spaced on either side of the carrier frequency, at intervals of 15 kHz, as in Fig. 5-162C), D, E, and F; and each sideband pair has an amplitude as shown in G. The center frequency is reduced in amplitude to 22.4% of the unmodulated value. The first sideband pair, at 99.985 MHz and 100.015 MHz, has an amplitude of 57.7% of the unmodulated carrier value; the second sideband pair, at 99.7 and 100.03 MHz, is 35.3% of the unmodulated carrier; and so on.

Spacing of Sidebands and Modulating Frequency. In Fig. 5-161, with a frequency deviation of 75 kHz and a modulating frequency of 15 kHz, the center frequency is reduced to less than 20% of its unmodulated amplitude. If the modulating frequency is reduced to 5 kHz with the same frequency deviation of 75 kHz (Fig. 5-163), the center frequency is reduced to only 1.4% of its unmodulated value. The sidebands are spaced every 5 kHz on either side of the center frequency, out to the 19th pair of sidebands; and all subsequent sidebands are less than 1% of the unmodulated carrier amplitude.

For the 15 kHz modulating frequency of Fig. 5-161, with a modulation index of 5, the total bandwidth is 240 kHz. In Fig. 5-163, with a modulating frequency of 5 kHz and a modulation index of 25, the total bandwidth occupied is 190 kHz. The bandwidth is greater than the deviation limits of ± 75 kHz, which is equal to a peak-to-peak deviation of 150 kHz. However, the sidebands above or below the limit are relatively small in amplitude and can be disregarded. In both figures the unmodulated carrier is shown in broken lines for comparison with the amplitudes of the FM sidebands.

Number of Sidebands vs Bandwidth. It should be obvious by now that there are definite relations between the amplitude of the modulating signal, its frequency, the frequency deviation it produces, and the total bandwidth occupied by the resultant FM wave. If the frequency deviation is kept constant, the number of sidebands increases as the modulating frequency decreases, and the total bandwidth of emission decreases as the modulating frequency decreases. The total bandwidth, however, can never be less than the bandwidth set by the peak-to-peak deviation alone, no matter how low the frequency of the modulating signal becomes. If the amplitude of the modulating signal increases and its frequency remains constant,

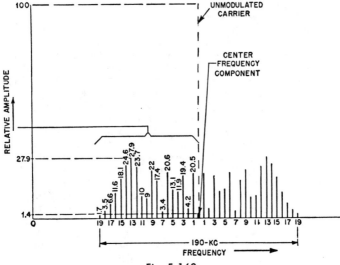

Fig. 5-163.

the deviation increases and the modulation index increases. This means that more energy goes into the outer sidebands and correspondingly more of them increase to significant amplitude. The result is an increase in the number of useful sidebands as well as an increase in bandwidth of emission.

Determining Bandwidth of Emission. The maximum bandwidth of an *AM* transmission is twice that of the maximum frequency present in the modulating wave. Since the bandwidth in an FM transmitter can exceed this by many times, the ratio of the bandwidth occupied to the absolute carrier frequency can be considerably larger than that of AM transmitters. When a very wide bandwidth is used (as in wideband FM), it is necessary to choose a carrier frequency sufficiently high that the bandwidth is a small percentage of the carrier frequency, to permit a reasonable number of assigned channels. The FM transmitter, however, can be adjusted so that the maximum bandwidth does not exceed that of an equivalent AM transmission—that is, for the production of only one pair of sidebands of significant amplitude. When the FM transmitter is adjusted for a deviation that produces a bandwidth equal to that produced by an equivalently modulated AM transmitter, it is called *narrowband* FM. With this narrow bandwidth, the transmitter can be operated at much lower frequencies (generally below 40 MHz).

Reasons for Preemphasis. In the transmitters used to convey speech, the deviation is the same for a given amplitude regardless of the frequency of the modulating signal. However, as signals pass through the transmitter, the receiver, and the space between them, certain amounts of unwanted noise and distortion are superimposed on the desired intelligence. This noise is distributed uniformly throughout the audible spectrum. Therefore, the ratio of the signal to the unwanted noise decreases in the higher frequencies, because the speech amplitudes in this range do not have the intensity that the lower frequencies have. Further, the distortion increases in the high-frequency portion of the spectrum. The high frequencies make the greatest contribution to intelligibility of speech waves, since the consonants, which form the majority of speech sounds, have their peak energy in this part of the audio bnd.

To avoid degrading the reproduction of consonants through poor signal-to-noise ratio in the upper end of the spectrum, a certain amount of added amplification (preemphasis) is provided for these frequencies in most transmitting equipment. The result of this process should not sound unnatural when received, and the reverse procedure (deemphasis) therefore is used at the receiver. This combination of preemphasis and deemphasis provides a more uniform signal-to-noise ratio throughout the audio range. A transmitter using preemphasis has a wider spectrum for speech than one without it. In general, the bandwidth of a speech signal deviating a transmitter 100% with preemphasis is about one-third greater than the deviation limits. If the deviation is 75 kHz, for example, the total bandwidth at 100% modulation is about 200 kHz (150+50).

5-119. *How is good stability of a reactance tube modulator achieved?*

The reactance tube modulator uses the characteristics of a vacuum tube (in an oscillator circuit) to control the reactance present in the tank of the oscillator. The stability of the oscillator essentially depends on the overall circuit. In other words, the greater the reactance change as a result of injected audio, the lower the stability. When the reactance tube modulator is operated at some submultiple of the intended transmitter output frequency, stability is enhanced, because the total variation of the tube's reactance is proportionately smaller than if the tube were actually operated at the transmitter output frequency.

5-120. *Explain, in a general way, why an FM deviation meter (modulation meter) would show an indication if coupled to the output of a transmitter that is phase-modulated by a constant-amplitude audio frequency. To what would this deviation be proportional?*

In FM or PM, deviation is proportional to audio amplitude (applied at the transmitter). When the amplitude of the input signal is held constant, the frequency deviation of the signal is constant, regardless of whether the transmitter is phase- or frequency-modulated. Thus, the deviation is proportional to the amplitude of the applied audio-frequency modulation.

5-121. *Draw a circuit diagram of each of the following stages of a phase-modulated FM transmitter (explain their operation and label the adjacent stages):*

- *Frequency multiplier (doubler) with capacitive coupling on input and output.*
- *Power amplifier with variable-impedance coupling to antenna, including circuit for metering grid and plate currents*
- *Speech amplifier with associated preemphasis circuit*

471

A complete transmitter using phase modulation is shown in Fig. 5-164. Each circuit element is shown in a broken-line box. The explanation of each functional element's operation is described elsewhere in this book (see index). A brief description of the functional elements is given below.

The *crystal oscillator* is used to generate the basic rf signal. This signal is processed through a phase modulator, which alters the phase of the applied oscillator signal in accordance with the intelligence arriving via the audio circuits.

The audio is processed first through a *preemphasis network*, which selectively attenuates certain frequencies. The speech amplifier provides the necessary audio amplification and impedance matching. An *audio correction* network is provided between the speech amplifier and phase modulator to shift the phase of the audio signal by 90°. This is required because the equivalent frequency deviation in PM is proportional to the audio modulating frequency. This effect is undesirable in indirect FM production, since the frequency deviation must be proportional to the amplitude of the audio signal. A simple *RC* network accomplishes this objective.

A *buffer* provides isolation between the multipliers and oscillator, thus lending additional frequency stability and rendering the oscillator independent from frequency shifting as a result of multiplier loading variations etc. The driver stage increases the processed signal to the level required by the final amplifier. The *final* or *power amplifier* delivers the resultant signal to the antenna through a simple pi-network antenna-matching system. The pi network does not discriminate against signals below operating frequencies. This makes it undesirable to use if the amplifier is driven directly by a frequency multiplier.

5-122. *What might be the effect on the transmitted frequency if a tripler stage in an otherwise properly aligned transmitter were slightly detuned?*

The transmitted frequency can be randomly phase-shifted as a result of a detuned tripler stage. This phase variation also is accompanied by frequency variation, the result of which is center-frequency instability and marked distortion of the received signal.

5-123. *Could the harmonic of an FM transmission contain intelligible modulation?*

In FM transmitters, frequency multiplication of the FM signal performs two functions: It increases the frequency of the signal to the value desired for transmission, in this way acting the same as a frequency multiplier in an AM transmitter; it also increases the *effective frequency deviation* of the FM signal. Thus, a harmonic of an FM signal does carry the modulation intelligence; however, the deviation of the harmonic will not be the same bandwidth as the deviation of the carrier frequency.

5-124. *Under what usual conditions of maintenance and repair should a transmitter be retuned?*

Transmitter tuning is a simple procedure and should be performed at any time there is change in the transmitter's components, when

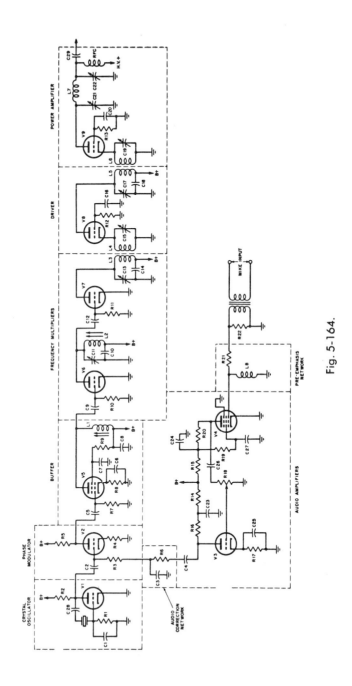

Fig. 5-164.

operating voltages have been altered, when the transmitter is connected to a different antenna, or when any tubes or transistors are substituted.

5-125. *If an indirect FM transmitter* **without modulation** *were within the carrier-frequency tolerance but* **with modulation** *were out of tolrance, what might be the possible cause?*

The cause might be any of the following or any combination of them:

1. Excessive deviation through improper adjustment, malfunctioning limiter, etc.
2. Multiplier stage out of tune.
3. Carrier shift from improperly balanced modulator. A symmetrically balanced modulator produces sidebands equal to the sum and difference of the audio signal and carrier frequencies, whereas the carrier is effectively canceled. An imbalance results in a carrier shift by the amount of asymmetry introduced by the balanced modulator.

5-126. *In an FM transmitter, what would be the effect on antenna current if the grid bias of the final power amplifier were varied?*

For optimum transfer of power to an antenna, it is highly desirable to have as efficient a transfer of power from the driver stage to the power amplifier as possible. Therefore, the grid tank circuit must provide an impedance match between the grid input impedance of the amplifier and the plate output impedance of the driver.

The impedance of a circuit normally is defined as the ratio of voltage to current in it; however, in the grid circuit of a class C amplifier, this ratio is far from constant. When the grid voltage goes highly negative, no current is drawn at all; when it is positive, a great deal of current flows. Therefore, the impedance of the grid circuit varies over a range from an extremely high to an extremely low value through the operating cycle. If the input impedance of the grid circuit is too high, the heavy current demanded by the extreme positive grid swing cannot be drawn. As a result, actual grid voltage and efficiency are reduced, and antenna current decreases proportionately. If the impedance of the grid tank circuit is too low, a great deal of power from the power stage is required to operate it, and the losses in the inductor consume a considerable amount of the applied power. Generally, a compromise value is used that is approximately equal to the ratio of the driving power in watts to the square of the grid current. The choice of values for the components in the grid tank circuit is determined by this impedance. The result usually is satisfactory regulation of the grid voltage, without excessive power loss.

5-127. *Explain briefly the principles involved in frequency shift keying (FSK). How is this signal detected?*

One of the most common of the nonspeech applications of FM is facsimile, involving the transmission of pictures, maps, and similar material, which are printed automatically at the receiver in response to signals from the transmitter. Radioteletype is another medium by which signals other than speech are transmitted. These media often use a system of FM known as *carrier modulation*, which consists of amplitude-modulating an rf carrier by an audio tone. The AM wave then is frequency-modulated and serves as a carrier for the applied signal.

In AM frequency shift keying, a keyer replaces the oscillator of a conventional CW transmitter. The keyer supplies a source of rf excitation that can be shifted slightly, either up or down (or both), to make a distinction between pulses and spaces.

During unmodulated (continuous wave) frequency shift operation, the transmitter operates with a specified carrier frequency. When a *mark* or a *pulse* is to be transmitted, the transmitter frequency is shifted slightly (usually downward). In the 3-level type of operation (which is not in common use at present), the frequency is shifted in one direction for a digital *1*, and in the opposite direction (by the same frequency deviation) to represent a digital *0*.

A beat frequency oscillator at the receiver allows generation of an audio tone whose frequency is proportional to the frequency shift of the transmitted carrier. Decoder circuits process the recovered audio signals to operate the teletypewriter.

5-128. *Assume that you have available the following instruments:*

> *VTVM*
> *Ammeter*
> *Heterodyne frequency meter (0.0002% error)*
> *Absorption-type wavemeter*
> *FM modulation meter*

> *Draw and label a block diagram of a voice-modulated (press-to-talk mike) indirect (phase-modulated) FM transmitter having a crystal multiplication of 12.*

1. *If the desired output frequency were 155.460 MHz, what would be the proper crystal frequency?*

2. *Consider the transmitter strip completely detuned; there are ammeter jacks in the control grid circuits of the multipliers and in the control grid and cathode circuits of the final amplifier. Explain in detail, step by step, a proper procedure for tuning and aligning all stages except the plate circuit of final power amplifier.*

3. *Assume a tunable antenna with adjustable coupling to the plate circuit of the final. With the aid of an ammeter in the cathode circuit of the final and a tube manual, describe a step-by-step method of obtaining maximum output power without damage to the tube.*

4. *If the final amplifier in (3) were a pentode, how would you determine the power input to the stage?*

5. *In (3), how would you determine if the final stage were self-oscillating; if so, what adjustments could be made?*

6. *Assume that the transmitter's assigned frequency is 155.460 MHz, with a required tolerance of ±0.0005%. What would be the minimum and maximum frequencies, as read on the frequency meter, that would insure that the transmitter is in tolerance?*

7. *Assume that the 1 MHz crystal oscillator of the frequency meter has been calibrated with WWV and that the meter is tunable to any frequency between each 1 MHz interval over a range of 20 to 40 MHz, with usable harmonics up to 640 MHz. Explain, in depth, what*

connections and adjustments would be made to measure the signal directly from the transmitter also by means of a receiver.

8. In checking the frequency deviation with the modulation meter, would you expect the greatest deviation by whistling or by speaking in a low voice into the microphone?

9. If the transmitter contained a means for limiting and were overmodulating, what measurements and adjustments could be made to determine the fault?

The block diagram of the phase-modulated transmitter is shown in Fig. 5-165. The frequencies of the various stages are shown in the appropriate blocks. The multipliers, grouped into a single block, provide a total multiplication of 12 through a process of doubling and tripling.

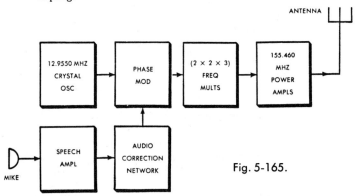

Fig. 5-165.

1. **Crystal Frequency**. The crystal frequency, as shown in the diagram, is 12.9550 MHz.

2. **Tuning**. The first step in the tuning process is to either disable the final amplifier or connect a dummy load to the antenna terminal. Assuming the final stage has a separate $B+$ supply, simply shut down the power to the final when tuning up the oscillator and multiplier stages. Insert the crystal into the oscillator crystal socket and apply power to the transmitter. (If crystal is oven mounted, wait at least 20 minutes before applying $B+$ to oscillator and multiplier circuits.)

Set the oscillator trimmer capacitor to the center of its range. Place absorption wavemeter near oscillator tank coil (with meter set to indicate in the 13 MHz region). Press mike switch and adjust trimmer for a frequency as close to 12.955 MHz as possible. If oscillator is also a frequency doubler, the wavemeter should be set to indicate in the 25−26 MHz range, and oscillator trimmer will be set to give indication of 2×12.955. Connect ammeter (microammeter or milliammeter) to grid circuit of subsequent multiplier stage and adjust oscillator output for maximum indication. As you go through the peak, you will note that on one side of the peak the output will fall off sharply; while it will diminish gradually on the other side. Back off the peak slightly on the gradual side.

Move the ammeter to the next multiplier and tune the stage for maximum deflection of the meter in its low-current range (usually 50 μA full scale). Each multiplier is adjusted with the meter in the grid circuit of the succeeding stage. Once the multipliers are tuned, connect the meter into the grid circuit of the final amplifier and adjust the output of the driver stage for maximum deflection. Connect a dummy load to the antenna terminal of the transmitter and switch on the $B+$. (The $B+$ will not be applied to the tube until the press-to-talk switch is operated.) Set the VTVM to indicate voltage (dc) and connect into the cathode circuit of the final amplifier. Key the mike switch and adjust the final output circuit for a dip in the meter reading. Connect the ammeter into the final's grid circuit and adjust the driver again for a maximum indication on the cathode-connected VTVM.

3. **Tuning to Antenna**. Adjust the variable antenna using the wavemeter. The antenna should be tuned to resonate at 155.46 MHz, and this should be accomplished before applying rf power to the antenna. Connect the VTVM into the cathode circuit of the final amplifier. Key the mike switch and adjust the plate tuning capacitor for a dip in the VTVM reading. When a dip is obtained, indicating resonance, adjust the loading capacitor in the final stage for a slightly greater indication; then follow up immediately by dipping the meter with the tuning capacitor. Continue with this process a few times, increasing the meter reading with the *loading* capacitor and tuning for a dip in the meter indication with the *tuning* capacitor.

The absorption wavemeter may be used as a field strength indicator for final touch-up, if desired. Remove power from the oscillator of this instrument and place it in the vicinity of the antenna. Key the transmitter and observe the indication while the variable antenna trimmer is adjusted slightly for an increase in the reading of the wavemeter. When this is accomplished, redip the final with the tuning capacitor.

4. **Power Input**. Since power input is equal to plate current multiplied by dc plate voltage, power may be determined by measuring these two values and making the necessary multiplication. Plate current, remember, is nothing more than electrons flowing through the chassis of the transmitter up through the cathode of the final amplifier, across the space charge and into the plate of the final amplifier. Thus, by placing the ammeter (milliammeter) in the cathode of the final, plate current is easily measured. The dc plate voltage should be measured at the power supply, since rf in the vicinity of a meter can render any readings inaccurate. The total wattage calculated using this system of measurement will come out a bit on the liberal side owing to the neglected currents that flow in the screen and control grid circuits. However, since this current represents only a small portion of the total power, it is usually wiser to leave this current out of the calculated figures just to be on the conservative side.

5. **Self-Oscillation**. When a stage self-oscillates, it is capable of producing an rf signal without excitation. To determine if self-oscillation is taking place in the final amplifier, simply remove

477

the excitation (drive) from the previous stage and use the wavemeter to check for the presence of rf.

6. **Tolerance**. The allowable error is 155.46×0.000005 (0.0005%). However, since the heterodyne frequency meter itself is not perfectly accurate, an allowance for the meter's error must be made. There are several ways for precisely determining the error capable of being introduced by the heterodyne frequency meter, but the simplest and safest method is simply to subtract the 0.0002% accuracy of the meter from the 0.0005% allowable tolerance, resulting in an allowable measured error of 0.0003%. In frequency this is 0.000003×155.46, or 466.38 Hz. In other words, the transmitter may be considered to be "on frequency" if measurement with the meter indicates any value within 466.38 Hz of the assigned frequency (155.46 MHz).

7. **Frequency Measurement**. The transmitter's signal should be coupled to the frequency meter. This will probably mean that a simple pickup antenna be placed in the vicinity of the antenna carrying the transmitter's signal. The oscillator of the heterodyne frequency meter should be adjusted to the highest frequency within its range that is a submultiple of the supposed transmitter frequency (such as 38.865 MHz), so that a signal will be radiated that is as strong at the fourth harmonic (155.460 MHz) as the transmitter signal. The setup of the instrument is shown in Fig. 5-166. Figure 5-167 shows a curve of the beat frequency plotted against the audible range of frequencies. When the difference frequency between the two signals is above the audible range, no sound is heard (the shaded area on the graph indicates the frequencies above audibility). As the two

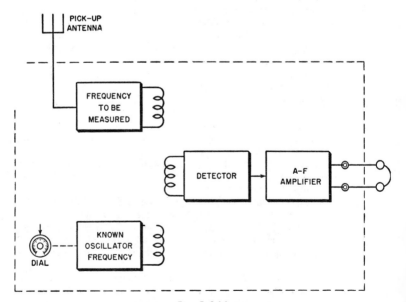

Fig. 5-166.

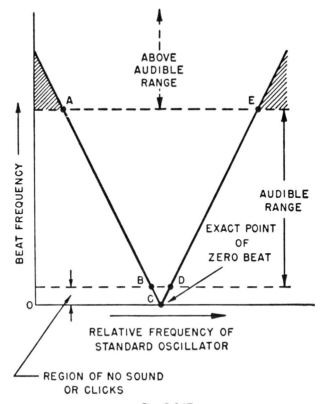

ABOVE
AUDIBLE
RANGE

A

E

BEAT FREQUENCY

AUDIBLE
RANGE

EXACT POINT
OF
ZERO BEAT

B D

C

0

RELATIVE FREQUENCY OF
STANDARD OSCILLATOR

REGION OF NO SOUND
OR CLICKS

Fig. 5-167.

frequencies are brought closer together (A on the curve), a high-pitched note is heard in the phones. This tone decreases in frequency as the frequencies get closer together. At point B the tone is replaced by a series of clicks. At C the clicks have stopped completely, and the heterodyne frequency meter is indicating the precise frequency of the transmitter under test. The heterodyne frequency meter may be read directly, in some cases (depending on the instrument's complexity); but more commonly, the meter indication consists of a series of dial readings, all of which have to be combined into a single multidigit number and compared against an entry in a special calibration book before the frequency represented by the number can be determined.

If a receiver is available, the process of frequency determination is simplified. Use the rf output capability of the heterodyne frequency meter to generate a signal that can be picked up by the receiver. The transmitter is then keyed. When the frequency meter's output signal is about the same strength as the signal radiating from the transmitter, the frequency meter is simply adjusted until a beat note is heard in the receiver. In this case the clicks are replaced by the varying tone. As the tone drops in pitch, the two signals are closing in on each other. At zero beat—the point where no tone is heard unless the frequency meter's dial is touched—the two signals are exactly on the same frequency.

8. **Deviation**. The greatest deviation will always occur when whistling, as opposed to speaking, into a microphone.

9. **Overmodulation**. To correct the problem of overmodulation in a transmitter equipped with a limiting control, simply connect a deviation meter for measurement of peak deviation and, while whistling into the microphone (which results in maximum deviation), adjust the limiting control for the required deviation (usually ± 5 kHz).

5-129. *Draw a schematic diagram of each of the following stages of a superheterodyne FM receiver. Explain the principles of operation and label adjacent stages.*

1. *Mixer with injected oscillator frequency*
2. *I-f amplifier*
3. *Limiter*
4. *Discriminator*
5. *Differential squelch circuit*

1. **Mixer with Injected Oscillator Signal**. Two triode mixer circuits are shown in Fig. 5-168. In sketch A the oscillator signal is injected along with the rf signal at the grid. In sketch B cathode injection is used. As far as the performance of the mixer is concerned, there is little to choose between the two methods of oscillator injection, except that

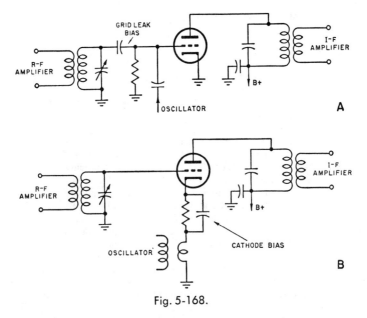

Fig. 5-168.

the grid loading with cathode injection is slightly greater. However, cathode injection gives better oscillator stability, since the load presented to the oscillator has a low impedance. The oscillator signal can be taken from a low-impedance point where varying loads do not affect the operating frequency.

If the operating frequency and the i-f are close together, the plate load impedance becoms sufficiently great to permit tuned-grid, tuned-plate oscillation, which causes instability. If this occurs, the stage must be neutralized.

The mixer beats the signal at the receiver's intermediate frequency.

2. **I-F Amplifier**. The "front end" of the FM receiver produces an output signal usually in the microvolt range, whereas the detector (discriminator) requires signals on the order of several volts for proper operation. Therefore, the i-f amplifiers must perform the required voltage amplification (or at least most of it). The i-f stages must amplify the signal between 100,000 and 1,000,000 times. They must also introduce sufficient selectivity to discriminate against stations operating on adjacent channels yet possess sufficient broadness that the outer sidebands of the FM signal remain essentially undistorted.

As shown in the partial schematic Fig. 5-169, the i-f signal is coupled into the string of i-f amplifiers by special transformers, with each transformer adding to the selectivity of the string. After amplification, the signal is passed to the detector (or discriminator). The final i-f amplifier shown in the schematic is a limiter and provides complete saturation of all moderately strong signals, so that no amplitude variations are present in any usable received signals.

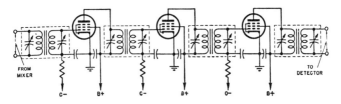

Fig. 5-169.

3.**Limiter**. Three 2-stage limiters are shown schematically in Fig. 5-170. Note the resemblance to the conventional i-f amplifierl; the principal difference is the addition of a grid-leak resistor and capacitor to provide bias. The limtier stages provide sufficient amplification for the incoming i-f signal that it saturates the tubes used for the stages. The idea of saturation is to so increase the level of incoming signals that further amplitude changes are not possible. Since the detector is made to respond only to frequency variations, the intelligence contained in the modulation is unimpaired. Similarly, variations in amplitude—from AM signals, noise, etc.—are eliminated, and the result is a minimum of such

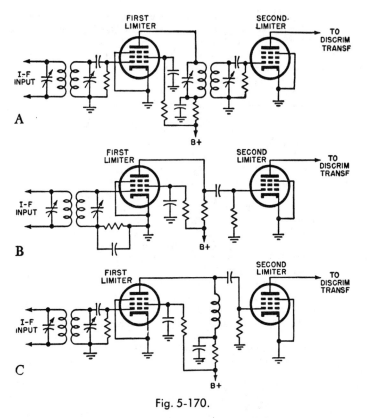

Fig. 5-170.

signals appearing at the speaker. Although a limiter does provide some amplification before its saturation point is reached, its main purpose is to limit the amplitude variations caused by fading and noise in the output voltage.

The response of an ideal limiter is shown in Fig. 5-171A. The tube must have a sharp cutoff characteristic. Very low values of screen voltage are used, and little bias is applied to the control grid. Therefore, large values of positive grid voltage quickly drive the tube to saturation, and large negative values drive it to cutoff. The transfer characteristic of the limiter is shown in Fig. 5-171B. An input signal varying greatly in amplitude with sharp pulses of noise superimposed is applied to the input of the limiter system. The varying voltage applied at the grid of the tube drives it to cutoff or saturation, so that the large variations in amplitude are clipped off.

4. **Discriminator**. A discriminator converts the frequency variation of an FM signal into audio variations. An FM discriminator known as a *cycle-counting detector* is shown in Fig. 5-172. In this circuit, selectivity is obtained through the use of a tuned first i-f at high frequency. The resistance-coupled circuit will pass a band of

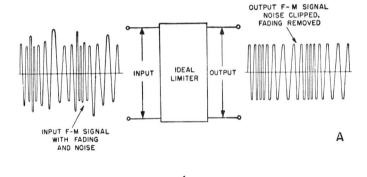

OUTPUT F-M SIGNAL
NOISE CLIPPED,
FADING REMOVED

INPUT F-M SIGNAL
WITH FADING
AND NOISE

A

Fig. 5-171.

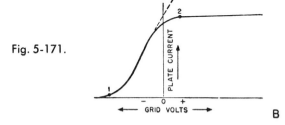

B

frequencies from low audio up to about 200 kHz. The essential operating feature of this discriminator is its response to the number of cycles provided by the 2-stage resistance-coupled limiter. The limiter produces a square wave, which is rectified by the duo-diode, the output of which is a series of negative-going pulses. As the frequency increases, the average rate of charge of the capacitor in the output circuit increases. Starting at a given center frequency, the charge on the capacitor fluctuates, depending on the departure of the signal from the center frequency. The resistor serves to lower the time constant so that the storage of charge can change fast enough to reproduce an audio signal.

5. **Differential Squelch Circuit**. The circuit of Fig. 5-173 shows the differential squelch system, which actually amplifies the no-signal noise in the receiver and uses this noise signal to cut off the receiver's audio amplifier circuits. When an incoming signal appears, the noise is *quieted*, thus releasing the squelch's hold on the audio section.

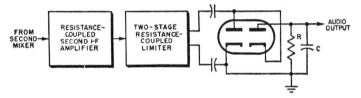

Fig. 5-172.

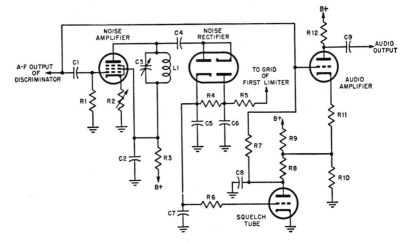

Fig. 5-173.

As shown, noise is amplified by a special amplifier, and the output is rectified by one section of the noise rectifier. The negative charge built up on C6 is applied to the grid of the first limiter through R5, reducing its gain. The positive peaks are rectified by the other half of the tube (hence the name of the squelch circuit), and a positive charge is built up on C5 and applied to the grid of the squelch tube through R6. The squelch tube conducts heavily, cutting off the aduio amplifier by making its grid highly negative.

5-130. *Draw a diagram of a ratio detector and explain its operation.*

The basic purpose of an FM detector is to rectify two i-f voltages whose amplitudes depend directly on frequency. In a *discriminator* these rectified voltages are then combined so that no voltage appears across their output at the center frequency of the i-f amplifier. A difference voltage proportional to the difference in frequency of the two applied i-f voltages is produced when the frequency of the i-f signal is above or below the center frequency. This detector is insensitive to changes in amplitude at the center frequency, but amplitude changes that are off center may cause the audio amplitude to vary somewhat. Therefore, whenever a discriminator is used, it must be preceded by a limiter. This added complexity can be avoided by a *ratio detector* circuit, which splits the rectified voltages in such a way that their ratio is directly proportional to the ratio of the applied voltages—which themselves vary with frequency.

When the sum of the rectified voltages from the transformer is maintained at a constant value, the ratio between them must also remain constant; in addition, the individual rectified voltages must remain constant. Output, then, is independent of amplitude variations in the signal, and no limiter is necessary. A simplified ratio detector circuit is presented in Fig. 5-174A. This sketch shows both diodes connected so that their outputs add, instead of subtracting as in a conventional discriminator. Capacitors C_L across the load resistors have a large value of capacitance and are charged by the output voltage of the rectifiers. This tends to make the total voltage across the load constant over the period of the time constant R_L-C_L, since a large capacitor across the combined loads maintains an average signal amplitude that is adjusted automatically to the required operating level. The rectified output must not vary at audio frequency, and the time constant of the capacitor and the load resistors must be great enough to smooth out such changes. This time constant is approximately 0.2 sec. The basic phase comparison circuit and the appropriate vector diagram of the audio detector and phase discriminator are the same.

In the circuit for a practical ratio detector (Fig. 5-174B), voltages $E1$, $E2$, and $E3$ are obtained in the same way as in the modified phase discriminator. Therefore, the applied voltage to the diodes also is the same. The diodes are connected in series and the current through load resistor R_L is always in the same direction. Consequently, the load resistor acquires the polarity shown, when the current flows from the plate of $D1$ to the cathode of $D2$. When an unmodulated signal is applied to the primary of the transformer, equal and opposite voltages

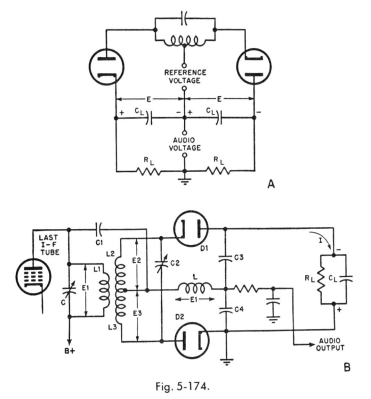

Fig. 5-174.

485

$E2$ and $E3$ are developed across the secondary in respect to the centertap. These voltages are rectified by the diodes, with the output voltage across the load resistor equal to their sum, or $E2+E3$; the large capacitor (C_L) is charged to this constant voltage. The time constant of R_L and C_L is long in comparison to the lowest audio frequency.

Since the voltage across C_L is constant, the sum of the voltages across $C3$ and $C4$ also must remain fixed. When the carrier frequency shifts with modulation, however, the voltages across $C3$ and $C4$ change; but the sum of their voltages stays fixed at the amplitude of the charge on the load capacitance (C_L). When the frequency decreases, $C4$ acquires a greater charge than $C3$; when the frequency increases, $C4$ loses charge to $C3$. Therefore, the voltage between the centertap of the two capacitors and ground varies as the ratio of the voltages across $C3$ and $C4$, the ratio depending on the instantaneous frequency. A variable voltage whose amplitude depends on the frequency deviation of the carrier consequently can be applied to the audio output. As the rate of variation increases with frequency deviation, the voltage at the centertap changes frequency, producing a higher audio frequency. Any amplitude variation in the input signal to the transformers—no matter where the carrier is in its swing—also tends to change the voltage across $C3$ and $C4$. The voltage across the RC network, however, cannot change rapidly enough to follow the amplitude modulations, and the ratio of the voltage across $C3$ and $C4$ do not change enough to produce an audio output.

The rectified voltage across the load circuit of the ratio detector adjusts itself to the amplitude of the input signal, and there is no minimum level where amplitude variations can still appear in the output. No matter how weak the signal is, the amplitude variations are removed to some extent by the constant charge on the capacitor. However, if signals of greater strength are tuned in, the charge on the capacitor is increased, and the total voltage across $C3$ and $C4$ is increased. As a consequence, ratio detectors produce audio output that is proportional to the average strength of the received signal. Ratio detectors can operate with as little as 100 mV of input, which is much lower than that required for limiter saturation, and less i-f gain is required. This receiver also is relatively quiet when no signal is received, since tube and transistor noise is not amplified as much.

As shown by the curves in Fig. 5-175, the tuning characteritic of the ratio detector has much lower side responses than the discriminator because they contain appreciable amplitude modulation, which is rejected in the load circuit. The disadvantages of the ratio detector are its greater susceptibility to impulse noise and fading, greater difficulty in alignment, and more complicated transformer design.

5-131. *Explain how spurious signals can be received or created in a receiver. How could this be reduced in sets having sealed untunable filters?*

Since a mixer is nothing more than a low-level modulator, the tuned input circuit can combine many signals with the fundamental of the local oscillator, or any of its harmonics, to produce an i-f output. If all

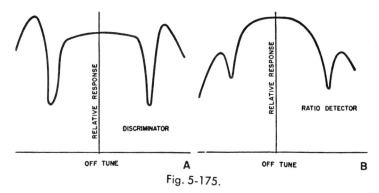

RELATIVE RESPONSE

RELATIVE RESPONSE

DISCRIMINATOR

RATIO DETECTOR

OFF TUNE **A** OFF TUNE **B**

Fig. 5-175.

but the desired signal are greatly attenuated before reaching the mixer input, and the oscillator is operating with low harmonic content, the response to spurious signals is minimized. This response depends on the selectivity in the input circuit of the mixer and in the preceding rf stage. The overall selectivity of the two stages is the product of the individual selectivities. If the response at a frequency far away from resonance is specified in decibels below that at resonance, the response of the two stages is the sum of the individual responses in decibels.

The most important spurious response is the *image frequency*, which combines with the local oscillator to produce a spurious i-f sideband. If the local oscillator is higher in frequency than the desired channel by 1 MHz, for example; the image response frequency is 1 MHz higher, or 2 MHz above the desired channel. If a strong carrier appears at the image frequency, it interferes with the desired station. The higher the intermediate frequency, the farther away the image is from the operating frequency and the greater its attenuation in the tuned circuits ahead of the mixer.

Spurious responses of less importance than the image frequency can occur at many different frequencies where harmonics of the local oscillator beat with undesired signals (and their harmonics) to produce the i-f signals. Many other possible spurious responses such as intermodulation are troublesome when the receiver is operated in the vicinity of a strong transmitter. It is difficult in some instances to determine the cause of a particular response in a receiver.

In all mixers a certain amount of coupling exists between circuits that introduce the rf signal to the tube and those that introduce the local oscillator signal. When the i-f is low compared with the operating frequency, the frequency of the oscillator and that of the mixer input circuit are very close together. If a strong signal appears in the mixer input circuit while the receiver is tuned to a weak signal on an adjacent channel, the stronger one will tend to cause the oscillator to shift frequency and lock in with it. This results in failure of reception of the weak signal, and is called *capturing*, or *pulling*. The degree of oscillator frequency pulling is dependent on the i-f, the coupling between the oscillator and input circuits, and the basic stability of the oscillator itself. The condition is aggravated with avc applied to the

487

mixer. In general, coupling between the oscillator and input circuits is greater at high frequencies, where oscillators tend to be less stable. Mixers have varying degrees of isolation between the oscillator and i-f circuits. Therefore, the oscillator-mixer combination designed for use at high frequencies is strongly influenced by the degree of isolation. Converters, because of the association of oscillator and mixer in a single tube envelope, generally are the worst offenders in regard to pulling.

Where extremely good selectivity is required, the standard double-tuned i-f transformer is not satisfactory. Even in double-conversion receivers there can be enough residual response in the adjacent channel to make reception difficult when a powerful local transmitter is operating while the receiver is tuned to a weak, distant station. Two methods designed to overcome this difficulty are the triple-tuned i-f transformer and the bandpass filter, the latter of which is a fixed, untunable, usually sealed, filter. The triple-tuned transformers have two ordinary windings inductively coupled to each other, but the output of the secondary is fed into a third parallel resonant circuit through a capacitor. In this way the coupling of the three circuits can be arranged for good gain and very sharp selectivity. A sufficient number of these stages provides good attenuation of the adjacent channel.

The other method is more complicated but produces better overall results. The output of the second mixer is fed into a bandpass filter that contains several tuned circuits. This filter produces a nearly ideal selectivity characteristic. Following the filter is a 3-stage resistance-coupled i-f amplifier, which, in turn, drives the detector. The gain ahead of the filter is deliberately kept low, and the strong adjacent-channel station therefore cannot cross-modulate the weak station to which the receiver is tuned. The filter selects the weak station and rejects the strong one before there is any appreciable voltage gain. All of the voltage gain takes place in the resistance-coupled stages, which receive only the weak signal from the filter, the strong adjacent-channel station being almost completely rejected.

5-132. *Describe, step-by step, a proper procedure for aligning an FM double-conversion superheterodyne receiver.*

All FM receivers contain a large number of tuned circuits, which must be adjsuted correctly if the unit is to function properly. Vibration, humidity, or temperature changes may cause the resonant circuits to drift off frequency in the field. Also, when a critical part is replaced, the associated resonant circuit may change frequency. The process of adjusting the tuned circuits of the receiver for optimum performance is called alignment.

The rf, i-f, and detector circuits of any superheterodyne receiver must be aligned to their proper frequencies. It is possible to accomplish a rough alignment by applying a signal at the antenna terminals and peaking the tuned circuits of the receiver until maximum output appears from the audio-frequency stages. This method is very unsatisfactory; however, in an emergency, with no servicing equipment available, the performance of the receiver can be restored to something approaching normal operation by this procedure.

The basic alignment procedure for any particular unit is given in detail in the manual that accompanies it. That is, all the manufacturers of commercial two-way FM transceivers publish recommended alignment procedures that are unique to their own lines. The procedures given here indicate general steps applicable to most FM receivers and therefore cannot be regarded as service information for any particular unit. The basic alignment procedure is to begin with the FM detector circuit and tune the i-f amplifiers or limiters one by one, working toward the mixer and finally dealing with the rf circuits.

The two systems of alignment in common use are the *meter* method and the *visual alignment* method. The meter method uses a signal generator that covers both the i-f and the entire rf range tuned by the receiver and a vacuum-tube voltmeter (or its semiconductor equivalent). The visual alignment technique uses an FM signal generator that covers the rf and i-f ranges, an oscilloscope, and sometimes a stable cw signal generator. In general, an FM receiver can be aligned more quickly and easily and with far more accuracy by the visual method than by the meter method. The disadvantage of the visual method lies in the complexity of the test equipment and the difficulty in obtaining all of the necessary testing devices in the field. The meter method of alignment uses the variations of dc voltage that take place in different parts of the receiver circuit when the tuning is changed. A steady carrier is applied from the signal generator to the circuit under test, and changes in voltage with tuning are observed on the meter. The visual method of alignment traces the actual response curves of the circuit under test on the screen of an oscilloscope. The tuned circuits are adjusted until the curves have the required amplitude and shape. The FM signal generator sweeps through the frequency band covered by the stage under test, and the oscilloscope traces a curve that corresponds to the output of that stage in synchronism with the FM generator.

5-133. *Discuss the cause and prevention of interference to radio receivers installed in motor vehicles.*

Even though most sources of interference are of a pulsing nature—which makes them equivalent to AM components—FM receivers are susceptible to these noises. Mobile interference stems from the making and breaking of electrical contacts in the ignition system; the high-frequency contacting of generator and alternator brushes; and the repetitive contacting of all types of small electrical motors, such as windshield wipers, electric fuel pumps, air conditioners, and car heaters. These sources produce *spark gap*-type signals that radiate from the devices themselves; they also produce transients which may propagate through the wiring of the vehicle.

Eliminating these interference sources is a matter of shielding, using better and more effective grounds, and incorporating filter-type inductors in the lines that supply power to interference sources. At the receiver an improvement can often be noted after carefully installing bypass capacitors in strategic locations.

489

5-134. Describe the difference between positive (p-type) and negative n-type) semiconductors with respect to:

- *The direction of current when an external voltage is applied*
- *The internal resistance when an external voltage is applied*

Current Flow. In an *npn* transistor, with bias voltages properly applied, the *n*-type emitter injects free electrons into the *p*-type base, where they are attracted across the second junction by the positive voltage present there. Because of the applied bias, current across the first junction finds a low-resistance path; current there remains essentially the same as in the first junction. The electron flow in an *npn* transistor is depicted in Fig. 5-176.

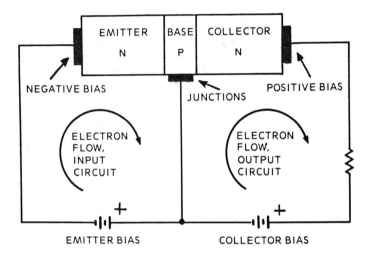

Fig. 5-176.

While conventional bipolar transistors can have either of two basic configurations, *npn* or *pnp*, the practical consideration we are concerned with is the polarity of the voltages that will be applied in the circuit where the transistor will be used. **All voltage biases for the *npn* must be reversed for the *pnp* transistor.** The above description of the operation of the *npn* applies to the *pnp* with certain changes. For example, we saw that the path of electron flow was from the emitter, across the base, and to the collector in an *npn* transistor. With a *pnp* transistor, we have to substitute some word for *electrons* if the direction of flow of the charge carriers is to be the same regardless of transistor polarity. Therefore, when we speak of *pnp* transistors, we speak of *hole* movement from the emitter, across the base, and to the collector (when we speak of *npn* transistors, we speak of *electron* movement over this same path). **What it boils down to is that the major charge carriers in an *npn* transistor are electrons; in a *pnp*** transistor, the major charge carriers are *holes (a hole is the absence of electrons, or the need for an electron to provide a balance)*.

Internal Resistance. A bipolar transistor typically consists of a slab of semiconductor material divided into threee sections. The two outer sections are doped with certain impurities to give them either a positive or negative characteristic. The basic semiconductor material is itself *intrinsic*, or neutral, and is usually composed of germanium or silicon. The center section of the intrinsic material is doped with a different impurity, so that it exhibits a characteristic polarity that is opposite to that of the two outer sections.

The three sections are sandwiched into the semiconductor slab. The areas where the sections meet are called *junctions* and it is the behavior of these junctions that governs the performance of the transistor itself. A single junction has the characteristic of a conventional diode; that is, it permits current to flow in one direction and restricts the flow of current in the other direction. But whatever happens in one junction greatly affects what happens in the other so long as there is a complete circuit in both the input and output stages of the transistor and the intermediate element is common to both, as in Fig. 5-176.

With the application of voltage to the input circuit, a current flows through the base—emitter junction. The action of the transistor is such that the same quantity of current (or some close approximation of it) is caused in the output circuit, which has a higher series internal resistance than the input circuit.

5-135. *What is the difference between forward and reverse biasing of transistors?*

Figure 5-177 is a plot of current versus voltage applied to a practical *pn* junction. Note that current flow in the forward-bias direction is quite high (measured in milliamperes). However, current in the reverse-bias direction, although low (measured in microamperes) is not zero (as might be expected). The reverse-bias current occurs because some acceptor ions and their associated holes occur in the *n*-type material (germanium or silicon), and some donor ions and their associated excess electrons occur in the *p*-type material. The holes found in *n*-type material and the excess electrons found in *p*-type material are called *minority carriers* because they are so few in number compared to the *majority* carrers (holes in *p*-type and excess electrons in *n*-type material). ·

When the *pn* junction is biased in the reverse direction for the majority carriers (electrons in *n* material and holes in *p* material), the *pn* junction is biased in the forward direction for the minority carriers. The internal mechanism of conduction for the minority carriers when forward-biased (majority carriers reverse-biased) is identical with that for forward-biased majority carriers.

Note (Fig. 5-177) that when a very high reverse bias is applied, a high reverse current flows. This high current is not due to the normal minority current carriers; a breakdown of the crystal structure occurs. Observation of Fig. 5-177 reveals that a *pn* junction biased in the forward direction is equivalent to a low-resistance element (high current for a given voltage). The *pn* junction biased in the reverse

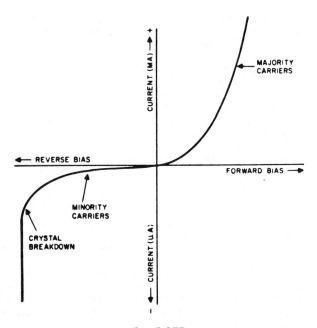

CURRENT (MA)

+

MAJORITY
CARRIERS

REVERSE BIAS

FORWARD BIAS

MINORITY
CARRIERS

CRYSTAL
BREAKDOWN

CURRENT (μA)

I

Fig. 5-177.

direction is equivalent to a high-resistance element (low current for a given voltage). For a given current the power developed in a high-resistance element is greater than that developed in a low-resistance element. (Power is equal to the current squared, multiplied by the resistance value, or $P \doteq I^2R$.) If a crystal containing two *pn* junctions were prepared, a signal could be introduced into the *pn* junction biased in the reverse direction (high resistance). This would produce a power gain of the signal when developed in an external circuit. Such a device would transfer the signal current from a low-resistance circuit to a high-resistance circuit. Contracting the terms *transfer* and *resistor* results in the term *transistor*.

5-136. *Show connections of external batteries, resistive loads, and signal sources as would appear in a properly fixed-biased common-emitter transistor amplifier.*

The common-emitter amplifier is the most popular transistor amplifier circuit. As shown in Fig. 5-178, its tube-type equivalent is the conventional common-cathode arrangement. The common-emitter circuit has the highest gain of all the amplifier types. The output waveform is an inverted duplicate of the input signal. The principal difference between the input and output waveforms is that the output waveform is considerably higher in amplitude than the input. It is, however, important to remember that the output is shifted in phase from the input by precisely 180°.

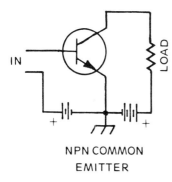

NPN COMMON
EMITTER

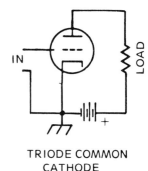

TRIODE COMMON
CATHODE

Fig. 5-178.

5-137. *The following are excerpts from a transistor handbook describing the characteristics of a pnp alloy-type transistor as used in a common-emitter circuit. Explain the significance of each item.*

Collector-to-base voltage (emitter open) .... $-40V$ *max*
Collector-to-emitter voltage (base-to-emitter voltage = 0.5V) .. $-40V$
Emitter-to-base voltage .... $-5.0V$ *max*
Collector current .... *10 mA max*
Transistor dissipation at ambient temperature of 25°C for operation in
free air .... *120 mW max*
Transistor dissipation at case temperature of 25°C for operation with
heatsink .... *140 mW max*
Ambient temperature range (operation and storage) $-65°C$ *to* $+100°C$

Ratings. Transistors have maximum ratings that cannot be exceeded if normal operation is to be expected. Similarly, many of a transistor's parameters require a *minimum* value of voltage, current, etc., which must be maintained if the specifications of the device are to be meaningful. It should be noted that any maximum or minimum value stated on the specification should be considered the limit when all other specified values are "normal," or well within the specified limits. For example, if a transistor is operated at maximum voltage and maximum current at the same time, the device's maximum power dissipation capability will probably be exceeded.

Open-Emitter Collector Voltage. This voltage, designated as V_{cbo}, is the maximum voltage that can be applied between the base and collector without exceeding the collector—base junction breakdown point. Here, the base is considered to be reverse-biased (−40V), and the emitter is open.

Collector-to-Emitter Voltage. This voltage, designated V_{ce}, is the dc collector-to-emitter breakdown voltage when the collector is reverse-biased with respect to the emitter and the emitter junction is reverse-biased through a specified circuit by 0.5V.

Emitter-to-Base Voltage. This voltage, designated V_{ebo}, represents the dc emitter-to-base breakdown voltage with the emitter reverse-biased with respect to base and the collector open.

493

Collector Current. This rating specifies the maximum collector current (dc) that can be maintained without overheating the transistor. It is a particularly significant specification with power transistors. The low collector current of 10 mA would mean the transistor is restricted to small-signal applications.

Free Air Dissipation. Without adequate heatsinking, the transistor referred to in the question has the ability of dissipating no more than 120 mW. With some external means for dissipating the transistor's heat, this rating may be exceeded, as noted below.

Heatsinking. Most power transistors are used with some external device designed to carry heat away from the semiconductor. When such an additional heatsink is used, the device's efficiency is improved and its thermal dissipation rating can be exceeded, sometimes by as much as 25%. The 140 mW rating states that any heatsink that does not allow the transistor's case temperature to exceed 25° can be used to increase the transistor's dissipation rating to 140 mW rather than 120 mW.

Ambient Temperature Range. Transistors will perform in accordance with their specifications only when they are operated or stored at temperatures within an established range. The limits given, −65°C to +100°C, define this storage and operating spectrum.

5-138. *Draw a circuit diagram of a method of obtaining self-bias, with one battery, without current feedback, in a common-emitter amplifier. Explain the voltage drops in the resistors.*

The single battery shown in the circuit of Fig. 5-179 directly produces the required reverse-bias voltage in the collector−base circuit. To understand the method by which the forward bias between the emitter and base is produced by the single battery, a knowledge of the internal

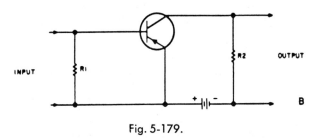

Fig. 5-179.

structure of the transistor is required. Forward bias for the *pnp* transistor requires the base to be negative with respect to the emitter. In a *pnp* transistor the collector is at the highest negative potential; the emitter is at the highest positive potential. The base is between the two and must assume a voltage between the two. Thus, the base must be less positive than the emitter or, in other words, negative with respect to the emitter. This condition satisfies the requirement of polarity necessary to produce a forward bias. The magnitude of the voltage between the emitter and the base must be very small compared to that between the collector and the base. Internally, the two *pn* junctions act as a voltage divider. The *pn* junction between the collector and base represents a high resistance and develops the larger voltage drop. The *pn* junction between emitter and base represents a low resistance and develops a low voltage.

5-139. *Draw a circuit diagram of a common-emitter amplifier with emitter bias. Explain its operation.*

One method of obtaining good current stability in a common-emitter amplifier is by using near-zero base resistance and swamping a resistor as shown in Fig. 5-180A. Resistor R_E is the swamping resistor; the secondary of transformer $T1$ offers a very low dc resistance in the base circuit.

A fixed emitter−base bias can be obtained in a single-battery common-emitter amplifier by means of a voltage divider. (This is shown in Fig. 5-180B.) The voltage divider consists of resistors R_F and R_B. The voltage developed across R_B contributes part of the emitter−base voltage. The current stability factor in this circuit is equal to the ratio of the combined value of R_B and R_F (the base ground-return resistance) to the emitter resistance. The lower the base ground-return resistance and the higher the emitter resistance, the better the current stability.

A circuit employing negative voltage feedback to improve current stability is shown in Fig. 5-180C. If the collector current (I_C) rises, the collector becomes less negative because of the larger dc drop in resistor R_C. As a result, less forward bias (negative base to positive emitter) is coupled through resistor R_F to the base. Reduced forward bias then reduces the collector current.

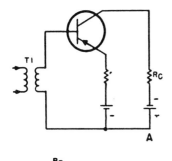

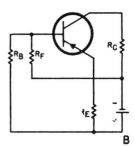

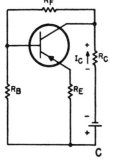

Fig. 5-180.

5-140. *The value of the alpha cutoff frequency of a transistor is primarily dependent on what one factor? Does the value of alpha cutoff frequency normally have any relationship to the collector-to-base voltage?*

The collector-to-emitter capacitance of the transistor affects alpha cutoff frequency more than any other single factor. This reactive element (sometimes referred to as the *barrier capacitance*) varies with changes in collector or emitter voltages and with temperature. In high-frequency oscillators, when the collector—emitter capacitance becomes an important factor, the effect of changes in the capacitance may be minimized by inserting a relatively large swamping capacitor across the collector-to-emitter electrodes. The total capacitance of the two in parallel results in a circuit that is less sensitive to variations in voltage. The added capacitor may be part of a tuned circuit.

The use of a common bias source for both collector and emitter electrodes maintains a relatively constant ratio of the two voltages. In effect, a change in one voltage is somewhat counteracted by the change in the other, since an increased collector voltage causes an increase in the oscillating frequency, and an increased emitter voltage causes a decrease in the oscillating frequency. Since the collector-to-base voltage has an effect on the capacitance of the collector junction, this voltage also tends to affect the alpha cutoff frequency.

5-141. *Why is stabilization of a transistor amplifier usually necessary? How would a thermistor be used in this respect?*

It has been established that the bias current of the transistor is temperature sensitive. Specifically, emitter current increases with an increase in temperature. Emitter current stabilization can be achieved by use of external circuits using temperature-sensitive elements. There are several temperature-sensitive electrical elements. One such element is the *thermistor* (contraction of the words *thermal* and *resistor*). The thermistor has a negative temperature coefficient of resistance; that is, its resistance value decreases with an increase in temperature.

The circuit shown in Fig. 5-181 employs a thermistor to vary the emitter voltage with temperature, to minimize temperature variations in the emitter current. This circuit contains two voltage dividers, the first consisting of resistors R4 and R1, and the second consisting of resistor R2 and thermistor RT1. The first voltage divider permits the application of a portion of battery collector voltage to the base terminal and ground (common return). The base terminal voltage is developed across resistor R1 and is in the forward-bias direction. The second voltage divider applies a portion of battery voltage (V_C) to the emitter terminal. The emitter terminal voltage is developed across resistor R1 and is in the forward-bias direction. The forward bias applied to the base terminal is larger than the reverse bias applied to the emitter terminal, so that the resultant base—emitter bias is always in the forward direction.

With an increase in temperature, the collector current would normally increase if the transistor were not stabilized. The increase in collector current can be prevented by reducing the forward bias. This

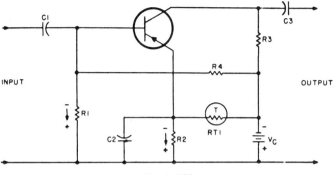

Fig. 5-181.

is acomplished by the voltage divider consisting of resistor $R2$ and thermistor $RT1$. As the temperature increases, the resistance of thermistor $RT1$ is decreased, causing more current to flow through the voltage divider. The increased current raises the negative potential at the emitter connection of resistor $R2$. This action increases the reverse bias applied to the emitter and decreases the net emitter–base forward bias. As a result, the collector current is reduced. Similarly, decreasing the temperature would cause the revere actions and prevent the decrease of collector current.

Capacitor $C1$ blocks the dc voltage of the previous stage and couples the ac signal into the base–emitter circuit. Capacitor $C2$ bypasses the ac signal around resistor $R2$. Resistor $R3$ is the collector load resistor and develops the output signal. Capacitor $C3$ blocks the dc collector voltage from, and couples the ac signal to, the following stage.

5-142. *Draw simple schematic diagrams of the following transistor circuits and explain their principles of operation. Use only one voltage source; state typical component values for low-power, 10 MHz operation:*

- *Colpitts oscillator*
- *Class B push-pull amplifier*
- *Common-emitter amplifier*
- *Pnp transistor directly coupled to an npn type*

Colpitts. Figure 5-182 illustrates a transistor Colpitts oscillator circuit. Regenerative feedback is obtained from the tank circuit and applied to the emitter of the transistor. Base bias is provided by resistors R_B and R_F. Resistor R_C is the collector load resistor. Resistor R_E develops the emitter input signal and also acts as the swamping resistor. The tuned circuit consists of capacitors $C1$ and $C2$ in parallel with transformer winding 1–2. Capacitors $C1$ and $C2$ form a voltage divider. The voltage developed across $C2$ is the feedback voltage. Either or both capacitors may be adjusted to control the frequency and the amount of feedback voltage. For minimum feedback loss the ratio of the capacitive reactance of $C1$ to $C2$ should be approximately equal to the ratio of the output impedance to the input impedance of the transistor. Component values might be

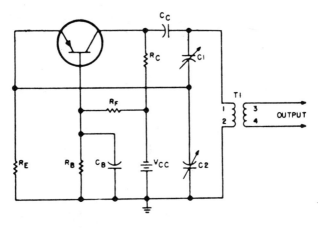

Fig. 5-182.

approximately as follows: $R_B = 22K$; $R_E = 12K$, $R_C = 47K$, $R_F = 22K$, $C_B = 0.022$ μF, C1 and C2 = values complementary to T1 primary, to give resonance at 10 MHz.

Class B Push-Pull Amplifier. Figure 5-183 shows a simplified circuit of a class B amplifier. The emitter–base junctions are zero-biased. In this circuit each transistor conducts on alternate half-cycles of the input signal. The output signal is combined in the secondary of the output transformer. Maximum efficiency is obtained even during idling (no input signal) periods, because neither transistor conducts during this period.

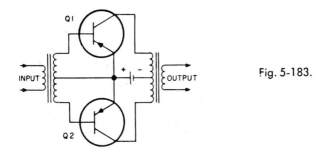

Fig. 5-183.

An indication of the output current waveform for a given signal current input can be obtained by considering the dynamic transfer characteristic for the amplifier. It is assumed that the two transistors have identical dynamic transfer characteristics. This characteristic, for one of the transistors, is shown in Fig. 5-184A. The variation in output (collector) current is plotted against input (base) current under load conditions. Since two transistors are used, the overall dynamic transfer characteristic for the push-pull amplifier is

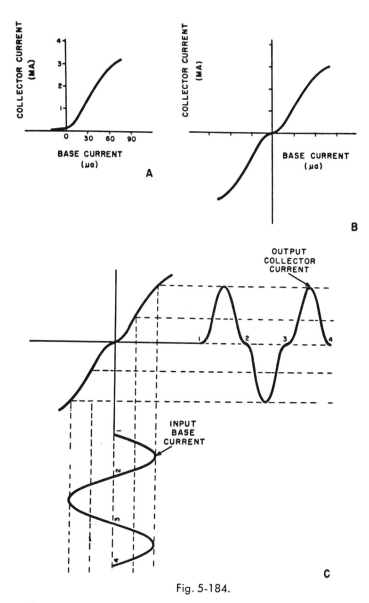

Fig. 5-184.

obtained by placing two of the curves back-to-back (Fig. 5-184B). Note that the zero line of each curve is lined up vertically to reflect the zero-bias current. In sketch C points on the base current (a sine wave) are projected onto the dynamic transfer characteristic. The corresponding points are determined and projected as indicated to form the output collector current waveform.

Common-Emitter Amplifier. The circuit of Fig. 5-185 shows two common-emitter amplifiers in cascade. All component values are given. This direct-coupled 10W high-fidelity amplifier uses special techniques to overcome thermal drift and loading problems. Temperature stabilization is achieved with effective base bias of the first stage, and loading problems are avoided by employing a self-balancing bias arrangement wherein subsequent amplifier stages are locked into the first stage. The diode in the circuit is another temperature stabilizing device. Connected from the base of the 2N1924 to the collector of the 2N1925, it balances out emitter—base resistance changes in the early stages. Effective thermal stabilization in any early amplifier stage makes light work of doing the same job further down the line.

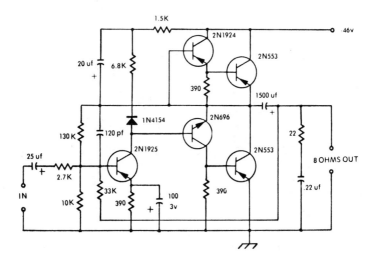

Fig. 5-185.

Use of dc feedback serves to cancel unwanted signal variations such as those caused by drift and collector current increases from temperature rises. When the phase relation between the input and output signals is reversed, the output signal reaches its peak at the same time the input reaches its null. Feeding back a portion of an output signal this way is called *negative feedback*. While negative feedback reduces the gain of the amplifier, it reduces distortion from any of the amplifier stages being used.

Cross-Polar Coupling. The direct-coupled amplifier shown in Fig. 5-186 is used for amplification of dc signals and very low frequencies. In the circuit shown, an *npn* transistor is connected directly to a *pnp* transistor. The direction of current is shown by the arrows. If the collector current of the first stage is larger than the base current of the second stage, then a collector load resistor (R1) must be connected as indicated.

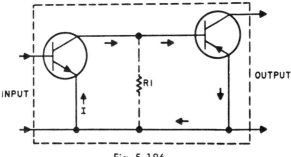

Fig. 5-186.

Because so few circuit parts are required in the direct-coupled amplifier, maximum economy can be achieved. However, the number of stages that can be directly coupled is limited. Temperature variation of the bias current in one stage is amplified by all the stages. causing severe temperature instability.

5-143. *Discuss etched wiring (printed circuits) with respect to the following:*

- *Determination of wiring breaks*
- *Excessive heating*
- *Removal and installation of components*

Wiring Breaks. Wiring breaks are probably a great deal more common than generally suspected. Fortunately, the large majority of boards can be subjected to relatively simple continuity checks, using nothing other than an ohmmeter. Printed circuit (PC) boards typically have wire routes on the lower side, and components mounted on the other side. If such a board is itself a module—that is, if it can be readily unplugged and disconnected form the "mother" assembly of which it is a part—looking for wire breaks is simply a matter of observing the conductive paths when the board is free. Lengthy paths can be traced quickly by touching the test prods of the ohmmeter to the extreme ends of each route to be checked. If absence of continuity is observed, one of the prods is moved closer to the other until the break is found.

Breaks in the printed wiring can ordinarily be repaired by bridging a length of wire across the gap. The wire should be stripped of its insulation, tinned thoroughly with solder, and then tacked down quickly into position, with a minimum of solder applied with a low-wattage iron (which has a small tip) to avoid bridging other paths inadvertently.

Wiring breaks can also be spotted—with more difficulty—while the board is connected into its circuit and with power applied. Using this approach, it is usually advisable to have a "map" of the board as well as a chart showing voltages that should appear at key points. (A PC board map is a drawing of the board with conductive paths shown in shaded screening. Generally, such maps also bear partial or complete schematics, since incorporation of the schematic does not compromise the readability of the map's shading.)

Excessive Heating. Unless the board is of particularly high-quality design—such as fabricated from epoxy–glass, Mylar, or some equally heat-resistant material—it is susceptible to the effects of overheating. Phenolic and pressed paper are about the only materials of which PC boards are typically made that will incur damage directly by overheating; however, there are indirect effects that may be attributable to excess heat. Typical of overheating problems are peeling conductor paths, resistors whose values are altered, and damaged semiconductors, in addition to the problems caused by molten solder bridging paths between conductors of the printed board.

To avoid damage from excessive heat, all components susceptible to heat damage should be soldered or desoldered with the aid of a heatsink—a device that grips the lead of a device between the spot where heat is applied and the body proper to absorb heat from soldering. Problems with molten solder can be avoided by using only the amount of solder necessary to effect a repair and by using a soldering iron that is of low-wattage design. If a conductive layer peels, the safest cure is to cut off the peeled piece with a sharp knife or razor blade, and bridge the area with a length of wire.

Component Considerations. Components can be quite difficult to remove from a circuit board once they have been installed. Particularly troublesome are components with more than one or two leads. When multilead devices must be installed, it is always a good idea to use a socket for the device rather than to solder the leads directly into the board. This way, removal of the device, should it become necessary, is reduced to nothing more than unplugging it from the socket.

Many manufactured electronic assemblies come equipped with transistors and integrated circuits that have been soldered into position. Removing these items can be an almost impossible task if the right tools are not available. In particular, ICs are difficult to remove after having been soldered into a PC board. The best bet, with ICs and multilead transistors, is to use a special desoldering tool that allows heating of all leads at once. Trying to heat and remove a lead at a time from a PC board can be like trying to lift oneself up by the bootstraps.

As mentioned above, active devices and those passive devices that are vulnerable to the effects of heating should be installed or removed with adequate protection for the device. Resistors tend to change value when overheated, and transistors tend to incur junction damage that renders them useless. Long-nose pliers are satisfactory for heatsinking though they do not afford the same degree of protection as the tiny gripping pliers designed for this purpose.

5-144. *What is a junction tetrode transistor? How does it differ from other transistors in base resistance and operating frequency?*

The highest frequency that can be amplified by a 3-terminal junction transistor is limited by the input capacitance and, particularly, the output capacitance of the transistor. One method for reducing these capacitances is to reduce the size of the transistor's semiconductor material. However, this method is physically limited because the semiconductor material must be large enough so that leads may be attached to the three regions. A second method is to restrict transistor action to a small portion of the semiconductor material, so that the effect of a small-size transistor with low input and output capacitance is obtained. To employ the latter method, a tetrode (4-terminal) transistor must be used.

A tetrode transistor is shown in Fig. 5-187. The tetrode transistor is constructed in the same manner as the 3-terminal (*pnp* or *npn*) junction transistor, except for the addition of a second terminal to the base region. Terminals *1*, *2*, and *3* are the conventional emitter, base, and collector terminals, respectively, and are biased in the same manner as in the 3-terminal transistor. Terminal *4* is the second connection to the base region. By placing a negative bias on terminal *4*, using battery V_{BB}, the indicated voltage gradient occurs within the base region. Note that forward bias (emitter more negative than base) occurs only over a small portion of the emitter−base junction. Current between base and collector also occurs over a small portion of the collector−base junction. Since the effective input and output capacitances involve only the active portions of the emitter−base junction and collector−base junction, respectively, these capacitance values are substantially reduced. The high-frequency response of the tetrode transistor, then, is substantially greater than that of the comparable 3-terminal transistor.

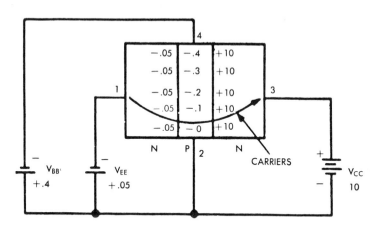

Fig. 5-187.

ANTENNAS

5-145.   Explain the voltage and current relationships in a one-wave antenna, in a half-wave antenna, and in a quarter-wave grounded antenna.

Half-Wave Antenna. The half-wave antenna is also known as a *Hertz antenna*. This type of antenna (Fig. 5-188) is composed of two quarter-wave sections. The electrical distance from the end of one line to the end of the other is λ/2 (one-half wavelength). If an rf voltage of the appropriate frequency is applied to the line, causing current to flow, the current will be maximum at the source end and minimum at the open end. The voltage will be maximum at the open ends and minimum at the center (source). In the drawing the curves represent relative values for currrent (I) and voltage (E). The farther from the antenna either curve is drawn, the larger the value at that spot on the antenna. Thus, current is shown to be maximum at the center (feed) point, while gradually diminishing to a very low value at the ends of the antenna. Voltage, whose minima and maxima are 90° out of phase with current, is quite low at the feed point and very high at the ends of the antenna. The fact that voltage and current are 90° apart in phase means that while current is at its peak, voltage is at a null, and vice versa.

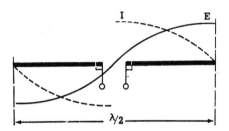

Fig. 5-188.

Quarter-Wave Grounded Antenna. The grounded quarter-wave antenna is also known as a *Marconi antenna*. The difference between the Marconi antenna and the Hertz (half wave) type is that the Marconi type requires a conducting path to ground, and the Hertz type does not.

A Marconi antenna used as a transmitting element is shown in Fig. 5-189. The transmitter is connected between the antenna and ground. The actual length of the antenna is λ/4 (one-quarter wavelength). However, this type of antenna, by virtue of its connection to ground, uses the ground surface as another

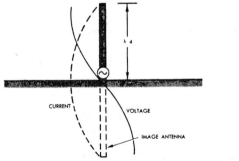

Fig. 5-189.

THE QUARTER WAVE GROUNDED ANTENNA IS CALLED THE "MARCONI."

quarter-wavelength member, making the antenna electrically a half-wavelength type. (See mirror image of Marconi antenna below radiator in Fig. 5-189.) This is so, because the earth is a good conductor and there is a reflection from the earth that is equivalent to the reflection that would be realized if another quarter-wave section were used. By use of the Marconi antenna, half-wave operation may be obtained. All of the voltage, current, and impedance relationships characteristic of a half-wave antenna will also exist in this antenna. The only exception to this is the input impedance, which is about 36.6Ω (half the impedance at the feed point of a half-wave antenna).

In the drawing, antenna current is shown as a broken-line curve. The solid curve represents the voltage. As with the Hertz antenna, voltage is essentially zero at the feed point and maximum at the end. Current is maximum at the feed point and diminishes to almost zero at the ends. If the values of voltage (or current) were taken at an infinite number of points along the antenna, the values, when plotted on graph paper, would form a portion of a sine wave.

One-Wave Antenna. A one-wave antenna is also known as a *harmonic*, or *long-wire*, antenna. An antenna of this type exhibits a current pattern as shown in the two sketches of Fig. 5-190. As shown, current is at a minimum at the ends and center of the antenna. Regardless of where the signal source is connected, the current minima and maxima retain their positions, as do voltage points, which are 90° out of phase with current.

The arrows shown directly below the antennas in the two sketches give the direction of current flow in the antenna wire. The left side of the antenna is of opposite polarity to the right half; and left-side current flows from left to right (despite the signal source position), while the right-side current flows from right to left.

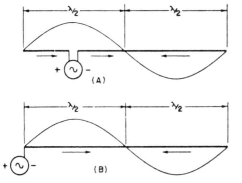

Fig. 5-190.

5-145. *What effect does the magnitude of the voltage and current at any point on a half-wave antenna (dipole) in free space have on the impedance at that point?*

In the induction field about an antenna, there are inductive and capacitive components. The value of these reactances and the value of the radiation resistance will affect the value of current in the antenna.

505

The combination of a reactive and a resistive opposition renders some impedance value for the antenna. This antenna impedance is similar to the characteristic impedance of a transmission line, and is called the *antenna input impedance*. The formulas that may be used to compute the values of this input impedance are as follows:

$$Z = E/I \qquad Z = R \pm jX$$

Any antenna, at resonance, presents a specific impedance at every point along its length. This can be seen by comparing the voltage and current values distributed along an antenna, as shown in Fig. 5-191A. Using the Ohm's law formula for impedance, it can be seen that **the highest impedance occurs where current is lowest, and vice versa.** Between points of highest and lowest impedance, antenna impedance values follow the curve of Fig. 5-191B.

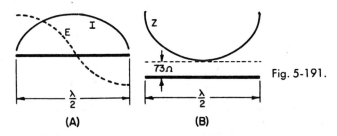

Fig. 5-191.

5-147. *How is the operating power of an AM transmitter determined using antenna resistance and antenna current?*

Operating power, from an extension of Ohm's law, is equal to **antenna current squared, multiplied by antenna resistance,** or $P = I^2R$.

Since a relationship exists between the antenna current and the power dissipated by the antenna, radiation resistance can be mathematically defined as the ratio of total power dissipated to the square of the effective value of antenna current, or $R = P/I^2$.

The radiation resistance varies with antenna length, as shown in the graph of Fig. 5-192. For a half-wave antenna, the radiation resistance measured at the current maximum (center of antenna) is about 73Ω. For a quarter-wave antenna, the resistance measured at

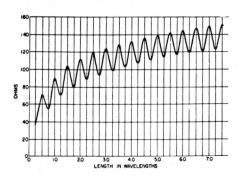

Fig. 5-192.

its current maximum is 36.6Ω. These are *free space* values; that is, the values of radiation resistance that would exist if the antenna were completely isolated, so that its radiation pattern was completely unobstructed.

For practical antenna installations the height of the antenna affects radiation resistance. Changes in radiation resistance occur because of ground reflections, which intercept the antenna and alter the amount of antenna current. Depending on their phase, the reflected waves may increase antenna current or decrease it. The phase of the reflected waves arriving at the end of the antenna, in turn, is a function of antenna height and orientation.

At some antenna heights it is possible for a reflected wave to induce antenna current in phase with transmitter current, so that the total antenna current increases. At other antenna heights the two currents may be 180° out of phase, so that total antenna current is less than if no ground reflection occurred.

With a given input power, if antenna current increases, the effect is as if radiation resistance decreased. Similarly, if the antenna height is such that the total antenna current decreases, the radiation resistance is increased. The actual change in radiation resistance of a half-wave antenna at various heights above ground is shown in Fig. 5-193. The radiation resistance of the horizontal antenna rises steadily to a maximum value of 90Ω at a height of about 3λ/8 (three-eighths wavelength). Then the radiation resistance falls steadily to 58Ω at a height of about 5λ/8. The resistance then continues to rise and fall around an average value of 73Ω, which is the free space value.

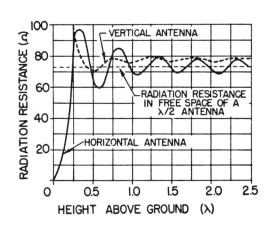

Fig. 5-193.

5-148. *What kinds of fields comprise the radiation field of a transmitting antenna, and what relationships do they have to each other?*

Current theory holds that there are two types of field produced by a driven antenna: *magnetic* and *electric*. The magnetic field is called an *H*-field and the electric field is referred to as an *E*-field. Since the current and voltage that produces these fields are 90° out of phase with

507

each other, the fields themselves are out of phase by the same angle, as shown in Fig. 5-194. Note that the 90° lag between the two radiated fields is shown by perpendicular line segments, with the vertical lines representing the E-field and the horizontal lines representing the H-field. (The sketch also references the left-hand rule for determining direction of a field associated with an inductor.)

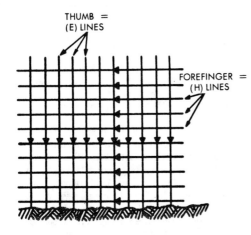

Fig. 5-194.

The relationship of the E and H fields as they are propagated in the radiation field is such that they are in phase in time and 90° out of phase in space. (*Radiation field* is the term used in modern theory to differentiate from *induction field*, associated with antennas but not related to propagation. Induction fields are of little concern for the purpose of the FCC exam.) Along the half-wave antenna the intensity of the field is not uniform. There are points along its length where the field is at a maximum and other points along its length where the field is minimum (Fig. 5-195).

The E-field is shown as the solid closed loops that exist on each side of the antenna. The H-fields, which are 90° out of phase in space, are shown as the circles that enclose either crosses or dots. (The dots represent field lines going into the page, and the crosses represent field lines emerging from the page.) The sine waves shown superimposed on the fields indicate the variation in electric flux intensity at various distances and angles away from the antenna.

In a direction perpendicular to the antenna, the fields are strongest. In a parallel direction—away from the antenna—that is, off the ends of the antenna—the fields are weakest. For this reason the half-wave antenna is said to be a directional antenna.

Because the current is greatest at the center of a dipole, maximum radiation takes place at this point; practically no radiation takes place from the ends. If this antenna could be isolated completely in free space, the points of maximum radiation would be in a plane perpendicular to the plane of the antenna at its center. The donut-shaped surface pattern is shown in Fig. 5-196A, and the

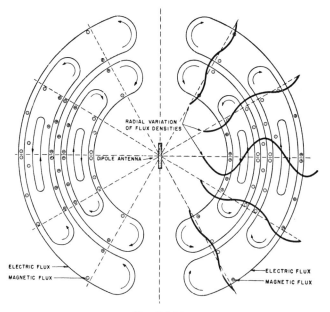

RADIAL VARIATION OF FLUX DENSITIES

DIPOLE ANTENNA

ELECTRIC FLUX
MAGNETIC FLUX

ELECTRIC FLUX
MAGNETIC FLUX

Fig. 5-195.

horizontal cross-section pattern is shown in Fig. 5-196B. Because a circular field pattern is created, the field strength is the same in any compass direction.

Theoretically, a vertical dipole in free space has no vertical radiation along its axis. However, it may produce a considerable amount of radiation at other angles measured to the line of the antenna axis. Figure 5-196C shows a vertical cross section of the radiation pattern of Fig. 5-196A. The radiation along OA is zero; but at another angle, represented by angle AOB, there is appreciable radiation. At a greater angle, AOC, the radiation is still greater. Because of this variation in field strength at different vertical angles, a field strength pattern of a vertical half-wave antenna taken in a horizontal plane must specify the vertical angle of radiation for which the pattern applies.

Figure 5-196D shows half of the donut pattern for a horizontal half-wave dipole. The maximum radiation takes place in the plane perpendicular to the axis of the antenna and crosses through its center.

The variation in radiation field intensity about an antenna can be shown graphically by polar diagrams, as in Fig. 5-197. Zero distance is assumed to be at the center of the chart, indicating the center of the antenna, and the circumference of the tangent circles is laid off in angular degrees. Computed or measured values of field strength then may be plotted radially in a manner that shows magnitude and direction for a given distance from the antenna. Field strengths in the

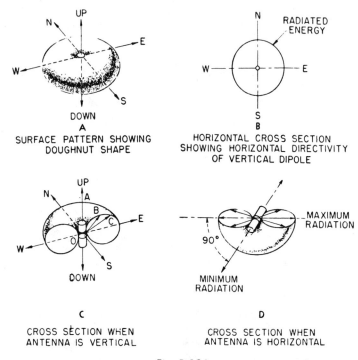

A
SURFACE PATTERN SHOWING
DOUGHNUT SHAPE

B
HORIZONTAL CROSS SECTION
SHOWING HORIZONTAL DIRECTIVITY
OF VERTICAL DIPOLE

C
CROSS SECTION WHEN
ANTENNA IS VERTICAL

D
CROSS SECTION WHEN
ANTENNA IS HORIZONTAL

Fig. 5-196.

vertical plane are plotted on a semicircular polar chart (not shown) and are referred to as *vertical polar diagrams.*

When antennas are close to the ground, vertically polarized waves yield a stronger signal close to the earth than do horizontally polarized waves. If the transmitting antenna is at least a wavelength above the ground, either type of polarization produces the same field intensity near the surface of the earth. With transmitting antennas several wavelengths above the ground, however, horizontally polarized waves produce a stronger signal close to the earth than can be achieved with vertical polarization.

5-149. *Can either of the two general fields that emanate from an antenna (radiation and induction fields) produce an emf in a receiving antenna? If so, how?*

With this question, we must back up a bit and cover some skipped-over theory. First, there are two general fields associated with an antenna, and these should not be confused with the two fields mentioned in answer to the preceding question. The *radiation field* is the general field that supports the two subfields described earlier as the electric and magnetic fields. The *induction field* is considered local to the antenna, even though it is indeed emanated (its intensity drops as the square of the distance from the antenna).

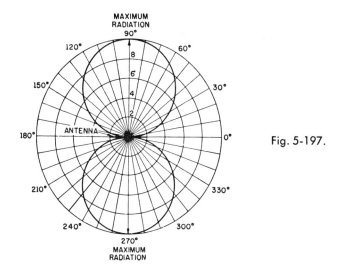

Fig. 5-197.

The propagated radiation field contains the electric and magnetic fields that are responsible for inducing a small voltage on the receiving antenna. The induced voltage "excites" the antenna, which is resonant at the frequency of the incoming radio wave, thus causing formation of a new induction field. Thus, the antenna may be thought of as a tuned circuit and, like any tuned circuit, it has the capability of absorbing energy so long as the energy supplied has the proper frequency.

The mechanism by which the voltage is produced on a receiving antenna may be likened to the manner in which radio waves are propagated from an antenna. The continuously reversing voltage (reversing at the rate represented by the frequency of resonance) causes electric and magnetic fields to build and collapse, thus creating a current in the antenna and associated transmission line.

5-150. *In speaking of radio transmissions, what bearing do the angle of radiation, density of the ionosphere, and frequency of emission have on the length of the skip zone?*

The ionosphere has many interesting characteristics. Some waves penetrate and pass entirely through it into space, never to return. Generally, the ionosphere also acts as a radio prism and refracts (bends) the sky wave back to the earth, as illustrated in Fig. 5-198.

The ability of the ionosphere to return a radio wave to the earth depends upon the angle at which the sky wave strikes the ionosphere, the frequency of the transmission, and ion density. When the wave from an antenna strikes the ionosphere at an angle, the wave begins to bend. If the frequency is "correct," the ionosphere is sufficiently dense, and the angle is "proper," the wave will eventually emerge from the ionosphere and return to the earth. If a receiver is located at either of the points (B) in Fig. 5-198, the transmission from point A will be received. (The antenna height in the figure is not drawn to

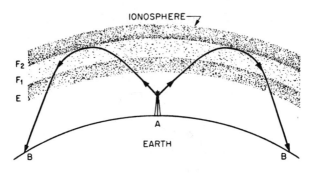

Fig. 5-198.

scale.) The sky wave in Fig. 5-199 is assumed to be composed of rays that emanate from the antenna in three distinct groups, which are identified according to the angle of elevation. The angle at which the rays of group *1* strike the ionosphere is too nearly vertical for the rays to be returned to the earth. The rays are bent out of line, but pass completely through the ionosphere and are lost.

The angle made by the rays of group *2* is called the *critical angle* for that frequency. Any ray that leaves the antenna at an angle greater than this angle will penetrate the ionosphere.

Group *3* rays strike the ionosphere at the smallest angle that will be refracted and still return to the earth. At any smaller angle the rays will be refracted but not return to the earth.

As the frequency increases, the *critical angle* decreases. Low-frequency fields can be projected straight upward and will be returned to the earth. The highest frequency that can be sent directly upward and still be returned to the earth is called the *critical frequency*. At sufficiently high frequencies, regardless of the angle at which the rays strike the ionosphere, the wave will not be returned to the earth. The critical frequency is not constant but varies, from one locality to another, with the time of day, with the season of the year, and with the sunspot cycle (at 11-year intervals).

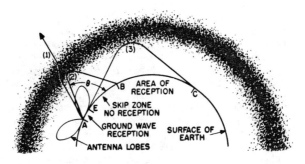

Fig. 5-199.

Because of this variation in the critical frequency, nomograms and frequency tables are issued that predict the *maximum usable frequency* (*muf*) for every hour of the day, for every locality in which transmissions are made.

The *skip zone* is the area in which a refracted signal from any given point can be heard. Generally, **when the angle of radiation is low and refraction occurs, the skip zone is at maximum**, as shown in Fig. 5-200. **By increasing the angle of radiation, the skip zone can be reduced**, assuming there is not excessive absorption of the waves by the ionospheric layers.

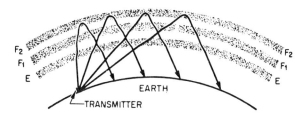

Fig. 5-200.

5-151. *How is it possible for a sky wave to "meet" a ground wave 180 out of phase?*

A sky wave is the portion of a radio signal that is radiated upward and refracted off the ionosphere. The ground wave is the portion of the signal that radiates in a horizontal plane and travels in a more or less line-of-sight manner, following generally the curvature of the earth. Occasionally, a receiver will be able to pick up signals that have traveled both routes. Since the signal that has traveled to the ionosphere and bounced back to earth has covered a considerably greater distance than the ground wave, it will arrive later than the signal that traveled the direct route. The ground wave may be any portion of a cycle out of phase, from a few degrees to nearly 360. When the two signals are out of phase by precisely 180, there is complete cancellation of both signals, or complete *fading*. Signals traveling both routes buck or bolster each other, depending on the phase relationship between them. The closer to 180 apart they are, the more signal cancellation takes place and the weaker the signal. The closer they are to being directly in phase, the stronger the signal (Fig. 5-201).

5-152. *What is the relationship between operating frequency and ground wave coverage?*

As the frequency decreases, ground wave coverage generally increases. Each frequency band has its own special uses. These uses depend on the nature of the waves—surface, sky, or space—and the effect that the sun, earth, ionosphere, and atmosphere have on them. It is difficult to establish fixed rules for the choice of a frequency for a particular purpose. Some general statements can be made, however.

513

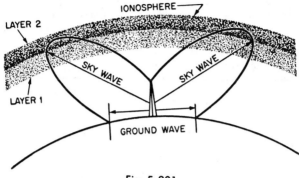

Fig. 5-201.

as to which frequency bands are best suited to the type of transmission to be made. For example, reliable worldwide communications is possible using high power and low frequencies. Some international communications systems and military broadcast stations use this combination of high power and low frequency.

5-153. *Explain the following terms with respect to antennas (transmission or reception):*

- *Field strength*
- *Power beam*
- *Physical length*
- *Electrical length*
- *Polarization*
- *Diversity reception*
- *Corona discharge*

Field Strength. Although the term could be applied to the magnitude of the transmitted energy, it is usually used in the context of reception. If a radiated electromagnetic field passes through a conductor, some of the energy in the field will set electrons in motion in the conductor. The intensity of this energy is referred to as the *field strength*. The electron flow set up constitutes a current that varies in accordance with the variations of the field. Thus, a variation of the current in a radiating antenna causes a similar varying current (of much smaller amplitude, of course) in a conductor at a distant location. Any intelligence being produced as current in a transmitting antenna will be reproduced as current in a receiving antenna. The characteristics of receiving and transmitting antennas are similar, so that a good transmitting antenna is also a good receiving antenna. **Field strength is the effective value of the electric field intentisy, in microvolts per meter, produced at a point by radio waves from a particular transmitting station.**

Power Beam. It is of course impossible for an antenna to radiate more power than a transmitter provides; however, when an antenna is used in such a manner as to concentrate a large portion of its energy into a restricted "beam," the antenna is said to have gain. The *power* *beam* of an antenna is the portion of the radiation pattern in which most of the transmitted energy is concentrated. The power beam of a directional antenna has a *power beamwidth*, expressed in degrees. This beamwidth is determined by measuring the field strength at the center of the beam for reference. The field strength diminishes as the receiving antenna is moved laterally from the center of this beamwidth. The number of circular degrees between half-power points constitutes the antenna's beamwidth.

A dipole's radiation pattern is bidirectional when it is mounted horizontally. An antenna—receiver combination, placed in the vicinity of such an antenna, is used to establish a 0 dB reference point in the center of the dipole's maximum radiation field. The gain of any beam-type antenna is determined by measuring the field strength at the receiver and comparing this strength with the strength of the field radiated from the dipole. If the antenna at the receiver shows an increase of 3 dB when the beam antenna is used for transmitting, the *effective radiated power* (ERP) of the transmitting antenna is said to have doubled. This 3 dB gain, it should be emphasized, only occurs in the transmitting antenna's power beam; the field strength at other points in the antenna's radiation pattern will be diminished by more than the amount required to produce the gain in the power beam.

Physical Length. The physical length of any antenna is the actual measured length of the antenna from end to end. The physical length of a half-wave antenna for a given frequency is derived as follows:

$$\lambda/2 \text{ (ft)} = \frac{300 \times 3.28 \times 0.95}{2f} = \frac{468}{f}$$

where f = frequency in megahertz. The numbers in the first portion of the equation are derived from these commodities:

300 = number of millions of meters per second that radio waves propagate
3.28 = number of feet in one meter
0.95 = velocity factor, or the ratio of wav velocity in antenna to velocity in free space

Electrical Length. The electrical length of an antenna is 5% longer than its physical length, because of differences in wave velocity in different media. The electrical length is the true measure of a portion of any wavelength used to calculate the physical length of an antenna. In other words, **the length of any wave traveling in free space is longer than the same wave traveling along an antenna. Antenna sizes are determined by calculating the electrical length, then deducting 5% to account for the velocity difference.**

If an antenna is constructed of very thin wire, and is isolated in space, its electrical length would correspond closely with its physical length. In practice, however, an antenna is never isolated completely from surrounding objects. For example, the antenna will be supported by insulators with a dielectric constant greater than 1.0. The dielectric constant of air is arbitrarily assigned a numerical value equal to 1. Therefore, the velocity of a wave along a conductor is always slightly less than the velocity of the same wave in free space, and the physical length of the antenna is less than the corresponding wavelength in space.

Polarization. Electromagnetic fields in space are said to be *polarized*, and the direction of the electric field is considered the direction of polarization. As the electric field is parallel to the axis of a half-wave dipole, the antenna is in the plane polarization. When the dipole is horizontally oriented, the radiated wave is horizontally polarized; when the dipole is mounted vertically, the radiated wave is vertically polarized. For maximum absorption of radiated energy, the receiving antenna must be polarized in the same plane as the transmitting antenna. *Cross polarization*—when the transmitting and receiving antennas are not polarized alike—causes the signal strength at the receiver to be at its minimum. The polarization of a wave tends to shift gradually as the distance between transmitting and receiving antennas increases. Occasionally, particularly when ionospheric refraction of a wave occurs, a wave that was propagated from a vertically polarized antenna will arrive at the receiving antenna with horizontal polarization.

Diversity Reception. One method that is sometimes used to help reduce the effects of fading in radio reception is to place two or more receiving antennas a wavelength or two apart, each antenna feeding its own receiver. The audio output of the various receivers are paralleled together. This process is known as *diversity reception*. The greater the number of antennas and receivers, the smaller the effects of fading become.

Corona Discharge. When a great deal of power is applied to an antenna, a considerably high voltage can be developed at the tips of the antenna. Sometimes, when ambient moisture builds up (fog, mist, etc.) in the vicinity of the antenna, arcing will occur between the moist air around the antenna tips and the antenna element itself. This arcing is referred to as *corona discharge*. Corona discharge occurs more frequently on antennas whose driven elements are pointed. Capacity hats, balled ends, and other blunting devices may be used to reduce corona discharges, which cause static and diminished signal strength at the receiver.

5-154.   *What would constitute the ground plane if a quarter-wave grounded whip antenna, one meter in length, were mounted on a metal roof of an automobile? Mounted near the rear bumper of an automobile?*

With the antenna centrally located atop the automobile, the ground plane would be the body of the car. At the frequency at which one meter is one-quarter wavelength, the car body ground would be fairly effective and the radiated signal would be omnidirectional in character. However, if the antenna were to be moved to the bumper, performance would change considerably. The car body would still serve as a ground plane, but it would only be effective for signals radiated in the direction represented by the mass of the car body; the antenna would be directional toward the front of the car. The ground itself (the pavement) would serve as a pseudo ground plane, but it is separated by some distance from the antenna feed point and does not have the conductivity of the car body. Thus, while the antenna would maintain its resonance, it would not perform as well over areas where the pavement was required to serve as the ground plane.

5-155. *Explain why a loading coil is sometimes associated with an antenna. Under this condition, would absence of the coil mean a capacitive antenna impedance?*

A loading coil is often used with simple antennas—usually mobile types—to increase the electrical length of the radiating element. Because of physical constraints associated with mobile and portable antennas, it is not practical to make the radiating element an appreciable fraction of a wavelength in physical size. A Marconi antenna for 27 MHz, for example, would require a radiator more than 8 ft in length. A loading coil in series with a much shorter radiator can be used to make an effective quarter-wave radiating element.

There is always a tradeoff to consider when using a loading coil with a radiator. The shorter the radiator used with a loading coil, the lower the efficiency of the antenna, for both receiving and transmitting. In theory, of course, a loading coil of the proper number of turns could be used in lieu of any radiator at all, because the antenna is, after all, the equivalent of a resonant circuit. However, while a tank circuit might easily load into a radiatorless coil, there would be no means by which the rf signals could propagate into the air, and there would be no effective capture area for signals to be received with such an arrangement.

To answer the second part of the question, absence of the coil in an otherwise resonant antenna would mean an antenna that is too short. If an antenna is shorter than the required length, the source end of the antenna will appear capacitive.

If an antenna is of the desired length—that is, if the electrical length approximately equals the physical length—the antenna will act as a resonant circuit, and will present to the source an impedance that will be a pure resistance. If the antenna is not of the proper length, the source will see an opposition other than the pure resistance offered under perfect conditions. The source may see an impedance that will look like a capacitive circuit or an inductive circuit, depending on whether the antenna is shorter or longer than the specified wavelength portion the antenna represents. **A Hertz antenna slightly longer than** $\lambda/2$ will act like an inductive circuit, and an antenna slightly shorter than $\lambda/2$ will appear to the source as a capacitive circuit. Any 2-wire open line longer than $\lambda/4$ appears electrically as a quarter-wave section with an additional section of open-circuited transmission line attached to it. The open section, which is capacitive in itself, will have its characteristics inverted and will appear to the source as an inductive circuit. Compensation for the additional length can be made by cutting the antenna down to proper length or by tuning out the inductive reactance (adding a capacitance in series). This added capacitive reactance will completely cancel the inductive reactance, and the source will then see a pure resistance, provided the proper size of capacitor is used.

If an antenna is shorter than the required length, the source end of the line will appear capacitive. The reason for this is the phase relationship between the current and the voltage at this shortened open-end line. The current leads the voltage by nearly 90° (a condition caused only by capacitance). Because of the reflection from the open end, the generator sees a capacitive load. This condition may be corrected by adding inductance in series with the antenna. Schematic representations of antennas having proper length, longer than normal length, and shorter than normal length are shown in Fig. 5-202.

5-156. *Will the velocity of signal propagation differ in different materials? What effect, if any, would this have on wavelength or frequency?*

The **velocity of propagation differs according to the medium** of propagation. Effectively, the result is a change in the electrical length of a wave. Consider conventional RG-8/U coaxial cable, for example—a standard transmission line used on many VHF transmitters and receivers. The *velocity factor* of this cable is approximately 66%; thus, the physical wavelength of a section of this cable is but 66% of the electrical length of an equivalent piece of bare wire hanging in free space or 66% the length of the transmitted wave in free space. In free space a radio wave propagates at the speed of light, or 300 million meters per second. In air the velocity is very slightly less. In transmission lines the velocity of propagation can be significantly less, and it must be taken into account when calculating physical lengths of rf-carrying conductors. For most half-wave antennas the velocity factor is 95%, which makes the physical length of such an antenna less than half the length of an actual wave in space.

5-157. *Discuss series and shunt feeding of quarter-wave antennas with respect to impedance matching.*

A shunt-fed quarter-wave antenna is often referred to as a *Marconi*, while a series-fed antenna might be referred to as an *ungrounded whip*, or simply a *vertical*. The shunt-fed antenna, typically used on frequencies below 2 MHz, is a vertical quarter-wave radiator whose lower end is grounded directly to the earth. The feed impedance is 36Ω (or slightly greater)—one-half the input impedance of a half-wave antenna. The effective current in the shunt-fed quarter-wave antenna is greatest at the base and minimum at the top, while the effective voltage is minimum at the base and maximum at the top. Normally the shunt-fed antenna has a small stud partway up the antenna, where the transmission line is connected. The reactance of the antenna may be tuned out with a series capacitor or inductor—this does not change the antenna configuration.

The series-fed quarter-wave vertical antenna for the same frequency as the case above consists of a vertical radiator insulated from the ground surface. Since the base is insulated from ground, this antenna may be fed right at the base. One form of the series-fed vertical consists of a quarter-wave radiator and a *counterpoise* connected to the radiator but insulated from the ground surface. The size of the counterpoise should be at least equal to, and preferably larger than, the size of the antenna.

The counterpoise and the surface of the ground form a large capacitor. Because of this capacitance, antenna current is collected in the form of charge and discharge currents. The end of the antenna

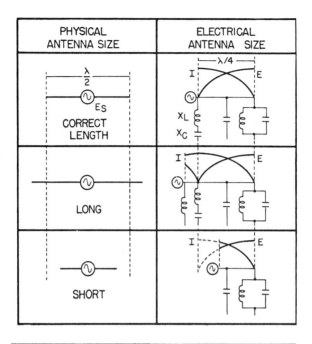

Fig. 5-202.

normally connected to ground is connected through the large capacitance formed by the counterpoise. If the counterpoise is not well insulated from ground. the effect is much the same as that of a leaky capacitor. with a resultant loss greater than if no counterpoise were used.

Although the shape and size of the counterpoise are not particularly critical. it should extend for equal distances in all directions. Contact between counterpoise and antenna is usually made from 8 to 12 ft above ground. When the antenna is mounted vertically. the counterpoise may have any simple geometric pattern. such as a group of spoke-like radials extending from the antenna feed point.

5-158. *Discuss the directivity and physical characteristics of the following types of antennas:*

- *Vee beam*
- *Corner reflector*
- *Parasitic array*
- *Stacked array*
- *Loop*

Vee-Beam. A vee beam (V-beam) is a long-wire antenna named by its configuration. It looks like a dipole whose central feed point has been pulled so that the legs assume the shape of a V. Usually. each leg is at least one wavelength from the feed point to the end: however. the V-beam antenna may be any number of wavelengths long. There are many different ways to orient the V-antenna: and it may be terminated for unidirectional radiation. or it may be unterminated for bidirectional use. A terminated V-beam is an antenna whose two end points are connected to ground through a resistor of 500Ω or 600Ω. An unterminated V-antenna's leg ends are isolated from ground. The gain and horizontal radiation angle are functions of the angle of the two legs. In the unterminated version the direction of radiation lies along a plane that intersects the apex of the antenna. and the gain is essentially the same in both directions along this plane. The terminated version performs best in one direction—the plane that is the vector of the two legs.

One version of the V-beam is the *tilted wire* type shown in Fig. 5-203. In this antenna the maximum field intensity is radiated in the

Fig. 5-203.

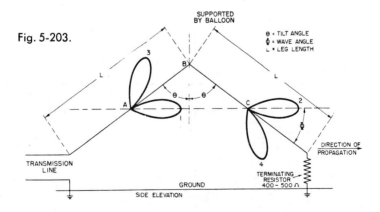

direction of the terminating resistor. In order that lobes *1* and *2* may properly comine in the desired direction of propagation, the distance *AC* is about λ/2 less than distance *ABC*. This arrangement causes the fields radiated at lobes *1* and *2* to be additive in the direction of propagation. The fields radiated at lobes *3* and *4* cancel. For efficient transmission, the tilt angle (*θ*) is equal to 90° minus the wave angle (*φ*).

Corner Reflector. In the corner reflector (Fig. 5-204) the driven element is usually a dipole placed at the center of the corner angle but at some distance from the vertex. The response pattern of this array not only depends on the corner angle but on the distance between the dipole and the reflector corner. If the dipole is located too far from the vertex, the response pattern will have several lobes. If it is brought in too close, the vertical response will be broadened, and the array will become more susceptible to ground-reflected signals.

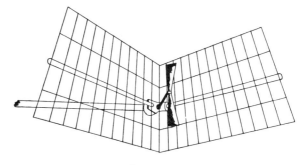

Fig. 5-204.

Parasitic Array. A parasitic array consists of a more or less conventional **dipole and a number of additional passive dipoles spaced at uncritical intervals along a boom** that bisects the plane of the driven element (dipole). The yagi antenna pictured in Fig. 5-205 shows the configuration of a fairly common form of this array. (The term *parasitic* is derived from the fact that only one element of the antenna is actually driven; the other elements are completely passive in nature and serve only to reinforce the signals emanating from or arriving at the antenna.)

The dipole labeled *radiator* in the drawing is the driven element. The *reflector* is a solid length of aluminum rod (usually) that is slightly longer than the driven element and placed approximately λ/4 behind it. Because of its length, the reflector reflects the largest percentage of the radiation striking it. The elements situated on the other side of the driven element are called *directors*. They are shorter than the driven element and serve to reinforce signals approaching from the driven element, adding to the net gain of the antenna itself.

Parasitic arrays are highly directional, depending on the number of elements, the spacing between elements, and the lengths of the directors. When the directors are all cut to the same size (slightly smaller than the driven element), the antenna has a very narrow

521

bandwidth; however, when each director is progressively smaller than the one nearer the radiator, the bandwidth is increased substantially (at the sacrifice of overall gain, of course).

Stacked Array. An array consists of at least two elements: a radiator and a reflector. If three elements are use, the third element becomes the director and is positioned on a boom as shown in Fig. 5-205. Interestingly, any two such arrays can be *stacked* to increase the net power gain of a single such array by 3 dB. In practice, the two antennas must be fed and spaced in such a manner that the output signals will be in phase with each other; otherwise, signal reinforcement will not take place and cancellation can occur.

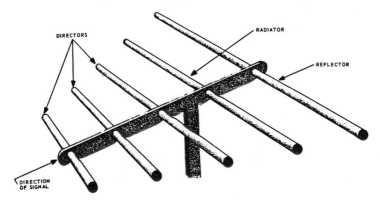

Fig. 2-205.

The simplest stacked array is shown in Fig. 5-206. This antenna consists of two dipoles stacked and properly phased. This arrangement is referred to as a *lazy H* because of the deployed antenna's resemblance to the letter *H*. The center terminals of each dipole are connected with a parallel wire, as shown. Each conductor of the transmission line is attached to this parallel wire at a point midway between the two dipoles to enhance the directivity, and directors may be added to achieve even greater directivity and gain.

Two identical stacked arrays may be connected together (stacked) and phased so that the overall gain of a single array is

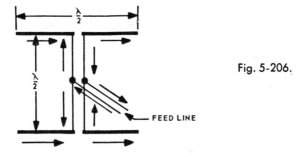

Fig. 5-206.

increased by 3 dB. Neglecting losses, each time the effective area of an antenna or array is doubled (by addition of another identical array), the power gain is increased by 3 dB.

Loop. A horizontally polarized loop antenna is virtually nondirectional. (The word *virtually* is used because there is a null in the pattern at the point where the loop is fed: otherwise the radiation pattern resembles the loop itself.) The pattern is that of the half-wave vertical antenna, the chief difference being that the E lines of force are horizontal rather than vertical.

The *vertical* loop exhibits a different pattern, resembling that of a horizontal half-wave antenna, as shown in Fig. 5-207. Looking straight down at a vertically mounted loop antenna, you would see a straight

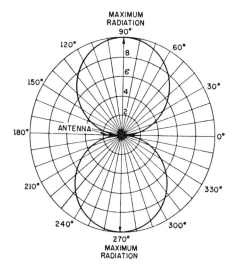

Fig. 5-207.

line along the plane of the antenna. This is represented by the horizontal line extending from 180° to 0° in the drawing. As shown, the antenna in this axis is essentially bidirectional, with a figure-8 pattern. There is a radiation null along both ends of the plane of the antenna, and major lobes perpendicular to this plane.

The radiation pattern is only shown in two dimensions. Actually, the figure-8 pattern can be thought of as a cross section of a donut-shaped field. Thus, the loop's angle of radiation is equal throughout its lobe area.

5-159. *Draw a sketch of a coaxial whip antenna; identify the positions and discuss the purpose of the following components: whip, insulator, skirt, trap, support mast, coaxial line, and input connector.*

The antenna is pictured in Fig. 5-208. The functions of each of the integral portions of the antenna are described in the drawing.

523

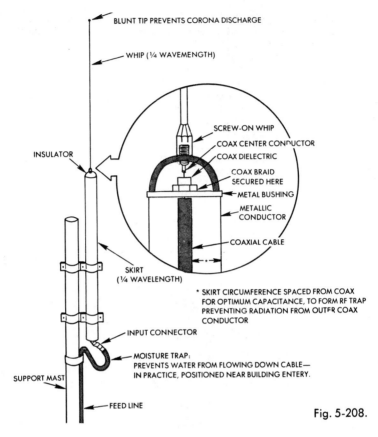

BLUNT TIP PREVENTS CORONA DISCHARGE

WHIP (¼ WAVEMENGTH)

SCREW-ON WHIP

COAX CENTER CONDUCTOR

COAX DIELECTRIC

COAX BRAID SECURED HERE

METAL BUSHING

METALLIC CONDUCTOR

INSULATOR

COAXIAL CABLE

SKIRT (¼ WAVELENGTH)

* SKIRT CIRCUMFERENCE SPACED FROM COAX FOR OPTIMUM CAPACITANCE, TO FORM RF TRAP PREVENTING RADIATION FROM OUTFR COAX CONDUCTOR

INPUT CONNECTOR

MOISTURE TRAP: PREVENTS WATER FROM FLOWING DOWN CABLE— IN PRACTICE, POSITIONED NEAR BUILDING ENTERY.

SUPPORT MAST

FEED LINE

Fig. 5-208.

5-159. *Why are insulators sometimes placed in antenna guy wires?*

Antenna guy wires have a way of being of just the right length to radiate a portion of the antenna's signal. When this occurs, antenna loading may be critical or unstable. Also, when the guy wires form a resonant length at a multiple of the transmitter frequency, harmonic radiation can be a serious problem for considerable distances from the transmitting site. To prevent these problems, antenna erectors break up the wires into uneven sections tied together with glass or ceramic insulators.

TRANSMISSION LINES

5-161. *What is meant by "characteristic impedance," or "surge impedance," of a transmission line? To what physical characteristics is it proportional?*

A transmission line typically consists of two parallel conductors spaced a specific distance from each other. The two leads carry current, of course, and so possess the property of *inductance*. And since the two wires are spaced conductors. they also possess the property of *capacitance*. Since the material of which each conductor is made has a specific conductivity. a transmission line possesses the property of resistance. The values of these properties determine the characteristic impedance.

A transmission line of infinite length would be considered as composed of an infinite number of capacitors and inductors. If a voltage were applied to the input terminals of the line. current would begin to flow: it would continue to flow as long as the capacitors and inductors were able to absorb electrical energy. Since there would be an infinite number of line sections. each having the properties depicted in the equivalent circuit of Fig. 5-209. the current would flow indefinitely. And if the infinite line were uniform. the impedance of any section of the line would be the same as the impedance offered to the circuit by any other portion of the line of the same unit length. Thus. the current would be of some finite value. If the current in the theoretical line and the voltage applied to it were known. the impedance of the line could be determined by application of Ohm's law. This value is referred to as the *characteristic. or surge. impedance* (Z_0).

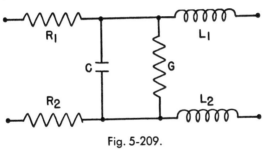

Fig. 5-209.

In practice. the impedance of a 2-wire line is proportional to the spacing between the wires. Actually. it is a function of the diameter of the wires. the dielectric material separating the two wires. and the conductivity of the wires. However. it is usually fairly easy to estimate characteristic impedance by simply observing the line. The greater the separation between conductors. the higher the impedance. As the diameter increases. the spacing must be increased proportionately to maintain the same impedance value.

Thus. the effect of increasing the spacing of the two wires is to increase the characteristic impedance. because the $L:C$ ratio is increased. Similarly. a reduction in the diameter of the wires also increases the characteristic impedance. The reduction in the size of the wire affects the capacitance more than the inductance. for the effect is equivalent to decreasing the size of the plates of a capacitor in order to decrease the capacitance. Any change in the dielectric material between the two wires also changes the characteristic impedance. If a change in the dielectric increases the capacitance between the wires. the characteristic impedance is reduced. The characteristic impedance of a 2-wire line with air as the dielectric may be obtained from the formula

$$Z_0 = 276 \log \frac{2D}{d}$$

where D is the spacing between the wires (center to center), and d is the diameter of one of the conductors.

The characteristic impedance of a concentric (coaxial) line with an air dielectric also varies with L and C. However, because the difference in construction of the two lines causes L and C to vary in a slightly different manner, the following formula must be used to determine the characteristic impedance of the coaxial line

$$Z_0 = 138 \log \frac{D}{d}$$

where D is the inner diameter of the outer conductor, and d is the outer diameter of the inner conductor.

5-162. *Why is the impedance of a transmission line an important factor with respect to matching of a transmitter to an antenna?*

When the transmission line's chracteristic impedance is the same as the terminating impedance of the transmitter as well as the input impedance of the antenna, the transmitter is effectively loading a transmission line of infinite length. That is, the antenna load appears purely resistive, and there is no reflection of part of the transmitter's output signal back down the line. When the impedances of these three elements (transmitter output tank, transmission line, and antenna input circuit) all are the same, the antenna system may be said to have a standing-wave ratio of 1:1; that is, for every wave put into the antenna, a wave is radiated into space without any portion being reflected back into the feed line. This is an idea that is never quite realized in practice, because of radiation resistance and losses in the system.

5-163. *What is meant by "standing waves"? Explain "standing-wave ratio." How can standing waves be minimized?*

Standing waves are difficult to explain because they involve a concept that cannot be observed. The theory can be simplified, however, by applying a fairly simple analogy. Suppose, for example, that radio waves *were* visible under certain conditions of illumination, and had the appearance of a sine wave superimposed on a full-wave antenna. Suppose also that we could strobe our "special illumination source" at a rate that matched the frequency of the signal being generated. Then, when the strobe "light" were aimed at our antenna, we would have the ability of seeing waves as they propagated from the antenna. Ideally, under this condition, the antenna being fed a continuous signal would appear to have full sine wave superimposed on it that did not move. Such a situation would be equivalent to having a standing-wave ratio of 1:1, which means that a wave is propagated into space for every wave that is fed into the antenna.

If, under this condition of hypothetical observation, the wave did not stand still, a less than ideal situation would be indicated. If the antenna were a shade too long. for exmple, or if there were a mismatch between the antenna and the transmission line, the wave would not be fully developed across the breadth of the antenna before a new wave tries to enter the antenna. As a consequence, part of the signal (lower in amplitude than the applied signal) would be reflected back toward the transmitter. In a mismatch situation the reflected signal travels back down the line at the same time other waves are antenna-bound. At the generator end (transmitter), another reflection takes place; part of the reduced-amplitude signal is dissipated across the final tank circuit or the antenna-matching network, while a smaller portion of the reflection is re-reflected back up the line but out of step (phase) with the original signal. The process is repeated with each wave applied to the transmission line, and the reflected components serve to cancel and interfere with the originally applied signal. At peak efficiency there is no reflected signal, and a wave is radiated into space at precisely the same time a new wave is developed across the antenna.

All the wave diagrams in Fig. 5-210 show the relationship that exists between the *incident* (applied) and the *reflected* wave in a transmission line that is terminated in an open circuit (the termination is not resistive at the line's characteristic impedance, but rather it is as a transmission line that has been disconnected from the antenna). The dark line shown superimposed on the waveform represents the standing waves. Standing waves are the instantaneous sum of both the incident and reflected waves. In the open transmission line the relationship between the incident and reflected wave is such that they are equal in amplitude and phase at the receiving end. The phase relationships in the figure may appear confusing, but it must be remembered that the incident wave is moving to the right while the reflected wave is moving to the left. In each of the diagrams shown, the instantaneous sum (standing waves) is plotted using the heavy dark line. In diagrams 2 and 6 the waveforms coincide, and at that point in time, the voltage is zero. If the diagrams are examined further, it is found that at a point one-quarter of the distance from the end and at a point three-quarters of the distance from the same end the voltage is zero at all times. Because of the zero stationary point, the waves are appropriately called "standing waves."

If an ac meter were used and current measurements were taken on the line, the current readings would only be of magnitude and not of polarity. If the values thus found were plotted on a graph, the current curve would appear as the positive-going waves illustrated in Fig. 5-211. This is the conventional picture of standing waves.

At the end of a transmission line terminated in an *open*, the current is zero and the voltage is maximum at the terminating end. This relationship may be stated in terms of phase. The voltage and current at the ends of an open-ended transmission line are 90° out of phase. At the end of a transmission line termianted in a *short*, the current is maximum and the voltage is zero. The voltage and current are again 90° out of phase. These current—voltage relationships are shown in the diagrams of Fig. 5-212. These phase relationships are important because they indicate how the line will act at different

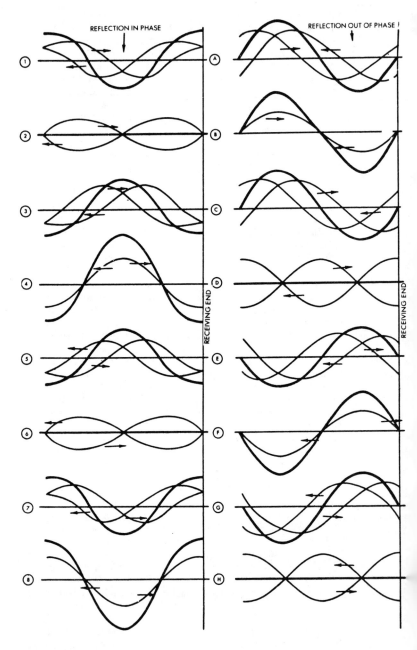

Fig. 5-210.

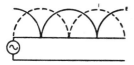

Fig. 5-211.

points along its length. A transmission line will have points of maximum and minimum voltage as well as points of minimum and maximum current. The position of these points can be accurately predicted if the applied freauerc· and type of line termination are known.

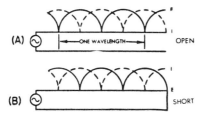

(A) ◀—ONE WAVELENGTH—▶ OPEN

(B) SHORT

Fig. 5-212.

5-164. *If standing waves are desirable on a transmitting antenna, why are they undesirable on a transmission line?*

A **standing wave** existing on an antenna is an indication that a wave is being radiated into space. **Standing waves on a transmission line represent barriers to signals** being applied to the antenna.

5-165. *What is meant by "stub-tuning"?*

When the transmission line does not match the input impedance of the antenna, a transformer may sometimes be used to change the effective impedance of the line to the extent required for a proper match. Since a quarter-wave section of transmission line is a 2:1 transformer, such sections are frequently used for this purpose. These small sections are called *stubs*, and when they are used at the termination point of a transmission line to match the termination impedance with the impedance of the line, the antenna is said to be stub tuned.

Because a transmission line has an impedance that varies over its entire length, regardless of the type of termination used, it is well suited for use as an impedance-matching device. The impedance of a quarter-wave section of transmission line shorted at one end varies widely over its length, as indicated by the diagrams of Fig. 5-213. At the shorted end the current is high and the voltage low; and the impedance of the shorted end is low. At the open end the conditions are reversed, and the impedance is high.

A 300Ω line may be matched to a 70Ω line without the creation of standing waves on either of the two lines to be matched, for example. Figure 5-213B shows how the connections for this case would be made. Energy from the 300Ω line sets up standing waves on the quarter-wave line. The connection made between the 300Ω line and the stub is made at a point where the impedance of the quarter-wave section (stub) is 300Ω. The 70Ω line is similarly adjusted to bring about an impedance match at the shorted end.

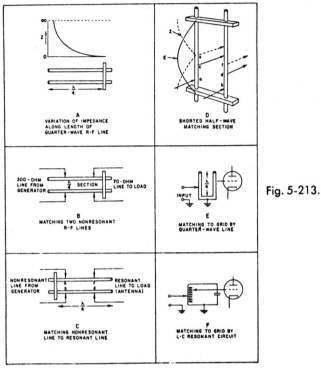

Fig. 5-213.

5-166. *What would be the considerations in choosing a solid-dielectric cable over a hollow, pressurized cable for use as a transmission line?*

In general, a hollow shell that is pressurized (with nitrogen) will be the better transmission line, because such a line will exhibit less loss per unit length and will be capable of handling greater power levels for any given conductor size. However, transmission lines of this type are considerably more susceptible to deterioration because of their vulnerability to external damage from bending, crushing, etc. The principal considerations in choosing between the two types of line should be: Will the transmission line be required to move after being installed? Will bends be required in the line between the antenna and the feed point (generator)? Will the transmission line be installed in an easily accessible place? (Pressurized line requires occasional checks to make sure the pressure has not dropped below the required value.)

In general, **solid dielectric cable should be used** in favor of pressurized cable **when the losses are not a significant factor, when the frequency is not appreciably high, when the transmission line is to be subjected to flexing** and, possibly, sharp bends, and when the line is to be mounted in a place where occasional inspection is not possible.

A very good solid-dielectric cable (such as aluminum-sheathed 50Ω Spir-O-Foam, which has an inert foam-type dielectric) performs quite well and exhibits a low loss. It requires some "plumbing" connections, but not to the same extent as the pressurized-line equivalent, which must be equipped with pressure gages that have to be monitored periodically. This type of solid-dielectric transmission line is a compromise between the flexible braided coaxial cable and the pressurized "pipeline" type of coax.

Losses in coaxial lines increase as the frequency goes up. Since losses are also a function of wavelength (the greater the number of wavelengths between the generator and the antenna, the higher the losses), the total tolerable losses must be considered when installing such a transmission line. Where losses are tolerable—both in receiving and transmitting—and the transmission line run is not excessive, a solid dielectric cable is usually preferable in terms of convenience of installation, cost, and freedom from care or upkeep. This is despite the fact that the relatively high-cost pressurized line does indeed perform considerably better than solid-dielectric cable when it is *properly* pressurized, periodically maintained, and installed with such care that bends and flexing are avoided.

FREQUENCY MEASUREMENTS

5-167. *Draw a simplified circit diagram of a grid-dip meter. Explain its operation and some possible applications.*

The *grid dipper* is now obsolete, having been replaced by transistor and FET dippers. Still, the question does appear in the exams, and it behooves the applicant to know the circuit and its applications.

With dip meters, it is possible to **determine the resonant frequency of an antenna system, to detect harmonics, and to check relative field strengths** (for example, in rotating an antenna for maximum signal strength). The meter may also be used as an **absorption frequency meter** when the oscillator of the dipper is not energized.

Basically, the grid-dip meter is a **calibrated oscillator which meters the grid current in the oscillator circuit**. With the oscillator functioning, energy is coupled from the tuned circuit to the circuit under test. The circuit under test is supplied a small amount of energy via a tank coil of the meter. Except for the field of the tank coil, the circuit under test is deenergized. Capacitors are adjusted to the point where the oscillator tank frequency is equal to the resonant frequency of the circuit under test. At resonance the grid current decreases, as indicated by the dip in the grid meter. The energy absorbed from the tank coil by the circuit under test decreases the ac component of plate voltage, thus causing a decrease in feedback energy from the plate to the oscillator grid. The grid voltage is driven less positive and the grid current decreases.

A simplified circuit of the grid-dip meter is shown in Fig. 5-214. Here, a Colpitts oscillator is used. A Colpitts oscillator uses two capacitors, C1 and C2, connected in series across the tank coil (L1), with the junction of the capacitors connected to the grounded end of the cathode resistor. Two coupling capacitors connect the tuned circuit to the plate and grid.

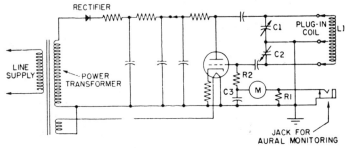

Fig. 5-214.

The meter is in series with the grid-leak resistors—the resistors being selected to produce a time constant with the grid capacitor $(C3)$. The grid capacitor becomes charged to a degree that cuts off oscillations until its charge leaks away through the meter and grid-leak resistor $(R1)$. Oscillations are restored for a period that depends on the time constant of $R2$ and $C3$. The net result is that the rf oscillations are modulated with an audio signal whose frequency is determined by the time constant. A jack is usually provided across resistor $R1$ for listening with a headphone to the audio signal, which changes in intensity. Some operators can detect small aural changes more readily than the amount of dip registered on the meter.

5-168. *Draw a simplified circuit diagram of an absorption wavemeter (with galvanometer indicator); explain its operation and some possible applications.*

Figure 5-215 shows an absorption wavemeter using a galvanometer to register changes in circuit current. When the wavemeter circuit is tuned to the same frequency as the unknown frequency of the device under test, a maximum circulatory current flows in the wavemeter

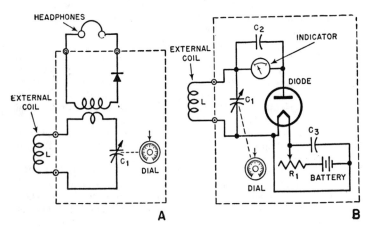

Fig. 5-215.

circuit. Since this circulatory current occurs at resonance and current is maximum in this condition. voltage drops appear across L, $C1$, and $C2$; the voltage drop across $C2$ causes the galvanometer to deflect. (The galvanometer may be replaced with an ordinary small lamp. which can be made to glow under maximum-current conditions.) As $C1$ is tuned to either side of resonance, the circulatory current becomes less and the meter indication diminishes (lamp grows dimmer).

In Fig. 5-216 the circulatory current is plotted against the wavemeter frequency for various degrees of coupling (between the resonant circuit of the device under test and the tank coil of the wavemeter). For accurate frequency measurements the external coil of the wavemeter is loosely coupled to the device under test. This accuracy is indicated by the sharpness of curve C at resonance. Although overcoupling. as shown in curve A. produces a greater circulatory current and meter deflection (or lamp brilliance). it results in inaccurate frequency measurements. Overcoupling results in a double-humped curve. wherein a maximum circulatory current is obtained on either side of resonance.

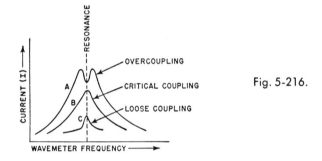

Fig. 5-216.

Wavemeters typically contain several external coils of the plug-in variety. Each coil represents a specific frequency range. and if the approximate frequency to be measured is known. the selection of the proper coil is simplified. Where the approximate frequency is unknown. each coil must be tried separately to obtain resonant indications. The tuning capacitor is of the air dielectric type. and the frequency range it covers determines the number of plug-in coils that are needed. A frequency standard. from which a fixed known-frequency signal can be obtained. is used to calibrate better wavemeters.

5-169. *Draw a block diagram of a secondary frequency standard. showing only those stages that would illustrate the principle of operation. Explain the functions of each stage.*

The counter-type frequency meter is a high-speed electronic counter with an accurate. crystal-controlled time base. This combination provides a frequency meter that automatically counts and displays the number of events or cycles occurring in a precise time interval. A simplified block diagram of a representative secondary standard is shown in Fig. 5-217.

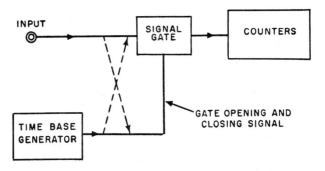

Fig. 5-217.

In addition to making direct frequency measurements, the counter can measure periods (dc to 100 kHz, for most basic instruments, and considerably higher with the addition of a *prescaler*), frequency ratios, and total events. A self-check feature enables an operator to verify instrument operation for most types of measurements. The internal oscillator is stable within a few parts in 100 million, generally. Thus, these counters make good secondary frequency standards.

For frequency measurements the signal is fed through a signal *gate* to a series of digital counters. A precision time interval obtained from the time-base section opens and closes the signal gate for an extremely accurate period of time (for example, one second). The counters count the number of cycles entering through the gate during the one-second interval and display the total. The answer is read directly as the number of kilohertz (or hertz, or megahertz) occurring during the period. The period of time the signal gate remains open is set by the frequency UNIT switch. For each position of this switch, the illuminated decimal point is automatically positioned so that the answer is always read directly. The answer is automatically displayed for a period of time determined by gate time or the setting of the DISPLAY TIME control on the front panel, whichever is greater.

To measure a period or time interval, the application of the two signals reverses, as shown by the dotted lines in Fig. 5-217. The period or time interval to be measured is connected to "open" and "close" the signal gate while one of the standard frequencies from the time base is passed through the signal gate to the counters. When measuring a period, one cycle of the incoming signal opens the gate, and the next cycle closes it. The number of cycles of the standard frequency from the time base that occurred during the period are then indicated on the counters. The standard frequencies obtained from the time base are selected so that the answer to the measured period will always be displayed directly in units of time (seconds, milliseconds, nanoseconds, or microseconds).

Provision is also made in the circuit to permit measurement of the average of 10 periods of the unknown frequency. Higher accuracy can thus be obtained than with single-period measurements.

The accuracy of frequency measurements is determined by an internal oscillator and by a possible error of plus or minus one digit—the least significant of the entire readout. (The least significant digit is at the extreme right of a displayed number.)

5-170. *Draw a block diagram of a heterodyne frequency meter. including the following stages: crystal oscillator. harmonic amplifier. variable-frequency oscillator. mixer. detector and af amplifier. and modulator. Show rf input as well as rf. af. and calibration outputs. Assume a bandswitching arrangement and a dial having arbitrary units and employing a vernier scale.*

- *Describe the operation of the meter.*
- *Describe. step by step. how the crystal could be checked against WWV using a suitable receiver.*
- *Under what conditions would the af modulator be used?*
- *Describe. step by step. how the unknown frequency of a transmitter could be determined by use of headphones and a suitable receiver.*
- *What would be meant by "calibration checkpoints"? When should they be used?*
- *If. in measuring a frequency. the tuning dial should show an indication between two dial frequency relationships in the calibration book. how could the frequency value be determined?*
- *How could this meter be used as an rf generator?*
- *Under what conditions would it be necessary to recalibrate the crystal oscillator?*

    1. **Operation**. The basic heterodyne frequency meter consists of a frequency-calibrated oscillator. which beats (heterodynes) against the frequency to be measured. As shown in Fig. 5-218. the input signal

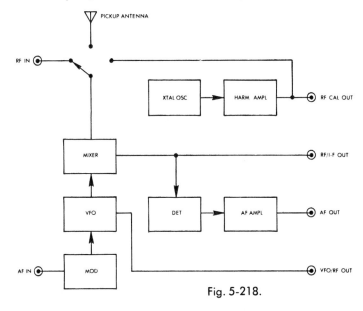

Fig. 5-218.

can be obtained through an integral receptacle or from a pickup antenna. The pickup antenna is coupled loosely to the device under test. The calibrated oscillator then is tuned so that the difference in frequency between the oscillator and the unknown frequency is in the audio range. This difference in frequency is known as the *difference*, or *beat frequency*; and when it is detected and amplified, it can be heard in the headphones (AF OUT in Fig. 5-218).

If the dial setting of the calibrated oscillator is tuned to the same frequency as the device under test, the difference frequency is zero, or at *zero beat*, and no audible sound is heard in the phones. When zero beat is obtained, the position of the pointer on the dial setting represents the unknown frequency.

Figure 5-219 shows a curve of the beat frequency plotted against the audible range of frequencies. When the difference frequency between the two signals is above the audible range, no sound is heard; the shaded area on the graph indicates the frequencies above audibility. As the two frequencies are brought closer to each other (*A* on the curve), a high-pitched note is heard in the headphones. This

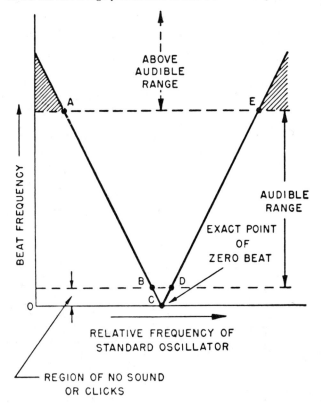

Fig. 5-219.

536

tone gradually decreases in frequency to a point (C) where it is replaced with a series of rapid clicks; the difference frequency is then only a few hertz. At C the clicks have stopped completely and the two original frequencies are equal to one another; this is the exact point of zero beat. Clicks are heard at rather infrequent intervals at point C. since it is difficult to maintain a condition of absolute silence in the phones over a prolonged interval of time because of a certain amount of circuit instability (which is unavoidable).

As the standard-oscillator frequency is varied beyond the zero-beat point. the number of clicks increases up to point D. A low-pitched tone is heard again at this point. and varying the frequency in the same direction causes a gradual increase in frequency until point E is reached. where the beat note is again inaudible.

Calibration Against WWV. The simplest method for checking the frequency meter's accuracy. when a high-frequency receiver is available. consists of coupling the oscillator to the receiver while monitoring the frequency of the appropriate WWV broadcast. The receiver is tuned precisely to WWV; then the crystal oscillator of the frequency meter is coupled to the receiver loosely via the RF CAL OUT jack on the meter. The crystal oscillator of the meter may be adjusted by means of a small internal trimmer capacitor in the crystal oscillator circuit. An on-frequency condition is obtained when the crystal oscillator is tuned so that a zero beat is produced in the receiver being used to accept the WWV signal and the signal from the heterodyne frequency meter.

AF Modulator. Where precision is required. listening for a zero beat is not sufficient. The human ear can only detect sounds greater than about 30 or 40 Hz; similarly. may reproducers are not capable of producing an audible signal at frequencies much below this range. The audio frequency modulator serves to extend the lower limit of hearing. in a sense. While the ear itself cannot detect a signal of 20 Hz or so. the effect of the 20 or 30 Hz difference is audible when an audio modulating signal is also present. The audio modulating signal. at a comfortable pitch. varies in amplitude at a rate that corresponds with the difference frequency between the two competing rf signals. Even a variation of a few hertz can be detected in this way.

Transmitter Frequency Measurement. See operation.

Calibration Checkpoints. The heterodyne frequency meter contains a stable crystal oscillator. which is used for calibrating the frequency of the variable-frequency oscillator (vfo). The crystal oscillator produces a number of harmonics. permitting calibration of the meter at various frequencies. These points of calibration are called *checkpoints*. and the frequencies at which they occur are given in a calibration book. which is used to determine the frequency of the dial setting.

Figure 5-220 shows a typical arrangement for calibrating a variable-frequency oscillator. Assume that the calibration book shows a crystal checkpoint at 3 MHz. The dial setting of the variable-frequency oscillator is adjusted to represent 3 MHz. If the second harmonic of the 1.5 MHz crystal oscillator (3 MHz) zero-beats

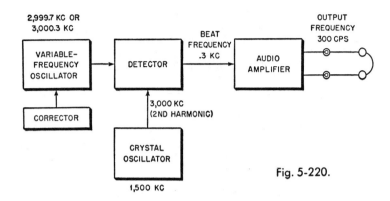

2,999.7 KC OR 3,000.3 KC

VARIABLE-FREQUENCY OSCILLATOR

CORRECTOR

DETECTOR

3,000 KC (2ND HARMONIC)

CRYSTAL OSCILLATOR

1,500 KC

BEAT FREQUENCY .3 KC

AUDIO AMPLIFIER

OUTPUT FREQUENCY 300 CPS

Fig. 5-220.

against the 3 MHz output of the variable-frequency oscillator, the output frequency is zero; there is no sound in the headphones, the vfo is already calibrated, and no compensating adjustment is necessary. However, if the output of the vfo is some other frequency than 3 MHz when the dial is set to 3 MHz, the variable-frequency oscillator must be calibrated. If it is set at 3 MHz and the actual frequency is 2.997 MHz or 3.0003 MHz, the output of the detector then will produce a beat frequency of 0.3 kHz, or 300 Hz, which can be heard in the headphones. The corrector control, usually a small variable capacitor, then is adjusted until the frequency of the vfo changes to 3 MHz. When this is done, no audible tone is heard in the headphones, and the vfo has been calibated. This procedure can be used for all checkpoints listed in the calibration book. Before making a correction in the calibration, the frequency meter should be turned on and allowed to warm up for 15−20 minutes to permit the operating temperature within the meter to stabilize.

Interpolating Frequency Readings. The relationship between the calibration book entries and the frequency is linear. If a reading is taken that falls between two entries, simply write the frequencies represented by the two entries that are adjacent to the dial setting. If the dial is halfway between the two entries, the frequency is halfway between the two representative frequency readings.

RF Generator. Most heterodyne frequency meters have a couple of output jacks, which may be used to obtain an rf signal from the heterodyne frequency meter. In the meter represented by the block diagram of Fig. 5-218, these two outputs are labeled RF I-F OUT and VFO/RF OUT. The VFO/RF OUT jack is supplied a signal from the variable-frequency oscillator of the meter, which itself may be varied to produce any frequency within the meter's range. The RF I-F OUT jack is supplied from the mixer, so its output is a resultant comprised of the signal produced by a combination of two frequencies supplied to the mixer.

Periodic Checking. To qualify as a secondary frequency standard, the frequency meter must be checked against a primary standard

(WWV) at regular intervals (not to exceed 6 months). However, it is an extremely good idea to make periodic checks more frequently than this, particularly when any of the operating conditions changes—such as location of the meter in the shop, variation of the source voltage, and when the meter is subjected to physical handling (as when transporting the meter to another location temporarily).

5-171. Draw a block diagram of an FM deviation meter, including the following stages: mixer, i-f amplifier, limiter, discriminator, and peak-reading voltmeter. Explain the operation of this instrument. Draw a circuit diagram and explain how the discriminator would be sensitive to frequency changes rather than amplitude changes.

As indicated in the block diagram of Fig. 5-221, a deviation meter is actually little different from an ordinary FM receiver. The chief difference is that an FM receiver contains a series of rf amplifiers ahead of the mixer and an audio amplifier stage following the FM detector (discriminator).

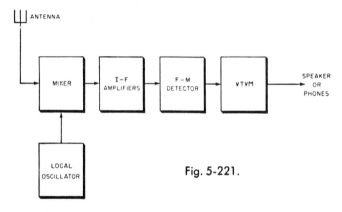

Fig. 5-221.

In operation, the rf signal from the transmitter is coupled loosely to the initial stage of the deviation meter (mixer) by means of a short length of wire attached to a connector at the mixer input. The transmitter should be modulated fully with a continuous tone of 1000 Hz, so that the transmitter's limiter stage clips the signal peaks slightly. The mixer combines the transmitted signal with the signal from the deviation meter's own local oscillator and produces an i-f signal that may be amplified and detected exactly in the manner of a conventional receiver. The i-f amplifier block of the deviation meter contains two special i-f amplifiers, called *limiters*, which saturate on almost all usable signals and remove any amplitude variations that may be present.

The constant-amplitude signal from the limiters in the i-f amplifier chain is coupled to the discriminator, whose output is an audio signal. The audio signal's level is directly proportional to the deviation of the transmitter's center frequency. By reading this level on a peak-reading voltmeter, an accurate indication of the transmitter's frequency deviation is obtained.

539

The response of an ideal limiter is shown in Fig. 5-222A. The amplifier stage must have a sharp cutoff characteristic. Very low values of screen voltage (where the amplifier stage is a tube) are used, and little bias is applied to the control grid. Therefore large values of positive grid voltage quickly drive the limiter tube to saturation, and large negative values drive it to cutoff. The transfer characteristic of the limiter is shown in sketch B. An input signal varying greatly in amplitude with the sharp pulses of noise superimposed on it is applied to the input of the limiter.

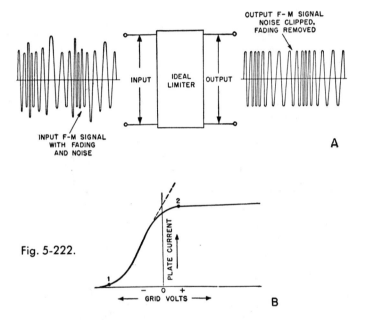

Fig. 5-222.

The varying voltage applied to the grid of the tube (or base of a transistor) drives it to cutoff or saturation, so that the large variations in amplitude are clipped off. In sketch B some amplification takes place for voltages between points 1 and 2, but the output is held constant beyond 2. Values more negative than point 1 are below cutoff and therefore do not appear in the output. For proper limiter action in a deviation meter, the lowest amplitude signal must swing at least from 1 to 2. The resultant output signal is square because the extreme positive and negative peaks have been clipped off in the limiter. And it is this clipped signal that is fed to the discriminator section and used to obtain the output voltage proportional to frequency deviation.

The basic purpose of the discriminator is to rectify two i-f voltages whose amplitudes depend directly on frequency. These rectified voltages then are combined so that no voltage appears across their output at the center frequency of the i-f amplifier. A *difference* voltage proportional to the difference in frequency of the two applied i-f voltages is produced when the frequency of the i-f signal is above or below the center frequency. This detector is insensitive to changes in amplitude at the center frequency, but changes in amplitude off center may cause the audio output to vary.

A simplified ratio detector circuit that might appear in a deviation meter is shown in Fig. 5-223A. This shows both diodes of the detector connected so that their outputs add instead of subtracting, as in a conventional discriminator circuit. Capacitors C_L across the load resistors have a large value of capacitance and are charged by the output voltage of the rectifier. This tends to make the total voltage across the load remain constant over the period of time constant R_L-C_L, since a large capacitor across the combined loads maintains an average signal amplitude that is adjusted automatically to the required operating level. The rectified output must not vary at an audio frequency, and the time constant of the capacitor and the load resistors must be great enough to smooth out such changes. This time constant is approximately 0.2 sec. The basic phase comparison circuit and the vector diagram of the ratio detector and phase discriminator are the same.

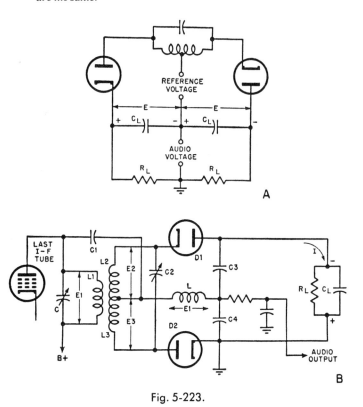

Fig. 5-223.

5-172. *Describe a usual method (and equipment used) for measuring the harmonic attenuation of a transmitter.*

When the output of a transmitter is to be measured directly for harmonic content and level of harmonic radiation. a wavemeter is typically used. If harmonic radiation from an antenna is to be measured. a field strength meter may be employed. Often a wavemeter may be used as a field strength meter by simple switching. The transmitter is coupled to the wavemeter loosely. and the transmitter output is reduced to the amount required to make the measurement. A reading is first taken with the wavemeter tuned to the fundamental output frequency of the transmitter under test. A new reading is then taken at the frequency representing the desired harmonic. Attenuation is calculated by comparing the two readings and is usually expressed in decibels.

5-173. *Why is it important that transmitters remain on frequency and that harmonics be attenuated?*

Obviously. a transmitter that drifts off frequency may cause needless interference to other users of the radio spectrum. Similarly. harmonics of any given fundamental frequency may fall on frequencies assigned to other services. Also. when a transmitter's output signal includes large amounts of harmonic radiation. it is a good indication that the transmit-signal waveform is being clipped by overmodulation.

When a receiver of a communications system is crystal-controlled and tuned to the frequency assigned by the FCC. maximum range and intelligibility will be realized as long as the companion transmitter is operating on that assigned frequency. When the transmitter drifts. however. the effective signal strength at the receiver is drastically reduced.

BATTERIES

5-174. *How does a primary cell differ from a secondary cell?*

In brief. **primary batteries are one-time batteries**: they are used and then discarded. **A secondary cell** may be used many times: each time its energy is expended. the battery **may be rejuvenated by recharging**. After a number of such charge—recharge cycles. the secondary cell must be replaced. A flashlight battery is an example of a primary cell. and an automobile battery is an example of a secondary cell.

5-175. *What is the chemical composition of the electrolyte of a lead—acid storage cell?*

The electrolyte of a lead—acid storage cell (secondary cell) is a diluted solution of sulfuric acid.

5-176. *What will be the result of discharging a lead—acid storage cell at an excessively high current rate?*

The battery will overheat. thereby accelerating the discharge rate and probably rendering irreparable damage to the cells. The capacity of a battery is reduced during periods of excessive heating.

Overheating causes sulfation, plate buckling, and gassing from electrolyte boiloff.

5-177. *If the charging current through a storage battery is maintained at the normal rate but its polarity is reversed, what will result?*

The answer depends to some extent of the rate of charge. If the battery is undergoing a *trickle charge*—that is, a charge equal to 0.1% of its own ampere-hour capacity—no damage to the battery should result from such abuse so long as the applied voltage is removed within a reasonable amount of time. However, under conditions of ordinary high-current charging, reverse-polarity current can cause cell buckling, overheating, and sulfation—all of which can cause premature exhaustion and permanent damage. Most significant, however, will be the *polarization* of cells, a phenomenon that results in permanent reversal of the polarity of individual cells, caused by trapped gases that serve to insulate the electrodes from the electrolyte internally.

5-178. *What is the approximate fully charged voltage of a lead−acid cell?*

The lead−acid cell's terminal voltage at full charge is approximately 2.1V.

5-179. *What steps may be taken to prevent corrosion of lead−acid storage cell terminals?*

1. Make certain battery terminals are shiny clean and free of grease.
2. Make certain the contact surface of the cable connectors are shiny clean and free of grease.
3. Attach connectors (cable) to battery terminals securely, allowing contact to be made over the greatest area possible; tighten well.
4. Apply a moisture-proof coating over the terminal connections. Silicone grease is exceptionally good for this, but ordinary household salve such as Vaseline works quite well.
5. Sprinkle baking soda (or equivalent neutralizing agent) over all exposed leads near the battery.

5-180. *How is the capacity of a battery rated?*

The battery's capacity is expressed in *ampere-hours*, and the number of ampere-hours is determined by the current and the amount of time required to bring the battery to a fully charged state after complete exhaustion. A battery that can be fully charged if supplied with a one-ampere current for a 10-hour period is rated at a 10 ampere-hours.

MOTORS AND GENERATORS

5-181. *What is meant by "power factor"? Give an example of how it is calculated. Discuss the construction and operation of dynamotors.*

Sometimes true power and apparent power are different. The product of current squared and resistance is equal to *true* power. *Apparent* power may be calculated by multiplying voltage times current or finding the product of current squared and impedance. The ratio of these two values of power represents the power factor and is a decimal fraction between 0 and 1. This value is the power actually consumed when compared to the total power available for use in a circuit. In mathematical terms the power factor may be written as

$$pf = \frac{P_{true}}{P_{apparent}} = \cos\theta$$

A dynamotor is a combination motor and generator. It has two armatures on a single shaft—a motor winding and a generator winding. The armatures turn in a common field. The motor is generally operated from a dc source such as a battery. (Until recent years most high-current $B+$ sources in vehicular communications systems were supplied by dynamotors powered from the vehicle battery. But the advent of semiconductors has made the dynamotor obsolete.)

5-182. *Describe the action and list the main characteristics of a shunt dc generator.*

The poles of a shunt dc generator retain some magnetism, called *residual magnetism,* when the machine is not in operation. This residual magnetism produces a weak magnetic field and, when the generator is started, a small voltage is induced in the armature and appears at the output terminals. Then, because the armature output voltage is connected across the field windings, a small current flows in the windings. This field current, in turn, strengthens the magnetic field; the output voltage rises accordingly, and a larger current flows in the windings. This action is cumulative, and the output voltage continues to rise to a point called *field saturation,* where no further increase in output voltage occurs.

If the initial direction of armature rotation is wrong, the cumulative action does not occur, since the small induced voltage opposes the residual field and there is no buildup of output voltage. Sometimes the field windings of a shunt generator are excited by a separate source. The terminal voltage of a shunt generator can be controlled by means of a rheostat inserted in series with the field windings. As the resistance is increased, the field current is reduced and, consequently, the generated voltage is reduced also. For a given setting of the field rheostat, either for a separately excited or self-excited machine, the terminal voltage at the armature brushes will be approximately equal to the generated voltage minus the IR drop produced by the load current in the armature. Consequently, the voltage available at the terminals of the machine will drop as the load is applied. This effect is greater in a self-excited generator than in a separately excited generator. Certain voltage-sensitive devices are available that automatically adjust the field rheostat to compensate for the variations in load, and when these devices are used, the terminal voltage remains essentially constant.

Shunt generators are used primarily in applications such as battery charging, when a constant voltage under varying current conditions is required. Separately excited shunt generators are often used in certain speed control systems.

5-183. *Name four causes of excessive sparking at the brushes of a dc motor or generator.*

Sparking at the brushes may be attributable to worn brushes, defective or open interpoles, damaged commutator, brushes not seated properly in their races, uneven wear on brushes and commutator so brushes do not contact commutator completely during each armature revolution, armature winding shorted (causing "welding"), or armature winding open (causing arcing).

5-184. *How may radio-frequency interference, often caused by sparking at the brushes of a high-voltage generator, be minimized?*

The first step is to minimize the sparking. The second step is to install the appropriate value of bypass capacitors from brushes to ground. Additional measures include installing series rf chokes and shielding the generator or the equipment in which the interference is being detected.

5-185. *How may the output voltage of a separately excited ac generator, at constant output frequency, be varied?*

The output voltage may be adjusted by means of a potentiometer connected in series with the field windings. The field windings carry dc to the generator from a separate voltage source. As the field voltage is decreased (by increasing the series resistance), the alternator's output voltage is reduced.

5-186. *What may cause a motor—generator bearing to overheat?*

The bearings of a motor—generator can overheat when they are operated without lubrication, when the motor—generator shaft is out of round, when the motor is operated at maximum load for excessive periods, when the bearings are not seated properly initially, when the bearings are showing signs of wearing out, when there is excessive friction during any part of the armature's cycle, or when the motor's speed is excessive.

5-187. *What materials should be used to clean the commutator of a motor or generator?*

If the dirt does not consist of grease or oil, dry, lint-free cloth is best for cleaning the commutator. Carbon tetrachloride, trichloroethylene, alcohol, and naphtha are all good cleaning agents if the commutator is greasy. The commutator should be dried thoroughly by wiping with a lint-free cloth before reinstallation in the generator housing.

5-188. *If the field of a shunt-wound dc motor were opened while the machine was running under no load, what would be the probable results?*

The speed of a shunt motor is dependent on the magnetic strength of the field; the higher the field strength, the slower the motor will turn. An open field would cut off the field current, and the motor speed would increase beyond the design point. Such operation could seriously damage the motor.

MIROWAVE EQUIPMENT

5-189. *Draw a diagram showing the construction and explain principles of operation of a traveling-wave tube.*

The traveling-wave tube has an electron gun that produces a stream of electrons that are kept in a tight beam with a magnetic focusing field supplied by a solenoid magnet. A cutaway view of the traveling-wave tube is shown in Fig. 5-224. The electrons are acelerated by two different means. Initially they are accelerated by the specially designed electron gun that originally produced them. In the electron gun, the heater boils off electrons from a parabola-shaped cathode. The paraolic shape tends to focus the electron stream. Small accelerator anodes increase the velocity. The result is a narrow beam that has the relative velocity of an electron accelerated by 1500V.

A positive potential on the helix and a collector anode at the end of the tube further accelerate the electrons. The electron beam is made to flow down the central axis of a long, loosely wound helix on its way to the collector. The beam is kept from spreading by the solenoid magnet surrounding the tube. The focusing system that is generally used is a long, wirewound, magnetic solenoid that completely surrounds the loosely wound helix portion of the tube. The axis of the solenoid magnetic field coincides with the axis of the helix.

The ability of this "magnetic lens" to keep the electron beam focused into a tight area is a direct function of the current through the magnet. The higher the solenoid current, the tighter the beam. If the magnetic field of the solenoid were lost for an instant, the electron beam would spread, intersect the helix, cause ionization, and destroy the traveling-wave tube. The weight of the electromagnet and associated power supply add to the bulk and complexity of the traveling-wave tube. The principal feature of the traveling-wave tube is its very broad bandwidth.

5-190. *Discuss the following with respect to waveguides:*

- *Relationship between frequency and size*
- *Modes of operation*
- *Coupling of energy into the waveguide*
- *General principles of operation*

Frequency—Size Relationship. The cross-sectional dimensions of a waveguide must be on the order of $\lambda/2$ (a half-wavelength) for it to contain electromagnetic fields properly. Thus, the higher the frequency to be transmitted via a waveguide, the smaller the dimensions required for the waveguide. A waveguide to be used at 1 MHz, for example, would be about 700 ft wide. Even at a frequency of 220 MHz or so, the waveguide would have to be about 4 ft wide, while at higher frequencies, such as 10 GHz (10,000 MHz), it need be only about an inch wide. Therefore, dimensions required by waveguides make them impractical for frequencies lower than about 3 GHz.

Another important consideration is the fact that energy will not be propagated through a waveguide when its dimension is $\lambda/2$ or less. The reason for this is that for any given waveguide there is a *cutoff frequency* below which it does not function as a power transfer device. This limits the frequency range of any system using waveguides.

Modes of Operation. Electric and magnetic fields exist simultaneously in the waveguide. In fact, the *H*-field causes a current, which, in turn, causes a voltage difference. This produces an E-field; and it, in turn, causes a current. This current creates an *H*-field, and so on. One field is dependent on the other, as energy is continually transferred from one field to the other.

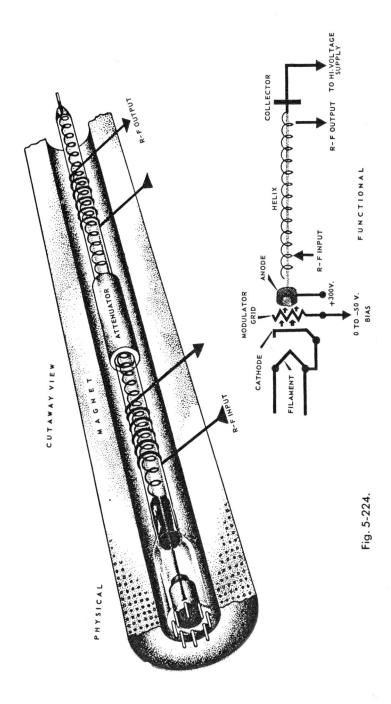

CUTAWAY VIEW

PHYSICAL

MAGNET

ATTENUATOR

R-F OUTPUT

R-F INPUT

COLLECTOR

TO HI-VOLTAGE SUPPLY

R-F OUTPUT

HELIX

ANODE

R-F INPUT

MODULATOR GRID

+300v.

0 TO -50 V. BIAS

CATHODE

FILAMENT

FUNCTIONAL

Fig. 5-224.

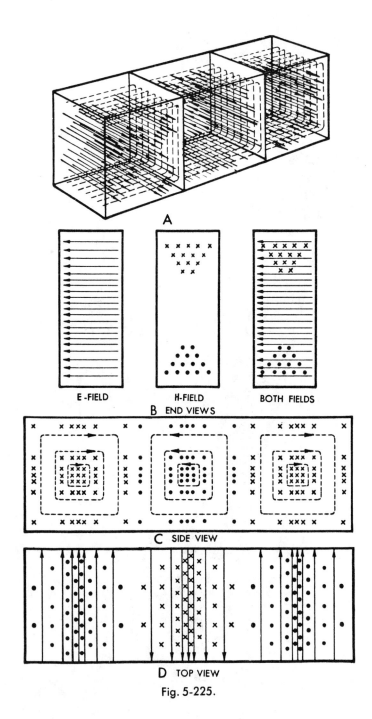

A

E-FIELD   H-FIELD   BOTH FIELDS

B   END VIEWS

C   SIDE VIEW

D   TOP VIEW

Fig. 5-225.

Figure 5-225A illustrates both fields in the waveguide. Since this picture is rather complicated, the presence and direction of the field is usually indicated in more simple diagrams, such as those shown in Fig. 5-225B, C, and D. In these diagrams the number of E-lines in a given area indicates the strength of the electrostatic field, while the number of H-lines in any given cross section indicates the strength of the magnetic field in that area.

The field configuration shown in Fig. 5-225 represents only one of the many ways in which fields are able to exist in a waveguide. Such a field configuration is called a mode of operation. In the case of the rectangular waveguide illustrated, the configuration is known as the *dominant mode*, since it is the easiest one to produce. Higher modes—that is, different field configurations—may occur accidentally or may be caused deliberately in a waveguide.

An example of another field configuration is developed in Fig. 5-226A. If the size of this waveguide were doubled over that of the waveguide shown in Fig. 5-225, the cross section would be a full wavelength rather than $\lambda/2$. The 2-wire conductor can be assumed to be $\lambda/4$ down from the top (or $\lambda/4$ up from the bottom). The remaining distance to the bottom is $3\lambda/4$. A three-quarter-wave section has the same high-impedance input as the quarter-wave section. Thus, the 2-wire line is properly insulated and will transfer energy. The field configuration will show a full wave across the wide dimension, as you can see in Fig. 5-226B.

This field configuration can be applied to a circular waveguide. The two conductors shown in Fig. 5-226C are assumed to be part of the waveguide wall. The remaining part of the wall forms the quarter-wave section. The quarter-wave section insulates the two conductors. This make it possible to transfer energy with minimum losses. The resulting field configuration shown in sketch D is the dominant mode for a waveguide with a circular cross section.

Coupling of Energy Into a Waveguide. A waveguide is a single conductor; therefore, it does not have the two connections that ordinary rf lines have, and it is necessary to use special devices to put energy into a waveguide at one end and remove it at the other. In a waveguide, as with many other electrical networks, *reciprocity* exists in an excitation system—that is, energy may be transferred either to the waveguide or from the waveguide with the same efficiency.

Waveguides may be excited by three principal methods: electric fields, magnetic fields, and electromagnetic fields. When a small probe is placed in a waveguide and fed with an rf signal, current will flow in the probe and set up an electrostatic field such as shown in Fig. 5-227A. This causes the E-lines to detach themselves from the probe and to form in the waveguide. When the probe is located in the right place, a field having considerable intensity will be set up. The best place to locate the probe is in the center, parallel to the narrow dimension and $\lambda/4$ away from the shorted end of the guide, as shown in Fig. 5-227C. This method of energy coupling is known as *electric field excitation*.

Another way of exciting a waveguide is by setting up a magnetic (H) field in the waveguide. This can be accomplished by placing a

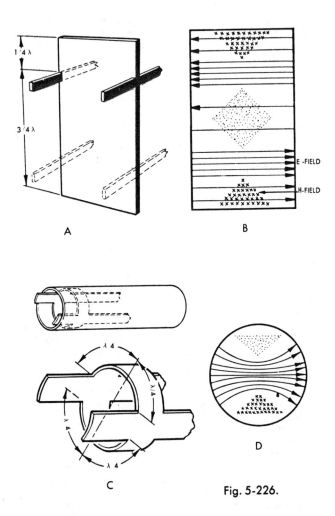

A

B

C

D

Fig. 5-226.

small loop that carries a high current in the waveguide. A magnetic field builds up around the loop. The field expands and fits the guide. If the frequency of the current is correct, energy will be transferred from the loop to the waveguide. A loop for transferring energy into a guide is shown at Fig. 5-228A and B. Notice that the loop is fed by a coaxial cable. The location of the loop for optimum coupling to the guide is at the place where the magnetic field that is to be set up will be of greatest strength. There are a series of places where this is true. Several are shown in Fig. 5-228C.

Another method for either putting energy into or removing it from waveguides, known as *electromagnetic excitation*, is through slots or openings. This method is sometimes used when very loose coupling is

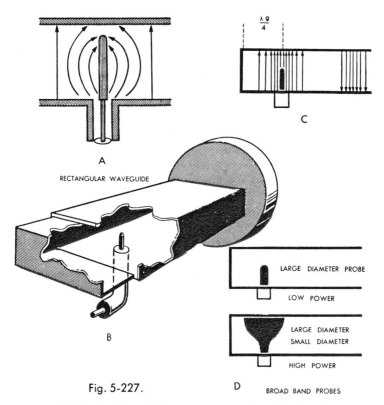

Fig. 5-227.

BROAD BAND PROBES

desired. In this method. energy enters the guide through a small aperture. as can be seen in Fig. 5-229C. Note that several other methods for electromagnetic excitation are shown also.

General Principles of Operation. To understand the action of a waveguide. assume that a waveguide has the form of a 2-wire line. In this condition there must be some means of supporting the two wires. Further. the support must be a nonconductor. so that no power will be lost by radiation leakage. An efficient way for both insulating and supporting the 2-wire line is shown in Fig. 5-230A. This line is spaced. insulated. and supported by porcelain standoff insulators. At communication frequencies the absorption of power by the dielectric material (insulators) causes them to ``look like'' a low resistance and capacitance.

The equivalent electrical circuit at higher frequencies is shown in Fig. 5-230B. For frequencies of 3 GHz and up. a better insulator than nonconducting porcelain insulators must be used. A superior high-frequency insulator for this purpose is a quarter-wave section of rf line. called a *metallic insulator*. Such an insulator is shown in Fig. 5-230C. As there are no dielectric losses in a quarter-wave section of rf line. the impedance at the open end (the junction of the 2-wire line) is very high.

551

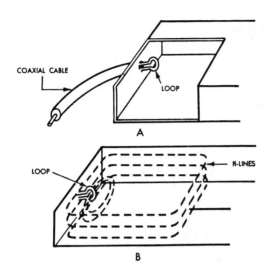

COAXIAL CABLE

LOOP

A

LOOP

H-LINES

B

Fig. 5-228.

WAVEGUIDE

H-FIELD

POSSIBLE LOCATION FOR LOOP

C

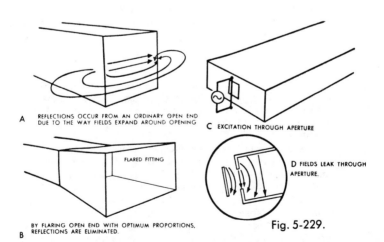

A REFLECTIONS OCCUR FROM AN ORDINARY OPEN END DUE TO THE WAY FIELDS EXPAND AROUND OPENING

C EXCITATION THROUGH APERTURE

FLARED FITTING

D FIELDS LEAK THROUGH APERTURE.

B BY FLARING OPEN END WITH OPTIMUM PROPORTIONS, REFLECTIONS ARE ELIMINATED.

Fig. 5-229.

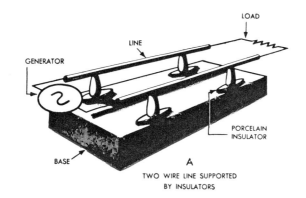

TWO WIRE LINE SUPPORTED
BY INSULATORS

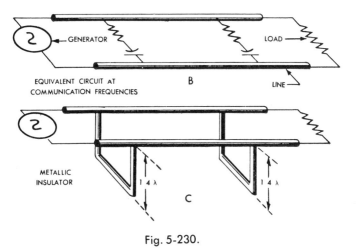

Fig. 5-230.

A metallic insulator can be placed anywhere along a 2-wire line. Figure 5-231A shows several on each side of 2-wire line. A point to note about this line is that the supports are $\lambda/4$ at only one frequency. This limits the high efficiency of the 2-wire line to one frequency only.

The use of several insulators results in the improved conductivity of a 2-wire line when the sections are connected together. This connection is made between the two adjacent insulators through a switch, as shown in Fig. 5-231B. When the switch is open, both quarter-wave sections are excited by the main line. In this condition there will be standing waves on the quarter-wave sections.

When the switch is connected to the same place on each section, the relative phase relationship of the voltages at the connection will be

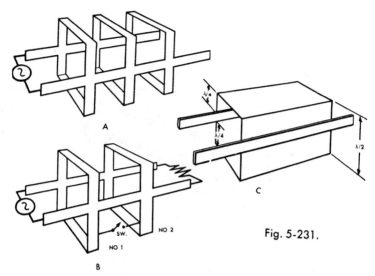

Fig. 5-231.

the same for each section. In this condition. the No. 1 section will be excited first by the generator. When the switch is closed. the No. 2 section will be partially excited by the No. 1 section through the switch connection. In this manner less energy from the main line is required to excite the No. 2 section. The parallel paths shown cause less resistance to exist along a given length of line. and energy is transferred with less copper loss.

When more wave sections are added to the line until each section makes contact with the next. the result is a rectangular box in which the line is at the center. as in Fig. 5-231C. The line itself is actually part of the wall of the box. The rectangular box thus formed is a waveguide.

5-191.   *How are cavities installed in vertical waveguides to prevent moisture from collecting? Why are long horizontal waveguides not desired?*

Cavities are installed in such a manner that moisture cannot get through the connection. In this sense. waveguide installations may be thought of as plumbing fixtures. Depending on the method of introducing energy into a waveguide. any of several techniques may be employed for preventing the accumulation of moisture or precipitation. The most effective method is *nitrogen pressurization*. This involves making all connections airtight and attaching pressure-monitoring gages to the plumbing. Pressurized nitrogen prevents moisture from forming inside the waveguide

Long horizontal waveguide runs are unsatisfactory because of the likelihood of moisture or dust particles forming at some place in the run. When such foreign matter accumulates. the efficiency of the waveguide is compromised and performance suffers.

5-192.   *Describe the physical structure of a klystron tube and explain how it operates as an oscillator.*

554

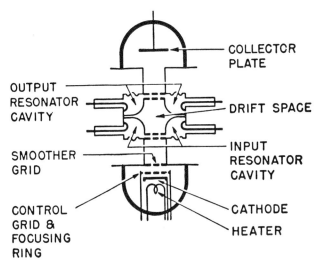

OUTPUT RESONATOR CAVITY

SMOOTHER GRID

CONTROL GRID & FOCUSING RING

COLLECTOR PLATE

DRIFT SPACE

INPUT RESONATOR CAVITY

CATHODE

HEATER

Fig. 5-232.

The klystron tube shown in Fig. 5-232 can operate as an amplifier or oscillator over a small tunable range. Its operation depends on the changes introduced in the velocity of a stream of electrons by alternately slowing it down and speeding it up, using the transit time between two points to produce an alternating current. This current delivers power to a resonant circuit in the form of a cavity.

The cathode emits a stream of electrons which is smoothed out to uniform velocity by the *smoother* grid. A radio-frequency field is applied to the grids of the input cavity resonator. This imposes a varying velocity on the stream, retarding or speeding it up. In the drift space, the electrons that have been speeded up will overtake those that have been slowed on an earlier cycle. This produces a still-stronger pulsation in the electron stream as it passes through the grids of the output cavity resonator. The latter takes power from the stream if it is tuned to the frequency of the pulsations. Therefore, amplification takes place between the input and output resonators. The tube can be used as an oscillator, of course, if some power from the output is coupled back to the input in phase.

Small tubes, called *reflex klystrons*, have been designed solely for use as local oscillators in microwave superheterodyne receivers. They use a single-cavity resonator, the electron stream passing through it twice—once in a forward direction and then reflected back through the cavity again. They can be tuned over a wide range of frequencies but have only limited power-output capability. This is the klystron most frequently used in microwave equipment.

5-193. *Explain the principles of operation of a cavity resonator.*

In ordinary radio work the conventional low-frequency resonant circuit consists of a coil and capacitor connected either in series or

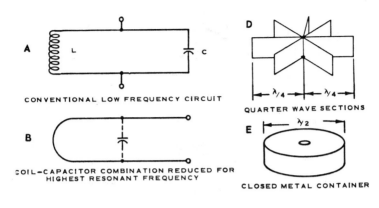

A — CONVENTIONAL LOW FREQUENCY CIRCUIT

B — COIL-CAPACITOR COMBINATION REDUCED FOR HIGHEST RESONANT FREQUENCY

D — QUARTER WAVE SECTIONS

E — CLOSED METAL CONTAINER

C

HALF TURN LOOP IN PARALLEL

Fig. 5-233.

parallel. as shown in Fig. 5-233A. To alter the resonant frequency. it is necessary to change either the capacitance or the inductance. or both. However. a frequency is reached where the inductance is a half-turn coil and where the capacitance consists only of the stray capacitance in the coil. In this circuit. the current handling capacity and breakdown voltage for the spacing would be low.

The current carrying ability of a resonant circuit may be increased by adding half-turn loops in parallel. This does not change the resonant frequency appreciably because it adds capacitance in parallel (which lowers the frequency) and inductance in parallel (which increases the frequency). As the effects of one cancel the effects of the other. the frequency remains about the same.

In Fig. 5-233C several half-turn loops are added in parallel. Sketch D shows several parallel quarter-wave Lecher lines. which are resonant when they are near a quarter wavelength. When more and more loops are added in parallel. the assembly eventually becomes a closed resonant box. as shown in sketch E. The box. called a *resonant cavity*. is a quarter-wave in radius (half-wave in diameter).

A resonant cavity displays the same resonant characteristics as a tuned circuit composed of a coil and capacitor. In it. there are a large number of current paths. This means that the resistance of the box to current flow is very low and that the Q of the resonant circuit is very high. While it is difficult to attain a Q of several hundred in a coil of wire. it is fairly easy to construct a resonant cavity with a Q of many thousands. Although a cavity is as efficient at low as at high frequencies. the large size required at low frequencies prohibit its use.

Troubleshooting

The FCC exam will include several questions of the multiple-choice type dealing with troubleshooting. Accordingly, this section is an edited and condensed version of the U.S. Navy's "6-step troubleshooting" technique, which should help not only in leading you to the right answers to the FCC test questions, but in tracking down real-life troubles in electronic equipment. Sample test questions based on actual circuits are included at the end of this section.

The Navy's 6-step troubleshooting procedure breaks down into these elements:

1. Symptom recognition
2. Symptom elaboration
3. Listing of probably faulty functions
4. Localizing the faulty function
5. Localizing trouble to the circuit
6. Failure analysis

STEP 1—SYMPTOM RECOGNITION

This is the first step in our logical approach to trouble analysis. To repair an equipment you must first determine whether it is functioning correctly or incorrectly.

A *trouble symptom* is a sign or indicator of some disorder or malfunction in an electronic equipment. *Symptom recognition* is the act of identifying such a sign when it appears.

Normal and Abnormal Performance

Since a trouble symptom is a manifestation of an undesirable change in equipment performance, we must have some standard of normal performance to serve as a guide. By comparing the present performance with the normal, you can recognize that a trouble symptom exists and make a decision as to just what the symptom is.

Your normal body temperature is 98.6°F. A change above or below this temperature is an abnormal condition—a trouble symptom. If you determine that your body temperature is 102°F, by comparing this with the normal you can say that the symptom is an excess temperature of 3.4°F. Thus, you have exactly defined the symptom.

The normal television picture is a clear, properly contrasted representation of an actual scene. It should be centered within the vertical and horizontal boundaries of the screen. If the picture suddenly begins to roll vertically, you should recognize this as a trouble symptom because it does not correspond to the normal performance which is expected.

Performance Evaluation

During the process of doing their assigned job, most electronic equipments yield information which an operator or technician can either see or hear. The senses of hearing and sight allow you to recognize the symptoms of normal and abnormal equipment performance. The display of information may be the sole job of the equipment, or it may be a secondary job to permit performance evaluation.

Electrical information, to be presented as sound, must be applied to a loudspeaker or a headset. A visual display results when the information is applied to a cathode-ray tube or to an indicating meter which is built into the equipment control panel and which can be viewed by the operator. Pilot lights also provide a visual indication of equipment operation.

As an example of how these various displays can be used to evaluate or monitor equipment performance, consider the plate-current or *tuning* meter, which monitors the plate current in the final stage of a broadcast transmitter. When the transmitter is tuned to the proper frequency, there should be a dip in the plate current meter. Tuning the transmitter corresponds to adjusting the capacitance of the parallel inductor—capacitor tank circuit so that the condition of parallel resonance exists at the desired freqency. Parallel resonane results in maximum impedance to plate current flow—hence, a very low value of plate current at this pont.

In the detuned condition, the plate current may be quite high, as shown in part A of Fig. 6-1. As the tuning control is adjusted to approach the proper frequency, the current will abruptly decrease, as shown in B. The lowest reading (C) will occur at the correct frequency if the equipment is performing normally.

Knowledge of the normal equipment displays will enable you to recognize an abnormal display, which provides the trouble symptoms we are concerned with in our first troubleshooting step.

Equipment Failure

Electronic equipment failure is the simplest type of trouble symptom to recognize. Equipment failure means that either the entire equipment or some part of it is not functioning and will, therefore, show no performance display. The absence of sound from a receiver when all controls are in their proper positions indicates failure. Similarly, the absence of a visible trace or picture

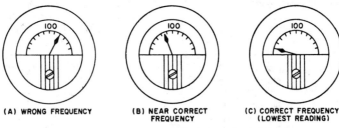

(A) WRONG FREQUENCY   (B) NEAR CORRECT FREQUENCY   (C) CORRECT FREQUENCY (LOWEST READING)

Fig. 6-1. Plate current indications during transmitter tuning process.

on the screen of a cathode-ray tube when all controls are properly set points to some form of equipment failure. If yo have observed the plate current reading on the tuning meter of a broadcast transmitter and the reading suddenly dropped to zero, you have observed an equipment failure.

Degraded Performance

Even if the audible and visual information is present, the equipment may not be performing normally. Whenever the equipment is doing its job, but is presenting the operator with information that does not correspond with the design specifications, the performance is said to be *degraded*. Such performance must be corrected just as quickly as an equipment failure. This performance may range from a nearly perfrect operating condition to the condition of barely operating.

STEP 2—SYMPTOM ELABORATION

As a second step, the symptom should be further defined. Most electronic systems have operational controls, additional indicating instruments other than the main indicating device, or other built-in aids for evaluating performance. These should be put to use at this point to see whether they will affect the symptom under observation or provide additional data that further defines the symptom.

Breaking out the test equipment and equipment diagrams and proceeding headlong into testing procedures on just the original recognition of a trouble symptom is an unrealistic approach. Unless you completely define a trouble symptom first, you can quickly and easily be led astray. The result, as before, would be loss of time, unnecessary expenditure of energy, and perhaps even a total dead-end approach. This step is the "I need more information" step in our systematic approach.

Symptom elaboration is the process of obtaining a more detailed description of the trouble symptom. Recognizing that the fluorescent screen of a cathode-ray tube is not lighted is not sufficient information for you to decide exactly what could be causing the trouble. This symptom could mean that the cathode-ray tube is burned out, that there is some disorder in the internal circuitry associated with this tube, the intensity control is turned down too low, or even that the equipment is not turned on. Think of all the time you may waste if you tear into the equipment and begin testing procedures when all you may need to do is flip a switch or plug in a power cord.

Similarly, recognizing an undesirable hum in a superheterodyne receiver as a trouble symptom could lead you in several directions if you do not obtain a more detailed description of the symptom. This receiver hum may be due to poor filtering action in the power supply, heater—cathode leakage, ac line voltage interference, or other internal or external faults.

It should be apparent by now that the primary reason for placing symptom elaboration as the second step in our logical procedure is that many similar trouble symptoms can be caused by a large number of equipment faults. To proceed efficiently, it s necessary to make a valid decision as to which fault is probably producing the specific symptom.

Use of Operating Controls

Operating controls are considered to be all front-panel switches, variable circuit elements, or mechanical linkages connected to internal circuit components which can be adjusted without going inside the equipment

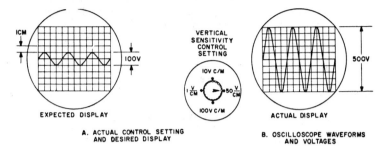

A. ACTUAL CONTROL SETTING AND DESIRED DISPLAY

B. OSCILLOSCOPE WAVEFORMS AND VOLTAGES

Fig. 6-2. Oscilloscope waveforms and voltages.

enclosure. These are the controls which the equipment operator must manipulate to supply power to the equipment circuits, to tune or adjust the performance characteristics, or to select a particular type of performance.

By their very nature, operating controls must produce some sort of change in the circuit conditions. This change will indirectly alter current or voltage values by the direct variation of resistance, inductance, or capacitance elements in the equipment circuitry. The information displays associated with the equipment—front-panel meters and other indicating devices—will enable you to see the changes which take place when the controls are operated.

Control manipulation can cause detrimental effects in equipment performance, as well as the desirable effects for which they are primarily intended. Manipulating controls in an improper order or allowing voltage and current values to exceed maximum design specifications may have resulted in the damage which brought about the original symptom. Unless you observe the proper precautions while investigating the symptom, even more damage to the equipment can result from the improper use of the operating controls.

Every electronic circuit component has definite maximum current and voltage limits below which it must be operated to prevent burnout or insulation breakdown. The meters placed on the front panel serve as an aid in determining voltage and current values at crucial points in the equipment circuitry. Operating controls should *never* be adjusted so that these meters indicate values above the maximum ratings.

Incorrect Control Settings

Incorrect operating-control settings will produce an apparent trouble symptom. We use the word *apparent* because the equipment may be operating perfectly, but because of the incorrect setting the information display will not correspond with the expected performance. An incorrect setting may be brought about by an accidental movement of the control or careless misadjustment. The discovery of such an incorrect setting permits sufficient elaboration of the trouble symptom to "fix" it immediately, thereby ending your troubleshooting project if you can verify that the incorrect setting was the only cause of the trouble symptom.

Assume that you are checking the voltage across the load resistor of an audio amplifier stage in a superheterodyne receiver with an oscilloscope. The waveform should be 100V from the positive peak to the negative peak, and you are trying to verify this amplitude in order to evaluate the amplifier stage performance. You intend to set the VERTICAL SENSITIVITY switch to 50 volts per centimeter and expect to see a consequent display waveform similar to that shown in Fig. 6-2A. However, in haste you accidentally set the vertical sensitivity switch to 10V/cm. As a result of this carelessness, the display you see is actually similar to that of B in the figure; and at first glance, you assume the amplitude is 500V since you think the switch is set at 50V/cm. Certainly, the first thought is that the amplifier is not functioning properly.

At this point your knowledge of amplifier operation hould be applied. Figure 6-3 is the circuit diagram for the amplifier you are checking. Immediately you should realize that, since the supply voltage for the amplifier is only 150V, it is an *operational inaccuracy* for 500V to exist across the load. The amplifier shown in the figure cannot produce an output voltage larger than its own plate supply voltage.

The next logical assumption is that the oscilloscope is in error. Since it is the vertical dimension which is apparently in error, this should immediately direct your attention to the VERTICAL SENSITIVITY control. Once you discover the error in control setting, you will realize that the display actually represents 100V p-p. Therefore, there is no real trouble symptom.

This application of equipment knowledge and logic should have enabled you to discover the error in less time that it took you to read this section. This represents a considerable savings over the time that would have been consumed if you had torn into the amplifier or oscilloscope looking for a nonexistent fault.

Aggravating the Trouble Symptom

If all controls are set at their correct positions but the symptom persists, it is still possible that an operating control is responsible for the trouble symptom. However, in this case, the trouble would have to fall in the general area of component failure. If a control is faulty, this may be immediately apparent—especially when it is a mechanical failure. However, additional information may be required to determine when a control has failed electronically, since the trouble symptom produced may also point to other electronic failures.

The specific intent is to aggravate the trouble symptom, if possible. By observing the changes this aggravation produces in the trouble symptom, you will be able to make a valid estimate as to just what is probably causing the panel meter readings and the displays produced by other front-panel devices.

As an example, consider the FREQUENCY RANGE switch on a broadcast transmitter. This control is a multiposition switch with each position connecting a different rf coil in parallel with the main tuning capacitor of the oscillator tank circuit. The value of each coil is such that it will cause the oscillator to vary over a different range of frequencies as the tuning capacitor is varied. If a weak-transmission symptom is reported, it is logical to try other frequency ranges by manipulating the selector switch. If normal transmission is achieved for any of the range positions, the fault probably lies either in the switch itself or in a few (perhaps only one) of the tuning coils. Such an observation would provide a quick location of the trouble area.

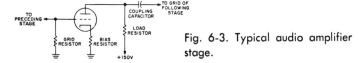

Fig. 6-3. Typical audio amplifier stage.

561

Further Aggravating the Trouble

In a receiver, if a mode selector switch can be changed from AM to FM operation, it is logical to check the receiver in both positions. If the symptom persists only in the AM mode, the circuitry associated with the FM mode can be eliminated as a probable cause later in our troubleshooting procedure.

If a broadcast transmitter uses plate modulation to add the audio signal to the rf signal, the degree of modulation will be controllable by a front-panel knob. The modulating signal is applied to the plate circuit of the rf amplifier through a coupling transformer. Between the input of this transformer and the microphone that gathers the voice information is an audio amplifier. The modulation control may vary the gain of this amplifier; hence, any additional undesirable changes in the trouble symptom produced by varying this control would point to faults in the audio units which preceded the modulation transformer.

The examples above represent only a small portion of the various controls associated with a transmitter or receiver. The controls and instrumentation associated with every type of equipment are specifically incorporated to provide information about that particular device. Therefore, it is necessary to understand the operation of the equipment in order to appreciate the aid which can be obtained by manipulating controls.

Data Recording and its Purpose

Symptom elaboration cannot be fully accomplished unless the observed displays can be completely evaluated. This means that the indications must be evaluated in relation to one another, as well as in relation to the overall operation of the equipment. The easiest method for accomplishing this evaluation is to have all data handy for reference by recording the information as it is obtained.

This will enable you to sit back a moment and think the information over before jumping to a conclusion as to where the trouble lies. It will also enable you to check the equipment manual and compare the information with detailed descriptions if this is necessary—a particularly useful technique for someone just becoming familiar with troubleshooting. Finally, by recording all control positions and the associated meter and indicator information, you can quickly reproduce the information and check to see that it is correct, as well as put the equipment in exactly the operating condition that you wish to test.

Whenever the adjustment of a control has no effect upon the symptom, this fact should also be recorded. This information may later prove to be just as important as any changes a control may produce in the trouble symptom.

Gaining further information about a trouble symptom by manipulating the operating controls and instruments will help you identify the probable faulty function required in the next step. This procedure will give you an estimate of where the trouble lies and will permit you to eventually classify the problem down to the exact item responsible.

If the trouble is cleared up by manipulating the controls, the trouble analysis *may* stop at this point. However, by using your knowledge of the equipment involved, you should find the reason why the specific control adjustment removed the apparent malfunction. This action is necessary to assure yourself, as well as the operator, that there are no additional faulty items which will produce the same trouble later.

In manipulating controls, you must be aware of the circuit area in which the control is located. Only those controls that will logically affect the indicated symptom should be adjusted

Whether or not you will proceed from step 2 to 3 (listing of probable faulty functions) or to step 5 (localizing trouble to the circuit) will depend on the number of units in the equipment or the complexity of a single-unit equipment.

STEP 3—LISTING OF PROBABLE FAULTY FUNCTIONS

The performance of the third step is dependent upon the information gathered in the two previous steps. Step 1, remember, was *symptom recognition*, that is, becoming aware of the fact that an equipment is performing its operational function in an abnormal manner. Step 2, *symptom elaboration*, allows you to use the operating controls and front-panel indicators to obtain as much information about the abnormality as you possibly can.

Step 3, listing of probable faulty functions, is applicable to equipments that contain more than one functional area, or unit. It allows you to mentally select the functional unit (or units) which probably contains the malfunction, as indicated by the information obtained in steps 1 and 2. The selection is made by stopping to think: "Where can the trouble logically be in order to produce the information I have gathered?"

The term *function* is used to denote an electronic operation performed by a specific area of an equipment. A transceiver, for example, may include the following functional areas: transmitter, modulator, receiver, and power supply. The combined functions cause the equipment to perform the electronic purpose for which it was designed.

Frequently, the terms *function* (an operational subdivision of an equipment) and *unit* (its physical subdivision) are synonymous. A functional unit may be located in one or more physical locations. For example, some components of a receiver, in a transceiver, may be located in the transmitter compartment. Normally, the physical location, such as a drawer containing a receiver, is referred to as a *unit*. A functional unit consists of all the components that are required for the unit to perform its function, whether these components are packaged in an individual drawer or in two drawers. Within this text the terms *function, units,* and *functional unit* will be used interchangeably, although in some equipment one or more circuits of a given function may have been built into a unit other than that bearing the title of the function.

Selection Logic

The technician who accomplishes the first two steps of our six-step procedure and then picks just any test or repair procedure in an attempt to correct the trouble is indeed a poor troubleshooter. He must first survey the information he has gathered; then, using his knowledge of equipment operation along with the aids provided in applicable technical manuals, he must make a technically sound decision as to what is probably causing the recorded symptoms.

The abnormal performance indications noted in steps 1 and 2 should also give you clues as to the probable location of an electronic malfunction. Electronic equipment can have as many as 10,000 circuits, or 70,000 individual parts. The probability of finding the faulty part by methodically checking each of the 70,000 parts in turn is highly remote. The size of the task can be reduced by a factor of seven by checking the outputs of each circuit rather than checking each part separately.

However, 10,000 tests is still a job of considerable magnitude. By dividing the 10,000 circuits into their normal groupings of electronic functional units—seven, a dozen, or two dozen—tests. Whether the equipment contains

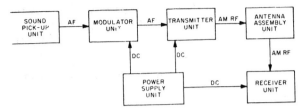

Fig. 6-4. Functional block diagram for AM transceiver set.

thousands. hundreds, or just a few circuits. logical reasoning dictates that the troubleshooting problem can be resolved more quickly and accurately by reducing the total circuits into a small number of groups.

Assume that we've divided the 10.000 circuits into 12 functional units. Locating the faulty unit might require 12 output tests unless you were lucky enough to find it before all units were tested. This still represents a departure from our basic logic. Whey should you test the turntable of a radio—television—phonograph console set if the picture on the TV tube is bad? You can predict that the trouble lies in the television receiver unit and confine your tests to that unit.

Functional Block Diagram

Electronic equipments and sets are subdivided into functional units. Each functional unit is generally contained with a single case or box or, in some instances. within drawers arranged in a rack comprising the overall set. The term *functional* is applied to these units because each one accomplishes a specific electronic function. The units are interconnected so that the individual functions will be performed in the proper sequence to accomplish the overall operational function of the set.

The equipment functional block diagram is an overall symbolic representation of the functional units within the equipment, as well as the signal flow paths between them.

Figure 6-4 is a typical functional block diagram. This particular diagram is for an AM transceiver composed of six separate units. Each unit performs an electronic function and conforms to the input—conversion—output (ICO) concept universally applied to all electronic circuits. units, and sets. Briefly. the function of each unit is:

1. The *transducer* (microphone) changes (converts) the sound information (input) to be transmitted into an electrical signal (output) of audio frequency (af).
2. The *modular unit* amplifies the af signal and applies it to the transmitter in such a manner as to cause the amplitude of the rf carrier signal to vary at an audio rate.
3. The *transmitter unit* provides the rf signal. as well as the proper boost for the power in the AM signal. to achieve the desired transmission range.
4. The *antenna assembly unit* converts the electrical AM signal into electromagnetic energy suitable for transmission through the atmosphere. When the transceiver is serving as a receiver. this unit converts the electromagnetic energy transmitted from another location into electrical signals to be applied to the receiver unit.
5. The *receiver unit* converts the AM signal received from another location into sound.

6. The *power supply unit* converts the line voltage into voltages suitable for powering the active devices tubes. transistors. ICs) in the system or subsystem.

There is no indication in the equipment functional block diagram as to how each function is accomplished. Thus. each functional unit may consist of a variety of circuits or stages. each performing its own electronic function. For example. the transmitter unit may contain an rf oscillator stage. a voltage amplifier stage. and several power amplifier circuits.

Notice that the connecting lines between the various functional blocks represent important signal flow connections. but that the diagram does not necessarily indicate where these connections can be found in the actual equipment circuitry.

Formulating a Faulty-Unit Selection

Making faulty-unit selections requires that you reach a decision as to the possible equipment area which could probably produce the trouble symptom and associated information. At this point in our six-step procedure. the trouble area will be restricted to a *functional unit* of the equipment. Thus. the functional block diagram is indispensable at this point.

Assume that you have found *no reception* as the trouble symptom for the transceiver whose functional block diagram is illustrated in Fig. 6-4. Manipulation of the receiver volume and tuning controls has no effect upon the no-reception condition. However. the POWER ON light and the dial lights of the receiver unit are all illuminated.

Out of the six functional units shown. only the power supply unit. the antenna assembly unit. and the receiver unit could possibly be at fault. since these are the only units associated with signal reception. Figure 6-5 shows the thought process involved in formulating a valid faulty-unit selection. The answers to the questions you must ask will be obtained from your knowledge of how the equipment operates and from your use of the technical diagrams depecting the equipment's circuitry. Most of them should come from a study of the functional block diagram.

First we consider the power supply unit and ask ourselves. "Would a failure or abnormal performance on the part of the power supply cause the original trouble symptom?" If the answer is "no." we can go on to consider another unit. If the answer is "yes." (as it is for the symptom given above). we

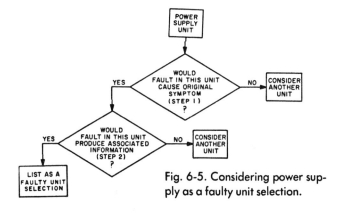

Fig. 6-5. Considering power supply as a faulty unit selection.

565

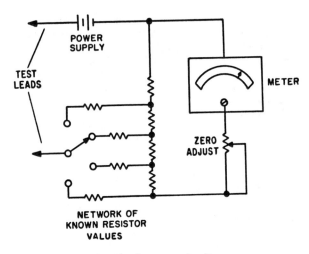

POWER SUPPLY

TEST LEADS

METER

ZERO ADJUST

NETWORK OF KNOWN RESISTOR VALUES

Fig. 6-6. Simple ohmmeter circuit.

ask ourselves. "Would a failure or abnormal performance on the part of the power supply produce the associated information obtained during symptom elaboration?" For this example the answer would be "yes." because the fact that the dial lights and POWER ON light are illuminated does not prove that the proper operating voltages are being produced. This is true because these lights are in the filament voltage circuit only. Therefore. we list the power supply unit as a faulty-unit selection. and we also note that the portion of this unit responsible for providing filament voltages is probably okay.

Next we consider the antenna assembly unit and receiver unit (separately) in the same manner. For the no-reception symptom and associated information given above. both of these units must also be listed as faulty-unit selections. A break in the antenna lead could easily cause our trouble. In this case every functional unit associated with receiving an external signal may be at fault. The number of selections can be reduced if the second step—symptom elaboration—yields more information about the trouble symptom.

The Exception to the Rule

There are some equipments which do not require a functional block diagram or a faulty-unit selection process. These equipments are relatively simple devices and consist of only one functional unit.

Figure 6-6 shows the circuit for a multirange ohmmeter. Equipment of this type represents almost an extreme in simplicity. For such equipment not only is a functional block diagram unnecessary. but troubleshooting step 3 (listing probably faulty function) and step 4 (localizing the faulty function) can be omitted entirely from our six-step procedure.

STEP 4—LOCALIZING THE FAULTY FUNCTION

The first three steps in our systematic approach to troubleshooting have dealt with the examination of both apparent and not-so-apparent equipment performance deficiencies. as well as a logical selection of the probable faulty functional units. Up to this point no test equipment other than the controls and indicating devices physically built into the equipment has been utilized. No dust covers or equipment drawers have been removed to provide access to any of the parts or internal adjustments. After evaluating the symptom information, you have made mental decisions as to the most probable areas in which the malfunction could occur.

Localizing the faulty function means that you will have to determine which of the functional units of the multiunit equipment is actually at *fault*. This is accomplished by systematically checking each faulty functional unit selection until the actual faulty unit is found. If none of the functional units in your list of selections display improper performance, it will be necessary for you to backtrack to step 3 and reevaluate the symptom information as well as obtain more information if possible. In some cases it may be necessary to return to step 2 and obtain additional symptom elaboration data.

At this point—step 4 in the troubleshooting sequence—you will bring into play your factual equipment knowledge and your skill in testing procedures. The utilization of standard or specialized test instruments and the interpretation of the test data will be very important *throughout* this and the remaining troubleshooting steps.

Testing a Faulty-Functional-Unit Selection

The factors to be considered in selecting the first test point, listed in their usual order of importance, are as follows:

1. The functional unit that will give the best information for simultaneously eliminating other untis, based upon the data obtained in steps 1, 2, and 3 of our procedure, provided that a certain unit is not obviously the cause.
2. Accessibility of test points—for example, a test point might be avoided as a first choice merely because the equipment must be disassembled to obtain access to this test point.
3. Past experience and history of repeated failures, provided that this factor is carefully weighed in the light of data obtained in steps 1, 2, and 3.

Test Results and Conclusions

Now that you have mastered the process of choosing the first faulty functional unit selection to test, you might ask, "Where do I go from here?" The answer, of course, depends upon the results of your first step.

There can be only two results—a *satisfactory* indication or an *unsatisfactory* indication. The latter may be in the form of no indication or a degraded indication. In any event, the result obtained should lead you to the next logical test.

Analyzing the Tests

Once the units have been isolated, what happens if the last check doesn't pinpoint the faulty unit? In this case you have either made an error in making one of your checks or the results of the check were misunderstood, leading you down the wrong path. This points up the importance of writing down your results. If you have the information written down, it is not difficult to look back and determine where you went astray.

Further Elaboration

If a final check shows the suspected units to be satisfactory, it will be necessary to reevaluate the information obtained from the previous checks. The question now is: How far back should you go?

You could ignore all the information and start over at the beginning with step 1. symptom recognition; however, this should not be necessary, because the fact that there is a trouble should have been pretty well established when the trouble was first reported. Returning to step 2, symptom elaboration, would allow you to reevaluate the meter readings or other indications that were present when the operating controls were manipulated. A return to step 3, listing of probable faulty functions, would permit a review of the list of faulty units previously prepared to insure that a possible faulty unit was not overlooked.

Trouble Verification

It is now necessary to reconsider whether a fault in this unit could logically produce the trouble symptom and fits the associated information obtained during symptom elaboration. To do this you will have to use the functional block diagram again.

To locate the faulty functional unit, we proceeded from symptom information to actual location. To verify the located functional unit we will proceed in the reverse direction. We will ask the question, "What trouble symptoms would this faulty unit produce?" Thus, equipment knowledge is very important.

If you will refer to Figure 6-4, you will be able to follow the logic in the example to be presented. Assume that the fault lies in the antenna assembly unit. It does not automatically switch over to the *receiver* function as it should. What trouble symptom would this failure produce?

First of all, we know that the symptom should occur only in the units associated with the receiver function. This would include the receiver unit. The modulator and transmitter units should be performing properly. The receiver should provide all normal responses, noise in the speaker, and the ability to vary the noise with the operating controls. However, no signal would be present.

If the original trouble symptom and the associated data collected during symptom elaboration fit the above expectations, we have verified the faulty functional unit.

Step 4 (localizing the faulty function) has been concerned with the testing of an equipment on a limited basis; that is, it has considered only those tests that are necessary to isolate a faulty functional unit. A logical application of equipment knowledge and symptom analysis, coupled with the three factors—simultaneous elimination of several functional units, test point accessibility, and past experience and history of repeated failure, enabled you to take the list of faulty functional unit selections made in step 3 and pick the most logical one for the first test. This same logic was then applied to the systematic selection of all subsequent test points. At each point, a new bit of information enabled you to narrow the trouble area until the faulty functional unit was located. The completion of this step as presented in this text should leave no doubt as to which functional unit is at fault.

STEP 5—LOCALIZING TROUBLE TO THE CIRUIT

To gain a better understanding of successive functional division, refer to Fig. 6-7. First, there is the equipment, or set, which is designed to perform an overall operational function. We see that steps 1 and 2 of our troubleshooting procedure are associated with this functional classification. The set is then divided into functional units, each designed to perform a major electronic function vital to the overall operational function. Steps 3 and 4 are associated

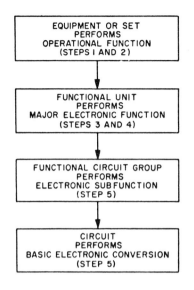

| EQUIPMENT OR SET PERFORMS OPERATIONAL FUNCTION (STEPS I AND 2) |

↓

| FUNCTIONAL UNIT PERFORMS MAJOR ELECTRONIC FUNCTION (STEPS 3 AND 4) |

↓

| FUNCTIONAL CIRCUIT GROUP PERFORMS ELECTRONIC SUBFUNCTION (STEP 5) |

↓

| CIRCUIT PERFORMS BASIC ELECTRONIC CONVERSION (STEP 5) |

Fig. 6-7. Functional divisions of equipment.

with this category. When there is only one functional unit, as in an ohmmeter, steps 3 and 4 are skipped.

The next division—the circuit group—is a convenient subdivision of the functional unit. The circuits and stages in the circuit group perform an electronic subfunction vital to the task assigned to the functional units. Our first concern in step 5 is to determine which of these groups is at fault. After this is done, we can go deeper into the equipment to isolate the final equipment division—the individual circuit.

The Correct Approach

Before you continue the troubleshooting procedures into step 5, you should pause and assimilate all of the data obtained at this point which may aid you in performing the next step. After completing step 4, you know that all of the inputs to the faulty function are correct and that one or more of the outputs is incorrect or nonexistent. The incorrect output waveforms obtained in step 4 should be analyzed to obtain any information which may indicate possible trouble areas within the functional unit. The original symptoms and clues obtained in the first two steps should not be discarded merely because steps 3 and 4 are completed. This information will be helpful throughout the troubleshooting procedure, and should be reviewed, together with all clues discovered in subsequent steps, before continuing to the next step.

Step 5 should be a continuation of the narrowing-down process, and the ICO principle should be employed in each part of this step. Each functional unit has a separate function within an equipment, and within each functional unit there may be two or more groups of circuits, each with a subfunction. This means that the input to each group (subfunction) is converted, and the output emerges in different form. An understanding of the conversions which occur within a functional unit makes it possible to logically select possible trouble areas within the unit. Testing is then performed to isolate the defective circuit group. The same principles are applied to the circuit group to locate the faulty circuit within the group.

Servicing Block Diagrams

The purpose of the servicing block diagram is to provide you with a pictorial guide for use in step 5. Figure 6-8 is such a diagram for the *receiver unit* of a transceiver set. There will also be a servicing block diagram for every other unit in the transceiver set—modulator. transmitter. and power supply. Occasionally. the entire equipment will be represented by one service block diagram.

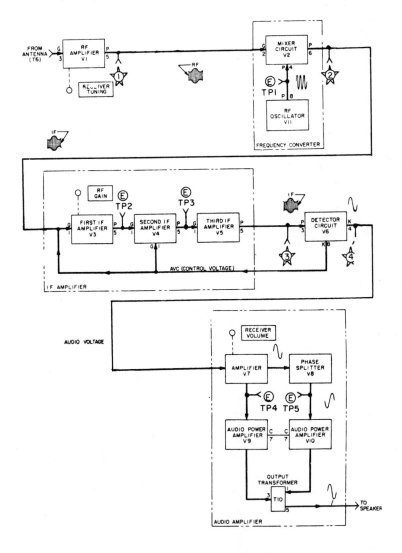

Fig. 6-8. Simplified servicing block diagram.

The use of a servicing block diagram is facilitated by the fact that all circuits within the functional unit are enclosed in heavy dashed lines, while circuits comprising a circuit group within the function are enclosed with light dashed lines. Within each dashed enclosure is the name of the functional unit or circuit group it represents. Main signal or data flow paths are represented by heavy lines, and secondary signal or data paths are represented by lighter lines. Notice in Fig. 6-8 that waveforms are given at several test points. Star test point symbols represent points which are useful for isolating faulty functional units, and circled test point symbols represent points which are helpful in locating faulty circuits or circuit groups.

Bracketing

Another aid to troubleshooting is the bracketing process, which provides the technician with a physical means of narrowing down the trouble area to a faulty circuit group and then to a faulty circuit.

Once the tests in step 4—localizing the faulty function—have been performed and the faulty unit isolated, the bracketing process begins by placing brackets (either mentally or with a pencil) at the good imput(s) and at the bad output(s) of the faulty function in the servicing block diagram. You know at this point that the trouble exists somewhere between the brackets. The idea is to make a test between the brackets and then move the brackets one at a time (either input or output bracket), and then make another test to determine whether the trouble is within the new bracketed area. This process continues until the brackets isolate the defective circuit.

The most important factor in bracketing is determining where the brackets should be moved in this narrowing-down process. This is determined on the basis of the technician's deductions from the analysis of systems and previous tests, the type of circuit paths through which the signal flows, and the accessibility of test points. All moves of the brackets should be aimed at isolating the trouble with a minimum number of tests.

Circuit Groups

You must be able to recognize circuit groups and to subdivide a block diagram of a functional unit into circuit groups before you can apply the bracketing procedure. A circuit group is one or more circuits which form a signal functional division of a functional unit of an equipment. A typical radio receiver contains the following circuit groups: rf amplifier, converter, i-f amplifiers, detector and audio amplifiers. A typical radio transmitter contains the following circuit groups: master oscillator, intermediate power amplifiers, and final power amplifier.

You can see that the circuit groups named above perform subfunctions in a receiver or transmitter and that their combined operations perform the complete function of the unit they constitute.

Signal Paths

The signals associated with a circuit group normally flow in one or more of four different types of signal paths. These include the linear path, convergent—divergent path, feedback path, and switching path.

The linear path is a series of circuits arranged so that the output of one circuit feeds the input of the following circuit. Thus, the signal proceeds straight through the circuit group without any return or branch paths. This is shown in part A of Fig. 6-9.

571

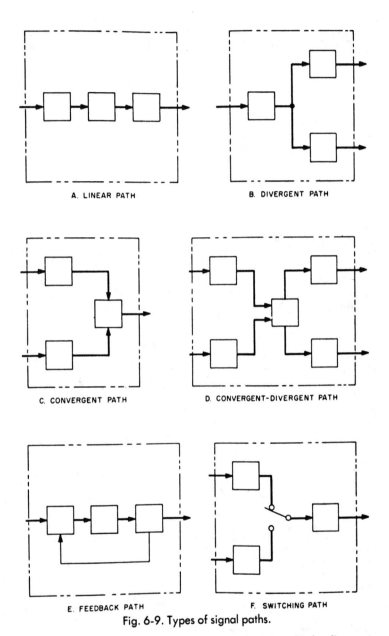

Fig. 6-9. Types of signal paths.

The convergent—divergent path may be any of three kinds: divergent, convergent, and the combined convergent—divergent. A divergent path is one in which two or more signals paths leave a circuit. as shown in *B*. When two or more signal paths enter a circuit. the path is known as a convergent path. An example is shown in *C*. A convergent–divergent path is one in which a circuit group or single circuit has multiple inputs and outputs. as shown in *D*. This type is not as common as the convergent path and the divergent path. The feedback path (Fig. 6-9E) is a signal path from one circuit to a preceding circuit. The switching path (Fig. 6-9F) has a switch for different signal paths.

Signal Substitution and Tracing

Signal substitution is a method of injecting an artificial signal into a circuit to check its performance. A radio receiver is an example of the equipment which can be tested by this method. If a signal generator is used to provide the proper signal at some test point in the receiver. a good output at the speaker indicates that the area between the test point and the speaker is free of trouble.

An example of the bracketing procedure is shown in Fig. 6-10. which represents a faulty functional uni . Step 4—localizing the faulty function—indicated a good input at test point *A* and a faulty output at test point *E*. indicating a trouble located between these two points.

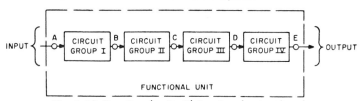

Fig. 6-10. Functional unit with input and output brackets.

Signal *tracing* would normally be used. since the signal at point *A* is known to be good. The signal at test point *C* would be the first logical place to check since this check would eliminate half of the circuit. (This will be discussed later in the text.) The signal at test point *C* can be checked by placing a meter or scope at this point. If the signal is satisfactory the *input* bracket would be moved from point *A* to point *C*. The next check. at point *D* would then isolate the defective circuit. If the test was satisfactory. the trouble would be in circuit group IV: if unsatisfactory. the trouble would be in circuit group II. Only the input bracket was moved. If the test at point *C* had been unsatisfactory. the *output* bracket would have been moved to this point. The next check. at test point *B*. would then isolate the defective circuit. If the signal is satisfoactory. the trouble would be in circuit group II: if unsatisfactory. the trouble would be in circuit group I. In this case. only the output bracket was moved.

If signal injection is used. a test signal would be injected at test point *C*. and the output checked at test point *E*. If the results are satisfactory. the *output* bracket is moved to point *C* and a signal is injected at test point *B* to isolate the defective circuit. If the signal is not correct at point *E*. the trouble should be isolated between points *C* and *E*. and the *input* bracket moved to point *C*. Injecting a signal at point *D* would then isolate the defective stage.

The first method of bracketing to be considered will be the method used for linear circuit arrangements. The best method of troubleshooting this type of circuit path is the *half-split method*. Assume that you have brackets at the input and output of a number of circuits or circuit groups in which thesignal path through all circuits is linear (Fig. 6-11A). Unless the symptoms point to one circuit in particular which might be the trouble source. the most logical place to move a bracket is to a convenient test point near the center of the

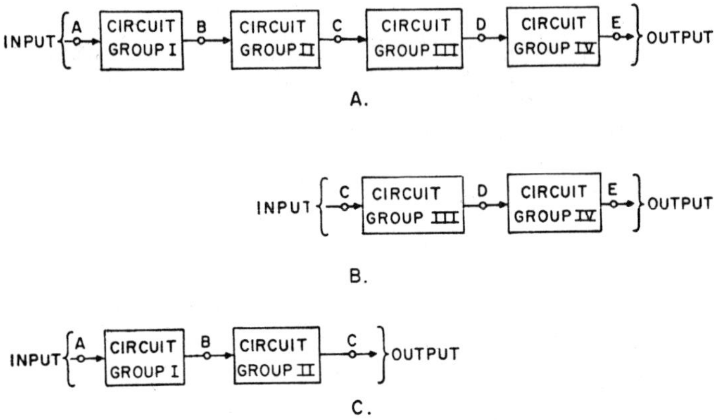

Fig. 6-11. Half-split method of bracketing.

bracketed area (point C. Fig. 6-11A). If a test indicates that the signal is good at this point. an input bracket should be left there (Fig. 6-11B). The brackets will then surround the second half of the linear circuit path. and the other half will be eliminated from the trouble area. If an incorrect signal is found at the test point. an output bracket placed at this point will show that the trouble exists in the first half of the linear circuit path (Fig. 6-11C). This process should be repeated with the area now enclosed with brackets until the brackets surround only one circuit. With the half-split method. a defective circuit can be located with a minimum of tests. By testing the circuits in sequence. the trouble may take many tests before being located.

It is unusual to find a complete functional unit with only one linear signal path; however. the half-split method can be applied to any part of a unit which contains a linear path. Convergent—divergent signal paths require a different technique. This type of signal path is not as easily recognized as linear paths; however. if you follow the definitions previously given. you should have little difficulty with this part of the procedure.

The next method of bracketing to be considered is applied to feedback signal paths. Before describing this method. a short discussion of the principles of feedback circuits will be necessary. As stated previously. a feedback signal path is one in which a signal is removed from some point in a circuit chain and applied to a point preceding its source. Since this feedback signal is combined with the original signal. it will tend to either increase or decrease the signal amplitude. If the feedback signal arrives back at the main signal path in phase with that signal. it is called *regenerative* feedback and will increase the gain of the circuit chain. When the feedback signal is out of phase with the main signal. it is called *degenerative* feedback and will decrease the circuit gain.

When troubleshooting any circuit with feedback paths. it is important to consider the type of feedback and the function of feedback in the circuit. Since a regenerative feedback path results in an increased circuit gain. a trouble in the feedback path results in a decreased output signal. Conversely. a trouble in a degenerative feedback path results in an increased output signal.

Another method of troubleshooting circuits containing feedback loops is to disable the feedback loop. This may be accomplished by disconnecting the feedback signal to ground. The first method is sometimes inconvenient. and the second method should be used only when it has been determined that shorting the signal to ground will not cause damage to the circuit.

Disabling the avc loop is convenient in the case of a receiver with an AVC ON-OFF switch. If a trouble is located in the circuit containing the avc loop, the switch can be used to determine whether the trouble still exists without avc.

The last type of signal path is the switching path. You have seen how electronic equipments are composed of various circuit chains interconnected to perform a desired task. Control of these circuits is usually accomplished by the use of switches placed directly in the circuits, or by remote switching relays.

To isolate faulty circuits along a switching branch, we initially test the final signal output for the branch following the switch. When the switch is a multiple-contact type, each contact may be connected to a different circuit branch. In this case, it may be necessary to place the switch in each position and check the final output of the branch associated with that position. If the symptoms and data point to one specific branch, it may not be necessary to check every switch position.

Once this test has been performed and the trouble is isolated to one or more branches, the suspected branches should be checked to locate the faulty branch. The next step is to apply the half-split, convergent—divergent, or feedback method, as required, to isolate the faulty circuit.

STEP 6—FAILURE ANALYSIS

This step places you in a position to replace or repair faulty circuit components so that the equipment can be returned to to optimum serviceability. However, locating the faulty part does not complete step 6. You will also be concerned with determining the cause of the failure. It is quite possible that still another failure occurred and, unless all faults are corrected, the trouble will recur at a later date. The final step in failure analysis requires that certain records be maintained. These records will aid you or some other technician in the future. They may also point out consistent failures which could be caused by a design error. When this step has been finished satisfactorily you can perform whatever repairs are necessary.

Schematic Diagrams

Schematic diagrams illustrate the detailed circuit arrangements of electronic parts (represented symbolically) which make up the complete circuits within the equipment or unit. These diagrams show what is inside the blocks on a servicing block diagram and provide the final picture of an electronic equipment.

Figure 6-12 shows the schematic diagram of the receiver unit for a transceiver set. The receiver unit differs slightly from the one illustrated by the functional diagram in Fig. 6-4. The frequency conversion function is accomplished in a single tube—there are no separate mixer and rf oscillator circuits. Only one i-f amplifier circuit is used.

These diagrams will be very helpful in making tests not shown directly on the servicing block diagram, as well as determining which branch of an isolated faulty circuit needs to be repaired. For example, to check the bias resistor of the phase splitter tube, $V6$, you could place the multimeter probes on pin 7 and the junction of $R19$ and $R21$. The value, as shown, should be 1000Ω.

Voltage and Resistance Charts

Once the faulty circuit has been isolated, the voltages and resistances of the various circuit branches must be measured to determine which

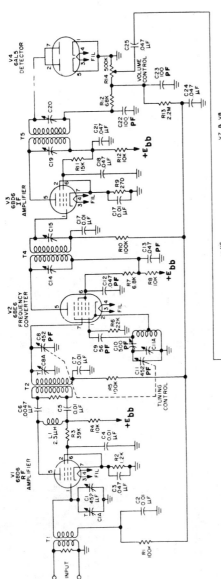
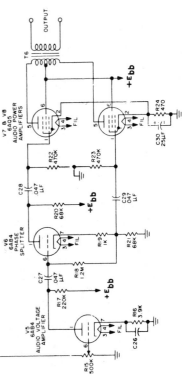

Fig. 6-12. Schematic diagram of receiver unit, transceiver set.

components within the circuit are at fault. The measurement results must be compared to *voltage and resistance charts* or tables in order to evaluate them. This information may appear on the apron of its associated foldout schematic diagram, or it may be on separate pages in the manual. The normal voltage and resistance reading to ground (or other point of significance) for each tube-socket transistor, or integrated-circuit pin is given. Also listed are the conditions necessary to observe the gain reading, such as control settings and equipment connections.

Types of Circuit Trouble

Regardless of the type of trouble symptom, the actual fault can eventually be traced to one or more of the circuit parts—resistors, capacitors, etc.—within the equipment. The actual faulty may also be classified by the degree of malfunction. The complete failure or abnormal performance of a part, or course, falls in line with the previous use of these terms. These types of faults are easily discovered.

There is a third degree of part malfunction which is not always so obvious. This is the *intermittent* part malfunction. *Intermittent* refers to something which alternately ceases and begins again. This same definition applies to electronic part malfunctions. The part operates normally for a period of time, then fails completely or operates on a degraded level for a while, and then returns to normal operation. The cyclic nature of this malfunction is an aid in determining that it exists; however, it is often difficult to locate the actual faulty part. This is true because of the fact that while you are testing the circuit in which this part lies, it may be operating normally. Thus you will pass it by as satisfactory, only to be faced with trouble again as soon as the cycle of operation completes itself.

Isolation of Faulty Parts

The first step in isolating a faulty part within a circuit is to apply the same ICO (input—conversion—output) method used in previous steps. The output signal should be analyzed to aid in making a valid selection of the parts or branch of the circuit which may cause the defective output The voltage, duration, and shape of the output waveform may be indications of possible open or shorted parts or out-of-tolerance values. This step performs two functions: It reduces to a minimum the number of test readings required; and it helps determine whether the faulty part, when located, is the sole cause of the malfunction.

The second step in isolating a faulty part is a visual inspection of the parts and leads in the circuit. Often this inspection will reveal burned or broken parts, or defective connections. Open filaments in electron tubes may also be spotted in this check.

Voltage measurements at transistor leads or at the pins of electron tubes can be compared with the normal voltages listed in available voltage charts to provide valuable aid in locating the trouble. This check will often help isolate the trouble to a single branch of a circuit. A separate circuit branch is generally associated with each pin connection of the transistor or electron tube. Resistance checks at the same points are also useful in locating the trouble. Suspected parts can often be checked by a resistance measurement.

When a part is suspected of being defective, a good part may be substituted for it in the circuit. You must keep in mind, however, that an undetermined fault in the circuit may also damage the substituted part. Another factor to consider before performing this step is that some circuits are critical. and substituting parts (especially transistors or tubes) may alter the circuit parameters.

In some equipment the circuits are specifically designed for the substitution process. For example. the plug-in circuit module is being employed in many electronic equipments. Once a trouble has been bracketed to a module. substitution of the module is the simplest method of correcting the fault.

Systematic Checks

Probable deductions should always be checked first. Next. because of the safety practice of setting a voltmeter to its highest scale before making measurements. the points having the highest voltages should be checked (transistor collector. and tube plate and screen grid). Then the elements having smaller voltages should be checked in the descending order of their applied voltage: that is. the transistor emitter and base. or the tube cathode and control grid.

Voltage. resistance. and waveform readings are seldom identical to those listed in the manual. The most important question concerning voltage checks is "How close is good enough?" In answering this question. there are many factors to consider. The tolerances of the resistors. which greatly affect the voltage readings in a circuit. may be 20%. 10%. or 5%: in some critical circuits. precision parts are used. The tolerances marked or color-coded on the parts are. therefore. one important factor. Transistors and electron tubes have a fairly wide range of characteristics and will thus cause variations in voltage readings. The accuracy of the test instruments must also be considered.

For proper operation. critical circuits require voltage readings within the values specified in the manufacturers technical manual: however. most circuits will operate satisfactorily if the voltages are slightly off. Important factors to consider are the symptoms and the output signal. If no output signal is produced at all. you should expect a fairly large variation of voltages in the trouble area. A trouble which results in a circuit performance just out of tolerance. however. may cause only a slight change in circuit voltages.

Locating the Faulty Part

The voltage and resistance checks discussed previously indicate which branch within a circuit is at fault. We must now isolate the trouble to a particular part (or parts) within the branch.

One procedure for accomplishing this is to move the test probe to the different points where two or more parts are joined together electrically and measure the voltage or resistance with respect to ground. Generally. however. the correct values (particularly voltage) will be difficult to determine from these points on a schematic diagram and may not be available elsewhere. Thus. we shall reserve this procedure for making resistance checks to locate shorts and openings in the branch. A better check to use when voltage readings are not not normal is a systematic check of the value of each resistor. capacitor. and inductor in the branch.

Common Malfunction Causes

Consider the transistor amplifier circuit shown in Fig. 6-13. Assume that our troubleshooting procedures have isolated the transistor as the cause of trouble—it is burned out. What could cause this? Excessive current can destroy the transistor by causing internal shorts or by altering the characteristics of the semiconductor material. which may be very

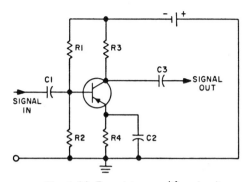

Fig. 6-13. Transistor amplifier circuit.

temperature sensitive. Thus, the problem reduces to a matter of determining how excessive current can be produced.

Excessive current could be caused by an excessively large input signal, which would overdrive the transistor. Such an occurrence would indicate a fault somewhere in the circuitry preceding the input connection. Power surges (intermittent excessive outputs) from the power supply could also cause the burnout. In fact, power supply surges are a common cause of transistor (and electron tube) burnout.

It is advisable to check for the conditions just mentioned before placing a new transistor in the circuit. Bias stabilization circuits are generally included (as in Fig. 6-13) to reduce the effect of excessive bias currents.

Some other malfunctions, along with their common causes, include:

1. Burned-out cathode resistors caused by shorts in electron tube elements.
2. Power supply overload caused by a short circuit in some portion of the voltage distribution network.
3. Burned-out transformer in shunt feed system caused by shorted blocking capacitor.
4. Burned-out fuses caused by power supply surges or shorts in filtering (power) networks.

In general, a degraded component characteristic can be traced to an operating condition which caused the maximum ratings of the component to be exceeded. The condition may be temporary and accidental, or it may be deeply rooted in the circuitry itself.

Bad tubes account for over 60% of all malfunctions in tube-type equipment. For this reason, the possibility of such a fault should be uppermost in your mind when you have reached this point in the six-step troubleshooting procedure.

As tubes age they undergo certain inherent changes. For example, there is a change in transconductance which generally lowers the gain of the tube. Also, the heater-to-cathode leakage current increases with age. This current is responsible for hum and other undesirable coupling effects between the heater and cathode. The period of time required for the leakage increase is shortened if the tube is frequently operated at a higher than normal temperature.

Other tube troubles include grid current variations, gas leakage, and improper usage (operation at excessive values). A consideration of these factors can locate multiple malfunctions, as well as prevent a future failure of similar nature.

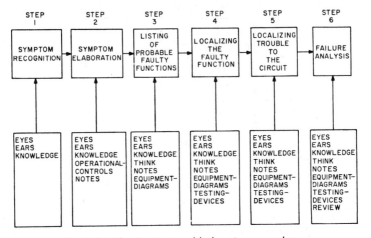

Fig. 6-14. The six-step troubleshooting procedure.

The six-step troubleshooting procedure is summarized in Fig. 6-14.

SAMPLE FCC QUESTIONS

The FCC test will include several circuit diagrams with marked components, similar to that shown in Fig. 6-15. The questions, all multiple-choice, are formulated to determine your degree of skill in troubleshooting. The following questions typify those you'll see on the exam.

1. *The diagram in Fig. 6-15 represents a tuned-plate, tuned-grid oscillator. What would the meter indication be if C1 were to short?*

    (a) Meter M1 would read higher.

    (b) Meter M2 would read lower.

    (c) Meter M1 would read lower.

    (d) Meter M2 would read zero.

    (e) None of the above—both meters would read normal.

By shorting capacitor C1, the input signal is removed, thus preventing current flow in the grid circuit and removing bias. With grid-leak bias, a positive potential is required to the grid before grid current can flow (and a flow of grid current is required to establish grid bias). Since C1 is shorted, the companion coil is shunted so that no voltage can be developed across it. The result, then, would be a reduced reading of meter M1. The circuit would not oscillate.

2. *If R1 in Fig. 6-15 should burn out, what would be the most likely indication?*

    (a) Meter M1 would read zero.

    (b) Meter M2 would read lower.

    (c) Meter M1 would read higher.

    (d) Meter M2 would read zero.

    (e) Both (b) and (c) above are true.

If you clearly understood the paragraph following the preceding question, you should have no trouble at all with this one. Resistor R1 must be in the grid circuit to establish operating bias. Without the resistor (a burned-out resistor is an open circuit), there will be no bias on the grid. Since oscillators operate

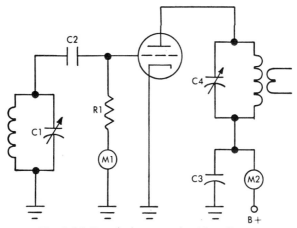

Fig. 6-15. Tuned-plate, tuned-grid oscillator.

class C, they require a large input signal swing to make conduction occur when biased properly. We can remove the bias but there will still be some interelectrode coupling during at least a portion of the operating cycle. The circuit may continue to oscillate (depending on tube's interelectrode capacitance, reflected reactance, etc.), but meter M1 would read zero.

3. *What would be the effect of a change in value of C2?*

 (a) Meter M2 will decrease.
 (b) Meter M1 will decrease.
 (c) Meter M2 will increase.
 (d) Meter M1 will increase.
 (e) Oscillating amplitude will change.

Changes in either the grid resistor or the grid coupling capacitor will affect the operating bias of the tube and will change the amplitude of oscillation. This is the only result we can be certain of, for the degree and extent of change dictate the reading of the meters in the circuit.

4. *What would be the result of detuning capacitor C4?*

 (a) Meter M1 decreases to zero.
 (b) Meter M2 decreases to zero.
 (c) Meter M2 increases.
 (d) Oscillation amplitude increases.
 (e) Feedback becomes degenerative.

Capacitor C4 is the plate tank load, and it must be in resonance for the circuit to operate in a stable condition. Remember that when a plate tank circuit is tuned to resonance, a dip in plate current occurs. When the tuning capacitor is moved from resonance in either direction, plate current increases. If the detuning is substantial, the tube will be destroyed from overcurrent. The answer, then, is (c).

5. *What would be the result of a leaky bypass capacitor C3?*

 (a) Meter M1 would read erratically.
 (b) Meter M2 would read erratically.
 (c) Oscillation would increase in amplitude.
 (d) Input tank circuit would shift frequency.
 (e) Meter M2 would increase.

Since B+ is supplied through the output tank coil, any leakage to ground on that line will increase the reading of M2—so long as C3 remains between the meter and the plate itself. If the power supply is unregulated, the leakage resistance in the bypass capacitor will act as a heavy drain on the B+ line, dropping the total voltage supplied to the plate. This would probably cause the frequency of the oscillator to shift, causing oscillation to be reduced in amplitude or checked altogether.

Appendix A

Extended Radio Operator Examination Program

The Federal Communications Commission and the Civil Service Commission are conducting a joint experiment to provide better service to applicants who are required to take FCC radio operator examinations. During the experiment, the number of locations where examinations are conductred will be substantially increased. The experiment includes only the areas served by the Anchorage, Chicago, Detroit, Honolulu, and Seattle FCC field offices. It should be emphasized *that this is an experiment* and it may not be possible to continue with this expanded service if the results of the experiment do not show it is justified.

You may wish to take your radio operator examination at one of the five FCC FIELD OFFICES involved in the experiment. An appointment is not required. Or it may be more convenient to take your radio operator examination at one of a number of other locations under the jurisdiction of these five FCC field offices. (An appointment is required.)

The five participating FCC field offices and their addresses are as follows:

Federal Communications Commission
Room G-63 U.S. Post Office Building
4th and G Street P.O. Box 644
Anchorage, Alaska 99510
Telephone: Area Code 907 272-1822

Federal Communication Commission
1054 Federal Building
Washington Blvd. and Lafayette Street
Detroit, Michigan 48226
Telephone: Area Code 313 226-6077

Federal Communications Commission
1872 U.S. Courthouse
219 South Dearborn Street
Chicago, Illinois 60604
Telephone: Area Code 312 353-5386

Federal Communications Commission
502 Federal Building
P.O. Box 1021
Honolulu, Hawaii 96808
Telephone: Area Code 808 546-5640

Federal Communications Commission
8012 Federal Office Building
First Avenue and Madison
Seattle, Washington 98174
Telephone: Area Code 206 442-7653

If you wish to take a radio operator examiniation at any of the five field office locations, you need only appear at the scheduled times. At the office you will complete the necessary application forms and pay the appropriate fee. Examinations are given at these field offices according to the following schedule.

Anchorage, Alaska	Commercial Radiotelephone Examinations	
	Monday through Friday	**8:00 AM to 3:30 PM**
	Commercial Radiotelegraph Examinations	
	Monday through Friday	**By Appointment Only**
	Amateur Examinations	
	Monday through Friday	**By Appointment Only**

Chicago, Illinois	Commercial Radiotelephone Examinations	
	Thursday	**9:00 AM and 1:00 PM**
	Commercial Radiotelegraph Examinations	
	Friday	**9:00 AM**
	Amateur Examinations	
	Friday	**9:00 AM**

Detroit, Michigan	Commercial Radiotelephone Examinations	
	Tuesday and Thursday	**9:00 AM and 1:00 PM**
	Commercial Radiotelegraph Examinations	
	Friday	**9:00 AM and 1:00 PM**
	Amateur Examinations	
	Friday	**9:00 AM and 1:00 PM**

Honolulu, Hawaii	Commercial Radiotelephone EXAMINATIONS	
	Tuesday and Thursday	**8:00AM**
	Commercial Radiotelegraph Examinations	
	Wednesday	**8:00 PM**

Examinations may be taken at other times if an appointment is made.

Seattle, Washington	Commercial Radiotelephone Examinations	
	Tuesday	**9:00 AM to 12:00 Noon**
	Commercial Radiotelegraph Examinations	
	Friday	**8:45 AM**
	Amateur Examinations	
	Friday	**8:45 AM**

Index

589

595